XPath™ 2.0 Programmer's Reference

Michael Kay

WILEY

Wiley Publishing, Inc.

XPath™ 2.0 Programmer's Reference

Published by
Wiley Publishing, Inc.
10475 Crosspoint Boulevard
Indianapolis, IN 46256
www.wiley.com

For general information on our other products and services please contact our Customer Care Department within the United States at (800) 762-2974, outside the United States at (317) 572-3993 or fax (317) 572-4002.

Trademarks: Wiley, the Wiley Publishing logo, Wrox, the Wrox logo, Programmer to Programmer, and related trade dress are trademarks or registered trademarks of John Wiley & Sons, Inc. and/or its affiliates. All other trademarks are the property of their respective owners. XSLT Copyright © 1994–2003 (Massachusetts Institute of Technology, European Research Consortium for Informatics and Mathematics, Keio University), All Rights Reserved. XPath is a trademark of Brocade Communication Systems, Inc. Wiley Publishing, Inc., is not associated with any product or vendor mentioned in this book.

Wiley also publishes its books in a variety of electronic formats. Some content that appears in print may not be available in electronic books.

Library of Congress Cataloging-in-Publication Data:

ISBN: 0-764-56910-4

Printed in the United States of America

10   9   8   7   6   5   4   3   2

Credits

Vice President and Executive Group Publisher
Richard Swadley

Vice President and Publisher
Joseph B. Wikert

Senior Acquisitions Editor
Jim Minatel

Editorial Manager
Kathryn A. Malm

Senior Production Editor
Gerry Fahey

Senior Development Editor
Emilie Herman

Production Editor
Felicia Robinson

Copy Editor
Techbooks

Media Development Specialist
Travis Silvers

Technical Editor
Wiley-Dreamtech India Pvt Ltd

Layout, Proofreading and Indexing
TECHBOOKS

To the Peacemakers

Contents

Contents

Contents

Contents

Contents

Contents

Contents

Contents

Acknowledgments

Firstly, I'd like to acknowledge the work of my colleagues on the W3C XSL and XQuery Working Groups, who worked together to create the XPath 2.0 language, and the many other experts inside and outside W3C who provided ideas and feedback. As a joint editor of the XSLT 2.0 specification I have to take responsibility not only for the imperfections in this book but also for some of the defects in the design of the language it describes. But although the specification lists a number of people as editors, most of the drafting was actually done by Don Chamberlin, and he therefore deserves the lion's share of the credit. Other individuals who played a key role in the creation of the language were James Clark, who laid the foundations with XPath 1.0, and Mary Fernandez, who chaired the task force that brought the two working groups together, and who frequently found a way to a solution when the groups appeared deadlocked. Ashok Malhotra managed the daunting task of defining the function library with commendable patience and persistence, and Scott Boag looked after the definition of the grammar. Many others, of course, contributed in many different ways.

I would like to thank the many readers of previous editions of *XSLT Programmer's Reference* who have provided feedback, criticism, and encouragement. Users of my Saxon implementation (a community that overlaps with the readers of the book) have also provided a great deal of stimulus. Without the knowledge that the book has been so widely appreciated, I would not have embarked on the daunting task of producing a new edition. Please keep the feedback coming, whether positive or negative.

The xsl-list at `http://www.mulberrytech.com/` has been a source of much inspiration. At first sight it might appear that the many novices who ask elementary questions are the main beneficiaries of this forum. In fact, however, the experienced users who answer the questions also gain a great deal: they learn from each other, and they learn from the beginners, who provide a constant insight into what users actually want to do with the language. There have been many occasions when I have used this knowledge in deciding what explanations to include in this book, and for that matter, in arguing for or against new language features in W3C meetings.

The bulk of this book was written while I was an employee of Software AG. I'd like to thank the company for allowing me to take this project on.

I must thank Wiley, who rescued this project when the old Wrox Press collapsed, and whose editor has applied a delicate touch both to reminding me of imminent deadlines and to correcting my prose.

And once again, I have to thank Penny and Pippa, who have sustained me through another winter in which I rarely left my desk.

About the Author

Michael Kay has been working in the XML field since 1997; he became a member of the XSL Working Group soon after the publication of XSLT 1.0, and took over as editor of the XSLT 2.0 specification in early 2001. He is also a member of the XQuery Working Group, and is a joint editor of the XPath 2.0 specification. He is well known not only through previous editions of this book, but also as the developer of the open-source Saxon product, a pioneering implementation of XSLT 2.0, XPath 2.0, and XQuery 1.0.

The author has recently formed his own company, Saxonica, to provide commercial software and services building on the success of the Saxon technology. Previously, he spent three years with Software AG, working with the developers of the Tamino XML server, a leading XQuery implementation. His background is in database technology: after leaving the University of Cambridge with a Ph.D., he worked for many years with the (then) computer manufacturer ICL, developing network, relational, and object-oriented database software products as well as a text search engine, and held the position of ICL Fellow.

Michael lives in Reading, England, with his wife and daughter. His hobbies include genealogy and choral singing (and once included chess). He has a croquet handicap of 9.

Introduction

Since XPath 1.0 was completed in November 1999, it has undoubtedly become one of the most important pieces of the XML jigsaw. From its origins as a sublanguage of XSLT, it has blossomed on its own merits as a freestanding language used wherever there is a need to select and reference nodes within XML documents. XPath 2.0 provides a substantial and long-awaited boost to the power of the language, and the significance of XPath as a component used by many other XML technologies is recognized by the fact that it now has a book all to itself.

This book is one of a pair: it is published together with a separate volume *XSLT 2.0 Programmer's Reference*. The two books together are derived from my earlier book *XSLT Programmer's Reference*, which covered XSLT 1.0 and XPath 1.0 in a single volume. There are two reasons for splitting the material into two volumes: one is that the languages have doubled in size, the other is that XPath is often used independently of XSLT. So this book is designed to be read either as a companion to *XSLT 2.0 Programmer's Reference*, or on its own.

The first edition of this book was published in the Spring of 2000, at the same time as the first complete XSLT implementations were appearing from companies such as Oracle, Microsoft, and IBM. The book quickly became recognized as the definitive reference on the XSLT and XPath languages, second only to the formal specifications from the World Wide Web Consortium (W3C). On the strength of the book, as well as my open-source XSLT implementation Saxon, I was invited to join the W3C Working Group developing the next version of the language, and I later became the editor of the XSLT 2.0 specification. I am also listed as one of the editors of the XPath 2.0 specification, though that is somewhat unfair to Don Chamberlin who does most of the hard work (the main reason I am on the list is that I prepared one of the early drafts of the specification). As a result of this history, I am writing with two hats. The general style of the book was set when I was writing as an outsider, a user of the W3C specifications with little idea how the decisions were made. I have tried to retain the objectivity of this perspective even though I am now only too aware of the tortuous debates and compromises that precede decisions on each language feature.

In the development of XPath 2.0, these debates were particularly vigorous because the language was developed not by a single working group, but by a joint task force of two working groups, each with different priorities and perspectives. The XSL Working Group came to the task with a natural tendency to defend the design decisions that had been made in XPath 1.0, and with expertise primarily in the area of document processing. The XQuery Working Group, on the other hand, consisted mainly of people with a background (in some cases a very distinguished background) in the design of database query languages, and with a natural tendency to criticize the features of XPath 1.0 that didn't fit the conventional wisdom as to what a database query language should look like.

The fact that the two groups decided to work together to produce a single XPath language, rather than two languages that were similar but different, is a credit to all the individuals concerned, and to the management of the World Wide Web Consortium (W3C) who believe strongly in consensus-building. The fact that it took four or five years to complete the process should come as no surprise; in fact, for some of us it is quite surprising that the process should have been completed at all.

You can guess at some of the debates that took place by reading between the lines of Chapter 1, where I discuss the technical characteristics of XPath as a language, and its relationships to other specifications in the XML family. Arguably the language that emerged at the end of the process is something of a hybrid, particularly in its approach to the vexed question of strong typing versus weak typing. However, I believe firmly that much of the success of XML is due to the fact that it is the first technology to cover the full range of information management requirements from free-form narrative documents to structured tabular data representation (with most things in practice falling somewhere in between these extremes). The Web created the requirement to handle all this information in a seamless way—think about a sports information site, or a holiday booking site—and XML arrived to meet this need. XPath, if it is to be useful across this wide spectrum, also needs to have a number of different personalities. I don't think this could have been achieved without bringing together people from different computing traditions whose ideas on language design principles sometimes differed widely.

One of the pleasures of XPath 1.0 (like XML itself) was the brevity of the specification: a mere 30 pages. I haven't tried to print the XPath 2.0 specification, but it is certainly vastly longer. What's more, it is split between multiple documents. The main language specification at `http://www.w3.org/TR/xpath20` points to subsidiary documents describing the data model, the function library, and the formal semantics, all at considerable length. As with a comparison between the US Constitution and the proposed EU Constitution, the length of the document tells us more about the number of people involved in defining it than about the benefits it offers. I would estimate that in reality the 2.0 language is about twice the size of XPath 1.0. Most of the new features are useful, though there is some redundancy to accommodate personal tastes (for example, some functions, such as `empty()` and `exists()`, can easily be expressed in terms of other functions). But whether the increased word count in the spec adds precision and clarity, or merely creates opportunities for errors and inconsistencies to creep in, is anyone's guess.

At the time of writing, the ink is not yet dry on the XPath 2.0 specification. The language went into its formal public consultation period on 12 November 2003, along with XSLT 2.0 and XQuery 1.0 (which is a superset of XPath 2.0). This three-month consultation generated over a thousand comments (over the family of specifications as a whole), which the working groups are still trawling through as I write in May 2004. These range from simple typos that are easily corrected, to offbeat ideas that have no chance of acceptance. In between these extremes are some tricky bugs and usability problems that need to be fixed. Many of these, however, are corner cases where the final decision is unlikely to affect many everyday applications (an example is the detail of how arithmetic overflow should be handled). There will certainly be a few changes to the language as a result of the public consultation, and as a result of implementation experience gathered during the Candidate Recommendation phase that still lies ahead, but my prediction is that these will be minor. Some changes already agreed have made it into this book. Where possible, we will draw attention to any further changes in the errata published at `http://www.wrox.com/`.

XPath 2.0 implementations have started to appear in products such as XMLSpy and Stylus Studio, as well as in XSLT 2.0 processors (where my own Saxon product currently has the field to itself). There are also surprisingly many early implementations of the XQuery 1.0 specification, which includes XPath 2.0 as a subset. Users, of course, have to make their own decisions about when to start moving forward.

Who This Book Is For

This book, as the title implies, is primarily a practical reference book for professional XPath developers. It assumes no previous knowledge of the language; however, it is not structured as a tutorial, and there will eventually be books on XPath 2.0 that provide a gentler approach for beginners. The difference with this book is that it doesn't just introduce you to the language, it takes you into all its hidden corners.

The book does assume a basic knowledge of XML and the architecture of the Web, and it is written for experienced programmers. There's no assumption that you know any particular language such as Java, Visual Basic or SQL, just that you recognize the concepts that all programming languages have in common. I know that many of my readers will be using XSLT, so there are many examples and notes that discuss the use of XPath in an XSLT context; however, you don't need to know XSLT in order to use XPath or to use this book.

I have tried to make the book suitable both for XPath 1.0 users upgrading to XPath 2.0, and for newcomers to XPath 2.0. This is easier to do in a reference book, of course, than in a tutorial. I have also tried to make the book equally suitable whether you work in the Java or .NET world.

As befits a reference book, a key aim is that the coverage should be comprehensive and authoritative. It is designed to give you all the detail, not just an overview of the 20% of the language that most people use 80% of the time. It's designed so that you will keep coming back to the book whenever you encounter new and challenging programming tasks, not as a book that you skim quickly and then leave on the shelf. If you like detail, you will enjoy this book; if not, you probably won't.

But as well as giving the detail, this book aims to explain the concepts, in some depth. It's therefore a book for people who not only want to use the language, but who also want to understand it at a deep level. Many readers of the earlier *XSLT Programmer's Reference* have written to me saying that they particularly appreciate these insights, and I have tried to retain this approach in the present volume.

What This Book Covers

This book aims to tell you everything you need to know about the XPath 2.0 language. It gives equal weight to the things that are new in XPath 2.0, and the things that were already present in version 1.0.

The book is about the language, not about specific products or APIs. The experience of XPath 1.0 is that there has been a very high level of interoperability between different XPath implementations, and if you can use one of them, then you can use them all.

If you are using XSLT 2.0, then you will want to use this book alongside the companion volume *XSLT 2.0 Programmer's Reference*. Since XSLT 2.0 has such a strong dependence on XPath 2.0, you really need both books. However, if you're using XPath 2.0 on its own, perhaps in conjunction with the DOM, then you can also use this book on its own.

XPath 2.0 is designed to work in conjunction with XML Schema. You don't have to use XML Schemas to use XPath 2.0, but there are some features in the language that aren't available unless you do. Chapter 3 gives a lightning tour of XML Schema from an XPath perspective, and if your job is to understand schemas written by other people rather than to write them yourself then this may be sufficient. But if you need to design and develop schemas yourself, there are other books that do the language justice.

How This Book Is Structured

The material in this book falls into two parts.

The first part, in Chapters 1 to 4, is concerned with explaining concepts. Chapter 1 is about the background to the language, about its relationship to other languages, and about its role and purpose.

Chapter 2 describes the data model—I'm a great believer in the idea that before you can understand how to manipulate data, you need to understand the structure of the data, which is what the data model tries to define. Chapter 3 examines the type system of the language, which defines which operations are applicable to which kinds of data. In the case of XPath 2.0, this is closely tied in with XML Schema, so the chapter starts with a survey of the key features of XML Schema. Chapter 4 then examines the XPath evaluation context. XPath is designed to operate as a sublanguage called from another language such as XSLT or Java, and the evaluation context is a formal way of describing the interface between XPath and its host language.

The second part of the book, in Chapters 5 to 11, contains reference information.

❑ Chapter 5 provides an introduction to the top-level constructs of the language, to its basic building blocks such as literals and function calls, and to the lexical rules for using whitespace and comments. The following chapters then each address one functional area.

❑ Chapter 6 covers the basic operators in the language for writing arithmetic and boolean expressions.

❑ The core of the XPath language, for version 2.0 as much as version 1.0, is the path expression, and these expressions are described in Chapter 7, along with three operators for combining the results of path expressions: union, intersect, and except.

❑ The main innovation in the XPath 2.0 data model is support for sequences, and Chapter 8 is devoted to a discussion of the operators that manipulate sequences, notably the «for» expression.

❑ When XPath is used in conjunction with XML Schemas, the type system plays an increasing role in the way XPath expressions are written. Expressions involving types are described in Chapter 9.

❑ Chapter 10 is the longest chapter in the book. It contains an alphabetical listing of all the functions in the core function library, which has expanded greatly since XPath 1.0

❑ Finally, Chapter 11 defines the syntax of XPath regular expressions as used in the three new functions matches(), replace(), and tokenize(). These facilities greatly boost the power of XPath to handle text matching and manipulation.

The appendices provide summary information for quick reference. Appendix A gives a summary of the language syntax (you can also use this as an index to locate the detailed description of each construct in the main body of the book). Appendix B is a table of operator precedences. Appendix C catalogs the areas of incompatibility between XPath 2.0 and XPath 1.0, and Appendix D lists error codes defined in the language specifications (which may or may not correspond to those produced by actual implementations).

What You Need to Use This Book

Because of the nature of XPath, and its role as a sublanguage, most of the examples found in this book are snippets of code rather than complete applications. They are there to show you what can be done, not really for you to try out for yourself (in particular, they are often shown without reference to any particular source document).

However, it's a good idea to try things for real as you meet them on the printed page, and I would encourage you to do this, either using the code as written, or making up your own variations that work with your own data files. There are XPath 2.0 processors in the latest versions of both XML Spy and

Stylus Studio. I personally found the one in Stylus Studio easier to work with, especially when you use it to select a few nodes in a large source document. Another good way of become familiar with XPath 2.0 is to use an XQuery processor such as Saxon or IPSI-XQ: there are a number of XQuery processors listed on the W3C XQuery home page at `http://www.w3.org/XML/Query`.

It's likely that you will find two kinds of XPath processor: a *basic* processor, and a *schema-aware* processor. However, the XPath specification doesn't itself define any conformance levels or subsets, it leaves this to the definitions of the host languages. XSLT 2.0 has defined this separation into two levels, and I think it's likely that XQuery will do the same. Other host specifications (for example, DOM) might define a different layering, but the distinction between facilities that require use of a schema and those that don't is likely to be a common theme. If you are particularly interested in the use of XPath with a schema, you will need to select a processor that supports this combination. One product that does so is the commercial version of Saxon, available from `http://www.saxonica.com/`.

Of course, it is likely that during the months after this book is published, XPath 2.0 processors will become available from other vendors. Most of the examples should run with any processor that conforms to the standards.

Other XPath Resources

Some of the sites that you might find useful for additional XPath information are:

- ❑ `http://www.w3.org/TR/xpath20`
  The latest version of the XPath 2.0 specification from the W3C, including references to the other specifications (such as the data model) on which it depends.

- ❑ `http://www.w3.org/Style/XSL/`
  Home page of the XSL Working Group

- ❑ `http://www.w3.org/XML/Query`
  Home page of the XQuery Working Group, including links to many XQuery implementations

- ❑ `http://www.mulberrytech.com/xsl/xsl-list`
  The home page of the xsl-list, a remarkably effective forum for all XSLT and XPath matters, from beginner's questions to advanced theoretical debates

Conventions

To help you get the most from the text and keep track of what's happening, we've used a number of conventions throughout the book.

> **Boxes like this one hold important, not-to-be forgotten information that is directly relevant to the surrounding text.**

Tips, hints, tricks, and asides to the current discussion are offset and placed in italics like this.

As for styles in the text:

- ❑ We *highlight* important words when we introduce them

- ❑ We show keyboard strokes like this: Ctrl+A

- ❑ We show code within the text as follows. Element names are written as `<html>` or `<xsl:stylesheet>`. Function names are written as `concat()` or `current-date()`. Other names (for example, of attributes or types) are written simply as `version` or `xs:string`. Fragments of code other than simple names are offset from the surrounding text by chevrons, for example, «`substring($a,1,1) = 'X'`». Chevrons are also used around individual characters or string values: as a general rule, if a string is enclosed in quotation marks, then the quotes are part of the code example, whereas if it is enclosed in chevrons, the chevrons are there only to separate the code from the surrounding text.

- ❑ Blocks of code are shown as follows:

```
In examples we highlight code with a gray background.
```

There are special conventions used for defining function signatures, but as these are used only in Chapter 10, they are described at the start of that chapter.

Source Code

Most of the examples in this book are in the form of small code fragments. In general, these fragments are incomplete, and are not intended to anything very useful on their own. You can build them into your own stylesheets or applications if you find them useful, but the idea is that you should use them as a source of ideas for writing your own code.

All of these examples are available for download at `http://www.wrox.com`. Once at the site, simply locate the book's title (either by using the Search box or by using one of the title lists) and click the Download Code link on the book's detail page to obtain all the source code for the book. Alternately, you can go to the main Wrox code download page at `http://www.wrox.com/dynamic/books/download.aspx` to see the code available for this book and all other Wrox books.

Because many books have similar titles, you may find it easiest to search by ISBN; for this book the ISBN is 0-764-56910-4.

Once you download the code, just unzip it with your favorite compression tool. Because most of the examples are very small, they have been collected together into a single XML document organized by chapter. (One way of using the collection of examples is to run them through an XPath 2.0 parser to see how many of the expressions it can handle correctly.)

Errata

We make every effort to ensure that there are no errors in the text or in the code. However, no one is perfect, and mistakes do occur. If you find an error in one of our books, like a spelling mistake or faulty piece of code, we would be very grateful for your feedback. By sending in errata you may save another reader hours of frustration and at the same time you will be helping us provide even higher quality information.

To find the errata page for this book, go to `http://www.wrox.com` and locate the title using the Search box or one of the title lists. Then, on the book details page, click the Book Errata link. On this page you can view all errata that have been submitted for this book and posted by Wrox editors. A complete book list including links to each's book's errata is also available at `www.wrox.com/misc-pages/booklist.shtml`.

On the errata page for this book you may also find information about any significant changes that have been made to the XPath 2.0 language after we went to press.

If you don't spot your error on the Book Errata page, go to `www.wrox.com/contact/techsupport.shtml` and complete the form there to send us the error you have found. We'll check the information and, if appropriate, post a message to the book's errata page and fix the problem in subsequent editions of the book.

p2p.wrox.com

For author and peer discussion, join the P2P forums at `p2p.wrox.com`. The forums are a Web-based system for you to post messages relating to Wrox books and related technologies and interact with other readers and technology users. The forums offer a subscription feature to e-mail you topics of interest of your choosing when new posts are made to the forums. Wrox authors, editors, other industry experts, and your fellow readers are present on these forums.

At `http://p2p.wrox.com` you will find a number of different forums that will help you not only as you read this book, but also as you develop your own applications. To join the forums, just follow these steps:

1. Go to `p2p.wrox.com` and click the Register link.
2. Read the terms of use and click Agree.
3. Complete the required information to join as well as any optional information you wish to provide and click Submit.
4. You will receive an e-mail with information describing how to verify your account and complete the joining process.

    You can read messages in the forums without joining P2P but in order to post your own messages, you must join.

Once you join, you can post new messages and respond to messages other users post. You can read messages at any time on the Web. If you would like to have new messages from a particular forum e-mailed to you, click the Subscribe to this Forum icon by the forum name in the forum listing.

For more information about how to use the Wrox P2P, be sure to read the P2P FAQs for answers to questions about how the forum software works as well as many common questions specific to P2P and Wrox books. To read the FAQs, click the FAQ link on any P2P page.

XPath 2.0 in Context

This chapter explains what kind of language XPath is, and some of the design thinking behind it. It explains how XPath relates to the other specifications in the growing XML family, and to describe what's new in XPath 2.0 compared with XPath 1.0.

The chapter starts with an introduction to the basic concepts behind the language, its data model and the different kinds of expression it supports. This is followed by a survey of new features, since I think it's likely that many readers of this book will already have some familiarity with XPath 1.0. I also introduce a few software products that you can use to try out these new features.

The central part of the chapter is concerned with the relationships between XPath and other languages and specifications: with XSLT, with XML itself and XML namespaces, with XPointer, with XQuery, and with XML Schema. It also takes a look at the way XPath interacts with Java and with the various document object models (DOM and its variations).

The final section of the chapter tries to draw out the distinctive features of the language, the things that make XPath different. The aim is to understand what lies behind the peculiarities of the language, to get an appreciation for the reasons (sometimes good reasons and sometimes bad) why the language is the way it is. Hopefully, with this insight, you will be able to draw on the strengths of the language and learn to skirt round its weaker points.

What Is XPath?

This is how the XPath 2.0 specification describes the language:

> XPath 2.0 is an expression language that allows the processing of values conforming to the [XPath] data model... The data model provides a tree representation of XML documents, as well as atomic values such as integers, strings, and booleans, and sequences that may contain both references to nodes in an XML document and atomic values. The result of an XPath expression may be a selection of nodes from the input documents, or an atomic value, or more generally, any sequence allowed by the data model. The name of the language derives from its most distinctive feature, the path expression, which provides a means of hierarchic addressing of the nodes in an XML tree.

So what is this trying to say?

Firstly, XPath is an expression language. It isn't described as a programming language or a query language, and by implication, it has less functionality than you would expect to find in a programming language or a query language. The most common kind of expression in XPath is one that takes an XML document as input, and produces a list of selected nodes as output: that is, an expression that selects some of the nodes in a document. XPath specializes in making it easy to access data in XML documents. However, XPath expressions are rather more general than this. «2+2» is a valid XPath expression, as is «matches($input,"[a-z]*[0-9]")».

The language is described in this summary primarily by reference to the kinds of data that it manipulates, that is, its data model. The question of what you are actually allowed to do with these data values is secondary. The data model for XPath 2.0 (which is shared also by the closely-related languages XSLT 2.0 and XQuery 1.0) provides essentially three building blocks, all mentioned in this summary:

❑ Atomic values of various types including strings, integers, booleans, dates, times, and other more specialized types such as QNames and URIs

❑ Trees consisting of nodes, which are used to represent the content of an XML document

❑ Sequences (or lists), whose items are either atomic values, or references to nodes in a tree. Sequences can't be nested.

We will be discussing this data model in considerable detail in Chapter 2. It's worth spending time on this, because understanding the data model is the key to understanding the language.

The expressions that you can write in XPath perform operations on these data values. XPath is a read-only language: it cannot create new nodes or modify existing nodes (except by calling functions written in a different language). It can however create new atomic values and new sequences. There's an important difference, which is that nodes (like objects in Java) have identity, whereas atomic values and sequences don't. There is only one number «2», and there is only one sequence «1,2,3» (or if you prefer, there is no way of distinguishing two sequences that both contain the values «1,2,3»), but there can be any number of distinct <a/> nodes.

Given that there are three broad categories of data values, there are similarly three broad categories of operations that can be performed:

❑ *Operations on atomic values*: These include a range of operators and functions for adding numbers, comparing strings, and the like. Example expressions in this category are «price * 1.1» and «discount > 3.0». Many of these operations are likely to be familiar from other more conventional languages, though there are a few surprises in store. Chapter 6 of this book describes these operations in detail.

❑ *Operations that select nodes in a tree*: The most powerful expression here, which forms the heart of XPath, is the path expression. An example of a path expression is «book[author="Kay"]/@isbn» which selects the «isbn» attributes of all the <book> elements that have a child <author> element with the value «Kay». Path expressions are analyzed in detail in Chapter 7, but I will have a few introductory words to say about them in this chapter.

❑ *Operations on sequences*: Here, the most important construct is the «for» expression. This applies an expression to every item in a sequence, forming a new sequence from the results. As an example, the result of the expression «for $i in 1 to 5 return $i*$i» is the sequence «1, 4, 9, 16, 25». (XPath variables are prefixed with a «$» sign to distinguish them from XML element names.) In practice, the items in the input sequence are more likely to be nodes: the expression «`for $n in child::* return name($n)`» returns a list containing the names of the child elements of the current node in the document. The «`for`» expression is referred to as a *mapping expression*, because it performs an item-by-item mapping from an input sequence to an output sequence. The «`for`» expression, and other operations on sequences, are described in Chapter 8 of this book.

We will now take a closer look at path expressions, which give XPath its distinctive flavor.

Path Expressions

A typical path expression consists of a sequence of steps, separated by the «`/`» operator. Each step works by following a relationship between nodes in the document. This is in general a one-to-many relationship. The different relationships are called axis. The most commonly used axis are:

- ❑ The `child` axis selects the children of the starting node, that is, the elements and text nodes (and perhaps comments and processing instructions) that are found between the begin and end tags of an element, assuming the starting node is an element.

- ❑ The `attribute` axis selects the attributes of an element.

- ❑ The `ancestor` axis selects all the elements that enclose the starting node in the XML document. The last ancestor is generally a node that represents the document itself: this is called the document node, and it is distinct from the node that represents the outermost element.

- ❑ The `descendant` axis selects the children of a node, the children of the children, and so on recursively, down to the leaves of the tree.

In the full form of a step, the axis name is followed by a construct called a `NodeTest` that indicates which nodes are to be selected. Often this consists simply of a node name, or it might be «`*`» to select all elements or attributes. So «`child::title`» selects the `<title>` elements that are children of the current node (there may be more than one), «`ancestor::*`» selects all the ancestor elements, and so on.

The «`/`» operator strings together a sequence of steps into a path. So, for example, «`child::book/child::chapter/attribute::status`» selects the «`status`» attributes of all the chapters of all the books that are children of the starting node.

In practice, steps are usually written using a shorthand syntax. Because the «`child`» axis is the one that's used most often, the prefix «`child::`» can be omitted. Attributes are also used frequently, so the prefix «`attribute::`» can be shortened to the mnemonic «`@`» sign. This means the path given in full above can be abbreviated to «`book/chapter/@status`».

The other common abbreviation is «`//`», which you can think of as searching the entire subtree below the starting node. For example, «`//figure`» selects all the `<figure>` elements in the current document. A more precise definition of this construct (and the others) is given in Chapter 7.

Any step in a path expression can also be qualified by a predicate, which filters the selected nodes. For example, «`book/chapter[@ed="John"]/@status`» returns the «`status`» attribute of all the chapters of all the books provided that the chapter has an attribute named «`ed`» whose value is «`John`».

Path expressions thus provide a very powerful mechanism for selecting nodes within an XML document, and this power lies at the heart of the XPath language.

Composability

As we've seen, the introduction to the XPath specification describes the language as an expression language, and this has some implications that are worth drawing out.

Expressions can be nested. In principle, any expression can be used in a position where a value is allowed. This theoretical freedom is slightly restricted by two factors: at a trivial level, you might have to enclose the expression in parentheses; more seriously, you can only use an expression that returns the right type of value. For example, you can't use an expression that returns an integer in a place where a sequence of nodes is expected. XPath values have a type, and the language has rules about the types of expressions. The type system of the language is unusual, because it is closely integrated with XML Schema. I shall have more to say about the type system in Chapter 3, and I will describe the language constructs that relate specifically to types in Chapter 9.

A language in which you can nest expressions in arbitrary ways is often referred to as being *composable*. Composability is regarded as a good principle of modern language design. Most languages have some restrictions on composability, for example in Java you can use an array initializer (a construct of the form «{1,2,3}») on the right-hand side of the «=» in a variable declaration, but you can't use it as an arbitrary expression. XPath has tried hard to avoid including any such restrictions—even to the extent of allowing you to do things that no one would ever want to do, like writing «--1», whose value is +1.

Closely allied with the idea of composability is the principle of *closure*. This term comes from mathematics. A closed group consists of a set of possible values (for example, the positive integers) and a set of possible operations, in such a way that every operation when applied to these values produces a new value that is also within the same space of possible values. If you take the positive integers together with the operators of addition and multiplication you have a (not very useful) closed group, but if you also allow subtraction and division the group is no longer closed, because the results are not always positive integers. In XPath the set of possible values is defined by the data model: as we have already seen, this allows nodes, atomic values, and sequences. The set of possible operations is defined by the expressions in the language, and the whole system is closed, because the result of every expression is also a value within the scope of the data model. Closure is a necessary property to achieve composability, because you can't use the result of one expression as the input to another unless the result is in the same value space.

What's New in XPath 2.0?

XPath 2.0 represents a major advance on version 1.0: the number of operators has doubled, and the number of functions in the standard function library has grown by a factor of four or five depending on how you do the counting. The changes to the core syntax are not so dramatic, but the introduction of a new type system based on XML Schema represents a pretty radical overhaul of the language semantics. The W3C working groups have also tried to define the language much more rigorously than XPath 1.0 was defined, with the result that the number of trees used when you print the spec has grown astronomically.

It's easy to list the new features in version 2.0 as a simple catalog of goodies. What's harder to do is to stand back and make sense of the total picture: Where is the language going? I'll try to answer the question posed in the section heading in both ways, first by listing the features, and then by trying to see if we can understand what it all means.

New Features in Version 2.0

Firstly, the XPath 2.0 data model offers new data types:

- ❑ XPath 1.0 had a single numeric data type (double precision floating point), XPath 2.0 offers in addition integers, decimals, and single precision

- ❑ There are new data types for dates, times, durations, and more

- ❑ It is also possible to exploit user-defined data types that are defined using XML Schema

- ❑ XPath 2.0 supports sequences as a data type. Sequences can contain nodes and/or atomic values. An important peculiarity of the XPath data model is that a singleton item such as an integer is indistinguishable from a sequence of length one containing that item.

The data model for representing XML documents has not actually changed very much, despite the fact that the description has grown from five pages to about 60. It still has the same seven kinds of node, namely document nodes (which were called root nodes in XPath 1.0), elements, attributes, text nodes, comments, processing instructions, and namespace nodes, and the relationship between them has not changed significantly. The main change is that element and attribute nodes can now have a type annotation. This is a label identifying the data type of the content of the element or attribute, which is determined by the definition of the element or attribute in the XML Schema that was used to validate the document. If the document has not been validated (which is still considered a perfectly respectable state of affairs) then the type annotation is set to one of the special values «xdt:untyped» for elements, or «xdt:untypedAtomic» for attributes.

Going hand-in-hand with the type annotation is the idea that an element or attribute node has a typed value: for example if the type annotation is «xs:integer», then the typed value will be an integer, while if the type annotation is «xs:NMTOKENS», then the typed value will be a sequence of «xs:NMTOKEN» values. Because the typed value is always a sequence of atomic values, the process of extracting the typed value of a node (which is performed implicitly by many XPath operations, for example equality comparison) is referred to as *atomization*.

Path expressions too have not changed very much since XPath 1.0. The biggest change is that the NodeTest (the part that follows the «axis::» if you write a step in full) can now test the type of the node as well as its name. For example, you can select all elements of type Person, regardless of the name of the element. This is very useful if you are using a schema with a rich type hierarchy in which many elements can be derived from the same type definition: many of the bigger and more complex XML vocabularies have this characteristic. It corresponds to the ability to use a generic supertype in an object programming language such as Java or C#, rather than having to list all the possible subtypes you are interested in.

Another significant change in path expressions is that you can use a function call in place of a step. This means that you can follow logical relationships in the XML document structure, not just physical relationships based on the element hierarchy. For example, if someone writes a function that finds all the orders for a customer, you can invoke this function in the middle of a path expression by writing «customer[@id="123"]/find-orders(.)/order-value». This means that the person writing this path expression doesn't necessarily need to know how the orders for a customer are found, and it means that the way that they are found can change without invalidating the expression. XPath itself does not allow you to write the find-orders() function—you can do this in either XQuery or XSLT, or perhaps in other languages in the future. Functions written in XQuery or XSLT can be invoked from anywhere within an XPath expression.

Outside the realm of path expressions, there's a raft of new operators in the language. These include:

❑ Operators «is», «<<», «>>» to test whether two expressions return the same node, or to test which of the two nodes is first in document order

❑ Operators «intersect» and «except» to find the intersection or difference between two sets of nodes

❑ Operators «eq», «ne», «lt», «le», «gt», «ge» to compare atomic values. These are provided alongside the XPath 1.0 operators «=», «!=», «<», «<=», «>», «>=» which allow sequences of values to be compared

❑ An integer division operator «idiv»

❑ An operator «to» which allows you to construct a range of integers, for example, «1 to 10».

The most important new syntactic constructs are:

❑ The «for» expression, which as we have already seen on page 8 is used to apply the same expression to every item in a sequence.

❑ The «if» conditional expression. For example, the expression «if (@price > 10) then "high" else "low"» returns one of the two strings "high" or "low" depending on the value of the «price» attribute.

❑ The «some» and «every» expressions. The expression «some $p in $products satisfies (every $o in $p/orders satisfies $o/value > 100)» returns true if there is at least one product all of whose orders are worth more than $100.

The function library has grown so much that it's hard to know where to begin. A full specification of all the functions is included in Chapter 10. The main highlights are:

❑ There are many new functions for handling strings, for example, to perform case conversion, to join a sequence of strings, and an ends-with() function to complement the XPath 1.0 starts-with().

❑ In particular, there are three functions matches(), replace(), and tokenize() that bring the power of regular expressions into the XPath language, greatly increasing its string-manipulation capabilities.

❑ All functions that perform comparison of strings can now use a user-specified collation to do the string comparison. This allows more intelligent localization of string matching to the conventions of different languages.

❑ There are new functions for aggregating sequences; specifically, max(), min(), and avg() are now available, alongside sum() and count() from XPath 1.0.

❑ There's a large collection of functions for manipulating dates and times.

❑ There are new functions for manipulating QNames and URIs.

Now let's try to stand back from the trees and examine the wood.

A Strategic View of the Changes

Is there any kind of unifying theme to these new features?

To find out, it helps to look back at the original requirements specification for XPath 2.0, which can be found at http://www.w3.org/TR/2001/WD-xpath20req-20010214 (there is also a later version, which describes how the requirements were met in the actual language design). It starts, very briefly, with a summary of the goals of the new version:

- ❑ Simplify manipulation of XML Schema-typed content

- ❑ Simplify manipulation of string content

- ❑ Support related XML standards

- ❑ Improve ease of use

- ❑ Improve interoperability

- ❑ Improve i18n support

- ❑ Maintain backward compatibility

- ❑ Enable improved processor efficiency

After this disappointingly brief introduction, it then launches into what is, frankly, a catalog of desired features rather than a true requirements statement (it never attempts to answer the question *Why is this needed?*). But the goals, and the way the detailed requirements are written, do give some clues as to what the working groups were collectively thinking about.

We'll talk more about the process by which XPath 2.0 was defined later in the chapter. For the moment, it's enough to note that it was produced jointly by two working groups: the XSL Working Group, who were responsible for XSLT and had produced the XPath 1.0 specification, and the XQuery Working Group who were interested in extending XPath to make it suitable as a query language for XML databases. This requirements statement, produced on St. Valentine's Day 2001, was the first fruit of the collaboration between the two groups. The thinking of the two groups at this stage had not converged, and if you read the document carefully, you can detect some of the tensions.

Let's try and read between the lines of the eight goals listed above. The ordering of the goals, incidentally, was probably not debated at length, but I think it is important psychologically as an indication of the relative priorities which some members at least attached to the various goals.

- ❑ *Simplify manipulation of XML Schema-typed content.* We've already seen that the introduction of a type system based on XML Schema is probably the most radical change in XPath 2.0. At this time, early in 2001, XML Schema was seen as absolutely central to W3C's future architectural direction. It was also central to the plans of many of W3C's member companies, such as Microsoft, Oracle, and IBM. Although James Clark (the designer of XSLT and XPath 1.0) was starting to make discontented noises about the technical qualities of the XML Schema specification, no one in the establishment really wanted to know. Everyone wanted XML Schema to be a success and was confident that it would indeed be a success, and it was self-evident that languages such as XPath for manipulating XML documents should take advantage of it.

    A great deal of the requirements document is given over to outline ideas of how the language might integrate with XML Schema. Looking at it now, it reads much more like a design sketch than a true requirements list.

❑ *Simplify manipulation of string content.* It was generally agreed that the facilities in XPath 1.0 for manipulating strings were too weak. Facilities were needed for matching strings using regular expressions, for changing strings to upper and lower case, and so on.

❑ *Support related XML standards.* This appears as a catch-all in the list of goals, but it reflects the fact that W3C specifications are not produced in isolation from each other. The different working groups spend a lot of time trying to ensure that their efforts are coordinated and that all the specifications work well together.

The actual requirements listed in the body of the document under the heading *Must support the XML Family of Standards* actually form a very motley collection, and some of them bear no relationship to this heading at all. The requirements that do make some sense in this category relate to the need to support common underlying semantics for XSLT 2.0 and XQuery 1.0, the need for a data model based on the InfoSet published by the XML Core Working Group (more on this on page 16), and the need for backward compatibility with XPath 1.0. Interestingly, this last requirement is classified as a *should* rather than as a *must*, which meant that backward compatibility could be sacrificed to meet other objectives.

❑ *Improve ease of use.* This heading was clearly seen as an open invitation for everyone to add their favorite features. So in this category we see things such as the need to add a conditional expression, the need to generalize path expressions, and the need for new string functions and aggregation functions. More fundamentally, there is also a subsection calling for consistent implicit semantics for operations that handle collections, and criticizing some of the design choices made in XPath 1.0 such as the way the «=» operator was defined over sets of nodes. Although these were described as *must* requirements, there was clearly no way of satisfying them without radical change to the language semantics, which would have had a devastating effect on backward compatibility. In the end, much of the debate of the next two years was spent finding an acceptable compromise to this problem.

One might imagine that a gathering of some of the brightest minds in the computer industry would not write "improve ease of use" as a goal without defining some way of measuring the ease of use of the language before and after the addition of these features. Sadly, one would be disappointed. A committee can do mindless things, regardless how bright the minds are that make it up.

❑ *Improve interoperability.* The word *interoperability* in W3C circles means the ability for different implementations of a specification to produce the same result.

I can't actually find any detailed requirements that support this goal, so it should be no surprise that XPath 2.0 actually allows a lot more freedom to implementers to introduce differences than XPath 1.0 did.

❑ *Improve i18n support.* Here i18n is shorthand for internationalization, the ability of the specification to support the needs of different languages and cultures worldwide. This is something the W3C takes fairly seriously (despite requiring editors of its specifications to write in English, with American spelling).

Again there is actually nothing concrete in the requirements to support this goal. The main new feature in XPath 2.0 that affects internationalization is the introduction of user-selected collations to support string comparison and sorting, but this feature does not actually appear explicitly in the requirements (instead, it found its way into XPath via the XSLT and XQuery requirements).

Two features that are notably lacking from XPath 2.0 are support for localized formatting of numbers and dates. For this, you need to turn to the additional function library provided by XSLT 2.0, which is available only when you use XPath expressions within an XSLT stylesheet.

❑   *Maintain backward compatibility.* As I've already mentioned, this appears as a *should* rather than a *must*. This has been a tension throughout the development of the language, as some XQuery people felt they wanted to be unconstrained by the past, whereas XSLT representatives felt a strong responsibility to their existing user base.

In the end, each decision was made on its merits. Incompatible changes were introduced only when the group as a whole felt that the gain was worth the pain. Some incompatibilities were inevitable, given the change in the data model and type system, but by and large gratuitous incompatibilities were avoided. Some of the worst conflicts were resolved by the introduction of the ability to run in backward compatibility mode (the infamous "mode bit", for those who have read Tracy Kidder's *Soul of a New Machine*). In many cases, the XPath 1.0 way of doing things was eventually retained because people came to see that it wasn't such a bad design after all.

❑   *Enable improved processor efficiency.* Once again, there is nothing in any of the requirements that explains how it is intended to contribute to this goal (and of course, there is again no measure of success). I think one could go through the requirements and explain how some of them might improve the performance of applications, but whether anyone actually was thinking this through at the time, I don't know.

Efficiency has frequently come up during the design discussions on language features, sometimes for good reasons and sometimes for bad. For example, designs were often rejected if they inhibited pipelining, that is, the ability to process a sequence of values without retaining all the values in memory. An example of such a rule that was present at one time was that the max() of a sequence should be the numeric maximum if all items in the sequence were numbers, or the string maximum otherwise. This means you need to read the whole sequence before you can compare the first two values, so this rule was rightly rejected. Quite often, however, vendors would come to the working group and ask for a feature to be changed simply because it looked difficult to implement (I've been guilty of this myself). Usually other implementors would squash such arguments, pointing out that alternative techniques were available. In general, a language design that is clean and simple from a user perspective turns out to be a better choice than one that developers find easy to implement.

One design decision that doesn't emerge clearly from this study of the requirements is the question of how big the language should be. There were (and are) differing views on this, and there is no obvious right answer that suits everyone. Some people wanted the language to be much smaller than it is, others to accommodate some of the XQuery features that have been left out, such as full FLWOR expressions. The final outcome is a compromise, but it is a compromise that has some rationale: in particular, the language includes sufficient power to make it *relationally complete,* as defined by E. F. Codd in the theory of the relational model. There is a mathematical definition of this term, and achieving this property gives reasonable confidence that the language will be powerful enough for most data retrieval tasks. However, this doesn't provide an absolute criterion for what should be included: for example, the decision not to include any sorting capability in XPath 2.0 could have gone either way.

I hope this summary gives a little bit of a feel of what the working groups were trying to achieve with the design of XPath 2.0. If it seems like something half-way between a carefully-thought out strategy and an ad hoc ragbag, then that's probably because it is. That's the way committees work.

XPath 2.0 Processors

At the time of writing there are three ways you can actually use XPath 2.0.

Firstly, you can use an XQuery 1.0 processor. There are quite a few XQuery processors available, and you can find them listed on the W3C home page for XQuery at `http://www.w3.org/XML/Query`. Since XPath 2.0 is a subset of XQuery 1.0, you can use any XQuery processor to execute XPath expressions. They vary considerably in the extent to which they implement the full specifications, and in how up-to-date they are with the latest drafts of the specifications. I haven't tried them all, and the situation changes from month to month, so I won't recommend any implementation in particular. One of the processors listed on the XQuery home page is my own Saxon implementation—Saxon is both an XSLT and an XQuery processor, with a common runtime engine supporting both languages, and this runtime also, of course, supports XPath 2.0.

Broadly speaking, the suppliers of these XQuery processors have either concentrated on building an industrial-strength XML database product, or they have concentrated on tracking the latest language standards. The more advanced a product is in terms of the language specification that it supports, the less advanced it is likely to be in terms of other database features such as updates, recovery, transactions, fast database loading capabilities, and so on.

One product that I have found very easy to install and use is IPSI-XQ, developed by the Fraunhofer Institut in Germany. An advantage that it has over Saxon is that it has a graphical user interface (Saxon can only be driven from the command line or from a Java API, which isn't very appealing when you're showing it off in a conference). You can get IPSI-XQ from `http://www.ipsi.fraunhofer.de/oasys/projects/ipsi-xq/index_e.html`. Figure 1-1 shows a simple query.

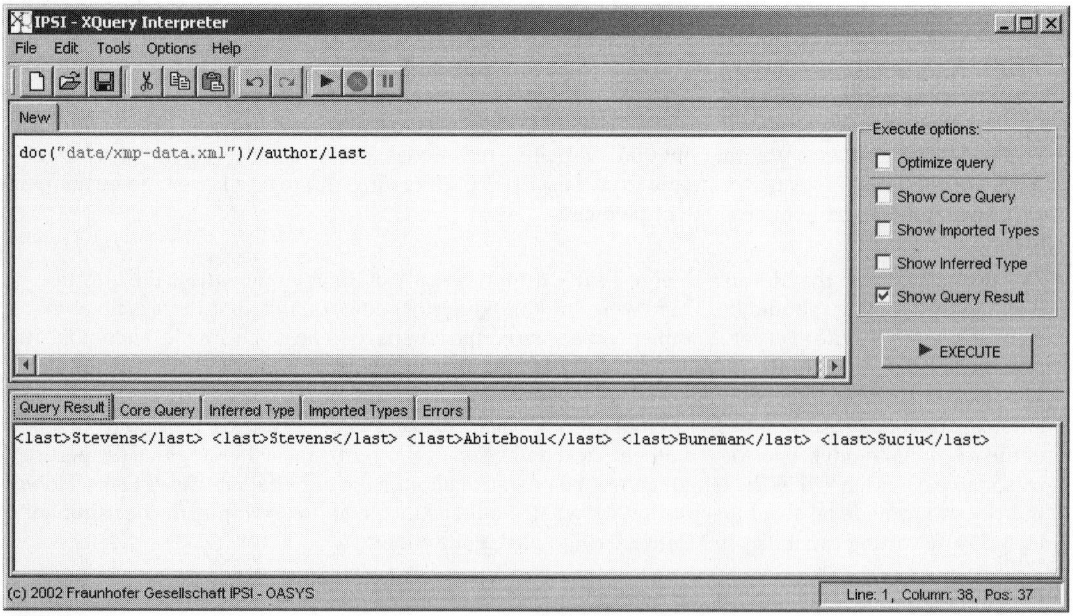

Figure 1-1

Usually when you use XPath 2.0, the program will be launched to process some particular source document. XQuery processors, however, are designed primarily to process multiple documents, so there is often no initial context for your expression. In this example the `doc()` function (which is described in Chapter 10 of this book) is used to select the document that you want to process, and everything else is selected within that document. The document selected in this query is found in the `examples` subfolder of the directory where IPSI-XQ is installed.

By comparison, there are relatively few pure XPath 2.0 products. The reason for this is that XPath isn't usually used on its own: it has always been designed as a specialized sublanguage that's intended for use in some kind of host environment.

One product that does include an XPath 2.0 processor is XML Spy. This is a commercial product, but you can get a free evaluation license for a limited period. You can download the code from `http://www.altova.com/`. Altova offers many different product configurations, so check that the one you are using includes the XPath 2.0 support.

To use the XPath 2.0 Analyzer within XML Spy, first load the document that you want to analyze. Then open up the XPath window, which you can do by selecting XML, then Evaluate XPath, from the menu. The default is to execute XPath 1.0: select the radio button labeled XPath 2.0 beta (by the time you read this, it may no longer be a beta release, of course).

You can then enter an XPath expression to run against the loaded document. The document I loaded was the text of Shakespeare's *Macbeth* in `macbeth.xml`, and my first attempt was the query «`distinct-values(//SPEAKER)`», which returned a somewhat alarming error message: "unexpected argument type, found First Witch". It turned out that this was because the `distinct-values()` function in the version of XML Spy I was using wasn't quite up-to-date with the latest version of the specs: this is a recurrent problem with all these products and will remain so until the final versions of the specifications are released. It appears that in XML Spy this query has to be written as shown in Figure 1-2.

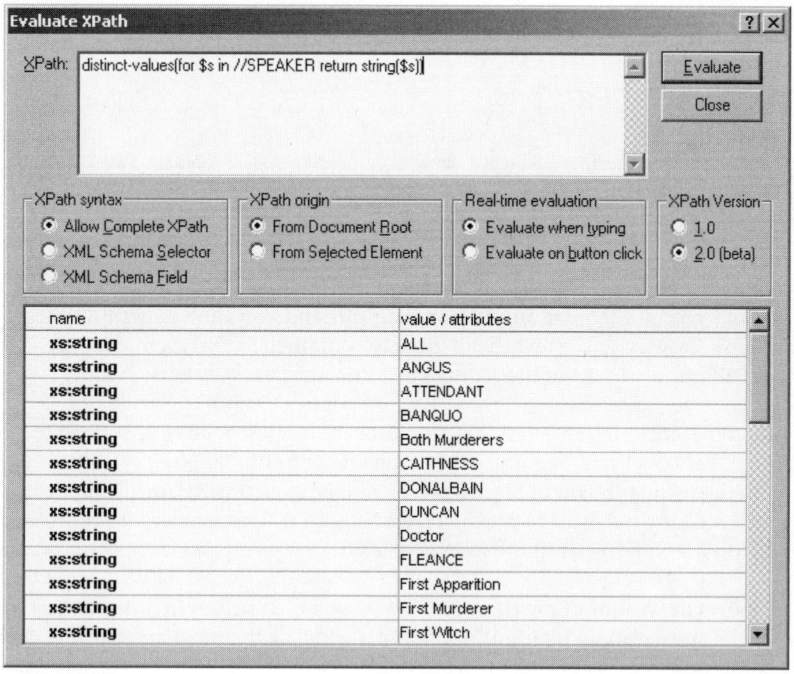

Figure 1-2

This expression uses the `distinct-values()` function, one of the many new functions available in XPath 2.0, to return a sequence that contains all the values appearing in a `<SPEAKER>` element anywhere in the document, with duplicate values removed. XML Spy appears to sort the results in alphabetical order, but the specification says that the order of the results is up to the implementation to decide.

Figure 1-3 shows another example using XML Spy. This one finds all the lines in the play containing the word "spot".

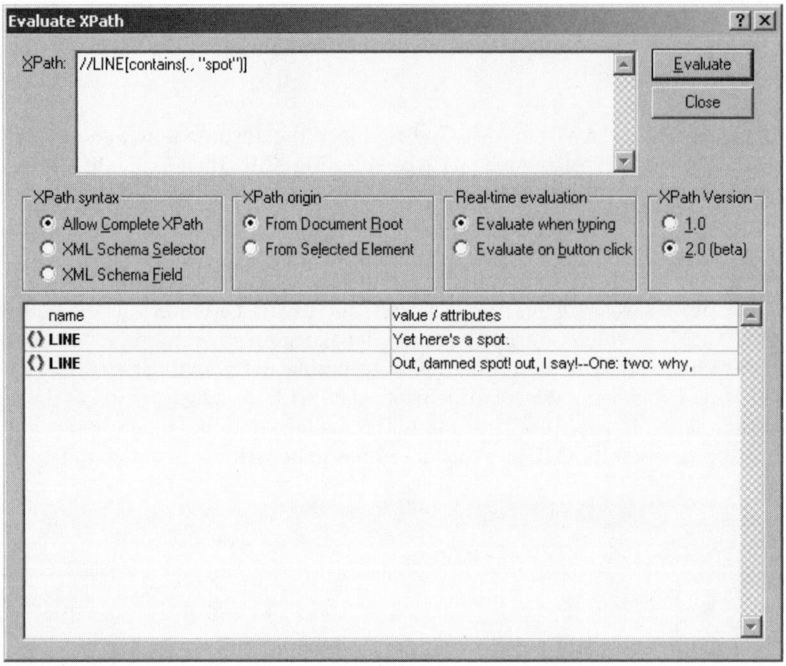

Figure 1-3

Since the result of every XPath expression is a sequence, it's not easy to get any formatted results out of this tool: you can't produce tabular output, for example, and you can't generate XML. If you select an element, XML Spy shows you the text that's directly contained in that element, even if there isn't any. No doubt the tool will improve a lot in the months to come: this is a very early beta.

Another product that includes an XPath 2.0 processor in its latest release is Stylus Studio (`http://www.StylusStudio.com`). I ran the same expression «`distinct-values(//SPEAKER)`» using Stylus Studio 5.1, with the results shown in Figure 1-4. Note that to enable XPath 2.0 support you need to click the button labeled v.2: by default, the product uses XPath 1.0. This version of Stylus Studio claims to support the XPath 2.0 working draft of November 2003.

This product shows the results of the `distinct-values()` function in order of first appearance: which works well for the speakers in a play, but might not always be the most appropriate choice.

In this particular example the results of the queries are strings. But if you enter an expression whose results are nodes in the source document, for example, the expression «`//SPEAKER[.="HECATE"]`»,

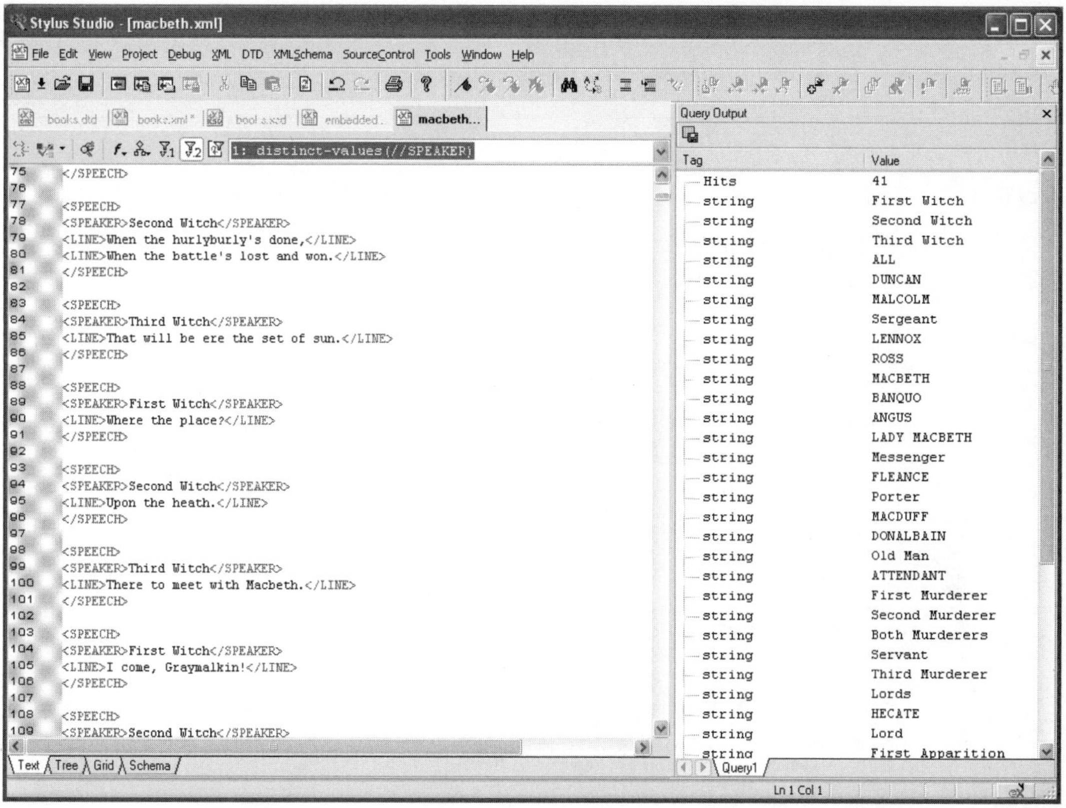

Figure 1-4

then the results will be shown in the right-hand pane as links, allowing you to click any node in the query results to locate the relevant element in the main editing window.

A tool that gives a much more graphic impression of how XPath works is the XPath Visualizer obtainable from http://www.vbxml.com/xpathvisualizer/. Unfortunately, however, this only supports XPath 1.0 at the time of writing. The tool works directly with Internet Explorer and its inbuilt XPath engine. To use it, unzip the download file into a suitable directory, and open the file XPathMain.htm. Then, browse to the source document you want to analyze, and click Process File. You can now enter XPath expressions, and see the nodes you have selected highlighted on the screen (use the arrow buttons to scroll to the next highlighted node). Figure 1-5 shows the same XPath expression as shown by XPath Visualizer.

One further XPath 2.0 implementation I have come across is Pathan 2: see http://software .decisionsoft.com/pathanIntro.html. This currently describes itself as an alpha release. It is a no-frills open-source implementation, that offers XPath only, and is designed as a component for integration into applications and tools.

The other way to use XPath 2.0 is from within XSLT 2.0. Currently, there are few XSLT 2.0 processors available: there is my own Saxon product (look for the latest release at http://saxon.sf.net/), and

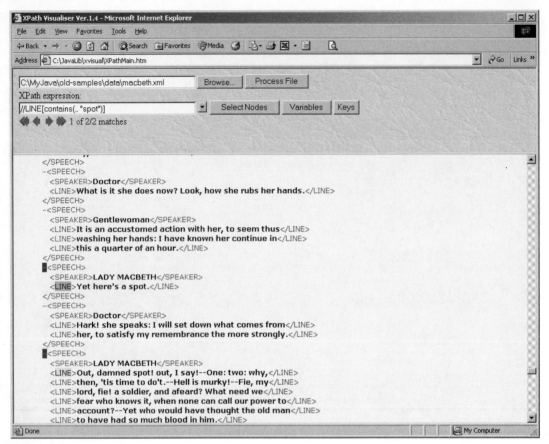

Figure 1-5

there is a beta release from Oracle, which has not been updated for some time (no doubt Oracle are waiting for the specifications to stabilize before they make their next shipment). Other processors are known to be under development, so keep an eye open for news. My companion book *XSLT 2.0 Programmer's Reference* explains the use of XSLT 2.0 in great detail, and XPath 2.0 plays a significant role in this.

Here's an example of a complete XSLT 2.0 stylesheet that uses XPath 2.0 features to get a count of all the words appearing in a document (perhaps the text of *Macbeth*), together with the frequency of each word:

```
<?xml version="1.0" encoding="iso-8859-1"?>
<xsl:stylesheet
    version="2.0"
    xmlns:xsl="http://www.w3.org/1999/XSL/Transform">

<xsl:output method="xml" indent="yes"/>

<xsl:template match="/">
    <wordcount>
```

```
      <xsl:for-each-group group-by="." select="
            for $w in tokenize(string(.), '\W+') return lower-case($w)">
        <xsl:sort select="count(current-group())" order="descending"/>
        <word word="{current-grouping-key()}"
              frequency="{count(current-group())}"/>
      </xsl:for-each-group>
    </wordcount>
  </xsl:template>

</xsl:stylesheet>
```

You can run this using the Saxon XSLT processor with a command such as:

```
java -jar c:\saxon\saxon8.jar macbeth.xml wordcount.xsl
```

to produce output which starts like this:

```
<?xml version="1.0" encoding="UTF-8"?>
<wordcount>
   <word word="the" frequency="735"/>
   <word word="and" frequency="567"/>
   <word word="to" frequency="405"/>
   <word word="i" frequency="373"/>
   <word word="of" frequency="348"/>
   <word word="macbeth" frequency="291"/>
   <word word="a" frequency="255"/>
   <word word="that" frequency="237"/>
   <word word="in" frequency="208"/>
   <word word="you" frequency="207"/>
   <word word="s" frequency="199"/>
   <word word="is" frequency="192"/>
   <word word="my" frequency="192"/>
```

This stylesheet uses a number of new XSLT 2.0 features, notably the `<xsl:for-each-group>` instruction which provides a long-awaited grouping facility for XSLT. It also makes heavy use of new constructs in XPath 2.0: the `tokenize()` function, which splits a string using a regular expression, the `lower-case()` function which converts text to lower case, and a «for» expression which applies the `lower-case()` function to every string in a sequence of strings.

Where XPath fits in the XML Family

XPath 2.0 is published by the World Wide Web Consortium (W3C) and fits into the XML family of standards, most of which are also developed by W3C. In this section, I will try to explain the relationship of XPath 2.0 to other standards and specifications in the XML family.

XPath and XSLT

XSLT started life as part of a bigger language called *XSL* (*Extensible Stylesheet Language*). As the name implies, XSL was (and is) intended to define the formatting and presentation of XML documents for display on screen, on paper, or in the spoken word. As the development of XSL proceeded, it became clear that this was usually a two-stage process; first a structural transformation, in which elements are selected, grouped and reordered, and then a formatting process in which the resulting elements are rendered as ink on paper, or pixels on the screen. It was recognized that these two stages were quite independent, so XSL was split into two parts, XSLT for defining transformations, and "the rest"—which is still officially called XSL, though most people prefer to call it XSL-FO *(XSL Formatting Objects)*—for the formatting stage.

Halfway through the development of XSLT 1.0, it was recognized that there was a significant overlap between the expression syntax in XSLT for selecting parts of a document, and the XPointer language being developed for linking from one document to another. To avoid having two separate but overlapping expression languages, the two committees decided to join forces and define a single language, XPath, which would serve both purposes. XPath 1.0 was published on the same day as XSLT 1.0, November 16, 1999.

XPath acts as a sublanguage within an XSLT stylesheet. An XPath expression may be used for numerical calculations or string manipulations, or for testing boolean conditions, but its most characteristic use is to identify parts of the input document to be processed. For example, the following instruction outputs the average price of all the books in the input document:

```
<xsl:value-of select="avg(//book/@price)"/>
```

Here the `<xsl:value-of>` element is an instruction defined in the XSLT standard, which causes a value to be written to the output document. The `select` attribute contains an XPath expression, which calculates the value to be written: specifically, the average value of the `price` attributes on all the `<book>` elements. (The `avg()` function is new in XPath 2.0.)

As this example shows, the XSLT and XPath languages are very intimately related.

In previous editions of this book I covered both languages together, but this time I have given each language its own volume, mainly because the amount of material had become too large for one book, but also because there are an increasing number of people who use XPath without also using XSLT. For the XSLT user, though, I'm afraid that at times you may have to keep both books open on your desk at once.

XPath and the InfoSet

XPath is primarily a language for extracting information from XML documents. However, the effect of an XPath expression isn't defined directly in terms of the lexical XML structure. XPath uses an abstraction of an XML document that consists, as we have seen, of a tree containing seven different kinds of nodes. This model itself is defined in terms of the XML Information Set, usually called the InfoSet, for short. In this section we'll take a quick look at the relationship of XPath to the InfoSet: we will return to this in more detail in Chapter 2.

XPath is designed to work on the information carried by an XML document, not on the raw document itself. The tree model is an abstraction of the original lexical XML, in which information that's deemed significant is retained, and other information is discarded. For example, you can see the attribute names and values, but you can't see whether the attribute was written in single or double quotes, you can't see what order the attributes were in, and you can't tell whether or not they were written on the same line.

One messy detail is that there have been many attempts to define exactly what constitutes the essential information content of a well-formed XML document, as distinct from its accidental punctuation. All attempts so far have come up with slightly different answers. The *XML Information Set* definition (or InfoSet), which may be found at `http://www.w3.org/TR/xml-infoset`, is the most definitive attempt to provide a common vocabulary for the content of XML documents.

Unfortunately, the InfoSet came too late to make all the standards consistent. For example, some treat comments as significant, others not; some treat the choice of namespace prefixes as significant, others take them as irrelevant. I shall describe in Chapter 2 exactly how XPath defines the tree model of XML, and how it differs in finer points of detail from some of the other definitions such as the Document Object Model or DOM.

Another more elaborate model of the information content of an XML document is the *post schema validation infoset* or PSVI. This contains the significant information from the source document, augmented with information taken from its XML Schema. It identifies which types in the schema were used to validate each element and attribute, and as such it underpins the notion of nodes having a type annotation and a typed value, which as we saw earlier are the two most important changes in the data model for XML documents introduced in version 2.0.

XML Namespaces

As far as XPath is concerned *XML namespaces* are an essential part of the XML standard. If a document doesn't conform with the XML Namespaces Recommendation, then you can't use it with XPath. This doesn't mean that the document actually has to use namespaces, but it does mean that it can't misuse them.

Here's a quick reminder of how namespaces work:

❑   Namespaces are identified by a Uniform Resource Identifier (URI). This can take a number of forms. The most common form is the familiar URL, for example `http://www.wrox.com/namespace`. The detailed form of the URI doesn't matter, but it is a good idea to choose one that will be unique. One good way of achieving this is to use the URL of your own Web site. But don't let this confuse you into thinking that there must be something on the Web site for the URL to point to. The namespace URI is simply a string that you have chosen to be different from other people's namespace URIs; it doesn't need to point to anything.

❑   The latest version of the spec, XML Namespaces 1.1, allows you to use an International Resource Identifier (IRI) rather than a URI. The main difference is that an IRI permits characters from any alphabet, whereas a URI is confined to ASCII. In practice, most XML parsers have always allowed you to use any characters you like in a namespace URI.

❑   Since namespace URIs are often rather long and use special characters such as «/», they are not used in full as part of the element and attribute names. Instead, each namespace used in a document can be given a short nickname, and this nickname is used as a prefix of the element and attribute names. It doesn't matter what prefix you choose, because the real name of the element or attribute is determined only by its namespace URI and its local name (the part of the name after the prefix). For example, all my examples use the prefix `xsl` to refer to the namespace URI `http://www.w3.org/1999/XSL/Transform`, but you could equally well use the prefix `xslt`, so long as you use it consistently.

❑   For element names, you can also declare a default namespace URI, which is to be associated with unprefixed element names. The default namespace URI, however, does not apply to unprefixed attribute names.

A namespace prefix is declared using a special pseudo.attribute within any element tag, with the form:

```
xmlns:prefix = "namespace-URI"
```

This namespace prefix can be used for the name of that element, for its attributes, and for any element or attribute name contained in that element. The default namespace, which is used for elements having no prefix (but not for attributes), is similarly declared using a pseudo-attribute:

```
xmlns = "namespace-URI"
```

It's important to remember when using XPath that the true name of an element is the combination of its local name (the part after any prefix) and the namespace URI. For example the name of the element `<a xmlns="http://ns.example.com/"/>` is the combination of the local name «a» and the namespace «`http://ns.example.com/`». A step in a path expression will only match this element if both the local name and the namespace URI match. The XPath expression doesn't have to use the same prefix as the element that's being matched, but the prefixes do have to refer to the same URI.

XML Namespaces 1.1 became a Recommendation on February 4, 2004, and XPath 2.0 can in principle work with either 1.0 or 1.1. Apart from the largely cosmetic change from URIs to IRIs mentioned earlier, the main innovation is the ability to undeclare a namespace, using a namespace undeclaration of the form «`xmlns:prefix=""`». This new feature doesn't have a great deal of effect on XPath itself, though it does create complications for XSLT and XQuery, which unlike XPath have instructions to create new nodes.

XPath and XPointer

One of the original reasons that XPath was defined in its own W3C specification, rather than as part of XSLT, was so that it could be used independently by the XPointer specification. Subsequently, XPointer has had a checkered history.

The intended role of XPointer is to define the syntax of fragment identifiers in URIs (that is, the part of the URI after the «#» sign) when referencing into the detail of an XML document. The theory is that the syntax of a URI fragment identifier depends on the media type of the resource identified by the URI. With the familiar HTML URIs, the fragment identifier is the value of an «id» or «name» attribute of an HTML element within the document. For XML, people wanted something more powerful. In particular, the hyperlinking community wanted to be able to reference into an XML document without requiring the document author to do anything special (like creating uniquely named anchors) to make this possible. XLink, the hyperlinking standard, and XPointer, which it used for defining cross-references, were closely coupled in everyone's minds. Hence the use of XPath as a general-purpose, powerful addressing mechanism.

XPointer remained work-in-progress for a long time. I don't know all the reasons for this, but I suspect that the main underlying cause was that it was too ambitious. In addition, I think that the success of the XSLT model for publishing content on the Web rather took the wind out of the sails of XLink. XSLT allows you to model your information in XML in any way that you like, and then convert it to HTML for presentation on the Web. If you are going to end up generating HTML as your presentation format, then it doesn't make much difference whether your XML represents inter-document relationships using XLink or in some other way. In fact, there's a strong argument for modeling relationships using tags that represent the meaning of the relationship, just as you do when modeling business objects and their properties. If an employee is represented by an `<employee>` element, and a department by a `<department>` element, then most people will choose to represent the relationship from an employee to a department using an element or attribute called «department», not by one called «xlink:href».

XLink managed to decouple itself from XPointer, and became a Recommendation on June 27, 2001. At that time, XPointer was a Last Call Working Draft, published six months earlier. The spec had retreated from Candidate Recommendation status because of technical problems with namespaces. An XPath expression contains element and attribute names such as «mf:product» that use namespace prefixes. The question is, where are these prefixes defined? Does it use the prefixes defined in the source document, or those defined in the target document? What happens if the XPointer is used in a free-standing URI reference, that isn't itself part of an XML document? This problem was discovered late in the day, and the language designers responded to this problem by going back to the drawing board, and devising an extension to XPointer that allowed the namespace prefixes to be defined within the XPointer itself.

Perhaps more importantly, XPointer hit a serious political problem in that it appeared to use a technique that Sun had patented. Sun proposed terms and conditions under which they agreed to license this patent, but the terms and conditions were not acceptable to everyone and this led to a fierce debate on patent policy in the W3C which overshadowed the original technical issues.

In the end, the XPointer specification was refactored into a number of separate modules. There is a framework specification which allows the definition of an extensible number of referencing schemes. The most basic scheme is to identify an element by its ID value, just as with an HTML fragment identifier. The next refinement is the element() scheme, which adds the ability to use hierarchic references: for example «element(/1/3)» refers to the third child of the first child of the root node. The full xpointer() scheme, which contains the original XPath-based syntax, has been languishing at Working Draft status since 2002 (see http://www.w3.org/TR/xptr-xpointer/) and since there is no longer an active Linking Working Group, it seems unlikely to progress further.

XPath and XQuery

XPath 2.0 is defined as a subset of XQuery 1.0; or to put it another way, XQuery has been designed as an extension of XPath 2.0. Unlike the embedding of XPath in XSLT, where there are two distinct languages with one invoking the other, XQuery is designed as a single integrated language that incorporates XPath as a subset. What this means in practice is that in XQuery (unlike XSLT), you can freely nest XQuery expressions and XPath expressions. For example, you can use an element constructor inside a path expression, like this:

```
<lookup><data/><data/></lookup>//data[code=$value]
```

XQuery is therefore more composable than XSLT (composability is the ability to construct any expression by combining simpler expressions), but the price it pays for this is that the syntax is not pure XML.

Although XQuery uses XPath as a subset, the XQuery specification doesn't actually refer to the XPath specification; rather it bodily copies the text of the XPath specification as part of the XQuery specification (this is all done, of course, by maintaining a single XML master document, with XSLT stylesheets used to generate the XPath and XQuery versions of the specification). The reason XQuery copies the XPath specification rather than referencing it is because XQuery doesn't simply allow you to use legal XPath expressions as subexpressions in your query, it also allows you to use XQuery expressions as operands to XPath constructs, thus changing the scope of the XPath language.

XPath and XML Schemas

As we have already seen, integration with XML Schema was listed as the first of the goals in the XPath 2.0 requirements document. Achieving this integration has created an enormous upheaval in the language semantics, and although this is something that will be a hidden change below the surface for many users, it does actually have a profound impact.

XPath 1.0 was a weakly typed language. It had types, but it had very few of them, and very few rules about what operations were applicable to what types of data. The general model was that if you supplied an integer where (say) a string was expected, the integer would be quietly converted to a string. Another example of a weakly typed language is JavaScript.

The conventional wisdom for database query languages is that they should be strongly typed. A strongly typed language has lots of rules about how you can use values, depending on their type. Many programming languages, such as Java, for example, are also strongly typed.

Although weak typing appears to be more user-friendly, it has many disadvantages. One of the main disadvantages is that the processor isn't able to do so much work at compile time, instead it has to make most of the decisions at runtime. One of the key roles of a database query language is to identify, while compiling the query, which indexes can be used to execute the query efficiently. Unlike optimization in a conventional language such as C or Java which might give you code that runs three or four times faster, optimization in a database query language can produce a thousand-fold improvement in speed, or more. Therefore, anything that can be done in the language design to give a query optimizer a better chance is considered a Good Thing.

Another difference is that in the weak typing world, the philosophy is generally to avoid runtime errors. XPath 1.0 works on the principle that if you ask a silly question, you get a silly answer. Ask it whether the string "apple" equals the boolean true, and the answer is yes. (If you ask whether the string "false" equals the boolean false, the answer, more surprisingly, is no). By contrast the philosophy in the strong typing world is that if you ask a silly question you get an error message. There are a number of reasons why this might be considered preferable, but one of the reasons is that if you ask a silly question against a multi-gigabyte database, it can take many hours to come up with the silly answer.

So the influence of database query language thinking led to pressure for XPath to become more strongly typed. This was one of the factors driving the adoption of XML Schema. The XSLT group were also pushing in this direction, however, for rather different reasons. It was recognized that when document types are managed for a large community of users, managing the schema (or DTDs) for the documents and managing the stylesheets are two activities that need to be closely coordinated. When the schema changes (as it does, frequently) then the stylesheet needs to change too. There is a clear correspondence between declarations in the schema and rules in the stylesheet. Therefore, it was argued, there ought to be some linkage between the schema and the stylesheet to make it easier to keep the two in sync, and to report errors if they were out of sync.

A move towards stronger typing didn't have to mean support for XML Schema, but given the way working groups in W3C review each others' work and meet to reconcile their differences, it was almost inevitable.

One of the big challenges was to introduce schema-derived types in such a way that they were an optional feature, so that users who had no schema (and perhaps no wish for one) could carry on as they were. The result is a language that is in some ways a strange hybrid between strong typing and weak typing. If this seems odd, it is worth reflecting that XML handles a vast spectrum from very highly structured data to very loosely structured documents, and that this ability to span the full range of information management requirements is one of its greatest strengths. So it shouldn't be surprising that XPath too is designed to handle a wide spectrum.

XPath, the DOM, and Java

The Document Object Model or DOM has origins that predate XML: it was originally the programming interface used to navigate your way around the objects on an HTML page, and was only later adapted so that it could handle XML as well. Later still, support for namespaces was bolted on. The DOM is a W3C specification that has grown considerably over the years. It is defined in a language-neutral way, but there are specific language bindings for a number of languages. Most users will be familiar either with the Microsoft implementation of the DOM, or with the Java language bindings.

Microsoft's MSXML product was probably the first to integrate an XPath processor into a DOM implementation. In fact, they did this before XPath was fully standardized, and in MSXML3 the default processor is still a non-standard variant of XPath (if you want real XPath, you have to ask for it specially, by setting the `selectionLanguage` property of the `Document` object to «XPath»).

The idea behind this interface is that instead of navigating your way laboriously to the required nodes in a DOM document using low-level methods such as `getFirstChild()`, `getNextSibling()`, `getAttribute()`, and so on, you should be able to select the set of nodes you want using a single call that supplies an XPath expression as an argument. In the Microsoft version of the interface, there are two methods that do this: `selectNode()` is used when you know that the XPath expression will select a single node in the tree, and `selectNodes()` is used when you want to select multiple nodes. The result is a `Node` or a `NodeList` respectively, which you can then manipulate using the normal DOM methods.

One of the drawbacks of this is that it doesn't allow you to use the full capability of XPath. If you want to count how many nodes satisfy a certain condition, for example, the only way to find out is to retrieve them all and then count them in the application. There is no way in this interface of invoking an XPath expression that returns a number, a string, or a boolean, as distinct from a node or a set of nodes.

Another limitation of the original Microsoft interface is that it doesn't allow you much control over the context of the XPath expression. For example, there is no way of supplying values of variables used in the expression. But set against these limitations, the API is delightfully simple to use.

Various Java implementations of the DOM also tried to provide XPath capabilities, many of them modeled directly on the Microsoft API, but some much more sophisticated. The Xalan XSLT processor, for example, provides an XPath API that works with the Xerces implementation of the DOM. This actually has two layers. The XPathAPI class provides a number of simple static methods such as `selectSingleNode()` and `selectNodeList()` which can be seen as parallels to the methods in Microsoft's API, though they are actually rather more complex (and therefore powerful). Underneath this is a much richer API that provides anything you could possibly want to control the execution of XPath statements, including, for example, the ability to compile expressions that can be evaluated later multiple times, with different settings for variables in the expression. This underlying API looks as if it was designed to provide the interface between the XSLT and XPath components of the Xalan product, so as you might expect it is a very rich and complex interface.

In the Java world there have been two serious attempts to provide alternatives to the DOM that are simpler, better integrated with Java, and more up-to-date in terms of XML specifications. One of these is JDOM (www.jdom.org), the other is called DOM4J (www.dom4j.org). Both have their merits and their band of enthusiastic followers. JDOM is pleasantly easy to use but has the major drawback that it uses concrete Java classes rather than interfaces, which means there is no scope for multiple implementations to coexist. DOM4J is a much richer API, which also means it is more complex. Both share the objective of being well integrated with the Java way of doing things, and both include XPath support as a standard part of the API.

A standard binding for XPath in the DOM came only with DOM level 3 (http://www.w3.org/TR/DOM-Level-3-XPath/), which became a W3C Candidate Recommendation in March 2003. (A Candidate Recommendation is rather like a beta release of software, which means that the specification is considered finished enough to ship, but might still have bugs that need fixing.) This is, of course, an interface to XPath 1.0 rather than XPath 2.0. Like the other DOM specifications, it includes an abstract interface defined in the CORBA IDL language, together with concrete interfaces for Java and JavaScript (or ECMAScript, to use its its official name). The Java interface treads a reasonable middle ground between simplicity and functionality: perhaps its most complex area is the way it delivers expression results of different types.

At the time of writing, there is an activity underway in the Java Community Process to define a standard Java API for XPath that will form part of JAXP 1.3 (JAXP is the Java API for XML Processing). Although this is not yet finalized, public previews have been made available (http://jcp.org/aboutJava/communityprocess/review/jsr206/index.html). This API does not simply endorse the DOM level 3 API. The main reasons for this decision appear to be that the designers wanted an API that was more Java-like (not just a Java binding of a CORBA IDL interface), that could be used with object models other than DOM, and that was easily extensible to handle XPath 2.0 in the future.

The net result of this is that there are quite a few different XPath APIs to choose from in Java. Hopefully, the JAXP 1.3 initiative will unify this, and will also succeed in its goal of being extensible to XPath 2.0, so that we end up with a single way of invoking XPath expressions from Java, that is independent of the choice of object model.

So much for the background and positioning of XPath 2.0. Let's look now at the essential characteristics of XPath 2.0 as a language.

XPath 2.0 as a Language

This section attempts to draw out some of the key features of the design of the XPath language.

The Syntax of XPath

The XPath syntax has some unusual features, which reflect the fact that it amalgamates ideas from a number of different sources.

One can identify three different syntactic styles within XPath expressions:

❑ *Conventional programming expressions*: This allows the same kind of expressions, infix operators, and function calls as many other programming languages; an example is an expression such as

«$x + 1 = round($y) mod 3». Such expressions trace their roots via programming languages such as Algol and Fortran back to the notations of elementary mathematics.

❑ *Path expressions*: These perform hierarchic selection of a node within a tree, an example is «/a/b//c». These expressions can be seen as a generalization of the syntax used by operating systems to identify files within a hierarchic filestore.

❑ *Predicate logic*: This includes the «for», «some» and «every» expressions, for example «for $i in //item[@price > 30] return $i/@code». These expressions, which are new in XPath 2.0, derive from the tradition of database query languages (SQL, the object database language OQL, and precursors to XQuery) which can be seen as adaptations of the notation of mathematical symbolic logic.

Some other factors that have influenced the design of the XPath syntax include:

❑ A decision that XPath should have no reserved words. This means that any name that is legal as an XML element name (which includes names such as «and» and «for») should be legal in a path expression, without any need for escaping. As a result, all names used with some other role, for example function names, variable names, operator names, and keywords such as «for» have to be recognizable by their context.

❑ In both the original applications for XPath (that is, XSLT and XPointer) the language was designed to be embedded within the attributes of an XML document. It therefore has no mechanisms of its own for character escaping, relying instead on the mechanisms available at the XML level (such as numeric character references and entity references). This also made the designers reluctant to use symbols such as «&&» which would require heavy escaping. This principle has been abandoned in XPath 2.0 with the introduction of the operators «<<» and «>>»; however, these operators are not likely to be used very often.

❑ There was originally an expectation that XPath expressions (especially in an XPointer environment) would often be used as fragment identifiers in a URI. As we have seen, this usage of XPointer never really took off—though there are XML database engines such as Software AG's Tamino that allow queries in the form of XPath expressions to be submitted in this way. This factor meant there was a reluctance to use special characters such as «#», «%», and «?» that have special significance in URIs.

Despite its disparate syntactic roots and its lexical quirks, XPath has managed to integrate these different kinds of expression surprisingly well. In particular, it has retained full composability, so any kind of expression can be nested inside any other.

An Embedded Language

XPath is designed as an embedded language, not as a stand-alone language in its own right. It is designed to provide a language module that can be incorporated into other languages.

This design assumption has two specific consequences:

❑ Firstly, the language does not need to have every conceivable piece of functionality. In the language of computer science, it does not need to be computationally complete. In more practical terms, it can be restricted to being able to access variables but not to declare them, to call functions but not to define them, to navigate around nodes in a tree but not to create new nodes.

❑   Secondly, the language can depend on a context established by the host language in which it is embedded. If an embedded language is to be well integrated with a host language, then they should share information so that the user does not need to declare things twice, once for each language. The information that XPath shares with its host language is called the context. This can be divided into information that's available at compile time (the static context), and information that's not available until runtime (the dynamic context). Both aspects of the XPath context are described in Chapter 4 of this book.

A Language for Processing Sequences

The striking feature of the XML data model is that the information is hierarchic. The relationship from an element to its children is intrinsically a one-to-many relationship. Moreover, the relationship is inherently ordered. Sometimes you don't care about the order, but it's part of the nature of XML that the order of elements is deemed to be significant.

This means that when you write an expression such as «author» (which is short for «child::author», and selects all the <author> elements that are children of the context node) then, in principle, the result is a sequence of elements. Very often you know that there will be exactly one author, or that there will be at most one, but in general, the result is a sequence of zero or more elements. The XPath language therefore has to make it convenient to manipulate sequences.

One of the notable consequences of this is the decision that the «=» operator should work on sequences. Suppose a book can have multiple authors. When you write an expression such as «book[author="Kay"]», you are selecting all the <book> elements that have «Kay» as one of their authors: the expression is a shorthand for «book[some $a in child::author satisfies $a="Kay"]». It would be very tedious if users had to write this extended expression every time, even in cases where they know there will only be one author, so the language builds this functionality into the semantics of the «=» operator. This feature is known by the rather grand name of *implicit existential quantification*. It's very convenient in many simple cases, though it can trip you up with more complex expressions, especially those involving negation.

When you apply this construct to an element that can only have zero or one occurrences, or to an attribute (which can never have more than one occurrence), the same definition comes into play. A test such as «book[discount>10]» will always be false when applied to a book that has no discount. This works in a very similar way to null values in SQL, except that it does not use three-valued logic. In SQL, the corresponding query is «select book where discount > 10». In this query, a book that has no discount (that is, where the discount is null) will not be returned. However, because of the way SQL defines three-valued logic, the query «select book where not(discount > 10)» will also fail to select any book whose discount is null. By contrast, XPath uses conventional two-valued logic, so the expression «book[not(discount>10)]» will return such books.

Some of the people on the XQuery working group whose background was in the design of database query languages were never very happy with the implicit semantics of the «=» operator in XPath, nor with the absence of three-valued logic. However, after much debate, these features of the XPath 1.0 semantics survived intact. The reason, I think, is that for SQL a cell in a table always contains either zero or one values, and "null" represents the zero case. For XML, a child element can have zero, one, or more occurrences within its parent, and (despite the invention of xsi:nil by the XML Schema people) the normal way of representing absent data in XML is by the absence of a child element or attribute, which means that selecting that element will return an empty sequence. The empty sequence in XPath therefore fulfils the same kind of role as the null value in the relational model, but in the context of a model that allows zero to many values, where SQL only allows zero or one.

XPath 1.0 only supported one kind of sequence, namely a set of nodes. Some people liked to think of this as an unordered collection, others as a sequence of nodes in document order, but this doesn't really make any real difference: it wasn't possible to represent a collection in an arbitrary user-defined order, such as employees in order of date of birth. XPath 2.0 has generalized this in two directions: firstly, sequences can now be in any order you like (and can contain duplicates), and secondly, you can have sequences of values (such as strings, numbers, or dates) as well as sequences of nodes.

Many of the operators in XPath 1.0 generalize quite nicely to support arbitrary sequences. For example, the «=» operator still matches if any item in the sequence matches, so you can write for example «@color = ("red", "green")» which will be true if the value of the color attribute is either red or green. Other operators, notably the «/» operator used in path expressions and the «|» operator used to combine two sets of nodes, only really make sense in the context of sets containing no duplicates, and these have not been generalized to work on arbitrary sequences.

Types Based on XML Schema

I've already discussed the relationship of XPath 2.0 to XML Schema, so I won't labor it again. But the type system of XPath is something that is highly distinctive, so it deserves a place as one of the key characteristics that gives the language its flavor.

I'll be exploring the type system in depth in Chapter 3. Here, I'll just give a few highlights, as a taste of things to come.

- ❑ We need to distinguish the types of the values that XPath can manipulate from the types that can appear as annotations on nodes.

- ❑ Atomic types can appear in both roles: You can declare an XPath variable of type integer, and you can also validate the content of an element or attribute as an integer, following which the element or attribute will be annotated with this type.

- ❑ Node kinds, such as element, attribute, and comment, appear as types of XPath values (I call these *item types*) but never as type annotations. You can't annotate an attribute as a comment, or even as an attribute, you can only annotate it with a simple type defined in XML Schema.

- ❑ Schema types divide into two groups: complex types, and simple types. Simple types divide further into atomic types, list types, and union types. All of these are either built-in types defined in the XML Schema specification, or user-defined types defined in a user-written schema. All of these can be used as type annotations on nodes, if the node has been validated against the appropriate type definition in the schema. But the only schema types that can be used for freestanding values, that is, for values that don't exist as the content of a node, are the atomic types.

- ❑ It's possible to have nodes that haven't been validated against any schema. These nodes are labeled as untyped in the case of elements, or untypedAtomic in the case of attributes.

- ❑ Whenever you use a node in an XPath expression in a context where an atomic value (or a sequence of atomic values) is expected, the typed value of the node is extracted. For example, if you write «@a + 1», the typed value of the attribute «a» is used. If this is a number, all is well.

If it's some other type such as string or date, the expression fails with a type error. But if the value is untyped, that is, if there is no schema, then weak typing comes into play: the value is automatically converted to the required type, in this case, to a number.

This is just a foretaste: the full explanations will appear in Chapter 3.

Summary

This introductory chapter offers an overview of XPath in general, and XPath 2.0 in particular. It tried to answer questions such as:

- ❑ What kind of language is it?
- ❑ Where does it fit into the XML family?
- ❑ Where does it come from and why was it designed the way it is?

We established that XPath is an expression language, and we looked at some of the implications of this in terms of the properties of the language and its relationship to other languages such as XSLT and XQuery. We tried to find some rationale for the large collection of new features that have been added to the language, and for the more fundamental changes to its underlying semantics.

Now it's time to start taking an in-depth look inside XPath 2.0 to see how it works. The next three chapters are about important concepts: the data model, the type system, and the evaluation context. Once you understand these concepts, you should have little difficulty using the language constructs that are introduced later in the book.

The Data Model

This chapter looks in some detail at the XPath data model, in particular the structure of the tree representation of XML documents. An important message here is that XPath expressions do not operate on XML documents as text, they operate on the abstract tree-like information structure represented by the text.

XPath is an expression language. Every expression takes one or more values as its inputs, and produces a value as its output. The purpose of this chapter is to explain exactly what these values can be.

One of the things an expression language tries to achieve is that wherever you can use a value, you can replace it with an expression that is evaluated to produce that value. So if «2+2» is a valid expression, then «(6-4)+(1+1)» should also be a valid expression. This property is called *composability*: expressions can be used anywhere that values are permitted. One of the important features that make a language composable is that the possible results of an expression are the same as the possible inputs. This feature is called *closure*: every expression produces a result that is in the same space of possible values as the space from which the inputs are drawn.

The role of the data model is to describe this space of possible values.

Changes in 2.0

The way in which an XML document is modeled as a tree has changed relatively little since XPath 1.0: the main change is that nodes can now be annotated with a type that is derived from validation against an XML Schema, and as a result, the content of a node can now be viewed as a typed value (which might be, for example, an integer, a string, or a sequence of dates, depending on the type annotation).

XPath 1.0 only supported three atomic types: boolean, double-precision floating point, and string. This has been generalized to allow all the types defined in XML Schema, though the host language may restrict this to a subset of these types.

XPath 1.0 supported node-sets (unordered collections of nodes, with no duplicates). XPath 2.0 generalizes this to support sequences, which are ordered and may contain duplicates, and which may contain atomic values as well as nodes.

Sequences

Sometimes object programming languages introduce their data model with the phrase "everything is an object". In the XPath 2.0 data model, the equivalent statement is that every value is a *sequence*.

By *value*, we mean anything that can be the result of an expression or an operand of an expression. In XPath 2.0, the value of every expression is a sequence of zero or more items. Of course XPath, like other languages, can use atomic values such as integers and booleans. But in XPath, an atomic value is just a special case of a sequence: it is a sequence of length one.

The items in a sequence are ordered. This means that the sequence (1, 2, 3) is different from the sequence (2, 3, 1). The XPath 2.0 data model does not have any direct means of representing unordered collections. Instead, where ordering is unimportant, it makes this part of the definition of an operator on sequences: for example, the `distinct-values()` function returns a number of values with no defined ordering, and with duplicates disallowed, but the result is still presented as a sequence. The ordering might sometimes be arbitrary and left to the implementation to determine, but there is always an ordering.

The items in a sequence are always numbered starting at 1. The number of items in a sequence (and therefore, the number assigned to the last item in the sequence) can be obtained using the `count()` function. (The functions available in XPath 2.0, such as `count()` and `distinct-values()`, are listed in Chapter 10.)

Sequences have no properties other than the items they contain. Two sequences that contain the same items are indistinguishable, so there is no concept of a sequence having an identity separate from its contents.

A sequence can be empty. Because two sequences that contain the same items are indistinguishable, there is no difference between one empty sequence and another, and so we often refer to *the* empty sequence rather than to *an* empty sequence. Empty sequences, as we shall see, are often used to represent absent data in a similar way to nulls in SQL.

The items in a sequence are either `atomic values`, or `nodes`. An atomic value is a value such as an integer, a string, a boolean, or a date. A node is a structural part of a tree; trees are used to represent the information in XML documents. We will examine atomic values and nodes in much greater detail later in the chapter. Most sequences either consist entirely of nodes, or entirely of atomic values, but this isn't always the case; it's quite legitimate (and occasionally useful) to have a sequence that consists, say, of two strings, an integer, and three element nodes.

The relationships between sequences, items, atomic values and nodes are summarized in the simple UML diagram in Figure 2-1.

> *UML (the Unified Modeling Language) provides a set of diagrammatic conventions for object-oriented analysis and design. For information about UML, see* `http://www.omg.org/technology/uml/index.htm`

This shows that:

❑   A sequence contains zero or more items

❑   An item is itself a sequence

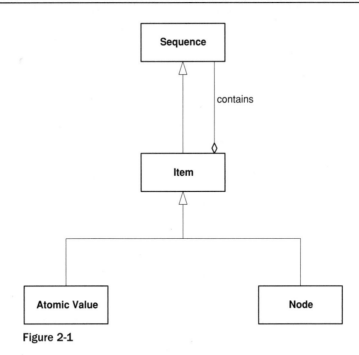

Figure 2-1

- ❑ An atomic value is an item
- ❑ A node is an item

Although we talk about a sequence containing nodes, this doesn't mean that a node can only be in one sequence. Far from it. It might be less confusing if we spoke of the sequence containing references to nodes rather than containing the nodes themselves, or if we used a verb other than "contains"—but sadly, we don't.

A sequence cannot contain or reference other sequences. This is an aspect of the data model that some people find surprising, but there are good reasons for it. The usual explanations given are:

- ❑ Sequences in the XPath data model are designed primarily to represent lists as defined in XML Schema. For example, XML Schema allows the value of an attribute to be a list of integers. These lists cannot be nested, so it wouldn't make sense to allow nested lists in the XPath model either.

- ❑ Sequences that contain sequences would allow trees and graphs to be constructed. But these would bear no relationship to the trees used to represent XML documents. In the XPath data model we need a representation of trees that is faithful to XML; we don't need another kind of tree that bears no relationship to the XML model.

The effect of this rule is that if you need a data structure to hold something more complicated than a simple list of items, it's best to represent it as an XML document. (This is easy when you are using XSLT or XQuery, which allow you to construct nodes in new trees at any time. It's less easy in XPath itself, which is a read-only language.)

The simplest way of writing an XPath expression whose value is a sequence is by using a comma-separated list: for example «1, 2, 3» represents a list containing three integers. In fact, as we will see in Chapter 8, the comma is a binary operator that concatenates two sequences. Remember that a single integer is a sequence. So «1, 2» concatenates the single-item sequence «1» and the single-item sequence «2» to create the two-item sequence «1, 2». The expression «1, 2, 3» is evaluated as «(1, 2), 3», and it concatenates the two-item sequence «1, 2» with the one-item sequence «3» to produce the three-item sequence «1, 2, 3». This definition of comma as an operator means that it is also possible to write sequences such as «$a, $b», which concatenates two arbitrary sequences represented by the variables $a and $b.

> *Sometimes a list of values separated by commas needs to be enclosed in parentheses to prevent ambiguity, for example when it is used as an argument in a function call. For details, see Chapter 8, page 240.*

Some of the important XPath operations defined on sequences are:

❑   «count ($S)» counts the items in a sequence

❑   «$S, $T» concatenates two sequences

❑   «$S [predicate]» selects those items in a sequence that satisfy some condition

❑   «$S [number]» selects the *N*th item in a sequence

❑   «for $item in $SEQ return f ($item)» applies the function «f» (which can actually be any expression) to every item in the sequence $SEQ, and returns the results as a new sequence. (In list processing languages, this is known as a *mapping* expression).

We will study these operators in much greater depth later in the book.

Sequences also play an important role in navigating trees, as we shall see. The result of a *path expression* such as «/book/chapter/section» is a sequence of nodes. All operators that apply to sequences in general (including those listed above) can therefore be used to manipulate sequences of nodes selected using path expressions.

In the next two sections, we'll look at the two kinds of item that can be found in a sequence, namely atomic values and nodes. We'll take atomic values first, because they are simpler.

Atomic Values

It's easiest to explain what an atomic value is by example: they are things like integers, floating-point numbers, booleans, and strings.

Every atomic value has a type (it is either an integer, or a string, or a boolean . . .). Broadly speaking, the types that are available are the 19 primitive types defined in XML Schema, such as xs:double, xs:string, or xs:date, which we will examine in the next chapter, and types derived from these.

An atomic value either belongs directly to one of these primitive types, or to a type that is defined by restricting one of these primitive types: this may be a built-in type such as xs:NMTOKEN, which is defined in the XML Schema specification itself as a restriction of xs:string, or a type defined in a user-written schema. For example, if you have a schema that defines `mf:part-number` as a restriction of `xs:string`, then you can have atomic values whose type is `mf:part-number`.

A type definition determines the set of possible values allowed for items of that type. For example, the type `xs:boolean` says that there are two possible values, called true and false. For a restricted type, the set of possible values is always a subset of the values allowed for its base type. For example, a type that is defined by restricting «`xs:integer`» might allow only the values 1 to 20.

An atomic value carries its type with it as a kind of label. If «`PY03672`» is an `mf:part-number`, then because of the way the type is defined, it is also an `xs:string`. This means it can be used anywhere that an `xs:string` can be used. However, its label still identifies it as an `mf:part-number`. Conversely, if you write the string literal «`"PY03672"`» in an XPath expression, the value will be labeled as an `xs:string`, and even though it meets all the rules that would make it a valid `mf:part-number`, you cannot use it in places where an `mf:part-number` is required, because it has the wrong label. To create a value labeled as an `mf:part-number`, you need to use the constructor function «`mf:part-number ("PY03672")`».

So the two properties of an atomic value are the value itself, and the type label. If two atomic values are the same in these two respects, then they are indistinguishable. Atomic values do not have any kind of identity separate from their value and their type; there is only one number 42, and only one string "Venice".

In particular, this means that atomic values are not in any way attached to a particular XML document. Atomic values can be extracted from nodes in an XML document, through a process called *atomization*, described on page 108; but once extracted, they have no residual connection with the document where they originated. Atomic values can also be derived quite independently of any document, for example as the result of an arithmetic expression.

The full set of primitive atomic types that are available in XPath (that is, types that are not derived by restriction from another type) has been left slightly open-ended. There is an assumption that by default, the 19 primitive types defined in XML Schema will be available. These are:

xs:boolean	xs:date
xs:decimal	xs:dateTime
xs:float	xs:time
xs:double	xs:duration
xs:string	xs:gYear
xs:QName	xs:gYearMonth
xs:anyURI	xs:gMonth
xs:hexBinary	xs:gMonthDay
xs:base64Binary	xs:gDay
xs:NOTATION	

*Throughout this book we will use the namespace prefix xs to refer to the namespace http://www.w3
.org/2001/XMLSchema, which is the namespace in which these types are defined.*

However, XPath is designed to be used in a wide variety of different environments, and host languages
(that is, specifications that incorporate XPath as a sublanguage) are allowed to tailor this list, both by
omitting types from the list and by adding to it. The actual list of atomic types that are available is
determined as part of the environment in which XPath expressions are compiled and executed, which we
will study in Chapter 4. XSLT 2.0, for example, defines a conformance level for a "basic XSLT processor",
which is designed to meet the needs of users who are not using XML schemas. This conformance level
restricts the set of primitive types supported to xs:boolean, xs:decimal, xs:double, xs:string,
xs:QName, xs:anyURI, xs:date, xs:dateTime, and xs:time.

The type xs:integer is unusual. On the one hand it has a special status in the XPath language (it is one
of the few types for which values can be written directly as literals). On the other hand, it is actually not a
primitive type, but a type that is derived as a restriction of xs:decimal. This is because the set of all
possible xs:integer values is a subset of the set of all possible xs:decimal values.

In fact there are four types for which XPath provides a syntax for defining literal constants:

Type	Example literals
xs:string	"New York", 'Moscow', ""
xs:integer	3, 42, 0
xs:decimal	93.7, 1.0, 0.0
xs:double	17.5e6, 1.0e-3, 0e0

*A number can always be preceded by a plus or minus sign when it appears in an XPath expression, but
technically the sign is not part of the numeric literal, it is an arithmetic operator.*

Values of type xs:boolean can be represented using the function calls false() and true(), listed in
the library of functions described in Chapter 10. Values of any other type can be written using constructor
functions, where the name of the function is the same as the name of the type. For example, a constant
date can be written as «xs:date("2004-07-31")».

There is one other type we need to mention in this section: the type xdt:untypedAtomic. The
namespace prefix «xdt» refers to the namespace http://www.w3.org/2003/11/xpath -
datatypes, which is defined not by XML Schema, but in the XPath specifications (the actual URI is
likely to change in successive drafts until the XPath specification is finalized). This type is used to label
values that have not been validated using any schema, and which therefore do not belong to any
schema-defined type. It is also, somewhat controversially, used to label values that have been validated
against a schema, in cases where the schema imposes no constraints. The set of possible values for this
type is exactly the same as the value space for the xs:string type. The values are not strictly strings,
because they have a different label (xdt:untypedAtomic is not derived by restricting xs:string).
Nevertheless, an xdt:untypedAtomic value can be used anywhere that an xs:string can be used. In

fact, it can be used anywhere that a value of any atomic type can be used, for example, it can be used where an integer or a boolean or a date is expected. In effect, xdt:untypedAtomic is a label applied to values whose type has not been established.

If an xdt:untypedAtomic value is used where an integer is expected, then the system tries to convert it to an integer at the time of use. If the actual value is not valid for an integer then a runtime failure will occur. In this respect xdt:untypedAtomic is quite different from xs:string, because if you try to use a string where an integer is expected, you will get a type error regardless whether it could be converted or not.

Nodes and Trees

We don't always want the input for an XPath expression to be XML in its textual form. We might want to access a document that has been constructed by an application in memory, or one that is stored in an XML database: in such cases, we don't necessarily want to put the document through an XML parser each time it is used. We might also want to access an XML view of data that isn't really an XML document at all: it might be rows in a relational database or (say) an LDAP directory, or an EDI message, or a data file using comma-separated values syntax. We don't want to spend a lot of time converting these into textual XML documents and then parsing them if we can avoid it, nor do we want another raft of converters to install.

XPath therefore defines its operations in terms of a representation of an XML document called the *tree*. The tree is an abstract data type. There is no defined API and no defined data representation, only a conceptual model that defines the objects in the tree, their properties and their relationships. The tree is similar in concept to the W3C Document Object Model (DOM), except that the DOM does have a defined API. Some implementers do indeed use the DOM as their internal tree structure. Others use a data structure that corresponds more closely to the XPath tree model, while some use internal data structures that are only distantly related to this model. It's a conceptual model we are describing, not something that necessarily exists in an implementation.

The objects in the tree are called nodes, and as we saw earlier, nodes are one of the two kinds of item found in an XPath sequence. Trees themselves technically are not values in the data model, in the sense that the value of an expression is never a tree as such. If you want to pass a tree as an argument to a function, what you actually do is to pass the root node of the tree. XPath expressions always manipulate nodes or sequences of nodes, and nodes always belong to trees, but the trees are really just abstract data structures made up of nodes.

As I mentioned, the XPath tree model is similar in many ways to the XML Document Object Model (DOM). However, there are a number of differences of terminology and some subtle differences of detail. I'll point some of these out as we go along.

XML as a Tree

In this section, I will describe the XPath tree model of an XML document, and show how it relates to textual XML files containing angle brackets.

This isn't actually how the XPath Data Model specification does it: it adopts a more indirect approach, showing how the data model relates to the XML InfoSet (an abstract description of the information content of an XML document), and the Post Schema Validation Infoset (PSVI), which is defined in the XML Schema specifications to define the information that becomes available as a result of schema processing. The InfoSet is described in a W3C specification at `http://www.w3.org/TR/xml-infoset/`. *The PSVI is described in the W3C Schema recommendations at* `http://www.w3.org/TR/xmlschema-1/`.

At a simple level, the equivalence of the textual representation of an XML document with a tree representation is very straightforward.

Example: An XML Tree

Consider a document like this:

```
<definition>
    <word>export</word>
    <part-of-speech>vt</part-of-speech>
    <meaning>Send out (goods) to another country.</meaning>
    <etymology>
        <language>Latin</language>
        <parts>
        <part>
            <prefix>ex</prefix>
            <meaning>out (of)</meaning>
        </part>
        <part>
            <word>portare</word>
            <meaning>to carry</meaning>
        </part>
        </parts>
    </etymology>
</definition>
```

We can consider each piece of text as a leaf node, and each element as a containing node, and build an equivalent tree structure, which looks like the Figure 2-2. I show the tree after the stripping of all whitespace nodes (in XSLT this can be achieved using the `<xsl:strip-space>` declaration; in other environments, it may be something you can control from the processor's API). In this diagram each node is shown with potentially three pieces of information:

❑   In the top cell, the *kind* of node

❑   In the middle cell, the *name* of the node

❑   In the bottom one, its *string-value*

For the document node and for elements, I showed the string-value simply as an asterisk: in fact, the string-value of these nodes is defined as the concatenation of the string-values of all the element and text nodes at the next level of the tree.

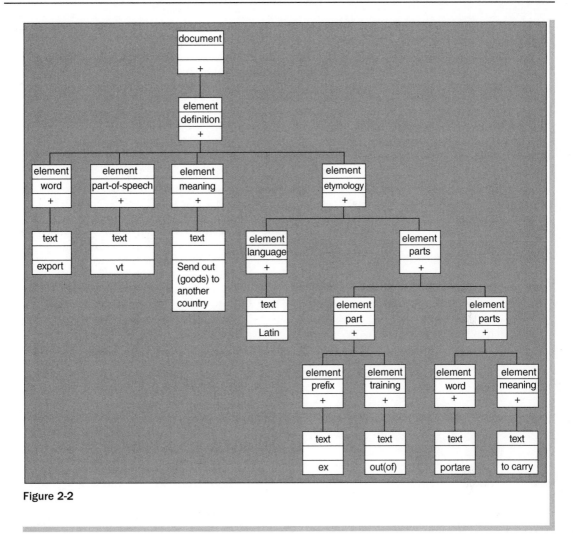

Figure 2-2

It is easy to see how other aspects of the XML document, for example, attributes and processing instructions, can be similarly represented in this tree view by means of additional kinds of node.

At the top of every tree there is a *root* node (trees in computer science always grow upside down). Usually the root will be a document node, but we will look at other cases later on.

> *The terminology here has changed since XPath 1.0. What was the root node in XPath 1.0 is now called a document node. In XPath 2.0, it is possible to have element nodes, or indeed any kind of node, that have no parent. Any node that has no parent, whatever kind of node it is, can be considered to be the root of a tree. So the term "root" no longer refers to a particular kind of node, but rather to any node that has no parent, and is therefore at the top of a tree, even if it is a tree containing just one node.*

The document node performs the same function as the document node in the DOM model, in that it doesn't correspond to any particular part of the textual XML document, but you can regard it as representing the XML document as a whole. The children of the document node are the top-level elements, comments, processing instructions and so on.

In the XML specification the outermost element is described as the "root or document element". In the XPath model this element is not the root of the tree (because it has a parent, the document node), and the term "document element" is not normally used, because it is too easily confused with "document node". I prefer to call it the "outermost element", because that seems to cause least confusion.

The XPath tree model can represent every well-formed XML document, but it can also represent structures that are not well-formed according to the XML definition. Specifically, in well-formed XML, there must be a single outermost element containing all the other elements and text nodes. This element can be preceded and followed by comments and processing instructions, but it cannot be preceded or followed by other elements or text nodes.

The XPath tree model does not enforce this constraint—the document node can have any children that an element might have, including multiple elements and text nodes in any order. The document node might also have no children at all. This corresponds to the XML rules for the content of an *external general parsed entity*, which is a freestanding fragment of XML that can be incorporated into a well-formed document by means of an entity reference. I shall sometimes use the term *well balanced* to refer to such an entity. This term is not used in the XPath specification; rather I have borrowed it from the rarely mentioned XML fragment interchange proposal (`http://www.w3.org/TR/xml-fragment.html`). The essential feature of a well-balanced XML fragment is that every element start tag is balanced by a corresponding element end tag.

Example: Well-balanced XML Fragment

Following is an example of an XML fragment that is well balanced but not well formed, as there is no enclosing element:

```
The <noun>cat</noun> <verb>sat</verb> on the <noun>mat</noun>.
```

The corresponding XPath tree is shown in Figure 2-3. In this case it is important to retain whitespace, so spaces are shown using the symbol ♦.

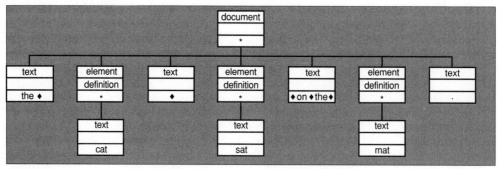

Figure 2-3

The string-value of the document node in this example is simply:

```
The cat sat on the mat.
```

In practice the input and output of an XSLT transformation will usually be well-formed documents, but it is very common for temporary trees constructed in the course of processing to have more than one element as a child of the document node.

Nodes in the Tree Model

An XPath tree is made up of nodes. There are seven kinds of node. The different kinds of node correspond fairly directly to the components of the source XML document:

Node Type	Description
Document node	The document node is a singular node; there is one for each document. Do not confuse the document node with the document element, which in a well-formed document is the outermost element that contains all others. A document node never has a parent, so it is always the root of a tree
Element node	An element is a part of a document bounded by start and end tags, or represented by a single empty-element tag such as <TAG/>. Try to avoid referring to elements as tags: elements generally have two tags, a start tag and an end tag
Text node	A text node is a sequence of consecutive characters in a PCDATA part of an element. Text nodes are always made as big as possible: there will never be two adjacent text nodes in the tree, because they will always be merged into one. (This is the theory. Microsoft's MSXML implementation, notoriously, doesn't always follow this rule)
Attribute node	An attribute node includes the name and value of an attribute written within an element start tag (or empty element tag). An attribute that was not present in the tag, but which has a default value defined in the DTD or Schema, is also represented as an attribute node on each separate element instance. A namespace declaration (an attribute whose name is «xmlns» or whose name begins with «xmlns:») is, however, *not* represented by an attribute node in the tree
Comment node	A comment node represents a comment written in the XML source document between the delimiters «<!--» and «-->»
Processing instruction node	A processing instruction node represents a processing instruction written in the XML source document between the delimiters «<?» and «?>». The *PITarget* from the XML source is taken as the node's name and the rest of the content as its value. Note that the XML declaration <?xml version="1.0"?> is not a processing instruction, even though it looks like one, and it is not represented by a node in the tree

Continues

Node Type	Description
Namespace node	A namespace node represents a namespace declaration, except that it is copied to each element that it applies to. So each element node has one namespace node for every namespace declaration that is in scope for the element. The namespace nodes belonging to one element are distinct from those belonging to another element, even when they are derived from the same namespace declaration in the source document

There are several possible ways of classifying these nodes. We could distinguish those that can have children (element and document nodes), those that can have a parent (everything except the document node), those that have a name (elements, attributes, namespaces, and processing instructions) or those that have their own textual content (attributes, text, comments, processing instructions, and namespace nodes). Since each of these criteria gives a different possible class hierarchy, the XPath data model instead leaves the hierarchy completely flat, and defines all these characteristics for all nodes. Where a characteristic isn't applicable to a particular kind of node, the data model generally defines its value as an empty sequence; though sometimes when you access the property from a real XPath expression what you actually get back is a zero-length string.

So if we show the class hierarchy in UML notation, we get the simple diagram shown in Figure 2-4.

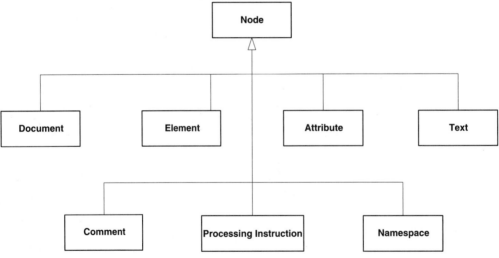

Figure 2-4

This diagram looks superficially similar to the tree we saw earlier, but this time I'm not showing a specific tree, I'm showing a class hierarchy: the boxes represent classes or types, and the arrow represents an *is-a-kind-of* relationship: for example a comment *is-a-kind-of* node. The earlier diagram was just one example of a particular tree, whereas now we are considering the structure of all possible trees.

I've already hinted at some of the properties and relationships of these nodes. Let's look at the properties and relationships in more detail, and then add them to the diagram.

The Name of a Node

In general, a node has a name. Nodes can (and often do) have simple names, but in the general case, node names are qualified by the namespace they are in.

An element or attribute name as written in a textual XML document is a *lexical QName*. (QName stands for Qualified Name.) A lexical QName has two parts: the prefix, which is the part of the QName before the «:» as written in the source XML, and the local part, which is the part of the QName after the «:». If there is no colon, the prefix is the zero-length string. For example, «xsl:stylesheet» is a lexical QName, with prefix «xsl» and local-name «stylesheet».

In the tree model, however, a name is represented by an *expanded QName*. This is represented by an atomic value whose type is xs:QName. The expanded QName also has two parts, though there is no explicit syntax for displaying it. The two parts are the namespace URI, and the local part. The namespace URI is derived from the prefix used in the source document, by finding the namespace declarations that are in scope where it is used, while the local name is again the part of the lexical QName after the «:». So the expanded QName corresponding to the lexical QName «xsl:stylesheet» has namespace URI http://www.w3.org/1999/XSL/Transform (assuming the standard namespace declarations are used), and local part «stylesheet».

The prefix itself is not officially part of the node name as represented in the tree model. When you look for a node with a particular name, it is only the namespace URI and the local name that the system is interested in, not the prefix.

The name of a node is accessible, as an xs:QName value, using the node-name() function defined in Chapter 10. The namespace URI and local-name parts of the name are also separately accessible (as strings) using the functions namespace-uri() and local-name().

Document nodes, comments, and text nodes have no name, and for these, the node-name() function returns the empty sequence. (Note that this differs from the DOM, where names such as «#comment» are used.)

For elements and attributes the node-name() function returns the name that appears in the source XML, after converting any namespace prefixes into namespace URIs.

The name of a processing instruction is the *PITarget* from the source XML: this contains a local name but no namespace URI, as processing instruction names are not subject to namespace rules.

The name of a namespace node is, by convention, the namespace prefix from the original namespace declaration (without the «xmlns:» part). For example, the namespace declaration «xmlns:acme= "http://acme.com/xml"» generates a namespace node with name «acme», while the default namespace declaration «xmlns="http://acme.com/xml"» generates a namespace node whose name is the zero-length string. The name of a namespace node, like the name of any other node, is an xs:QName; the namespace URI part of this xs:QName is always null, while the local-name part holds the namespace prefix.

There are occasions when the system has to generate a namespace prefix from the expanded name, specifically when you use the name() function described in Chapter 10, and when you serialize a tree to produce an XML document. On these occasions the system will allocate a prefix by looking at the namespace nodes on the tree. Usually, it will keep the same prefix as the one you used in the source document, but there are occasions when it may choose a different one. For example, this may happen if the tree contains two different prefixes representing the same namespace. However, the processor will always output a prefix that refers to the correct namespace URI.

The String Value of a Node

Every node has a string value, which is a sequence of Unicode characters. You can get the string value of a node using the `string()` function described in Chapter 10.

For a text node the string value is the text as it appears in the source XML document, except that the XML parser will have replaced every end-of-line sequence (for example, CRLF as used on Windows platforms) by a single new line (#xA) character.

For a comment, the string value is the text of the comment, minus the delimiters.

For a processing instruction, it is the *data* part of the source processing instruction, not including the white space that separates it from the *PITarget*. For example, given the processing instruction `<?ignore this?>`, the string value is «this».

For an attribute, the string value is the value of the attribute as written, modified by any whitespace normalization done by the XML parser and schema processor. The detailed rules for whitespace normalization of attributes depend on the attribute type.

For a document or element node, the string value is defined as the concatenation of the string values of all the element and text children of this node. Or, to look at it another way: the concatenation of all the PCDATA contained in the element (or for the document node, the entire document) after stripping out all markup. (This again differs from the DOM, where the `nodeValue` property in these cases is null.)

For a namespace node the string value is, by convention, the URI of the namespace being declared.

The string value of a node can be obtained by using the `string()` function described in Chapter 10. This should not be confused with the `xs:string()` constructor, which works differently when applied to a node: it extracts the typed value of the node, as described in the next section, and then converts the typed value to a string. This might not give precisely the same result. For example, if an attribute is declared in the schema as being of type `xs:decimal`, and the actual attribute is written as «a="146.50"», then the result of the `string()` function will be «146.50», while the result of the `xs:string()` constructor will be «146.5». This is because the `xs:string()` constructor takes the typed value (a decimal number) and converts it to a string using the standard rules for converting decimals to strings, which take no account of how the value was originally written in the source document. For the same reasons, if the attribute is declared as an `xs:boolean`, and the actual attribute is written as «ok="1"», then the result of «string(@ok)» will be the string «1», while the result of «xs:string(@ok)» will be the string «true».

In XPath 1.0, the string value of a node was used whenever a node was supplied as an argument to a function that expected a string. In XPath 2.0 in this situation, the atomization procedure is invoked, which gives the same result as the `xs:string()` constructor described above. If there's no schema, then the result is the same, because the typed value of the node will be the same as its string value (but labeled as `xdt:untypedAtomic`). In XPath 2.0, the only time the string value is used directly is when you explicitly call the `string()` function, and the result differs from the typed value only if the node has been validated using a schema.

The Typed Value of a Node

The typed value of a node reflects the content of the node as it appears after schema validation. The typed value is available using the data() function described in Chapter 10; it is also obtained implicitly as the result of the process of atomization, described on page 108.

Schema validation only really applies to element and attribute nodes, so let's get the other kinds of nodes out of the way first. For document nodes, text nodes, comment nodes, processing instruction nodes, and namespace nodes, the typed value is the same as the string value, which is defined in the previous section. However, for document nodes, namespace nodes, and text nodes, the value is labeled as xdt:untypedAtomic, while for comments and processing instructions it is labeled as xs:string. There is, as one might expect, some tortuous logic behind this apparently arbitrary distinction: labeling a value as xdt:untypedAtomic enables the value to be used in contexts where a value other than a string is required, whereas a value labeled as xs:string can only be used where that is the type expected. There are plausible scenarios where one might want to use the content of document nodes, namespace nodes, and text nodes in non-string contexts, but it's hard to think of similar justifications for comments and processing instructions.

Let's return to elements and attributes, which are the cases where the typed value comes into its own.

First of all, if you're working on a document that has no schema, or that has not been validated against a schema, or if you're using an XPath processor that doesn't support schema processing, then the typed value of an element or attribute is the same as the string value, and is labeled with the type xdt:untypedAtomic. This is very close to the situation with XPath 1.0, which didn't support schema processing at all. It means that when you use an expression that returns an element or attribute node (for example, path expressions like «title» or «@price»), then they take on the type expected by the context where you use them. For example, you can use «@price» as a number by writing «@price * 0.8», or you can use it as a string by writing «substring-after(@price, '$')». The typed value of the attribute, which is simply the string value as written in the source document, will be converted to a number or to a string as required by the context. If the conversion fails, for example, if you try to use the value as an integer when it isn't a valid integer, then you get a runtime error.

If you have processed the document using a schema, things get more interesting. The situation where the typed value is most useful is where the schema defines a simple type for the element or attribute (or in the case of elements, a complex type with simple content—which means that the element can have attributes, but it cannot have child elements). Simple types in XML Schema allow atomic values or lists of atomic values, but they don't allow child elements.

- ❑ The simple type may be an atomic type, such as xs:integer or xs:date, in which case the typed value will be the result of converting the string value to an xs:integer or xs:date value according to the rules defined by XML Schema. The value must be a valid xs:integer or xs:date, or it wouldn't have passed schema validation.

- ❑ The schema may also define the type as being a list, for example, a list of xs:integer or xs:date values. In this case the typed value is a sequence of zero or more atomic values, again following the rules defined in XML Schema.

- ❑ Another possibility is that the schema defines a union type, for example, it may allow either an xs:integer or an xs:date. The schema validator tries to interpret the value as an xs:integer (if that is the first possibility listed), and if that fails, it tries to validate it as an xs:date. The typed value returned by the data() function may then be either an xs:integer or an xs:date value.

❑ Lists of a union type are also allowed, so you can get back a sequence containing (say) a mixture of integers and dates.

For attributes, all types are simple types, so the above rules cover all the possibilities. For elements, however, there are additional rules to cover non-simple types:

❑ If the schema defines the element as having mixed content, then the typed value is the same as the string value, labeled as xdt:untypedAtomic. Note that the deciding factor is that the schema allows mixed content (a mixture of element and text node children), not that the element in question actually has mixed content: in reality it might have element children, or text children, or both or neither. This is identical to the rule for processing without a schema, which means that in many cases, narrative or document-oriented XML (as opposed to data-oriented XML) will be processed in exactly the same way whether there is a schema or not. Narrative XML is characterized by heavy use of mixed content models.

❑ If the schema defines the element as having empty content (that is, the element is not allowed to have either element node or text nodes as children, though it can have attributes) then the typed value is an empty sequence.

❑ If the schema defines the element as having an element-only content model (that is, it can contain element nodes as children but not text nodes), then there is no typed value defined, and attempting to retrieve the typed value causes an error. This error is classified as a type error, which means it may be detected and reported either at compile time or at evaluation time. The reason that this is an error is that the typed value must always be a sequence of atomic values, and there is really no way of doing justice to the content of a structured element by representing it as such a sequence. The content is not atomic, because it only makes sense when considered in conjunction with the names of the child elements. Element-only content models tend to feature strongly in "data-oriented" XML applications.

The specification includes some special rules concerning the handling of values of types xs:date, xs:time, and xs:dateTime. Essentially, these provide an exception to the rule that values are processed as defined in XML Schema. It was decided that XSLT and XQuery users would get upset if the timezone part of the original string value was simply discarded, causing two values like «15:00:00-05:00» and «14:00:00-06:00» to be treated as identical. Instead, the XPath data model provides that the timezone is retained as part of the typed value. Even though it plays no part in subsequent operations such comparisons or sorting, the original timezone is then available when the value is converted back to a string in a result document. The XSLT functions format-date(), format-time(), and format-dateTime() (described in *XSLT 2.0 Programmer's Reference*) also retain the original timezone in the displayed value.

The Type Annotation of a Node

As well as having a typed value, a node also has a type annotation. This is a reference to the type definition that was used to validate the node during schema processing. It is not available directly to applications, but it affects the outcome of a number of type-sensitive operations. For example, when you select all attributes of type xs:date by writing the path expression «//attribute(*, xs:date)» (this is described in Chapter 9), the system looks at the type annotations of the attributes to see which nodes qualify.

In the W3C specifications for the data model, the type annotation is modeled as an xs:QName holding the name of the type in the case where the type is a globally declared schema type, or an invented name in the case where it is locally declared (not all types defined in a schema need to be named). It's reasonable to treat this as polite fiction, designed to tie up loose ends in the specification in an area where the practical details will inevitably vary from one implementation to another. Any real schema-aware XPath processor will need to have some kind of access to schema information both at compile time and at runtime, but the W3C specifications have not tried to model exactly what this should look like. In practice, the type annotation on a node is likely to be implemented as some kind of pointer into the metadata representing the cached schema information. But for defining the semantics of constructs like «//attribute(*, xs:date)», it's enough to assume that the node contains just the type name.

The type annotation defines the type of the content of the node, not the type of the node itself. This is an important distinction, and we'll have more to say about it when we discuss the XPath type system in the next chapter.

You might imagine that the type annotation is redundant, because the typed value is itself an atomic value, and the atomic value itself has a label identifying its type. Very often, the type annotation of the node will be the same as the label on its typed value. However, this only works for nodes whose typed value is a single atomic value. In cases where the schema type is a list type, or a union type, the type annotation on the node is the name of the list or union type, which is not the same as the type of the individual atomic values making up the typed value. For example, if the schema type of an attribute is xs:IDREFS (which is defined as a list of xs:IDREF values), then the type annotation on the attribute node will be xs:IDREFS, but the items in the typed value will be labeled xs:IDREF. If the typed value is an empty sequence, there will be no items to carry a label, but the containing node can still be annotated as being of type xs:IDREFS.

There is, however, a strong relationship between the string value, the typed value, and the type annotation. In fact, with knowledge of the schema and access to a schema validator, the typed value can always be reconstructed from the string value and the type annotation.

If an element or attribute node has not been validated using a schema processor, then the type annotation will be xdt:untypedAtomic in the case of an attribute node, or xdt:untyped in the case of an element node.

For document, comment, processing-instruction, and namespace nodes, there is no type annotation (the value of the type annotation is an empty sequence). For text nodes, the type annotation is xdt:untypedAtomic (but I haven't been able to find anything in the language that makes use of this fact).

The Base URI of a Node

A node has a base URI. This should not be confused with its namespace URI. The base URI of a node depends on the URI of the source XML document it was loaded from, or more accurately, the URI of the external entity it was loaded from, since different parts of the same document might come from different XML entities. The base URI is used when evaluating a relative URI that occurs as part of the value of this node, for example an href attribute: this is always interpreted relative to the base URI of the node it came from.

It is possible to override this by specifying an explicit base URI using the xml:base attribute. For example, if an element has the attribute «xml:base="../index.xml"», then the base URI for this element, and for all its descendants provided they are in the same XML external entity, is the index.xml file in the parent directory of the file that would otherwise have provided the base URI.

The base URI is maintained explicitly only for document nodes, element nodes and processing instruction nodes. For attributes, text nodes, and comments, and for elements and processing instructions without an explicit base URI of their own, the base URI is the same as the URI of its parent node.

For a namespace node the base URI is « ( ) », the empty sequence. The system doesn't attempt to go to the parent node to find its base URI. This is rather a curiosity. The only time you might be interested in the base URI of a namespace node is if you are using the namespace URI as the URI of a real resource, for example a schema. But even then, the base URI will only be needed if this is a relative URI. W3C, after fierce debate, decided that a relative namespace URI was deprecated and implementation defined, so the working groups steered clear of defining an interpretation for it.

The fact that text nodes don't have their own base URI is a little ad hoc, since a text node need not come from the same external entity as its parent element, but it reflects the decision that text nodes should be joined up irrespective of entity boundaries.

The base URI of a node in a source document is used almost exclusively for one purpose: to resolve relative URI references when loading additional input documents using the `doc()` function, described in Chapter 10 (or in XSLT, the similar `document()` function, described in *XSLT 2.0 Programmer's Reference*). The base URI is accessible using the `base-uri()` function, which is also described in Chapter 10.

The Children of a Node

A node has a sequence of child nodes. This one-to-many relationship is defined for all nodes, but the list will be empty for all nodes other than document nodes and element nodes. So you can ask for the children of an attribute, and you will get an empty sequence returned.

The children of an element are the elements, text nodes, processing instructions, and comments contained textually between its start and end tags, provided that they are not also children of some lower-level element.

The children of the document node are all the elements, text nodes, comments, and processing instructions that aren't contained in another element. For a well-formed document the children of the root node will be the document element plus any comments or processing instructions that come before or after the document element.

The attributes of an element are not regarded as children of the element; neither are its namespace nodes.

The Parent of a Node

Every node, except a node at the root of a tree, has a parent. A document node never has a parent. Other kinds of node usually have a parent, but they may also be parentless. The parent relationship is *not* the exact inverse of the child relationship: specifically, attribute nodes and namespace nodes have an element node as their parent, *but they are not considered to be children of that element*. In other cases, however, the relationship is symmetric: elements, text nodes, processing instructions, and comments are always children of their parent node, which will always be either an element or the document node.

Two nodes that are both children of the same parent are referred to as being *siblings* of each other.

The Attributes of a Node

This relationship only exists in a real sense between element nodes and attribute nodes, and this is how it is shown on the diagram at the end of this section. It is a one-to-many relationship: one element has zero or more attributes. In fact, the relationship has-attribute is defined for all nodes, but if you ask for the attributes of any node other than an element, the result will be an empty sequence.

The Namespaces of a Node

This relationship only really exists between element nodes and namespace nodes, and this is how it is shown on the diagram. It is a one-to-many relationship: one element has zero or more namespace nodes. Like the attributes relationship, the relationship namespaces is defined for all nodes, so if you ask for the namespaces of any node other than an element, the result will be an empty sequence.

Note that each namespace node is owned uniquely by one element. If a namespace declaration in the source document has a scope that includes many elements, then a corresponding namespace node will be generated for each one of these elements. These nodes will all have the same name and string-value, but they will be distinct nodes for the purposes of counting and using the «is» operator (which tests whether its two operands are references to the same node: see Chapter 6).

Completing the UML Class Diagram

It's now possible to draw a more complete UML class diagram, as shown in Figure 2-5. In this version:

❑   I brought out PotentialParent and PotentialChild as separate (abstract) classes, to group those nodes that can be parents (document and element nodes) and those nodes that can be children (elements, text nodes, comments, and processing instructions). Note that elements fall into both categories. This grouping is for illustration only, and in reality the relationships hasChildren, hasAttributes, and hasNamespaces are available for all kinds of node, they just return an empty sequence when the node is not a document or element node.

❑   I identified the hasChildren relationship between an element or document node and its children.

❑   I identified the separate relationships between an element and its attributes, and between an element and its namespace nodes.

❑   I identified the additional class UnparsedEntity. This is not itself a node on the tree. It corresponds to an unparsed entity declaration within the document's DTD. Although unparsed entities are defined as part of the XPath data model, they are not accessible by any standard function in XPath itself; but they are exposed by the functions unparsed-entity-uri() and unparsed-entity-public-id() available in XSLT (see Chapter 7 of *XSLT 2.0 Programmer's Reference*).

It's worth mentioning that the XPath tree model never uses null values in the sense that SQL or Java use null values. If a node has no string-value, then the value returned is the zero-length string. If a node has no children, then the value returned is the empty sequence, a sequence containing no items.

Let's look briefly at some of the features of this model.

Names and Namespaces

XSLT and XPath are designed very much with the use of XML Namespaces in mind, and although many source documents may make little or no use of namespaces, an understanding of the XML Namespaces Recommendation (found in http://www.w3.org/TR/REC-xml-names) is essential.

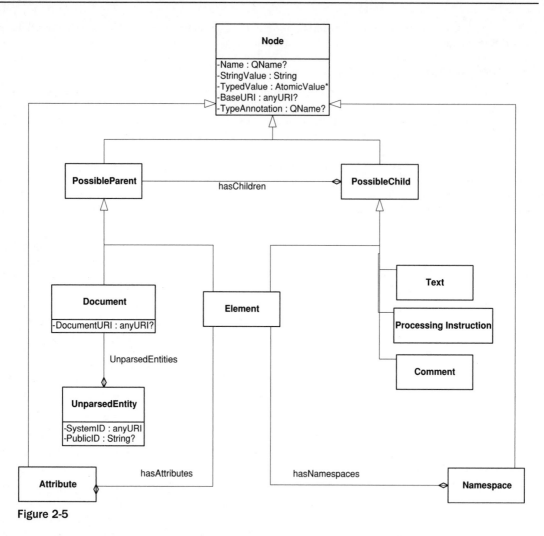

Figure 2-5

I'll start with an overview of how namespaces work, and then get into more detail of how they are represented in the XPath 2.0 data model.

Namespaces: An Overview

Expanding on the description in Chapter 1 (page 17), here's a summary of how namespaces work:

❑   A namespace declaration defines a namespace prefix and a namespace URI. The namespace prefix needs to be unique only within a local scope, but the namespace URI is supposed to be unique globally. Globally here really does mean globally—not just unique in the document, but unique across all documents around the planet. To achieve that, the advice is to use a URI based on a domain name that you control, for example, «`http://www.mega-utility.com/ namespace/billing`». XPath doesn't impose any particular rules on the URI syntax, though it's a good idea to stick to a standard URI scheme in case this ever changes: in most of our examples we'll use URIs beginning with «http://». To avoid any ambiguity, it's also best to avoid relative URIs such as «billing.dtd». After a fierce debate on the issue, W3C issued an edict deprecating the use of relative namespace URIs in XML documents, and stating that the effect of using them is implementation-defined. What this actually means is that they couldn't get everyone to agree. However, as far as most XPath processors are concerned, the namespace URI does not have to conform to any particular syntax. For example, «abc», «42», and «?!*» are all likely to be acceptable as namespace URIs. It is just a character string, and two namespace URIs are considered equal if they contain the same sequence of Unicode characters.

❑ The namespace URI does not have to identify any particular resource, and although it is recommended to use a URL based on a domain name that you own, there is no implication that there is anything of interest to be found at that address. The two strings «file:///c:/this.dtd» and «file:///c:/THIS.DTD» are both acceptable as namespace URIs, whether or not there is actually a file of this name; and they represent different namespaces even though when read as filenames they might identify the same file.

❑ The fact that every XSLT stylesheet uses the namespace URI http://www.w3.org/1999/XSL/Transform doesn't mean that you can only run a transformation if your machine has an internet connection. The name is just an elaborate constant, it's not the address of something that the processor has to go and fetch.

❑ A namespace declaration for a non-null prefix is written as follows. This associates the namespace prefix my-prefix with the namespace URI http://my.com/namespace:

```
<a xmlns:my-prefix="http://my.com/namespace">
```

❑ A namespace declaration may also be present for the null prefix. This is known as the default namespace. The following declaration makes http://your.com/namespace the default namespace URI:

```
<a xmlns="http://your.com/namespace">
```

❑ In the absence of such a declaration, an unprefixed element name is not in any namespace. I will often describe such a name as being in the null namespace, though this is not the officially correct terminology.

❑ The default namespace applies only to element names, not to attribute names; an unprefixed attribute name is always in the null namespace.

❑ You can undeclare the default namespace like this:

```
<a xmlns="">
```

This puts you back in the position you were in at the outermost level of the document: an element name with no prefix is in the null namespace.

❑ The latest version of the XML Namespaces Recommendation, version 1.1, also allows you to undeclare other namespaces, like this:

```
<a xmlns:my-prefix="">
```

This has the effect that the prefix becomes unavailable for use within this element. This feature is not yet widely implemented or used, but the XPath 2.0 data model allows for it.

❑   The scope of a namespace declaration is the element on which it appears and all its children and descendants, excluding any subtree where the same prefix is undeclared or redeclared to associate it with a different URI. This scope defines where the prefix is available for use. Within this scope, any name with the given prefix is automatically associated with the given namespace URI.

Namespaces in the Data Model

A namespace-qualified name is referred to as a QName. When a QName appears in a textual XML document, it is written in the form *prefix:local-part*. For example, in the name xsl:template, the prefix is «xsl» and the local part is «template». I refer to this form as a *lexical QName*. The real underlying name, however, is the combination of the namespace URI and the local part. When two names are compared, they are considered equivalent if they have the same namespace URI and the same local part; it is irrelevant whether or not they were written with the same prefix. The combination of a namespace URI and a local name is referred to as an *expanded QName*.

An expanded QName is never written directly in XPath, it is purely an internal value manipulated by the system. However, in some APIs and in error messages you might sometimes see expanded QNames written out in the form «{http://my.com/namespace}local-name». This format is sometimes called Clark notation, after James Clark, the editor of the XSLT 1.0 and XPath 1.0 specifications.

The job of converting element and attribute names from lexical QNames into expanded QNames is done by the XML parser. The namespace URI of the name is found from the innermost element that carries a namespace declaration of the relevant prefix. If a name has no prefix, then its namespace URI is considered to be the default namespace URI in the case of an element name, or a null URI in the case of an attribute name.

In the XPath data model, element and attribute nodes contain an expanded QName to represent the name of the element or attribute. In theory at least, no information is retained about the original prefix. (This doesn't stop an implementation keeping the prefix for use in diagnostics, just as it might also keep the line number of the element in the original XML file, but it's not part of the data model, and therefore the results of an XPath expression never depend on it.)

However, although prefixes are not present in element and attribute nodes, they are present elsewhere in the data model, namely in namespace nodes. A namespace node represents the binding of a namespace prefix to a namespace URI: it uses the node name to hold the prefix, and the string value of the node to represent the URI.

For any element, it is possible to determine all the namespace declarations in force for that element, by retrieving the associated namespace nodes. These are all made available as if the namespace declarations were repeated on that specific element. The application cannot determine where the namespace declaration actually occurred in the original document, but if there is a namespace node present for a particular element, then it follows that there was a namespace declaration either on that element or on some containing element.

Namespace undeclarations, for example «xmlns="" », or in XML Namespaces 1.1 «xmlns: ppp="" », are not represented as namespace nodes; rather they have the effect that the parser won't create a namespace node for the namespace that has been undeclared. Without the undeclaration, the parser would create a namespace node for that namespace for every element within its scope, whether the element uses it or not; the namespace undeclaration stops this happening.

Although the namespace declarations are originally written in the source document in the form of XML attributes, they are not retained as attribute nodes on the tree, and cannot be processed by looking for all the attribute nodes. Similarly, it is not possible to generate a namespace node on the result tree by creating an attribute with a name such as «xmlns:p»: such names are reserved for namespace declarations. In the data model, namespaces and attributes are quite distinct animals. XSLT 2.0 has a special instruction, <xsl:namespace>, for creating namespace nodes on the rare occasions that you need to do so.

Namespace Sensitive Content

Namespace nodes are needed because of the possibility that elements or attributes will contain namespace-sensitive content. If namespace prefixes were only ever used in element and attribute names, it would be quite enough to convert these into expanded QNames and discard the namespace prefixes, inventing new prefixes if necessary when the tree is turned back into textual XML.

Unfortunately, it is quite common for XML documents to contain references to element or attribute names within the content of the document. The obvious examples of XML documents that use this technique are XSLT stylesheets and XML schemas. When you see a stylesheet containing an attribute such as «select="html:table"», or a schema containing the attribute «type="xs:date"», you are looking at namespace-sensitive content. Similarly, the attribute «xsi:type="xs:short"» appearing in an instance document is using namespaces both in the attribute name and in the attribute content. Stylesheets and schemas are not the only XML documents to use this technique, but they are probably the ones you will encounter most frequently.

In general, the XML parser can't convert these values from lexical QNames to expanded QNames because it doesn't know that they are special. XML Schema has tried to address the problem by defining a data type «xs:QName» that declares the content of an element or attribute to be a QName, but this doesn't solve the whole problem, for a number of reasons:

- ❑ There can be namespace-sensitive content other than simple QNames; for example an attribute might contain an XPath expression, which is also namespace sensitive, but there is no schema-defined type for it.

- ❑ There are documents that have no schema.

- ❑ Although knowing the data type means that a schema processor can convert the lexical QName used in the string value of these attributes to the expanded QName used as the typed value, this only works if the schema processor knows the mapping of prefixes to namespace URIs. So if you want to be able to construct a tree and then pass it to a schema processor for validation, you need some way of representing the namespace information on the tree before this can work.

- ❑ The definition of the xs:QName data type says that an unprefixed QName is assumed (like an unprefixed element name) to be in the default namespace. (You need to read the errata of the XML Schema 1.0 specification to discover this.) Unfortunately, at least one heavy user of QName-valued attributes, namely the XSLT specification, had already decided that an unprefixed QName (like an unprefixed attribute name) should be in the null namespace. This means that if the attribute were defined as an xs:QName, a schema processor would allocate the wrong namespace URI. So you will find that in the schema for XSLT 2.0 (the schema that can be used to validate XSLT stylesheets), the xs:QName data type isn't actually used.

So, namespace nodes exist primarily so that namespace prefixes appearing in namespace-sensitive content can be handled. Although this might seem a minor requirement, they cause significant complications.

The way namespace nodes are represented in the data model hasn't changed significantly between XPath 1.0 and XPath 2.0. What has changed, though, is that namespace nodes are now semi-hidden from the application. To be precise, the only way that you could actually get your hands on a namespace node in XPath 1.0 was by using the namespace axis; and in XPath 2.0, the namespace axis has been deprecated, which means that some implementations may continue to support it for backward compatibility reasons, but they aren't required to. Instead, two functions have been provided, `in-scope-prefixes()` and `namespace-uri-for-prefix()`, that provide access to information about the namespaces that are in scope for any element. These functions are described in Chapter 10. The significance of this change is that it gives implementations the freedom to maintain namespace information internally in a form that is much more efficient than the formal description of namespace nodes in the data model would imply: remember that the data model is just a model, not a description of a real implementation.

The other use for namespace nodes is that they allow namespace prefixes on element and attribute names to be reconstituted when required. Strictly speaking, this is a luxury because the choice of prefix is arbitrary. In practice, however, we are all accustomed to seeing standard prefixes used for well-known namespaces, and we would find it much more difficult to read XML documents if randomly generated prefixes were used. There are two occasions on which namespace prefixes need to be reconstituted:

❑ When the `name()` function is used: this returns the name of a node as a lexical QName. The `name()` function, like all others in the standard library, is described in Chapter 10.

❑ When a tree representing an XML document is serialized, to create textual XML. Serialization can't be invoked directly from XPath, but is offered by host environments such as XSLT and XQuery.

In both cases the original prefix for an element or attribute can usually be reconstituted by examining the namespace nodes on the tree. There are exceptions, typically when the document maps two prefixes to the same namespace URI, but they are relatively rare in practice.

As far as XPath itself is concerned, don't worry too much about namespace nodes—all you need to know is that there are functions you can call to resolve namespace prefixes found in element or attribute content. When you construct new trees using XSLT or XQuery, however, understanding what namespace nodes are present on the new tree becomes rather more important.

IDs

An `ID` is a string value that identifies an element node uniquely within a document. If an element has an `ID`, it becomes easy and (one hopes) efficient to access that element if the `ID` value is known. Before XML Schemas came along, the `ID` always appeared as the value of an attribute declared in the DTD as being of type `ID`. XML Schema has retained this capability, but also allows the content of an element to be used as an ID value. This is done by declaring its type as `xs:ID`, which is a type derived by restriction from `xs:string`.

In the data model, every element has at most one `ID` value and (if the document is valid, which is not necessarily the case) every `ID` value identifies at most one element.

For example, in an XML dataset containing details of employees, each `<employee>` element might have a unique `ssn` attribute giving the employee's Social Security number. For example:

```
<personnel>
<employee ssn="SSN-123-45-6789">
   <name>John Doe</name>
   ...
</employee>
<employee ssn="SSN-123-45-6890">
   <name>Jane Stagg</name>
   ...
</employee>
</personnel>
```

As the ssn attribute is unique, it can be declared in the DTD as an ID attribute using the following declaration:

```
<!ATTLIST employee ssn ID #REQUIRED>
```

Alternatively, an ID attribute can be declared in a schema:

```
<xs:element name="employee">
  <xs:complexType>
    <xs:sequence>
       <xs:attribute name="ssn" type="xs:ID"/>
       ...
    </xs:sequence>
  </xs:complexType>
</xs:element>
```

Attributes of type ID are often given the name ID as a reminder of their role; unfortunately, this sometimes leads people to believe that the attribute name ID is somehow special. It isn't; an ID attribute is any attribute defined in the DTD or schema as having type ID, regardless of the attribute name.

An ID value is constrained to take the form of an XML NCName. This means, for example, that it must start with a letter, and that it must not contain characters such as «/», «:», or space.

Attributes can also be defined as being of type IDREF or IDREFS if they contain ID values used to point to other elements in the document (an IDREF attribute contains one ID value, an IDREFS attribute contains a whitespace-separated list of ID values). XPath provides a function, id() (see page 347), which can be used to locate an element given its ID value. This function is designed so that an IDREF or IDREFS attribute can be used as input to the function, but equally, so can any other string that happens to contain an ID. However, IDREF and IDREFS attributes are treated specially by the idref() function (see page 349), which follows IDREF links in the opposite direction—given an ID value, it finds all the nodes of type IDREF or IDREFS that refer to it.

There is a slight complication with the use of ID values, in that XPath is not constrained to process only valid XML documents. If an XML document is well formed (or merely well-balanced) but not valid, then values that are supposed to be IDs may be duplicated, and they might not obey the syntactic rules for an XML NCName. Similarly, attributes might be marked as IDREF attributes, but actually contain broken links (values that don't match the ID of any element in the document). The XPath specification says that if an ID value appears more than once, all occurrences except the first are ignored. If the ID value contains invalid characters such as spaces, the id() function will fail to find the element but will otherwise appear to work correctly. If you use ID values, it's probably a good idea to use a validating XML parser to prevent this situation occurring.

In XSLT there is a more flexible approach to finding elements (or other nodes) by content, namely keys. With keys you can do anything that IDs achieve, other than enforcing uniqueness. Keys are declared in the stylesheet using the <xsl:key> element, and they can be used to find a node by means of the key() function. For more details, see *XSLT 2.0 Programmer's Reference*.

Characters in the Data Model

In the XML Information Set definition (http://www.w3.org/TR/xml-infoset) each individual character is distinguished as an object (or *information item*). This is a useful model conceptually, because it allows one to talk about the properties of a character and the position of a character relative to other characters, but it would be very expensive to represent each character as a separate object in a real tree implementation.

The XPath model has chosen not to represent characters as nodes. It would be nice if it did, because the XPath syntax could then be extended naturally to do character manipulation within strings, but the designers chose instead to provide a separate set of string-manipulation functions. These functions are described in Chapter 10.

A string (and therefore the string-value of a node) is a sequence of zero or more characters. Each character is a Char as defined in the XML standard. Loosely, this is a Unicode character. More precisely, it is one of the following:

❑   One of the four whitespace characters tab #x9, linefeed #xA, carriage return #xD, or space #x20.

❑   An ordinary 16-bit Unicode character in the range #x21 to #xD7FF or #xE000 to #xFFFD.

❑   An extended Unicode character in the range #x10000 to #x10FFFF. In programming languages such as Java, and in files using UTF-8 or UTF-16 encoding, such a character is represented as a *surrogate pair*, using two 16-bit codes in the range #xD800 to #xDFFF. But as far as XPath is concerned, it is one character rather than two. This affects functions that count characters in a string or that make use of the position of a character in a string, for example the functions string-length(), substring(), and translate(). Here XPath differs from Java, which counts a surrogate pair as two characters.

> *Unicode surrogate pairs are starting to be increasingly used for specialist applications. For example, there is a full range of musical symbols in the range #x1D100 to #x1D1FF. Although these are unlikely to be used when typesetting printed sheet music, they are very important in texts containing musical criticism. They also have some of the most delightful names in the whole Unicode repertoire: Who can resist a character called* Tempus Perfectum cum Prolatione Perfecta? *If you're interested, it looks like a circle with a dot in the middle.*

Note that line endings are normalized to a single newline #xA character, regardless of how they appear in the original XML source file.

It is not possible in a stylesheet to determine how a character was written in the original XML file. For example, the following strings are all identical as far as the XPath data model is concerned:

❑   >

❑   >

- ❑ >

- ❑ >

- ❑ >

- ❑ `<![CDATA[>]]>`

The XML parser handles these different character representations. In most implementations, the XPath processor couldn't treat these representations differently even if it wanted to, because they all look the same once the XML parser has dealt with them.

What Does the Tree Leave Out?

The debate in defining a tree model is about what to leave out. What information from the source XML document is significant, and what is an insignificant detail? For example, is it significant whether the CDATA notation was used for text? Are entity boundaries significant? What about comments?

Many newcomers to XSLT ask questions like "How can I get the processor to use single quotes around attribute values rather than double quotes?" or "How can I get it to output « » instead of « »?" The answer is that you can't, because these distinctions are considered to be things that the recipient of the document shouldn't care about, and they were therefore left out of the XPath tree model.

Generally, the features of an XML document fall into one of three categories: definitely significant, definitely insignificant, and debatable. For example, the order of elements is definitely significant: the order of attributes within a start element tag is definitely insignificant; but the significance of comments is debatable.

The XML standard itself doesn't define these distinctions particularly clearly. It defines certain things that must be reported to the application, and these are certainly significant. There are other things that are obviously significant (such as the order of elements) about which it says nothing. Equally, there are some things that it clearly states are insignificant, such as the choice of CR-LF or LF for line endings, but many others about which it stays silent, such as choice of «"» versus «'» to delimit attribute values.

One result of this is that different standards in the XML family have each made their own decisions on these matters, and the XPath data model is no exception.

The debate arises partly because there are two kinds of application. Applications that want only to extract the information content of the document are usually interested only in the core information content. Applications such as XML editing tools tend also to be interested in details of how the XML was written, because when the user makes no change to a section of the document, they want the corresponding output document to be as close to the original as possible.

To resolve these questions and get some commonality across the different standards, the W3C defined a common model of the information in an XML document: the so-called XML Information Set (or *InfoSet*, as it is often referred to). This is available at http://www.w3.org/TR/xml-infoset.

The XML information set as finally defined includes 17 different information items, listed below. In earlier drafts of the Infoset specification, some of these were classified as core information items, and others, by implication, as non-core. This classification obviously proved too controversial, because it disappeared in the final version of the specification. However, it's interesting to look back at the drafts to see how they classified different features.

The 17 kinds of information item are as follows:

❑   *Originally classified as core:* Document, Element, Attribute, Processing Instruction, Unexpanded Entity, Character, Notation, Namespace Declaration.

❑   *Originally classified as non-core:* Comment, Document Type Declaration, Internal Entity, External Entity, Unparsed Entity, Entity Start Marker, Entity End Marker, CDATA Start Marker, CDATA End Marker.

Even after removing the distinction between core and non-core information, the Infoset specification is not written in a prescriptive style. The only conformance rules it imposes are that other specifications must explain which information items are made available to the application and which aren't.

Another attempt to define the core information content of an XML document appears in the specification of Canonical XML (http://www.w3.org/TR/xml-c14n). This specification approaches the question from a different angle: it tries to define rules for deciding when two lexically different XML documents have the same information content. To do this, it defines a transformation that can be applied to any XML document to turn it into canonical form; and if two documents have the same canonical form, they are considered equivalent.

The process of turning a document into canonical form is summarized as follows:

1.   The document is encoded in UTF-8

2.   Line breaks are normalized to #xA

3.   Attribute values are normalized, depending on the attribute type

4.   Character references and parsed entity references are expanded

5.   CDATA sections are replaced with their character content

6.   The XML declaration and document type declaration (DTD) are removed

7.   Empty element tags (<a/>) are converted to tag pairs (<a></a>)

8.   Whitespace outside the document element and within tags is normalized

9.   Attribute value delimiters are set to double quotes

10.   Special characters in attribute values and character content are replaced by character references

11.   Redundant namespace declarations are removed

12.   Default attribute values defined in the DTD are added to each element

13.   Attributes and namespace declarations are sorted into alphabetical order

This specification has a gray area too: canonical form may or may not retain comments from the original document. So in place of the Infoset definition, we have an alternative definition of core XML information: namely, information that is retained when a document is turned into canonical form.

Figure 2-6 illustrates the resulting classification: the central core is information that is retained in canonical form; the "peripheral" ring is information that is present in the Infoset but not in canonical XML; while the outer ring represents features of an XML document that are excluded from the information set entirely.

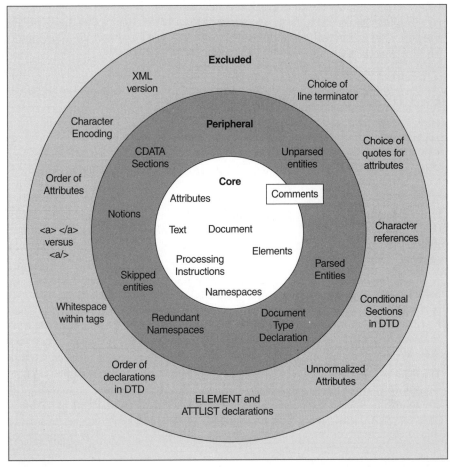

Figure 2-6

The choice of information items that are present in the XPath tree model, and which therefore are accessible to an XPath expression, follows the core as shown in the above diagram fairly closely, but there are some very small differences of detail:

- ❑ The XPath model includes comments, which are optional information items in Canonical XML.

- ❑ Canonical XML retains namespace prefixes as originally defined in the source document. In practice most XSLT and XPath processors will also retain namespace prefixes, but in theory, according to the specification, the name() function in XPath can return any namespace prefix so long as it maps to the correct namespace URI.

- ❑ The XPath model retains the base URI as a property of a node: this property is not retained in Canonical XML.

The way in which the textual content of an item is modeled differs between XPath and the Infoset: the Infoset describes each character as an individual information item, whereas the XPath model concatenates adjacent characters into a property called the string-value of a node. In the case of character content within elements this also requires the inclusion of text nodes in the model. However, this is purely a difference in the way the data is described: the information content of both models is the same. The reason the Infoset makes each character a separate information item is that it allows CDATA section boundaries and entity reference boundaries to be placed between the characters. These information items are not retained in Canonical XML, nor are they visible in the XPath model.

From Textual XML to a Data Model

I've explained the data model so far in this chapter by relating the constructs in the data model (such as element nodes and text nodes) to constructs in a textual XML document.

This isn't actually how the W3C specs define it. There are two important differences:

❑   The W3C specifications don't describe the model in terms of textual XML, they describe it in terms of the XML Infoset, which we examined in the previous section, together with the PSVI (Post Schema Validation Infoset), which describes an augmented Infoset containing not only the information in the raw XML, but also the additional information that becomes available as a result of schema validation.

❑   Although the W3C specifications describe a mapping from the Infoset and PSVI to the XPath data model, this mapping is non-normative (which is standards-speak for saying that it's not officially part of the standard). Products aren't required to provide any particular way of constructing an XPath data model from raw XML. This was also true in XSLT 1.0, and it is an issue that has caused some controversy, because it means there is no guarantee that two XPath processors will give the same answer when applied to the same source document.

The main reason for putting this mapping outside the conformance boundary of the specification is to allow XPath to be used in as wide a variety of contexts as possible, for example in environments where the data model is not constructed from textual XML at all, but is rather a view of non-XML information. Unfortunately, this also means that where the data model is constructed in the conventional way by parsing textual XML files, different processors are allowed to do it in different ways.

Examples of the variations that have arisen in this area between different 1.0 processors are:

❑   The standard way of building a data model using Microsoft's MSXML processor, if all options are set to their default values, causes whitespace-only text nodes to be removed from the model. The standard mapping keeps these nodes present. Microsoft's decision has some rationale: in many cases the extra whitespace nodes simply get in the way, they make the XPath user's life more difficult, and they take up space for no useful reason. Unfortunately, there are some cases where the whitespace is actually significant, and more importantly, this decision means that it's not uncommon for an XSLT stylesheet to produce a different result under MSXML than the result produced under every other processor.

❑   One XSLT vendor (Fourthought: see www.fourthought.com) decided that it would be a good idea to expand any XInclude directives in the source XML as part of the process of building the data model. There is nothing in the spec to say whether XInclude should be expanded or not, and it's something that some users might want to happen and other users might not want to happen. So they were entirely within their rights to make this decision. But again, it creates a problem because different processors are no longer compatible.

With the XPath 2.0 data model, there is additional scope for variations between processors. Because the model is designed to support XQuery as well as XSLT, the range of possible usage scenarios is greatly increased. Many XQuery vendors aim to offer implementations capable of searching databases containing hundreds of gigabytes of data, and in such environments performance optimization becomes a paramount requirement. In fact, database products have traditionally treated performance as a more important requirement than standards conformance, and there are indications that this culture is present among some of the XQuery vendors. Examples of the kind of variations that may be encountered include the following:

❑   Dropping of whitespace text nodes.

❑   Storing only the typed value of elements and attributes, and not the string value. This means that the `string()` function would reconstitute a string value from the typed value, rather than returning the value that was present in the original textual XML. Such products will not always be able to return the value as originally written: for example an integer value «+0100» will be returned as «100», and a boolean value written as «0» will be returned as «false».

❑   Dropping comments and processing instructions, especially when they are contained within simple-valued elements. Vendors storing the data in "shredded" form in a relational database have particular difficulty coping with values such as:

    `<birth>1914-09<!-- or 06? -->-28</birth>`

    or a list of values such as:

    `<readings>23.6 18.2 12.5 <!--rest added by MHK--> 18.6 19.3</readings>`

❑   Dropping unused namespace declarations.

It remains to be seen how most vendors will handle these problems. Hopefully, vendors will offer any optimizations as an option that the user can choose, rather than as the default way that source XML is processed when loading the data.

Controlling Serialization

XPath itself does not produce new trees, and so it is not concerned with how trees in the data model get converted back into textual XML—a process generally referred to as *serialization* (though it must not be confused with serialization as defined in programming languages such as Java). This is a matter for the XSLT and XQuery specifications, which do produce new trees. The suite of W3C specifications includes one devoted to serialization. This was originally part of the XSLT specification, but it was extracted into a separate spec to make it reusable; it allows any language that uses the XPath data model to invoke the same serializer. I have covered this material in the companion book *XSLT 2.0 Programmer's Reference*. But in this chapter, it's worth taking a look at how serialization tackles the information that I have classified as peripheral or excluded.

A tree constructed using XSLT or XQuery contains only the core information present in the XPath data model. The serializer, however, gives a little bit of extra control over how the result tree is converted into a textual XML document. Specifically, it allows control over:

- ❑ Use of CDATA sections
- ❑ XML version
- ❑ Character encoding
- ❑ The standalone property in the XML declaration
- ❑ DOCTYPE declaration

Some of these things are considered peripheral in our classification above, and some are in the excluded category. The features that can be controlled during serialization do not include all the peripheral information items (for example, it is not possible to generate entity references, except by using a rather low-level facility called *character mapping*), and they certainly do not include all the excluded features. There is no way of controlling the order in which attributes are written, or the choice of <a/> versus <a></a> to represent empty elements, the disposition of whitespace within a start tag, or the presence of a newline character at the end of the document.

In short, the set of things that you can control in the serialization stage of processing bears some resemblance to the classification of features in the Information Set and in Canonical XML, but not as much resemblance as one might expect. Perhaps if the Information Set had been defined earlier, there would be greater consistency between the different W3C specifications.

To underline all this, let's list some of the things you can't see in the input tree, and some of the things you can't control in a textual XML output file.

Invisible Distinctions

In the table below, the constructs in the two columns are considered equivalent, and in each case you can't tell as a stylesheet writer which one was used in the source document. If one of them doesn't seem to have the required effect, don't bother trying the other because it won't make any difference:

Construct	Equivalent
`<item/>`	`<item></item>`
`&gt;`	`&#62;`
`<e>&quot;</e>`	`<e>"</e>`
`<![CDATA[ a < b ]]>`	`a &lt; b`

`<a xmlns="one.uri">`
`  <b/>`
`</a>`
	`<a xmlns="one.uri">`
	`  <b xmlns="one.uri"/>`
	`</a>`

`<rectangle x="2" y="4"/>`	`<rectangle y='4'`
	`         x='2'`
	`/>`

In all these cases, except CDATA, it's equally true that you have no control over the format of the output. Because the alternatives are equivalent, you aren't supposed to care which is used.

Why make a distinction for CDATA on output? Perhaps because where a passage of text contains a large number of special characters, for example in a book where you want to show examples of XML, the use of character references can become very unreadable. It is after all one of the strengths of XML, and one of the reasons for its success, that XML documents are easy to read and edit by hand. Also, perhaps, because there is actually some controversy about the meaning of CDATA: there have been disputes, for example, about whether «<![CDATA[ ]]>» is allowed in circumstances where XML only permits whitespace.

DTD Information

The XPath 1.0 designers decided not to include all the DTD information in the tree. Perhaps they were already anticipating the introduction of XML Schemas, but in any case, support for DTDs is certainly no better in XPath 2.0 than it was in 1.0.

The XPath processor (but not the application) needs to know which attributes are of type ID or IDREF/IDREFS, so that the relevant elements can be retrieved when the id() or idref() function is used (these functions are described in Chapter 10). In the case of a schema-aware processor, XPath 2.0 determines this information as a result of schema validation: the information is implicit in the type annotation of element and attribute nodes. For processors that are not schema-aware, or in the case of documents that have a DTD but no schema, the question is somewhat fudged in the specifications. XSLT 2.0, for example, says that with a non-schema-aware processor, all attributes are annotated as being of type xdt:untypedAtomic; but at the same time, it encourages implementations to support the id() and idref() functions based on information obtained from the DTD, when available.

For XSLT users, the best advice is probably to steer clear of id() and idref(), and define keys instead using the <xsl:key> declaration. The result is more likely to be portable, and in any case, keys offer much more flexibility.

Document Order

Nodes within a tree have an ordering, called document order. Where two nodes come from the same tree, their relative position in document order is based on their position in the tree, which in turn is based on the ordering of the underlying constructs in the original textual XML document. For example an element precedes its children in document order, and sibling nodes are listed in the same order as they appear in the original source document. By convention an element node is followed by its namespace nodes, then its attributes, and then its children, but the ordering of the namespace nodes among themselves, and of the attribute nodes among themselves, is unpredictable.

Where two nodes come from different trees, they still have a document order, but it is not predictable what it will be. In fact, any sequence of nodes can be sorted into document order, whether the nodes come from the same document or different documents, and if you sort the same sequence into document order more than once you will always get the same result, but in the case of nodes from different documents, you can't predict which one will come first. The spec does say, however, that nodes from different documents will not be interleaved: a node from document A will never come after one node from document B and before another node from document B.

There are a number of XPath expressions that always return nodes in document order. These include all path expressions (any expression using the «/» operator), step expressions such as «ancestor::*», and expressions using the operators union (or «|»), intersect, and except. If you want to sort a sequence

$seq into document order, you can do this with the trivial path expression «$seq/.», or by forming a union with the empty sequence: «$seq|()».

XPath 2.0 also includes an operator to test whether one node is before or after another in document order: the expression «$a << $b» returns true if node $a is before $b in document order.

When a node is copied, for example using the XSLT instruction <xsl:copy-of>, the new node has a new position in document order that is quite unrelated to the position of the old node.

Summary

This chapter explained the data model that underpins the XPath 2.0 language, as well as XSLT 2.0 and XQuery 1.0. All values that form the inputs and outputs of XPath expressions can be described using this data model.

The key features of the model are:

❑ Every value is a sequence (even if it is a sequence of length one). There are two kinds of item in a sequence, atomic values and nodes.

❑ Atomic values belong to one of the primitive types defined in XML Schema, or to a subtype of one of these primitive types.

❑ Nodes are the building blocks of the tree model used in XPath, and relate to concepts defined in the XML standards: they are similar, but not completely identical, to nodes in the DOM model.

In the next chapter we will look at the XPath 2.0 type system in more detail.

3

The Type System

The XPath data model (which we studied in the previous chapter) and the type system, which forms the subject of this chapter, are very closely related topics. In fact, one could say that the data model provides the top-level types in the type system (sequences, nodes, atomic values), and the rest of it is just filling in the detail. However, in order to understand the detail of the XPath type system (which is shared with XSLT and XQuery) we need to understand something about XML Schema, on which it is based.

This chapter starts with a quick tour of XML Schema. This won't be a tutorial on how to write a schema—there are other books devoted to that subject. Rather, we'll concentrate on understanding XML Schema from an XPath perspective.

After the introduction to XML Schema, we look at how this ties together with the XPath data model presented in the previous chapter to form the type system for the XPath language.

Finally, we look at the role that the type system plays in the XPath language: how does it affect the expressions that you can write, and the results that they produce?

What Is a Type System?

Before beginning our tour of XML Schema, let's make sure that when we talk about a type system, we're talking the same language.

Every programming language has some kind of type system. A language manipulates values, and the values are of different types. At the simple level, they might be integers, booleans, and strings. Then the language might support various kinds of composite types, for example, arrays or records or lists. Most modern languages also allow users to define their own types, on top of the basic types provided "out of the box".

So at the first level, types are used to classify the values that can be manipulated by expressions in the language, and the type system defines the basic types provided by the language and the facilities for defining new types built by combining and refining existing types.

Types serve two main purposes. Firstly, they define a set of permissible values. For example, if you say that a function expects a positive integer as its first argument, then the phrase "positive integer" tells you what the valid values for the first argument are.

Secondly, a type defines a set of possible operations. Integers can be added, lists can be concatenated, booleans can be manipulated using the operators «and», «or», and «not».

Not only does the type tell you whether a particular operation is permitted on a value of that type, it determines how that operation will be performed. So integers, strings, dates, and high school grades can all be sorted into order, but the way they are sorted depends on their type. Operations that are performed in different ways depending on the type of their operands are called *polymorphic* operations (from Greek words meaning *many shapes*).

Types are useful in programming languages for a number of reasons:

❑   Types allow errors to be detected, including programming logic errors and data errors. Because a type defines a set of permissible values, the system can give you an error message when you try to use a value that is not permissible. And because a type defines a set of allowed operations, the system can also give you an error message if you try to apply an operation to the wrong kind of value.

❑   Types allow polymorphic operations to be defined. At a simple level, this allows «A < B» to mean different things depending on whether A and B are numbers or dates or strings. At a more sophisticated level, it allows the kind of inheritance and method overriding which is such a powerful tool in object-oriented programming.

❑   Types allow optimization. To make expressions in a language such as XPath run as fast as possible, the system does as much work as it can in advance, using information that is available at compile time from analysis of the expression itself and its context. A lot of the reasoning that can be done at this stage is based on analysis of the types of values that the expression will process. For example, XPath has a very powerful «=» operator, in which the operands can not only be any type of value (such as integers or strings) but can also be sequences. Handling the general case, where both operands are arbitrary sequences containing items of mixed types, can be very expensive. In most cases the operands are much simpler, for example two integers or two strings. If the system can work out in advance that the operands will be simple (and it often can) then it can generate much more efficient code and save a lot of work at runtime.

The thinking on types has changed quite considerably between XPath 1.0 and XPath 2.0. In 1.0, there were very few types, and very little type checking. Almost all operations were permitted, and runtime errors were very rare. That sounds good on the surface, but what it actually means is that if you make a mistake, you don't get an error message, you just get the wrong answer back (or no answer at all, which can be even more bewildering). This approach to language design generally goes under the name *dynamic typing* or *weak typing* and it is found most often in scripting languages such as JavaScript and Perl. XPath 2.0 has made a significant shift toward the other approach to language design, based on *static typing* or *strong typing*, which is more characteristic of compiled languages such as C or Java. It has to be said that not everyone is happy with the change, though there are good reasons for it, essentially the fact that XPath (and its big sister, XQuery) are starting to be used to tackle much bigger problems where a more robust engineering approach is needed.

Actually, the really innovative thing about XPath 2.0 is that it tries to accommodate multiple approaches to typing within a single language. Because XML itself is used to handle a very wide spectrum of different kinds of document, from the very rigidly structured to the very flexible, XPath 2.0 has been designed to accommodate both very flexible and dynamic approaches, where you have no idea what the data is going to look like in advance, to highly structured queries where the structure of the data is regular and predictable and the expression can be optimized to take advantage of the fact. That's the theory, anyway; in practice, as one might expect, there are a few wrinkles.

Enough of this introduction to type systems in programming languages; let's take a look at XML Schema, which provides the underlying foundation for the XPath type system.

XML Schema: An Overview

The primary purpose of XML Schema is to enable documents to be validated: a schema defines a set of rules that XML documents must conform to, and enables documents to be checked against those rules. This means that organizations using XML to exchange invoices and purchase orders can agree on a schema defining the rules for these messages, and both parties can validate the messages against the schema to ensure that they are okay. So the schema, in effect, defines a type of document, and this is why schemas are central to the type system of XPath.

In fact, the designers of XML Schema were more ambitious than this. They realized that rather than simply giving a yes or no answer, processing a document against a schema could make the application's life easier by attaching labels to the validated document indicating, for each element and attribute in the document, which schema definitions it was validated against. In the language of XML Schema, this document with validation labels is called a *Post Schema Validation Infoset* or PSVI. The XPath data model is based on the PSVI, but it only retains a subset of the information in the PSVI: specifically, the type annotations attached to element and attribute nodes, which we described in the previous chapter.

We'll start by looking at the kinds of types that can be defined in XML Schema, starting with simple types and moving on to progressively more complex types.

Simple Type Definitions

Let's suppose that many of our messages refer to part numbers, and that part numbers have a particular format such as ABC12345. We can start by defining this as a type in the schema:

```
<xs:simple-type name="part-number">
  <xs:restriction base="xs:token">
    <xs:pattern value="[A-Z]{3}[0-9]{5}"/>
  </xs:retriction>
</xs:simple-type>
```

Part number is a simple type because it doesn't have any internal node structure (it doesn't contain any elements or attributes). I have defined it by restriction from xs:token, which is one of the built-in types that come for free with XML Schema. I could have chosen to base the type on xs:string, but xs:token is probably better because with xs:string, leading and trailing whitespace is considered significant, whereas with xs:token, it gets stripped automatically before the validation takes place. The particular restriction in this case is that the value must match the regular expression given in the <xs:pattern> element. The syntax of regular expressions in XML Schema is a subset of the syntax allowed in XPath expressions, which is given in Chapter 11. This particular regular expression says that the value must consist of exactly three letters in the range A–Z, followed by exactly five digits. (For COBOL diehards, that means «PIC A(3)9(5)»).

Having defined this type, I can now refer to it in definitions of elements and attributes. For example, I can define the element:

```
<xs:element name="part" type="part-number"/>
```

This allows documents to contain <part> elements whose content conforms to the rules for the type called part-number. Of course, I can also define other elements that have the same type, for example:

```
<xs:element name="subpart" type="part-number"/>
```

Note the distinction between the name of an element and its type. Many element declarations in a schema (declarations that define elements with different names) can refer to the same type definition, if the rules for validating their content are the same. It's also permitted, though we won't go into the detail just yet, to use the same element name in different places within a document with different type definitions.

We can also use the same type definition in an attribute, for example:

```
<xs:attribute name="part-nr" type="part-number"/>
```

As we will see later in the book, we can use path expressions in XPath that select elements or attributes of a particular type. Once a document has been validated using this schema, elements that have been validated against the declarations of part and subpart given above, and attributes that have been validated against the declaration named part-nr, will carry the type annotation part-number, and they can be selected using a path expression such as

```
//element(*, part-number)
```

This selects all elements in a document that have the type annotation part-number. If further types have been defined as restricted subtypes of part-number (for example, Boeing-part-number) those will be selected too. The «*» indicates that we don't care what the name of the element is, only what its type is.

XPath also allows you to test whether a variable contains an element or attribute of a particular type:

```
if ($param instance of attribute(*, part-number)) ...
```

This tests whether the value supplied in $param is an attribute node annotated as a part-number. We'll study these XPath expressions in detail in Chapter 9.

One final point before we move on to look at complex types. Simple types in XML Schema are not the same thing as atomic types in the XPath data model. This is because in the schema, a simple type allows a sequence of values. For example, it is possible to define the following simple type:

```
<xs:simpleType name="colors">
  <xs:list>
    <xs:simpleType>
      <xs:restriction base="xs:NCName">
        <xs:enumeration value="red"/>
        <xs:enumeration value="orange"/>
```

```
                <xs:enumeration value="yellow"/>
                <xs:enumeration value="green"/>
                <xs:enumeration value="blue"/>
                <xs:enumeration value="indigo"/>
                <xs:enumeration value="violet"/>
            </xs:restriction>
        </xs:simpleType>
    </xs:list>
</xs:simpleType>
```

There are actually two type definitions here. The inner type is anonymous, because the
<xs:simpleType> element has no name attribute. It defines an atomic value, which must be an
xs:NCName, and more specifically, must be one of the values «red», «orange», «yellow», «green»,
«blue», «indigo», or «violet». The outer type is a named type (which means it can be referenced from
elsewhere in the schema), and it defines a list type whose individual items must conform to the inner type.

This type therefore allows values such as «red green blue» or «violet yellow» or even «red red
red». The values are written in textual XML as a list of color names separated by spaces, but once the
document has been through schema validation, the typed value of an element with this type will be a
sequence of xs:NCName values.

The term *simple type* in XML Schema rules out types involving multiple attribute or element nodes, but it
does allow composite values consisting of a sequence of atomic values.

Elements with Attributes and Simple Content

One thing that might occur quite frequently in an invoice or purchase order is an amount in money: there
might be elements such as:

❑   <unit-price currency="USD">50.00</unit-price>

❑   <amount-due currency="EUR">1890.00</amount-due>

What these two elements have in common is that they have a currency attribute (with a particular
range of allowed values), and content that is a decimal number. This is an example of a *complex type*. We
defined part-number as a simple type because it didn't involve any nodes. The money-amount type is
a complex type, because it involves both a decimal number and an attribute value. We can define this by
declaring two elements in the schema with the same type:

```
<xs:simpleType name="currency-type">
  <xs:restriction base="xs:token">
    <xs:enumeration value="USD"/>
    <xs:enumeration value="EUR"/>
    <xs:enumeration value="GBP"/>
    <xs:enumeration value="CAD"/>
  </xs:restriction>
</xs:simpleType>

<xs:complexType name="money-amount">
  <xs:simpleContent>
    <xs:extension base="xs:decimal">
```

```
        <xs:attribute name="currency" type="currency-type"/>
      </xs:extension>
    </xs:simpleContent>
  </xs:complexType>
```

Here we have defined two new types in the schema, both of them named. The first defines the type of the currency attribute. We could have used the same name for the attribute and its type, but many people prefer to keep the names of types distinct from those of elements and attributes, to avoid confusing the two. In this case I've chosen to define it (again) as a subtype of xs:token, but this time restricting the value to be one of four particular world currencies. In practice, of course, the list might be much longer. The currency-type is again a simple type, because it's just a value, it doesn't define any nodes.

The second definition is a complex type, because it defines two things. It's the type of an element that has a currency attribute which conforms to the definition of the currency-type, and which has content (the text between the element start and end tags) that is a decimal number, indicated by the reference to the built-in type xs:decimal. This particular kind of complex type is called a *complex type with simple content*, which means that elements of this type can have attributes, but they cannot have child elements.

Again, the name of the type is quite distinct from the names of the elements that conform to this type. We can declare the two example elements above in the schema as follows:

```
<xs:element name="unit-price" type="money-amount"/>

<xs:element name="amount-due" type="money-amount"/>
```

But although the type definition doesn't constrain the element name, it does constrain the name of the attribute, which must be «currency». If the type definition defined child elements, it would also constrain those child elements to have particular names.

Again, we can use an XPath expression to select all the elements that have been annotated by a schema processor as conforming to this type:

```
//element(*, money-amount)
```

In an XSLT 2.0 stylesheet, this also means we can write a template rule for processing elements of this type, which means that all the logic for formatting money amounts can go in one place. For example, we could write:

```
<xsl:template match="element(*, money-amount)">
  <xsl:value-of select="@currency, format-number(., '#,##0.00')"/>
</xsl:template>
```

This would output the example <amount-due> element as «EUR 1,890.00». (The format-number() function is available only in XSLT, and is described in Chapter 7 of *XSLT 2.0 Programmer's Reference*).

Elements with Mixed Content

The type of an element that can contain child elements is called a *complex type with complex content*. These essentially fall into two categories, called *mixed content* and *element-only content*. Mixed content allows intermingled text and child elements, and is often found in narrative XML documents, allowing markup such as:

```
<para>The population of <city>London</city> reached
  <number>5,572,000</number> in <year>1891</year>, and had risen
  further to <number>7,160,000</number> by <year>1911</year>.</para>
```

The type of this element can be declared in a schema as:

```
<xs:complex-type name="para-type" mixed="true">
  <xs:choice minOccurs="0" maxOccurs="unbounded">
    <xs:element ref="city"/>
    <xs:element ref="number"/>
    <xs:element ref="year"/>
  </xs:choice>
</xs:complex-type>
```

In practice, the list of permitted child elements is often much longer than this, and a common technique is to define *substitution groups* that allow a list of such elements to be referred to by a single name. We look more closely at substitution groups on page 73.

Narrative documents tend to be less constrained than documents holding structured data such as purchase orders and invoices, and while schema validation is still very useful, the type annotations generated as a result of validation aren't generally so important when the time comes to process the data using XPath expressions: the names of the elements are usually more significant than their types. However, there is plenty of potential for using the types, especially if the schema is designed with this in mind.

When schemas are used primarily for validation, the tendency is to think of types in terms of the form that values take. For example, it is natural to define the element <city> (as used in the example above) as a type derived by restriction from xs:token, because the names of cities are strings, perhaps consisting of multiple words, in which spaces are not significant. Once types start to be used for processing information (which is what you are doing when you use XPath), it's useful also to think about what the value actually means. The content of the <city> element is not just a string of characters, it is the name of a geographical place, a place that has a location on the earth's surface, that is in a particular country, and that may figure in postal addresses. If you have other similar elements such as <county>, <country>, and <state>, it might be a good idea to define a single type for all of them. Even if this type doesn't have any particular purpose for validation, because it doesn't define any extra constraints on the content, it can potentially be useful when writing XPath expressions because it groups a number of elements that belong together semantically.

Elements with Element-Only Content

This category covers most of the "wrapper" elements that are found in data-oriented XML. A typical example is the outer <person> element in a structure:

```
<person id="P517541">
  <name>
    <given>Michael</given>
    <given>Howard</given>
    <family>Kay</family>
```

```
    </name>
    <date-of-birth>1951-10-11</date-of-birth>
    <place-of-birth>Hannover</place-of-birth>
  </person>
```

The schema for this might be:

```
<xs:element name="person" type="person-type"/>

<xs:complexType name="person-type">
  <xs:sequence>
    <xs:element name="name" type="personal-name-type"/>
    <xs:element name="date-of-birth" type="xs:date"/>
    <xs:element name="place-of-birth" type="xs:token"/>
  </xs:sequence>
  <xs:attribute name="id" type="id-number"/>
</xs:complexType>

<xs:complexType name="personal-name-type">
  <xs:sequence>
    <xs:element name="given" maxOccurs="unbounded" type="xs:token"/>
    <xs:element name="family" type="xs:token"/>
  </xs:sequence>
</xs:complexType>

<xs:simpleType name="id-number">
  <xs:restriction base="xs:ID">
    <xs:pattern value="[A-Z][0-9]{6}"/>
  </xs:restriction>
</xs:simpleType>
```

There are a number of ways these definitions could have been written. In a so-called *Russian Doll* schema, the types would be defined inline within the element declarations, rather than being given separate names of their own. The schema could have been written using more top-level element declarations, for example the <name> element could have been described at a top level. When you use a schema for validation, these design decisions mainly affect your ability to reuse definitions later on when the schema changes. When you are using a schema to describe types that can be referenced in XPath expressions, however, they also affect the ease of writing these queries.

In choosing the representation of the schema shown above, I made a number of implicit assumptions:

- ❑ It's quite likely that there will be other elements with the same structure as <person>, or with an extension of this structure: perhaps not at the moment, but at some time in the future. Examples of such elements might be <employee> or <pensioner>. Therefore, it's worth describing the element and its type separately.

- ❑ Similarly, personal names are likely to appear in a number of different places. Elements with this type won't always be called <name>, so it's a good idea to create a type definition that can be referenced from any element.

- ❑ Not every element called <name> will be a personal name, the same tag might also be used (even in the same namespace) for other purposes. If I was confident that the tag would always be used for personal names, then I would probably have made it the subject of a top-level element declaration, rather than defining it inline within the `<person>` element.

❑ The elements at the leaves of the tree (those with simple types) such as `<date-of-birth>`, `<place-of-birth>`, `<given>`, and `<family>` are probably best defined using local element declarations rather than top-level declarations. Even if they are used in more than one container element, there is relatively little to be gained by pulling the element declarations out to the top level. The important thing is that if any of them have a user-defined type (which isn't the case in this example) then the user-defined types are defined using top-level `<xs:simpleType>` declarations. That's what I have done for the `id` attribute (which is defined as a subtype of `xs:ID`, forcing values to be unique within any XML document), but I chose not to do the same for the leaf elements.

Defining a Type Hierarchy

Using top-level type definitions in this way becomes very handy in XPath when you have many different elements using the same type definitions. I've come across an example of this in action when handling files containing genealogical data. A lot of this data is concerned with recording events: events such as births, baptisms, marriages, deaths, and burials, but also many other miscellaneous events such as a mention in a newspaper, enrollment at a school or university, starting a new job, receiving a military honor, and so on. Traditionally, this data is recorded using a file format called GEDCOM, which predates XML by many years, but has a similar hierarchic structure in which different kinds of information are represented by tagged records that can contain other tagged records in a very extensible way. As a result, this structure can very easily be translated directly into XML and manipulated using XML tools such as XPath and XSLT.

The GEDCOM specification defines about thirty kinds of event such as BIRTH, DEATH, and MARRIAGE, and then provides a general catch-all EVENT record for anything else you might want to keep information about. All these records have a common structure: they allow information about the date and place of the event, the sources of information about the event, the participants and witnesses, and so on. In other words, they are all different elements with the same type.

In XPath 1.0, the only way of referring to elements was by name. This meant that if you wanted to select all the events for a person in order of date, you had to know all the element names representing events, and write a union expression of the form «BIRTH|DEATH|MARRIAGE|...» to select them. This is tedious to say the least, and it is also inextensible: when new kinds of event are introduced, the XPath expression stops working.

XPath 2.0 introduces the ability to refer to elements by type: you can now write an expression of the form «element(*, EVENT)» which selects all elements of type EVENT. The «*» indicates that you don't care what the name of the element is, you are interested only in its type. This is both more convenient and more flexible than listing all the different kinds of event by name.

You can go beyond this, and define a type hierarchy. In a genealogical database, in addition to recording events in a person's life, you can also record properties of a person such as their occupation, religion, state of health, or (if you want) their height or eye color. GEDCOM hasn't modeled these particularly well: it treats them as events, which isn't a particularly good fit. They have a lot in common with events, in that you want to record the evidence for the information, but they tend to be independent of place and to be applicable over some extended period of a person's life. So in an ideal world we would probably model these using a separate type called, say, ATTRIBUTE (not to be confused with XML attributes, of course). The things that EVENT and ATTRIBUTE have in common could be defined in a third type from which both of these inherit: let's call this DETAIL. Then in an XPath expression I can find all the events and all the attributes for a person with the single expression «element(*, DETAIL)».

This same technique can also be used with narrative XML structures. For example, in the DTD for XHTML you find the following definitions:

```
<!ELEMENT h1 %Inline;>
<!ATTLIST h1
   %attrs;
   >
<!ELEMENT h2 %Inline;>
<!ATTLIST h2
   %attrs;
   >
<!ELEMENT h3 %Inline;>
<!ATTLIST h3
   %attrs;
   >
<!ELEMENT h4 %Inline;>
<!ATTLIST h4
   %attrs;
   >
```

This immediately tells you that the four elements <h1>, <h2>, <h3>, and <h4> have the same type (we don't know from this fragment what the permitted contents and attributes of the elements are, but they are clearly all the same). If these elements are defined with a common type in a schema, then you can start to write generic XPath code to handle all of them in the same way.

You also find type hierarchies in the structure of narrative documents. Looking again at the DTD for XHTML, we find:

```
<!ELEMENT q %Inline;>
<!ATTLIST q
   %attrs;
   cite          %URI;          #IMPLIED
   >
```

This tells us that a <q> element has the same structure as the elements such as <h1> and <h2> shown above (and many others that we didn't show) with the difference that an extra optional attribute, cite, is allowed. The only slightly tricky question here is, which one is a subtype of the other?

The W3C has published a (non-normative) schema for XHTML at http://www.w3.org/TR/xhtml1-schema/. It's instructive to look at its design.

The schema defines the <h1> and <h2> elements (and many others) as follows:

```
<xs:element name="h1">
   <xs:complexType mixed="true">
      <xs:complexContent>
```

```
        <xs:extension base="Inline">
          <xs:attributeGroup ref="attrs"/>
        </xs:extension>
      </xs:complexContent>
    </xs:complexType>
</xs:element>

<xs:element name="h2">
  <xs:complexType mixed="true">
    <xs:complexContent>
      <xs:extension base="Inline">
        <xs:attributeGroup ref="attrs"/>
      </xs:extension>
    </xs:complexContent>
  </xs:complexType>
</xs:element>
```

Note that both elements have been defined with anonymous type definitions, rather than by reference to a named type definition. From the point of view of XPath, this is unfortunate: it means that the types are unnamed (so you can't refer to them in an XPath expression), and also the two elements technically have different types, which means you can't get as much value as you might out of type checking. For example, you can't define a variable in XSLT or XQuery whose declared type allows it to take either of these two elements, or others with the same structure, but nothing else. It would have been much better if this schema had been written as:

```
<xs:element name="h1" type="gen-inline">
<xs:element name="h2" type="gen-inline">

<xs:complexType name="gen-inline" mixed="true">
  <xs:complexContent>
    <xs:extension base="Inline">
      <xs:attributeGroup ref="attrs"/>
    </xs:extension>
  </xs:complexContent>
</xs:complexType>
```

It would also have made the schema quite a bit shorter!

However, all is not lost. Although the two elements have different types, they are both derived by extension from a common type named `Inline`. This type is defined like this:

```
<xs:complexType name="Inline" mixed="true">
  <xs:choice minOccurs="0" maxOccurs="unbounded">
    <xs:group ref="inline"/>
    <xs:group ref="misc.inline"/>
  </xs:choice>
</xs:complexType>
```

The two `<xs:group>` elements identify long lists of element names that can appear in the content of any element using this type definition.

When we look for the <q> element, we find this definition:

```
<xs:element name="q">
  <xs:complexType mixed="true">
    <xs:complexContent>
      <xs:extension base="Inline">
        <xs:attributeGroup ref="attrs"/>
        <xs:attribute name="cite" type="URI"/>
      </xs:extension>
    </xs:complexContent>
  </xs:complexType>
</xs:element>
```

This is exactly the same as the definitions of the <h1> and <h2> elements seen earlier, with the addition of the extra `cite` attribute.

So in this particular schema, we find that <h1>, <h2>, and <q> are all defined as subtypes of a common supertype, `Inline`. This means that the XPath expression «element(*, Inline)» will find all three of them (and many others). But there is no named type that distinguishes <h1> and <h2> on the one hand, and <q> on the other, although their types are clearly different.

You will often find yourself working with XML Schemas that were designed, like this one, primarily for validation. If you get the chance to design the schema with XPath processing in mind, you can often do a little better. I've already shown you how I would have defined <h1> and <h2> with a common type named `gen-inline`.

The <q> element could then be defined by extending the `gen-inline` type:

```
<xs:element name="q">
  <xs:complexType mixed="true">
    <xs:complexContent>
      <xs:extension base="gen-inline">
        <xs:attribute name="cite" type="URI"/>
      </xs:extension>
    </xs:complexContent>
  </xs:complexType>
</xs:element>
```

I could have defined this as another top-level named type, but in this case, the extra attribute is very specific to this element, so it doesn't seem worth the trouble.

So the main difference in this structure is that I've introduced one extra type, `gen-inline`, which extends the existing `Inline` type by adding the standard attributes in the attribute group named `attrs`. (These attributes include `id`, `class`, `style`, `title` and quite a few others).

This extra type is likely to prove very useful in a system that does strict static type checking, which I will be discussing later in the chapter. In a system with strict static type checking, the expression «element(*, Inline)/@title» (which is trying to select the `title` attribute of every element whose type is `Inline`) will give you an error, because the type `Inline` doesn't define this attribute; but the expression «element(*, gen-inline)/@title» would succeed, because my gen-inline type does include this attribute. Strict static typing is potentially very useful to detect the kind of spelling mistakes which otherwise simply lead to an XPath expression producing wrong answers. But if you want to use this feature, you will probably need to pay much more careful attention to your schema design to make it usable.

I raised the question earlier whether the type of the <q> element should be a subtype or a supertype of the type used for elements such as <h1> and <h2>. As we saw, in the published XHTML schema they are actually sibling types (they are both subtypes of Inline). In my own schema, I defined <q> using an unnamed subtype of the gen-inline type used for the <h1> and <h2> elements.

Logically, one could argue that the possible content of an <h1> or <h2> element is a strict subset of the possible content of a <q> element (it can include anything a <q> can contain except for the extra cite attribute), and that therefore the type of <h1> and <h2> should be a subtype of the type used for <q>. On that basis, instead of defining the type for <q> as an extension of the type for <h1> and <h2>, we would define the type for <h1> and <h2> as a restriction of the type for <q>. It's possible to do this in XML Schema, especially where the only difference is to prohibit an attribute from appearing (there is special syntax <xs:attribute name="cite" use="prohibited"> that makes it possible). Usually, though, this isn't the way schemas grow. We tend to refine existing structures by adding elements and attributes to them, and in XML Schema, refining complex types by extension is generally a lot simpler than refining them by restriction. So that's what you will tend to find has been done.

Building a type hierarchy by looking at the elements and seeing what child elements and attributes they have in common isn't really the right way to do it. This is a bottom-up approach to classification. One reason it doesn't work well is that it can give many possible answers: for example, should you group A with B because they have the same attributes, or group A with C because they have the same child elements? It's much better to create the type hierarchy as a result of top-down analysis, the kind of object modeling that's commonly used when designing databases. If you take this approach, then <employee> becomes a subtype of <person> not because they have similar content models but rather because every employee is a person : you appeal to your knowledge of the classification of things in the real world. It's much harder to do this when looking at the kind of markup you find in XHTML, but it can still give you useful answers. This approach tells you, for example, that <sub> and <sup> go together because they are both concerned with character-level formatting, and <ol> and <ul> go together because they both define lists.

This leads on to another classification tool available in XML Schema, namely substitution groups, which forms the subject of the next section.

Substitution Groups

The type of an element or attribute tells you what can appear inside the content of the element or attribute. Substitution groups, by contrast, classify elements according to where they can appear.

As we've already seen, there is a schema for XSLT 2.0 stylesheets published as part of the XSLT Recommendation. Let's look at how this schema uses substitution groups. I'm not concerned here with the actual effect of any specific XSLT elements, it just makes an interesting case study of a schema.

Firstly, the schema defines a type that is applicable to any XSLT-defined element, and which simply declares the standard attributes that can appear on any element:

```
<xs:complexType name="generic-element-type">
  <xs:attribute name="extension-element-prefixes" type="xsl:prefixes"/>
  <xs:attribute name="exclude-result-prefixes" type="xsl:prefixes"/>
  <xs:attribute name="xpath-default-namespace" type="xs:anyURI"/>
  <xs:attribute ref="xml:space"/>
  <xs:attribute ref="xml:lang"/>
  <xs:anyAttribute namespace="##other" processContents="skip"/>
</xs:complexType>
```

There's a good mix of features used to define these attributes. Some of them use built-in types (xs:anyURI), some use user-defined types defined elsewhere in the schema (xsl:prefixes), two of them (xml:space and xml:lang) are defined in a schema for a different namespace. The <xs:anyAttribute> at the end says that XSLT elements can contain attributes from a different namespace, which are not validated. (Perhaps it would be better to specify lax validation, which would validate the attribute if and only if a schema is available for it).

Every XSLT element except the <xsl:output> element allows a standard version attribute (the <xsl:output> element is different because its version attribute is defined for a different purpose and has a different type). So the schema defines another type that adds this attribute:

```
<xs:complexType name="versioned-element-type">
  <xs:complexContent>
    <xs:extension base="xsl:generic-element-type">
      <xs:attribute name="version" type="xs:decimal" use="optional"/>
    </xs:extension>
  </xs:complexContent>
</xs:complexType>
```

The XSLT specification classifies many XSLT elements as *instructions*. This is not a structural distinction based on the attributes or content model of these elements (which in fact varies widely), it is a distinction based on the way they are used. In particular, instruction elements are interchangeable in terms of where they may appear in a stylesheet: if you can use one instruction in a particular context, you can use any instruction. This calls for defining a substitution group:

```
<xs:element name="instruction"
            type="xsl:versioned-element-type"
            abstract="true"/>
```

Note that although the substitution group is defined using an element declaration, it is not defining a real element, because it specifies «abstract="true"». This means that an actual XSLT stylesheet will never contain an element called <xsl:instruction>. It is a fictional element that exists only so that others can be substituted for it.

What this declaration does say is that every element in the substitution group for <xsl:instruction> must be defined with a type that is derived from xsl:versioned-element-type. That is, every XSLT instruction allows the attributes extension-element-prefixes, exclude-result-prefixes, xpath-default-namespace, xml:space, xml:lang, and version. This is, in fact, the only thing that XSLT instructions have in common with each other, as far as their permitted content is concerned.

Individual instructions are now defined as members of this substitution group. Here is a simple example, the declaration of the <xsl:if> element:

```
<xs:element name="if" substitutionGroup="xsl:instruction">
  <xs:complexType>
    <xs:complexContent mixed="true">
      <xs:extension base="xsl:sequence-constructor">
        <xs:attribute name="test" type="xsl:expression" use="required"/>
      </xs:extension>
    </xs:complexContent>
  </xs:complexType>
</xs:element>
```

This shows that the <xsl:if> element is a member of the substitution group whose head is the abstract <xsl:instruction> element. It also tells us that the content model of the element (that is, its type) is defined as an extension of the type xsl:sequence-constructor, the extension being to allow a test attribute whose value is of type xsl:expression—this is a simple type defined later on in the same schema, representing an XPath expression that may appear as the content of this attribute.

The type xsl:sequence-constructor is used for all XSLT elements whose permitted content is a *sequence constructor*. A sequence constructor is simply a sequence of zero or more XSLT instructions, defined like this:

```
<xs:complexType name="sequence-constructor">
  <xs:complexContent mixed="true">
    <xs:extension base="xsl:versioned-element-type">
      <xs:group ref="xsl:sequence-constructor-group"
                minOccurs="0" maxOccurs="unbounded"/>
    </xs:extension>
  </xs:complexContent>
</xs:complexType>

<xs:group name="sequence-constructor-group">
  <xs:choice>
    <xs:element ref="xsl:variable"/>
    <xs:element ref="xsl:instruction"/>
    <xs:group ref="xsl:result-elements"/>
  </xs:choice>
</xs:group>
```

The first definition says that the xsl:sequence-constructor type extends xsl:versioned-element-type, whose definition we saw earlier. If it didn't extend this type, we wouldn't be allowed to put <xsl:if> in the substitution group of <xsl:instruction>. It also says that the content of a sequence constructor consists of zero or more elements, each of which must be chosen from the sequence-contructor-group. The second definition says that every element in the sequence-contructor-group is either an <xsl:instruction> (which implicitly allows any element in the substitution group for <xsl:instruction>, including of course <xsl:if>), or an <xsl:variable>.

The <xsl:variable> element is not defined as a member of the substitution group because it can be used in two different contexts, either as an instruction or as a top-level declaration in a stylesheet. This is one of the drawbacks of substitution groups: they can't overlap. The schema defines all the elements that can act as declarations in a very similar way, using a substitution group headed by an abstract `<xsl:declaration>` element. It's not possible for the same element, `<xsl:variable>`, to appear in more than one substitution group, so it has been defined in neither, and needs to be treated as a special case.

If you need to use XPath 2.0 to access an XSLT stylesheet (which isn't as obscure a requirement as it may seem, there are many applications for this) then the classification of elements as instructions or declarations can be very useful. For example, you can find all the instructions that have an attribute in the Saxon namespace with the expression:

```
//schema-element(xsl:instruction)[@saxon:*]
```

assuming that the namespace prefix «saxon» has been declared appropriately. Here the leading «//» indicates a search of the whole document, the expression «schema-element(xsl: instruction)» selects elements that are either named `<xsl:instruction>`, or are in the substitution group with `<xsl:instruction>` as its head element, and the expression «[@saxon:*]» is a filter that selects only those elements that have an attribute in the «saxon» namespace.

The penalty of choosing a real schema for our example is that we have to live with its complications. As we saw earlier, the `<xsl:variable>` element isn't part of this substitution group. So we might have to extend the query to handle `<xsl:variable>` elements as well. We can do this by writing:

```
/*/(schema-element(xsl:instruction)|xsl:variable)[@saxon:*]
```

A detailed explanation of this expression has to wait until much later in the book: the «/» and «|» operators, and the predicate in square brackets, are all described in Chapter 7, while the construct «schema-element(xsl:instruction)» is explained in Chapter 9.

To sum up this section: substitution groups not only are a very convenient mechanism for referring to a number of elements that are substitutable for each other in the schema, but also provide a handy way of referring to a group of elements in XPath expressions. This is particularly true where the elements don't have much in common with each as far as their internal structure is concerned. But they do have one limitation, which is that elements can only belong directly to one substitution group (or to put it another way, substitution groups must be properly nested, they cannot overlap).

This completes our tour of XML Schema which was conducted very much from an XPath perspective. The rest of the chapter builds on this understanding to show how the XPath type system works, and how it is related to the types of XML Schema.

Atomic Types

The place where the XPath and XML Schema type systems come together most closely is in the definition of the atomic types, and that's the area we will look at next.

Notice that we're talking here about atomic types rather than simple types. In XML Schema, we use an `<xs:simpleType>` declaration to define any type other than a complex type, that is, any type that doesn't permit attributes or child elements. Attributes always have simple types, and elements may have simple types if they don't allow child elements or attributes. But simple types are not necessarily atomic types, because they allow lists. For example, consider the type definition (again taken from the schema for XSLT 2.0):

```
<xs:simpleType name="prefixes">
  <xs:list itemType="xs:NCName" />
</xs:simpleType>
```

This defines a simple type whose value allows a list of names (the type xs:NCName defines a name that follows the XML rules: NCName means no-colon-name). An example of an attribute conforming to this type might be «a="h1 h2 h3"». This is a simple type, but it is not an atomic type. Atomic types do not allow lists.

XML Schema also allows simple types to be defined as a choice; for example, a simple type might allow either a decimal number, or the string «N/A». This is referred to as a union type. Like list types, union types are simple types but they are not atomic types.

Atomic types come from a number of sources.

XML Schema defines 19 primitive types and 25 derived types that can be used in any schema: these are referred to as the XML Schema built-in types. They include commonly used types such as xs:boolean and xs:string, and some that are decidedly obscure like xs:gYearMonth and xs:NOTATION. These types are all in the XML Schema namespace http://www.w3.org/2001/XMLSchema.

There is also a second namespace for schema-defined datatypes, called http://www.w3.org/2001/XMLSchema-datatypes. Frankly, this namespace is best forgotten. It doesn't provide anything that you don't get by using the ordinary XML Schema namespace, and it creates some technical problems because the types in this namespace are not exact synonyms of the types in the ordinary namespace. My advice is, don't go anywhere near it.

XPath 2.0 adds four more atomic types: xdt:dayTimeDuration, xdt:yearMonthDuration, xdt:anyAtomicType, and xdt:untypedAtomic. The last two are rather special, so I shall cover them separately.

You can define your own atomic types in a schema. A type becomes available for use in XPath expressions through a piece of magic called the XPath Static Context, which we will examine in more detail in Chapter 4. This really means that the binding between an XPath expression and a schema is something outside the control of the XPath specification itself. In XSLT, for example, it is controlled using an <xsl:import-schema> declaration in the stylesheet, but in other XPath environments, it may be controlled in a different way.

Implementors can also add their own atomic types. There are a number of reasons they might want to do this. The most likely reason is to make it easier for XPath expressions to make calls on external functions, for example, functions written in C# or Java. The XPath specification doesn't say how this is done, and leaves it to implementors to define. Another reason implementors might want to add extra data types is to support XPath access to some specialized database, for example, an LDAP directory. XPath is defined in terms of a data model with an obvious relationship to XML, but there is no reason why other sources of data cannot be mapped to the data model equally well, and doing this effectively might involve defining some custom types. (I mentioned LDAP because it is a hierarchic database, which provides a particularly good fit to the XPath data model.) Generally, any extra types added by the implementor will have names that are in some implementation-controlled namespace.

In the sections that follow, I will describe the built-in atomic datatypes in a number of groups. These are my own categories, not anything that comes from the specifications themselves:

- ❑ *The major atomic datatypes*: `xs:anyURI`, `xs:boolean`, `xs:date`, `xs:dateTime`, `xs:decimal`, `xs:double`, `xs:integer`, `xs:QName`, `xs:string`, `xs:time`, `xdt:dayTimeDuration`, and `xdt:yearMonthDuration`. These are the only atomic data types that are directly supported in the XPath library of functions and operators for anything but the most trivial of operations. They are therefore the ones you are most likely to be using most of the time. In XSLT 2.0, these are the only ordinary types that every XSLT processor is required to support.

- ❑ *The minor atomic datatypes*: These are defined as primitive types in XML Schema, but they are not well supported by XPath, and you are unlikely to use them very often. These are `xs:gYear`, `xs:gYearMonth`, `xs:gMonth`, `xs:gMonthDay`, `xs:gDay`, `xs:duration`, `xs:float`, `xs:hexBinary`, `xs:base64Binary`, and `xs:NOTATION`.

- ❑ *The derived numeric datatypes*: These are defined by restriction from the `xs:integer` type. They all define integers with a limited range of values, for example, `xs:positiveInteger`, `xs:short`, `xs:unsignedByte`.

- ❑ *The derived string datatypes*: These are defined by restriction from `xs:string`. They include types like `xs:token` and `xs:NCName` that restrict the syntax of the string and define the treatment of whitespace.

- ❑ *The type* `xdt:untypedAtomic`: This represents values whose type is unknown, because the value has not been validated by a schema processor. This is a chameleon type, whose values can be used freely in any context, provided that the value can be converted at runtime to the type that's expected.

There are two ways to use these atomic types in XPath.

- ❑ You can use them in a schema to define the types of elements and attributes. When you do this, the result of validating an XML document against this schema will be that the elements and attributes acquire a type annotation of the appropriate atomic type, and the typed value of the nodes (which is what you typically get when you use the node as input to an operation such as addition) will be the atomic value of the relevant type.

- ❑ You can manipulate atomic values of these types in your XPath expressions. For example, if you compare two strings, the result is a boolean, that is, a value of type `xs:boolean`. This value has never been anywhere near an XML document, let alone an XML Schema validator, but it is an `xs:boolean` all the same.

The Major Atomic Types

This section describes the most important atomic types used in XPath expressions, in alphabetical order. These types are chosen because they are the ones that are supported in the standard library of functions and operators defined in XPath, in particular the functions listed in Chapter 10. If you are using an XSLT 2.0 processor with no schema support, these will be the only data types available, and even if you are using XML Schemas, they are probably the types you will use 95% of the time.

xs:anyURI

This type is intended to hold URIs, in the widest sense of the term. This includes:

❑ Absolute URIs such as «http://www.w3.org/»

❑ Relative URIs such as «../index.html»

❑ URI References, that is URIs with a fragment identifier at the end, separated by a «#» character: for example «http://www.w3.org/TR/xpath20#Introduction» or simply«#Introduction»

❑ Unescaped URIs such as «file:///My Documents/biog.doc». Technically, this is not a URI because it contains a space character. To make it into a URI, the space must be escaped so it appears as «file:///My%20Documents/biog.doc». A number of specifications such as XML Linking explicitly allow a URI to be held in its unescaped form (because it isn't a real URI until it is escaped, I sometimes refer to it as a *wannabe-URI*). And although these aren't real URIs, XML Schema explicitly allows them to appear in an xs:anyURI value.

Most data types in XML Schema are rather specific about exactly what is allowed in the value space of the data type (for example, xs:boolean has two values, true and false), and how these values may be written in a source document (the lexical representation: with xs:boolean the values «0», «1», «true», and «false» are permitted). Most types also define a *canonical lexical representation* for each value in the value space, which is the representation that will be chosen when a typed value is converted to a string.

For the xs:anyURI type, these definitions have been fudged. Though the wording makes it clear that the intention is for xs:anyURI items to hold a URI as defined in the relevant internet RFCs (see for example http://www.ietf.org/rfc/rfc2396), they stop short of saying that a schema validator is expected to check that the contents actually conform with these rules. There is good reason for this reticence: many commonly used URIs don't actually conform with the rules in the RFC, and in any case, the rules in the RFC are not always clear.

I have read some books on XML Schema that suggest that in the value space of xs:anyURI, the value is always escaped (as in the example «file:///My%20Documents/biog.doc») and that conversion from the lexical form used in a source document to the value space should therefore cause this escaping to happen. This would mean that when you compare two xs:anyURI values, differences caused by one of them being escaped and the other not don't matter. This is one interpretation of the spec, but I think it is an imaginative one, and in practice schema processors appear to allow any string to be used as an xs:anyURI value, and to leave the string unchanged when converting it to its internal representation.

The functions described in Chapter 10 that use URIs actually model URIs as strings rather than as xs:anyURI values. The W3C working groups made this decision for two reasons:

❑ As we have seen, XML Schema is less than clear about the precise rules for the xs:anyURI data type

❑ Because an xs:anyURI is not a string, it is very inconvenient to manipulate, as none of the string-handling functions such as substring-before(), concat(), and matches() are available. You can't even legally compare an xs:anyURI value to a string literal. You end up having to do frequent conversions between an xs:anyURI value and an equivalent xs:string, and this starts to get tedious.

My advice would be *don't use this data type in XPath expressions*. By all means use it when writing a schema, to document the fact that a particular element or attribute is designed to hold a URI, but as soon as you read such an element or attribute into your XPath expression, convert it to a string and then manipulate it as a string. Conversions between data types are described in Chapter 9.

xs:boolean

This is the simplest data type defined in XML Schema. It has two values in the value space, referred to as `true` and `false`, and each of these has two permitted lexical representations: «1» and «true», «0» and «false».

Although it's so simple there are some interesting quirks in the way XML Schema and XPath handle this data type.

❑ As far as XML Schema is concerned, the `xs:boolean` data type has no ordering. But in XPath, there is an ordering: `false` is considered to be less than `true`. XPath 2.0 has taken this position largely for backward compatibility with XPath 1.0, and also because it can actually be useful: for example a stylesheet might use the expression «age < 18» as a sort key, which will output the adults first, then the children.

❑ There are two ways of converting a string to a boolean. An XML Schema processor interprets «1» and «true» as true, «0» and «false» as false. This behavior also occurs when you use a «cast as xs:boolean» expression (described in Chapter 9), or the `xs:boolean()` constructor, which is shorthand for the `cast` expression.

But if you use the `boolean()` function (or `fn:boolean()` if you want to write it with a namespace prefix), as described in Chapter 10, then a zero-length string translates to `false`, and everything else to `true`. This is also the result you get if you do an implicit conversion of a string to a boolean by using a string in a context such as «if (S) then A else B», where S is a string.

Again, the difference is partly historic: the XPath 1.0 rules were invented before XML Schema came along. But the convention of equating a zero-length string to `false` also has a long history in weakly typed programming languages, and is very convenient in some recursive algorithms that need to terminate when the argument is a zero-length string.

xs:date

The `xs:date` type represents a date. The lexical representation of the date (that is, the way it appears in a textual XML document) is always the representation defined in the ISO 8601 standard, that is YYYY-MM-DD (for example, «1999-11-16» for November 16, 1999). This format is chosen because it is unambiguous; the theory is that XML documents should represent information in a neutral form that is independent of how different users might want to see the information formatted.

XPath 2.0, in fact, does not provide any direct capability for formatting dates and times in a user-friendly way. This functionality is present only in XSLT, through the `format-date()` function. The `format-date()` function is described in *XSLT 2.0 Programmer's Reference*, in Chapter 7.

A rather quirky feature of the `xs:date` data type is that as well as holding the date itself, it can also hold a timezone. This is something that ISO 8601 itself doesn't allow. The idea is that a date actually represents a period of 24 hours starting at midnight in a particular timezone, and ending at the following midnight in the same timezone. The date November 16, 1999 represents a different period of 24 hours in New York from the period it represents in London, Tokyo, or Los Angeles, so the schema designers came up with the idea of adding a timezone to the date to indicate exactly when the date begins and ends. In the lexical representation, the timezone is added after the date part, for example «1999-11-16-05:00» represents a date in the timezone that is five hours behind UTC (the timezone used in the Eastern United States during the winter months). The timezone is optional; it is also possible to have a date value with no timezone, in which case the precise beginning and end of the 24-hour period represented by the value are considered to be unknown.

XML Schema doesn't define how dates are represented internally in the system, but it does define a *value space* for every data type. If two different lexical values translate into the same value in the value space, then they are completely equivalent (to the extent that when you copy an element or attribute, the original lexical representation won't necessarily be retained). For dates (as distinct from times) the XML Schema and XPath specifications agree that the timezone is part of the value space: that is, «1999-11-16-05:00» represents a different xs:date value from «1999-11-16+01:00».

This gives the problem of deciding whether a date that specifies a timezone (for example «1999-11-16-12:00») comes before or after a date that doesn't specify a timezone (for example «1999-11-16») when you want to perform comparison operations or sorting. If both dates have timezones, the answer is clear enough: the dates are sorted in order of their starting instants. And if neither have timezones, you can assume that they relate to the same timezone. But if one has a timezone and the other doesn't, it's not obvious what the answer should be. XML Schema took a rather purist view, saying that dates are *partially ordered*, which means that for some pairs of dates you don't know which one comes first. For an expression language like XPath, partial ordering is a nightmare: the system has to come up with some kind of answer. The answer chosen was that the system environment contains an implicit timezone that can be used as a default, and when dates with no timezone have to be compared or sorted, the system will assume that they refer to this implicit timezone. We look more closely at the implicit timezone when we examine the XPath evaluation context in the next chapter.

The operations you can perform on a date include:

❑   Comparing and sorting dates

❑   Converting dates to and from strings

❑   Extracting the component parts of a date (year, month, day, timezone)

❑   Adding a duration to a date (or subtracting a duration) to get another date

❑   Determining the difference between two dates, as a duration

❑   Converting the value to an xs:dateTime (the result is the starting instant of the date)

❑   In XSLT only, formatting a date for human consumption (for example, as «Wednesday 16th November»)

Dates held using this data type are always supposed to be Gregorian dates, even if they predate the introduction of the Gregorian calendar (which happened at different times in different countries). In principle, historic events are supposed to have their dates adjusted to represent them using the modern calendar.

Negative dates (BC dates) are supported, but they are a minor disaster area in XML Schema. According to XML Schema, the year zero is not allowed, and the year before 0001 is represented as −0001. However, shortly before XML Schema was published, a new edition of ISO 8601 came out that stated that the year before 0001 should be represented as 0000. The Schema specification hasn't changed to match this, but it includes a note saying that it might change in the future. It's hard to see how such a change can be made, however, as it would affect the meaning of data in existing documents, and the results of queries. In practice, I would advise against using this data type for historical dates. For most applications it's probably better to represent them using their original calendar.

xs:dateTime

The xs:dateTime type represents the combination of a date and time, that is, it represents an instant in time. The lexical representation is again based on ISO 8601, for example it might be «2004-04-12T13:05:00Z» to represent five minutes past one in the afternoon of 12th April 2004, in the timezone Z (Z represents Coordinated Universal Time, abbreviated to UTC, and often still referred to by its older name of Greenwich Mean Time or GMT).

The seconds part of an xs:dateTime can contain a fractional part. The number of significant digits that are retained is implementation-defined, but must be at least three.

As with xs:date, the complications with dates and times are all to do with timezones (if only the world could agree to synchronize its clocks, the problem would disappear). XML Schema takes the view that the value space of xs:dateTime represents instants in time, and that «2004-04-12T13:05:00Z» and «2004-04-12T08:05:00-05:00» are the same instant in time (five past one in London is five past eight in New York), and are therefore indistinguishable.

The XSLT and XQuery working groups didn't feel it was acceptable that the original timezone information written in the source XML document should be simply thrown away. It didn't seem right, for example, that a transformation that copies a source document containing the value «2004-04-12 T08:05:00-05:00» should produce the value «2004-04-12T13:05:00Z» in the result document. Although it's right to consider the two values as being equal (in the same way that 1 and 01 are equal) it seems that there is some information content in the timezone that the user probably wants to hold on to. So, after much agonizing and debate between the working groups, the XPath data model defines a value space that retains the original timezone as well as the "instant in time". This doesn't affect the test whether two xs:dateTime values are equal, but it does affect other operations, for example the operation of converting an xs:dateTime value to a string (which will reconstitute the original timezone).

Like xs:date values, xs:dateTime values don't need to specify a timezone, and XPath adopts the same solution: they are assumed to apply to an implicit timezone taken from the evaluation context.

The operations you can perform on an xs:dateTime include:

- ❑ Comparing and sorting dateTimes
- ❑ Converting dateTimes to and from strings
- ❑ Extracting the component parts of a dateTime (year, month, day, hour, minutes, seconds, timezone)
- ❑ Adding a duration to a dateTime (or subtracting a duration) to get another dateTime
- ❑ Determining the difference between two dateTimes, as a duration
- ❑ Extracting the date or time part separately

❑ Adjusting the timezone: that is, creating an equivalent dateTime with or without a timezone, or with a different timezone (see the adjust-dateTime-to-timezone() function on page 297)

❑ In XSLT only, formatting a dateTime for human consumption (for example, as «Wednesday 16th November, 1.30p.m.»)

xs:decimal

The xs:decimal data type represents numbers that can be accurately expressed in decimal notation. This type is useful for values such as amounts of money, where the actual value space is discrete rather than continuous, and where the rounding errors that arise with binary formats such as xs:double and xs:float are undesirable.

In a user-defined subtype of xs:decimal, the values can be restricted in terms of the total number of allowed digits, and the number of digits allowed after the decimal point. If the built-in type xs:decimal is used without restriction, the number of digits allowed must be at least 18, though it can be greater than this if the implementation chooses. Some implementations may use an unlimited-precision representation (Saxon does, for example).

Any numeric literal written with a decimal point in XPath 2.0 (but without using exponential notation) represents an xs:decimal value, for example the literal «3.50». Note that this represents exactly the same xs:decimal value as the literal «3.5»: in general, trailing zeros after the decimal point will be lost when xs:decimal values are manipulated, which can be a bit awkward when you are handling amounts of money. For example, the result of «2.44 + 2.56» is displayed as «5». XSLT has a function format-number() that allows you to control the way values are formatted, for example you can use a picture of «0.00» to ensure that there are always two digits after the decimal point. But there is no equivalent to this in XPath or XQuery.

XPath 2.0 offers a full range of arithmetic operators and functions on xs:decimal values. These are summarized in the entry for xs:double which follows this entry. The arithmetic operators are described in more detail in Chapter 6, and the functions are listed in Chapter 10. When you apply these operators and functions to xs:decimal operands, the result is generally also an xs:decimal. In the case of operators with two operands you can mix xs:decimal with other numeric types; if the other operand is an xs:float or xs:double then the xs:decimal is converted to an xs:float or xs:double as appropriate, and the result will also be an xs:float or xs:double.

The main operation that can cause problems is division. The division operator in XPath is div, because «/» is reserved for use in path expressions. Division by zero is a fatal error. When you perform a division that does not have an exact decimal result, for example «10 div 3.0», the precision of the result is implementation-defined. One implementation might give you 3.333333, another might give you 3.333333333333. An implementation could even claim to be conformant if it gave you the answer 3, though it might not prove popular in the marketplace if it did that.

When a decimal number is displayed as a string, it is shown as an integer if there are no significant digits after the decimal point. So the result of «2.5+2.5» is displayed as «5».

xs:double

The xs:double type represents double-precision floating point numbers. This was the only numeric data type supported in XPath 1.0, and it is therefore the default for some operations where backward compatibility is important: in particular, if you apply numeric operations to the value of a node in a schemaless document, the system will try to convert the contents of that node to an xs:double value.

An xs:double is a double-precision (64-bit) floating-point number, and its behavior is defined to follow the IEEE 754 standard. This standard (*IEEE Standard for Binary Floating-Point Arithmetic. ANSI/IEEE Std. 754-1985*) has been widely implemented by many microprocessors for some years, but it is only through its adoption in the Java language that it has become familiar to high-level language programmers. If you understand how floating point behaves in Java, the contents of this section will be quite familiar; if not, they may be rather strange.

XPath 2.0 introduces the ability to use scientific notation for floating-point numbers, either on input or on output. If you want to enter the number one trillion, you can now write 1.0E12. In fact, if you want to write an xs:double as a literal in an XPath expression, you must write it in scientific notation, otherwise it will be treated as an xs:decimal (if it has a decimal point) or as an xs:integer (if not).

On output, that is when you convert an xs:double to a string, scientific notation is used only if the absolute value is smaller than 0.000001, or greater than 1,000,000. This means that most everyday numbers will be formatted in ordinary decimal notation on output. In XSLT, you can control the format of numeric output more precisely by using the format-number() function, which is defined in *XSLT 2.0 Programmer's Reference*.

In general, I recommend using xs:double for numbers that are on a continuous scale (for example, distances, weights, or temperatures), and using xs:decimal for numbers that represent discrete quantities, such as sums of money. But this is only rough guidance.

IEEE 754 defines the following range of values for a double-precision number:

Value	Description
Finite nonzero values	These are values of the form $s \times m \times 2x$, where s (the sign) is +1 or −1, m (the mantissa) is a positive integer less than 2^{53}, and x (the exponent) is an integer between −1075 and 970, inclusive
Positive zero	This is the result of subtracting a number from itself. It can also result from dividing any positive number by infinity, or from dividing a very small number by a very large number of the same sign
Negative zero	This is the result of dividing any negative number by infinity. It can also result from dividing a positive number by minus infinity, or from dividing a very small negative number by a very large positive number, or vice versa
Positive infinity	This is the result of dividing any positive number by zero. It can also result from multiplying two very large numbers with the same sign. Note that division by zero is not an error: it has a well-defined result
Negative infinity	This is the result of dividing any negative number by zero. It can also result from multiplying two very large numbers with different signs
NaN	Not a Number. This is the result of attempting to convert a non-numeric string value to a number. It can also be used to mean "unknown" or "not applicable", like the SQL null value

These values cannot all be written directly as XPath constants. However, they can be expressed as the result of expressions, for example:

Value	XPath expression
Negative zero	−0e0
Positive Infinity	1 div 0e0
Negative Infinity	−1 div 0e0
NaN	number("NaN")

Technically, negative numbers cannot be written directly as constants: «−10» is an expression rather than a number, but in practice it can be used anywhere that a numeric constant can be used. The only thing you need to be careful of is that a space may be needed before the unary minus operator if you write an expression such as «$x div -1».

Except for NaN, number values are *ordered*. Arranged from smallest to largest, they are:

- ❑ Negative infinity
- ❑ Negative finite non-zero values
- ❑ Negative zero
- ❑ Positive zero
- ❑ Positive finite non-zero values
- ❑ Positive infinity

This ordering determines the result of less-than and greater-than comparisons, and in XSLT it determines the result of sorting using <xsl:apply-templates> or <xsl:for-each> with a sort key specified using <xsl:sort data-type="number">.

NaN is *unordered*, so the operators «<», «<=», «>», and «>=» return false if either or both operands are NaN. However, when <xsl:sort> is used to sort a sequence of numeric values that includes one or more NaN values, NaN values are collated at the start of the sequence (or at the end if you choose descending order).

Positive zero and negative zero compare equal. This means that the operators «=», «<=», and «>=» return true, while «!=», «<», and «>» return false. However, other operations can distinguish positive and negative zero; for example, «1.0 div $x» has the value positive infinity if $x is positive zero, and negative infinity if $x is negative zero.

The equals operator «=» returns false if either or both operands are NaN, and the not-equals operator «!=» returns true if either or both operands are NaN. Watch out for the apparent contradictions this leads to; for example, «$x=$x» can be false, and «$x<$y» doesn't necessarily give the same answer as «$y>$x».

The simplest way to test whether a value $x is NaN is:

```
if ($x!=$x) then ...
```

If this seems too obscure for your taste, then provided you know that $x is numeric you can write:

```
if (string($x)='NaN') then
```

If you are familiar with null values in SQL, some of this logic might seem familiar, but there are some subtle differences. For example, in SQL the condition «null=null» has the value null, so that «not(null=null)» is also null; while in XPath «NaN=NaN» is false, so that «not(NaN=NaN)» is true.

XPath provides a number of operators and functions that act on numeric values:

❑   The numerical comparison operators «<», «<=», «>», and «>=». Note that within a stylesheet, you may need to use XML escape conventions to write these, for example, «<» in place of «<».

❑   The numerical equality operators «=» and «!=».

❑   The unary minus operator «-».

❑   The multiplicative operators «*», «div», and «mod».

❑   The additive operators «+» and «-».

❑   The number() function, which can convert from any value to a number.

❑   The string() function, which convert a number to a string.

❑   The boolean() function, which converts a number to a Boolean.

❑   The abs() function returns the absolute value of a number.

❑   The functions round(), ceiling(), floor(), and round-half-to-even(), which convert a number to an integer.

❑   The aggregate functions sum(), avg(), max(), and min() which produce a single xs:double value when applied to a sequence of xs:double values.

Operators on numbers behave exactly as specified by IEEE 754. XPath is not as strict as Java in defining exactly what rounding algorithms should be used for inexact results, and in what sequence operations should be performed. In fact XPath 2.0 is more liberal than XPath 1.0, in that it allows any of the options permitted by IEEE 754 to be chosen. These include, for example, producing an error on overflow rather than returning positive or negative infinity.

Many implementations, however, are likely to follow the Java rules. In this case, numeric operators and functions never produce an error. An operation that overflows produces positive or negative infinity, an operation that underflows produces positive or negative zero, and an operation that has no other sensible result produces NaN. All numeric operations and functions with NaN as an operand produce NaN as a result. For example, if you apply the sum() function to a sequence, then if the sequence contains a NaN value, the result of the sum() function will be NaN.

xs:integer

The xs:integer data type supports the positive and negative natural numbers. Neither XML Schema nor XPath 2.0 dictate what the maximum value of an integer is. XML Schema has a rule that implementations must support at least 18 decimal digits. But one of the subtypes of xs:integer, namely xs:unsignedLong, supports values in the range 0 to 18,446,744,073,709,551,615. This requires 20 digits, so an implementation that stops at 18 is going to struggle to pass some of the conformance tests.

Unlike all the other types that I classify as major types, xs:integer is not a primitive type but a derived type. It is derived by restriction from xs:decimal. This means that every valid xs:integer is also a valid xs:decimal, and anywhere that an xs:decimal can be used, an xs:integer can be substituted. The actual nature of the restriction is that the xs:integer type contains all xs:decimal values that have no significant digits after the decimal point.

The xs:integer type follows the pattern of the other numeric types, in that all the arithmetic operators and functions, when applied to an xs:integer argument (or to two xs:integer operands) produce an xs:integer as their result.

The main exception to this is division. XPath 2.0 provides two division operators. The div operator treats integer operands as xs:decimals, and produces an xs:decimal result (so «5 div 2» is 2.5). The idiv operator (for integer division) produces an xs:integer result, so «5 idiv 2» is 2. Closely related to this is the avg() function: the average of a sequence of xs:integer values is an xs:decimal.

xs:QName

The xs:QName type is a rather specialized type whose values hold XML qualified names.

An xs:QName has two forms. In its lexical form, it consists of either a simple local name (such as «product»), or a local name qualified by a namespace prefix (such as «mfg:product». In its expanded form, it consists of two components: a namespace URI (possibly null) and a local name.

There is no direct string representation of the expanded value, though in some interfaces (for example in the Java JAXP interface) expanded QNames are represented in a notation devised by James Clark, of the form «{namespace-uri}local-name», for example «{http://www.mfg.org/ns}product».

This type is unusual (and, one might add, a great nuisance) because it is not possible to translate between the lexical form and the internal value space without having additional context information. A schema validator gets this context information from the namespace declarations that surround the element or attribute where the QName appears. For XPath (and XSLT and XQuery) processors, which have the job of extracting parts of a document and copying them into different places, this dependency on context information causes no end of hassle: it isn't safe to copy a QName to a new location unless you also copy its context information. This is why the spec devotes so much attention to the arcane matter of namespace nodes. It's also for this reason that there are restrictions on what you can do with an xs:QName—for example, it is the only type (apart from xs:NOTATION, which is another oddity) that you cannot convert to a string.

One of the ideas behind defining xs:QName as a primitive type in XML Schema was so that the XML infrastructure would know which parts of the document have dependencies on namespace declarations, and would therefore be able to ensure that the relevant namespace declarations are kept around when data is copied. Unfortunately this doesn't work, because you can have namespace-sensitive data in a document without declaring it as an xs:QName. For example, if your document contains XPath expressions (which it will do if it happens to be a stylesheet, but it's not uncommon to find them in other kinds of document as well) then it will necessarily contain namespace-sensitive content that isn't flagged as such, because an XPath expression is more complex than a simple xs:QName.

In fact, one of the paradoxes is that although the presence of the xs:QName type in XML Schema is often attributed to the fact that XSLT stylesheets use QNames in the content of attributes, the schema for XSLT 2.0 stylesheets doesn't actually use the xs:QName type. This is because there's a small but important difference in the rules. XML Schema specifies (you have to read the errata to find this out) that when an xs:QName is written with no namespace prefix, it uses the default namespace, in the same way as element names with no prefix. But XSLT specifes that when its QNames are unprefixed, they have a null namespace URI, in the same way as unprefixed attribute names—the default namespace is not used. Although an XML Schema processor would get the right answer in testing the validity of the attributes if they were declared with the xs:QName type, it would give the wrong answer to an application that asked for the typed value of the attribute. I labor this point for two reasons: firstly, because it shows one of the pitfalls of the xs:QName data type, and more importantly, because it shows how types in XML Schema, once you start using them in XPath (or XSLT or XQuery) are about much more than validity checking, they also define the conversion from the lexical values appearing in the input to the typed values seen by the application.

What operations does XPath support on xs:QName values?

❑ You can compare two QNames for equality. This sounds trivial, but it is probably the most important reason for using them. The comparison checks both the namespace URI and the local name, and it ignores the prefix. Moreover, the proper rules are used for this comparison; it's not subject to the uncertainties that arise when comparing strings, for example whether accents are significant and whether lower-case compares equal to upper-case. For example, the test:

```
node-name(.) = expanded-QName("http://www.mfg.org/ns", "product")
```

is comparing two xs:QName values. This is much more reliable than the test:

```
name(.) = "mfg:product"
```

which could go wrong for two reasons: it's dependent on the choice of namespace prefix, which shouldn't make any difference, and it's doing a string comparison using the default collation, which might compare strings such as «product» and «Product» as equal if that's the way it's been set up. There's more detail on collations in the next section, which discusses the xs:string data type.

❑ You can construct an expanded QName from the namespace URI and local-name using the expanded-QName() function shown above, and you can extract these two components using the rather clumsily-named functions local-name-from-QName() and namespace-uri-from-QName().

Although you cannot convert a QName directly to a string, you can convert a string to a QName. For example, you can write «xs:QName("mfg:product")», which will produce the expanded QName whose local-name is «product», and whose namespace URI is the namespace URI corresponding to the «mfg» prefix. The way this correspondence is established is outside the control of XPath itself: it is part of the static context of an XPath expression. In XSLT stylesheets, for example, it is established by the namespace declarations in the stylesheet surrounding the place where the XPath expression appears.

❑   Note that this construct allows the lexical QName to be constructed at runtime (if that weren't true, there wouldn't be much point in it), for example it allows you to write something like:

```
xs:QName(concat("mfg:", local-name($e)))
```

For this to work, the system has to know the original namespace context at runtime, not only at compile time. It's therefore a rather expensive feature of the language that some implementors complain about a great deal.

> **Watch out for changes in the rules here: this part of the XPath specification is still being hotly debated.**

xs:string

A string value in XPath is any sequence of zero or more characters, where the alphabet of possible characters is the same as in XML: essentially the characters defined in Unicode.

String values can be written in XPath expressions in the form of a literal, using either single quotes or double quotes, for example «'John'» or «"Mary"». In theory, the string literal can contain the opposite quote character as part of the value, for example «"John's"». In practice, certainly in XSLT, XPath expressions are written within XML attributes, so the opposite quote character will generally already be in use for the attribute delimiters. For more details, see the section *StringLiteral* in Chapter 5, page 144.

There is no special null value, as there is in SQL. Where no other value is appropriate, a zero-length string or an empty sequence is used. These are not the same thing: an empty sequence is a sequence containing no items («count($x)» returns 0), while a zero-length string is a sequence containing a single item, whose type is xs:string and whose value has a string-length of zero («count($x)» returns 1, «string-length($x)» returns 0). However, although zero-length strings and empty sequences aren't the same thing, most of the functions in the standard library (see Chapter 10) give the same answer when an empty sequence is supplied as the input as when a zero-length string is supplied.

> *The specifications try always to use the term zero-length string for the value «" "», to avoid any possible confusion, but occasionally the terms null string and empty string slip in by mistake.*

The actual set of Unicode characters permitted in XML changes between XML 1.0 and XML 1.1. At the time of writing, the XPath 2.0 specifications leave it to the implementor to decide which version of XML to align with.

In XML 1.0, the only ASCII control characters permitted (codes below x20) are the whitespace characters x09, x0A, and x0D (tab, newline, and carriage return). In XML 1.1, all control characters other than x00 are allowed, though you have to write them using XML character references rather than in their native encoding. For example, the BELL character, which in former times was used to ring the bell on a teletype machine, but nowadays is more likely to result in an irritating electronic beep, is represented as «&x07;». The requirement to use this form is because some of these control characters have special meaning in communications protocols that may be used to carry XML documents. The exclusion of the x00 character (sometimes called NUL) is probably a concession to programmers writing XML parsers and related software in C, where this character is treated as a string delimiter. It also has the effect—probably deliberate—that you still can't use XML directly to convey binary data, you have to encode it as characters. As we will see (on page 94), XML Schema provides two data types to help with this, `xs:hexBinary` and `xs:base64Binary`.

Unicode was originally defined so that all characters would fit in two bytes (the highest code point was 65,535), but it has since outgrown that limit, and now defines characters using code points up to 1,114,111. In programming languages such as Java, there is poor support for Unicode characters above 65,535, and they appear in the application as a *surrogate pair*: two `char` values that have to be processed as a pair. (There are plans to provide library support for higher codepoints in JDK 1.5, but the basic data types `char` and `String` won't be changed). In XPath, you don't have to worry about surrogate pairs. Each character, even those above 65,535, is counted as a single character. This affects functions such as `string-length()`, which count the number of characters in a string, and `substring()`, which extracts the characters at particular positions in the string.

Strings may be compared using the «=» and «!=» operators, as well as «<», «>», «<=», and «>=». The exact way in which these work is context-dependent. Strings are always compared using a collation, and it is up to the collation to decide, for example, whether the two strings «naive» and «naïve» are equal or not (spot the difference). XPath itself doesn't define what the default collation is (and neither does XSLT), it leaves the choice to the user, and the way you select it is going to depend on the configuration options for your particular XPath processor. If you want more control over the choice of a collation, you can use the `compare()` function, which is described in detail in Chapter 10 (see page 310).

The handling of the «<» and «>» operators is not backward compatible with XPath 1.0. In XPath 1.0, these operators, when applied to two strings, attempted to convert both strings to numbers, and compared them numerically. This meant, for example, that «"4"="4.0"» was false (because they were compared as strings), while «"4">="4.0"» was true (because they were compared as numbers). In XPath 2.0, if you want to compare strings as numbers, you must convert them to numbers explicitly, for example, by using the `number()` function.

The library of functions available for handling strings is considerably expanded from XPath 1.0. It includes:

- ❑ `concat()` and `string-join()` to concatenate strings with or without separators
- ❑ `contains()`, `starts-with()`, and `ends-with()` to test whether a string contains a particular substring
- ❑ `substring()`, `substring-before()`, and `substring-after()` to extract part of a string
- ❑ `upper-case()` and `lower-case()` to change the case of characters in a string
- ❑ `string-length()` to find the length of a string
- ❑ `normalize-space()` to remove unwanted leading, trailing, and inner white space characters
- ❑ `normalize-unicode()` to remove differences in the way equivalent Unicode characters are represented (for example, the letter «ç» with a cedilla can be represented as either one Unicode character or two)

Perhaps the most powerful addition to the string-handling capability in XPath 2.0 is the introduction of support for regular expressions, familiar to programmers using languages such as Perl. Regular expressions provide a powerful way of matching and manipulating the contents of a string. They are used in three functions:

- ❑   `matches()` tests whether a string matches a particular regular expression. For example «`matches("W151TBH", "^[A-Z][0-9]+[A-Z]+$")`» returns `true`. (This regular expression matches any string consisting of one uppercase letter, then one or more digits, and then one or more letters.)

- ❑   `replace()` replaces the parts of a string that match a given regular expression with a replacement string. For example, «`replace("W151TBH", "^[A-Z]([0-9]+)[A-Z]+$", "$1")`» returns «`151`». The «`$1`» in the replacement string supplied as the third argument picks up the characters that were matched by the part of the regular expression written in parentheses.

- ❑   `tokenize()` splits a string into a sequence of strings, by treating any character sequence that matches the regular expression as a separator. For example, «`tokenize("abc/123/x", "/")`» returns the sequence «`"abc", "123", "x"`».

All these functions are described in detail in Chapter 10. The syntax of regular expressions is described in Chapter 11.

xs:time

The `xs:time` data type represents a time of day, for example, 12:15:00. Like an `xs:dateTime`, it can represent the fractional number of seconds to an arbitrary precision determined by the implementation (at least three decimal digits are required), and it can optionally incude a timezone. A time with a timezone is written, for example, as «`12:15:00+01:00`» to indicate a timezone one hour ahead of UTC (as used in much of continental Europe during the winter months, and in Britain during the summer).

Like `xs:date` and `xs:dateTime` values, `xs:time` values without an explicit timezone are assumed to apply to an implicit timezone taken from the evaluation context.

Operations you can perform on an `xs:time` include:

- ❑   Comparing and sorting times
- ❑   Converting times to and from strings
- ❑   Extracting the component parts of a time (hour, minutes, seconds, timezone)
- ❑   Adding a duration to a time (or subtracting a duration) to get another time
- ❑   Determining the difference between two times, as a duration
- ❑   Combining the time with a date to create an `xs:dateTime` (there is actually no direct way of achieving this, but it can be done by combining the other functions available)
- ❑   Adjusting the timezone: that is, creating an equivalent time with or without a timezone, or with a different timezone (see the `adjust-time-to-timezone()` function on page 297)

Although timezones are complex enough already, one problem that the XPath model doesn't tackle is daylight savings time (also known as summer time). If you want to use `xs:time` values to represent, say, a schedule of flights departing from Logan airport in Boston, then you probably want to use the value «`13:15:00`» to mean "a quarter past one, in Boston's time zone". Specifying this as

«13:15:00-05:00» would be incorrect, because for half the year Boston is five hours behind UTC, and for the other half it is only four hours behind. My recommendation in this situation would be not to store a timezone with the value itself, but to use some other way of representing the information (for example, a timezone attribute on the containing element). Alternatively, it might be better to hold all times internally in UTC (sometimes called Zulu time) and only convert them to a local timezone for display purposes.

A particular problem that is unique to xs:time values is comparison and sorting, because the natural ordering is cyclic. For example, most people would agree that 18:00:00 is before 23:59:00, but is it before 00:00:00? And is 20:00:00-05:00 (8 p.m. in New York) before or after 00:30:00+00:00 (half past midnight in London)?

There is no correct answer to this question, but the rule that XPath has adopted is at least reasonably simple. The answer is: if the value has no timezone, assume it is in the implicit timezone defined by the evaluation context; then adjust both values to UTC, and compare them according to the number of seconds that have elapsed since midnight. The effect of this rule is that 18:00:00-05:00 (6 p.m. in New York) is after 22:00:00-05:00 (10 p.m. in New York), which might not be what you expected. This arises because the corresponding UTC values are 23:00:00Z and 03:00:00Z, respectively. For an answer that makes more sense to the residents of New York, the pragmatic solution is to convert both values to strings, and compare them as strings.

xdt:dayTimeDuration and xdt:yearMonthDuration

XML Schema provides a primitive data type xs:duration, which we will discuss briefly on page 95. A duration represents a period of time, expressed in years, months, days, hours, minutes, seconds, and fractions of a second.

Durations that mix these different units are difficult to handle because the length of a month is variable. For example, what should be the result of comparing a duration of one month with a duration of 30 days? XML Schema addressed this problem by defining a partial ordering for durations, which means that some durations are clearly longer than others, but for some pairs of durations (like the example just cited), the relative magnitude is undefined.

The idea of a partial ordering makes life rather difficult for a language like XPath. Operations like «=» and «<» need to produce a yes-or-no answer, introducing a "maybe" would complicate the language immensely. For this reason, XPath decided to introduce two new duration types, which are defined as subtypes of xs:duration. The xdt:dayTimeDuration handles durations expressed in days, hours, minutes, seconds, and fractions of a second, while xdt:yearMonthDuration handles durations in years and months. These behave much more cleanly: an xdt:dayTimeDuration is just a decimal number of seconds, and an xdt:yearMonthDuration is just an integer number of months.

You can manipulate these two duration subtypes using arithmetic operators and functions: for example you can add and subtract two durations to give another duration, you can multiply or divide a duration by a number to get another duration, and you can divide one duration by another to get the ratio between the two durations as a number (more specifically, as an xs:double). You can also use functions such as sum() and avg() to get the total or average of a sequence of durations.

I personally prefer to use numbers for most of these operations. There's no reason why you can't use an xs:double to represent a duration in seconds, just as you would use one to represent a distance, a weight, a temperature or a voltage. Many calculations in fact become easier when you represent durations as numbers: for example, there is no way to divide a distance by a duration to obtain an average speed, except by converting the duration to a number. Similarly, if you want to work out how much to pay someone who has worked for five hours at $10/hour, it's no use multiplying the duration five hours by 10: the answer will be 2 days and 2 hours, not $50.

Where the duration types do prove useful is when they are used in conjunction with dates and times. You can add a duration to a date or time to get another date or time, and you can subtract one date or time from another to get a duration.

Durations are written lexically in the notation defined by the ISO 8601 standard. The general form is the letter «P», followed by one or more of the components *n*Y for the years, *n*M for the months, *n*D for days, *n*H for hours, *n*M for minutes, and *n*S for seconds. A «T» is used as a separator between the days and the hours. All the values are integers except for the seconds, which may be fractional. Zero components may be omitted (though at least one component must be present), and a negative duration may be written with a leading minus sign. So «P10Y6M» is 10 years 6 months, while «PT10H30M» is 10 hours, 30 minutes. XML Schema treats the values «P12M» and «P1Y» as distinct (an enumeration facet that permits one of these forms will not permit the other), but XPath treats them as equal, and will not retain any distinction between the two forms when converting the typed value back to a string value.

XPath provides no functions to format durations in a user-friendly output representation. Instead there are six functions years-from-duration(), months-from-duration(), days-from-duration(), hours-from-duration(), minutes-from-duration(), and seconds-from-duration() which allow the components to be extracted. These will be the components after normalizing the value: for example if the duration is supplied as «P18M», then extracting the components will give you one year and six months. If the duration is negative, then all the components will be supplied as negative numbers.

The Minor Atomic Types

The previous section covered the major data types of XPath 2.0, the ones that are well supported by functions and operators in the language: specifically, xs:anyURI, xs:boolean, xs:date, xs:dateTime, xs:decimal, xs:double, xs:integer, xs:QName, xs:string, xs:time, xdt:dayTimeDuration, and xdt:yearMonthDuration.

In this section I will briefly survey what I call the minor atomic datatypes. These are defined as primitive types in XML Schema, but they are not well supported by XPath, and you are unlikely to use them very often. These are xs:gYear, xs:gYearMonth, xs:gMonth, xs:gMonthDay, xs:gDay, xs:duration, xs:float, xs:hexBinary, xs:base64Binary, and xs:NOTATION.

The Partial Date Types

This category refers to the five types xs:gYear, xs:gYearMonth, xs:gMonth, xs:gMonthDay, and xs:gDay. They essentially represent dates in which one or two of the components are missing.

It has to be said that these types have been treated with a certain amount of derision by commentators. I have heard them referred to as the *gHorribleKludge* data types, or (after the pronunciation of "gDay"), the *Strine* data types. I have yet to see them used in a real application, and it does seem fairly extraordinary that these types, even if someone finds them useful, should be considered as primitive types on the same level as string, boolean, and double. For my part, if I want to design an XML database that includes information about the vintage years of my favorite wines, I think I can do it without using the xs:gYear data type, let alone an xs:gYear with a timezone.

But for better or worse, they are there—so we might as well describe them and move on.

The lexical representation of these values follows ISO 8601 conventions, using hyphens to represent missing components. ISO 8601 does not allow timezones on these values, this is an extra addition by the XML Schema working group. The allowed formats are shown using examples in the table below.

Type	Without timezone	With timezone
xs:gYear	2004	2004+08:00
xs:gYearMonth	2004-07	2004-07+08:00
xs:gMonth	-07	-07+08:00
xs:gMonthDay	-07-31	-07-31+08:00
xs:gDay	-31	-31+08:00

For the xs:gYear and xs:gYearMonth types, an optional leading minus sign is allowed to indicate BC dates.

The format of xs:gMonth values was shown incorrectly in the published XML Schema Recommendation as «-MM-». The error was corrected in a subsequent erratum, but in the meantime it has found its way into many books on XML Schema and a number of software products.

XPath 2.0 allows conversion of these values to and from strings. It allows them to be compared with each other using the «=» and «!=» operators, but they cannot be sorted or compared using «<» and «>». Comparison uses the implicit timezone if the value itself has no timezone. This means that two xs:gYear values are not equal to each other if they are in different timezones. (If you ever come across an application that relies on this, let me know.)

XPath 2.0 also allows casting from an xs:dateTime or xs:date to any of these five types: the relevant components (including the timezone) are extracted, and the other components are discarded. The full rules for casting between different data types are given in Chapter 9.

Binary Data Types

XML Schema supports two data types for holding binary data (for example, images or sound clips). These are xs:base64Binary and xs:hexBinary. Binary data cannot be held in an XML document directly, so it is always encoded as characters, and these two data types support the two most popular encodings.

Base 64 encoding is defined by reference to Internet mail standards in RFC 2045 (http://www.ietf.org/rfc/rfc2045.txt), though the format was originally described in RFC 1421. The basic idea is that the binary stream is split into 24-bit chunks (three bytes), and each chunk is then considered as four groups of 6 bits. Each 6-bit group is then considered to be the code representing a character in an alphabet of 64 characters, and this character is used to represent the value in the lexical representation. The 64-character alphabet consists of A–Z, a–z, 0–9, «+», and «/». One or more «=» characters may occur at the end to indicate padding to a whole number of 8-bit bytes, and newlines may appear to break up the total sequence (according to the RFC, the maximum line length is 76 characters).

The hexBinary encoding is simpler but less compact: it simply takes each octet of the binary stream, and represents it as two hexadecimal digits.

XPath 2.0 doesn't offer any very useful functionality for these two data types. In particular, it doesn't provide you with any way to convert the values to or from an actual stream of octets. What you can do is to compare the values for equality, convert them to and from strings, and convert between the two data types, in either direction.

Single-Precision Floating Point

Unlike the other data types that I've classified as minor, xs:float is well supported by functions and operators in XPath 2.0; in fact any operator or function that can be applied to an xs:double can also be applied to an xs:float.

There is no numeric literal for xs:float values, you have to create them using a constructor function, for example «xs:float(3.14159)».

The real reason I have classified xs:float as a minor data type is that I can't see any reason why anyone should want to use it. Compressing a floating point number into 32 bits made sense in the 1960s, but it makes little sense nowadays, and the loss of precision when performing numeric calculations is far too severe for most applications to justify the space saving. The only justification I have heard for including this type in XML Schema is for compatibility with other (older) type systems such as SQL.

In XML Schema, xs:float is not defined as a subtype of xs:double. Its value space is a strict subset of xs:double, but the working group decided to make it a primitive type apparently because of the difficulty of defining the nature of the restriction, which would have required the invention of new facets. In XPath, however, xs:float can be considered for most practical purposes to be a subtype of xs:double. It won't pass explicit tests such as «$F instance of xs:double» that it would pass if it were a true subtype, but you can pass an xs:float value to any function or operator that expects an xs:double, and it will be converted automatically (this particular kind of conversion is referred to as numeric promotion).

When you mix xs:float and xs:double in a calculation, the result is xs:double. If you mix xs:float and xs:decimal, however, the result is xs:float.

The xs:duration Data Type

The xs:duration type is one of the primitive data types in XML Schema, but as we've already seen, XPath decided to avoid the difficulties it posed by introducing the two subtypes xdt:yearMonth Duration and xdt:dayTimeDuration. You can still use the xs:duration type in your schema and in your documents, but there is very little support for it in XPath. In fact, you can't even compare one xs:duration to test whether it is equal to another. The only operations that are allowed are a few conversions: you can convert a string to an xs:duration, and convert an xs:duration to a string. You can also convert an xs:duration to an xdt:yearMonthDuration or xdt:dayTimeDuration, which is done by removing the components that aren't applicable to the target type.

The xs:NOTATION Data Type

The xs:NOTATION data type is perhaps the weirdest primitive type in the whole armoury. It's provided to give backward compatibility with a rarely used feature in DTDs.

In a DTD you can define an unparsed entity like this:

```
<!ENTITY weather-map SYSTEM "weather.jpeg"
    PUBLIC "-//MEGACORP//WEATHER/" NDATA JPEG>
```

This example refers to a binary file weather.jpeg, and the NDATA part tells you that its format is JPEG. The keyword NDATA can be read as "Non-XML Data".

This declaration is only valid if JPEG is the name of a notation defined somewhere in the DTD, for example:

```
<!NOTATION JPEG SYSTEM "image/jpeg" >
<!NOTATION GIF SYSTEM "image/gif" >
```

The theory is that the system identifier tells the application what the name JPEG actually means. Unfortunately, there is no standardization of the URIs you can use here, so this doesn't work all that well in practice. I've used the registered media type (or MIME type) for JPEG as if it were a URI, but this isn't universal practice.

Elsewhere in the DTD you can define an attribute whose value is required to be one of a number of specified notations, for example:

```
<!ELEMENT map EMPTY>
<!ATTLIST map
   format NOTATION (JPEG|GIF) "JPEG"
   src ENTITY #REQUIRED
>
```

This defines an element, <map>, whose content is empty, and which has two attributes: a format attribute of type NOTATION, whose value must be JPEG or GIF, with the default being JPEG, and a src attribute, whose value must be the name of an unparsed entity defined in the DTD.

You can't actually declare unparsed entities in a schema (for that, you need to continue using a DTD), but you can declare attributes whose values must be entity names or notation names. The schema equivalent to the DTD declarations above would be:

```
<xs:notation name="JPEG" system="image/jpeg"/>
<xs:notation name="GIF" system="image/gif"/>

<xs:element name="map">
  <xs:complexType>
    <xs:attribute name="format" type="image-notation" default="JPEG"/>
    <xs:attribute name="src" type="xs:ENTITY"/>
  </xs:complexType>

<xs:simpleType name="image-format">
  <xs:restriction base="xs:NOTATION">
    <xs:enumeration value="JPEG"/>
    <xs:enumeration value="GIF"/>
  </xs:restriction>
</xs:simpleType>
```

Note that you can't declare an attribute whose type is xs:NOTATION, it must be a subtype of xs:NOTATION that is restricted to a specific list of allowed values. This all mirrors the rules for use in DTDs, and is all designed to ensure that users whose document types make use of unparsed entities and notations aren't prevented from taking advantage of XML Schema.

Although notations were added to XML Schema for backward compatibility reasons, the schema working group added an extra feature: they made notation names namespace-aware. In the schema above, the notation name «JPEG» is interpreted as a local name defined within the target namespace of the containing schema. If the target namespace is anything other than the null namespace, then the notation name actually used in the source document (and in the <xs:enumeration> elements) will need to be qualified with a namespace prefix.

So, how is xs:NOTATION supported in XPath 2.0? The answer is, minimally. There are two things that are allowed:

❑   You can compare two xs:NOTATION values to see if they are equal, or not equal

❑   You can cast an xs:NOTATION value to a string.

Casting a string to an xs:NOTATION is not allowed. This means that there is actually no way of constructing an xs:NOTATION value from scratch within an XPath expression: the only way you can get one is by reading the content of an attribute whose type annotation is xs:NOTATION.

This completes our survey of the "minor" types: that is, the types that are defined in XML Schema as primitive types, but which have fairly specialized applications (to put it politely). The next two sections deal with the two families of derived types that are predefined in XML Schema: the derived numeric types, and the derived string types.

Derived Numeric Types

XML Schema defines a range of types defined by restriction from xs:integer. They differ in the range of values permitted. The following table summarizes these types, giving the permitted value range for each one.

Type	Minimum	Maximum
xs:byte	-128	127
xs:int	-2147483648	2147483647
xs:long	-2^{63}	$2^{63}-1$
xs:negativeInteger	no minimum	-1
xs:nonNegativeInteger	0	no maximum
xs:nonPositiveInteger	no minimum	0
xs:positiveInteger	1	no maximum
xs:short	-32768	32767
xs:unsignedByte	0	255
xs:unsignedInt	0	4294967295
xs:unsignedLong	0	$2^{64}-1$
xs:unsignedShort	0	65535

The type hierarchy for these types is shown in Figure 3-1.

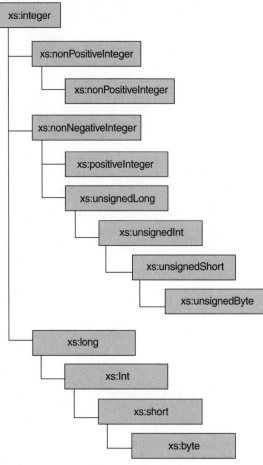

Figure 3-1

The range of values permitted in an xs:integer is unspecified. The specification says that at least 18 digits must be supported, but since the maximum value of an xs:unsignedLong is 18,446,744,073,709,551,615 it is clear that 18 digits is not actually sufficient. Some implementations may allow arbitrary precision integers.

I'm not a great enthusiast for these types. Their ranges are matched to the capacity of bits and bytes in the hardware, rather than to value ranges that actually occur in the real world. If you want to hold a percentage, and its value is an integer in the range 0 to 100, I would recommend defining a data type with that specific range, rather than using an off-the-shelf data type such as unsignedByte. This then leaves the question of which type to derive it from. There are 10 types in the above list that you could choose from. My own choice would be to derive it directly from xs:integer, on the grounds that any other choice is arbitrary.

As far as schema validation is concerned, it really doesn't matter very much what the type hierarchy is: if you define your percentage data type with a minInclusive value of 0 and a maxInclusive value of 100, then the validator will do its work without needing to know what type it is derived from. When it comes to XPath processing, however, the type hierarchy starts to become more significant. For example, if a function is defined that accepts arguments of type xs:positiveInteger, then a value of type my:percentage will be accepted if my:percentage is derived by restriction from xs:positiveInteger, but not if my:percentage is derived from xs:int. The fact that every valid percentage is also a valid xs:int doesn't come into it: the value is substitutable only if the type is defined as a subtype of the required type in the type hierarchy.

In the standard function library, there are a number of functions that return integers, for example count(), position(), and month-from-Date(). There are also a few functions that require an integer as one of the arguments, for example, insert-before(), remove(), and round-half-to-even(). All these functions are described in Chapter 10. In all cases the type that appears in the function signature is xs:integer, rather than one of its subtypes. In many cases a subtype could have been used, for example count() could have been defined to return an xs:nonNegativeInteger, position() could have been defined to return xs:positiveInteger. But this wasn't done, and it's interesting to see why.

Firstly, consider functions that accept an integer as an argument, such as remove(). Here the integer represents the position of the item to be removed. This could have been defined as an xs:positiveInteger, since the only values that make sense are greater than zero (positions in a sequence are always numbered from one). But if this was done then the function call «remove($seq, 1)» would give a type error, on the curious grounds that 1 is not an xs:positiveInteger. This is because, when you supply a value in a context where a particular type is required, the type checking rules rely on the label attached to the value, they don't consider the value itself. The type label attached to the integer literal «1» is xs:integer, and xs:integer is not a subtype of xs:positiveInteger, so the call fails.

Secondly, consider functions that return an integer, such as month-from-date(). Here the result is always in the range 1 to 12. So the result could have been defined as an xs:byte, or an xs:integer, or an xs:positiveInteger, or several other types. Alternatively, a new type xdt:month-value could have been defined with the specific range 1 to 12. Defining it as xs:byte would have been helpful to people who want to use the returned value in a call to a function that expects an xs:byte, while defining it as an xs:positiveInteger would have helped people who want to call functions that expect that type. Defining a custom type just for this purpose would have been overkill. It's not possible to please everyone, so the plain vanilla type xs:integer was chosen to stay neutral.

The fact of the matter is that numeric ranges don't naturally fall into a hierarchy, and type checking by looking at the labels rather than the actual value doesn't work particularly well in this situation. Choosing a type such as xs:int may give performance advantages on some systems compared with xs:long, but they are likely to be miniscule. My advice would be either to define a type that reflects the actual semantics of the value, for example percentage or class-size or grade, or just use the generic type xs:integer. If you write general-purpose functions (which is strictly speaking outside the scope of XPath, and takes you into XSLT or XQuery territory), then declare the expected type as xs:integer, and check the validity of the actual value within the code of your function.

Some people advocate defining numeric types for different units of measure, for example inches or centimeters. If you find this useful to document the intended usage, then that's fine, but don't expect the type system to do anything clever with the values as a result. It won't stop you adding an inches value to a centimeters value, for example. My personal preference is to model units of measure as complex types, typically using an element whose content is the numeric value, and with a fixed, defaulted attribute to denote the unit of measure. Subtypes are designed to be used where values of the subtype are substitutable for values of the parent type, which means they aren't appropriate if you want to restrict the operations that are permissible.

Derived String Types

As well as types derived from `xs:integer`, the standard repertoire of types that come as standard with XML Schema include a family of types derived from `xs:string`. The type hierarchy is shown in Figure 3-2.

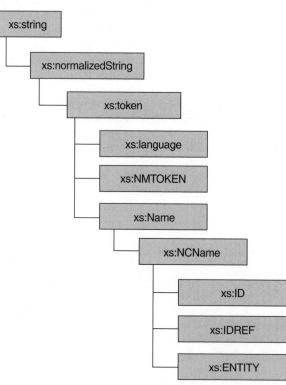

Figure 3-2

Most of these types restrict the set of characters that are allowed to appear in the string, but they also have other purposes:

❑ Some affect the way that whitespace within the value is normalized

❑ Some such as `xs:ID` and `xs:IDREF` trigger special validation rules that apply to the document as a whole

The processing of whitespace within an element or attribute value is controlled in XML Schema using the `xs:whiteSpace` facet on the data type. There are three possible values: `preserve`, `replace`, and collapse. These work as follows:

- preserve leaves the value intact.

- replace replaces each tab, carriage return, or newline character with a single space.

- collapse removes leading and trailing whitespace, and replaces any sequence of internal whitespace characters by a single space character. (*Whitespace* here means any of the characters x09, x0A, x0D, and x20, while *space* means the character x20.)

Validation of a source document against a schema only happens after XML parsing is complete, so this level of whitespace processing only comes into play after the XML parser has already done its work. The XML parser replaces any end-of-line sequence (for example, x0Dx0A) by a single newline character (x0A), unless it is written using character references such as «», and it also normalizes attribute values using the replace rule above. Specifying preserve in the schema won't stop the XML parser replacing tabs in an attribute value by spaces, unless you write them as «	».

In practice, you choose the whitespace processing you want not by specifying an explicit xs:whiteSpace facet, but by deriving your type definition from xs:string if you want preserve, xs:normalizedString if you want replace, and xs:token if you want collapse. (The type xs:token is a notorious misnomer, it actually represents a sequence of tokens separated by whitespace, and the assumption is that it makes no difference which whitespace characters are used as separators.)

You can restrict the allowed values for a string using the xs:pattern facet, which provides a regular expression that the value must match. The pattern is applied to the value after whitespace processing has been carried out.

> Patterns can also be used for data types other than strings, but they are rather blunt instruments. For example, if you try to define a subtype of **xs:decimal** with the pattern «[0-9]+\.[0-9]{2}», which states that there must be two digits after the decimal point, then any attempt to cast a value to this type is likely to fail— the system isn't clever enough to add trailing zeros to the value just because the pattern requires them.

Oddly, XML Schema doesn't define a data type for strings in which spaces are not allowed, such as part numbers. It's often handy to define such a type as a user-defined type, from which many other application-oriented types can be derived. You can define it like this:

```
<xs:simpleType name="my:singleToken">
  <xs:restriction base="xs:token">
    <xs:pattern value="[^\s]+"/>
  </xs:restriction>
</xs:simpleType>
```

This pattern also restricts the value to contain at least one non-space character (a zero-length string is not allowed).

The meaning of each of the data types is summarized in the table below.

Type	Usage
xs:string	Any sequence of characters, in which whitespace is significant
xs:normalizedString	Any sequence of characters, in which whitespace acts as a separator, but no distinction is made between different whitespace characters
xs:token	A sequence of tokens separated by whitespace
xs:language	A value that follows the rules for the xml:lang attribute in XML
xs:NMTOKEN	A sequence of characters classified as name characters in the XML specification. This includes letters, digits, «.», «-», «_», and «:», and a few other special characters
xs:Name	An NMTOKEN that starts with a character classified as an initial name character in the XML specification. These include letters, «_», and «:»
xs:NCName	A Name that does not include a «:» (a no-colon-name)
xs:ID	The value of an ID can be any valid NCName, but it is constrained to be unique among all the ID values in a document
xs:IDREF	The value of an IDREF can be any valid NCName, but it is constrained to be the same as some ID value somewhere in the same document
xs:ENTITY	The value of an ENTITY can be any valid NCName, but it is constrained to the same as the name of an unparsed entity defined in the DTD

XPath 2.0 doesn't handle any of these types specially, it just treats them as strings. If you try to cast a value to one of these types, it will first apply the whitespace rules for that type, and it will then check that the value conforms to the rules for the type. (This means for example, that calling «xs:token($s)» has pretty well the same effect as calling «normalize-space($s)»; the only difference is that in the first case, you end up with a value labeled as an xs:token, and in the second case, it is labeled xs:string.)

> Confusingly, the **normalize-space()** function (which is carried forward from XPath 1.0 and is described in Chapter 10 of this book), *collapses* whitespace, while the **xs:normalizedString** data type in XML Schema *replaces* whitespace.

The special validation rules for xs:ID, xs:IDREF, and xs:ENTITY are not invoked when you create atomic values of these types, they only make sense in the context of validating an entire document. Since XPath only reads documents (it never writes them or validates them) this means they have very little value in a pure XPath context.

This concludes our tour of the built-in atomic data types defined in XML Schema. Before finishing, we need to look at the special data type xdt:untypedAtomic, and at the three list data types xs:NMTOKENS, xs:IDREFS, and xs:ENTITIES.

Untyped Atomic Values

It might seem perverse to have a type called xdt:untypedAtomic, but that's the way it is. This isn't a type defined by XML Schema, it is a type used to label data that hasn't been validated against an XML Schema.

XML is a technology whose unique strength is its ability to handle everything from completely unstructured data, through semi-structured data, to data that has a completely rigid and formal structure. XPath needs to work with XML documents that fit anywhere in this spectrum. Indeed, it's not unusual to find documents where one part is rigidly structured, and another is completely free form.

One way of handling this would be to say that everything that isn't known to have a specific data type is simply labeled as a string. But to enable more accurate type checking of expressions and queries, the language designers wanted to be more precise than this, and to distinguish data that's known to be a string because it has been validated against a schema, from data that's handled as a string because we don't know any better.

The value space of xdt:untypedAtomic is the same as that of xs:string; in other words, any sequence of Unicode characters permitted in XML can be held as an xdt:untypedAtomic value. So in terms of the values they can represent, there's no difference between xdt:untypedAtomic and xs:string. The difference is in how the values can be used.

xdt:untypedAtomic is a chameleon type: it takes its behavior from the context in which it is used. If you use it where a number is expected, it behaves like a number; if you use it where a date is expected, it behaves like a date, and so on. This can cause errors, of course. If the actual value held in the xdt:untypedAtomic value isn't a valid date, then using it as a date will fail.

In XPath 1.0, all data extracted from a source document was untyped in this sense. In some ways this makes life easy for the programmer, it means that you can do things like «@value + 2» without worrying about whether @value is a number or a string. But occasionally, this freedom can lead to confusion. For example, in XPath 1.0, «boolean(@value)» tests whether the value attribute exists; «boolean(string(@value))» tests whether it exists and is not an empty string, while «boolean(number(@value))» tests whether it exists and has a numeric value that is not zero. To make these kind of distinctions, you need to understand the differences between data types.

With XPath 2.0, if your source documents have gone through schema validation, the elements and attributes will be annotated with a data type. This label tells the system what operations are legitimate on the data type, and may also be used to select different ways of implementing the same operation. For example, testing «@A < @B» will give different results depending on whether the attributes A and B have been defined in the schema as strings, numbers, or durations.

Data labeled as xdt:untypedAtomic continues to behave as all data did in XPath 1.0, it has no intrinsic type of its own, and is converted to whatever the default type is for the context in which it is used. If you supply an xdt:untypedAtomic value as an argument to a function call, it is converted (cast) to the type defined in the function signature. If you use it as an operand of an arithmetic operator such as «+» then the system tries to convert it to a number (actually, an `xs:double`). If you use it as an operand of «=» or «<» then it first tries to convert it to the type of the other operand, which means that «@A > 4» and «@A > '4'» may give you different answers (if the attribute value is «10», for example, the first test will return `true`, the second `false`). If both operands are of type `xdt:untypedAtomic`, then they will be compared using the rules for strings.

One thing that can trip you up if you aren't using schemas, and are therefore used to most of your data being untyped, is that the result of an operation is never untyped. This means, for example, that you can write «concat("Chapter", @chap-num)», and the value of @chap-num will be treated as an `xs:string`, which is what the `concat()` function requires. You can also write «@chap-num + 1», and «@chap-num» will be treated as a number, which is what the «+» operator requires. But you can't write «concat("Chapter", @chap-num + 1)», because the result of «@chap-num + 1» is not untyped, it is an `xs:double`, and the `concat()` function requires an `xs:string`. You have to do the conversion explicitly, like this: «concat("Chapter, string(@chap-num + 1))».

Values can be labeled as `xdt:untypedAtomic` even when they come from a document that has been validated against a schema, if the validation rules in the schema caused that part of the document to be skipped. This situation can arise with documents that are part rigid structure, part free form.

Although untyped values arise most commonly when you extract the value of an unvalidated node in a source document, you can also construct an untyped value explicitly, in the same way as any other atomic value, by using a constructor function or cast. For example, the function call «xdt:untypedAtomic (@date)» extracts the value of the @date attribute, and returns an untyped value regardless whether the original attribute was labeled as a date, as a string, or as something else. This technique can be useful if you need to process data that might or might not have been validated, or if you want to exploit the chameleon nature of `xdt:untypedAtomic` data by using the value both as a string and as a date.

NMTOKENS, IDREFS, and ENTITIES

This section of the chapter is about atomic types, but it would not be complete without mentioning the three built-in types defined in XML Schema that are not atomic, namely `xs:NMTOKENS`, `xs:IDREFS`, and `xs:ENTITIES`. These all reflect attribute types that were defined in DTDs, and are carried forward into XML Schema to make transition from DTDs to schemas as painless as possible.

In the sense of XML Schema, these are simple types, but they are not atomic types. XML Schema distinguishes complex types, which can contain elements and attributes, from simple types which can't. Simple types can be defined in three ways: directly by restricting an existing simple type, by list, which allows a list of values drawn from a simple type, or by union, which allows a choice of values from two or more different simple types. But when it comes down to actual values, an instance of a simple type is either a single atomic value, or a list of atomic values. Single atomic values correspond directly to atomic values in the XPath data model, as described in the previous chapter, while lists of atomic values correspond to sequences.

If an element or attribute is defined in the schema to have a list data type such as `xs:NMTOKENS`, then after validation the element or attribute node will have a type annotation of `xs:NMTOKENS`. But when an XPath expression reads the content of the element or attribute node (a process called atomization), the result is not a single value of type `xs:NMTOKENS`, but a sequence of values, each of which is an atomic value labeled as an `xs:NMTOKEN`.

For example, you can test an attribute to see whether it is of type xs:NMTOKENS like this:

```
if (@A instance of attribute(*, xs:NMTOKENS)) ...
```

or you can test its value to see if it is a sequence of xs:NMTOKEN values like this:

```
if (data(@A) instance of xs:NMTOKEN * ) ...
```

What you cannot do is to test the attribute node against the sequence type «xs:NMTOKEN*», or the value contained in the attribute against the list type «xs:NMTOKENS». Both will give you syntax errors if you attempt them. For more information on using the «instance of» operator to test the type of a value, see Chapter 9.

Schema Types and XPath Types

The preceding discussion about list types demonstrates that while the XPath type system is based on XML Schema, the types defined in XML Schema are not exactly the same thing as the types that XPath values can take. This is best illustrated by looking at the two type hierarchies and seeing how they compare. The type hierarchy in XML Schema is shown in Figure 3-3.

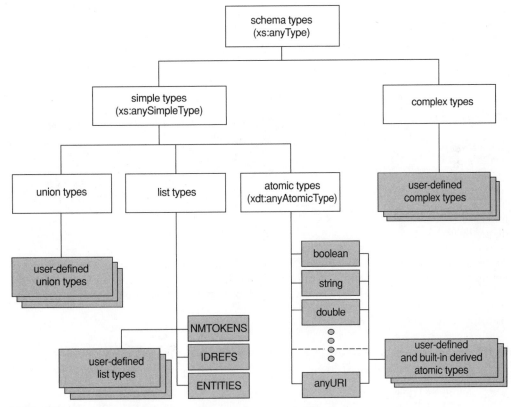

Figure 3-3

This type hierarchy contains all the types that can be used as type annotations on nodes. The boxes that are shown shaded are concrete types, so they can be used directly; the unshaded boxes are abstract types, which can only be used via their subtypes. Some of the abstract types are named, which means you can refer to them in an XPath expression (for example, you can write «element (*, xs:anySimpleType)» which will match any element whose type annotation shows that its type is a simple type). Others are unnamed, which means you cannot refer to them directly.

There is another type hierarchy, which represents the types of XPath items. This type hierarchy is shown in Figure 3-4.

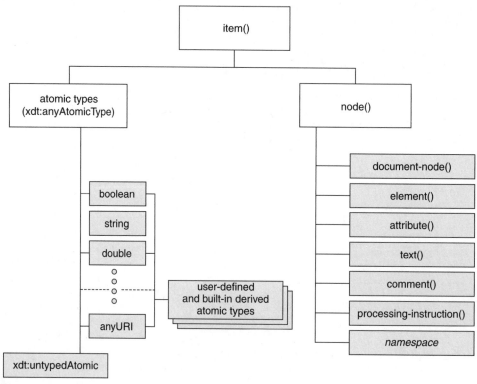

Figure 3-4

This reflects the structure we described in the previous chapter: every item in an XPath sequence is either a node or an atomic value; there are seven kinds of node, and the atomic types are either the built-in atomic types defined in the XML Schema specification, or user-defined atomic types.

Comparing these two diagrams:

- ❑ Atomic types appear in both. Atomic types can be used either as annotations on nodes, or as the type of a free-standing XPath item.

- ❑ Complex types, list types, and union types appear on the first diagram, but not the second. These types can be used as node annotations, but you can never have a free-standing XPath item that belongs directly to one of these types.

❑   Node kinds appear on the second diagram only. You can have an item in an XPath sequence that is an element or a comment or a processing instruction, but these types never appear as type annotations on element or attribute nodes.

It's a little unfortunate that the boxes on both these diagrams are all referred to as types, when we are actually dealing with two different (but overlapping) categories: I call the first category *schema types*, and the second category *item types*. The W3C specification for functions and operators attempts to depict both of these categories on a single type hierarchy diagram, but in my view this is likely to confuse more people than it enlightens. Apart from anything else, when you do this you find that xdt:anyAtomic Type, which appears on both diagrams, has two different supertypes.

Item types and schema types are used in different ways in XPath:

❑   You can test whether an item $V belongs to a particular item type T by writing «$V instance of T».

❑   You can test whether a node $N has a type annotation that is a particular schema type S by writing «$N instance of attribute(*, S)» or «$N instance of element(*, S)».

Because atomic types such as xs:integer belong to both categories, they can be used in either of these two ways. But item types such as «comment()» can only be used in the first of these roles, while non-atomic schema types such as xs:IDREFS can only be used in the second role.

The Type Matching Rules

The purpose of a type system in a language, as we saw, is to define which operations are legitimate for which types of value. In this section we will examine the way that XPath defines these rules.

It's easiest to start with the rules for function calling. You can't define your own functions in XPath itself, but you can call functions written in other languages such as XSLT and XQuery, as well as the functions provided in the core function library that comes with the language. Each of these functions has a signature, which defines the types of each of the arguments expected by the function. The rules described in this section define whether or not a particular value can be used in a function call, given a particular type used in the function signature.

For example, the signature of the function remove() is given in Chapter 10 as follows:

Argument	Data type	Meaning
sequence	item()*	The input sequence
position	xs:integer	The position of the item to be removed
Result	item()*	*A sequence containing all the items in the input sequence except the item at the specified position*

This shows that the function expects two arguments. The names of the arguments are irrelevant: these names are purely for reference within the documentation, they are not used in an actual function call. The important thing here is the data type expected for each argument.

The first argument has a type of «item()*». There are two parts to this: the item type, and the cardinality. The item type in this case is «item()», which is the most general item type of all, and accepts any node or atomic value. The cardinality is «*», which means that the argument can be a sequence containing zero, one or more items. Taken together, this means that the first argument of remove() can be any sequence whatsoever.

The second argument has a type of xs:integer. There is no cardinality specified, which means that the default cardinality is used: the effect of this is that the sequence supplied as the argument value must contain exactly one item. The item type for this argument is xs:integer, which means that the supplied value must be an atomic value labeled as an xs:integer, or as a subtype of xs:integer (for example, it might be labeled as an xs:positiveInteger). Supplying any other value would lead to a type error, which might be reported either when the expression is compiled, or when it is subsequently evaluated.

Actually, the type system is not quite as rigid as this. Instead of supplying an xs:integer for the second argument, you can also supply:

❑ An untyped atomic value, provided that it takes a form that can be converted to an integer.

❑ A node, provided that the typed value of the node is either an xs:integer, or an untyped atomic value.

However, you cannot supply a string (even a string that obviously contains an integer, such as «"17"»), and you cannot supply a value of a different numeric type, such as xs:decimal or xs:double. You can use an xs:integer where an xs:double is expected, but not the other way around.

When the function call expects an atomic value and the supplied value is a node, the system goes through a process called *atomization* to extract the typed value of the node. Atomization is applied to the supplied value (a sequence) to produce a derived value (the atomized sequence). The rules are:

❑ Any atomic value in the supplied sequence is added to the atomized sequence unchanged.

❑ For any node in the supplied sequence, the typed value is extracted, as described in Chapter 2 (see page 41). The typed value is in general a sequence of zero or more atomic values, and the values in this sequence are added to the atomized sequence. If the node has not been validated against a schema, these atomic values will be untyped (they will have the type label xdt:untypedAtomic); if they have been validated, they are likely to have some other type such as xs:integer or xs:date.

❑ For some kinds of node, extracting a typed value is not possible: specifically, this is true for elements that are labeled with a type that has complex element-only content. Supplying such a node where the function expects an atomic value is an error, and the XPath evaluation will fail.

The atomized sequence is then checked against the type given in the function signature. The cardinality of the sequence as a whole must match the cardinality constraints given in the function signature, and each item in the sequence must match the item type given.

The detailed syntax for describing the allowed type of each function argument is given in Chapter 9, where it is referred to as a sequence type descriptor. The detailed rules for deciding whether a particular value is allowed as an argument to a function call, and the way it is converted to the required type when necessary, are given in Chapter 5, in the section describing function calls on page 160.

Function calls are not the only place in XPath where a value needs to be checked against a required type. Many of the operators in the language, such as «+», «-», and «|», also have rules saying what type of operands are acceptable. These rules are based on the rules for function calls, but they are slightly different because XPath allows operators to be polymorphic: that is, the same operator can mean different things depending on the types of the arguments supplied. This is not currently allowed for function calls. For each operator, the rules are therefore slightly different, and they are described in this book in the section dealing with each operator. The non-trivial examples are the «=» family of operators and the arithmetic operators, which are all described in Chapter 6.

In XSLT 2.0, the function calling rules are also used to describe what happens when you assign a value to a variable, or to a parameter of a template. For example, suppose a template is declared like this:

```
<xsl:template name="do-something">
  <xsl:param name="input" as="xs:integer *"/>
  <xsl:sequence select="sum($input)"/>
</xsl:template>
```

This template has a signature in exactly the same way that a function has a signature, and the «as» attribute of the <xsl:param> element defines the required type of the parameter value, which in this case must be a sequence of integers. The same rules are used as in XPath function calls, for example, it is okay to supply a node whose type annotation indicates that it contains a sequence of integers, but it is not okay to supply a string.

The same is true of XSLT variable declarations. If you write:

```
<xsl:variable name="input" as="xs:integer *" select="my:function(12)"/>
```

then the system checks that the result of the expression in the «select» attribute is a sequence of integers, or that it can be converted to a sequence of integers by atomization and/or casting of untyped atomic values, and fails with a type error if not.

> *XQuery chose not to use the function calling rules for variable assignment, but instead applies a stricter criterion. When you write in XQuery «let $x as xs:integer* := my:function(12)» then the result of «my:function(12)» must actually be a sequence of integers; no conversions such as atomization, or casting of untyped atomic values, are permitted in this context.*

Static and Dynamic Type Checking

As I said in the introduction to this chapter, one of the major purposes of the type system in a programming language is to enable programming errors to be detected and corrected. The best time to do this, where possible, is at compile time.

Very often, you will compile and execute an XSLT stylesheet, or an individual XPath expression, as a single indivisible operation. You may therefore feel that there isn't much difference between detecting an error at compile time and detecting it at runtime. Indeed, if you use XPath expressions from a programming language such as Java, it's likely that the XPath expressions won't be compiled until the Java program is executed, so in a sense all errors become runtime errors. However, there is still a big difference, because an error that's detected at compile time doesn't depend on the input data. This means that it will be reported every time you process the XPath expression, which means it can't remain lurking in the code until some chance condition in the data reveals a latent bug that got through all your tests.

I had a real-life example of this recently. In Chapter 12 of the companion book, *XSLT 2.0 Programmer's Reference*, there is a stylesheet whose task is to perform a knight's tour of the chessboard: a tour, starting from a user-specified square, in which the knight visits every square on the chessboard exactly once. I published an XSLT 1.0 version of this stylesheet in the previous edition of the book, and I have also written an XQuery 1.0 version which is published with the Saxon software distribution. Part of the algorithm involves backtracking when the knight gets stuck in a blind alley; however, I never found a way of testing the backtracking, because in every case I tried, the knight got all the way around the board without ever getting stuck. In fact, I said in the book that although I couldn't prove it, I believed that the backtracking code would never be invoked.

Three years after I first wrote the code, one of my readers discovered that if the knight starts on square f1, it gets stuck on move 58 and has to retrace its steps. (The same user has since reported that this is the only starting square where this happens.) The way he made the discovery was that in the XQuery version of the algorithm, the backtracking code was wrong. I had coded two arguments to a function call the wrong way around, and when the function call was executed, this was detected, because one of the values had the wrong type. So type checking detected the error, but static type checking (that is, compile time checking) would have detected it three years earlier.

But static type checking also has a downside: it makes it much harder to cope with unpredictable data. With strict static type checking, every expression must satisfy the compiler that it can never fail at runtime with a type error. Let's see what happens if, for example, you have a price attribute whose value is either a decimal number, or the string «N/A». You can define this in XML Schema as follows:

```
<xs:attribute name="price">
  <xs:simpleType>
    <xs:union memberTypes="xs:string price-NA/>
  </xs:simpleType>
</xs:attribute>

<xs:simpleType name="price-NA">
  <xs:restriction base="xs:string">
    <xs:enumeration value="N/A"/>
  </xs:restriction>
</xs:simpleType>
```

Now let's suppose that you want to find the average price of those products where the price is known. Your first attempt might look like this:

```
avg( product/@price[. != "N/A"] )
```

This looks sensible, but under strict static type checking, it will fail to compile. There are two reasons. Firstly, you can't compare a number with a string, so the expression «. = "N/A"» isn't allowed, on the grounds that the value of «.» (that is, the typed value of the price attribute) might be a number. Secondly, although you and I can tell that all the attributes that get through the filter in square brackets will be numeric, the compiler isn't so clever, and will report an error on the grounds that some of the items in the sequence being averaged might be strings rather than numbers.

The first of these two errors will be reported even if type checking is delayed until runtime, so in this case the static type checker has done us a service by reporting the error before it happened. The second error is a false alarm. At runtime, all the attribute values being averaged will actually be numeric, so the error of including a string in the sequence will never occur.

This example is designed to illustrate that static type checking is a mixed blessing. It will detect some errors early, but it will also report many false alarms. The more you are dealing with unpredictable or semi-structured data, the more frequent the false alarms will become. With highly structured data, static type checking can be a great help in enabling you to write error-free code; but with loosely structured data, it can become a pain in the neck. Because XML is designed to handle such a wide spectrum of different kinds of data, the language designers therefore decided that static type checking should be optional.

Whether you use static or dynamic type checking, the first error in our example above will need to be corrected. The simplest way to do this is to force the value of the attribute to be converted to a string before the comparison, like this:

```
avg(product/@price[string(.) != "N/A"])
```

For the other error (the false alarm) we don't need to take any further action in the case of a system that only does dynamic type checking. However, if we want the expression also to work with systems that do static type checking, we will need to change it. We don't need to invoke any data conversion in this case, because the values are already numbers; instead, we need to tell the system to delay its type checking until runtime. This can be done using the «treat as» expression, which is described in detail in Chapter 9. The code then looks like this:

```
avg(data(product/@price[string(.) != "N/A"]) treat as xs:decimal*)
```

The phrase «treat as xs:decimal*» can be read as an assertion about the value of the expression. The programmer is asserting that the value of the preceding expression will be a sequence of xs:decimal values. To make this assertion work, we have to call the data() function to extract the values of the price attributes; without this, the value of the expression would be a sequence of attribute nodes, not a sequence of xs:decimal values, so the assertion would fail.

There's another way of correcting the expression that will satisfy both the static and the dynamic type checkers. The actual intent of the expression is to select all the values of the price attribute that are numeric, and we can do this directly, and much more elegantly, by writing:

```
avg( product/attribute(price, xs:decimal) )
```

The construct «attribute(price, xs:decimal)» is a sequence type descriptor that is satisfied only by an attribute node whose name is price and whose type annotation is xs:decimal. Selecting the attributes this way kills both the type errors with one stone. It avoids comparing the numeric values to a string, and it tells the static type checker that all the selected attributes will be of type xs:decimal, which means it is safe to average them. This kind of expression is described in detail in Chapter 9.

I don't know how many XPath 2.0 implementations will offer static type checking. Most of the enthusiasm for the feature comes from XQuery vendors, because stronger type checking can make a real difference when optimizing queries over very large databases. I suspect that most XPath 2.0 vendors will leave this feature out; but time alone will tell.

Looking back at the example:

```
avg(product/@price[. != "N/A"])
```

it might have occurred to you that under XPath 1.0, apart from the fact that the avg() function was not available, this would have worked quite happily, with neither static or dynamic errors. That's because XPath 1.0 treated all data in source documents as being untyped. You could compare the value of an attribute to a string, and it would treat it as a string, and you could then take an average, and it would treat the same value as a number. You can do the same thing in XPath 2.0, simply by switching off schema processing: if there is no schema, or if you switch off schema processing, then the attributes are going to be treated as xdt:untypedAtomic values, and will adapt themselves to whatever operation you want to perform, just as with XPath 1.0. If you like this way of working, there is nothing to stop you carrying on this way. However, you should be aware of the consequences: many programming errors in XPath 1.0 go undetected, or are very difficult to debug, because the system in effect tries to guess what you meant, and sometimes guesses wrong. For example, if you compare a string to a number using the «=» operator, XPath 1.0 guesses that you wanted a string comparison (so «4 = "04"» is false), while if you compare a string to a number using the «<=» operator, XPath 1.0 guesses that a numeric comparison was intended (so «4 <= "04"» is true). Sooner or later, this is going to trip you up. With a schema-aware XPath 2.0 processor you have to be explicit about whether you want a string comparison or a numeric comparison, by explicitly converting one of the operands to the type of the other.

The XPath 2.0 Recommendation distinguishes static type checking from dynamic type checking. A product that offers static type checking is pessimistic: it assumes that if things can go wrong, they will go wrong. For example, if the operand of «+» is known at compile time to be either a string or an integer, the compiler will report a failure, because the pessimistic assumption is that sooner or later, the actual value of the operand will turn out to be a string.

Another kind of static type checking is permitted, but is not described explicitly in the specification, which I will call optimistic static type checking. Here, you will only get an error message at compile time if the system knows that an expression cannot possibly succeed. An example of such an expression is:

```
current-date() = "2004-01-01"
```

Here the operand on the left will always be an xs:date, and the operand on the right will always be an xs:string. Comparison of a date to a string can never succeed, so even an optimistic type checker can report the error at compile time. To correct the error, you need to write:

```
current-date() = xs:date("2004-01-01")
```

It's worth pointing out that neither static nor dynamic type checking can catch all errors. Going back to my knight's tour where two parameters to a function call were coded in the wrong order, the error was only caught because the two arguments had different types. If both arguments had had a type of xs:integer, say, the function call would have succeeded, and the query would have gone on to produce garbage output.

A great deal depends in practice on how carefully you specify your types. Specifying the types of function parameters and of variables is done at the XSLT or XQuery level rather than within XPath itself, but it is this type information that forms the basis of the type checking performed by the XPath processor. If you choose not to specify any types at all, this is rather like declaring every Java variable or function with the generic type Object: you will get no compile time errors, but an awful lot of runtime errors. I find that it's good programming discipline always to declare the types of variables and of function arguments. However, it's generally best to avoid over-constraining them. It can be tempting to declare types such as xs:positiveInteger rather than xs:integer if the value will always be positive; but as we've seen, this doesn't just constrain the value to be positive, it means that it actually has to be labeled as an `xs:positiveInteger`. The value represented by the XPath numeric literal «3» is an `xs:integer`, but it is not an `xs:positiveInteger`, because it has the wrong type label. So I tend to steer clear of using such types, because they create too much inconvenience.

Summary

The type system is probably the most innovative and the most controversial aspect of XPath 2.0, and is very different in concept from the type system of XPath 1.0. We started this chapter with a brief rationale for introducing a type system based on XML Schema, and we ended the chapter with a discussion of the different forms of type checking that XPath 2.0 processor can apply, and some hints and tips to enable you to choose the right options.

In between, we took a lightning tour of the facilities of XML Schema from an XPath perspective, and looked in detail at each of the built-in atomic types defined in the XML Schema specification. We then saw how the type hierarchy in XML Schema relates to the type hierarchy in the XPath data model: they are strongly related, but they are not the same thing.

We also outlined how the type checking rules operate when calling an XPath function.

We're now moving towards the section of the book that provides detailed reference information for each construct in the XPath language. The reference section occupies Chapters 5 through 10. Before we get there, however, there is one more preliminary to be covered, which is the XPath *context*. The XPath context defines the environment in which an XPath expression is evaluated, and formalizes the interface between XPath and the outside world. This will be the subject of the next chapter.

The Evaluation Context

XPath was designed as an expression language that could be embedded in other languages. The first such language was XSLT, but it was always envisaged that this would only be one of many host languages. Subsequent experience has shown that this did indeed happen: XPath (sometimes in the form of a restricted subset) has been used not only within XSLT and XPointer, but within a variety of programming languages such as Java and Perl, and also as a sublanguage for expressing constraints within XML Schema.

To make XPath suitable for this role as a sublanguage, there needs to be a clear interface between XPath and the host language. This interface specifies what information is provided by the host environment to the XPath environment, and the sum total of this information is referred to as the *evaluation context*.

The evaluation context can be split into two halves: information that is available at compile time (while the XPath expression is being parsed and checked for static errors), and information that is available only at runtime. These two parts are called the static context and the dynamic context, and they are described in the two sections of this chapter.

An XPath host language such as XSLT will always contain a section describing how the static and dynamic context for XPath expressions are set up. Some aspects of the context may be under user control, some may have fixed values, and other parts may be completely implementation defined. This will vary from one host language to another. As far as XPath is concerned, it doesn't matter whether the information is fixed in the host language specification or whether it is provided by the vendor or by the user: the information is there somehow, and is available for use.

As I describe each part of the evaluation context in this chapter, I will also explain how it is initialized when the host language is XSLT. This serves two purposes. If you are using XSLT (as many XPath users are) then the information is directly useful. If you are using some other host language, then it serves as a concrete example of how the facility can be used.

The Static Context

The static context contains information that's needed while performing the analysis or compilation phase on an XPath expression.

In many environments, XPath is a "load and go" technology: you submit an expression as a string, and it is compiled and executed straight away. In this case, the distinction between the static context and the dynamic context isn't all that important. In other environments, however, there is a distinction. XSLT stylesheets are often compiled once and then executed many times, and the XPath expressions within the stylesheet will typically be compiled when the stylesheet is compiled (usually not into machine code, but into some intermediate form that a runtime interpreter can later process). So it's worth making the distinction between the two phases even if they are often combined.

The various parts of the static context are described in the sections that follow.

XPath 1.0 Compatibility Mode

This value is a boolean: compatibility mode is either on or off. Compatibility mode will be switched on when users want the effect of an XPath expression to be as close as possible to the effect that the same expression would have had under XPath 1.0.

In XSLT, compatibility mode for XPath expressions in a stylesheet is switched on by setting the «version» attribute to «1.0», either on the <xsl:stylesheet> element, or on an inner element in the stylesheet if it is required only for certain expressions and not for others. If the stylesheet specifies «version="2.0"», the 1.0 compatibility mode will be off.

XPath processors (and XSLT processors) are not obliged to offer XPath 1.0 compatibility mode. This is because there may be new XPath 2.0 host languages that never supported XPath 1.0, and users of such host languages would have no need for backward compatibility. Also, the language is designed for longevity, and there might come a time in the future when vendors find that their customers no longer need the backward compatibility option; it would make little sense to deprive such vendors of their conformance badge.

Setting XPath 1.0 compatibility mode does not mean that everything in the language is 100% backward compatible. Because the type system in XPath 2.0 has changed so much, this would be very difficult to achieve. Appendix C contains a list of the incompatibilities that remain: most of them are corner cases that few users are likely to encounter, but one or two are more significant.

So what exactly changes if you set 1.0 compatibility mode? The following rules are applied only when in this mode:

❑ In a function call, if the expected type of an argument is «xs:string» or «xs:string?», then the supplied value of the argument is converted to a string by calling the string() function. If the supplied value is a sequence then this atomizes the sequence and discards all items after the first. It then casts the remaining value to a string (the casting rules are given in Chapter 9).

❑ In a function call, if the expected type of an argument is «xs:double» or «xs:double?», then the supplied value of the argument is converted to a number by calling the number() function. If the supplied value is a sequence then this atomizes the sequence and discards all items after the first. It then casts the remaining value to an xs:double (the casting rules are given in Chapter 9).

The current draft of the specification is a little unclear as to exactly when this rule applies. The intent is that it should apply to functions like round(), floor(), and ceiling(), whose signature describes the argument as numeric, with either no occurrence indicator or an occurrence indicator of «?».

❑ In a function call, if the expected type of an argument is one of «node()», «node()?», «item()», or «item()?», and if the supplied value is a sequence containing more than one item, then all items after the first are discarded.

❑ In an arithmetic expression using an operator such as «+», «*», or «mod», if either of the operands (after atomization) is a sequence containing more than one item, then all items after the first are discarded. If the operands are of the wrong type for the operator (which means they are not numbers, and they are not one of the combinations of date, time, and duration that can be handled by the arithmetic operator in question), then the operands are converted to xs:double values by applying the number() function. This may mean that the result of the arithmetic expression is returned as NaN (not-a-number) rather than raising an error.

❑ In a general comparison, that is, an expression using one of the operators «=», «!=», «<», «<=», «>», «>=», if one of the operands is numeric then the other operand is converted to an xs:double value by applying the number() function.

What lies behind these rules is that XPath 1.0 was a weakly typed language, in which the arguments of function calls and operators were implicitly converted to the required type. XPath 2.0 has a much richer type system, in which such implicit conversion would often give unexpected results. So with XPath 2.0, you have to do the conversions you want explicitly. But this creates a backward compatibility problem. The rules given above are designed to minimize this problem, by catering for all the cases that could actually arise with a 1.0 expression. The reason that strings and numbers are treated differently from other types is that they are the only atomic types that were supported in XPath 1.0—except for booleans. And in the case of booleans, weak typing continues to apply in XPath 2.0: every value can be converted to a boolean when it is used in a context such as the condition of an «if» expression, by taking its *effective boolean value*. The rules for this are described on page 165.

The following table illustrates some expressions whose results differ when running in backward compatibility mode.

Expression	Compatibility Mode	
	On	Off
contains(3.14, ".")	true	type error
"apple" + "pear"	NaN	type error
"apple" < 3	false	type error
@a < "42" where @a has the untyped value "7"	true (numeric comparison)	false (string comparison)

In-Scope Namespaces

Many XPath expressions contain prefixed QNames. The names of elements and attributes can be prefixed, as can the names of variables, functions, and types. A prefix in such a name means nothing by itself: to know what type the name «xs:integer» refers to, you have to know what namespace URI is bound to the prefix «xs». It isn't possible to define the binding of a prefix to a namespace URI within the XPath expression itself, so instead it has to be part of the context. It's part of the static context so that the XPath processor can work out at compile time what all names appearing in the expression are actually referring to.

This part of the static context is modeled as a set of (prefix, URI) pairs. No prefix may appear more than once. It's an error if the XPath expression contains a QName whose prefix isn't present in this list.

In XSLT, because a stylesheet is an XML document, the in-scope namespaces for an XPath expression are defined by writing namespace declarations such as «xmlns:xs="http://www.w3.org/2001/XML Schema"» in a containing element (often, but not necessarily, the <xsl:stylesheet> element). The namespace prefixes you can use within an XPath expression are precisely those that you could use in an element name or attribute name appearing in the same place in the stylesheet.

Each stylesheet module has its own static context, so a global variable declared in one module as:

```
<xsl:variable name="this:color" select="'red'" xmlns:this="http://module1/ns"/>
```

might be referenced in another module as:

```
<xsl:attribute name="bgcolor" select="$that:color"
               xmlns:that="http://module1/ns"/>
```

For other host languages, a different way of establishing the namespace context might be used. XQuery, for example has its own syntax for declaring namespaces, as does XPointer. In XQuery some namespaces (such as the XML Schema namespace) are hardwired, and others can be declared in the query prolog using syntax such as:

```
declare namespace saxon = "http://saxon.sf.net/";
```

In XPointer the syntax is:

```
xmlns(xs=http://www.w3.org/2001/XMLSchema)
```

When XPath is used from a programming language such as Java, there will generally be some method in the API that allows a namespace to be declared. In some APIs it is possible to declare namespaces implicitly by nominating a node in a source document, indicating that all the namespaces that are in scope for that node should be considered to be in scope for the XPath expression.

Default Namespaces

When a QName that has no namespace prefix is used, default namespaces come into play.

In XPath 1.0, the rule was simple: no prefix means no namespace. That is, unprefixed names always referred to objects whose namespace URI was null. In XPath 2.0 there is more flexibility. The static context potentially contains two defaults, for use with different kinds of name:

❑   The default namespace for elements and types, as the name implies, is used to qualify any name within the XPath expression that is recognized as an element name or a type name. In path expressions, it is always possible to distinguish element names by means of the axis on which they appear: if the axis is the attribute or namespace axis, then unprefixed names are considered to be in no namespace, whereas on any other axis, the namespace URI for an unprefixed name is taken from this default. The default is also used for element names appearing in a test such as «element(invoice, *)», and for the names of types, in constructs such as «attribute (*, part-number)».

Note that if a default namespace is set, then it becomes impossible to refer to names that are in the null namespace. If you need to refer to such names, you will need to ensure that this item in the context is not set.

❑ The default namespace for functions is used to qualify unprefixed names used in function calls, for example «f()». Most XPath users will probably want to follow the convention that calls to functions in the standard library are unprefixed, while calls to user-defined, vendor-defined, or third-party functions carry a namespace prefix that defines their origin. However, if you prefer to prefix calls on the standard functions and leave calls to user functions unprefixed, the choice is up to you (as far as XPath is concerned, anyway).

❑ For other kinds of name, for example attribute names and variable names, there is no default namespace. For these names, no prefix always means no namespace.

In XSLT, the default namespace for elements and functions does *not* come from the default namespace declaration in the stylesheet. Setting a default namespace using «xmlns="http://www.example .com/"» does not affect the meaning of unprefixed names within path expressions (or in XSLT match patterns, which follow the same rules). Instead, in XSLT 2.0 only, you can use the special attribute «xpath-default-namespace» to define this part of the static context.

As for the default namespace for functions, XSLT doesn't allow you to set this at all. When XPath is used within XSLT stylesheets, the default namespace for functions is always the namespace containing the core function library.

The rules for other host languages may well be different. XQuery, for, example, sets the default namespace for elements and types using the XML-like syntax «xmlns="http://www.example.com/"», and allows you to choose any namespace you like as the default namespace for functions.

In-Scope Schema Definitions

This part of the static context represents the schema information that is available at the time an XPath expression is compiled. Technically, it consists of:

❑ A set of named top-level type definitions (simple and complex types)

❑ A set of named top-level element declarations

❑ A set of named top-level attribute declarations

Type definitions, element declarations, and attribute declarations are referred to collectively as schema components (there is apparently a good reason why types are "defined" whereas elements and attributes are "declared", but the explanation I was given was pretty tortuous).

The specifications don't say exactly what information can be extracted from these definitions, this is left to the implementation to sort out. In theory XPath itself, because it doesn't actually validate elements against the schema, doesn't need to know very much about them at all. All it needs to be able to do is to look at the type annotation on a node and decide whether the node is or is not an instance of a given type in the schema, which it can do by knowing the names of the types and the type hierarchy. In practice of course, XPath implementations can use a lot more information than this for optimization purposes.

XPath itself isn't concerned with where these definitions come from. It's the job of the host language to decide which types are made available in the context. In practice there's a minimum set of types that must be available, because the XPath functions and operators need them: this set corresponds roughly to the set of types that a basic XSLT processor will make available, but it's XSLT that defines this set, not XPath itself.

In XSLT, the schema components provided in the static context include:

❑   Some or all of the built-in types of XML Schema. In the case of a schema-aware processor this includes all the built-in types, but in the case of a basic (non-schema-aware) processor it is a much smaller subset.

❑   Schema components from schemas imported using the <xsl:import-schema> declaration in the stylesheet. This declaration can only be used if the processor is schema-aware.

❑   Other implementation-defined types needed to support vendor extensions, for example, the ability to call external Java methods.

For example, if you want to reference components from the OpenGIS schema for geographical coordinate systems, you might write in your stylesheet:

```
<xsl:import-schema namespace="http://www.opengis.net/gml" schema-location=
       "http://schemas.opengis.net/gml/3.0.1/base/coordinateSystems.xsd"/>
```

You would then be able to use XPath expressions that reference components in this schema, for example:

```
<xsl:if test=". instance of element(*, gml:CoordinateSystemAxisType)">
```

A different host language, however, could make schema components available in a different way entirely. There is no obligation on the host language to put this under user control.

An XPath expression cannot make explicit reference to types (for example, in an «instance of» expression, described in Chapter 9) unless those types are present in the static context. This also applies to element declarations named in a «schema-element(N)» test, and to attribute declarations named in a «schema-attribute(N)» test. (These constructs are all defined in Chapter 9.) Elements and attributes that are named in the ordinary way within a path expression, however, do not need to have a declaration present in the static context.

The set of schema components that are present in the static context may be a subset of those available at runtime. This is an issue that caused the working groups a great deal of grief: what happens if the XPath expression calls the doc() function to load a document, and that document is validated using a schema (perhaps the schema named in its xsi:schemaLocation attribute) that wasn't supplied as part of the static context for the XPath expression? The problem arises when you write an XPath expression such as «doc('abc.xml')/a/b instance of xs:integer». To evaluate this, the XPath processor needs to look at the type annotation on the <b> element and determine whether this type is a subtype of xs:integer. How is it supposed to know?

In fact, it's not just expressions like this that need the type information. A simple comparison such as «if (doc('abc.xml')/a/b = $x) then ...» uses the typed value of the <b> element, and to determine how to do the comparison, the processor needs to know the type.

The answer the working group came up with is to invoke magic (or, in the phrase that was used at the time, a "winged horse"). The practical reality is that in many cases the XPath processor will have a fairly intimate relationship with the XML parser and/or the XML schema validator. In such cases, the XPath processor probably has access to all the schema information that was used when validating the document. It would be very difficult to formalize all this information as part of the evaluation context, so all that the specification says is that if such information is available, the XPath processor can use it to evaluate expressions like this. If the information isn't available, then the document must be rejected.

There are very many different scenarios for how documents are parsed, validated, and queried. In a typical XSLT environment, the parsing and validation usually happen just before the transformation starts. In an XML database, however, parsing and validation happen when the document is loaded into the database, which may be months or years before the query is executed. The XPath specification tries to cope with this variety of different usage scenarios, but in doing so, it inevitably introduces some aspects of the language that are implementation-defined.

You can avoid these problems by explicitly importing all the schemas that are used to validate documents used by your XPath expressions.

In-Scope Variables

The static context for an XPath expression includes a list of the variables that can be referenced. The information available at this time includes the name of the variable and its type, but not the actual value. It's up to the host language how these variables are declared: in XSLT, for example, they are declared using <xsl:variable> and <xsl:param> elements in the stylesheet. The scoping rules are also defined by the host language: for example, XSLT specifies that global variables are available to any XPath expression anywhere in the stylesheet (in any module), while local variables are available only within XPath expressions contained in an attribute of an element that is a following-sibling of the variable declaration, or a descendant of a following-sibling. So the stylesheet parameter:

```
<xsl:param name="start" as="xs:integer?" required="no"/>
```

adds a variable with name «start» and type «xs:integer?» to the static context of every XPath expression in the stylesheet.

The name of a variable is a QName: that is, it contains a namespace URI and a local name. In practice, it's quite unusual to put variables in a namespace, but it is permitted. It's more common to see this with XQuery, which associates namespaces with modules, so that variables exported by a module will carry the namespace of that module.

It is an error for the XPath expression to refer to variables that aren't present in the static context. In a system that does static type checking, it's also a static error to use a variable in a way that is inconsistent with its type. In systems that do dynamic type checking, such errors are reported only if they occur when the XPath expression is evaluated.

This aspect of the static context differs from all the other aspects in that it can vary for different parts of a single XPath expression. The static context for a nested subexpression may include variables declared in containing «for», «some», or «every» expressions, as well as the variables made available by the host language. The XPath expressions that declare new variables are all listed in Chapter 8.

In-Scope Functions

The static context for an XPath expression also includes a list of the functions that can be called from within the expression. Each function is identified uniquely by its name (a QName, containing a namespace URI and local name) together with its *arity*, which is an integer indicating how many parameters the function has. Two functions with the same name but different numbers of parameters are regarded as being completely distinct functions.

The information that's needed about each function at compile time, apart from the name and arity, is the function signature. The function signature defines the type of each of the function's parameters, as well as the type of its result. This information enables the XPath processor to decide at compile time whether a function call is legitimate: it can check firstly that a function with the right name and number of arguments actually exists, and secondly, (if the processor does static type checking) that the arguments are each of the correct type. Even when the processor doesn't do static type checking, the signature is useful for optimization, because it enables the processor to generate code to convert the supplied values to the required type.

Like other aspects of the static context, the way in which the in-scope functions are populated is defined by the host language. In most host languages, the function library is likely to include at least:

- ❑ The functions defined in the core library: that is, the functions listed in Chapter 10 of this book.

- ❑ A constructor function corresponding to each atomic type in the in-scope schema definitions. These functions are used to construct an instance of the corresponding atomic type, for example, the function «xs:date('2004-06-01')» can be used to construct a date.

However, if a host language wanted to restrict the function library, it could choose to do so. For example, a host language might choose to support the whole function library with the exception of the doc() and collection() functions.

In XSLT, the in-scope functions include the two categories above, together with:

- ❑ A number of standard functions defined within the XSLT specification, for example format-number(), format-date(), and generate-id(). These are described in Chapter 7 of *XSLT 2.0 Programmer's Reference*.

- ❑ User-defined functions written in the stylesheet using the <xsl:function> declaration.

- ❑ Extension functions, for example, functions written as Java methods. The way in which extension functions are made available in the static context depends on the implementation. For example, XSLT processors written in Java generally provide an implicit binding to Java methods, in which the namespace URI of the function identifies a Java class name, and the local name identifies the method name within a class. In such cases the set of in-scope functions for the XPath processor effectively includes every public method in every class on the Java classpath. Other XSLT processors require an explicit binding of extension functions in the stylesheet, for example through a vendor-defined declaration such as <msxsl:script>. In these cases, the functions added to the static context are those that are explicitly declared. (Extension functions are fully described in Chapter 8 of *XSLT 2.0 Programmer's Reference*).

In principle, it's a static error if the XPath expression contains a call on a function that isn't present in the static context. However, XSLT fudges this slightly by masking the error in certain circumstances. This is to allow you to write conditional code that calls different extension functions depending on which XSLT processor you are using. Under these circumstances, the error won't actually be reported until the function call is executed at runtime.

As we saw above, function names contain a namespace URI and a local name. In an actual function call, the function name is written using an optional namespace prefix and a local name. If the prefix is absent, then the function is assumed to belong to the default namespace for functions, which we described earlier in this chapter on page 119. Usually, (and always in XSLT) the default namespace for functions will be the namespace for the core function library. In the current (November 2003) drafts this is `http://www.w3.org/2003/11/xpath-functions`, but the final namespace URI will be known only when the specifications reach Candidate Recommendation status. The XPath specification allows any namespace URI to be chosen as the default, but the host language doesn't have to pass this flexibility on to the user.

If there is a default namespace for functions (and as we've seen, there usually will be), then it becomes impossible to refer to functions that aren't in any namespace, because there is no way of associating a namespace prefix with names in the null namespace. The practical consequence of this is that if you import a schema with no target namespace, you will not be able to call constructor functions for the atomic types defined in that schema. Instead you will have to use the more verbose «cast as» syntax, which is described in Chapter 9. For example, if you have an atomic type called «percentage», you will have to write «98 cast as percentage» rather than «percentage(98)».

Although constructor functions are named after atomic types, they use the default namespace for functions, not the default namespace for elements and types. For example if the default namespace for elements and types is «http://ns.acme.com/», and there is an atomic type «part-number» defined in the schema for this namespace, then you will be able to refer to the type without using a prefix: for example «"AXZ98532" cast as part-number». But when you use the constructor function, the default namespace for functions applies, so you will typically need to use a namespace prefix in this case: «acme:part-number("AXZ98532")».

Collations

The static context for XPath expressions includes a set of collations, one of which is marked as the default collation. A collation is essentially a set of rules for comparing and sorting strings. One collation might decide that «pass» and «Paß» are equal, another that they are distinct.

As far as XPath is concerned, collations are defined outside the system, and a collation is treated as a black box. The XPath processor knows which collations exist (because they are listed in the static context) but it doesn't know anything about their characteristics, beyond the fact that it can use the collation to compare two strings.

Collations are identified by URIs. These are like namespace URIs, in that they don't necessarily identify real resources on the Web: they are just globally unique names, ensuring that collations defined by one vendor can't be confused with those defined by a different vendor. There is only one collation whose name has been standardized, namely:

```
http://www.w3.org/2003/11/xpath-functions/collation/codepoint
```

Like other URIs defined in the draft specifications, this name will only be finalized when the specs become Candidate Recommendations. This collation compares strings character by character, using the numeric values assigned to each character in the Unicode standard. So, for example, «"Z" < "a"» is true when using this collation, because the numeric code for «Z» is 90, and the code for «a» is 97.

As with other aspects of the static context, it's up to the host language to say what collations are available and how they are defined. In this area, however, XSLT as a host language has nothing to say: it leaves it entirely up to the implementation. Many implementations are likely to devise a scheme whereby URIs identify collations provided by the programming language environment, by a database system, or by the operating system.

In Java, for example, you can define a collator by creating an object of class `java.text.Collator`. You can obtain a collator for a particular Locale, which will give you the basic rules for a language (for example «ä» collates after «z» in Swedish, but not in German). You can then parameterize the collator: for example you can set its strength, which determines whether or not it ignores accents and case, and you can control whether it applies Unicode normalization to the characters before comparison: this process recognizes that there are alternative ways of coding the same character in Unicode, either as combined characters (one codepoint representing lower-case-c-with-cedilla) or as separate characters (separate codepoints for the «c» and the cedilla). Saxon allows you to specify a collation URI that specifies these parameters explicitly, for example the URI

```
http://saxon.sf.net/collation?lang=de;strength=secondary;
```

requests a collation suitable for German («lang=de») in which secondary differences between characters (in practice this means case) are considered significant, but tertiary differences (in practice, accents) are not. So «"A"="a"» is false but «"a"="ä"» is true. However, this way of constructing a collation URI is peculiar to Saxon, and other products will have their own conventions.

If you want to write XPath expressions that are portable between products, it's a good idea to assign your chosen collation URI to a variable in the host language, and to reference it using the variable within the XPath expression itself.

The default collation is the one that's used in simple comparisons such as «@a = "potato"». It's worth thinking carefully about your choice of default collation. Generally speaking, if you're searching for text then you want to cast the net wide, which means you want a weak collation (one that treats «A» and «ä» as equal). But if you're sorting, you want to make fine distinctions, which means you need a strong collation. Sorting algorithms look first for primary differences between words («a» versus «b»), then for secondary differences («a» versus «A»), and then for tertiary differences («a» versus «ä») . So you will usually want the sort algorithm to take all these differences into account.

Having said this, it's worth noting that XPath doesn't actually do sorting. If you want to sort data, you need XSLT or XQuery. XPath provides many functions for comparing strings, including comparing whether one string is less than another, but it can't actually sort a collection of strings into order.

It's also interesting to note that although XPath defines the set of collations as part of the static context, there's nothing in the XPath language definition that uses this information at compile time. Collations are used only at runtime, and requesting a collation that doesn't exist is defined as a dynamic error rather than a static error. The reason collations are in the static context is a carry-over from XQuery. XQuery defines sorting of sequences using an «order by» clause in which the collation must be known at compile time. The reason for this restriction is that XQuery systems running on large databases need to make compile-time decisions about which indexes can be used to access the data, and this can only be done by comparing the sort order requested in the query against the collation that was used when constructing the index.

Base URI

When an XPath expression calls the doc() function to load a document, the argument is a URI identifying the document. This may either be an absolute URI (for example, «http://www.w3.org/TR/doc.xml») or a relative URI such as «index.xml». If it is a relative URI, the question arises, what is it relative to? And the answer is: it is relative to the base URI defined in the static context.

Where XPath expressions are contained within an XML document, as happens with XSLT, it's fairly obvious what the base URI should be: it's essentially the URI of the document containing the XPath expression. (This isn't a completely clear-cut concept, because a document might be reachable by more than one URI. The thinking comes from the way URLs are used in a Web browser, where any relative URL in an HTML page is interpreted relative to the URL that was used to fetch the page that it contains. Generalizing this model has proved a fairly tortuous business.)

Where XPath expressions arise in other contexts, for example, if they are generated on the fly within a C++ program, it's far less clear what the base URI should be. So XPath delegates the problem: the base URI is whatever the host language says it is. The context dependency is made explicit by identifying the base URI as part of the static context, and as far as XPath is concerned, the problem disappears.

It's again worth noting that there is nothing in the XPath language semantics that causes the base URI to have any effect at compile time. It is used only at runtime, and then only when certain functions are used (including not only doc(), but also collection() and base-uri()). The reason it's defined as part of the static context is the expectation that it will be a property of the document containing the text of the XPath expression.

Statically Known Documents and Collections

Later in the chapter (see page 131) we'll be looking at how the available documents and collections form part of the dynamic context of an XPath expression. Normally, one might expect that nothing is known at compile time about the documents that the query might access when the time comes to execute it. However, this isn't always the case, especially in a database environment. This information in the static context acknowledges that in some environments, an XPath expression might be compiled specifically to execute against a particular source document or collection of source documents, and that the system might be able to use this knowledge at the time it compiles the expression.

This is especially the case in a system that does static type checking. One of the difficulties with static type checking arises when the XPath expression contains a construct such as:

```
doc("invoice.xml")/invoice/line-item[value > 10.00]
```

To perform strict static type checking on this expression, the system needs to know what the data type of «value» is. If «value» were a date, for example, then the expression would be in error (you can't compare a date with a number) and the type checker would have to report this. But how can we know what the type of «value» is, if we don't know in advance what type of document «invoice.xml» is?

The specification makes provision for some documents and/or collections to be recognized by the system at compile time. For example, you might compile an XPath expression against a particular database, and you might know that all the documents in that database, or in some part of that database, have been validated against a particular schema. This knowledge might allow the system to know that the example expression above is type-safe. Without this knowledge, to get this query past a system that does static type checking you would need to change it to:

```
doc("invoice.xml")/invoice/line-item
        [(value treat as xs:decimal) > 10.00]
```

This is obviously very inconvenient. It's no surprise that most of the vendors who are planning to implement static type checking in their products are generally running in a database environment where the schemas are all known in advance.

This discussion probably affects XQuery much more than it does XPath. Most vendors of XML databases will be using XQuery rather than XPath as the query language (though some are offering XPath as a stop-gap). There's nothing intrinsic to the argument, however, that makes it only relevant to XQuery, and that's why this information is also part of the static context in XPath.

The Dynamic Context

We've now finished our tour of the static context, which contains all the information available at compile time about the environment in which an XPath expression will run. We'll now look at the information that's available at execution time.

In principle, all the information that was available in the static context remains available to the XPath processor when evaluating the query. The dynamic context supplements this with additional information. In practice, however, the XPath processor is free to discard information that it will not need at runtime. For example, it may not need to know the names of variables at runtime, it only needs to know where the values of the variables will be held.

The following sections look at the different parts of the dynamic context in turn.

The Focus

The *focus* is a collective term used to describe three important pieces of information in the dynamic context: the context item, the context position, and the context size.

The most important of these is the context item. Consider the simple path expression «@code». This selects an attribute named «code». But an attribute of what? This expression only makes sense if the context item identifies an element node. The expression then selects the «code» attribute of that element. When an XPath expression like this is embedded in some host language, it is the job of the host language to define how the context item is initialized.

The term *context node* is often used to mean "the context item, assuming it is a node". Very often the context item will be a node, but it can also be an atomic value such as a string or a number.

In an XSLT template rule, for example, the context node is the node that was matched by the template rule. So if you write:

```
<xsl:template match="product">
  <xsl:value-of select="@code"/>
</xsl:template>
```

then the XPath expression «@code» is evaluated with the matched <product> element as the context node.

To see the effect of the context position and size, it's probably easiest to look at an <xsl:for-each> instruction in XSLT, for example:

```
<xsl:for-each select="author">
  <xsl:value-of select="."/>
  <xsl:if test="position() != last()">, </xsl:if>
</xsl:for-each>
```

The XPath expression «.», used in the <xsl:value-of> instruction, simply selects the context item. (The <xsl:value-of> instruction then writes a text node containing the value of this item converted to a string.)

The function position() returns the value of the context position, and the function last() returns the value of the context size. In an <xsl:for-each> instruction, each item in the selected sequence (here, each <author> element) is processed in turn. While each item is being processed, it becomes the context item, and its position in the sequence of items being processed becomes the context position. Positions are always numbered starting at one. The context size is the number of items in the sequence, which of course is the same for each of the items. So the test <xsl:if test="position() != last()">, </xsl:if> outputs a comma after every item except the last.

XSLT also initializes the context position and size when a sequence of nodes is processed using <xsl:apply-templates>.

In other host languages, for example, in APIs for invoking XPath, it's quite common that there is no provision for setting the context position and size, only the context item. There is no obligation on the host language to provide this capability. It can choose always to set the context position and size to one, or to leave them undefined (in which case it's an error to use the functions position() or last()).

The context item will very often be a node, but in principle it can be any kind of item, that is, a node or an atomic value. In XSLT 2.0, for example, you can use the <xsl:for-each> instruction to process a sequence of strings, and within such an instruction the context item will be a string. If you then use a path expression that relies on the context item being a node (for example, a path expression such as «@code»), it will fail with an error.

The focus is initialized by the host language on entry to an XPath expression, but the focus can change when evaluating a subexpression. There are two constructs in XPath that change the focus: the path expression «A/B», and the filter expression «S[P]». Path expressions are described in full detail in Chapter 7 of this book, and filter expressions in Chapter 8. Let's take the filter expressions first.

In fact there are two very similar constructs of the form S[P] that use predicates in square brackets, and we'll explain the difference between them in Chapters 7 and 8. For the purpose of this discussion, there is no distinction—they both handle the focus in the same way.

In this construct, «S» is a sequence (that is, it's some expression whose value is a sequence—and as every expression evaluates to a sequence, this actually means it can be any expression whatsoever). «P» is a predicate, which filters the sequence by selecting only those items that match a given condition. So if we write «author[@surname="Smith"]» we are selecting those <author> elements that have a «surname» attribute whose value is «Smith».

Within the predicate, just as within an <xsl:for-each> instruction in XSLT, the context item is the item from the sequence that's being tested; the context position is the position of that item in the sequence being filtered (counting from one); and the context size is the number of items in the sequence. This means, for example, that you can select the first half of the sequence by writing:

```
$sequence[position() * 2 <= last()]
```

There is a special rule for predicates, namely that if the value of the predicate is a number N, then it is treated as a shorthand for the condition «[position() = N]», which selects the Nth item in the sequence.

For path expressions of the form «A/B», the rules are the same as the rules for predicates. The expression B is evaluated once for each node in the sequence produced by evaluating A, and while B is being evaluated, that node is the context item, the position of that node in the sequence is the context position, and the number of items in the sequence is the context size. However, it's very hard to construct a useful path expression that actually uses position() or size() on the right-hand side of the «/» operator, because both the operands of «/» have to be sequences of nodes. Using them inside a predicate such as «A/B[last()]» doesn't count, of course, because the focus changes again once you're inside the predicate.

It's also important to be aware that certain expressions *don't* change the focus. Specifically, the focus is not changed within a «for», «some», or «every» expression (these expressions are described in Chapter 8). So the expression

```
«sum(for $i in //item return @price * @quantity)»
```

is incorrect (at any rate, it doesn't do what you probably intended), because the context item doesn't change within this expression, which means that relative path expressions «@price» and «@quantity» are not evaluated relative to each item in turn. The way you should write this is:

```
«sum(for $i in //item return $i/@price * $i/@quantity)»
```

A path expression such as «//item» is often referred to as an absolute path expression, which can easily give the impression that its value doesn't depend on the context item. This isn't entirely true. Such an expression selects nodes starting from a document node, but this document node is selected as the node at the root of the tree containing the context node. So when the context item changes, if it selects a node in a different document, then the result of «//item» changes too. This also means (which can come as a surprise) that when the context item isn't a node, an expression such as «//item» gives you an error. For example, this means you can't write:

```
«tokenize(sentence, "\s+")[not(. = //stopword)]»
```

because by the time you're in the predicate, the context item is one of the strings produced by the `tokenize()` function, which means there is no context node, and therefore no root for «`//stopword`» to select from. The solution to this problem is to assign the result of the expression «`//stopword`» (or perhaps the root node from which it navigates) to a variable.

Dynamic Variables

The dynamic context of an XPath expression also holds the values of all the variables that are defined in the static context. The name *dynamic variables* is not a very happy choice, since it would appear to suggest that some variables are static and others are dynamic. In fact, the set of variables that are available to the expression is known statically; the names and types of these variables are part of the static context, and the values of the variables are part of the dynamic context. Each of these variables must have a value by the time the expression is evaluated, it is not possible for a variable to be "null" or "uninitialized". The closest thing to a null value is the value «`()`», the empty sequence.

The value of each variable will always conform to its type. If the static type of the variable is «`xs:decimal`», for example, the value can be an instance of «`xs:decimal`» or an instance of «`xs:integer`» (which is a subtype of «`xs:decimal`») but it cannot be an «`xs:string`» or an «`xs:float`».

The way that the variable acquires its value is up to the host language. In many languages there will not be a meaningful distinction between declaring a variable (in the static context) and giving it a value (in the dynamic context). In XSLT there is no distinction in the case of <`xsl:variable`>, but there is in the case of <`xsl:param`>. In the example on page 121 we showed a stylesheet parameter declared as:

```
<xsl:param name="start" as="xs:integer?" required="no"/>
```

The value supplied to this parameter when the stylesheet is invoked becomes part of the dynamic context for every XPath expression in the stylesheet. If no value is supplied, the dynamic context contains the default value, which in this case is the empty sequence, «`()`».

Function Implementations

For every function defined in the static context of the expression, there must be an implementation available so that the function can be called and can return a result.

I don't think this is saying anything very profound, so I will move on. It does make the point that although the signatures of the in-scope functions must be known when the XPath expression is compiled, there is scope for substituting different implementations of the function at runtime.

Current Date and Time

The specification tries to ensure that all the information that an XPath expression can depend on is included formally as part of the context. An XPath expression that uses the functions `current-date()`, `current-time()`, or `current-dateTime()` depends on the current date and time, so this is modeled as part of the dynamic context.

XPath is designed on the basis that functions are always pure functions, and a characteristic feature of a pure function is that when you call it repeatedly, it returns the same result each time. The current date and time in the dynamic context are therefore defined not to change during the execution of an XPath expression. In fact, in XSLT, they are defined not to change during the execution of an entire stylesheet. This means that the functions are not useful for applications such as performance instrumentation; they are intended rather for recording the approximate time at which a stylesheet or query was executed, and for use in business logic calculations such as displaying a date three days from today.

Implicit Timezone

The handling of timezones caused a great deal of trouble in the design of the XPath functions and operators.

In XML Schema, it's defined that a value of type xs:dateTime represents an instant in time. The value written as «2004-01-31T22:00:00-05:00» represents 10 p.m. on 31st January in the US East Coast timezone; this is the same instant in time as 3 a.m. on 1st February in the UK, which is written as «2004-02-01T03:00:00Z». So as far as XML Schema is concerned, these two values are identical and indistinguishable.

If XSLT and XQuery had taken the same view, the result would be that copying a document (a null transformation) would change the value «2004-01-31T22:00:00-05:00» in the input document so it appeared as «2004-02-01T03:00:00Z» in the result document. The working groups felt that users would not be happy with this: they felt that the timezone conveys meaningful information, and should be retained.

XML Schema also allows values to be specified without a timezone, for example, as «2004-01-31 T22:00:00». This can be interpreted as meaning that the timezone is unknown, but this interpretation makes life very complicated when dates and times are compared with each other: it means, for example that «2004-01-31» is definitely earlier than «2004-02-05», but it's uncertain whether «2004-01-31» is earlier than «2004-02-01», because if the first date is used in a part of the world whose timezone is «-12:00», it refers to the same period of 24 hours as the second date in a place whose timezone is «+12:00». Such uncertainty causes havoc with query languages, and so XPath took a different approach. Instead of interpreting the absence of a timezone as meaning that the timezone is unknown, it interprets it as meaning that an implicit timezone should be assumed. Typically, where possible, this will be the timezone in the place where the user is located, or failing that, the timezone in the place where the computer is located. However, XPath doesn't worry itself with how the implicit timezone is set up: it simply says that there is one, leaves it to the host environment to initialize it, and goes on to specify how it is used when performing operations on dates and times.

Some host languages might choose to specify how the implicit timezone is initialized: in Java, for example, it could have a defined relationship to the current locale. XSLT however chooses to pass the buck on to the implementation. It's likely that many implementations will use the timezone setting from the computer on which the XSLT processor is running, which may or may not give useful results.

The implicit timezone is used behind the scenes by a number of operators that manipulate dates and times, but it is also available explicitly to the XPath user through the function implicit-timezone(), which is included in Chapter 10.

Available Documents and Collections

One of the aims in defining the evaluation context for XPath is to list all the things in the environment that can affect the result of an XPath expression. Two of the most environment-dependent constructs in the language are the doc() function, which loads a document using a URI, and the collection() function, which similarly identifies a collection of documents using a URI (this function is primarily intended for use with XML databases).

In the XSLT 1.0 specification there was a fairly detailed description of how the document() function (the precursor to the doc() function in XPath 2.0) was supposed to work. It described in some detail the process of URI resolution, the way in which the URI was dereferenced to fetch a resource from the Web, the requirement for this resource to contain well-formed XML, and the way that the media type of the resource affected the interpretation of any fragment identifier in the URI.

But at the same time, the specification said that the input to the XSLT processor was a tree, following the rules in the data model, and that nothing in the specification should constrain the way in which the tree was constructed.

There's clearly a tension between these two definitions, and this revealed itself, during the life of the specification, in some practical problems. Notoriously, the Microsoft XSLT processor took the second statement at face value, and stripped spaces from the source document by default, which meant that it often produced different results from other XSLT processors. Another XSLT processor decided to expand XInclude directives in the source document by default. Both of these decisions were entirely conformant according to the specification, and yet they led to practical interoperability problems.

Even more extreme effects can be achieved by exploiting the URIResolver interface in the Java JAXP API (which Microsoft has emulated in the System.Xml.Xsl framework classes under the name XmlResolver). This allows the user to nominate a routine that will intercept all requests for a URI from the doc() function, and take over the job of delivering a document in response to the request. This means, for example, that you can call the doc() function with the URI «special://prime/100» and return a document containing the first 100 prime numbers, constructed algorithmically. This mechanism is undoubtedly useful, but it rather makes a mockery of any detailed description in the language specification of how the doc() function is supposed to work.

There was a great deal of debate in the working groups about whether the specification should be tightened up to ensure that the results of the new doc() function were interoperable across all processors, or whether they should be relaxed completely to acknowledge that the process of getting from a URI to a tree is entirely under the control of the implementation (and possibly the user). In the end, the latter approach was chosen, recognizing the reality that since the specification couldn't stop people from inventing things like Java's URIResolver, it might as well acknowledge the fact.

The way that this idea has actually been expressed in the spec may seem a little confusing. It simply says that the dynamic context of an XPath expression provides a mapping from URIs onto document nodes. The easiest way to read this is by thinking of the mapping as being an external function rather like the Java URIResolver: if you give it a URI, it comes back with a document node. This function might go out to the Web, retrieve an XML document, parse it, validate it, and turn it into a tree in the data model. Or, it might return a document node that represents a virtual document, which is actually a collection of data in a relational database. Or, it might construct an XML document containing the first 100 prime numbers. Quite simply, anything goes.

This approach maximizes flexibility at the expense of interoperability. You simply can't be sure any more that the same call on the doc() function will produce the same results on two different implementations. The hope is, however, that market forces will ensure that most products support the obvious mappings from URIs to documents, even though these mappings are no longer mandatory, and might not be provided by XPath processors designed to operate in specialized environments. To encourage this, the data model specification describes a mapping from the XML InfoSet to the XPath data model. Implementations aren't constrained to use this mapping, but if they choose to use it, then a reasonable degree of interoperability should follow.

As well as the doc() function which returns a document node corresponding to a URI, XPath 2.0 also provides the collection() function which returns a collection of documents (actually, a sequence). While there is a great deal of precedent and user expectation for the way in which URIs will map to individual documents, there is very little precedent for the concept of a document collection identified by URI, and it's likely therefore that different processors will interpret this concept in very different ways. There is a tendency, however, for good ideas to be copied from one implementation to another, so perhaps conventions will start to appear. However, the concept of collections is really intended as an abstraction of an XML database, or part of an XML database, and since the system architecture of different XML databases is highly variable, there might well remain radical differences in the way that the concept of a collection is realized.

As with other aspects of the context, the host language gets a say in the matter. For example, a host language could say that the set of available documents and collections is always empty, and thus constrain XPath expressions to operate on a single document, or on documents accessible through variables. But in the case of XSLT, little more is said on the subject. The only thing that XSLT adds is a specification of the document() function, which continues to be available in XSLT and is now defined in terms of the simpler XPath 2.0 doc() function.

Summary

In this chapter we described all the contents of the XPath evaluation context, including both the static and the dynamic context. The context is important because it establishes the interface between XPath and a host language such as XSLT, and it identifies all the external information that may affect the result of an XPath expression.

This concludes the introductory part of this book, which explained all of the important concepts behind the specification of the XPath language. The next chapter starts the reference section of the book, which contains detailed specifications of every language feature.

5

Basic Constructs

This chapter defines the basic constructs of the XPath language. The complete grammar of the language is summarized in Appendix A, and for convenience I have split the constructs of the language across five chapters, as follows:

Chapter	Scope
5	Notation used for describing the grammar Overall structure of the language Lexical rules (including comments and whitespace handling) Literals Variable references Parenthesized sub-expressions Context item expression «.» Function calls Conditional expressions: «if»
6	Arithmetic operators: «+», «-», … Value comparison operators: «eq», «lt», … General comparison operators: «=», «<», … Node identity and ordering operators: «is», «<<», «>>» Boolean operators: «and», «or»
7	Path expressions: «/», «//» Steps and axes Union, intersect, and except operators
8	Sequence concatenation operator: «,» Numeric range operator: «to» Filter expressions «a[b]» Mapping expressions: «for» Quantified expressions: «some» and «every»

Continues

Chapter	Scope
9	SequenceType production «instance of» «castable as» «cast as» «treat as»

As with other programming languages, the syntax is defined in a set of *production rules*. Each rule defines the structure of a particular construct as a set of choices, sequences, or repetitions.

I took the formal production rules directly from the XPath specification document (`http://www.w3.org/TR/xpath20`), but reordered them for ease of explanation, and I made minor changes to the typography and to some of the production names for ease of reading. I also pulled in those rules from the XML and XML Namespaces standards that the XPath syntax references. I've tried to do this in a way that leaves the original rule clearly recognizable, so you can relate it to the original specification if you need to. However, I tried to include in this book all the information you need from the XPath specification, so this should only be necessary if you need to see the precise wording of the standard.

Notation

The XPath specification, by and large, uses the same syntax notation as the rest of the family of XML specifications. This is often referred to as extended BNF, though the number of variations you find on the BNF theme can be a little bewildering. I have stuck fairly closely to the notation used in the XPath 2.0 specification, though I have allowed myself a little typographic license in the hope that this adds clarity.

As in the rest of the book, I used French quotation marks «thus» (also known as chevrons or guillemets) to surround pieces of XPath text that you write: I chose this convention partly because these marks stand out more clearly, but more importantly to distinguish these quotation marks unambiguously from quotation marks that are actually part of the expression. So if I say, for example, that literals can be enclosed either in «"» or «'» marks, then it's clear that you don't actually write the chevrons. XPath syntax doesn't use chevrons with any special meaning (though like any other Unicode character, you can use them in string literals and comments), so you can be sure that any chevron you see is not to be included in the expression.

An unusual feature of the XPath 2.0 grammar is the way certain symbols are grouped together. For example, the syntax of a cast expression is given in the XPath Recommendation as:

```
CastExpr ::= UnaryExpr ( <"cast" "as"> SingleType )?
```

This indicates that a cast expression consists of a `UnaryExpr` optionally followed by the compound symbol «cast as» and a `SingleType`. These compound symbols behave in some ways like one lexical token, and in some ways like two. You can think of XPath 2.0 either as having a rather unusually powerful lexical analyzer, in which compound symbols such as «cast as» are recognized as single tokens, or you can think of it as having a grammar that requires lookahead; the purpose of the angle brackets in the production rule is to show that the parser can only go down this path in the grammar if both words «cast» and «as» are present, which means that if it finds «cast» followed by something other than «as», it has to do some backtracking. This really doesn't affect users of the language very much at all, it's mainly a complication that implementors of an XPath parser need to be aware of. I've therefore used a notation for these compound symbols which I hope is less distracting: I write this example as «cast as», where the space between the two parts of the symbol indicates that whitespace characters (and comments, if you really want) is allowed between the two words. So in Chapter 9, you will find that the above production rule appears as:

```
CastExpr ::= UnaryExpr ( «cast as» SingleType )?
```

In this example the whitespace is necessary to avoid the two words being read as a single token. In other cases such as «for $» and «if (», the whitespace is optional.

The whitespace characters allowed as separators in XPath expressions are the same as in XML: space (x20), tab (x09), newline (x0A), and carriage return (x0D).

The notations used in production rules are as follows:

Construct	Meaning
«abc»	The literal characters abc
xyz	A construct that matches the production rule named xyz
P|Q	A choice of P or Q
P?	Either P, or nothing
P*	Zero or more repetitions of P
P+	One or more repetitions of P
[i-n]	One of the characters in the range «i» to «n» inclusive
«abc xyz»	A compound symbol consisting of the token «abc» followed by the token «xyz»
(P)	A sub-expression

The production rules in XPath implicitly define the precedence of the different operators. For example the rule for OrExpr defines it as a sequence of AndExpr operands separated by «or» operators. This is a convenient way of defining that the «and» operator binds more tightly than «or». The precedence order of all the operators is summarized in Appendix B.

One consequence of this style of definition is that the simplest OrExpr consists of a single AndExpr with no «or» operator present at all. This leads to all sorts of surprises. For example because of the way the grammar is written, «3» is not just an IntegerLiteral, it is also a FilterExpr, a RelativePathExpr, a MultiplicativeExpr, a TreatExpr, and quite a few other things besides. This means that I can't use the term OrExpr when I want to refer specifically to an expression that uses an «or» operator. Instead, I'll refer to this as "an «or» expression." This distinction works quite well in most cases, and if there's any risk of confusion then I'll try to spell out exactly what construct I'm talking about.

Although the production rules in XPath define the operator precedence, they do not impose any type checking. This follows the practice of most modern language specifications, where rules for type checking are regarded as being enforced in a second phase of processing, after the raw parsing of the syntax. It would be hard to define all the type checking rules in the grammar, because many of them operate at a distance. Since the type-checking rules can't all be defined in the grammar, the language designers decided to go to the other extreme, and define none of them in the grammar.

This means that the grammar allows many kinds of expression that are completely nonsensical, such as «3 | 'bread'» (where «|» is the set union operator). It's left to the type-checking rules to throw this out: the rules for the «|» operator say that its operands must be of type «node() *», that is, sequences of nodes. Think of an analogy with English—there are sentences that are perfectly correct grammatically, but still nonsense: "An easy apple only trumpets yesterday."

Where to Start

Some people prefer to present the syntax of a language bottom-up, starting with the simplest constructs such as numbers and names, while others prefer to start at the top, with a construct like Program or Expression. In the previous edition of this book I presented the rules alphabetically, which works for a reasonably small language, but would require rather a lot of jumping around now that the language has grown to occupy a whole book of its own, rather than a single chapter in an XSLT book.

So what I've chosen to do this time around is to start at the top, with the section *Expressions*, which is really just an opportunity to provide an overview of the grammar, and then work bottom-up, starting with the basic building blocks of the language in this chapter, and progressing through the other operators in the next four chapters. Each of these chapters describes a reasonably self-contained set of expressions that you can write in XPath. There's no obviously logical order to these, but I decided to present the simpler operators and expressions first, to make life as easy as possible if you decide to read the chapters sequentially. This also corresponds broadly with the order in which material is presented in the XPath specification itself.

> *If you want to find where in the book a particular construct is described, you might find the syntax summary in Appendix A helpful.*

Many languages distinguish the lexical rules, which define the format of basic tokens such as names, numbers, and operators, from the syntactic rules, which define how these tokens are combined to form expressions and other higher-level constructs.

The XPath specification includes both syntactic and lexical production rules, but they are not quite as cleanly separated as in some languages. The main distinction between the two kinds of rule is that whitespace can be freely used between lexical tokens but not within a lexical token. I will try to identify clearly which constructs are considered to be lexical tokens as we come across them in the grammar.

Expressions

The top-level construct in XPath (the entry point to the list of productions) is called Expr. This is described with the following syntax:

Expression	Syntax
Expr	ExprSingle («,» ExprSingle)*
ExprSingle	ForExpr | QuantifiedExpr | IfExpr | OrExpr

These rules indicate that an Expr is a list of ExprSingle expressions separated by commas, and an ExprSingle is either a ForExpr, a QuantifiedExpr, an IfExpr, or an OrExpr.

Here are some examples of the constructs mentioned in these rules:

Construct	Example
Expr	1 to 3, 5, 7, 11, 13
ExprSingle	*any of the examples below*
ForExpr	for $i in 1 to 10 return $i*$i
QuantifiedExpr	some $i in //item satisfies exists($i/*)
IfExpr	if (exists(@price)) then @price else 0
OrExpr	@price > 3 or @cost < 2

I'll cover the «,» operator (which concatenates two sequences), together with the ForExpr and the QuantifiedExpr in Chapter 8, which is all about expressions on sequences. The IfExpr (which allows you to write conditional «if..then..else» expressions) is covered in this chapter, on page 165, and the OrExpr, which allows you to use the boolean «or» operator, and provides the entry point to most of the rest of the XPath syntax, is described in Chapter 5.

The ExprSingle construct has a special role in the grammar. Because the «,» symbol is overloaded (it's used both as an operator for concatenating two lists, and also as a syntactic delimiter in constructs such as a function call) there are places where you might expect the grammar to allow any Expr to appear, but where in fact only an ExprSingle is allowed. This means that if you want to use a «,» operator in such contexts, you have to enclose the expression in parentheses.

The constructs IfExpr, ForExpr, and QuantifiedExpr are syntactically unusual in the XPath grammar because they start with keywords and contain multiple sub-expressions. In a conventional language, they would probably be called statements rather than expressions. Nevertheless, they are true expressions, in the sense that they can be evaluated to produce a result, and they can appear anywhere in the grammar where an expression is required.

The OrExpr starts a list of productions that contains all the conventional expressions of the language, as follows:

Expression	Syntax
OrExpr	AndExpr («or» AndExpr)*
AndExpr	ComparisonExpr («and» ComparisonExpr)*
ComparisonExpr	RangeExpr ((ValueComp | GeneralComp | NodeComp) RangeExpr)?
RangeExpr	AdditiveExpr («to» AdditiveExpr)?
AdditiveExpr	MultiplicativeExpr ((«+» | «-») MultiplicativeExpr)*
MultiplicativeExpr	UnionExpr ((«*» | «div» | «idiv» | «mod») UnionExpr)*
UnionExpr	IntersectExceptExpr ((«union» | «|») IntersectExceptExpr)*
IntersectExceptExpr	InstanceOfExpr ((«intersect» | «except») InstanceOfExpr)*
InstanceofExpr	TreatExpr («instance of» SequenceType)?
TreatExpr	CastableExpr («treat as» SequenceType)?
CastableExpr	CastExpr («castable as» SingleType)?
CastExpr	UnaryExpr («cast as» SingleType)?
UnaryExpr	(«-» | «+»)* PathExpr

These expressions all have a similar form: each defines an expression in terms of expression in the row below combined with particular infix or prefix operators. These operators are all described in the following chapters, according to the role that they play.

At the level of PathExpr, the syntax starts to become rather more specialized again, which shouldn't be surprising because path expressions are the characteristic feature of the XPath language that gives it its special flavor. Chapter 7 is devoted to path expressions, where you will find the full syntax.

Below the level of path expressions, the most primitive expressions in the language are referred to as primary expressions. At that level we will pick up the story again in this chapter, on page **000**.

As explained in Chapter 1, XPath is a read-only expression language. It's a general principle of XPath that expression evaluation is free of side effects: evaluating an expression isn't going to change the values of any variables, write information to log files, or prompt the user for their credit card number. Therefore evaluating the same expression more than once, in the same context, shouldn't make any difference to the answer or to the final output, and equally it shouldn't make any difference in which order expressions are evaluated. As a result, the XSLT and XPath specifications generally say nothing about order of evaluation.

The only way side effects can occur from evaluating an expression is if the expression calls user-written (or vendor-written) extension functions, because the XPath specification doesn't constrain what an extension function can do. Equally, it makes no guarantees about when, and in what order, extension functions are called.

Examples

Examples of expressions occur throughout this book. Here is a selection, brought together to indicate the variety of constructs that fall under this heading:

Expression	Description
`$x + ($y * 2)`	Returns the result of multiplying `$y` by two and adding the value of `$x`
`//book | //magazine`	Returns a sequence of nodes containing all of the `<book>` and `<magazine>` elements in the same document as the context node. (This could also be written, perhaps more efficiently, as «`//(book|magazine)`»)
`substring-before(author, ' ')`	Finds the value of the first `<author>` child of the context node, and returns that part of the value that precedes the first space character
`chapter and verse`	Returns the `xs:boolean` value `true` if the context node has a child `<chapter>` element and also a child `<verse>` element
`93.7`	Returns the decimal value `93.7`
`sum(for $i in // product return $i/price * $i/qty)`	Returns the result of multiplying the values of price and qty for every `<product>` element in the document, and summing the results
`avg( // (product)[position()<=5]) /price)`	Returns the average `<price>` of the first five `<product>` elements in the document

Lexical Constructs

An XPath 2.0 expression is written as a sequence of Unicode characters. Every character that's available in XML 1.0 can be used in an XPath expression, and possibly characters that are available in XML 1.1 as well, though that's been left up to the implementation to decide.

XPath itself isn't concerned with how these characters are encoded. XPath expressions will often be embedded in other languages such as XSLT, or they may be constructed as runtime character strings using a programming language such as Java or JavaScript. Any escape conventions local to the host language will be applied before the XPath parser gets to see the expression, and the syntax described in the XPath Recommendation (and in this book) is the syntax after such escapes have been expanded. For example:

❑ When XPath expressions are written in an XSLT stylesheet, the escaping conventions of XML apply. This means, for example, that a «<» character must be escaped as «<» and an ampersand as «&». Since XPath expressions are invariably written inside an attribute value in the stylesheet, the delimiting quotation marks of the attribute value (usually «"», but you can choose «'» if you prefer) must also be escaped, typically as «"» or «'», respectively. It's also worth remembering that the XML parser normalizes whitespace in an attribute value, so if you want to write an expression that tests whether some element in your source document contains a tab character, you should write this as `<xsl:if test="contains(x,` `'&#x09;')">`. As far as XPath is concerned, an XPath expression can contain a tab character inside a string literal (and indeed, that's what it sees in this example), but to get the tab character past the XML parser, you need to escape it.

❑ Similarly, when XPath expressions are written within character strings in a host language such as Java, you will need to use the escaping conventions of that language: for example a backslash needs to be written as «\\» and a quotation mark as «\"».

XPath is an unusual language in that it has no reserved words. Unembellished names in an XPath expression, such as «table» and «author», refer to elements or attributes in the source document that have these names. Since there are no restrictions on what you can call the elements in your source document (other than the characters that can be used), XPath has been designed so there are no restrictions on the names that can appear in the XPath expression. The result is that other names (for example, the names of variables and functions, as well as language keywords) have to be either embellished in some way, or recognized by the context in which they appear. There are several ways the grammar achieves this:

❑ Names of variables are always preceded by a «$» sign, for example «$x» (whitespace is allowed between the «$» and the «x», though it is rarely used in practice).

❑ Names of functions are always followed by a left parenthesis, for example, «not(». Again, whitespace is allowed before the «(». Some syntactic keywords use the same convention. For example «if» in a conditional expression is always followed by «(», and node tests such as «element()» are also written with parentheses. (This node test matches any element node; if you leave out the parentheses, then it matches only elements that have the name «element».)

❑ Some operators, such as «and», «or», and «div», are written as keywords, but they are recognized as keywords only if they appear in a context where an operator is expected. The language is carefully arranged so that there is no ambiguity, and you can happily write constructs such as «and or or» to test whether there is an element called «and» or an element called «or» in your source document.

- ❑ Some operator names consist of doubled keywords, such as «instance of» or «castable as». These are recognized only if they appear as a pair.

- ❑ The keywords «for», «some», and «every», which introduce expressions described in Chapter 8, are recognized by virtue of the fact that they are always followed by a «$» sign (which in turn introduces the name of a variable).

As with most languages, the first stage in processing an XPath expression is lexical analysis, also known as tokenizing. The first stage of identifying the tokens is done fairly mechanically, and does not depend in any way on the context. At each stage, the longest sequence of characters that could comprise a single token is read. There are a few places where this can lead to surprises, for example «x+1» is read as three tokens, whereas «x-1» is read as a single token. This is because XML names can contain a «-» character but not a «+» character. To ensure that «x-1» is read as a subtraction rather than as a single name, you need a space before the «-» for example «x - 1». You also need to be careful with the humble «.» character, which can appear in several different roles in XPath: as a decimal point within a number, as a separator character within a name, and as a symbol in its own right, representing the context item. So, for example if you write «$a is .» (which tests whether variable $a refers to the context node) then you need a space between the «is» and the «.».

Once the text has been split into tokens, the tokens are classified. It is at this stage that the decision is made whether a name such as «div» is being used as an element name in a path expression, as a function name, as a variable name, or as an operator or keyword. As we have seen, the decision on how to classify a token may depend on the tokens that precede and follow it. It's likely that many parsers will also group together compound tokens such as «cast as» at this stage, though the details of how this is done are left entirely to the implementation.

The following sections present the basic lexical constructs found within an XPath expression.

Comments

Comments may appear in an XPath expression anywhere that whitespace may appear. Comments begin with «(:» and end with «:)», which feels slightly comical until you get used to it. But it means that comments are quite distinctive visually, and they read well because they look parenthetical.

Here is an example of a comment within an XPath expression:

```
if (string(@x))
then (: attribute x exists and is non-empty :) @x
else "none"
```

Was it really necessary for XPath to invent a completely new syntax for comments? Well, none of the obvious candidates would work. The C/Java convention is heavily reliant on symbols such as «/» and «» which are already overloaded in XPath. The SQL convention of «--» doesn't work because it's perfectly legal to have two adjacent hyphens in an XML name. The XML syntax of <!--x--> doesn't work in an expression that's embedded in an XML attribute in a stylesheet. Because of XML attribute normalization, anything that attaches significance to line endings is ruled out. Curly braces were tried at one stage, but they are easily confused with the delimiters for attribute value templates in XSLT, or the equivalent embedded expressions in XQuery (and they were a new invention anyway). So smileys it is …*

XPath 2.0 comments can be nested. This allows you to comment-out a section of code even if it already contains comments. So for example the following expression is legal, and evaluates to 3:

```
3 (: +
   if (number(@x))
   then (: attribute x exists and is non-zero :) @x
   else 0
 :)
```

To achieve this, the production rules for comments are given as follows:

Symbol	Syntax
ExprComment	«(:» (ExprCommentContent | ExprComment)* «:)»
ExprCommentContent	Char

The way this rule works is that within a comment, you can have a sequence of things, each of which is either a character or a comment. Since the system always looks for the longest matching construct, if it sees «(:» within a comment then it will interpret this as the start of a nested comment, rather than as two ordinary characters.

Changes in XPath 2.0

XPath 1.0 provided no way of writing comments within an expression. The facility has become necessary because with the introduction of conditional expressions, «for» expressions, and the like, XPath 2.0 expressions can be much longer and more complex.

Numeric Literals

Numeric literals represent constant numbers. There are three types of number that can be written as constants within an XPath 2.0 expression: these correspond to the types xs:integer, xs:decimal, and xs:double. The type of the value is inferred from the way it is written. The rules are shown in the table below:

Symbol	Syntax
IntegerLiteral	Digit+
DecimalLiteral	(«.» Digit+) | (Digit+ «.» Digit*)
DoubleLiteral	((«.» Digit+) | (Digit+ («.» Digit*)?)) («e» | «E») («+» | «-»)? Digit+
Digit	[0-9]

That is to say:

- ❑ A sequence of one or more digits, with no decimal point or «e» or «E», is interpreted as an integer literal. For example «0», «23» and «0034» are all integer literals.

- ❑ A sequence of one or more digits, with a decimal point among the digits or at the beginning or end, is interpreted as a decimal literal. Examples are «1.50», «.001», and «3.».

- ❑ A literal in scientific notation (or to be pedantic, in Fortran notation) is interpreted as an xs:double value. It starts with the mantissa, which may take the same form as either an integer or a decimal literal, followed by the letter «E» in upper or lower case (there is no distinction between the two, though upper case «E» is always used on output), followed by an exponent expressed as an integer, optionally preceded by a plus or minus sign. Examples are «0e0», «0.314159e+001», and «1.E-6».

The production rule for Digit is written as a *regular expression* and means that Digit is a sequence of one or more characters, each in the range 0 to 9. The square brackets do not mean that the construct is optional, as in some other syntax notations; rather they indicate a range of characters.

You may be wondering why a leading minus sign is not allowed at the front of a numeric literal. The answer is that it is allowed, but it's not part of the literal, so it's not included in these rules. You can write «-1», but this is technically not a numeric literal, it is an arithmetic expression using a unary minus operator. This operator is described in Chapter 6.

The actual value of the literal is defined in a way that guarantees consistency with the interpretation of values of type xs:integer, xs:decimal, or xs:double by XML Schema. These rules aren't as clear-cut as you might imagine; for example, if you specify a decimal value with more decimal places than are supported by your implementation, it's not obvious whether the processor is supposed to reject the value or to round it. The XML Schema working group is still debating this point nearly three years after the specification was published.

There's a significant change in this area from XPath 1.0, where all numeric values were treated as double-precision floating point. In XPath 1.0, the literal «1.5» represented an xs:double, in XPath 2.0, it is an xs:decimal. This can affect the precision of numerical calculations. The chances are that the only applications that will notice the change are those that are numerically fairly sophisticated (for example, an XSLT stylesheet that does trigonometrical calculations to produce SVG output). If you have such an application, it may be worth replacing any literals of the form «1.5» by «1.5e0» when you migrate to XPath 2.0.

It's worth mentioning here that the rules for output of numbers are not the same as the rules for input. When a number is converted to a string, the results are determined by the casting rules given in Chapter 9. To summarize these:

- ❑ An xs:integer value is output as an integer, for example, «42» or «-315»

- ❑ An xs:decimal value with no fractional part is output as if it were an integer, with no decimal point. If it has a fractional part, it is output with at least one digit before and after the decimal point, and no other insignificant leading or trailing zeros. Examples of xs:decimal output are «42», «-315», «18.6», «0.0015».

- ❑ An xs:double or xs:float value that's within the range 1e-6 to 1e+6 (one millionth to one million, positive or negative) is output in the same way as a decimal. Outside this range, exponential notation is used, with one significant digit before the decimal point. Examples of xs:double output are «42», «315», «18.6», «0.0015», «1.003e12», «8.752943e13».

These rules have the effect that you often don't need to know whether the numbers you are dealing with are integers, decimals, or doubles. For example, if @width is an attribute in a schema-less document whose value is «width="17"», then the value of «string(@width + 1)» is «18»; you never need to know that the result of the addition was actually an xs:double (the rules for arithmetic involving mixed types are in Chapter 6).

If you want more control over the formatting of numeric output, XSLT has a function format-number() which offers detailed control. There's nothing comparable in XPath itself, but you can get rid of surplus decimal digits by using the round-to-half-even() function described in Chapter 10.

Examples

Expression	Description
86	The xs:integer value eighty-six
3.14159	An xs:decimal value representing π to five decimal places
1.0E-6	The xs:double value one-millionth

Changes in XPath 2.0

XPath 1.0 supported the lexical forms now used for integer literals and decimal literals, but interpreted the values as double-precision floating point. There was no support in XPath 1.0 for scientific notation.

String Literals

A StringLiteral represents a constant string.

Symbol	Syntax
StringLiteral	(«"» ([^"])* «"»)+ | («'» ([^'])* «'»)+

Unless you are familiar with regular expressions you may find this production rule difficult to read. The original in the XPath Recommendation is even more cryptic, and I have replaced it with a form that I find simpler to explain.

What it is saying is actually quite simple; a StringLiteral is either a sequence of any characters other than double-quotes, enclosed between double-quotes, or a sequence of any characters other than single-quotes, enclosed between single-quotes. For example, «"John"», or «'Jane'», or «"don't"» or «'I said "go"!'».

In both cases you can put several of these sequences together end-to-end (the «+» sign indicates repetition). This has the effect of doubling the delimiting quote character, which provides an escaping mechanism allowing you to use the delimiter within the string. For example you can write «'O''Connor'» to represent the string «O'Connor».

A `StringLiteral` is a lexical token. Whitespace within a `StringLiteral` is allowed, and is significant (whitespace characters are part of the value). If you are using XPath expressions within an XML document, then some care is needed when using tab, carriage-return, and newline characters within a literal, because the XML parser is required to replace these by space characters before the XPath expression parser ever gets to see them, as part of the process of *attribute value normalization*. You can use character references such as «	», «
», and «» to prevent this happening. However, character references such as this are recognized only if the XPath expression is preprocessed by an XML parser. They are not recognized when the expression is written as a string in a Java or C# program.

Examples

The following examples assume XPath is being used in a free-standing environment with no need to escape special characters:

Expression	Description
`"John's"`	The string «John's»
`'"'`	A string consisting of a single character, the double quotation mark
`'O''Reilly'`	The string «O'Reilly»

The following examples assume XPath expressions are contained in an attribute within an XML document, for example an XSLT stylesheet:

XSLT Attribute	Description
`select="'John''s'"`	The string «John's». The character used as the string delimiter can be escaped by doubling it
`select="'&quot;'"`	A string consisting of a single character, the double quotation mark. The character used as the XML attribute delimiter can be escaped by using an XML entity or character reference
`select="'Don''t say &quot;yes&quot;'"`	The string «Don't say "yes"». This combines the two escaping techniques from the previous examples

Changes in XPath 2.0

The ability to include the string-delimiter character within the string by doubling it is new in XPath 2.0. The convention has been adopted from SQL, and has the advantage of being backward-compatible with XPath 1.0.

XSLT Usage

Handling the two kinds of quotation mark in XPath expressions written within stylesheets can be tricky, even with the new escape convention introduced in XPath 2.0. You can often circumvent the problems (and produce clearer code) by using variables. For example, instead of writing:

```
<xsl:if test="@input = 'Don''t say &quot;yes&quot;'">
  ...
</xsl:if>
```

write instead:

```
<xsl:variable name="s" as="xs:string">
  <xsl:text>Don't say "yes"</xsl:text>
</xsl:variable>
<xsl:if test="@input = $s">
  ...
</xsl:if>
```

Within XML text nodes, apostrophes and quotation marks can be written literally without escaping—there is no need to use the entity references «'» and «"».

I find it quite useful to have two global variables available in a stylesheet, as follows:

```
<xsl:variable name="apos" as="xs:string">'</xsl:variable>
<xsl:variable name="quot" as="xs:string">"</xsl:variable>
```

This makes it possible to use the variables «$apos» and «$quot» to construct strings using the concat() function, for example:

```
<xsl:value-of select="concat($quot, @input, $quot)"/>
```

Names

Names are used within an XPath expression to refer to elements and attributes in a source document, and to refer to objects such as variables, functions, and types.

Expression	Syntax
QName	(Prefix «:»)? LocalPart
Prefix	NCName
LocalPart	NCName
NCName	(Letter | «_») (NCNameChar) *
NCNameChar	Letter	Digit	«.»	«-»	«_»	CombiningChar	Extender

The productions `QName` and `NCName` are actually defined in the XML Namespaces Recommendation, not in XPath itself. This ensures that any name that can be used for an element or attribute in a source document can also be used in an XPath expression.

Informally, an `NCName` starts with a letter or underscore, and continues with zero or more `NCNameChars`, which may be letters, digits, or the three punctuation characters dot, hyphen, and underscore. The «`Letter`» and «`Digit`» categories include a wide variety of characters and ideographs in non-Latin scripts as well as accented Latin letters, while the «`CombiningChar`» and «`Extender`» categories cover accents and diacritics in many different languages.

The rules for `Letter`, `Digit`, `CombiningChar`, and `Extender` are given in the XML specification. The definitions are in the form of long lists of Unicode characters, and little would be gained by repeating them here. The basic principle is that if a name is valid in XML, then it is also valid in XPath.

In nearly all contexts, the kind of name that is allowed in XPath is a `QName`. This means a lexical `QName` as defined in the XML Namespaces Recommendation, which either takes the form «`prefix:local-name`» where both the prefix and the local-name are `NCNames` (no-colon names), or the simpler form «`local-name`» in which the prefix is omitted. If a prefix is present then it must always be one that has been declared in the static namespace context for the XPath expression, as described in Chapter 4. If no prefix is present, then the interpretation depends on what kind of name it is. If it is used where an element name is expected, then it is taken to refer to the default namespace for elements, which is also defined in the static context of the expression. If it is used where an attribute name is expected, then the local-name is assumed to be a name that is not in any namespace.

As in XML, names are case-sensitive, and names are only considered to match when they consist of exactly the same sequence of characters (or more strictly, the same Unicode code-points). This is true even when the Unicode standards describe characters as equivalent, for example different ways of writing accented letters.

Examples

The following are examples of valid `NCNames`:

A
alpha
π
א
_system-id
iso-8859-1
billing.address
Straßenüberführung
ΕΛΛΑΣ
_...------_..._

I did see an example recently of an XML document that used «⏘» on its own as an element name, but it is not something I would recommend.

XSLT Usage

QNames are also used in XSLT stylesheets in a number of other contexts, outside the scope of XPath expressions. They are used both to refer to elements in the source document (for example, in `<xsl:preserve-space>` and `<xsl:strip-space>`) and to name and refer to objects within the stylesheet itself, including variables, templates, modes, and attribute sets.

There are also some situations where QNames can be constructed dynamically as a result of evaluating an expression. They are used, for example, in `<xsl:element>` and `<xsl:attribute>` to generate names in the result document, and in the `key()` and `format-number()` functions to refer to objects (keys and decimal-formats, respectively) defined in the stylesheet. QNames constructed at runtime are never used to match names in the source document, and they are never used to match template names, variable names, mode names, or attribute set names in the stylesheet; these references must all be fixed names.

A QName is used in XPath for matching the names of nodes in the source document.

Whether the QName is written statically in the stylesheet, or whether it is constructed dynamically, if the name has a prefix then the prefix must be declared by a namespace declaration on some surrounding element in the stylesheet module.

For example:

```
<xsl:apply-templates select="math:formula" xmlns:math="http://math.org/"/>
```

Here the namespace is declared on the actual element that uses the prefix, but it could equally be any ancestor element.

The actual element in the source document does not need to have the tag «`math:formula`», it can use any prefix it likes (or even the default namespace) provided that in the source document the element name is in the namespace URI «`http://math.org/`».

If the QName does not have a prefix, then the rules are more complicated, and there are three possibilities:

❑ In the case of a name used as the name of a literal result element in the stylesheet, or the name passed as an argument to the XSLT `element-available()` function, the namespace that's used is the one declared using a default namespace declaration in the stylesheet, in the form «`xmlns="some.uri"`». If there is no such declaration, the name is assumed to be in no namespace.

❑ In the case of a name used as an element name or type name in an XPath expression, or in certain other contexts such as:

  ❑ an XSLT pattern

  ❑ the `elements` attribute of `<xsl:strip-space>` or `<xsl:preserve-space>`

  ❑ the `as` attribute of elements such as `<xsl:function>` and `<xsl:variable>`

  ❑ the `type` attribute of instructions such as `<xsl:element>`

the name is assumed to be in the namespace declared using the `xpath-default-namespace` attribute on the `<xsl:stylesheet>` element. This can also be overridden on any other element in the stylesheet. If there's no such declaration, the name is assumed to be in no namespace.

A name is being "used as an element name" if it appears in an axis step (see Chapter 7) whose axis is anything other than the attribute or namespace axis. Some names appearing in the `SequenceType` production used to describe types also fall into this category.

❑ Names used to refer to attribute and namespace nodes, as well as the names of variables, functions, and stylesheet objects such as modes, keys, and named templates, are always considered to be in no namespace when they are unprefixed.

The reasoning behind these rules is that names of elements in the stylesheet use the standard XML default namespace «`xmlns=" "`»; names of elements in the source document use the special default `xpath-default-namespace`, and names of objects other than elements never use a default namespace.

> **A QName with no prefix appearing in an XPath expression never uses the default namespace defined in the source document.**

It's a common mistake to forget this. Your source document starts as follows:

```
<html xmlns="http://www.w3.org/1999/xhtml">
```

and your stylesheet starts:

```
<?xml version="1.0"?>
<xsl:stylesheet xmlns:xsl="http://www.w3.org/1999/XSL/Transform"
    xmlns="http://www.w3.org/1999/xhtml"
    version="2.0">

<xsl:template match="html">
```

Why doesn't the template rule for «`match="html"`» fire when the `<html>` element is encountered? The answer is that the default namespace (declared with «`xmlns="..."`») applies to unprefixed `QNames` in the source document, but it doesn't apply to unprefixed `QNames` appearing in expressions and match patterns in the stylesheet. You either need to write:

```
<?xml version="1.0"?>
<xsl:stylesheet xmlns:xsl="http://www.w3.org/1999/XSL/Transform"
    xmlns:xhtml="http://www.w3.org/1999/xhtml"
    version="1.0">

<xsl:template match="xhtml:html">
```

or you need to define an `xpath-default-namespace`:

```
<?xml version="1.0"?>
<xsl:stylesheet xmlns:xsl="http://www.w3.org/1999/XSL/Transform"
```

```
      xpath-default-namespace="http://www.w3.org/1999/xhtml"
      version="2.0">

  <xsl:template match="html">
```

What's worse, your source document might actually not start with:

```
  <html xmlns="http://www.w3.org/1999/xhtml">
```

but rather with:

```
  <!DOCTYPE html SYSTEM "http://www.w3.org/TR/xhtml1/DTD/xhtml1-strict.dtd">
  <html>
```

Here it's not obvious that the `<html>` element is actually in a namespace. But it is, because hidden away inside the DTD is the sneaky little definition:

```
  <!ELEMENT html (head, body)>
  <!ATTLIST html
    %i18n;
    id      ID      #IMPLIED
    xmlns   %URI;   #FIXED 'http://www.w3.org/1999/xhtml'
  >
```

which has the effect of adding the namespace declaration «xmlns="http://www.w3.org/1999/xhtml"» to the `<html>` element whether you asked for it or not. This means that a bare «match="html"» in your stylesheet won't match this element; you need to match the namespace as well.

Operators

There is no hard-and-fast rule about exactly what constitutes an operator in the XPath language; but this is a good place to provide a general overview of the different kinds of operator.

We can classify as first-order operators all the operators that take one or more expressions as their operands, and produce a result that is obtained by evaluating the operands, and combining the values of the operands in some way. The first-order operators are listed in the table below, in precedence order. Operators listed on the same row of the table have the same precedence.

Operator	Effect
,	sequence concatenation
or	boolean disjunction (A or B)
and	boolean conjunction (A and B)
eq ne lt le gt ge = != < <= > >= << is >>	ordering comparison between single values ordering comparison between sequences ordering/identity comparison between nodes

Operator	Effect
to	constructs a sequence of consecutive integers
+ -	addition, subtraction
* div idiv mod	multiplication, division, modulus
| union	union of two sequences considered as sets of nodes
intersect except	intersection and difference of sequences considered as sets of nodes

Some of these operators are written as symbols, some as words. Where words are used, they are not reserved words: they are recognized as operators by virtue of where they appear in an expression. This means that it is quite legitimate to write an expression such as «div div div» in which the first and final words represent names of elements in the source document, and the middle word is a «div» operator.

The symbols «*» and «/» double as operators and as expressions in their own right. In an operator context, «*» means multiplication, but in an expression context, it selects all the child elements of the context node. If the context node is the element <a>2</a>, then the expression «*+*» evaluates to «4». In fact «*» also has a third role, as an occurrence indicator after a type name, as in «xs:integer*».

As operators are tokens, they may always be preceded and followed by whitespace, and must not include any embedded whitespace. In some cases it is necessary to precede or follow an operator by whitespace to ensure it is recognized. This applies not only to the named operators (such as «and» and «or»), but also to the minus sign «--» which could be mistaken for a hyphen if written with no preceding space.

The numeric comparison operators are written here as XPath sees them; when they appear in an XSLT stylesheet the special characters «<» and «>» should be written «<» and «>», respectively.

The second group of operators can be classified as type operators. These take two operands, one of which is a value, the other a type. The operators in this category are:

❑ «instance of»

❑ «cast as»

❑ «castable as»

❑ «treat as»

The fact that they are all written as compound symbols helps to make the grammar unambiguous. Again, none of these words are reserved in any way. All these operators, together with the syntax for describing a type, are fully described in Chapter 9.

The final group of operators are best described as higher-order operators. These are characterized by the fact that they don't simply evaluate their operands and combine the resulting values: each has its own rules for how the different subexpressions contribute to the final result. These operators have custom syntax that doesn't always look like a conventional operator at all. They are shown in the table below:

Expression	Meaning
for $x in E1 return E2	Evaluates E2 once for every value in E1, concatenating the resulting sequences
some $x in E1 satisfies E2	Returns true if E2 is true for any item in E1
every $x in E1 satisifes E2	Returns true if E2 is true for every item in E1
if (E1) then E2 else E3	Evaluates E2 or E3 depending on the value of E1
E1 / E2	Evaluates E2 once for every value in E1, returning a sequence of nodes in document order
E1 [E2]	Returns those items in the sequence E1 for which E2 evaluates to true

This concludes our survey of the lexical constructs in an XPath expression. We will now look at the basic syntactic building blocks, which are referred to as primary expressions.

Primary Expressions

Primary expressions are the most basic kinds of expression in XPath, and ultimately, all XPath expressions are constructed by combining primary expressions using various operators. The following sections in this chapter describe each kind of primary expression. These are described by the syntax:

Expression	Syntax
PrimaryExpr	Literal | VariableReference | ParenthesizedExpr | ContextItemExpr | FunctionCall
Literal	NumericLiteral | StringLiteral
NumericLiteratal	IntegerLiteral | DecimalLiteral | DoubleLiteral

We have already covered numeric and string literals earlier in the chapter. The rest of the chapter therefore concentrates on the four other kinds of primary expression: variable references, parenthesized expressions, the context item expression, and function calls.

The only real thing that these different kinds of PrimaryExpr have in common is the context in which they can be used.

According to the syntax rules, any PrimaryExpr can be followed by a predicate to form a FilterExpr, so for example «17[1]» and «'Berlin'[3]» are both legal. And in fact, in XPath 2.0 these expressions are not only syntactically legal, they also make sense semantically: a single item such as «17» or «'Berlin'» is a sequence of length one, and applying a predicate to it can either return that item, or an empty sequence. Filter expressions are described in Chapter 8.

Examples

Expression	Description
23.5	A NumericLiteral is a PrimaryExpr
'Columbus'	A StringLiteral is a PrimaryExpr
$var	A VariableReference is a PrimaryExpr
contains(@name, '#')	A FunctionCall is a PrimaryExpr
(position() + 1)	A parenthesized expression is a PrimaryExpr

The notable omission from the list of primary expressions is AxisStep: an axis step such as «child::node()» is not a PrimaryExpr, even though it contains no other expressions. This ensures that an expression such as «para[1]» is unambiguously a PathExpr, with the predicate «[1]» taken as part of the Step, rather than it being a FilterExpr consisting of a PrimaryExpr «para» followed by a Predicate «[1]». It is possible to turn an AxisStep into a PrimaryExpr by putting it in parentheses, so «(para)[1]» is a FilterExpr. In this case the meaning is the same, but this will not always be the case.

Variable References

A VariableReference is a reference to a variable. The variable may be declared in an enclosing «for», «some», or «every» expression, as described in Chapter 8; or it may be defined in the evaluation context for the XPath expression. In XSLT this means that it may be declared in an <xsl:variable> or <xsl:param> element in the stylesheet.

Expression	Syntax
VariableReference	«$» QName

The use of a «$» sign is necessary to distinguish a variable reference from a reference to an element in the source document: «para» selects a child <para> element in the source, while «$para» is a reference to a variable.

Whitespace is allowed between the $ sign and the QName, though it is rarely used (it was not permitted in XPath 1.0).

Usage

The QName must match the name of a variable that is in scope at the point where the expression containing the variable name appears. A variable can be declared either within a containing «for», «some», or «every» expression, or by the context in which the XPath expression appears. In XSLT this means the name will be exactly the same as the name attribute of the relevant <xsl:variable> or <xsl:param> element; note however that if the name contains a namespace prefix, it is the namespace URI that must match, not necessarily the prefix.

The value of the variable reference is whatever value has been assigned to it by the matching «for», «some», or «every» expression, or (in the case of XSLT stylesheets) the matching <xsl:variable> or <xsl:param> declaration. The value may be of any type: any sequence containing nodes, atomic values, or a mixture of both.

A variable reference can be used anywhere in an XPath expression where a value is required. It cannot be used to represent concepts of the language other than values, for example you can't use a variable in place of a name, a node type, or an axis. Nor can you use a variable to hold an entire expression.

A common misunderstanding about variables is to write a path expression such as:

```
/booklist/book/$property
```

thinking that if the value of **$property** is the string "title", then this is equivalent to writing

```
/booklist/book/title
```

That's not the way variables in XPath work. You can do this sort of thing in a shell scripting language, where variables work by textual substitution: in that kind of language the content of the variable can hold any part of an expression.

In XPath, variables hold values, not pieces of an expression. The actual meaning of the above expression is

```
/booklist/book/"title"
```

which isn't very meaningful, and will give you a type error saying that the expression on the right-hand side of the «/» operator must return a sequence of nodes, not a string.

The way to achieve the desired effect is to write:

```
/booklist/book/*[local-name() eq $property]
```

Some processors (including Saxon and Xalan) offer an **evaluate()** extension function, which allows you to construct an XPath expression at runtime, from a string which might be held in a variable. But this capability is not present in the standard.

It's relatively unusual to see variables whose name includes a namespace prefix. It can be useful, though, if you want to write a general-purpose reusable library module in XSLT or XQuery; you can then define global variables to hold constants visible to users of the library, and putting these in a specific namespace will help to ensure that there are no naming conflicts. In fact, XQuery requires that global variables exported from a module are declared in the namespace associated with that module.

Examples

```
$x

$lowest-common-denominator

$ALPHA

$my-ns-prefix:param1

$π
```

Parenthesized Expressions

A `ParenthesizedExpr` either consists of an expression enclosed in parentheses, or it consists of an empty pair of parentheses, used to represent the empty sequence.

Expression	Syntax
ParenthesizedExpr	«(» Expr? «)»

When the contained `Expr` is present, parentheses have the same effect in XPath as in most other languages; they change the order of evaluation, so that the enclosed expression is evaluated first, regardless of the normal operator precedence.

Parentheses are sometimes needed around an expression that uses the «,» operator (which denotes list concatenation), to avoid the «,» being interpreted as a separator between the arguments in a function call or the clauses of a «for» expression. For example, to find the maximum of two numbers $i and $j, you need to write «max(($i, $j))», to make it clear that the function is being called with one argument (a sequence) and not with two. The «,» operator is described in detail in Chapter 8. Because «,» has the lowest precedence of any operator, it is generally necessary to use parentheses with it. However, if it is used at the top level of an XPath expression, the parentheses are not needed. For example, one can write in XSLT:

```
<xsl:apply-templates select="title, author, abstract, body"/>
```

to process the four selected elements in the order indicated.

If there is no contained expression, that is, if the `ParenthesizedExpr` is written as «()», then its value is the empty sequence. For example, the expression «$a union ()» returns the union of the sequence $a and the empty sequence; this has the effect of returning all the nodes in $a, in document order and with duplicates removed. The «union» operator (which can also be written «|») is described in Chapter 6.

One special case where the meaning of parentheses may not be immediately apparent is in conjunction with predicates. Predicates are used to filter the items in a sequence, for example, «$seq[. >= 0]» selects all the items in the sequence $seq whose value is greater than zero. As explained in Chapter 7, the meaning of a predicate is subtly different when it appears as part of an axis step. The result of this distinction is that:

- ❑ «ancestor::node()[1]» selects the innermost ancestor of the context node (that is, its parent)
- ❑ «(ancestor::node())[1]» selects the outermost ancestor of the context node (that is, the root of the tree).

For a more complete explanation of this distinction see the sections on *Axis Steps* in Chapter 7, and *Filter Expressions* in Chapter 8.

Another rather specialized use for parentheses is to remove syntactic ambiguities when using the «/» symbol as an expression referring to the document node at the root of the current tree. When «/» is followed by a name, or by the symbol «*», then it is assumed to be the start of an absolute path expression. This means that if you want to follow «/» with a named operator, you need to enclose it in parentheses, for example:

```
if ((/) instance of document(schema-element(mf:invoice))) then ...
```

or

```
if ((/) intersect $nodes) then ...
```

Another way of disambiguating «/» in such expressions is to write it as «/.».

Changes in XPath 2.0

The syntax «()» to represent an empty sequence, and the use of the «,» operator to perform sequence concatenation, are new in XPath 2.0.

Because a Step in a path expression is now a general expression (see Chapter 7), it becomes possible in XPath 2.0 to use parentheses in a path expression such as «book/(chapter|appendix)/title».

Context Item Expressions

The ContextItemExpr is simply the expression «.»:

Expression	Syntax
ContextItemExpr	«.»

The context item may either be a node or an atomic value, or its value may be undefined. If the value is undefined, then evaluating the expression «.» causes an error.

At the outermost level of an XPath expression, the value of the context item is established by the calling environment. For example, in XSLT it is determined by the innermost `<xsl:for-each>` or `<xsl:apply-templates>` iteration. Where XPath expressions are evaluated from a host language such as Java or C#, the calling API often provides the application with a way to set the initial context item.

Internally within an XPath expression, there are two constructs that change the context item. Within a predicate P of an expression such as «`$SEQ[P]`», the predicate is evaluated for each item in `$SEQ` in turn, with that item as the context item; and on the right-hand side of the «`/`» operator, in a path expression such as «`E1/E2`», the context item for evaluating E2 is set to each item in E1 in turn.

> The value of the context item is not changed in the body of a «`for`» expression (described in Chapter 8). It is therefore wrong to write something like:
>
> ```
> sum(for $x in //item return ./@price * ./@qty)
> ```
>
> Instead, you need to write:
>
> ```
> sum(for $x in //item return $x/@price * $x/@qty)
> ```

Changes in XPath 2.0

In XPath 1.0, the «`.`» symbol was an abbreviation for the `Step` «`self::node()`». This restricted its value to being a reference to a node (never an atomic value), and it also imposed certain other restrictions, for example it was not possible to apply a predicate to «`.`». In XPath 2.0 you can use constructs such as «`.[*]`» which returns the context item only if it is a node that has a child element.

In XPath 1.0, «`.`» was never undefined—it always had a value, and the value was always a single node. In XPath 2.0, there are many situations in which it can be undefined, for example it is undefined on entry to a function body written in XSLT or XQuery.

Usage

The two places where «`.`» is commonly used are:

❑ With the operator «`//`» in a relative path expression such as «`.//A`», which (loosely speaking) selects all the descendant `<A>` elements of the context node. The «`.`» is necessary here because if the expression started with «`//`» it would select all descendants of the root node.

❑ On its own, to perform operations on the value of the context item. This usually arises in expressions such as «`.=3`» or «`string-length(.)`» where we want to test the value of the context node, or in the XSLT instruction `<xsl:value-of select="."/>`, which outputs the atomized value of the context item to the result tree.

Some people also like to use the «`.`» operator for clarity at the start of a relative path expression such as «`./TITLE`», but in fact this is precisely equivalent to «`TITLE`» on its own.

In XPath 2.0, if you want to remove duplicates from a sequence of nodes $seq, and sort them into document order, you can write «$seq/.», or equivalently, «./$seq». The sorting and deduplication is part of the defined behavior of the «/» operator.

Function Calls

A FunctionCall invokes a function. This may be one of the system-defined functions described in Chapter 10, or it may be a vendor- or user-supplied function.

Each built-in or user-defined atomic type also has a corresponding constructor function available for constructing values of that type (for example, «xs:date('2004-02-29')» constructs a date).

There may also be additional functions described in a host language in which XPath is embedded—for example, XSLT defines further functions available for use from XPath expressions contained in XSLT stylesheets (for details, see Chapter 7 of *XSLT 2.0 Programmer's Reference*).

Expression	Syntax
FunctionCall	FunctionName «(» (Argument («,» Argument)*)? «)»
FunctionName	QName
Argument	ExprSingle
ExprSingle	ForExpr | QuantifiedExpr | IfExpr | OrExpr |

The syntax of a function call consists of the function name, which is in general a QName, followed by the list of zero or more supplied arguments, in the usual way.

Each argument must be an ExprSingle. This basically means any XPath expression, so long as it does not contain a top-level «,» operator. If you want to supply a list of values separated by commas as a single argument, you must enclose it in parentheses. Note the difference between:

```
concat("A", " nice", " cup", " of", " tea")
```

which calls the concat() function with five separate arguments, each one a single string, and:

```
string-join(("A", "nice", "cup", "of", "tea"), " ")
```

which calls the string-join() function with two arguments, the first one being a sequence of five strings, and the second a string containing a single space character. These two function calls are both legal, and as it happens they both have the same effect. Both the functions are described in Chapter 10. The concat() function is exceptional in that it allows an arbitrary number of arguments to be supplied.

The arguments themselves can be expressions such as «/», «.» or «@*», which may look a bit strange at first encounter. For example, the function call «exists(/*)» returns true if the context node is in a tree whose root is a document node that has an element node as a child.

Identifying the Function to be Called

The set of functions that is available for calling is defined in the static context for the XPath expression, as described in Chapter 4. This means that it is known at compile time whether a particular function name is valid or not. Normally, you can therefore expect a compile time error if you call a function that does not exist.

The function name is a QName. Like other QNames, it is written as a lexical QName (with an optional prefix and a local name, separated by a colon), and this lexical QName is expanded using the namespace declarations that are in scope for the XPath expression. So the expanded name of the function consists of a namespace URI and a local-name. The XPath static context includes a default namespace URI for function names, which will usually be quite separate from the default namespace URI for other kinds of name. Throughout this book I have assumed that the default namespace URI for functions will normally be the namespace containing the standard library of functions listed in Chapter 10, and that functions such as count() and exists() may therefore be called with unprefixed names. This namespace URI, in the current draft of the specifications, is http://www.w3.org/2003/11/xpath-functions. It is possible to use a different default namespace for your functions, but in this case you will need to use an explicit prefix (conventionally «fn:», but this is up to you) in all calls on the standard functions.

> *XSLT 2.0 doesn't allow you to select any namespace other than the standard* http://www.w3.org/2003/11/xpath-functions *namespace as the default namespace for functions; it does, however, allow you to use a specific prefix bound to this namespace if you wish.*

The function name is recognized in the XPath syntax by virtue of the fact that it is followed by a left parenthesis. This means that certain unprefixed names used as keywords in the language are not available for use as function names, specifically attribute(), comment(), document-node(), element(), empty(), if(), item(), node(), processing-instruction(), schema-attribute(), schema-element(), text(), type(), and typeswitch(). This list includes one name, typeswitch(), which is not actually used as a keyword in XPath, but is reserved to retain compatibility with XQuery.

The set of functions that is available for calling will generally include the following:

- ❑ The core library of XPath functions described in Chapter 10 of this book.

- ❑ Additional functions defined by the host language in which XPath is embedded, for example, the XSLT functions described in Chapter 7 of *XSLT 2.0 Programmer's Reference*.

- ❑ Constructor functions corresponding to the built-in atomic types in XML Schema, for example, xs:date() and xs:float(). For details of these functions, see Chapter 9.

- ❑ Constructor functions corresponding to user-defined atomic types in any imported schema. These are also described in Chapter 9.

- ❑ Additional functions made available by the vendor of the XPath processor. These should be in a namespace controlled by that vendor. An example is the function saxon:evaluate() offered by the Saxon product. For details, see the documentation supplied by the vendor.

❑   User-written functions, written in XSLT or XQuery. The XPath language itself does not provide any mechanism for defining functions (only for calling them) but XPath processors may well provide a way of linking to a library of XSLT or XQuery functions even when XPath expressions are being executed outside that environment.

❑   User-written functions (known as extension functions in XSLT, external functions in XQuery) written in an unrelated programming language, such as Java, C#, or JavaScript. The mechanisms for linking to such functions, and for converting values between the XPath data types and those of the target language, have been left to implementors to define.

It is not possible to write functions in XPath itself. For this, you need XSLT 2.0, XQuery 1.0, or potentially some other language that supports the capability. XPath only provides the ability to call such functions, not to define them.

A number of useful third-party function libraries have become available for XSLT 1.0 processors (see for example http://www.exslt.org and http://fxsl.sf.net/) and this process can be expected to accelerate now that functions can be written in both XSLT 2.0 and XQuery 1.0.

Functions, at least in theory, are uniquely identified by their expanded QName (that is, namespace URI and local name) and their *arity*—that is, the number of arguments. The idea is that the static context contains a list of functions that are available to be called, and it cannot contain two functions with the same name and the same arity. There is no overloading of functions, in the sense that you can't have two functions with the same name and the same number of arguments, distinguished only by the types of the arguments.

Products that allow you to call Java methods are quite likely to provide some kind of overloading in practice, if one can extrapolate from what XSLT 1.0 processors do. The specification leaves enough latitude to allow this: all aspects of external calls are essentially implementation-defined. Conceptually, a product can satisfy the letter of the law by claiming that for each possible Java method name and number of arguments, there is a single function in the static context, and it is this notional function that decides which of several Java methods to call, based on the types of the arguments supplied.

Converting the Arguments and the Result

At compile time, every function in the static context has a known signature defining the types of the arguments and the type of the result. It's probably best to put this in concrete terms by showing example functions written in XSLT or XQuery. For example, consider a function that calculates the total sales of a product (the actual logic isn't important).

Here is the XSLT 2.0 implementation:

```
<xsl:function name="mf:product-sales" as="xs:decimal">
  <xsl:param name="product" as="schema-element(mf:product)"/>
  <xsl:sequence select="sum($product//sale[@product-code eq $product/code])"/>
</xsl:function>
```

And here is the equivalent in XQuery 1.0:

```
declare function mf:product-sales ($product as schema-element(mf:product))
        as xs:decimal {
    sum($product//sale[@product-code eq $product/code])
};
```

In both cases, we have defined the function name as `mf:product-sales` (we'll assume that the namespaces have been declared properly), and we have defined it to take a single argument, which is an element conforming to the schema-defined element declaration `mf:product`. This means the element will either be a valid `mf:product`, or will be a member of its substitution group; the detailed meaning of the syntax «`schema-element(mf:product)`» is given in Chapter 9. The return type of the function is declared to be an `xs:decimal`.

> *There's no formal link between the namespaces used for functions and the namespaces used for elements, attributes, and schema-defined types. But with functions which, like this one, are very specific to a particular element type, I think it's a useful convention to put the function in the same namespace as the element type.*

An XPath expression that invokes this function might look like this:

```
//mf:product[mf:product-sales(.) gt 100000]
```

This expression returns a sequence containing all the `<mf:product>` elements that have total sales in excess of 100,000.

In this example, the required type of the argument was a single node, and the result type of the function was a single atomic value. It is also possible, of course, for functions to take sequences as their arguments, or to return sequences as their result. In general, the required type of an argument has two parts: the required cardinality, and the required item type. The required cardinality is shown by an occurrence indicator after the type, and may be one of:

Occurrence Indicator	Meaning
(none)	Exactly one item
*	Any number of items
+	One or more items
?	Either one item, or none

The required item type defines a type that each item in the supplied value must conform to. This may be a very generic type, such as «`node()`», or a very specific type, such as «`element(mf:product)`» or «`xs:unsignedByte`». If no required type is specified for an argument, the implicit default is «`item()*`». This allows any sequence of items, in other words any value at all.

The XPath processor is required to check that the arguments supplied in the function call are of the right type. The rules it applies are as follows.

1. First, the name of the function and the number of arguments are used to locate the signature of the function to be called. An error occurs if no suitable function can be located. Once the signature has been located, each argument in the function call is checked against the declared type of the corresponding parameter in the signature, using the rules below.

2. Each supplied argument is evaluated, to produce a value, which in general is a sequence that may contain atomic values, nodes, or a mixture of the two. (Note, however, that the processor isn't obliged to evaluate an argument that isn't used—this means that errors may go undetected.)

3. If the required item type is `xdt:anyAtomicType` or a subtype of this (that is, if the function expects atomic values for this argument, rather than nodes), then the following steps are carried out:

    ❑ The supplied sequence is atomized. Atomization replaces each node in the supplied sequence by its typed value (which may itself be a sequence), and leaves any atomic values in the sequence unchanged.

    ❑ If any of the values in the atomized sequence are of type `xdt:untypedAtomic` (which will normally be the case when the values are extracted from elements and attributes that have not been validated against any schema), then the system attempts to convert them to the required type by casting. The rules showing what casts are possible are given in Chapter 9, but they essentially follow the rules defined in XML Schema—if the required type is `xs:date`, for example, then the `xdt:untypedAtomic` value must have the form of a valid lexical `xs:date` value. If the cast isn't possible, the error is fatal.

    ❑ If the required type is a numeric type (`xs:double`, `xs:float`, `xs:decimal`, or a type derived from any of these by restricting the allowed set of values), and if the supplied value is also numeric, then type promotion is attempted. For example, it is acceptable to supply an `xs:integer` value where an `xs:double` is expected. Numeric type promotion is described in detail in Chapter 6, because it plays an important role for arithmetic operators.

4. At this stage, a final check is made that the argument value is now a valid instance of the required type. For this to be true, each item in the sequence must be an instance of the required item type, and the number of items in the sequence must match the required cardinality. The detailed rules are the same as those for the «instance of» operator, which is described in Chapter 9. If the value doesn't conform as required, a type error is reported.

5. If all is well, the function is called, and the result of the function call expression (as you would expect) is the value returned by the function, which will always conform to the type given in the function signature.

Changes in XPath 2.0

The rules given in the previous section impose much stricter type checking than XPath 1.0, which always attempted to convert the supplied arguments to the required type. XPath 2.0 effectively retains this behavior only when the value you supply is a node in a document that has not been schema-validated. This might be because you are using a processor that isn't schema-aware, or because you chose not to validate the document, or because the node in question is defined by a schema to be in part of a document that is skip-validated (which for practical purposes means that any content is allowed).

There are other cases where function calls would have succeeded in XPath 1.0, but will fail under these stricter rules. An example is a function call such as «contains(position(), "o"». The arguments to the `contains()` function must be of type `xs:string`, but the result returned by the `position()` function is of type `xs:integer`. XPath 1.0 would cheerfully convert the integer to a string, but XPath 2.0 is stricter—if you intend a conversion to take place, you must invoke it explicitly, for example, by calling the `string()` function.

To ensure that most XPath 1.0 expressions can be carried forward to XPath 2.0 without breaking under these stricter rules, XPath 2.0 defines a backward compatibility mode that relaxes the rules. If you are running in XSLT, the backward compatibility mode is invoked whenever the stylesheet (or some element in the stylesheet surrounding the XPath expression in question) specifies the attribute «version= "1.0"». When XPath is invoked in other ways, the mechanism for switching on backward compatibility mode is defined by the design of the API you are using (it's not mandatory for every implementation to offer this feature).

Backward compatibility mode changes the function calling rules by adding an extra rule before rule 3 in the list above. This rule is essentially in two parts:

❑   If the required cardinality of the parameter is zero or one (that is, if the parameter doesn't permit a sequence of more than one item), then all items in the supplied value after the first are discarded.

❑   If the required item type is a string or number type, then the supplied value is converted to a string or number using the string() or number() function as appropriate.

These rules apply only where the required type of the parameter fits into the XPath 1.0 type system. For example, if the required type is xs:date, no extra conversions are performed. More specifically, the first rule (which discards all but the first item in a sequence) applies only where the required item type is «item()», «node()», xs:string, or a numeric type such as xs:double. The second rule applies only if the required item type is xs:string or a numeric type.

Although the XPath 1.0 type system also included a boolean data type, there is no special treatment of xs:boolean in the backward compatibility rules. That's because the only XPath 1.0 function that actually expected a boolean argument was the not() function, and this function in XPath 2.0 has been defined in a way that is fully backward compatible.

XPath 1.0 never defined any rules for calling external user-defined functions, so backward compatibility in that area is entirely a matter for implementors.

Side Effects

None of the standard functions have side effects; they don't change the values of variables, they don't produce any output, and they don't change any settings in the browser or the operating system. They don't even create any new nodes, though both XSLT and XQuery allow you to write functions that can be called from XPath to create new nodes.

There is nothing to stop an extension function from having side-effects; for example, an extension function could print a message or increment a counter, or even do something more radical such as modify the source document or the stylesheet itself. However, extension functions with side effects are likely to be rather unpredictable, since there is nothing to say in which order things happen. For example, you can't assume that global variables are evaluated in any particular order or that they are evaluated only once; and a global variable that is never accessed might never be evaluated at all.

Functions can have side-effects even it you think of them as read-only. You might imagine that if you write an extension function ext:read() that reads a line of input from the console, then the expression «(ext:read(), ext:read())» will read two lines, and return them in order. You could be in for a surprise. The system might read two lines, and return them out of order; or it might read a single line, and return two copies of it. This is because calling the ext:read() function has the side-effect of changing the current reading position in a file connection. Implementations might try to be more helpful than this, but you can't rely on it.

The closest that the standard library comes to a function with side-effects is the `trace()` function, which is supposed to produce diagnostic output. Like other functions in the standard library, this is described in Chapter 10. However, the specification gives so much latitude in terms of the way this is implemented that it would be quite legitimate for an implementation to do nothing when it encounters this function call. You might well find that with an optimizing processor, the output produced by multiple calls on the `trace()` function bears very little relationship to the expected order of execution.

Functions that create new nodes are something that the formal semantics of the language does try to handle in a sanitary way. XPath itself, when confined to the standard function library, is a read-only language, but both XSLT and XQuery do allow functions that create and return new nodes. For example, in XSLT:

```
<xsl:function name="f:make" as="element()">
  <e/>
</xsl:function
```

or in XQuery:

```
declare function f:make() as element() {
  <e/>
};
```

These functions create all sorts of complexities in the language semantics, for example it is no longer possible to take a function call out of a loop and execute it once only. It also means that the expression «f:make() is f:make()» is false. Frankly, in XSLT stylesheets I would advise against writing such functions—generally, I think it's good coding practice in XSLT to use XSLT instructions and templates when creating nodes in the result tree, and to use XPath expressions and functions when reading information from the source tree. XQuery doesn't have this distinction between instructions and expressions, so the same function mechanism has to serve both purposes. But you need to use it with care.

Examples

Expression	Description
`true()`	A call on a standard function that always returns the `xs:boolean` value `true`
`string-length($x)`	A call on a standard function that expects a string, and returns the number of characters it contains. The actual value supplied can be a node, provided its type is either `xs:string` or `xdt:untypedAtomic`. If `$x` is a non-string value, such as an `xs:anyURI`, a type error occurs, unless you are running in backward compatibility mode
`count(*)`	A call on a standard function that evaluates the path expression «*» (which returns all element children of the context node) and returns a number indicating how many nodes there are in this sequence
`xt:intersection ($x, $y)`	A call on an extension function. It is identified as an extension function by the presence of a prefix «xt:» which must correspond to a namespace declaration that is in scope. The rules for locating an implementation of this extension function are implementor-defined

Conditional Expressions

A conditional expression corresponds to the «if..then..else» construct found in some form in almost every programming language. A condition is evaluated, and based on the result, the expression returns the result of evaluating either the «then» or the «else» branch.

Expression	Syntax
IfExpr	«if (» Expr «)» «then» ExprSingle «else» ExprSingle

The «else» branch is constrained to be an ExprSingle (an expression containing no top-level comma) because a trailing comma would be ambiguous when the expression appears, for example, as an argument in a function call. The «then» branch is constrained to be an ExprSingle purely for symmetry. Any expression can be used as the condition, and although it would be unusual for this expression to use the «,» operator, there is no reason to disallow it.

Note that both branches (the «then» and the «else») must be present. It's quite common to write «else ()» to return nothing (an empty sequence) when the condition is false, but you have to write this explicitly.

The expression used as the condition to be tested (inside the parentheses) is evaluated to give its *effective boolean value*. Unusually, XPath 2.0 doesn't apply strict type checking to this expression, rather it defines a set of rules allowing any value to be converted to the xs:boolean values true or false. The rules are that every value is treated as true, except the following:

❑   The empty sequence

❑   A singleton xs:boolean value false

❑   A singleton zero-length xs:string or xdt:untypedAtomic value

❑   A singleton xs:double, xs:float, or xs:decimal that is numerically equal to zero

❑   A singleton xs:double or xs:float NaN (not-a-number) value.

There is no atomization applied to any nodes in the sequence. This means that if the value includes one or more nodes, the result is true, regardless of the contents of the node. Even if «@married» is an attribute whose typed value is the xs:boolean value false, the result of the expression «if (@married) then "yes" else "no"» is the string «yes». If you want to test the contents of the node, rather than testing for its existence, use the data() function to atomize it explicitly, or write the test in the form «if (@married = true()) then ..».

Note that the effective boolean value of a sequence doesn't simply test whether the sequence is empty, because of the special cases for a singleton sequence. If you want to test whether a sequence is empty, use the empty() or exists() functions described in Chapter 10.

These rules for forming the effective boolean value are consistent with the rules used in other XPath contexts where a true/false value is required. These include:

❑   The operands of «and» and «or» (see Chapter 6)

- ❑ The argument of the functions `boolean()` and `not()` (see Chapter 10)
- ❑ The expression used as a predicate within square brackets in an axis step or filter expression, so long as the value is not numeric (see Chapters 7 and 8)
- ❑ The expression in the «`satisfies`» clause of «`some`» and «`every`» expressions (see Chapter 8)

The same rules are also used in XSLT 2.0, in evaluating the `<xsl:if>` and `<xsl:choose>` instructions.

A significant feature of these rules is that the processor can determine the effective boolean value of any sequence without looking further than the second item in the sequence. This makes the algorithm very efficient.

However, the rules are not the same as the rules in XML Schema for converting a string to an `xs:boolean` value. In XML Schema, the valid lexical representations of the `xs:boolean` value `false` are «`0`» and «`false`», while the valid lexical representations of `true` are «`1`» and «`true`». The XML Schema rules are used in XPath 2.0 in the following circumstances:

- ❑ By the expression «`$S cast as xs:boolean`»
- ❑ By the `xs:boolean()` constructor function (note the difference from the `boolean()` function in the core library, sometimes written as `fn:boolean()` to emphasize the difference)
- ❑ When an `xdt:untypedAtomic` value is implicitly converted to an `xs:boolean` value in the course of a function call, where one of the function arguments has a required type of `xs:boolean`.

Conditional expressions are one of the few places in the XPath language where you get a guarantee that an expression will or will not be evaluated. Specifically, if the condition is true then the «`else`» branch will not be evaluated, while if it is false, the «`then`» branch will not be evaluated. This means you can safely use expressions that could otherwise cause errors, for example:

```
if ($cols ne 0) then (count($items) idiv $cols) else ()
```

I personally prefer putting in the explicit test «`$cols ne 0`» rather than writing «`if ($cols)..`» and relying on the fact that zero is treated as false.

Changes in XPath 2.0

Conditional expressions are new in XPath 2.0. In the context of an XSLT stylesheet, they often make it possible to replace a cumbersome `<xsl:choose>` instruction. For example, the following:

```
<xsl:variable name="color">
  <xsl:choose>
    <xsl:when test="$day='Sunday'">white</xsl:when>
    <xsl:otherwise>red</xsl:otherwise>
  </xsl:choose>
</xsl:variable>
```

can now be replaced with:

```
<xsl:variable name="color"
              select="if ($day eq 'Sunday') then 'white' else 'red'"/>
```

The rules for calculating the effective boolean value of an expression have been carefully chosen to be compatible with the rules for converting strings, numbers, or node-sets to booleans in XPath 1.0, while at the same time generalizing them to handle an arbitrary sequence. If they seem arbitrary, blame history.

Examples

Expression	Description

`if (@x)`
`then @x`
`else 0`
	Returns the attribute node @x if it exists, or the `xs:integer` value zero otherwise. (This can also be expressed as «(@x,0)[1]»)

`if ($area/sales)`
`then avg($area/sales/@value)`
`else number('NaN')`
	Returns the average sales value for the selected area if there were any sales, or the not-a-number value NaN otherwise

`if (normalize-space(.))`
`then string(.)`
`else ()`
	Returns the context item converted to a string if it contains any non-whitespace characters, otherwise returns the empty sequence. This relies on the fact that `normalize-space()` returns a zero-length string (which is treated as `false`) if all the characters in the string are whitespace

Summary

XPath expressions are used in XSLT to select data from the source document and to manipulate it to generate data to place in the result document. XPath expressions play the same role for XML as the SQL SELECT statement plays for relational databases—they allow us to select specific parts of the document for transformation, so that we can achieve the required output. Their use is not restricted to XSLT stylesheets—they can also be used with XPointers to define hyperlinks between documents, and many DOM implementations allow XPath expressions to be used to find nodes within the DOM.

This chapter provided an introduction to the basic constructs in XPath expression: an overview of the grammar and the lexical rules, and explanation of some of the basic constructs such as literals, variable references, function calls, and conditional expressions.

The next four chapters explore the language in more depth. Chapter 6 looks at the basic operators for aruthmetic, boolean comparisons, and testing identity and ordering of nodes. Chapter 7 describes path expressions and the operations for combining sets of nodes to form their union, intersection, or difference. Chapter 8 examines expressions on sequences, notably the «for» expression, which provides a general mapping capability to construct one sequence by applying an expression to each item of an input sequence. Then, Chapter 9 discusses operations on types.

Finally, Chapter 10 is a catalog of all the functions in the core library, and Chapter 11 gives the syntax for regular expressions, which are used in three of these functions.

Operators on Items

This chapter defines the simple operators available for use in XPath expressions. This is inevitably a rather arbitrary definition, but these operators seem to have enough in common to justify putting them together in one chapter. All these operators return single items (as distinct from sequences)—in fact, all of them except the arithmetic operators in the first section return a boolean result.

More specifically, this chapter describes the following families of operators:

❑   Arithmetic operators, «+», «-», «*», «div», and «mod»

❑   Value comparison operators «eq», «ne», «lt», «le», «gt», «ge»

❑   General comparison operators «=», «!=», «<», «<=», «>», «>=»

❑   Node comparison operators «<<», «is», and «>>»

❑   Boolean operators «and» and «or»

Many of these operators behave in much the same way as similar operators in other languages. There are some surprises, though, because of the way XPath handles sequences, and because of the way it mixes typed and untyped data. So don't skip this chapter just because you imagine that everything about these operators can be guessed.

Path expressions, which are used to select nodes within an XML document and which can be considered the defining feature of the XPath language, will be described in Chapter 7, while Chapter 8 is devoted to operations used to process sequences. The tour of the language syntax finishes in Chapter 9, which describes operations on types. Chapter 10 contains a full description of all the functions available in the standard function library.

Arithmetic Operators

These operators are normally used to perform numeric calculations on numbers, which may be of any of the numeric types: xs:integer, xs:decimal, xs:float, or xs:double. They are also overloaded to perform calculations on dates and durations.

Note that this section only describes arithmetic operators built in to the XPath syntax. These operators are complemented by a range of arithmetic functions in the standard function library, described in Chapter 10. The functions in this library include `abs()`, `ceiling()`, `floor()`, `round()`, `round-to-half-even()`, `sum()`, `max()`, `min()`, and `avg()`.

Syntax

The syntax of expressions using the arithmetic operators is defined by the following syntax productions in the XPath grammar.

Expression	Syntax
AdditiveExpr	MultiplicativeExpr ((«+» | «-») MultiplicativeExpr) *
MultiplicativeExpr	UnionExpr ((«*» | «div» | «idiv» | «mod») UnionExpr) *
UnaryExpr	(«-» | «+») * PathExpr

The priority of operators is indicated by the grammar. Unary «+» and «-» have a higher priority (bind more tightly) that the multiplicative operators «*», «div», «idiv», and «mod», which in turn have higher priority than the binary forms of «+» and «-». In between union operators and unary operators, there is a long list of operators with intermediate priority, such as «intersect» and «cast as». A full list of operator priorities, showing how these operators relate to others, is given in Appendix B.

There are two division operators: «div» for exact division, and «idiv» for integer division. The precise rules for these are described below. The «mod» operator gives the remainder when one number is divided by another. The reason that the «/» symbol isn't used for division is that this would conflict with its use in path expressions, which are described in Chapter 7.

When using the minus operator, take care that it does not get confused with a hyphen within a name. If it immediately follows a name, use a space to separate it. Note that «price-discount» (without spaces) is a single hyphenated name, whereas «price - discount» (with spaces) performs a subtraction. If in doubt, use spaces to separate an operator from the surrounding tokens: it never does any harm.

If there are several operators with the same priority, they are evaluated from left to right. For example «5-2-2» means «(5-2)-2», which evaluates to «1».

Type Promotion

There are special rules for arithmetic operators to determine the type of the result of the expression, based on the types of the operands.

If the operands have the same type, then in general the result is the same type as the operands. So, for example, the sum of two xs:integer values is an xs:integer, while the result of multiplying two xs:double values is an xs:double. The exception to this rule is the «div» operator, when the operands are xs:integer values: in this case, the result is an xs:decimal. For example, the result of «5 div 2» is the xs:decimal value «2.5».

The phrase "the same type" in this rule means the underlying numeric type: one of xs:integer, xs:decimal, xs:float, or xs:double. If you add two xs:short values, the result will be an xs:integer, not an xs:short. (At any rate, it's not guaranteed to be an xs:short; the only requirement on the implementation is that the result must be an xs:integer, and of course returning an xs:short would satisfy that requirement, so long as the result of the operation is in the range of values that xs:short can handle.)

If you use these operators to combine two values that are of different types, type promotion kicks in. This defines a pecking order among the four numeric types: xs:double wins over xs:float, xs:float over xs:decimal, and xs:decimal over xs:integer. If you mix two types, then the loser in this pecking order is first converted to the type of the winner, and the result has the same type as the winner. So, for example, the result of the expression «2.5 + 1» is the xs:decimal value «3.5», because «2.5» is an xs:decimal and «1» is an xs:integer, and xs:decimal is higher in the pecking order.

Changes in XPath 2.0

The main change affecting these operators is the increased range of data types they can handle. In XPath 1.0, all numbers were handled as double-precision floating point, and the operators were not overloaded to handle any other data types.

In XPath 1.0, the arguments supplied to the function were automatically converted to numbers, using the rules for the number() function (which is described in Chapter 10). This means, for example, that the result of «1+true()» would be 2 (true() converts to 1), and the result of «"apple"+"pear"» would be NaN (any non-numeric string converts to the special not-a-number value NaN, and adding two NaNs gives NaN). These conversions are still carried out in XPath 2.0 if you run with backward compatibility enabled. This will happen, for example, in the case of XPath expressions contained in an XSLT stylesheet that specifies «version="1.0"». The main advantage of this behavior is that you never get a runtime error (only NaN results), and if this is important to you, you can achieve the same effect in XPath 2.0 by using the number() function explicitly, even without backward compatibility enabled.

The «idiv» operator is new in XPath 2.0. It does integer division, and is particularly useful when calculating how many rows and columns you need for a table: for example if you have $N items to arrange in 3 columns, then the number of rows needed is «($N+2) idiv 3». Although the result is always an integer, the operands don't have to be integers: for example, the result of «3.6 idiv 1.5» is «2». In fact, a handy use of this operator is to convert any number $x to an integer by writing «$x idiv 1».

Despite the availability of a backward compatibility mode, not everything is 100% guaranteed to give the same answer as with XPath 1.0. Firstly, many calculations will use decimal rather than floating-point arithmetic, so the precision of the result may be different. This also means that you may get failures where previously you got NaN or Infinity as a result. Trying to add things that aren't numbers might also give you different results. But these are edge cases, and most common-or-garden XPath expressions should continue to work unchanged.

Unary plus has been added to the language largely so that any value accepted as the lexical value of a number by XML Schema is also accepted as a valid constant value in an XPath expression. XML Schema accepts «+1.0» as a legal representation of a number, so XPath 2.0 accepts it too.

The relative precedence of the union operator «|» and unary minus has changed since XPath 1.0. In 1.0, the expression «-@price|@cost» was interpreted as «-(@price|@cost)», whereas it now means «-@price | -@cost», which will give a type error on the grounds that the operands of «|» must be nodes.

Effect

The detailed rules for these operators are as follows. The rules are given here on the assumption that the special rules for XPath 1.0 backward compatibility are not in force; the changes that apply under backward compatibility mode are described later.

1. The operands are atomized, as described on page 108 in Chapter 3. This means that nodes are replaced by their typed values: for example, if one of the operands is the attribute node «@price», then the typed value of this attribute is extracted.

2. If, after atomization, either operand is an empty sequence, then the result of the operation is also an empty sequence. For example, if the context node has no price attribute, then the result of «@price * 0.8» is the empty sequence, «()».

3. If either operand after atomization is a sequence of more than one item, a type error is raised. For example, if you write the expression «price * 0.8» and the context node has more than one child element called <price>, a type error ensues. The significance of it being a type error is that it may be reported either at compile time or at runtime, as discussed in the section on *Static and Dynamic Type Checking* in Chapter 3 (Page 109).

4. If either operand is an xdt:untypedAtomic value, then it is converted (using the casting rules) to an xs:double. This situation will normally occur when the operand as written is a node in a schema-less document. For example, suppose the expression is «@price * 0.8», and there is no schema, and the price attribute in the source document is written as «price= "129.99"». Then the attribute value will be converted to the xs:double value 1.2999e2, and the result of the multiplication will also be an xs:double. Note the difference with numeric literals, described on page 142 in Chapter 5—in the case of a value contained in an untyped node, it is always converted to an xs:double when used as an operand of «*», regardless of whether it is written in exponential notation or not.

> The conversion to an **xs:double** uses the casting rules (described in Chapter 9), not the rules of the **number()** function. This means that if the value isn't a valid number, the expression will fail with a runtime error, rather than returning the value **NaN**

5. If the operands are now of an acceptable type for the operator, the calculation is carried out. In the case of numeric operands, all combinations of numeric values are acceptable, and the values are first promoted to a common type as described in the section *Type Promotion* above. The only other kinds of operands that are acceptable are certain combinations of dates, times, and durations, which are described in the section *Arithmetic using Durations* below. The calculation may succeed or fail (the most obvious example of a failure is division by zero); if it fails, a runtime error is reported.

6. If the operands are of the wrong type, then a type error is raised. For example, this will happen if one of the operands is an xs:boolean or xs:string value.

There are two differences to these rules when backward compatibility is in force. Firstly, in step 3, instead of reporting an error when there is more than one item in the sequence, all items except the first are discarded. Secondly, after step 4, if the operands aren't of acceptable types for the operator (for example, if one of them is an xs:string or an xs:boolean), then both operands are converted to xs:double values using the number() function. This means that the result will also be of type xs:double. If the value of an operand isn't numeric, the answer comes out as NaN rather than an error. This conversion isn't done for the «idiv» operator, because this operator is new in XPath 2.0, so backward compatibility problems don't arise.

Arithmetic Using Numbers

This section describes some of the corner cases that can arise when doing numeric arithmetic.

Integer Arithmetic

With integer operands, there are few surprises.

❑ Division by zero is a fatal error, whether you use the «div» or «idiv» operator.

❑ The language spec doesn't define the maximum size of an integer, though it does say it must be at least 18 decimal digits, which should be enough for most purposes. Every conforming implementation is required to provide an option to detect integer overflow and report it as a fatal error. It's also permissible to provide a mode where arithmetic wraps around (as it does in many programming languages like Java and C). If both options are available, the spec doesn't say which should be the default. The thinking is that some users will want to pay the cost of the runtime error detection, whereas others will prefer raw speed.

The result of dividing two integers using the «div» operator is an xs:decimal value, but the spec doesn't say what the precision of the result should be. For example, if you write «10 div 3» then one system might produce the answer «3.333» while another produces «3.3333333333333333».

The «mod» operator, which gives the remainder from an integer division, can be confusing when negative numbers are involved. I find the following rules of thumb helpful:

❑ The result is positive if the first operand is positive, negative if it is negative.

❑ The result depends only on the absolute value of the second operand, not on its sign.

It's also useful to think of the «mod» operator in conjunction with «idiv». Thus:

Expression	Result	Expression	Result
20 mod 3	2	20 idiv 3	6
20 mod –3	2	20 idiv –3	–6
–20 mod 3	–2	–20 idiv 3	–6
–20 mod –3	–2	–20 idiv –3	6

In all cases (except where $y is zero) the result of «($x idiv $y) * $y + ($x mod $y)» is $x.

Decimal Arithmetic

Decimal arithmetic is useful because it avoids the rounding errors that arise with floating point calculations. This is particularly true when handling values that are discrete rather than continuous, of which the most obvious example is money.

Again, the language spec doesn't define the maximum precision that can be held in an xs:decimal value. This is more likely to be a problem with xs:decimal than with xs:integer, and it means that different products are likely to give different answers to the same calculation (though hopefully, only a little bit different!).

The main problem is with division. Even systems that support indefinite-precision xs:decimal values (as Saxon does, for example) have to make a decision as to how many digits to record in the result of «10 div 3», and the spec offers no clues.

As with integer arithmetic, division by zero is a fatal error.

The rules for handling overflow are subtly different from the rules for integers. In the case of xs:decimal, overflow (that is, calculation of a result that is too big for the system to handle, whatever this limit might be) must be reported as an error. So unlike the situation with integers, there is no prospect of the system giving you a spurious result by wrapping around.

Another situation that can arise with xs:decimal values is underflow. This happens when the result of a computation is smaller than the smallest value that can be recorded, but greater than zero. Equally, of course, it could be a very small negative number. For example, if you multiply 0.00000001 by itself, and the system can only handle 10 decimal places after the decimal point, you will get an underflow. The rule in this case is that the result returned must be the xs:decimal value 0.0.

Floating-Point Arithmetic

Floating-point arithmetic (whether using single precision xs:float, or double-precision xs:double) is defined by the rules of the IEEE 754 specification. These rules are summarized in Chapter 3.

The XPath 1.0 specification tied the definition of floating-point arithmetic pretty closely to the same rules as were adopted in Java. But in fact, the IEEE 754 specification offers a number of options, and XPath 2.0 gives implementors a bit more freedom to select which options to provide. In particular, the specification allows for errors to be raised on overflow or underflow conditions, whereas the XPath 1.0 profile always returned positive or negative infinity in the overflow case, and positive or negative zero for underflow. So in corner cases, the behavior may not be exactly the same as with XPath 1.0, and not quite so consistent across different processors.

The unary minus operator is defined to change the sign of the operand. This is subtly different from subtracting the operand from zero, because it means that «-0e0» represents negative zero rather than positive zero. There's very little difference between the two: about the only way of telling them apart is by a test such as «1 div $x > 0», which returns true if $x is positive zero (the division gives positive infinity), but false if $x is negative zero. There has been a certain amount of confusion over the fact that XML Schema does not recognize the value negative zero. You can write «-0e0» in a source document, but it means exactly the same as writing «+0e0». This is because XML Schema doesn't recognize the concept of two values being equal but distinguishable. For practical purposes the distinction between the two values is rarely important, and it doesn't really matter that it is lost once you write the results away to an XML document. Its only significance is that it preserves a useful difference in the intermediate results of complex calculations.

Floating point arithmetic can always give you rounding errors, because there are values that can be written accurately in decimal notation that can't be expressed accurately in binary. So, for example, the result of the expression «1.0E-3 * 1.0E-4» might not be displayed as «1.0E-7» as you would expect, but as «1.0000000000000001E-7». You can round it to the number of decimal places required using the round-half-to-even() function described in Chapter 10, or in XSLT, by using the format-number() function described in *XSLT 2.0 Programmer's Reference*, Chapter 7.

Examples of Numeric Arithmetic

Expression	Description
$X + 1	The result of adding 1 to the value of the variable $X
last()-1	One less than the position of the last node in the context list
@margin*2	Twice the value of the margin attribute of the context node. This will work only if the margin attribute either has a numeric type, or is untyped and has a value that can be interpreted as a number
ceiling(count(item) div 3)	One-third of the number of child <item> elements of the context node, rounded upwards. (Useful if you are arranging the items in three columns)
$seq[position() <= last() idiv 2]	Selects the first half of the items in the sequence $seq, rounded down. For example, if there are 11 items in the sequence, it selects the first five
item[position() mod 2 = 0]	Selects the even-numbered child <item> elements of the context node. (Again, this can be useful if you are arranging items in a table)

Continues

Expression	Description
count($list) mod 5 + 1	The number of items in the sequence $list modulo 5, plus one. The result will be a number in the range 1 to 5.
- @credit	The negated numeric value of the credit attribute of the context element node. If the context node has no credit attribute, or if its value is not numeric, the result of the expression is «()» (the empty sequence), unless backward compatibility mode is set, in which case it is NaN (not a number)
1---1	A not very useful but perfectly legal way of writing the value zero. The first minus sign is a binary subtraction operator; the next two are unary minus signs

Arithmetic Using Durations

As well as being used for conventional arithmetic using numbers, the arithmetic operators are also used to perform certain operations on dates, times, and durations. Not all combinations make sense; for example, it's sensible to add 3 days to a date, but it isn't sensible to add two dates.

There's a table in the XPath 2.0 specification that lists all the combinations of operators and operands that are permitted, and the number that involve dates, times, and durations is alarmingly large. But appearances are deceptive: on closer examination, it turns out that these are all permutations on a small number of themes. The number of permutations is large because it involves:

❑ *Three date/time types*: xs:date, xs:dateTime, and xs:time

❑ *Two duration types*: xdt:yearMonthDuration and xdt:dayTimeDuration

❑ Symmetric operations, e.g. duration + date as well as date + duration

In fact, all the options boil down to five basic categories:

Expression	Meaning
date/time +|- duration	Returns a date/time that is a given duration after or before the supplied date/time. For example, 2004-12-31 plus three days is 2005-01-03
duration +|- duration	Adds or subtracts two durations to give another duration. For example, one hour plus two hours is three hours
duration *|div number	Multiplies a duration by a numeric factor, or divides it by a numeric factor, to give another duration. For example, one month times 3 is three months
date/time - date/time	Determines the interval between two dates/times, as a duration. For example, 2005-01-03 minus 2004-12-31 is three days

Expression	Meaning
duration div duration	Determines the ratio between two durations, as a number. For example PT12H divided by PT10M is 72

In each of these cases the following rules hold:

- ❑ If the operator is «+» or «*» (but not if it is «-» or «div») then the operands may be written in either order.

- ❑ Subtracting a positive duration is the same as adding a negative duration (a negative duration is written, for example, as «-P3D» to represent minus three days).

- ❑ The duration must be either an xdt:dayTimeDuration or an xdt:yearMonthDuration. The first kind is equivalent to an exact number of seconds, the second to an exact number of months. The primitive type xs:duration can't be used for arithmetic, because the variation in the length of a month creates too many uncertainties.

- ❑ Multiplying a duration by a number such as 0.5 is the same as dividing it by 2.0.

The following sections examine each of the four cases in a bit more detail.

Date/Time plus Duration

This section covers the following combinations of operands:

Operand 1	Operand 2	Result
xs:date	xdt:yearMonthDuration	xs:date
xs:date	xdt:dayTimeDuration	xs:date
xs:dateTime	xdt:yearMonthDuration	xs:dateTime
xs:dateTime	xdt:dayTimeDuration	xs:dateTime
xs:time	xdt:dayTimeDuration	xs:time

The allowed operators are «+» and «-». If the operator is «+», then the operands may appear in either order; if it is «-», then the date/time must be the first operand and the duration the second. Subtracting a positive duration has the same effect as adding a negative duration, and vice versa.

The decision to allow arithmetic using the two subtypes xdt:yearMonthDuration and xdt:dayTimeDuration, while not allowing it using the parent type xs:duration, is slightly perverse, since any xs:duration value can be decomposed into an xdt:yearMonthDuration and an xdt:dayTimeDuration. But by now, you should be used to the idea that the handling of durations in XML Schema and XPath has a few rough edges.

Let's start by seeing how to add an xdt:dayTimeDuration to an xs:dateTime. This is reasonably straightforward. An xdt:dayTimeDuration represents an exact number of seconds. When you add this to an `xdt:dateTime` you get the value that represents the instant in time that is this number of seconds later (or earlier, if the duration is negative) than the original, in the same timezone. (The specification, which is done by reference to an algorithm given in an appendix of the XML Schema Recommendation, is careful to ignore the leap seconds that can be inserted arbitrarily into the calendar to handle variations in the earth's speed of rotation.)

If you're adding an `xdt:dayTimeDuration` to an `xs:date`, rather than to an `xs:dateTime`, you can get the right answer by considering the `xs:dateTime` at `00:00:00` on the date in question, and then ignoring the time part of the result.

If you're adding the duration to an `xs:time`, the result is taken modulo 24 hours. For example, `03:00:00` plus `P1D` is `03:00:00`, and `03:00:00` plus `PT36H` is `15:00:00`.

If you're adding an `xdt:yearMonthDuration` to an `xs:date`, the rules are slightly more complicated. What is 31st January plus one month? The answer given by the specification is that it is 28th February, or 29th February if it's a leap year.

Adding an `xdt:yearMonthDuration` to an `xs:dateTime` is the same as adding it to the date part of the `xs:dateTime`, and returning the time portion unchanged. Adding an `xdt:yearMonthDuration` to an `xs:time` is not allowed, because it would always return the value unchanged.

Duration plus Duration

You can only add or subtract two durations of the same type. The allowed combinations of operands are:

Operand 1	Operand 2	Result
`xdt:yearMonthDuration`	`xdt:yearMonthDuration`	`xdt:yearMonthDuration`
`xdt:dayTimeDuration`	`xdt:dayTimeDuration`	`xdt:dayTimeDuration`

The operator can be either «+» or «-».

The rules are reasonably obvious (at any rate, they appear to be obvious to the writer of the specification, which simply says that the result is the sum or difference of the two durations). Remember that an `xdt:yearMonthDuration` is equivalent to an `xs:integer` number of months, and an `xdt:dayTimeDuration` is equivalent to an `xs:decimal` number of seconds. The addition and subtraction of two durations, whether they are positive or negative in sign, thus reduces to simple arithmetic on numbers.

For example, subtracting `PT6H` (6 hours) from `P1D` (one day) gives `PT18H` (18 hours).

Only binary «+» and «-» can be used with durations: the unary «+» and «-» operators, for no particularly good reason, are constrained to work only with numbers. The easiest way to turn a positive duration into an equivalent negative duration is to multiply it by «-1», as described in the next section.

Duration times Number

An `xdt:dayTimeDuration` or `xdt:yearMonthDuration` can be multiplied or divided by a number, to give another duration of the same type. The operand combinations are:

Operand 1	Operand 2	Result
xdt:yearMonthDuration	xs:double xs:float xs:decimal	xdt:yearMonthDuration
xdt:dayTimeDuration	xs:double xs:float xs:decimal	xdt:dayTimeDuration

The operator can be «*» (multiply) or «div» (divide). If the operator is «*», the operands can appear in either order; if it is «div», then the numeric operand must be the second operand.

The effect of the operation is equivalent to converting the duration to a number of months or seconds, performing a numeric multiplication or division, and then converting the result back to a duration.

At the time of writing the specification actually requires the numeric operand to be a double, other numeric types cause a type error. I'm assuming this bug will be fixed.

Date/Time minus Date/Time

There are a number of operators that subtract date/time values to give a duration. These don't cover all possible cases, so they are supplemented by additional functions.

The cases covered by the subtraction operator «-» are:

Operand 1	Operand 2	Result
xs:date	xs:date	xdt:dayTimeDuration
xs:dateTime	xs:dateTime	xdt:dayTimeDuration
xs:time	xs:time	xdt:dayTimeDuration

If the first operand represents an instant in time later than the second operand, then the result will be a positive duration; if it represents an earlier instant in time, then the result will be a negative duration.

The operation works by taking the normalized value of each date/time operand, that is, the time converted to UTC timezone. If the date/time was supplied without a timezone, then it is assumed to represent a date/time in the implicit timezone defined by the evaluation context (see Chapter 4).

For operands of type xs:dateTime, the result is the duration corresponding to the number of seconds that separate the two instants in time.

For operands of type xs:date, the result is the difference between the starting instants of the two dates. Since the dates can be in different timezones, the result is not necessarily an integer number of days.

For operands of type xs:time, the values, after normalization to UTC, are assumed to represent two times occurring on the same date. The value will therefore be positive if the UTC-normalized value of the first time is greater than the UTC-normalized value of the second time. This can lead to surprises; for example, the value of «xs:time("23:00:00 - 05:00") - xs:time("18:00:00-05:00")» is the negative duration «-PT19H». This is because after normalization to UTC, the expression is equivalent to «xs:time("04:00:00Z") - xs:time("23:00:00Z")».

The function subtract-dateTimes-yielding-dayTimeDuration(), which is described in Chapter 10, has exactly the same effect as the subtraction operator «-».

The function subtract-dateTimes-yielding-yearMonthDuration() is used to find the interval between two xs:dateTime values in months, and the function subtract-dates-yielding-yearMonthDuration() finds the interval between two xs:date values in months. The result is the largest number of whole months that can be added to the second xs:date value to give an xs:date that is on or before the first xs:date value. If the first xs:date is earlier than the second, it is the largest number of months that can be subtracted from the second xs:date to give an xs:date that is on or after the first xs:date.

Duration divided by Duration

It is possible to divide an xdt:dayTimeDuration by another xdt:dayTimeDuration, or an xdt:yearMonthDuration by another xdt:yearMonthDuration, to obtain a double. The division operator must be «div» («idiv» is not supported). The result is equivalent to converting both the durations into a number of months or seconds and performing a numeric division.

Here are some examples:

Expression	Result
xdt:dayTimeDuration("P10D") div xdt:dayTimeDuration("PT6H")	40
xdt:dayTimeDuration("-P1D") div xdt:dayTimeDuration("PT1S")	−86400
xdt:yearMonthDuration("P1M") div xdt:yearMonthDuration("P1Y")	0.083333333 . . .

This operation actually provides the easiest way to convert a duration into a number of months, days, or seconds. To convert an xdt:dayTimeDuration to seconds, for example, just divide it by xdt:dayTimeDuration("PT1S"). This is useful when you need to perform calculations that are not directly supported by the operations available on durations. Examples include:

❑ Dividing a distance by a duration to obtain an average speed.

❑ Multiplying the number of hours worked by the hourly rate to obtain the amount of money due.

❑ Determining the day of the week for a given date.

The following code illustrates how to display the day of the week, supplied in the variable `$date`:

```
("Sunday", "Monday", "Tuesday", "Wednesday", "Thursday", "Friday", "Saturday")
    [1 + (($date - xs:date("1901-01-06")) div xdt:dayTimeDuration("P1D") mod  7)]
```

The ability to divide one duration by another is a late addition to the XPath specification, so to run this example with Saxon you will need version 8.0 or later. In XSLT 2.0 you can display the day of the week using the `format-date()` function, described in Chapter 7 of *XSLT Programmer's Reference*.

Value Comparisons

XPath 2.0 has introduced a completely new set of operators for comparing single atomic values. These are shown in the table below:

Operator	Meaning
eq	equals
ne	not equals
lt	less than
le	less than or equal to
gt	greater than
ge	greater than or equal to

These were introduced primarily because they have much cleaner and more predictable behavior than the XPath 1.0 operators «=», «!=», «<», «<=», «>», and «>=». The XPath 1.0 operators are still available, and are described later in this chapter under the heading *General Comparisons* on page 188.

The real driver for introducing these new operators was not really the requirements of XPath users, but the needs of XQuery, which is a superset of XPath 2.0. XQuery needs to be able to search large databases, and if you want to search a terabyte of data then you need to take advantages of indexes. This means you need to be able to rearrange the query as written by the user into a form that can take advantage of the indexes known to be available, and this rewriting of an expression into a different form is only possible if the operators have very clean mathematical properties. For example, a very useful property that makes rearranging expressions possible is called *transitivity*, which means that if «A=B» and «B=C» are both true, then you know that «A=C» will also be true. Unfortunately, this isn't the case for the «=» operator in XPath 1.0. For example, in XPath 1.0, «1=true()» and «true()="true"» are both true, but «1="true"» is false.

But although these operators were introduced specifically to enable XQuery optimization, I think it's a good idea to get into the habit of using them for most routine comparisons. You probably won't see any very visible performance benefit for the average XSLT stylesheet, but you may find that you make fewer errors because the behavior of the operators is simpler and more predictable.

In the XPath syntax, the two kinds of comparison operator, as well as the three operators «is», «<<», and «>>» which we will meet later in this chapter (see page 196), are presented like this:

Expression	Syntax
ComparisonExpr	RangeExpr ((ValueComp | GeneralComp | NodeComp) RangeExpr) ?
ValueComp	«eq» | «ne» | «lt» | «le» | «gt» | «ge»
GeneralComp	«=» | «!=» | «<» | «<=» | «>» | «>=»
NodeComp	«is» | «<<» | «>>»

This means that all 15 operators listed here have the same priority. For all these operators the result of the expression is always an xs:boolean value. The reference to RangeExpr in the syntax can be ignored for now: it just refers to the next kind of expression in operator precedence order, which happens to be the range expression (of the form «1 to 10») described in Chapter 8.

The biggest difference between the value comparison operators and the general comparison operators described on page 188 is that the value comparison operators always compare two atomic values with each other, whereas the general comparison operators can be used to compare sequences.

Permitted Operand Types

The detailed effect of the comparison depends on the types of the two operands. These must be compatible with each other. There are some data types that can be compared using the «eq» and «ne» operators, but not the «lt», «le», «gt», or «ge» operators. An example is xs:QName—you can test whether two xs:QName values are equal to each other, but not whether one is less than the other.

The permitted operand types for value comparisons are summarized in the two tables that follow. Both operands must have the same type (as defined by a row in the table). Comparing two values whose types don't match (for example comparing an integer to a string) doesn't give you a result of false, it is a type error. This means the error may be reported either at compile time or at runtime, as discussed in Chapter 3.

The first table is for «eq» and «ne», and shows for each data type how the comparison is done.

Data type	Definition of «eq»
xs:string	The two strings are compared using the default collation established in the static context for the expression. Collations are described in detail on page 123. In consequence, the results may be quite different in different environments, for example in one context the strings «Strasse» and «Straße» may be equal, in another context they may be unequal

Data type	Definition of «eq»
Numeric	Any two numeric values can be compared (xs:integer, xs:decimal, xs:float, or xs:double). If they are of different types, one value is first promoted to the type of the other in the same way as for arithmetic operators (see page 170). They are then tested for numeric equality (this means, for example, that «1.00» and «01» will compare equal). There are a couple of special cases with floating point numbers: positive and negative zero are considered equal to each other, but NaN (not a number) is not equal to any other number, in fact it is not even equal to itself
xs:boolean	Two xs:boolean values are equal if they are both true, or both false
xs:dateTime	Two xs:dateTime values are equal if they represent the same instant in time. This means that if both include a timezone, they are adjusted so that they are in the same timezone (conventionally UTC, but any timezone would do). Although the XPath data model retains the original timezone attached to the value, it plays no part in the comparison: the two xs:dateTime values «2004-01-01T02:00:00Z» and «2003-12-31T21:00:00-05:00» (2 a.m. in London and 9 p.m. in New York) are considered equal. If either or both of the values has no timezone, it is considered to represent a time in the implicit timezone defined by the XPath evaluation context, as described in Chapter 4. If implicit timezones are set depending on the locale or preferences of the individual user, this means that two xs:dateTime values that appear equal for one user might appear not equal for another—but this can only happen in the situation where one of the values has an explicit timezone and the other does not
xs:date	In most cases it is likely that xs:date values will be stored without a timezone, in which case the test whether two dates are equal is straightforward. If a date does have a timezone, then it is a significant part of the value, and dates will only be considered equal if they have the same timezone; though if one of them has a timezone and the other does not, the implicit timezone is used in the comparison in the same way as for xs:dateTime values
xs:time	Values of type xs:time are compared in the same way as xs:dateTime values. That is, the values are compared after adjusting to UTC, using the implicit timezone from the context in the case of an xs:time value with no explicit timezone. For example, «02:00:00Z» and «21:00:00-05:00» (2 a.m. in London and 9 p.m. in New York) are considered equal
xs:gYear xs:gYearMonth xs:gMonth xs:gMonthDay xs:gDay	Values of these types are comparable only with other values of the same type. Since all of these types allow an optional timezone, they follow the same rules as xs:date. In fact, one way of defining equality is by converting the values to xs:date values by supplying arbitrary values for the missing components, and then comparing the resulting dates

Continues

Data type	Definition of «eq»
xs:QName	Two xs:QName values are equal if they have the same namespace URI (or if both have no namespace URI) and if they have the same local name. Both the URI and the local name are compared in terms of Unicode codepoints, no collation is used
xs:anyURI	Two xs:anyURI values are equal if they are identical, character for character. A working group in W3C spent a great deal of time trying to come up with a more sophisticated definition of URI equality (for example, one that recognized which parts of the URI are case-sensitive and which are not) but the task proved too difficult, so XPath uses the simplest possible definition
xs:base64Binary xs:hexBinary	Although these two types share the same value space, it is not possible to compare one with the other directly: you have to cast the value first. For each of the types, values are equal if they consist of the same sequence of octets
xs:NOTATION	The value space of xs:NOTATION is the same as the value space of xs:QName, and xs:NOTATION values are compared in the same way as xs:QName values
xs:duration	The xs:duration type in XML Schema is the only type for which no equality operator has been defined in XPath. If you try to compare two xs:duration values (or even to compare an xs:duration with itself) you will get an error. The reason for this is essentially a lack of consensus as to whether two xs:duration values such as «P1Y» (one year) and «P12M» are equal or not: according to the XML Schema specification, they are distinct. It's expected that there will be revised definitions of the duration data types in the next version of XML Schema, and in the meantime, the XSLT and XQuery groups decided that the safest thing was to wait and see what emerged, rather than risk creating legacy that would be regretted later. The signal that this is sending is that XPath 2.0, for all practical purposes, does not support the xs:duration data type.
	However, as described in Chapter 3, XPath 2.0 has defined two subtypes of xs:duration called xdt:yearMonthDuration and xdt:dayTimeDuration. These basically handle the durations that are well-behaved, in that they consist either of an exact number of months, or an exact number (not necessarily an integer number) of seconds. These types do away with the problems caused by the variable length of a month, and equality on these types is defined in terms of the length of the duration rather than its representation: so «P1Y» equals «P12M», and «PT1800S» equals «PT12H»

The «ne» operator is the exact inverse of «eq»: if an «eq» comparison raises an error, then «ne» also raises an error; if «eq» returns true, then «ne» returns false, and if «eq» returns false, then «ne» returns true. This is true even for peculiar cases like NaN: if the value of $x is NaN, then «$x eq $x» is false, while «$x ne $x» is true. Another reassuring feature of these operators is that if «$a eq $b» is true, then «$b eq $a» is also true. (It's worth mentioning these things because as we'll see later in the chapter, when it comes to the «=» and «!=» operators it's best not to make any assumptions).

The other four operators in this group, «lt», «le», «gt», and «ge», work only for data types that are ordered. The data types that have an ordering, and the way the ordering works, are defined in the table below.

Data type	Definition of ordering
xs:string	The ordering of strings is determined by a collation, in the same way as equality comparison. These operators use the default collation established in the XPath evaluation context, as described in Chapter 3. There's actually a tension between equality comparison and ordering comparisons: for testing equality, you often want a *weak* collation, for example one that compares «yes» and «YES» as equal. But for ordering, you often want to put the strings in some kind of order, even if it's fairly arbitrary, so you want «yes» either to be less than «YES», or greater than it (that is, you want a *strong* collation). If you want to use different collations for different operations, you can achieve this by using the compare() function described in Chapter 10, but for the «eq» and «lt» family of operators, you have to choose a single collation that may be a compromise
Numeric	Any two numeric values can be compared (xs:integer, xs:decimal, xs:float, or xs:double). If they are of different types, one value is first promoted to the type of the other in the same way as for arithmetic operators (see page 170). They are then tested for numeric order (this means, for example, that «10» is greater than «2»)
xs:boolean	The value false is considered, quite arbitrarily, to be less than true
xs:dateTime	One xs:dateTime value is considered less than another if it represents an earlier instant in time. As with equality testing, the two values are adjusted to a common timezone, using the implicit timezone from the evaluation context if the value does not have its own timezone. The effect is, for example, that «2004-01-01T01:00:00Z» is less than «2003-12-31T23:00:00-05:00»
xs:date	In XML Schema, xs:date values are described as being partially ordered. This means that for some pairs of dates, one of them is clearly earlier than the other, but for other pairs (in particular, a pair of dates in which one has a timezone and the other does not) it's impossible to decide. Putting such a rule into a query language would have been impossibly complex, so instead the decision is made by interpreting all dates without a timezone as being in the implicit timezone defined by the evaluation context. The rule is that one date is less than another if it starts earlier than the other one starts, even if the two dates overlap: for example, «2004-01-01+10:00» is less than «2004-01-01Z» because the New Year starts earlier in Sydney than it does in London

Continues

Data type	Definition of ordering
xs:time	Values of type xs:time present a particular problem for ordering, because the values are actually cyclic. Converting both values to the UTC timezone produces some strange results, for example, it means that «18:00:00-05:00» is greater than «20:00:00-05:00», because the equivalent UTC times are «23:00:00Z» and «01:00:00Z», respectively. But for want of a better way of defining it, this is what XPath does. There are various strategies you can use to avoid this problem: if the times being compared are in the same timezone, then a simple approach is just to convert them to strings and compare the strings
xs:gYear xs:gYearMonth xs:gMonth xs:gMonthDay xs:gDay xs:QName xs:anyURI xs:base64Binary xs:hexBinary xs:NOTATION	These types have no ordering defined. Using any of the operators «lt», «le», «gt», «ge» with values of these types is a type error
xs:duration	As with equality comparisons, xs:duration values themselves are not considered to be ordered, so the operators «lt», «le», «gt», and «ge» are not available. This removes the problem of deciding whether 30 days is less than, equal to, or greater than one month. The two XPath subtypes of xs:duration, namely xdt:yearMonthDuration and xdt:dayTimeDuration, are much more well behaved. The effect of comparing them is the same as converting the value to a number of months, or a number of seconds, and comparing the two numbers. This means, for example, that «PT36H» (36 hours) is greater than «P1D» (one day)

In nearly all cases the four operators have the obvious relationship to each other: for example, if «$a lt $b» is true, then «$a le $b» is also true, as is «$b gt $a». The one exception is the xs:double (and xs:float) value NaN. If NaN appears as either operand of any of these four operators, or as both operands, then the result is always false.

Type Checking for Value Comparisons

The operands in a value comparison are processed according to the following rules. These rules apply to all six operators. Note that there are no special backward-compatibility rules here, because these operators were not available in XPath 1.0.

1. Each of the operands is atomized, as described on page 108 in Chapter 3. This means that when you supply a node as the argument, the typed value of the node is extracted.

2. If either operand (after atomizing) is a sequence containing more than one value, then a type error occurs.

3. If either operand (after atomizing) is an empty sequence, the result is an empty sequence.

4. If either of the values, after atomizing, is of type xdt:untypedAtomic (which will generally be the case if the value has been extracted from an element or attribute in a schema-less document), then it is converted to a string (a value of type xs:string). This is true even if the other operand is a number.

5. If the two values are not comparable then a type error occurs. This can happen because their types are incompatible with each other (for example one is an xs:string and the other an xs:decimal), or it can happen because both values belong to a type for which equality or ordering is not defined, such as xs:QName.

6. Otherwise, the values are compared according to the ordering rules for their data type, as described in the table in the previous section.

There are a couple of controversial decisions reflected in these rules.

The first is that either operand is allowed to be an empty sequence. The specification has vacillated on this question in successive drafts.

The main argument in favor of allowing an empty sequence is that the empty sequence should behave like null values in SQL: any operator or function that has «()» as an argument should return «()» as a result. This also makes it easier to handle optional elements and attributes. This principle has not been followed systematically throughout the language, but it is followed by most of the operators. At one stage the language design also included SQL-like three-valued logic, but this was dropped, largely because it was incompatible with XPath 1.0. In most cases, XPath 1.0 and now also XPath 2.0 treats absent data in almost exactly the same way as SQL, but without relying on three-valued logic. For example, in an expression such as «//item[@code eq 3]», items that have no code attribute will not be selected. Equally, if you write «//item[@code ne 3]», items that have no code attribute will not be selected. (In both cases, the value of the predicate is an empty sequence, and the effective boolean value of an empty sequence is false). But unlike SQL, the XPath expression «//item[not(@code = 3)]» does select items with no code attribute. The SQL rule that «not(null)» returns «null» has no parallel in XPath.

The argument in favor of disallowing an empty sequence was to maximize the freedom of the optimizer to rearrange predicates, so as to make use of indexes. Although the current rules do not compromise transitivity, they do make other rewrites impossible, for example, the expressions «A ne B» and «not(A eq B)» are no longer equivalent.

The other controversial decision is that xdt:untypedAtomic values are converted to strings regardless of the type of the other operand. Taking again the example «@code eq 3», this means you will get a type error if the source document has no schema, because you can't compare a string to a number. This rule was introduced in order to make equality transitive. For example, suppose @code is an untyped attribute whose string value is «4.00». Then «@code eq "4.0"» and «@code eq 4.0e0» would both be true (one is a string comparison and the other a numeric comparison), and since «4.0 eq 4.0e0» is true, transitivity would then require that the string comparison «"4.0" eq "4.0e0"» is also true. This clearly isn't feasible; as strings, these values are not the same thing.

Examples of Value Comparisons

Expression	Description
`$x eq 2`	This is `true` if $x is a sequence of exactly one item, and that item is an instance of `xs:double`, `xs:float`, or `xs:decimal` (or a type derived from these by restriction) that is numerically equal to 2. It is also `true` if the single item in $x is a node whose typed value is one of these numeric types, and is numerically equal to 2. The result is `false` if the item in $x is a different numeric value, and it is effectively false if $x is empty. If $x contains more than one item, or contains a non-numeric value, the result is an error
`count($x) gt 2`	This is true if the number of items in the sequence $x is 3 or more, and is false otherwise. No type error can occur in this case, because the value returned by the `count()` function will always be an integer, and `count()` accepts any type of value as its argument
`@x eq "yes"`	This is true if the context node has an attribute named x, and the type of that attribute is either `xs:string` or `xs:untypedAtomic` or a type derived from `xs:string` by restriction, and the value of the attribute compares equal to the string «yes» under the rules of the default collation (which is context-dependent). If the attribute doesn't exist then the effective value is false. If the attribute has a different type, the result is a type error
`@retirement-date ge current-date()`	This is true if the context node has an attribute named `retirement-date`, and the type of that attribute is `xs:date` or a user-defined type defined as a restriction of `xs:date`, and the value of the attribute is the same as or after the current date. In the unlikely event that the `retirement-date` attribute has a timezone associated with it, this will be taken into account in the comparison; if not, the implicit timezone is used, which will always be the same as the timezone used in the result of the `current-date()` function. If the `retirement-date` attribute does not exist the effective result is false. If the attribute has any type other than `xs:date`, including the case where it has type `xdt:untypedAtomic`, a type error occurs

General Comparisons

The term *general comparisons* is used for expressions involving the six operators «=», «!=», «<», «<=», «>», and «>=». These operators are retained and generalized from XPath 1.0. As we shall see, they are considerably more powerful than their counterparts used in value comparisons, but this also means that they may be rather more expensive, and they can also lead to a few surprises—they don't always give the answer you expect.

The syntax for these operators has already been given, because they are combined into the same production rules as the simpler operators «eq», «ne», «lt», «le», «gt», and «ge», which are given on page 181.

General comparisons are more powerful than value comparisons in two ways:

❑ General comparisons allow either or both operands to be sequences (of zero, one, or many items), whereas value comparisons require the operands to be single items.

❑ General comparisons are more flexible in the way they handle untyped atomic values (that is, data from schema-less documents). In particular, the way an untyped value is handled depends on the type of the value that it is being compared with.

In addition, general comparisons have special rules for use when backward compatibility mode is selected (in XSLT, this depends on whether the version attribute is set to «1.0» or «2.0»).

> Remember that if you are embedding your XPath expressions in an XML document—for example an XSLT stylesheet—then the «<» character must be escaped as «<». Many people also like to escape «>» as «>», though this is not strictly necessary.

Changes in XPath 2.0

Despite the special rules for handling backward compatibility mode, the general comparison operators are probably the area where incompatibilities between XPath 1.0 and XPath 2.0 are most likely to be encountered. This is mainly because of the generalization of the data model to handle sequences, and also because of the increased range of data types. XPath 1.0 only supported four data types (string, number, boolean, and node-set). Given two operands, and allowing for symmetry, there were therefore 10 possible combinations of operand types, and each of these was described separately. Because there was little consistency to the XPath 1.0 rules, generalizing them to handle a much richer set of data types proved difficult.

The incompatibility that you are most likely to hit is when comparing strings, or untyped nodes. In XPath 1.0, an equality comparison («=») between two nodes (all nodes were untyped in those days) treated both values as strings, while an ordering comparison («<») treated them as numbers. This led to oddities such as the fact that «"2"="2.0"» was false, while «"2"<="2.0"» and «"2">="2.0"» were both true. This has been swept away in XPath 2.0; if you compare two strings, or untyped values, using any of these operators, then they are compared as strings, using the default collation defined in the XPath evaluation context. So if you have an expression such as «@discount < @max-discount», and the element in question is <e discount="5" max-discount="10"/>, then XPath 1.0 would return true, while XPath 2.0 returns false. The solution is to make sure that if you want a numeric comparison, you force it by converting the values explicitly to numbers, for example, by using the number() function (which is described in Chapter 10).

(Note that this problem only occurs if both values are strings. It's much more common to see expressions in which one value is a string and the other is a number, for example, «@price > 10.00», and these continue to work as before.)

Another incompatibility occurs when comparing a sequence of nodes to a boolean value. In XPath 1.0, «$node-set = true()» was true if the node-set was non-empty. In XPath 2.0, a sequence compares equal to true if, after atomization, it contains an item that is equal to true. This is a pretty radical change in meaning, but fortunately this kind of expression occurs very rarely in practice.

Rules for General Comparisons

I will present the rules first, and then discuss their consequences.

1. Each of the operands is atomized. This means that if the operand starts out as a sequence of nodes, the process turns it into a sequence of atomic values. There may be more atomic values than nodes (if some of the nodes are defined in the schema to contain a list), or fewer (if some of them contain empty lists). The original operand may contain atomic values as well as nodes, and the atomization process leaves these atomic values alone.

2. The remaining rules are applied to compare each pair of items from the two sequences, taking one value in the pair from the first sequence, and the other value from the second sequence. This means that if one sequence contains four items, and the other contains five, then each item in the first sequence must be compared with each item in the second, giving 20 comparisons to be done in total. If any of these comparisons is true, the result of the general comparison is true. If they are all false, the result is false. If any of the comparisons fails with an error, the general comparison as a whole fails. However, it's not defined in what order the comparisons are done, so if there's a pair of items for which the comparison is true, and another pair for which it raises an error, then the final result might be either true or an error.

3. Considering each pair of items from the two sequences in turn, if one item of the pair is an xdt:untypedAtomic value (typically, a value extracted from a node in a schema-less document), then it is converted to a more specific type. If both items in the pair are xdt:untypedAtomic values, then they are both converted to xs:string values. If only one item is an xdt:untypedAtomic value, then it is converted to the type of the other item. There is a special rule when the second item is numeric: in this situation the xdt:untypedAtomic value is always converted to an xs:double value. This caters for a situation such as comparing the untyped value «2.1» with the xs:integer value «2»; it would be unreasonable to convert the value «2.1» to an integer before doing the comparison.

4. There is now a further rule that comes into play only when backward compatibility mode is enabled. This is that if one of the items in the pair is numeric, and the other is not, then the non-numeric item is converted to an xs:double using the casting rules. This can only succeed if the value is a string or a boolean, in all other cases, the conversion will raise an error. In consequence, a comparison such as «"23"=23» is allowed, and can succeed, under the backward compatibility rules. In pure XPath 2.0 mode, comparison of a string to a number is not allowed; you have to convert one of the operands explicitly to the type of the other, to make it clear whether a string comparison or a numeric comparison is intended.

5. Finally, after any conversions defined in steps 3 and 4, the two items are compared using the rules for the corresponding value comparison operator: that is, one of «eq», «ne», «lt», «le», «gt», and «ge», depending on whether the original operator was «=», «!=», «<», «<=», «>», or «>=». If the result of this comparison is true, then no further work is needed, and the result of the whole general comparison expression is true. If the result is false, however, the process moves on to the next pair of values.

In rule 4, the use of the casting rules rather than the number() *function is a bug, and will hopefully be fixed. The difference is that casting raises an error if the value is not numeric, whereas the* number() *function returns* NaN *(not-a-number). Since this rule is only there for backward compatibility, it should use the* number() *function.*

Fortunately, it's quite rare in practice for both operands to be sequences of more than one item. This case can get very expensive, though there are plenty of ways an XPath processor can avoid actually doing M×N comparisons. It's made more complicated by the fact that the conversion rules apply separately to each pair of items. This means that if you have the comparison «@a = (12, "pineapple")», where the node «@a» is untyped, then the untyped value has to be converted to a number to be compared with the number 12, and to a string to be compared with the string "pineapple". In the general case, it isn't possible to do all the conversions upfront, before starting the pairwise comparison.

The more type information you can supply at compile time, the more likely it is that the XPath processor will actually know in advance that it doesn't have to deal with these complications, because they can't actually arise. For example, if you are writing a function in XSLT or XQuery that has a parameter $p, and the function contains the test «if ($p=3) then . . .», then declaring the parameter as an xs:integer (if that's what it is) can make a world of difference—if you don't declare its type, then the processor is going to have to assume the worst, which is that it might be an arbitrary mixture of typed nodes, untyped nodes, integers, strings, dates, and anything else the caller of the function cares to throw at it. But if you declare it as an xs:integer then the compiler can quietly replace the complex «=» operator with the much simpler and presumably faster «eq» operator. Alternatively, if you know that $p will be an integer, you can write the expression using the «eq» operator directly.

A much more common case in practice is where either or both operands can be empty sequences. These can hold some surprises, so it is well worth studying the rules carefully, even if they seem complicated. Just to warn you of the dangers that lie in wait for the unwary, here are some particular elephant traps:

- ❑ You can't assume that «$X=$X» is true. It usually will be, but if «$X» is an empty sequence, it will be false.

- ❑ You can't assume that «$X!=3» means the same as «not($X=3)». When «$X» is a sequence, the first expression is true if any item in the sequence is not equal to 3, while the second is true if no item in the sequence is equal to 3.

- ❑ You can't assume that if «$X=$Y and $Y=$Z», then «$X=$Z». Again, sequences are the culprit. Two sequences are considered equal if there is a value that both have in common, so «(2,3)=(3,4)» is true, and «(3,4)=(4,5)» is true, but «(2,3)=(4,5)» is false.

In this strange Orwellian world where some values seem to be more equal than others, the one consolation is that «$X=$Y» always means the same as «$Y=$X».

Comparing Sequences

Where a sequence $N is compared with a string 'mary', the test «$N='mary'» is effectively a shorthand for "if there is an item $n in $N such that $n eq 'mary'". Similarly, the test «$N!='mary'» is effectively a shorthand for "if there is an item $n in $N such that $n ne 'mary'". If $N contains two items, whose values are "mary" and "john", then «$N='mary'» and «$N!='mary'» will both be true, because there is a node that is equal to 'mary' and another that is not. If $N is an empty sequence, then «$N='mary'» and «$N!='mary'» will both be false, because there is no item that is equal to 'mary', but there is also no item that is not equal to 'mary'.

Note that when the operand is a sequence of nodes, we are only concerned with the nodes that are members of the sequence in their own right. The children of these nodes are not members of the sequence.

XSLT Example: Node-Set Comparisons

Consider the following piece of XML:

```
<booklist>
    <book><author>Adam</author><title>Penguins</title></book>
    <book><author>Betty</author><title>Giraffes</title></book>
</booklist>
```

Suppose we create a variable whose value is a node sequence containing all <book> elements, as follows:

```
<xsl:variable name="all-books" select="//book"/>
```

And now suppose we do the following test:

```
<xsl:if test="$all-books = 'Adam'"/>
```

If there is no schema, then the result is false, because the sequence $all-books contains two <book> nodes, and neither has a value of "Adam". The first <book> element has the value "AdamPenguins", and the second has the value "BettyGiraffes". The fact that one of them has a child whose value is "Adam" is of no consequence, the child is not a member of the sequence $all-books.

If there is a schema, and the schema defines the type of the <book> elements as being a complex type with element-only content, then this expression will raise an error. This is because the equality comparison tries to atomize the nodes supplied in its operands, and atomizing an element defined to have element-only content is an error.

An interesting consequence of the rules for comparing sequences is that if $N is an empty sequence, the result of the test «$N=$N» is false, because there is no item in the first sequence whose value is equal to that of an item in the second sequence.

It is very easy to trip up on these rules, by assuming for example that <xsl:if test="@name!='James'"> means the same as <xsl:if test="not(@name = 'James')">. It doesn't; if there is no name attribute, the first test is false, while the second is true.

Generally speaking, it is best to steer clear of the «!=» operator unless you know exactly what you are doing. Use «not(x=y)» instead; it is more likely to match the intuitive meaning.

One situation where «!=» can be useful with sequences, however, is to test whether all items in a sequence have the same value. For example, writing <xsl:if test="not($documents//

version!=1.0)"> tests whether there is any node in the sequence «$documents//version» whose numeric value is not 1.0.

XPath 2.0 provides two constructs, the «some» and «every» expressions that make such conditions on sequences easier to express. For example, you could also write the above test as:

```
<xsl:if test="every $d in $documents//version
              satisfies $d eq 1.0">
```

The «some» and «every» expressions are described in Chapter 8.

It is important to remember that an equality test compares the typed values of the nodes, not their identity. For example, «..=/» might seem to be a natural way of testing whether the parent of the context node is the root of the tree. In fact this test will also return true if the parent node is the outermost element, because in a well-formed (and schema-less) tree the value of the outermost element is the same as the value of the document node. Not only is the test wrong, it could also be very expensive: the value of the root contains all the text in the document, so you might be constructing two strings each a million characters long and then comparing them. XPath 2.0 provides an operator for comparing nodes by identity: you can write this test as «.. is /». The «is» operator is described under *Node Comparisons* on page 196.

The rules for comparing two sequences using «=» apply equally when comparing two sequences using an operator such as «<»: the comparison in this case is true if there is some value in the first sequence that is less than some value in the second sequence, under the rules for the «lt» operator. If all the values in the two sequences have the same data type, then the result actually follows the rules the following table, where max() and min() represent the maximum and minimum numeric values of items in the sequence.

Expression	Result
M < N	True when min(M) < max(N)
M <= N	True when min(M) <= max(N)
M > N	True when max(M) > min(N)
M >= N	True when max(M) >= min(N)

Comparisons Involving Document Nodes

When one of the operands of an EqualityExpr is the document node at the root of a tree, it follows the rules described above for sequences. However, such a sequence will always contain exactly one node, so in many ways the actual behavior is much more like that described for strings, where the string in question is the string value of the document node—that is, the concatenation of all the text nodes in the document.

Trees can arise in various ways. The root expression «/» refers to a tree; so does the result of the doc() function.

In XSLT you can construct a temporary tree using an <xsl:variable> or <xsl:param> element with no select attribute. For example, the value of the variable <xsl:variable name="pi">3.14159 </xsl:variable> is the root node of a temporary tree.

One difference from the source document tree is that the source tree usually represents a well-formed XML document, whose root node has a single element child and no text node children, whereas a temporary tree only has to be well-balanced: the root may have any number of element nodes and text nodes as its children. The pi example is a tree consisting of a document node that has a single text node as a child.

If you compare a tree-valued variable with a string, the result will be true if the string-value of the root of the tree is equal to the string. So a simple tree valued variable declared as

```
<xsl:variable name="city">Osaka</xsl:variable>
```

behaves just like a string declared as

```
<xsl:variable name="city" select="'Osaka'"/>
```

In both cases «$city='Osaka'» will be true and «$city='Tokyo'» will be false.

A tree-valued variable can also be more complex, for example:

```
<xsl:variable name="tree">A <emph>very</emph> important person</xsl:variable>
```

The tree in this example is a root node with three child nodes: a text node for "A♦" (where ♦ represents a space character), an <emph> element node, and a text node for "♦important♦person". The string value of this variable is the string «A♦very♦important♦person». An «=» or «!=» comparison with $tree will give the same result as a comparison with this string.

When a document has been validated using a schema, XPath 2.0 doesn't allow atomization of an element node defined with element-only content. If you want to achieve the effect of concatenating all the text within such an element, you have to use the string() function explicitly. However, the same rule doesn't apply to document nodes. Document nodes can always be atomized, whether or not the document has a schema, and the result is always a string (technically, an xdt:untypedAtomic value) containing all the textual content of the document.

To summarize, where one of the operands of the «=» or «!=» comparison is the document node at the root of a tree, the result of the comparison will be the same as comparing an xdt:untypedAtomic value containing all the text of the document.

These rules actually mean that for most purposes, an XSLT variable defined as:

```
<xsl:variable name="city">Johannesburg</xsl:variable>
```

behaves in exactly the same way as the string variable:

```
<xsl:variable name="city" select="'Johannesburg'"/>
```

However, because the value is actually untyped, it can also be compared with (say) a number or a date. So an XSLT variable declared as:

```
<xsl:variable name="pi">3.14159</xsl:variable>
```

can be used in a comparison «[$x > $pi]», which will be interpreted as a numeric comparison if $x is numeric. If $pi were a string it would be an error under XPath 2.0 (except when in backward compatibility mode) to compare it with a number.

Examples of General Comparisons

Expression	Description
@width = 3	Tests whether the width attribute of the context node, after converting to a number, has the numeric value 3. If there is no width attribute, the result will be false. If the width attribute exists and is typed as numeric, the result will be true if and only if the numeric value is equal to three. If the width attribute exists and is untyped, the result will be true if the width attribute can be converted to a number equal to 3, for example if it is «3» or «3.00».
	If the width attribute is defined in the schema as a list-valued attribute, then the result is true if any of the values in this list is equal to 3
@width = @height	Tests whether the width attribute and the height attribute of the context node have the same typed value. If both are untyped, they are compared as strings: this means that if width is «3» and height is «3.00», the result will be false. It will also be false if either or both attributes are absent. If you want a numeric comparison, use the number() function (described in Chapter 10, page 393) to force a conversion.
	If either or both of the attributes are defined in the schema as being list-valued, then the comparison is true if the two lists have any value in common
@width != $x	If there is no width attribute the result will be false.
	If the attribute width is untyped, then if the variable $x holds a numeric value, a numeric comparison is performed; if it holds a string value, a string comparison is performed. The result will be true if the values are different.
	If the attribute width is typed, then an error will occur if the type is incompatible with the type of $x.
	If $x holds a sequence, the result will be true if there is any item in the sequence whose typed value is not equal to the width attribute, using string comparison; it will be false if the sequence is empty.
	If the schema-defined type of the width attribute is a list type, then the comparison is performed with each item in that list considered individually
count(*) > 10	True if the context node has more than ten element children

Continues

Expression	Description
`sum(SALES) < 10000`	`True` if the sum of the numeric values of the `<SALES>` children of the context node is less than 10,000
`position() < last() div 2`	`True` if the context position is less than half the context size, that is, if the position of this node is less than half way down the list of nodes being processed
`not(//@temp <= 0.0)`	`True` if all values of the `temp` attribute in the document are numeric, and greater than zero

Node Comparisons

This section describes the three operators «`<<`», «`is`», and «`>>`», which are used to compare nodes. The «`is`» operator tests whether the two operands evaluate to the same node; the operators «`<<`» and «`>>`» test whether one node is before or after another in document order.

The syntax has already been covered under *Value Comparisons* on page 181: these operators are defined by the same production rule that defines the value comparison operators (the «`eq`» family) and the general comparison operators («`=`» and friends).

For all three operators, each operand must be either a single node or an empty sequence. If either operand is an empty sequence, the result is an empty sequence (which will be treated as `false` if it is used in a boolean test such as a predicate). If either operand is a sequence containing more than one item, or an item other than a node, then a type error is reported.

The «is» Operator

The «`is`» operator tests whether both operands evaluate to the same node. The nodes must be identical; it's not enough to have the same name or the same value, they must actually be the same node.

> *The Data Model specification struggles when it tries to define the concept of node identity. There are good reasons for this: it doesn't fit well into a language that in most other respects is purely functional. For example, if you write a function `f()` in XSLT or XQuery that creates and returns a new element node, then the expression «`f() is f()`» returns false, because each time `f()` is called, it creates a node with distinct identity. This breaks the rule that applies to all other XPath function calls, namely that calling the same function repeatedly with the same arguments and the same evaluation context always returns the same result.*

Here's an example of how the «`is`» operator can be used. Sometimes you have a sequence of elements such as:

```
<H1/><p/><p/><p/><H1/><p/><p/><H1/><p/><p/>
```

and you need to select all the `<p/>` elements that follow a particular `<H1>` element, up to the next `<H1>` element. (I have shown all the elements as empty because we're not interested in their content for this example.) Let's suppose that the variable `$H` identifies the `<H1>` element where you want to start. The expression «$H/following-sibling::p» selects all the <p> elements after the start element, but it doesn't stop when it reaches the next <H1>. You want to select only the <p> elements whose immediately preceding <H1> element is $H. Here is the expression to do this:

```
$H/following-sibling::p[preceding-sibling::H1[1] is $H]
```

Another way of solving this problem would be to write:

```
$H/following-sibling::p except $H/following-sibling::H1/following-sibling::p
```

but I think the solution using the «is» operator is likely to be more efficient. (The «except» operator is described in Chapter 7, on page 234.)

In XSLT 2.0, problems like this can also be tackled using the construct <xsl:for-each-group group-starting-with="H1">. *See Chapter 5 of* XSLT 2.0 Programmer's Reference *for details.*

The operators «<» and «>»

The operators «<» and «>» test whether one node is before or after another in document order. For example, «$A « $B» is true if and only if $A precedes $B in document order. The concept of document order is described in Chapter 2, on page 59.

There is no requirement that the two nodes should be in the same document. Document order is defined as an ordering of all the nodes encountered, across all documents. If nodes are in different documents, then you can't predict which one will be first in document order, but although the answer is arbitrary, it will be consistent within a single run.

These two operators can be particularly useful in XQuery, since some XQuery implementations do not provide axes such as preceding-sibling, following-sibling, preceding, or following. If you are using an XQuery implementation that doesn't offer the following-sibling axis, then you can find the following siblings of a node $N using the expression «$N/../node()[. >> $N]».

Consider again the problem given in the previous section, where the input has the form:

```
<H1/><p/><p/><p/><H1/><p/><p/><H1/><p/><p/>
```

Another way of finding all the <p> elements that follow an <H1> element identified by the variable $H is:

```
$H/following-sibling::p[not($H/following-sibling::H1[1] << .)]
```

This selects those <p> elements provided that they are before the next <H1> element. Note the careful construction of the predicate, which is designed to work even when $H does not have a «following-sibling::H1». It works because when one of the operands of «<» is an empty sequence, the result of the comparison is an empty sequence, which is treated as false. If the expression were written:

```
$H/following-sibling::p[$H/following-sibling::H1[1] >> .]
```

then it would not select any <p> elements after the last <H1> element.

Changes in XPath 2.0

These three operators are new in XPath 2.0.

In XPath 1.0 the only way to test whether two variables $A and $B referred to the same node was to write something like «count($A|$B) = 1». This relies on the fact that the union operator «|» removes duplicate nodes. If you see this construct when upgrading existing code to XPath 2.0, using the «is» operator will almost certainly be more efficient.

In an XSLT 1.0 stylesheet, nodes could also be compared for identity using the expression «generate-id($A) = generate-id($B)». Again the «is» operator is more direct and more likely to be efficient.

Boolean Expressions

This section concludes the chapter with a description of the operators «and» and «or».

There is no «not» operator in XPath, it's provided as a function instead, and is described in Chapter 10, on page 391.

Expression	Syntax
OrExpr	AndExpr («or» AndExpr) *
AndExpr	ComparisonExpr («and» ComparisonExpr) *

The syntax shows that the «and» operator binds more tightly than «or», so that «A and B or C and D» means «(A and B) or (C and D)». Personally, I prefer to use parentheses to avoid any doubt.

The fact that an AndExpr is defined in terms of a ComparisonExpr just means that the family of operators including «=» and «eq» are next in precedence order after «and». These operators were described earlier in this chapter.

An «or» expression returns true if either of its operands is true, while an «and» expression returns true if both of its operands are true.

The operands of «and» and «or» are converted to xs:boolean values by taking their effective boolean value. This applies the same rules as for the conditional («if») expression described in Chapter 5, and the boolean() function, described in Chapter 10. For example, a string is false if it is zero-length, and a sequence is false if it is empty.

XPath 1.0 defined that the right-hand operand of «and» or «or» wasn't evaluated if the result could be established by evaluating the first operand (that is, if the first operand was false in the case of «and», or true in the case of «or»). The reason for this rule was to give clearly defined behavior in the event of errors occurring. In XPath 2.0, the language designers have decided to sacrifice some of this predictability in favor of giving the implementation maximum freedom to rearrange expressions so that indexes can be used. For example, suppose you write an expression like this, to select all the male employees who are retiring today:

```
//employee[@sex='M' and @retirement-date=current-date()]
```

The XPath 1.0 rules say that you can't look at the retirement date until you've established that the employee is male. But if you have a hundred thousand employees, and they are indexed on their date of retirement, then the most efficient strategy would be to use the index, find the employees who are retiring today, and then select those among them who are male. The reason the rules were changed in XPath 2.0 is to allow systems to use this more efficient strategy.

Suppose you know that for female employees only (for some reason) the value of the retirement-date attribute might not be a date at all, but the string value «standard». A schema can be defined using a union type that allows the value to hold either a date, or this special value. The XPath 1.0 rules guaranteed that you would never look at the retirement-date attribute of female employees while evaluating the expression, which would mean that you can never get the error that occurs when comparing the string «standard» to a date. The XPath 2.0 rules don't give you this guarantee. To protect yourself against the failure, you could write:

```
//employee[if (@sex='M')
        then @retirement-date = current-date()
        else false()]
```

Unlike the «and» and «or» operators, the «if» expression does give you a guarantee: if the condition is false, the «then» branch will not be executed. Similarly, if the condition is true, the «else» branch will not be executed.

Another situation where these rules matter is if one branch contains a call on an external function that has side effects. Writing such functions is something that's been left very much implementation-defined, but many XPath implementations will allow calls to external routines, and once they allow that, it's impossible to prevent such functions having arbitrary side-effects. If you want to prevent a subexpression being evaluated because it has side-effects, the only reliable way to ensure this is with an «if» expression: don't rely on «and» and «or».

Note that there are no null values in XPath, as there are for example in SQL, and there is therefore no need for three-valued logic to handle unknown or absent data. Instead, you may need to test explicitly for absent values, as shown in some of the examples below.

Examples

Expression	Description
$x > 3 and $x < 8	True if the value of variable $x is greater than 3 and less than 8
@name and @address	True if the context node has both a name and an address attribute. (Both the operands are sequences of nodes, which are converted to the xs:boolean true if they contain at least one node, and to false if they are empty)

Continues

Expression	Description
`string(@name) and string(@address)`	True if the context node has both a `name` and an `address` attribute and if neither is a zero-length string. (Both the operands are strings, which are converted to the `xs:boolean` `true` if their length is non-zero. If an attribute is absent, the sequence will be empty, and its string value will therefore be the empty string)
`true()`	A trivial `AndExpr` consisting of a single function call
`$x = 5 or $x = 10`	True if the variable `$x` has the value 5 or 10. This could also be written as «`$x = (5, 10)`».
`@name or @id`	True if the context node has a `name` attribute, an `id` attribute, or both
`not(@id) or @id=""`	True if the context node has no `id` attribute or if it has an `id` attribute and the value is an empty string
`//para[position()=1 or position()=last()]`	Selects the `<para>` elements that are either the first or the last (or the only) `<para>` children of their parent node

Summary

This chapter described the following groups of XPath operators:

- ❑ Arithmetic operators, «+», «-», «*», «div», and «mod»
- ❑ Value comparison operators «eq», «ne», «lt», «le», «gt», «ge»
- ❑ General comparison operators «=», «!=», «<», «<=», «>», «>=»
- ❑ Node comparison operators «<<», «is», and «>>»
- ❑ Boolean operators «and» and «or».

Many of these operators behave in a way that is likely to be familiar from other languages, though there are differences because of the different data model, in particular, the fact that everything in XPath is a sequence.

The next chapter describes the most distinctive feature of the XPath language, namely path expressions. Unlike the operators in this chapter, these are quite unique to XPath.

7

Path Expressions

This chapter defines the syntax and meaning of *path expressions*. Path expressions are the most distinctive feature of the XPath language, the construct that gives the language its name. The chapter also describes other constructs in the language that are closely associated with path expressions, in particular *steps* and *axes*, and the «union», «intersect», and «except» operators.

Path expressions are used to select nodes in a tree, by means of a series of steps. Each step takes as its starting point a node, and from this starting point, selects other nodes.

Each step is defined in terms of:

- ❑ An *axis*, which defines the relationship to be followed in the tree (for example, it can select child nodes, ancestor nodes, or attributes)

- ❑ A *node test*, which defines what kind of nodes are required, and can also specify the name or schema-defined type of the nodes

- ❑ Zero or more *predicates*, which provide the ability to filter the nodes according to arbitrary selection criteria.

Path expressions, because they are so commonly used, allow many useful syntactic abbreviations. In order to get the concepts across clearly, I will start by using only the full, verbose syntax for path expressions (I will call these *full path expressions*), and will then go on to introduce the abbreviations later in the chapter.

Because they are closely associated with processing the results of path expressions, this chapter also describes the operators used to combine two sets of nodes by taking their union, intersection, or difference.

Examples of Path Expressions

Before describing the different kinds of path expression in more detail, it may be helpful to look at some examples.

Expression	Description
para	This PathExpr consists of a single AxisStep, which selects all the <para> element children of the context node
@title	This RelativePathExpr selects all the title attributes of the context node. The result will either be empty or contain a single attribute node
book/author/first-name	This RelativePathExpr selects the <first-name> elements that are children of the <author> elements that are children of the <book> elements that are children of the context node
para[@id]	This PathExpr consists of a single AxisStep that contains a Predicate. It selects all the <para> element children of the context node that have an id attribute
para/@id	This is a RelativePathExpr consisting of two AxisSteps separated by the «/» operator. It selects the id attributes of all the <para> element children of the context node. This differs from the previous example in that the result is a sequence of attribute nodes rather than a sequence of element nodes
/*/para	This absolute path expression selects all the <para> element children of the containing document element (that is, of the outermost element of the document containing the context node). The «*» is a wildcard that selects all elements on the chosen axis
$paragraphs	This expression, like every other primary expression (for example, «2+2»), is technically a PathExpr. But that's a technicality; we'll reserve the term *path expression* for a PathExpr that either contains either a «/» operator, or an AxisStep, or both
$sections/body	This PathExpr selects all <body> element children of nodes in the sequence identified by the variable $sections. A type error occurs if $sections contains an item that isn't a node. The results will be in document order even if the original sequence $sections isn't in document order
$sections[3]/body	This PathExpr selects all <body> element children of the third node in the sequence identified by the variable $sections
$sections/.	This PathExpr selects all the nodes that are present in the value of the variable $sections, but with duplicates removed, and sorted into document order. The only effect of the «/.» in this case is to force the reordering and deduplication

Expression	Description
`/contract/ clause[3]/ subclause[2]`	This absolute path selects the second `<subclause>` of the third `<clause>` of the `<contract>` that is the document element. If the document element is not a `<contract>`, or if any of the other components are missing, it produces an empty sequence
`//figure`	The absolute path selects all the `<figure>` elements in the document. (See page 229 for advice about the possible poor performance of this construct)
`city[not(@name= preceding-sibling::city/ @name)]`	This `RelativeExprPath` selects all the child `<city>` elements of the context node that do not have a name attribute that is the same as the name attribute of a preceding `<city>` element with the same parent. It thus selects a set of child `<city>` elements with unique names

The `PathExpr` construct is without doubt the most complex construct in the XPath language. The actual production rules are quite complicated and hard to follow, but they are there to make path expressions easy to write, especially if you are familiar with UNIX-style path names for directories and files. Most of the syntactic complications arise from the range of abbreviations that are permitted, so we will first cover the full, regular syntax, and then introduce the abbreviations later.

Changes in XPath 2.0

In XPath 2.0, the syntax of path expressions has been generalized so that any expression can be used as a step in a path, so long as it returns a sequence of nodes. For example, «doc('a.xml')/id('Z123')» is now a valid path expression. This makes «/» behave in a similar way to other binary operators.

In XPath 1.0, path expressions were defined to return a node-set, that is, a set of nodes with no duplicates, in no particular order. XSLT 1.0, however, always processed the resulting nodes in document order. The XPath 2.0 data model does not support node-sets as such, but by redefining path expressions to return a sequence of nodes in document order with no duplicates, the result is effectively the same.

There are new facilities in XPath 2.0 to select nodes according to their schema-defined type, rather than selecting them only by name. These facilities are described in detail in Chapter 9.

The constructs «.» and «..» can now be followed by predicates.

The axes are unchanged from XPath 1.0, with one exception: the namespace axis has been deprecated. This means that XPath 2.0 implementations may or may not make this axis available. All the information that was available by using the namespace axis in XPath 1.0 (that is, the ability to find all the namespaces declared for any given element) can now be obtained through two new functions: `in-scope-prefixes ()` and `namespace-uri-for-prefix()`. These functions are described in Chapter 10. The reason for replacing the namespace axis with these functions is to allow implementations more flexibility to implement namespaces efficiently. Modeling the information using namespace nodes imposed burdens on the implementation that offered no real benefit to users, for example, the ability to do union and intersection operations on sets of namespace nodes, and the ability to get back from a namespace node to its parent element.

It is now possible to select nodes with a given local-name, regardless of their namespace. This is done using the syntax «*:local-name», which mirrors the syntax «prefix:*» that is used to select all nodes in a given namespace, regardless of their local-name.

The operators «except» and «intersect» are new in XPath 2.0, and the keyword «union» has been introduced as a synonym for «|». The alternative spelling «union» has been added because it is familiar from SQL, and because the operator «|» can get rather lost visually when it used to combine the results of two complex «for» expressions. This applies especially to XQuery, where the operator may often be used to combine the results of two FLWOR expressions that might each be a dozen lines long (FLWOR expressions are XQuery's equivalent to the SELECT statement of SQL).

Full Path Expressions

A PathExpr is an expression for selecting a set of nodes by following a path (a sequence of one or more steps) from a given starting point. The starting point may be either the context node, or the root node of the tree containing the context node. You can also use path expression to select nodes starting from an arbitrary sequence of nodes given, say, by the value of a variable or the result of a function call.

The result of a path expression is always a sequence (possibly an empty sequence) of nodes, and the nodes are always returned with no duplicates, and in document order. The concept of document order is explained in Chapter 2, on page 59.

Syntax

Expression	Syntax
PathExpr	(«/» RelativePathExpr?) | («//» RelativePathExpr) | RelativePathExpr
RelativePathExpr	StepExpr ((«/» | «//») StepExpr)*

This production indicates that there are four forms a path expression can take, namely:

- ❑ «/» (a *root expression*)
- ❑ «/» RelativePathExpr (an *absolute path*)
- ❑ «//» RelativePathExpr (an *abbreviated absolute path*)
- ❑ RelativePathExpr (a *relative path*)

However, the one starting with «//» is simply an abbreviation, so we'll leave it until later in the chapter (see *The «//» Abbreviation*, on page 228). This leaves three, which I will cover in the following sections: root expressions on page 205, absolute paths on page 206, and relative paths on page 208. The names are my own: I had to invent some section headings as there are no suitable names in the XPath specification itself.

If we were strict about it, we could also classify «/» as an abbreviation for the expression «root() treat as document-node()», and expressions of the form «/A» as abbreviations for «(/)/A». We won't do that, but the exercise does reveal that all path expressions really boil down to expressions of the form «A/B» where A and B are arbitrary expressions. So most of the discussion about the meaning of path expressions is actually a discussion about the meaning of the binary «/» operator.

An arithmetic expression such as «A+B+C» can be decomposed into the form «(A+B)+C)», and defined in terms of a binary «+» operator that takes two operands. Similarly, a path expression of the form «A/B/C» can be decomposed into «(A/B)/C)», which means that the result of a path expression is defined entirely in terms of the meaning of the binary «/» operator. There is a difference, however: The «/» operator is a higher-order operator, because the expression used as its right-hand operand is evaluated repeatedly, once for every item in the sequence selected by the first operand.

The Root Expression «/»

I've invented the term *root expression* to refer to the expression «/», when used on its own. This doesn't actually have a name in the XPath syntax, and I feel it's important enough to give it one.

The meaning of this expression is: the node that is the root of the tree containing the context node, provided that this is a document node.

It's defined in the language specification as being equivalent to the expression:

```
«root(.) treat as document-node()»
```

This means that it selects the same node as the root() function described in Chapter 10, when given the context node «.» as an argument, but raises an error if this node isn't a document node (the «treat as» expression is covered in Chapter 9).

Various errors can arise if you use the «/» expression inappropriately:

❑   It's an error if there is no context item. This happens, for example, at the outer level of a function body in XSLT or XQuery.

❑   It's an error if there is a context item but the context item isn't a node. This happens if you are in a predicate that's being used to filter a sequence of atomic values (see *Filter Expressions* in Chapter 8), or it can happen in XSLT if you are using the `<xsl:for-each>` instruction to process a sequence of atomic values.

❑   It's an error if the context item is in a tree whose root is something other than a document node. In XPath 1.0, every tree had a document node at its root, in fact, it was called a root node rather than a document node because there was no distinction. But the XPath 2.0 data model allows you to have orphaned trees with no document node. Commonly these will have an element as their root. They can also have other kinds of node as the root, for example an attribute or text node, but in this case the tree can only contain one node.

❑   The language could have been designed so that «/» was a synonym of the function call «root(.)», which selects the root of the tree whatever kind of node it is. The designers decided not to do this, to avoid the surprises that can otherwise occur if you find yourself at a different kind of node from the one you were expecting. This decision also has the advantage that the type of the expression «/» is known more precisely: it always returns a document node, which means that it is always safe to use it in contexts (such as a call to a user-defined function) where a document node is the required type.

The symbol «/» is unusual because it is used both as an operator and as an expression in its own right. This can lead to some syntactic ambiguities; for example, the expression «/ union /*» looks as if it is trying to find the union of the two node sequences «/» and «/*», but actually it is an absolute path expression whose first step is «child::union» («union» is a legitimate element name) and whose second step is «child::*». If «/» is followed by something that could be a legitimate step in a path expression, then that's the interpretation that's chosen. Adding whitespace after the «/» doesn't make any difference. What you need to do if you want the other interpretation is to put the «/» in parentheses, thus: «(/) union /*».

This ambiguity was actually present, and unremarked-upon, in XPath 1.0, though it arose less frequently because there weren't many operators in XPath 1.0 that could sensibly be applied to «/» as an operand. The «|» operator does not cause any ambiguities because it cannot be confused with an element name.

Absolute Paths

An absolute path represents a path starting at the root node of the tree that contains the context node.

This syntax is familiar to anyone who has used UNIX filenames, though it is not actually very logical. I find it helpful to think of the «/» at the start of an absolute path expression as being a unary version of the binary «/» operator. This means that an absolute path «/X» can be considered as an abbreviation for the expression «(/)/X», in the same way as «-3» is an abbreviation for «(0)-3». That is, the «/» is really just a binary operator with a defaulted first operand. The implicit first operand in this case is the node selected by the root expression «/». After this expansion, an absolute path behaves in exactly the same way as a relative path, which is described in the next section.

A consequence of these rules is that an absolute path such as «/X» will throw an error in all the cases where the root expression «/» throws an error. Specifically:

❑ It's an error if there is no context item.

❑ It's an error if there is a context item but the context item isn't a node.

❑ It's an error if the context item is in a tree whose root is something other than a document node.

Abbreviated absolute paths, which take the form «//X», are discussed in the section *The «//» Abbreviation*, on page 228.

The term *absolute* is rather a misnomer, since absolute paths always select nodes starting at the root of the document containing the context node. In fact, XPath 2.0 no longer uses the term. But it's handy to have a name for the things, and the idea is not that different from an absolute URI like file:///c:/temp.xml, which although it's called an absolute URI, always selects files on your local machine. Absolute, like global, is a relative term.

There's a good reason for the restriction that an absolute path expression can only be used to select within a tree that's rooted at a document node. If it were allowed to start from any kind of node, there would be some strange surprises. For example, if the root of the tree were an element node named <A>, then the expression «/A» would not select that element. This expression is an abbreviation for «(/)/child::A», so it would select all elements named A that are children of the root element, but not the root element itself. Rather than allow such surprises to occur, the working group decided to make this an error. If you want to select relative to the root of a non-document tree, you can always do this with a relative path expression whose first step is a call to the root() function, described in Chapter 10. For example, you can select all the A elements in a tree, even an A element that is the root of the tree, with the expression «root(.)/descendant-or-self::A».

If you want to start from the root of a different document than the one containing the context node, the simplest approach is to write a path expression whose first component is a variable reference identifying the root of the tree you want to make your selection from. This happens frequently in XSLT. If you are writing a stylesheet that loads several source documents using the doc() function, there is no direct way of selecting the root of the principal source document when the context node is in a different one. To solve this problem it is useful to include in your stylesheet a global variable declaration of the form <xsl:variable name="input" select="/"/>. You can then refer to the root of the principal document at any time as «$input», and you can select other nodes in this tree with relative path expressions of the form «$input/A/B».

Examples of Absolute Paths

Expression	Description
/	Selects the root node of the document containing the context node, provided it is a document node
/price-list	Selects the document element within the current document, provided its name is <price-list>. (*Current document* here and in the other examples means the tree containing the context node, assuming that the tree is rooted at a document node)
/*	Selects the document element within the current document, whatever its name
/child::node()	Selects all nodes that are immediate children of the document root, that is, the document element plus any comments or processing instructions that come before or after the document element. (However, note that the <?xml version="1.0"?> at the start of a document is *not* a processing instruction; in fact it is not a node at all, and is not accessible using XPath)
/*/xsl:*	Selects all element nodes with names in the namespace associated with the «xsl:» namespace prefix that are immediate children of the document element. (If applied to an XSLT stylesheet, this would select all the top-level XSLT declarations)
//figure	This abbreviated absolute path expression selects all the <figure> elements in the current document

Relative Paths

A relative path expression is used to select nodes relative to the context node, using one or more steps. We have already seen the syntax:

Expression	Syntax
RelativePathExpr	StepExpr ((«/» | «//») StepExpr)*
StepExpr	AxisStep | FilterExpr

Effect

The syntax rule above tells you that a RelativePathExpr consists of one or more steps separated by the path operator «/» or the shorthand path operator «//». We'll look at the «//» operator later, on page 228, and concentrate for now on «/».

In XPath 2.0, many of the syntactic restrictions on path expressions were removed. The «/» symbol is now a genuine binary operator, that takes arbitrary expressions as its operands. There is a restriction that the expressions must evaluate to sequences of nodes, but that's enforced in the same way that any operator restricts the types of its operands—through the type rules, not by restricting the language syntax.

So although we tend to think of a path expression as a sequence of steps, for example, «A/B/C/D», we can actually understand the meaning of path expressions simply by defining the meaning of the operator «/», just as we can understand expressions like «A+B-C+D» by defining the meaning of the operators «+» and «-». As with other operators, the expression «A/B/C/D» can be evaluated from left to right, as «((A/B)/C)/D», and in fact it is entirely legitimate to use parentheses in this way. In the vast majority of cases the «/» operator is associative, which means that «(A/B)/C» gives you the same answer as «A/(B/C)», and this explains why you don't often see parentheses being used in this way. However, there are a few exceptional cases where «/» is not associative, as we shall see.

So what exactly does the «/» operator do?

I will explain this in terms of an expression «E1/E2», where E1 and E2 are arbitrary expressions but constrained by the type rules to return sequences of nodes. This expression is evaluated as follows:

- ❑ E1 is evaluated to produce a sequence of nodes; let's call this S1.

- ❑ For each node in S1, the expression E2 is evaluated. The context for evaluating E2 has this node from S1 as the context node. It also has the position of this node in the sequence S1 as the context position, and the number of nodes in S1 as the context size, but in practice it's very rare to write an expression on the right-hand side of «/» that depends on the context position or size.

- ❑ Each time E2 is evaluated, it produces a sequence of nodes (if it doesn't, a type error is reported). All the nodes produced when E2 has been evaluated once for every node in S1 are bundled together into a single sequence. Duplicate nodes are then removed, and the remaining nodes are sorted into document order.

- ❑ The resulting sequence of nodes forms the result of the path expression «E1/E2».

The most common kind of expression to use as an operand of «/» is a *step*. Let's look at a simple example where both operands are steps: the expression «child::book/attribute::isbn». (I'm deliberately using the verbose syntax here, the abbreviated form is «book/@isbn».) So E1 in this example is the expression «child::book», which selects all the elements that are children of the context node and have the name «book». It's possible that the context node doesn't have any <book> children, of course, in which case this will give you an empty sequence, and when that happens, the result of «E1/E2» is also an empty sequence. But let's suppose it selects three books. For each one of these <book> elements, the E2 expression (in our case «attribute::isbn») is evaluated, with that <book> as the context node. The step expression «attribute::isbn» selects the attribute node whose name is isbn and whose parent node is the context node. So assuming that each <book> element actually has an isbn attribute, the final result contains three attribute nodes, one for each of the three books. In this case there won't be any duplicate nodes to get rid of, and the final result will be the sequence of three attribute nodes in document order.

It's worth noting that although «/» is now a regular operator in the sense that there are no syntactic restrictions on its operands, it does have some slightly unusual properties. Most operators work by evaluating both their operands, and then combining the results in some way. This operator evaluates the expression on the right repeatedly. Operators and functions that work like this are often called higher-order operators, and if you've used functional programming languages before, you will recognize «/» as behaving like a *map* or *apply* operator in such languages; it maps the sequence that's the result of the first expression by applying the second expression to each item in that sequence.

Another interesting thing about the «/» operator is that there's very little point using an expression on the right-hand side if its result doesn't depend in some way on the context node. However, there is no rule that enforces this as a constraint. You can write an expression such as «$N/$M» if you like, so long as both the variables $N and $M are sequences of nodes. If you follow through the rules given above, you'll see that the result contains all the nodes in $M, in document order, except in the case where $N is empty, in which case the final result is empty. During the design stage, some people in the working group wanted to disallow such expressions. But on the whole, it's not a good principle in language design to disallow things just because they don't seem useful. On that basis, you would stop people writing «$X+0», or «$X*1».

Examples of Relative Paths

Expression	Description
ancestor::CHAPTER	This is a RelativePathExpr consisting of a single Step. It selects the ancestors of the context node that are elements with the name <CHAPTER>
TITLE	This is a RelativePathExpr consisting of a single Step: this time the Step is an AbbreviatedStep. It selects the children of the context node that are elements with the name <TITLE>
descendant::PARA/@style	This is a RelativePathExpr consisting of two Steps. The first Step selects the descendants of the context node that are <PARA> elements; the second Step is an AbbreviatedStep that selects the style attributes of these elements

Continues

Expression	Description
section[1]/clause[3]	This is a RelativePathExpr consisting of two Steps, each of which includes a positional predicate. The first Step selects the first <section> element that is a child of the context node, the second Step selects the third <clause> element that is a child of the selected <section>
chapter/section/para/sentence	This RelativePathExpr selects every <sentence> element that is a child of a <para> element that is a child of a <section> element that is a child of a <chapter> element that is a child of the context node
doc('a.xml')/id('Z123')	This example illustrates that the operands of the «/» operator do not have to be AxisStep expressions. This example selects the document with a particular relative URI, and using the resulting document node as the context node, then selects the element with a particular ID value
book/(chapter|appendix)	This is another example that uses an operand that is not an AxisStep. For each selected <book> element, it evaluates the expression «(chapter|appendix)», which selects all the child <chapter> and <appendix> elements of the book, in document order

Associativity of the «/» Operator

I mentioned that in the vast majority of cases the «/» operator is associative, which means that «(A/B)/C» returns the same result as «A/(B/C)». For those with insatiable curiosity, there are only two examples that I know of where this is not the case:

❑   The expression is not associative if one of the steps creates new nodes. There is no expression in XPath itself that creates new nodes, but an XPath expression can contain a function call to a function written say in XSLT or XQuery that creates such nodes. And in XQuery, steps in a path expression can construct nodes directly, for example, you can write «<p q="2"/>/@q». If we use the XQuery syntax for illustration, we can see that «$A/../<B/>» eliminates duplicate nodes in the result of «$A/..», and therefore the number of <B> elements in the result is equal to the number of distinct nodes that are parents of nodes in $A. But the expression «$A/(../<B/>)» creates one <B/> element for every node in $A that has a parent. So the number of <B> elements returned in the two cases is different.

❑   The expression is not associative if one of the steps uses the position() or last() functions. For example, consider the expression «A/remove($S, position())». The remove() function, described in Chapter 10, returns the sequence of items supplied in its first argument, except for the item whose position is given in the second argument. This means that if A contains exactly one node, then the result is all the nodes in $S except the first. But if A contains two nodes, then the result is the union of «remove($S, 1)» and «remove($S, 2)», which (think about it carefully) contains all the nodes in $S. Now if we extend this to the expression «A/B/remove($S, position())» we can see that the result should contain all the nodes in

$S except when «A/B» contains exactly one node, because the expression should be evaluated as «(A/B)/remove($S, position())». But if it were written the other way, as «A/(B/remove($S, position))», the first node in $S would be dropped only if every A has exactly one B child.

These examples are fairly pathological, but you might like to try them out on your chosen XPath processor to see how well it handles them (I can tell you that at the time of writing, Saxon sometimes gets these wrong). There may well be much simpler path expressions in which «/» is not associative, but I haven't discovered them yet!

Document Order and Duplicates

There are three kinds of expression in XPath 2.0 whose result is always guaranteed to be a sequence of nodes in document order, with no duplicates. They are all covered in this chapter. Specifically, they are:

❑ Any expression using the unary or binary path operator «/»

❑ Any axis step (even an axis step like «preceding-sibling::*» that uses a reverse axis delivers its results in forwards document order)

❑ Any expression using one of the binary operators «union», «intersect», and «except».

The elimination of duplicates is always based on node identity, not value.

Many simple path expressions would always return results in document order anyway, and would never select duplicates. In these cases, the system doesn't have to do any extra work to satisfy this rule. For example, any path expression that does downward selection using the child axis will naturally retrieve the nodes in document order. But it's easy to come up with path expressions that don't have this property, for example, «following-sibling::*/..» selects the parents of all the following siblings; and of course they all have the same parent, so after eliminating duplicates this expression returns at most a single node.

Generally, the automatic sort into document order is a choice that avoids surprises, especially when processing loosely structured text: if an expression selects a number of text nodes in a document, then document order is the order that is most likely to retain the meaning. The only situation that can sometimes be confusing is when you write an expression such as «$sorted-employees/name» where the sequence in $sorted-employees has been carefully sorted into some logical order (for example, sorting employees by length of service). You can't do this kind of sorting in XPath alone, but it's easily done in XSLT or XQuery. In this situation, the «/» operator destroys the ordering, and gives you the names of the employees in document order. The solution in this case is to use a «for» expression instead of a path expression, as described in Chapter 8.

There is no specific function in XPath to take an existing sequence and reorder it in document order, but you can achieve this easily by writing the dummy path expression «$seq/.», or if you prefer, by taking the union with the empty sequence, «$seq|()».

Steps

This section discusses the expressions called steps. Steps are often used as operands of the «/» operator in a path expression, which is how they got their name (a path consists of many steps). But in fact, a step is an expression in its own right, and it can be used on its own without any need for a «/» operator. We've also seen that XPath 2.0 allows the operands of «/» to be any kind of expression, they are no longer constrained to be steps. So the «/» operator and steps have become quite decoupled in the semantics of the language. However, they are so often used together that it makes sense to retain the term path expression to describe any expression that uses either a «/» operator or a step or both.

A step selects a set of nodes that are related in some way to the context node: for example, the children, the parent, or the following siblings of the context node. The relationship in question is called an axis. An axis is essentially a one-to-many relationship between nodes. If you prefer, you can think of it as a function which takes a single node as input, and produces a sequence of related nodes (for example, the children, the attributes, or the ancestors of that node) as output. Because axes are used so frequently and could be said to be the core feature of the XPath language, we don't use the standard function call syntax, but the underlying theory can be expressed in purely functional terms.

A step has three parts: the axis, the node test, and the predicates. The axis and the predicates can be defaulted, but the node test is always present. The three parts of a step are discussed in more detail in the sections that follow: axes on page 215, node tests on page 220, and predicates on page 230. In this section, we'll start with an overview.

A step is based on a particular axis, and it can also choose to filter the nodes that are present on the axis. There are two kinds of filter that can be used, alone or in combination:

❑ A node test allows nodes to be selected according to the kind of node, the name and namespace of the node, and (as we shall see in Chapter 9) the type annotation of the node, as determined by schema validation.

❑ The step can also include general-purpose predicates, which can specify an arbitrary boolean condition that a node must satisfy, or can select nodes at particular positions in the sequence returned by the axis.

The next section gives the syntax of steps.

Syntax of Steps

Expression	Syntax
AxisStep	(ForwardStep | ReverseStep) PredicateList
PredicateList	Predicate *
Predicate	«[» Expr «]»
ForwardStep	(ForwardAxis NodeTest) | AbbrevForwardStep
ReverseStep	(ReverseAxis NodeTest) | AbbrevReverseStep

Expression	Syntax
ForwardAxis	«child ::» | «descendant ::» | «attribute ::» | «self ::» | «descendant-or-self ::» | «following-sibling ::» | «following ::» | «namespace ::»
ReverseAxis	«parent ::» | «ancestor ::» | «preceding-sibling ::» | «preceding ::» | «ancestor-or-self ::» |

The split between forward and reverse axes in this grammar is cosmetic. It's presented this way because there are semantic distinctions in the way predicates are evaluated in the two cases, and it's nice when semantic distinctions can be related clearly to syntactic distinctions.

The abbreviations for steps will be covered later (see page 226). For the moment, we'll concentrate on the unabbreviated syntax in which the axis names are spelt out in full.

Effect

A step can be used to follow any axis and to find any kind of node.

The step itself is defined in terms of a simpler concept, the axis. Each axis returns a set of nodes relative to a specific origin node, for example, its previous siblings or its ancestors. The step returns a subset of the nodes on this axis, selected by the kind of node, the name of the node, the schema-defined type of the node, and the predicate expressions.

The NodeTest supplies any restrictions on the node kind, name, and type of the selected nodes, while the predicate expressions provide arbitrary boolean conditions that the nodes must satisfy, or positional filters that constrain their relative position.

The result of a step is always a sequence of nodes (possibly an empty sequence) with no duplicates, in document order. This is true even if the axis is one of the reverse axes, such as preceding-sibling, that selects nodes that are before the context node in document order.

For example, the step «ancestor::node()», given any starting node, finds all the ancestors of that node. When the step is used in a path expression such as «$n/ancestor::node()», it returns a sequence containing all the ancestors of all the nodes in $n. The sequence will be in document order, which means that the outermost ancestor (the root of the tree) will appear first in the result.

To understand the meaning of positional predicates in the step it is often useful to think of an axis as retrieving nodes in a particular order, but the formal definition doesn't require this. Instead these predicates are defined in terms of a number assigned to each node. For a forward axis (as shown in the syntax above), the nodes are numbered to show their relative position in document order, while for a reverse axis, they are numbered in reverse document order. The effect of positional predicates (such as «booklist/book[3]») is to select those nodes whose number matches the value of the predicate. This means that if the axis is a forward axis, the positional predicate «[3]» will return the node that is third in document order; if it is a reverse axis, the same predicate will return the node that is third in reverse document order.

So the evaluation of the step function, for a given context node, proceeds as follows:

1. All the nodes on the selected axis are found, starting at the context node.

2. Those that satisfy the node test (that is, those of the required node kind, name, and type) are selected.

3. The remaining nodes are numbered from 1 to n in document order if the axis is a forward axis, or in reverse document order if it is a reverse axis.

4. The first (leftmost) predicate is applied to each node in turn. When evaluating the predicate, the context node (that is, the result of the «.» expression) is that node, the context position (the result of the position() function) is the number assigned to the node in stage 3, and the context size (the result of the last() function) is the largest number allocated in stage 3. A numeric predicate such as «[2]» or «[last()-1]» is interpreted as a shorthand for «[position()=2]» or «[position()=last()-1]», respectively. The node is selected if the predicate is true, and is discarded if the predicate is false.

5. Stages 3 and 4 are repeated for any further predicates.

Examples of Steps

Expression	Description
child::title	Selects child elements of the context node named <title>
title	Short form of «child::title»
attribute::title	Selects attributes of the context node named title
@title	Short form of «attribute::title»
ancestor::xyz:*	Selects ancestor elements of the context node whose names are in the namespace with prefix «xyz»
*[@width]	Selects all child elements of the context node that have a width attribute
text()[starts-with(.,'The')]	Selects every text node that is a child of the context node and whose text content starts with the characters «The»
*[@code][position()<10]	Selects the first nine child elements of the context node that have a code attribute
*[position()<10][@code]	Selects from the first nine child elements of the context node those that have a code attribute

Expression	Description
`self::*[not(@code = preceding-sibling::* /@code)]`	Selects the current element node provided that it does not have a code attribute with the same value as the code attribute of any preceding sibling element
`namespace::*`	Selects all the namespace nodes that are in scope for the context node. If the context node is not an element, the result will be empty
`self::item`	Selects the context node if it is an `<item>` element, or an empty sequence otherwise. This is usually used in a predicate, for example «`*[not(self::item)]`» selects all the children of the context node except those that are `<item>` elements. This relies on the rules for *effective boolean value*, whereby an empty sequence is treated as false
`comment()`	Selects all comment nodes that are children of the context node
`@comment()`	Short for «`attribute::comment()`», this selects all comment nodes on the attribute axis. The attribute axis can only contain attribute nodes, so this will always return an empty sequence; nevertheless it is a legal step

Axes

An *axis* is a path through the document tree, starting at a particular node (which I'll call the origin) and following a particular relationship between nodes. There are 13 axes defined in XPath, as follows:

ancestor
ancestor-or-self
attribute
child
descendant
descendant-or-self
following
following-sibling
namespace
parent
preceding
preceding-sibling
self

This section explains the meaning of each of the axes, first with a textual definition, and then with a diagram.

Axis	Description
`ancestor`	Selects all the nodes that are ancestors of the starting node. The first node on the axis is the parent of the origin node, the second is its grandparent, and so on; the last node on the axis is the root of the tree

Continues

Axis	Description
ancestor-or-self	Selects the same nodes as the ancestor axis, but starting with the origin node rather than with its parent
attribute	If the origin node is an element, this axis selects all its attribute nodes, in some arbitrary order. Otherwise, it selects nothing
child	Selects all the children of the origin node, in document order. For any node except a document node or element node, this selects nothing. Note that the children of an element node do not include its attributes or namespace nodes, only the text nodes, element nodes, processing instructions and comments that make up its content
descendant	Selects all the children of the origin node, and their children, and so on recursively. The resulting nodes are in document order. If the origin is an element, this effectively means that the descendant axis contains all the text nodes, element nodes, comments and processing instructions that appear in the original source document between that element's start and end tags, in their original sequence
descendant-or-self	This is the same as the descendant axis, except that the first node selected is the origin node itself
following	This selects all the nodes that appear after the origin node in document order, excluding the descendants of the origin node. If the origin is an element node, for example, this effectively means that it contains all the text nodes, element nodes, comments and processing instructions in the document that start after the end tag of the origin element. The following axis will never contain attribute or namespace nodes
following-sibling	This selects all the nodes that follow the origin node in document order, and that are children of the same parent node. If the origin is a document node, an attribute node, or a namespace node, then the following-sibling axis will always be empty
namespace	If the origin node is an element, this axis selects all the namespace nodes that are in scope for that element; otherwise it is empty. The order of the namespace nodes is undefined. The namespace nodes correspond to namespace declarations (xmlns="x" or xmlns:y="z") on the element itself or on one of its ancestor elements, but excluding any namespace declaration that cannot be used on this element because it is masked by another declaration of the same namespace prefix. For more information about namespace nodes see Chapter 2
parent	This axis selects a single node, the parent of the origin node. If the origin node is a document node, or any other node that happens to be the root of a tree, then the parent axis is empty

Axis	Description
preceding	This selects all the nodes that appear before the origin node, excluding the ancestors of the origin node. If the origin is an element node, this effectively means that it contains all the text nodes, element nodes, comments and processing instructions in the document that finish before the start tag of the origin element. The preceding axis will never contain attribute or namespace nodes
preceding-sibling	This selects all the nodes that precede the origin node, and that are children of the same parent node. If the origin is a document node, an attribute node, or a namespace node, then the preceding-sibling axis will always be empty
self	This selects a single node, the origin node itself. This axis will never be empty

The various axes can also be shown diagrammatically. In each case in the table below the diagram shows the origin node in dark shading, while the nodes on the axis are numbered in the sequence they appear on the axis. The diagram does not show attribute and namespace nodes, and the attribute and namespace axes are therefore excluded from the table.

Axis	Diagram
ancestor	
ancestor-or-self	

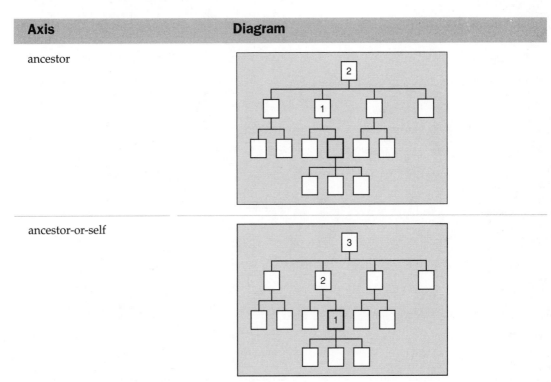

Continues

Axis	Diagram
child	
descendant	
descendant-or-self	
following	

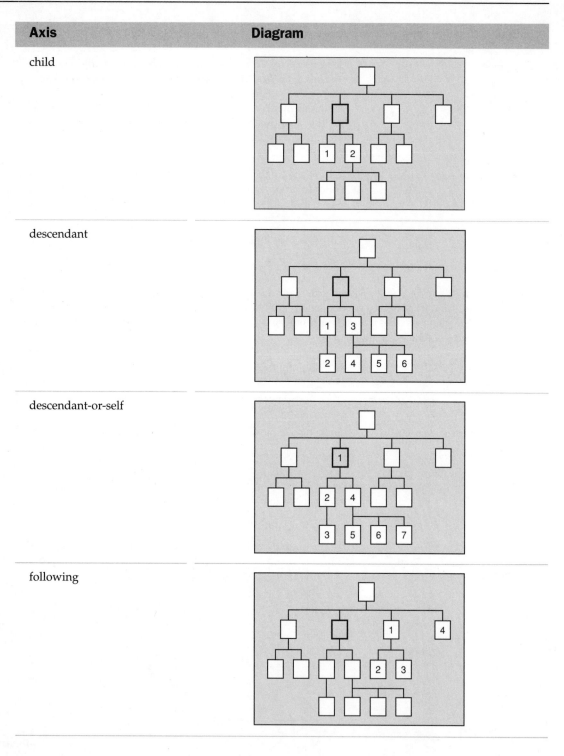

Axis	Diagram
following-sibling	
parent	
preceding	
preceding-sibling	

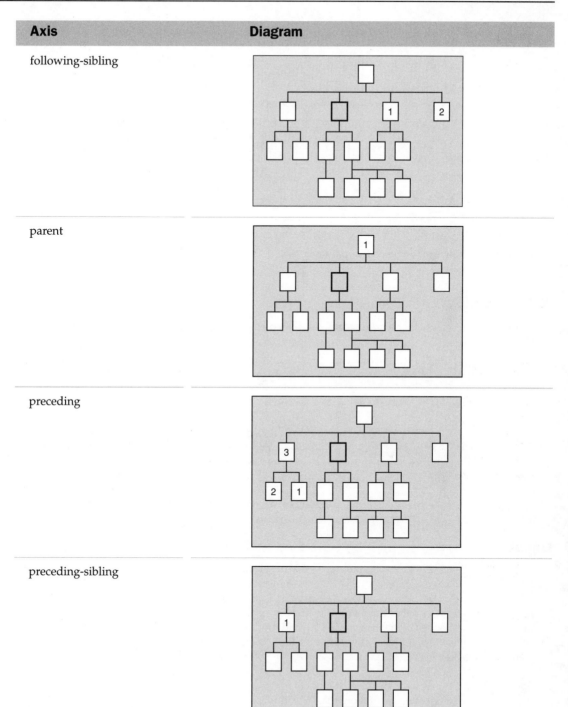

Continues

Axis	Diagram
self	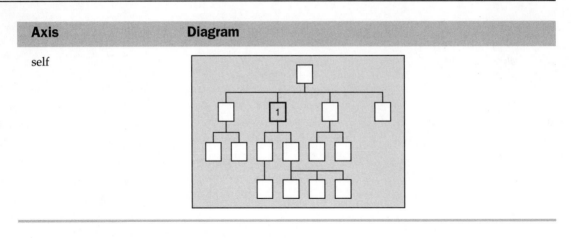

For details of how axes are used in a path expression, and examples, see Step on page 211.

Node Tests

A NodeTest tests whether a node satisfies specified constraints on the type of node or the name of the node.

Expression	Syntax
NodeTest	NameTest | KindTest

A NodeTest is either a NameTest or a KindTest. A NameTest selects nodes by name, while a KindTest allows selection based on the kind of node and also (in the case of elements and attributes) its schema-defined type.

Specifying a NameTest implicitly causes selection of a particular kind of node: attributes for the attribute axis, namespaces for the namespace axis, and elements in all other cases.

Usage

A NodeTest is used in an AxisStep to specify the name and/or kind of the nodes to be selected by the Step.

In general you specify either the name of the nodes, or their kind. If you specify a NameTest, this implicitly selects nodes of the principal node kind for the axis used in the Step. For the attribute axis, this selects attribute nodes; for the namespace axis, it selects namespace nodes, and for all other axes, it selects element nodes.

Specifying node() as the KindTest selects all nodes on the axis. You must specify node() if you want the AxisStep to select nodes of more than one kind.

Specifying processing-instruction() or comment() or text() as the KindTest selects nodes of the specified type. It doesn't make sense to specify any of these on the attribute or namespace axes, because they can't occur there. These nodes are unnamed, except for processing instructions, which is why there is an option in this single case to specify both the node kind and the node name required.

Examples of Node Tests

Expression	Description
TITLE	This NameTest selects all <TITLE> elements, unless it is used with the attribute axis (in the form «attribute::TITLE» or «@TITLE»), when it selects the TITLE attribute, or with the namespace axis (as «namespace::TITLE»), when it selects the namespace node whose prefix is TITLE
news:article	This NameTest selects all nodes with local name «article» within the «news» namespace. These may be attribute nodes or element nodes, depending on the axis. There must be an enclosing element in the stylesheet that declares the «news» prefix, by having an attribute of the form «xmlns:news="urn:newsml:iptc.org:20001006: NewsMLv1.0:1"». The node in the source document must have a name that uses this namespace URI, but it does not need to use the same prefix
MathML:*	This NameTest selects all nodes whose names are in the MathML namespace. These may be attribute nodes or element nodes, depending on the axis. There must be an enclosing element in the stylesheet that declares this prefix, by having an attribute of the form «xmlns:MathML="http://www.w3.org/1998 /Math/MathML"»
*	This NameTest selects all elements, unless it is used with the attribute axis (in the form «attribute::*» or «@*») when it selects all attributes, or with the namespace axis (as «namespace::*»), when it selects all namespaces
text()	This NodeTest selects all text nodes on the relevant axis
processing-instruction()	This NodeTest selects all processing instructions on the relevant axis. Note that the XML declaration at the start of the document is *not* a processing instruction, even though it looks like one
processing-instruction ('ckpt')	This NodeTest selects all processing instructions with the name (or PITarget as the XML specification calls it) «ckpt»: for example the processing instruction <?ckpt frequency=daily?>
node()	This NodeTest selects all nodes on the relevant axis

Name Tests

As we have seen, a NodeTest is either a NameTest or a KindTest. This section describes NameTests. A NameTest is either a name, or a generic name specified using wild cards.

Syntax

Expression	Syntax
NameTest	QName | Wildcard
Wildcard	«*» | NCName«:*» | «*:»NCName

Note that a `NameTest` cannot contain embedded whitespace.

Usage

In general, a `NameTest` will match some names and will not match others.

The `NameTest` «*» matches any name. (But when used as an expression on its own, «*» is short for «child::*», which selects all child elements of the context node. The fact that the result is restricted to element nodes only is because «*», when used in an `AxisStep`, selects only nodes of the principal node kind for the axis, and for all axes except the attribute and namespace axes, the principal node kind is element nodes.)

> **A surprising effect of this rule is that in XSLT you can't write:**
>
> ```
> <xsl:copy-of select="@*[not(self::title)]"/>
> ```
>
> **to copy all attributes of an element except the title attribute. Why? Because the principal node kind for the self axis is element nodes, so if the context node is an attribute named title, «self::title» won't select it. Instead, write:**
>
> ```
> <xsl:copy-of select="@* except @title"/>
> ```
>
> **The «except» operator is described in the section** *Combining Sets of Nodes*, **on page 234.**

The `NameTest` «xyz:*» matches any name whose namespace is the one currently bound to the namespace prefix «xyz». It is not necessary that the name being tested should use the same prefix, only that the prefix should refer to the same namespace URI.

A `NameTest` of the form «*:code» matches any node whose local-name is code, regardless of its namespace (it will match names in any namespace, as well as names that are in no namespace).

The `NameTest` «xyz:code» matches any name whose namespace is the one currently bound to the namespace prefix «xyz», and whose local part is «code». It is not necessary that the name being tested should use the same prefix, only that the prefix should refer to the same namespace URI.

The interpretation of a NameTest such as «code» (with no namespace prefix) depends on the context.

❑ If it is used with any axis other than the attribute or namespace axes, then it selects elements whose name is in the namespace identified in the XPath context (see Chapter 4) as the default namespace for elements. (Note that in XSLT, this is established using the xpath-default-namespace attribute, typically on the <xsl:stylesheet> element. It is not established by writing a default namespace declaration of the form «xmlns="some.uri"».)

❑ If it is used with the attribute or namespace axis, then it selects nodes whose namespace URI is null.

> If your source document uses a default namespace declaration such as «xmlns=
> "some.uri"», then a <code> element in the source document will not be selected
> by an XPath expression such as «//code», even if the stylesheet contains the same
> namespace declaration «xmlns="some.uri"». This is because in the XPath
> expression, the default namespace is ignored. You will either need to specify an
> explicit namespace declaration such as «xmlns:x="some.uri"» and refer to the
> element as «//x:item», or to declare an xpath-default-namespace in the
> stylesheet.

Note that if a default namespace for elements has been set up, then the only way to select those elements whose namespace URI is null is to include a predicate that tests the result of the namespace-uri() function.

Examples of Name Tests

Expression	Description
*	Matches any name. If «*» is used on its own, it represents the step «child::*», which selects all child elements of the context node, regardless of their name
xt:*	Matches any name in the namespace bound to the prefix «xt». If «xt:*» is used on its own, it represents the step «child::xt:*», which selects all child elements of the context node that are in the namespace bound to the prefix «xt»
title	Matches a node whose local name is name «title» and whose namespace URI is null, unless a default namespace for elements has been established in the context (and then, only when the axis is not the attribute or namespace axis)
wrox:title	Matches the name that has local part «title» and whose namespace is the namespace currently bound to the prefix «wrox»
*:title	Matches any name whose local part is «title», whether or not it is in a namespace

Kind Tests

As we have seen, a NodeTest is either a NameTest or a KindTest. NameTests were described in the previous section; this section describes KindTests. A KindTest represents a constraint on the kind of nodes that are selected by an AxisStep.

Expression	Syntax
KindTest	DocumentTest | ElementTest | AttributeTest | PITest | CommentTest | TextTest | AnyKindTest
PITest	«processing-instruction (» (NCName | StringLiteral)? «)»
DocumentTest	«document-node (» ElementTest? «)»
CommentTest	«comment (» «)»
TextTest	«text (» «)»
AnyKindTest	«node (» «)»

The constructs ElementTest and AttributeTest are used primarily to test the schema-defined type of a node. These constructs are explained together with other type-related constructs on page 281 in Chapter 9.

Note that the names «comment», «text», and so on cannot be used as function names, but apart from this, they are not reserved words. It is quite possible to have elements or attributes called «text» or «node» in your source XML document, and therefore you can use «text» or «node» as ordinary names in XPath. This is why the names are flagged in a KindTest by the following parentheses, for example, «text()». The syntax rules are written so that the keyword and the following left parenthesis are treated as a compound symbol by the XPath parser, which in effect means that the parser does a look-ahead for the «(» before deciding whether the keyword such as «text» is to be interpreted as a NameTest or as a KindTest.

There are three ways you can select processing instructions. The simple test is «processing-instruction()», which selects any processing instruction node regardless of its name. If you want to select processing instructions named «xml-stylesheet», say, then you can write either «processing-instruction("xml-stylesheet")» or «processing-instruction(xml-stylesheet)». The two are equivalent: the syntax with quotes is retained for compatibility with

XPath 1.0, while the syntax without quotes is introduced for symmetry with the «element(...)» and «attribute(...)» tests described in Chapter 9.

Usage

A KindTest can be used within an AxisStep to restrict the Step to return nodes of a particular kind. The keywords «comment», «text», and «processing-instruction» are self-explanatory: they restrict the selection to nodes of that particular kind. The keyword «node» selects nodes of any type, and is useful because a Step has to include some kind of NodeTest, so if you want all the nodes on the axis, you can specify node(). For example, if you want all child nodes, specify «child::node() ». Remember that although «node()» as a NodeTest selects any kind of node, «node()» as a Step means «child::node()» and therefore selects only children of the context node. If you want to select attributes as well, write «@*|node()».

If you want to select all elements, you can use the KindTest element(), and if you want to select all attributes, you can use attribute(). However, it is more usual in these cases simply to use the NodeTest «*». Specifying «*» selects the nodes of the principal node kind for the selected axis, which will always be elements in the case of an axis that can contain elements, and attributes in the case of an axis that can contain attributes. The KindTests element() and attribute() are generally used with parameters that specify the schema-defined type of the required elements or attributes, as described in Chapter 9.

Similarly, the KindTest document-node() can be used without parameters to select all document nodes. But you won't see this used much in practice, because the document node can be selected using the simpler syntax «/», discussed earlier in this chapter on page 205. With parameters, the document-node() KindTest can be used to test for the document node containing an element of a particular schema-defined type—again, this is described in Chapter 9.

There is no specific way of selecting namespace nodes. But all the nodes on the namespace axis are namespace nodes, so the expressions «namespace::*» and «namespace::node()» both work fine, provided that your implementation supports use of the namespace axis.

Examples of Kind Tests

These examples show some different KindTests, used in the context of a containing path expression.

Expression	Description
parent::node()	Selects the parent of the context node, whether this is an element node or the root node. This differs from «parent::*», which selects the parent node only if it is an element. The expression «parent::node()» is usually abbreviated to «..»
//comment()	Selects all comment nodes in the document
child::text()	Selects all text node children of the context node. This is usually abbreviated to «text()»
@comment()	A strange but legal way of getting an empty node-set: it looks for all comment nodes on the attribute axis, and of course finds none

Abbreviations

Until now we have been looking at the full syntax for path expressions, though some of the examples actually used abbreviations. This section describes the various abbreviations that make path expressions easier to write. The abbreviations that are available are:

❑   The ability to omit the axis name (and the following «::») when using the child axis (or, in one specific case, when using the attribute axis)

❑   The use of «@» as an abbreviation for the attribute axis

❑   The ability to select the parent of a node using the shortcut «..»

❑   The use of the operator «//» to select descendant nodes.

In XPath 1.0, the expression «.» was considered to be an abbreviation for the step «self::node()». In XPath 2.0 this is no longer the case, because «.» can also be used when the context item is an atomic value rather than a node. For this reason, «.» is now classified as a primary expression in its own right, and is covered with the other kinds of primary expression in Chapter 5.

Defaulting the Axis Name in a Step

A full step is written in the form:

```
axis-name «::» NodeTest Predicates?
```

Since the most common axis is the child axis, it is possible to omit the «child::» part and write the step in the abbreviated form:

```
NodeTest Predicates?
```

For example, the path expression «employee/name/first-name» consists of three steps, each of which has been abbreviated in this way. It is short for «child::employee/child::name/child::first-name».

Most people writing XPath expressions use this abbreviation all the time without really thinking about it. In fact, it's rare to see «child::» spelled out explicitly. But I do sometimes like to write the full form to alert the reader to what's going on. For example, the expression «record[*]» selects all <record> elements that have one or more child elements. I sometimes write this as «record[child::*]» so that anyone reading the code can see more clearly what it means. The full syntax for the expression, of course, is «child::record[child::*]», and you could spell it out even more explicitly by writing «child::record[exists(child::*)]». (The exists() function is in Chapter 10).

There's one exception to the general rule that if you don't specify an axis, you get the child axis. This is when you use a NodeTest of the form «attribute(...)» or «schema-attribute(...)». This kind of NodeTest is used when testing the schema-defined type of an attribute node; it is described in detail in Chapter 9. Because the NodeTest makes it clear that you are looking for attributes rather than child elements, the system in this case chooses the attribute axis as the default. This avoids you having to write «attribute::attribute(*)» or «@attribute(X)», both of which read rather oddly, though they are both legal and logical.

The «@» Abbreviation

When the «@» sign appears in front of a NodeTest, it indicates that you are selecting nodes using the attribute axis. It is short for «attribute::».

What this means in practice is that in a path expression «A/@B», B is referring to an attribute of A, while in the path expression «A/B», B is referring to a child element of A.

Again, this abbreviation is ubiquitous among XPath developers, and it's rare to see «attribute::» written out in full. In fact, the «@» in front of an attribute name has become so familiar that people often think of it as being almost part of the name. I'm probably not the only one who has found myself typing <person @id="B123"> in an XML document (which, of course, will be thrown out by an XML parser).

> Take care when using the «self::» axis. You can write «self::title» to test whether the context node is a <title> element, but you can't write «self::@title» to test whether it is a title attribute. This is because «@» is short for «attribute::», and «self::attribute::title» doesn't make sense: you can either look on the self axis, or the attribute axis, but not both at once.

Examples

Expression	Description
@category	The full form of the expression would be «attribute::category»
title	The full form of the expression would be «child::title»

The «..» Abbreviation

The construct «..» appearing as an abbreviated step is short for «parent::node()». As such, it selects the parent of the context node. If the context node has no parent (that is, if it is the root of a tree), then it selects an empty sequence.

This notation is found most commonly at the start of a relative path expression. For example «../@name» selects the name attribute of the parent of the context node. It is possible to use «..» anywhere in a path expression, though the need rarely arises. For example, «//title/..» selects all elements in the document that have a child element called <title>. The same result could be achieved, perhaps more naturally, by writing «//*[title]».

Note that every node except a root node has a parent.

This means that «/..» is always an empty sequence. In XPath 1.0, there was no direct way of representing an empty sequence, and so you may see this notation used when an empty sequence is needed, perhaps as the default value of a parameter in an XSLT template rule. In XPath 2.0 it's more natural to write this as

«()». Indeed, an XPath 2.0 processor that implements the static typing feature (see Chapter 3) may well give you an error if you write «/..», kindly pointing out to you that it will never select anything.

Writing «not(..)» is a simple way of testing whether the context node is the root.

As explained in Chapter 2, the element containing an attribute is considered to be the parent of the attribute, even though the attribute is not a child of the element. So you can select all elements containing an attribute named ID with an expression such as «//@ID/..» (though «//*[@ID]» achieves the same thing and might be more efficient). Unlike biological relationships, in XPath the "parent" and "child" relationships are not the inverse of each other. The same applies to namespace nodes.

In XPath 1.0 the expression «..» could not be followed by a predicate: you could not write <xsl:if test="..[@color='black']">. This was probably an oversight by the language designers, and the restriction has been lifted in XPath 2.0. As you would expect, this expression tests whether the parent element node has a color attribute whose value is «black».

Examples in Context

Expression	Effect
exists(..)	Tests whether the context node has a parent (in other words, whether it is the root of a tree)
../@name	Selects the name attribute of the parent of the context node

The «//» Abbreviation

Colloquially, «//» in a path expression means "find all descendants". More formally, whether it appears at the start of a path expression or as a binary operator, it is equivalent to writing «/descendant-or-self::node()/».

The expression «//A» is often used to select all <A> elements in the document.

How does this work? The expression «//A» means «/descendant-or-self::node()/ child::A», which selects all <A> elements whose parent is either the document node or a descendant of the document node, looking as always within the tree that contains the context node. Since every element has a parent that meets these criteria, it selects all <A> elements. Similarly, «//@B» means «/descendant-or-self::node()/attribute::B», which selects all B attributes in the current document.

The significance of the abbreviation becomes apparent when predicates are involved. The expression «//para[1]» expands to «/descendant-or-self::node()/child::para[1]», which selects every <para> element that is the first child of its parent. If you only want the first <para> element in the entire document, you can get this by writing «(//para)[1]».

The «//» abbreviation can also be used as an operator anywhere that «/» can appear. Another useful form of expression is «.//A», which selects all <A> elements that are descendants of the context node. Again, the official meaning is «./descendant-or-self::node()/child::A». The «./» in this expanded expression is redundant: people often write path expressions such as «./A/B», but the

«./» is pure noise. At any rate, it's pure noise when the expression after the «./» is an AxisStep (in other cases, it may trigger reordering and deduplication, in the same way as adding «/.»). But with «//», the leading «.» becomes necessary to indicate that you want to start the selection at the context node, not at the root.

Expressions using «//» can be expensive to evaluate, because the XPath processor will often have to search the whole document to find the selected nodes. If you can specify a more restricted search it is generally a good idea to do so—for example, if you know that all the <book> elements are children of the document element, then specifying «/*/book» will generally be much more efficient than writing «//book». Of course, actual performance characteristics of different products may vary.

Examples in Context

Expression	Description
//figure	Selects all <figure> elements in the document
//book[@category= 'fiction']	Selects all <book> elements in the document that have a category attribute with the value « fiction»
//*/*	Selects all element nodes that have an element as a parent, in other words all elements except those that are immediate children of the root node. Here «*» is a NameTest that matches any element
//book/title	Selects all <title> elements that have a <book> element as their parent
chapter//footnote	Selects all <footnote> elements that are descendants of a <chapter> element that itself is a child of the context node
.//footnote	Selects all <footnote> elements that are descendants of the context node
doc('lookup.xml') //entry	Selects all <entry> elements within the document identified by the relative URI lookup.xml. The doc() function is described in Chapter 10, page 329
$winners//*/@name	Selects the name attribute of all elements that are descendants of a node that belongs to the node-set identified by the variable $winners
.//..	This strange but perfectly legal expression combines «//» which finds the descendants of a node, and «..» which finds its parent. The effect is to find all nodes that are the parent of a descendant of the context node, plus the parent of the context node itself
chapter//footnote	Selects all <footnote> elements that are descendants of a <chapter> element that itself is a child of the context node

Comparing the «//» Operator with «/descendant::»

Consider the two expressions «$chapters//diagram[1]» and «$chapters/descendant::diagram[1]»:

«$chapters//diagram[1]» means «$chapters/descendant-or-self::node()/child::diagram[1]», that is, every <diagram> element that is the first <diagram> child of its parent element and that is a descendant of a node in $chapters.

«$chapters/descendant::diagram[1]» means the first <diagram> element (taking them in document order) that is a descendant of a node in $chapters. Another way of writing this is «($chapters//diagram)[1]».

To see the difference, consider the following source document:

```
<chapter>
    <section>
        <diagram nr="12"/>
        <diagram nr="13"/>
    </section>
    <diagram nr="14"/>
    <section>
        <diagram nr="15"/>
        <diagram nr="16"/>
    </section>
</chapter>
```

With this document, if the variable $chapters contains only the outer <chapter> element, «$chapters//diagram[1]» will select diagrams 12, 14, and 15, while both «$chapters/descendant::diagram[1]» and «($chapters//diagram)[1]» will select diagram 12 only.

Predicates

We saw earlier that a step has three parts: an axis, a NodeTest, and optionally a list of predicates. A predicate is a qualifying expression used to select a subset of the nodes in a sequence. The predicate may be any XPath expression, and it is written in square brackets.

Expression	Syntax
PredicateList	Predicate *
Predicate	«[» Expr «]»

There are two very similar constructs in XPath that use predicates. They can be used in an AxisStep, to qualify the nodes selected by the axis, and they can be used in a FilterExpr, to filter any sequence. We will talk about the more general filter expressions in Chapter 8, and concentrate here on the use of predicates with an AxisStep. The meaning of the two cases is very similar, and it's easy to use them without always being aware of the difference.

For example:

Expression	Description
para[position()>1]	Here the predicate «[position()>1]» is being applied to the Step «para», which is short for «./child::para». It selects all the <para> element children of the context node except the first. Because the expression is an AxisStep, the results are guaranteed to be in document order and to contain no duplicates
$para[position()>1]	Here the predicate «[position()>1]» is being applied to the value of the variable-reference «$para». The expression selects all items in the sequence except the first. The result does not have to be in document order (it can contain atomic value as well as nodes, so document order would not make sense) and it can contain duplicates. The items in the result are returned in their original order

In both cases the effect of a predicate is to select a subset of the items in a sequence. There's a significant difference when a predicate is used with a path expression of more than one step. For example:

Expression	Description
chapter/para[1]	Here the predicate «[1]» is being applied to the Step «para», which is short for «./child::para». It selects the first child <para> element of each child <chapter> element of the context node
(chapter/para)[1]	This is a FilterStep where the predicate «[1]» is being applied to the sequence of nodes selected by the path expression «chapter/para». The expression selects a single <para> element, the first child <para> of a <chapter> that is a child of the context node

In effect, the predicate operator «[ ]» has higher precedence (it binds more tightly) than the path operator «/».

Another distinction between the two cases is that in the case of a FilterExpr, the items are always considered in their original order when evaluating the predicate. In the case of an AxisStep, the nodes are considered in the order of the relevant axis. This is explained in more detail below.

A predicate may be either a boolean expression or a numeric expression. These are not distinguishable syntactically; for example the predicate «[$p]» could be either. The distinction is only made at runtime. (That's the official rule, anyway. If an optimizer can work out in advance whether the value is numeric or boolean, then it will. It's a good idea to declare the types of your variables and parameters, which will make the optimizer's job easier.)

The following table shows some examples of boolean predicates:

Expression	Description
section [@title='Introduction']	Here the predicate is a conventional boolean expression. This example selects every child \<section\> element that has a title attribute with the value «Introduction»
section[title]	The predicate is true if the relevant section has at least one child \<title\> element
title[substring- before(.,':')]	The PredicateExpr evaluates to true if the string-value of the title has one or more characters before its first colon: that is, if the substring-before() function returns a non-empty string
book[not(author= preceding- sibling::author)]	The PredicateExpr here is true if the author of the book is not the same as the author of some preceding book within the same parent element. The effect of this expression is to select the first book by each author

If the value of the predicate is a number (that is, if its type label is xs:decimal, xs:integer, xs:float, or xs:double, or some subtype of these), it is treated as a numeric predicate. If it is of any other type, it is converted to an xs:boolean value using the *effective boolean value* rules described in Chapter 5 (these are the same as the rules for the boolean() function). So for example, the predicate «[@sequence-number]» is true if the context node has a sequence-number attribute, and is false otherwise. The actual numeric value of the attribute sequence-number is immaterial: the value of «@sequence-number» is a sequence of nodes, so it is treated as «[boolean(@sequence-number)]». If you want to use the sequence number attribute as a numeric predicate, write «[number(@sequence-number)]».

A numeric predicate «[P]» is simply a shorthand for the boolean predicate «[position()=P]», so you could also achieve the required effect by writing «[position()=@sequence-number]».

Note that the rules for recognizing a predicate as a number are very strict. For example, a string written as «"20"» is not considered to be a number: it's the type label on the value that matters, not the format of the value itself. Equally, the XSLT variable declared in the example below is not a number, it is the document node at the root of a temporary tree (see the \<xsl:variable\> topic in Chapter 5 of *XSLT 2.0 Programmers Reference* for further explanation):

```
<xsl:variable name="index">3</xsl:variable>
```

If you want to use this value as a predicate, either write it so the value of the variable is a number:

```
<xsl:variable name="index" select="3"/>
```

(but don't write «select="'3'"», because that would make it a string); or force it to a number in the predicate:

```
<xsl:value-of select="item[number($index)]"/>
```

or write the boolean predicate in full:

```
<xsl:value-of select="item[position()=$index]"/>
```

As explained in Chapter 4, every expression is evaluated in a particular context. The context in which the predicate is evaluated is not the same as the context for the expression that it forms part of. The predicate is applied separately to each node selected by the axis, and each time it is evaluated:

❑ The context node (the node selected by «.») is the node to which the predicate is being applied.

❑ The context position (the result of the position() function) is the number assigned to that node within the sequence of nodes.

❑ The context size (the result of the last() function) is the number of nodes in the sequence.

As we saw earlier the number assigned to a node selected by an AxisStep depends on the direction of the axis used in that AxisStep. Some axes (child, descendant, descendant-or-self, following, following-sibling) are forward axes, so the position() function numbers the nodes in document order. Other axes (ancestor, ancestor-or-self, preceding, preceding-sibling) are reverse axes, so position() numbers them in reverse document order. The self and parent axes return a single node, so the order is irrelevant. The ordering of nodes on the attribute and namespace axes is undefined, so positional predicates on these axes don't make much sense, though they are permitted.

The following table shows some examples of positional predicates.

Expression	Description
para[1]	The first <para> child element of the context node
para[last()]	Selects the last <para> child element of the context node
para[position()!=1]	Selects all <para> child elements of the context node, other than the first
para[position()=1 to 5]	Selects the first five <para> elements. This works because the «=» operator returns true if the left-hand operand (position()) contains a value that is equal to one of the items in the right hand operand (1 to 5), which is true if position() is in the range 1 to 5
para[last()-1]	Returns the last but one <para> child of the context node
para[3.2]	Returns an empty sequence. The value 3.2 is treated as a numeric predicate. The value of position() will never be equal to 3.2, so no elements are selected
para[position()]	Selects all child <para> elements. The predicate expands to «[position()=position()]», which is always true
para[position()-1]	Returns an empty sequence. The predicate expands to «[position()=position()-1]», which is always false

Continues

Expression	Description
para[number(@nr)]	Returns every child <para> element that has a nr attribute whose numeric value is equal to the position of the <para> element in the sequence. This rather perverse example illustrates that specifying a numeric predicate gives no guarantee that at most one node will be selected

An AxisStep can contain a sequence of zero or more predicates. Specifying two separate predicates is not the same thing as combining the two predicates into one with an «and» operator. The reason is that the context for the second predicate is different from the context for the first. Specifically, in the second predicate, the context position (the value of the position() function) and the context size (the value of the last() function) consider only those nodes that successfully passed through the previous predicate. What this means in practice is shown in the examples below:

Expression	Description
book[author="P. D. James"][1]	The first book that was written by P. D. James
book[1][author="P. D. James"]	The first book, provided that it was written by P. D. James
book[position()=1 and author="P. D. James"]	The first book, provided that it was written by P. D. James. This is the same as the previous example, because in that example the second predicate is not dependant on the context position

Combining Sets of Nodes

Until now this chapter has been all about path expressions. This section describes operators that combine two sets of nodes. Although these aren't technically path expressions, they are invariably used in conjunction with path expressions, so it's useful to deal with them at the same time. The operators are:

❑   Union, written «union» or «|», which includes a node in the result if it is present in either of the two supplied sets, eliminating any duplicates

❑   Intersection, written «intersect», which includes a node in the result if it is in both the two sets

❑   Difference, written «except», which includes a node in the result if it is in the first set and is not in the second.

XPath 2.0 does not actually support sets (that is, collections with no intrinsic order and with duplicates disallowed) in its data model. Instead, sets of nodes are simulated using sequences. The actual type of the operands for the `union`, `intersect` and `except` operators is «`node()*`», which allows any sequence of nodes. This is also the type of the result. But semantically, these operators ignore any duplicates in the input sequence, and they ignore the order of the nodes in the input sequence. The result sequence will never contain any duplicates, and the results will always be in document order.

As with path expressions, when we talk about duplicate nodes in this section, we are always talking about multiple references to the same node, that is, we are concerned with node identity, not with the values contained in the nodes. Unfortunately the XPath 2.0 data model talks about sequences containing nodes, when it really means that sequences contain references to nodes. I personally feel uncomfortable talking about a sequence containing two nodes that have the same identity, which is the language used in the specification: I find it much more natural to talk about a sequence containing two references to the same node, because there aren't two nodes, there is only one.

There have been many debates about whether the node-sets of XPath 1.0 were true sets or not, given that (in XSLT at any rate) the nodes were always processed in document order. The answer is that they were indeed true sets, because it was not possible to have distinct collections such as (A, B), (B, A), and (A, B, B, A). There was only one collection in the XPath 1.0 model that could contain the nodes A and B, and the fact that the nodes were always processed in a canonical order doesn't change this.

In XPath 2.0, it is possible to have distinct sequences such as (A, B), (B, A), and (A, B, B, A). However, the operators described in this section treat these sequences as if they were identical. So these operators are using sequences to simulate node-sets, and I shall therefore use the term node-sets to describe these values.

Syntax

Expression	Syntex
UnionExpr	IntersectExceptExpr ((«union» | «|») IntersectExceptExpr)*
IntersectExceptExpr	PathExpr ((«intersect» | «except») PathExpr)*

This syntax shows that the «union» operator (which has «|» as a synonym) binds less tightly than the «intersect» and «except» operators. So the expression «A union B intersect C» means «A union (B intersect C)». As always, there is no shame in adding extra parentheses if you're not sure about the rules (or even if you are).

Both operands to the union, intersect, and except operators must be sequences of zero or more nodes. A type error will occur if this isn't the case. The input sequences don't have to be in any particular order, and they are allowed to contain duplicates; the original order and the duplicates will have no effect on the result.

Examples

Expression	Description
`*/figure	*/table`	Returns a node-set containing all the grandchildren of the context node that are `<figure>` or `<table>` elements. This can also be written «`*/(figure|table)`»
`book[not(@publisher)]	book[@publisher='Wrox']`	Returns all the `<book>` children of the context node that either have no `publisher` attribute, or that have a `publisher` attribute equal to "Wrox". Note that the same result could be achieved, perhaps more efficiently, by using the «`or`» operator in the predicate
`(.|..)/title`	Returns all the `<title>` elements that are immediate children of either the context node or the parent of the context node
`sum( (book|magazine)/@sales)`	Returns the total of the `sales` attribute values for all the `<book>` and `<magazine>` children of the context node
`(//* | //@*) [.='nimbus2000']`	Returns a node-set containing all the element and attribute nodes in the document whose string value is «`nimbus2000`»
`following::para intersect $chap//*`	Returns all `<para>` nodes that are after the context node in document order, provided that they are descendants of the node in variable `$chap`
`key('a', 'Gilbert') intersect key('a', 'Sullivan')`	The `key()` function is defined in XSLT to select nodes using a defined index. This expression selects nodes that are indexed both under «`Gilbert`» and under «`Sullivan`»
`exists(. intersect $arg)`	Returns `true` if the context node is included in the sequence `$arg`
`@* except @note`	Selects all the attributes of the context node except the `note` attribute

Usage

The «`intersect`» operator is also useful for testing whether one node is a member of a given set of nodes. For example, the following expression tests whether node $N is a descendant of node $A:

```
if ($N intersect $A/descendant::node()) then ...
```

This works because if $N is among the descendants of $A, the intersection will contain $N, and the effective boolean value of a sequence containing one node is `true`. If $N is not among the descendants of $A, the intersection will be empty, and the effective boolean value of an empty sequence is `false`.

The «except» operator is useful when there is a need to process all the child elements of a node, or all its attributes, except for certain specific exclusions. For example, the XSLT instruction

```
<xsl:copy-of select="@* except @last-changed"/>
```

copies all the attributes of the context node to the result document except for the last-changed attribute (if there is one).

Set Intersection and Difference in XPath 1.0

XPath 1.0 provided no equivalent to the «intersect» and «except» operators. In XPath 1.0, if you want to form the intersection between two node-sets $p and $q, the following rather tortuous expression achieves it:

```
$p [ count( . | $q ) = count( $q ) ]
```

This selects the nodes in $p that are also in $q. They must be in $q, because their union with $q has the same number of nodes as $q itself.

Similarly, the following XPath 1.0 expression finds the nodes that are in $p and not in $q:

```
$p [ count( . | $q ) != count( $q ) ]
```

If you see these constructs when you are upgrading XPath 1.0 code, you can confidently replace them with the XPath 2.0 constructs:

```
$p intersect $q
$p except $q
```

which are not only a lot easier to understand, but will probably be much more efficient as well.

Some XSLT 1.0 processors also provided extension functions to implement set intersection and difference, for example, the functions defined in the EXSLT library (http://www.exslt.org). These have been superseded by the new operators.

Summary

XPath expressions are used to select data from the source document and to manipulate it to generate data to place in the result document. Path expressions play the same role for XML as the SQL SELECT statement plays for relational databases—they allow us to select specific parts of the document for transformation, so that we can achieve the required output.

This chapter has provided a full description of the meaning of path expressions, the «/» operator, steps, axes, node tests, and predicates, and it also covered the other operations defined on sequences of nodes, namely the union, intersect, and except operators.

The next chapter will describe constructs in the XPath language that operate on any kind of sequence, whether it contains nodes, atomic values, or a mixture of the two.

Sequence Expressions

One of the most notable innovations in XPath 2.0 is the ability to construct and manipulate sequences. This chapter is devoted to an explanation of the constructs in the language that help achieve this.

Sequences can consist either of nodes, or of atomic values, or of a mixture of the two. Sequences containing nodes only are a generalization of the node-sets offered by XPath 1.0. In the previous chapter we looked at the operators for manipulating node-sets, in particular, path expressions, and the operators «union», «intersect», and «except».

In this chapter we look at constructs that can manipulate any sequence, whether it contains nodes, atomic values, or both. Specifically, the chapter covers the following constructs:

- ❑ *Sequence concatenation operator:* «,»

- ❑ *Numeric range operator:* «to»

- ❑ *Filter expressions:* «a[b]»

- ❑ *Mapping expressions:* «for»

- ❑ *Quantified expressions:* «some» and «every»

First, some general remarks about sequences.

Sequences (unlike nodes) do not have any concept of identity. Given two values that are both sequences, you can ask (in various ways) whether they have the same contents, but you cannot ask whether they are the same sequence.

Sequences are immutable. This is part of what it means for a language to be free of side effects. You can write expressions that take sequences as input and produce new sequences as output, but you can never modify an existing sequence in place.

Sequences cannot be nested. If you want to construct trees, build them as XML trees using nodes rather than atomic values.

A single item is a sequence of length one, so any operation that applies to sequences also applies to single items.

Sequences do not have any kind of type label that is separate from the type labels attached to the items in the sequence. As we will see in Chapter 9, you can ask whether a sequence is an instance of a particular sequence type, but the question can be answered simply by looking at the number of items in the sequence, and at the type labels attached to each item. It follows that there is no such thing as (for example) an "empty sequence of integers" as distinct from an "empty sequence of strings". If the sequence has no items in it, then it also carries no type label. This has some real practical consequences, for example, the sum() function, when applied to an expression that can only ever return a sequence of xs:duration values, will return the integer 0 (not the zero-length duration) when the sequence is empty, because there is no way at runtime of knowing that if the sequence hadn't been empty, its items would have been durations.

Functions and operators that attach position numbers to the items in a sequence always identify the first item as number 1 (one), not zero. (Although programming with a base of zero tends to be more convenient, Joe Public has not yet been educated into thinking of the first paragraph in a chapter as paragraph zero, and the numbering convention was chosen with this in mind.)

This chapter covers the language constructs that handle general sequences, but there are also a number of useful functions available for manipulating sequences, and these are described in Chapter 10. Relevant functions include: count(), deep-equal(), distinct-values(), empty(), exists(), index-of(), insert-before(), remove(), subsequence(), and unordered().

The Comma Operator

The comma operator can be used to construct a sequence by concatenating items or sequences. We already saw the syntax in Chapter 5, because it appears right at the top level of the XPath grammar:

Expression	Syntax
Expr	ExprSingle («,» ExprSingle)*
ExprSingle	ForExpr | QuantifiedExpr | IfExpr | OrExpr

Although the production rule ExprSingle lists four specific kinds of expression that can appear as an operand of the «,» operator, these actually cover any XPath expression whatsoever, provided it does not contain a top-level «,».

Because the «,» symbol also has other uses in XPath (for example, it is used to separate the arguments in a function call, and also to separate clauses in «for», «some», and «every» expressions, which we will meet later in this chapter), there are many places in the grammar where use of a general Expr is restricted, and only an ExprSingle is allowed. In fact, the only places where a general Expr (one that contains a top-level comma) is allowed are:

❑   As the top-level XPath expression
❑   Within a parenthesized expression

- ❑   Within the parentheses of an «if» expression
- ❑   Within square brackets as a predicate

Neither of the last two is particularly useful, so in practice the rule is: if you want to use the comma operator to construct a list, then it must either be at the outermost level of the XPath expression, or it must be written in parentheses.

For example, the max() function expects a single argument, which is a sequence. If you want to find the maximum of three values $a, $b, and $c, you can write:

```
max(($a, $b, $c))
```

The outer parentheses are part of the function call syntax; the inner parentheses are needed because the expression «max($a, $b, $c)» would be a function call with three parameters rather than one, which would be an error.

> *XPath does not use the JavaScript convention whereby a function call with three separate parameters is the same as a function call whose single parameter is a sequence containing three items.*

The operands of the «,» operator can be any two sequences. Of course, a single item is itself a sequence, so the operands can also be single items. Either of the sequences can be empty, in which case the result of the expression is the value of the other operand.

The comma operator is often used to construct a list, as in:

```
if ($status = ('current', 'pending', 'deleted', 'closed')) then ...
```

which tests whether the variable $status has one of the given four values (recall from Chapter 6 that the «=» operator compares each item in the sequence on the left with each item in the sequence on the right, and returns true if any of these pairs match). In this construct, you probably aren't thinking of «,» as being a binary operator that combines two operands to produce a result, but that's technically what it is. The expression «A,B,C,D» technically means «(((A,B),C),D)», but since list concatenation is associative, you don't need to think of it this way.

The order of the items in the two sequences is retained in the result. This is true even if the operands are nodes: there is no sorting into document order. This means that in XSLT, for example, you can use a construct such as:

```
<xsl:apply-templates select="title, author, abstract"/>
```

to process the selected elements in a specified order, regardless of the order in which they appear in the source document. This example is not necessarily processing exactly three elements: there might, for example, be five authors and no abstract. Since the path expression «author» selects the five authors in document order, they will be processed in this order, but they will be processed after the <title> element whether they precede or follow the title in the source document.

Examples

Here are some examples of expressions that make use of the «,» operator to construct sequences.

Expression	Effect
`max(($net, $gross))`	Selects whichever of $net and $gross is larger, comparing them according to their actual data type (and using the default collation if they are strings)
`for $i in (1 to 4, 8, 13) return $seq[$i]`	Selects the items at positions 1, 2, 3, 4, 8, and 13 of the sequence $seq. For the meaning of the «to» operator, see the next section
`string-join((@a, @b, @c), "-")`	Creates a string containing the values of the attributes @a, @b, and @c of the context node (in that order), separated by hyphens
`(@code, "N/A")[1]`	Returns the code attribute of the context node if it has such an attribute, or the string "N/A" otherwise. This expression makes use of the fact that when the code attribute is absent, the value of @code is an empty sequence, and concatenating an empty sequence with another sequence returns the other sequence (in this case the singleton string "N/A") unchanged. The predicate in square brackets makes this a filter expression: filter expressions are described later in this chapter, on page 244
`book/(author, title, isbn)`	Returns a sequence containing the <author>, <title>, and <isbn> children of a <book> element, *in document order*. Although the «,» operator retains the order as specified, the «/» operator causes the nodes to be sorted into document order. So in this case the «,» operator is exactly equivalent to the union operator «|»

Numeric Ranges: The «to» Operator

A range expression has the syntax:

Expression	Syntax
RangeExpr	AdditiveExpr («to» AdditiveExpr)?

The effect is to return a sequence of consecutive integers in ascending order. For example, the expression «1 to 5» returns the sequence «1, 2, 3, 4, 5».

The operands do not have to be constants, of course. A common idiom is to use an expression such as «1 to count($seq)» to return the position number of each item in the sequence $seq. If the second operand is less than the first (which it will be in this example if $seq is an empty sequence), then the range expression returns an empty sequence. If the second operand is equal to the first, the expression returns a single integer, equal to the value of the first operand.

The two operands must both evaluate to single integers. You can use an untyped value provided it is capable of being converted to an integer: for example you can write «1 to @width» if width is an attribute in a schema-less document containing the value «34». However, you can't use a decimal or a double value without converting it explicitly to an integer. If you write «1 to @width+1», you will get a type error, because the value of «@width+1» is the double value 35.0e0. Instead, write «1 to xs:integer(@width)+1». or «1 to 1 + @width idiv 1».

It's an error if either operand is an empty sequence. For example, this would happen if you ran any of the examples above when the context node did not have a width attribute. Supplying a sequence that contains more than one item is also an error.

If you want a sequence of integers in reverse order, you can use the reverse() function described in Chapter 10. For example, «reverse(1 to 5)» gives you the sequence «5,4,3,2,1». In an earlier draft of the specification you could achieve this by writing «5 to 1», but the rules were changed because this caused anomalies for the common usage «1 to count($seq)» in the case where $seq is empty.

Although the semantics of this operator are expressed in terms of constructing a sequence, a respectable implementation will evaluate the sequence lazily, which means that when you write «1 to 1000000» it won't actually allocate space in memory to hold a million integers. Depending how you actually use the range expression, in most cases an implementation will be able to iterate over the values one to a million without actually laying them out end-to-end as a list in memory.

Examples

Here are some examples of expressions that make use of the «to» operator to construct sequences.

Expression	Effect
for $n in 1 to 10 return $seq[n]	Returns the first 10 items of the sequence $seq. The «for» expression is described later in this chapter, on page 247
$seq[position() = 1 to 10]	Returns the first 10 items of the sequence $seq. This achieves the same effect as the previous example, but this time using a filter expression alone. It works because the «=» operator compares each item in the first operand (there is only one, the value of position()), with each item in the second operand (that is, each of the integers 1 to 10), and returns true if any of them matches. It's reasonable to expect that XPath processors will optimize this construct so that this doesn't actually involve 10 separate comparisons for each item in the sequence.
	Note that you can't simply write «$seq[1 to 10]». If the predicate isn't a single number, it is evaluated as a boolean, and the effective boolean value of the sequence «1 to 10» is true, so all the items will be selected

Continues

Expression	Effect

`string-join(`
`for $i in 1 to $N`
`return " ", "")`
	Returns a string containing $N space characters

`for $i in 1 to`
`count($S) return`
`($S[$i], $T[$i])`
	Returns a sequence that contains pairs of corresponding values from the two input sequences $S and $T. For example, if $S is the sequence (`"a"`,`"b"`,`"c"`) and $T is the sequence (`"x"`,`"y"`,`"z"`), the result will be the sequence (`"a"`,`"x"`,`"b"`,`"y"`,`"c"`,`"z"`)

Filter Expressions

A filter expression is used to apply one or more `Predicates` to a sequence, selecting those items in the sequence that satisfy some condition.

Expression	Syntax
`FilterExpr`	`PrimaryExpr Predicate*`
`Predicate`	«`[`» Expr «`]`»

A `FilterExpr` consists of a `PrimaryExpr` whose value is a sequence, followed by zero or more `Predicates` that select a subset of the items in the sequence. Each predicate consists of an expression enclosed in square brackets, for example «`[@name='London']`» or «`[position()=1]`».

The way the syntax is defined, every `PrimaryExpr` is also a trivial `FilterExpr`, including simple expressions such as «`23`», «`'Washington'`», and «`true()`».

Since in XPath 2.0 every value is a sequence, it is possible to apply predicates to any value whatsoever. For example, it is legitimate to write «`1[$param]`». This returns the value «`1`» if $param is `true`, or an empty sequence if $param is `false`.

Each predicate is applied to the sequence in turn; only those items in the sequence for which the predicate is true pass through to the next stage. The final result consists of those items in the original sequence that satisfy each of the predicates, retaining their original order.

A predicate may be either a numeric predicate (for example «`[1]`» or «`[last()-1]`»), or a boolean predicate (for example «`[count(*) gt 5]`» or «`[@name and @address]`»). If the value of the expression is a single number, it is treated as a numeric predicate; otherwise it is converted, if necessary, to an `xs:boolean`, and is treated as a boolean predicate. The conversion is done using the rules for computing the *effective boolean value*, which are the same rules as are used for the condition in an «`if`» expression (described in Chapter 5 on page 117) or for the operand of the `boolean()` function (described in Chapter 10 on page 304), except that if the value is a single number—which might be an integer, decimal, float, or double—then the predicate is treated as a numeric predicate rather than a boolean predicate.

If the value of the predicate contains nodes, there is no automatic atomization of the nodes (that is, the values of the nodes are not extracted). In fact, if the value of the predicate contains one or more nodes, then its effective boolean value is always true. This means, for example, that «person[@isMarried]» selects any <person> element that has an isMarried attribute, irrespective of the value of that attribute. If you want to test the value of the attribute, you can atomize it explicity using the data() function, or you can use a comparison such as «person[@isMarried=true()]».

A numeric predicate whose value is N is equivalent to the boolean predicate «[position() eq N]». So, for example, the numeric predicate «[1]» means «[position() eq 1]», and the numeric predicate «[last()]» means «[position() eq last()]».

It's important to remember that this implicit testing of position() happens only when the predicate expression actually evaluates to a single number. For example, «$paras[1 or last()]» does not mean «$paras[position()=1 or position()=last()]», because the result of evaluating «1 or last()» is a boolean, not a number (and as it happens, it will always be true). Similarly, «book[../@book-nr]» does not mean «book[position()=../@book-nr]», because the result of «../@book-nr» is a node, not a number.

> *A neat way to force the node to be atomized in such cases is to use the unary «+» operator: write* «book[+../@book-nr]».

A consequence of the rule is that if the predicate is a number that is not equal to an integer, the result will be an empty sequence. For example, «$S[last() div 2]» will select nothing when the value of last() is an odd number. If you want to select a single item close to the middle of the sequence, use «$S[last() idiv 2]», because the idiv operator always returns an integer.

In nearly all practical cases, a numeric predicate selects either a single item from the sequence, or no items at all. But this is not part of the definition. To give a counter-example, «$x[count(*)]» selects every node whose position is the same as the number of children it has.

As discussed in Chapter 4, every XPath expression is evaluated in some context. For an expression used as a predicate, the context is different from the context of the containing expression. While evaluating each predicate, the context is established as follows:

❑ The *context item* (the item referenced as «.») is the item being tested

❑ The *context position* (the value of the position() function) is the position of that item within the sequence of items surviving from the previous stage

❑ The *context size* (the value of the last() function) is the number of items surviving from the previous stage.

To see how this works, consider the filter expression «$headings[self::h1][last()]». This starts with the sequence of nodes that is the value of the variable «$headings» (if this sequence contains items that are not nodes, then evaluating the predicate «self::h1» will raise an error). The first predicate is «[self::h1]». This is applied to each node in «$headings» in turn. While it is being applied, the context node is that particular node. The expression «self::h1» is a path expression consisting of a single AxisStep: it selects a sequence of nodes. If the context node is an <h1> element this sequence will contain a single node—the context node. Otherwise, the sequence will be empty. When this value is converted to a boolean, it will be true if it contains a node, and false if it is empty. So the first predicate is actually filtering through those nodes in «$headings» that are <h1> elements.

The second predicate is now applied to each node in this sequence of <h1> elements. In each case the predicate «[last()]» returns the same value: a number indicating how many <h1> elements there are in the sequence. As this is a numeric predicate, a node passes the test when «[position()= last()]», that is, when the position of the node in the sequence (taken in its original order) is equal to the number of nodes in the sequence. So the meaning of «$headings [self::h1] [last()]» is "the last <h1> element in the sequence $headings."

Note that this isn't the same as «$headings [last()] [self::h1]», which means "the last item in $headings, provided it is an <h1> element."

The operation of a Predicate in a FilterExpr is very similar to the application of a Predicate in an AxisStep (which we studied in Chapter 7, on page 230), and although they are not directly related in the XPath grammar rules, you can often use Predicates without being fully aware which of these two constructs you are using. For example, «$para[1]» is a FilterExpr, while «para[1]» is an AxisStep. The main differences to watch out for are firstly, that in a path expression the predicates apply only to the most recent Step (for example, in «book/author[1]» the «[1]» means the first author within each book), and secondly, that in a filter expression the items are always considered in the order of the supplied sequence (whereas in an AxisStep they can be in forward or reverse document order depending on the direction of the axis).

Examples

Expression	Description
$paragraphs[23]	This FilterExpr consists of a VariableReference filtered by a Predicate. It selects the 23rd item in the sequence that is the value of variable $paragraphs, taking them in the order of that sequence. If there is no 23rd item, the expression returns an empty sequence
key('empname', 'John Smith')[@loc='Sydney']	This FilterExpr comprises a FunctionCall filtered by a Predicate. The key() function is available only in XSLT. Assuming that the key «empname» has been defined in the containing stylesheet to select employees by name, it selects all employees named John Smith who are located in Sydney
(//section|//subsection) [title='Introduction']	This FilterExpr consists of a parenthesized UnionExpr filtered by a Predicate. It selects all <section> and <subsection> elements that have a child <title> element with the content «Introduction»

Expression	Description
`(//@href/doc(.))` `[pricelist][1]`	This `FilterExpr` first selects all documents referenced by URLs contained in `href` attributes anywhere in the source document, by applying the `doc()` function to the value of each of these attributes. The «`/`» operator causes any duplicates to be removed, as described in Chapter 7. From this set of documents it selects those whose outermost element is named `<pricelist>`, and from these it selects the first. The order of nodes that are in different documents is not defined, so if there are several price lists referenced, it is unpredictable which will be selected

Where a predicate is used as part of a `FilterExpr` (as distinct from an `AxisStep`), the items are considered in their original sequence for the purpose of evaluating the `position()` function within the predicate. There are some cases where the order of the sequence is not predictable, but it is still possible to use positional predicates. For example the result of the `distinct-values()` function is in an undefined order, but you can still write «`distinct-values($in)[1]`» to obtain one item in the sequence, chosen arbitrarily.

The «for» Expression

The «`for`» expression is one of the most powerful new features in XPath 2.0, and is closely related to the extension to the data model to handle sequences. Its effect is to apply an expression to every item in an input sequence, and to return the concatenated results of these expressions.

The syntax also allows several sequences to be provided as input, in which case the effect is to apply an expression to every combination of values taken one from each sequence.

The syntax as given in the XPath 2.0 Recommendation is rather clumsy, because the grammar is designed to share as many production rules as possible with XQuery, and the «`for`» expression in XPath can be regarded as a cut-down version of XQuery's much richer FLWOR expressions. For this book, I've rewritten the syntax in the way it would probably have been presented if XQuery didn't exist.

Expression	Syntax
ForExpr	«for $» VarName «in» ExprSingle («,» «$» VarName «in» ExprSingle)* «return» ExprSingle
VarName	QName

An `ExprSingle` is any XPath expression that does not contain a top-level «`,`» operator. If you want to use an expression containing a «`,`» operator, write it in parentheses. For example the expression «`for $i in (1,5,10) return $i+1`» returns the sequence «`2,6,11`».

The notation «for $» indicates that for the purposes of parsing, the word «for» must be followed by a «$» sign to be recognized as a keyword. The two parts of this compound symbol can be separated by whitespace and comments.

We'll look first at «for» expressions that operate on a single sequence, and then move on to the more general case where there are multiple input sequences.

Mapping a Sequence

When used with a single sequence, the «for» expression applies the expression in the «return» clause to each item in the input sequence. The relevant item in the input sequence is accessed not as the context item, but as the value of the variable declared in the «for» clause.

These variables are referred to as range variables, to distinguish them from variables supplied from outside the XPath expression, such as variables declared in an XSLT stylesheet. The term comes originally from the branch of mathematical logic called predicate calculus, and has been adopted in a number of programming languages based on this underlying theory.

In most cases the expression in the «return» clause will depend in some way on the range variable. In other words, the «return» value is a function of the range variable, which means we can rewrite the «for» expression in the abstract form:

```
for $x in $SEQ return F($x)
```

where «F($x)» represents any expression that depends on $x (it doesn't have to depend on $x, but it usually will).

What this expression does is to evaluate the expression «F($x)» once for each item in the input sequence $SEQ, and then to concatenate the results, respecting the original order of the items in $SEQ.

In the simplest case, the return expression «F($x)» returns one item each time it is called. This is illustrated in Figure 8-1, where the function «F($x)» in this example is actually the expression «string-length($x)».

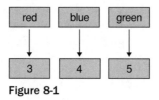

Figure 8-1

We say that the expression «for $x in $SEQ return string-length($x)» *maps* the sequence «"red", "blue", "green"» to the sequence «3,4,5».

In this case, the number of items in the result will be the same as the number of items in the input sequence.

However, the return expression isn't constrained to return a single item, it can return any sequence of zero or more items. For example, you could write:

```
for $s in ("red", "blue", "green") return string-to-codepoints($s)
```

The function `string-to-codepoints()`, which is part of the standard library defined in Chapter 10, returns for a given string, the Unicode code values of the characters that make up the string. For example, «`string-to-unicode("red")`» returns the sequence «`114,101,100`». The result of the above expression is a sequence of 12 integers, as illustrated in Figure 8-2.

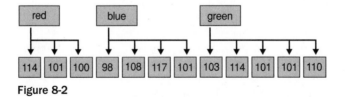

Figure 8-2

The integers are returned in the order shown, because unlike a path expression, there is nothing in the rules for a «`for`» expression that causes the result sequence to be sorted into document order. Indeed, document order is not a meaningful concept when we are dealing with atomic values rather than nodes.

Examples

Expression	Description
`for $i in 1 to 5` `return $i*$i`	Returns the sequence «`1,4,9,16,25`». This example is a one-to-one mapping
`for $i in 0 to 4` `return 1 to $i`	Returns the sequence «`1,1,2,1,2,3,1,2,3,4`». This example is a one-to-many mapping. Note that for the first item in the input sequence (0), the mapping function returns an empty sequence, so this item contributes nothing to the result

For Expressions and Path Expressions

The items in the input sequence of a «`for`» expression can be atomic values or nodes, or any mixture of the two. When applied to a sequence of nodes, «`for`» expressions actually behave in a very similar way to path expressions. The expression:

```
for $c in chapter return $c/section
```

returns exactly the same result as the path expression:

```
chapter/section
```

However, there are some significant differences between «`for`» expressions and path expressions:

❑   In a path expression, both the input sequence and the step expression are required to return nodes exclusively. A «`for`» expression can work on any sequence, whether it contains nodes or atomic values or both, and it can also return any sequence.

- ❑ Path expressions always sort the resulting nodes into document order, and eliminate duplicates. A «for» expression returns the result sequence in the order that reflects the order of the input items.

- ❑ In a path expression, the context item for evaluating a step is set to each item in the input sequence in turn. In a «for» expression, the range variable fulfils this function. The context item is not changed. Nor are the context position and size (position() and last()) available to test the position of the item in the input sequence.

A common mistake is to forget that «for» expressions don't set the context node. The following example is wrong (it's not an error, but it doesn't do what the writer probably intended):

```
(:wrong:) sum(for $i in item return @price * @qty)
```

The correct way of writing this is:

```
(:correct:) sum(for $i in item return $i/@price * $i/@qty)
```

Generally speaking, there is usually something amiss if the range variable is not used in the «return» expression. However, there are exceptions to this rule. For example, it's quite reasonable to write:

```
string-join(for $i in 1 to $n return "-", "")
```

which returns a string containing $n hyphens.

It's also often (but not invariably) a sign of trouble if the value of the return expression depends on the context item. But it's not actually an error: the context item inside the return expression is exactly the same as the context item for the «for» expression as a whole. So it's legal to write an expression such as:

```
chapter/(for $i in 1 to 10 return section[$i])
```

which returns the first 10 sections of each chapter.

Combining Multiple Sequences

The «for» expression allows multiple input sequences to be defined, each with its own range variable. For example, you can write:

```
for $c in //customer,
    $o in $c/orders,
    $ol in $o/line
return $ol/cost
```

The simplest way to think about this is as a nested loop. You can regard the «,» as a shorthand for writing the keywords «return for», so the above expression is equivalent to:

```
for $c in //customer
return
    for $o in $c/orders
```

```
    return
       for $ol in $o/line
       return $ol/cost
```

Note that each of the range variables can be referenced in the expression that defines the input sequence for the next range variable.

In the example above, each iteration is rather like a step in a path expression; it selects nodes starting from the node selected in the containing loop. But it doesn't have to be this way. For example, you could equally write an expression such as:

```
for $c in doc('customers.xml')//customer,
    $p in doc('products.xml')//product
            [$c/orders/product-code = $p/code]
   return $c/line/cost
```

It's still true that this is equivalent to a nested-loop expression:

```
for $c in doc('customers.xml')//customer
return
    for $p in doc('products.xml')//product
            [$c/orders/product-code = $p/code]
   return $c/line/cost
```

The other way to think about this, particularly if you are familiar with SQL, is as a relational join. The system isn't actually obliged to evaluate the «for» expression using nested loops (this applies whether you write it in the abbreviated form using multiple range variables separated with commas, or whether you use the expanded form shown above). Instead, the optimizer can use any of the mechanisms developed over the years in relational database technology to evaluate the join more rapidly. There's no guarantee that it will do so (in practice, I think XQuery implementations are likely to put a lot of effort into join optimization, while XPath implementations might be less ambitious), so you need to use potentially expensive constructs like this with some care.

Saxon, at the time of writing, will try to move sub-expressions out of a loop if they don't depend on the range variable. So the expression «doc('products.xml')//product» will probably only be evaluated once, and the expression «$c/orders/product-code» will only be evaluated once for each customer. But after this, every product code in the customer file will be compared with every product code in the product file. In XSLT, you can avoid this overhead by using keys: see the description of the <xsl:key> declaration and the key() function in XSLT 2.0 Programmer's Reference.

Example

Expression	Description

`count(`
`   for $i in 1 to 8,`
`      $j in 1 to 8`
`   return f:square($i,$j))`
	Assuming that «f:square(row, column)» returns an integer identifying the piece that occupies a square on a chessboard, or an empty sequence if the square is unoccupied, this expression returns all the pieces on the board

Examples in XMLSpy

The XMLSpy 2004 product (see http://www.altova.com/) includes a beta release of an XPath 2.0 processor that shows the results of an expression using a graphical user interface. In this section I will provide a couple of examples that illustrate the results of «for» expressions using that product.

I'm using the sample document ipo.xml that comes with the product: look in the Purchase Order folder. This consists of an outer element <ipo:purchase-order> with various namespace declarations, then addresses for shipping and billing:

```
<shipTo export-code="1" xsi:type="ipo:EU-Address">
   <name>Helen Zoe</name>
   <street>47 Eden Street</street>
   <city>Cambridge</city>
   <postcode>126</postcode>
</shipTo>
<billTo xsi:type="ipo:US-Address">
   <name>Robert Smith</name>
   <street>8 Oak Avenue</street>
   <city>Old Town</city>
   <state>AK</state>
   <zip>95819</zip>
</billTo>
```

This is followed by an <items> element containing a number of items with the general format:

```
<item partNum="833-AA">
   <productName>Lapis necklace</productName>
   <quantity>2</quantity>
   <price>99.95</price>
   <ipo:comment>Need this for the holidays!</ipo:comment>
   <shipDate>1999-12-05</shipDate>
</item>
```

(Altova took this example from the XML Schema primer published by W3C, but apparently failed to realize the subtlety that UK postcodes are alphanumeric.)

Let's look first at the classic problem of getting the total value of the order. In this expression (Figure 8-3) I'll first list all the individual price and quantity elements, and then their sum.

The total is shown in the bottom line.

XMLSpy takes the namespace context for the XPath expression from the namespaces declared in the source document, so to get this to work, I had to add the namespace declaration «xmlns:xs="http://www.w3.org/2001/XMLSchema"» to the <ipo:purchaseOrder> element.

The second example from XMLSpy uses a join, and just to show that joins don't arise only from data-oriented XML, I've chosen an example that uses narrative XML as its source. Specifically, it uses the XML source of the XPath 1.0 specification, which happens to be included in XMLSpy as a sample document.

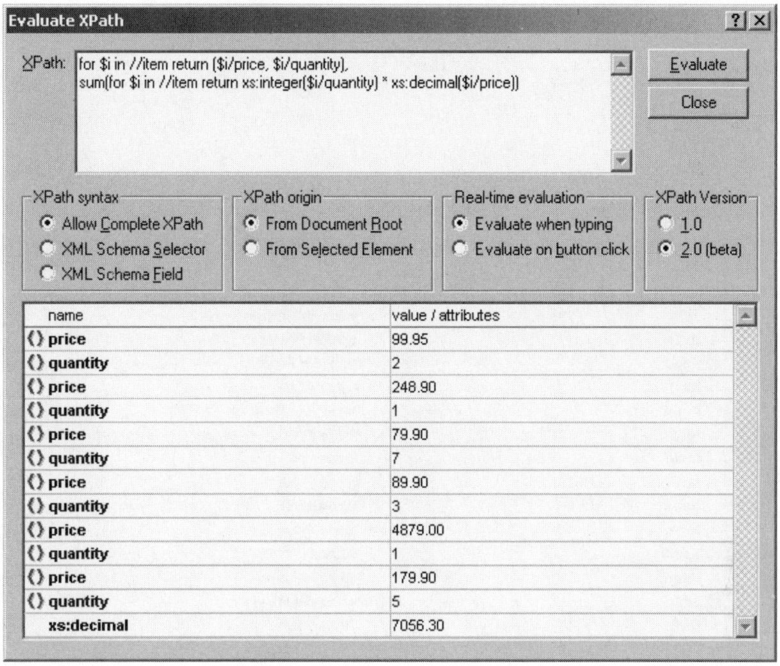

Figure 8-3

The DTD for this document type allows term definitions to be marked up using a `<termdef>` element such as:

```
<termdef id="dt-document-order" term="Document Order">There is an
ordering, <term>document order</term>, defined on all the nodes in the
document corresponding to the order in which the first character of
the XML representation of each node occurs in the XML representation
of the document after expansion of general entities.</termdef>
```

References to a defined term can be marked up using a `<termref>` element. This example shows a `<termref>` that happens to be nested inside another `<termdef>`:

```
<termdef id="dt-reverse-document-order" term="Reverse Document
Order"> <term>Reverse document order</term> is the reverse of
<termref def="dt-document-order">document order</termref>.</termdef>
```

There is a relationship between the `<termref>` element and the `<termdef>` element, by virtue of the fact that the def attribute of a `<termref>` must match the id attribute of a `<termdef>`. The stylesheet used to construct the published XPath specification turns this relationship into a hyperlink. Where there is a relationship, there is potential for performing a join, as Figure 8-4 shows.

The output here is not particularly visual. It shows a sequence of pairs, each pair containing first, a defined term (the term attribute of a `<termdef>` element), and secondly, the heading (`<head>` element) of the innermost `<div1>`, `<div2>`, or `<div3>` section that contains a reference to that term. The reason that this is shown as a one-dimensional list rather than as a table is of course that it *is* a list: the XPath 2.0

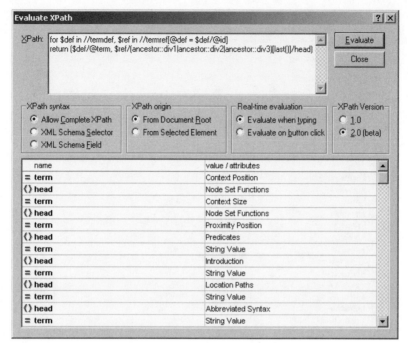

Figure 8-4

data model does not allow construction of trees, or of nested sequences, that would allow a table to be represented more directly. In practice, you would either use a custom application to present the data, or you would embed this XPath expression in an XSLT stylesheet or XQuery query that allows you to construct the output as XML or (say) HTML. The resulting display would probably look something like this:

Term	Section containing Reference
Context Position	Node Set Functions
Context Size	Node Set Functions
Proximity Position	Predicates
String Value	Introduction
String Value	Location Paths
String Value	Abbreviated Syntax

The «some» and «every» Expressions

These expressions are used to test whether some item in a sequence satisfies a condition, or whether all values in a sequence satisfy a condition.

The syntax is like this:

Expression	Syntax
QuantifiedExpr	«some $» | «every $» VarName «in» ExprSingle («,» «$» VarName «in» ExprSingle) * «satisfies» ExprSingle
VarName	QName

The name *quantified expression* comes from the mathematical notations on which these expressions are based: the «some» expression is known in formal logic as an existential quantifier, while the «every» expression is known as a universal quantifier.

As with the «for» expression, these two expressions bind a range variable to every item in a sequence in turn, and evaluate an expression (the «satisfies» expression) for each of these items. Instead of returning the results, however, a quanitified expression evaluates the effective boolean value of the «satisfies» expression. In the case of «some», it returns true if at least one of these values is true, while in the case of «every», it returns true if all of the values are true. The range variables can be referenced anywhere in the expression following the «satisfies» keyword, and the expression following the «in» keyword can use all variables declared in previous clauses of the expression (but not the variable ranging over that expression itself).

For example:

```
some $p in //price satisfies $p > 10000
```

is true if there is a <price> element in the document whose typed value is a number greater than 10,000, while:

```
every $p in //price satisfies $p > 10000
```

is true if every <price> element in the document has a typed value greater than 10,000.

The result of the expression (unless some error occurs) is always a single xs:boolean value.

The «satisfies» expression is evaluated to return a boolean value. This evaluation returns the *effective boolean value* of the expression, using the same rules as for the boolean() function and the condition in an «if» expression. For example, if the result of the expression is a string, the effective boolean value is true if the string is not zero-length. The expression will almost invariably reference each one of the range variables, although the results are still well defined if it doesn't.

> As with «for» expressions, «some» and «every» expressions do not change the context item. This means that the following is wrong (it's not an error, but it doesn't produce the intended answer):
>
> ```
> (:wrong:) some $i in //item satisfies price > 200
> ```
>
> It should be written instead:
>
> ```
> (:correct:) some $i in //item satisfies $i/price > 200
> ```

Note that if the input sequence is empty, the «some» expression will always be `false`, while the «every» expression will always be `true`. This may not be intuitive to everyone, but it is logical—the «every» expression is true if there are no counter-examples, for example, it's true that every unicorn has one horn, because there are no Unicorns that don't have one horn. Equally, and this is where the surprise comes, it is also true that every Unicorn has two horns.

In fact these two expressions are interchangeable: you can always rewrite

```
every $s in $S satisfies not(C)
```

as:

```
not(some $s in $S satisfies C)
```

If there is only a single range variable, you can usually rewrite the expression

```
some $s in $S satisfies $s/C
```

as

```
exists($S[C])
```

which some people prefer, as it is more concise. If the sequence $S consists of nodes, you can also leave out the call on the `exists()` function, for example, you can rewrite:

```
if (some $i in //item satisfies $i/price * $i/quantity > 1000) ...
```

as:

```
if (//item[price*quantity > 1000]) ...
```

The difference is a matter of taste. The «some» expression, however, is more powerful than a simple predicate because (like the «for» expression) it can handle joins, using multiple range variables.

The XPath 2.0 specification describes the semantics of the «some» and «every» expressions in a rather complicated way, using a concept of "tuples of variable bindings". This happened because the XPath 2.0 specification is generated by subsetting XQuery 1.0, whose core construct, the FLWOR expression, makes use of this concept already. It would have been possible to specify «some» and «every» in a much simpler way for XPath users. In fact, the expression:

```
some $s in $S, $t in $T, $u in $U satisfies CONDITION
```

has exactly the same effect as the expression:

```
exists(for $s in $S, $t in $T, $u in $U return boolean( CONDITION ))[.]
```

while the expression:

```
every $s in $S, $t in $T, $u in $U satisfies CONDITION
```

has exactly the same effect as the expression:

```
empty(for $s in $S, $t in $T, $u in $U return not( CONDITION ))[.]
```

The rather unusual predicate «[.]» selects all the items in a sequence whose effective boolean value is true. In the first case, the result is true if the result of the «for» expression contains at least one value that is true, while in the second case, the result is true if the result of the «for» expression contains no value that is false.

(The functions exists() and empty() are described in Chapter 10. The exists() function returns true if the supplied sequence contains one or more items, while empty() returns true if the sequence contains no items.)

Examples

Expression	Description
some $i in //item satisfies $i/price gt 200	Returns true if the current document contains an <item> element with a <price> child whose typed value exceeds 200
some $n in 1 to count($S)-1 satisfies $S[$n] eq S[$n+1]	Returns true if there are two adjacent values in the input sequence $S that are equal
every $p in //person satisfies $p/@dob castable as xs:date	Returns true if every <person> element in the current document has a dob attribute that represents a valid date, according to the XML Schema format YYYY-MM-DD
some $k in //keyword, $p in //para satisfies contains($p, $k)	Returns true if there is at least one <keyword> in the document that is present in at least one <para> element of the document
every $d in //termdef/@id satisfies some $r in //termref satisfies $d eq $r/@def	Returns true if every <termdef> element with an id attribute is referenced by at least one <termref> element with a matching def attribute

Quantification and the «=» Operator

An alternative to using the «some» expression (and sometimes also the «every» expression) is to rely on the implicit semantics of the «=» operator, and other operators in the same family, when they are used to compare sequences. As we saw in Chapter 6, these operators can be used to compare two sequences, and return true if any pair of items (one from each sequence) satisfies the equality condition.

For example, the expression:

```
//book[author="Kay"]
```

means the same as

```
//book[some $a in author satisfies $a eq "Kay"]
```

Similarly, the expression:

```
//book[author=("Kay", "Tennison", "Carlisle")]
```

means the same as:

```
//book[some $a in author,
           $s in ("Kay", "Tennison", "Carlisle")
       satisfies $a eq $s]
```

It's a matter of personal style which one you choose in these cases. However, if the operator is something more complex than straight equality—for example, if you are comparing the two values using the `compare()` function with a non-default collation—then the only way to achieve the effect within XPath is to use a «some» or «every» expression.

Errors in «some» and «every» Expressions

Dynamic (runtime) errors can occur in «some» and «every» expressions just as in any other kind of XPath expression, and the rules are the same. But for these expressions the rules have some interesting consequences that are worth exploring.

Let's summarize the rules here:

❑ If a dynamic error occurs when evaluating the «satisfies» expression, then the «some» or «every» expression as a whole fails.

❑ As soon as the system finds an item in the sequence for which the «satisfies» expression is true (in the case of «some») or false (in the case of «every») then it can stop the evaluation. It doesn't need to look any further. This means that it might not notice errors that would be found if it carried on to the bitter end.

❑ The system can process the input sequence in any order that it likes. This means that if there is one item for which evaluating the «satisfies» expression returns true, and another for which it raises an error, then you can't tell whether the «some» expression will return true or raise the error.

Some systems might deliberately choose to exploit these rules by evaluating the error cases last (or pretending to do so) so as to minimize the chance of the expression failing, but you can't rely on this.

What does this mean in practice? Suppose you have an attribute defined in the schema as follows:

```
<xs:attribute name="readings">
  <xs:simpleType>
    <xs:list>
      <xs:simpleType>
        <xs:union>
```

```
        <xs:simpleType base="xs:decimal"/>
        <xs:simpleType base="xs:string"/>
          <xs:enumeration value="n/a"/>
        </xs:simpleType>
      </xs:union>
    </xs:simpleType>
  </xs:list>
</xs:simpleType>
</xs:attribute>
```

Or to put it more simply, the attribute's typed value is a list of atomic values, each of which is either a decimal number or the string value «n/a». For example, the attribute might be written «readings="12.2 -8.4 5.6 n/a 13.1"».

Now suppose you want to test whether the set of readings includes a negative value. You could write:

```
if (some $a in data(@readings) satisfies $a lt 0) then ...
```

The chances are you will get away with this. Most processors will probably evaluate the condition «$a lt 0» against each value in turn, find that the condition is true for the second item in the list, and return true. However, a processor that decided to evaluate the items in reverse order would encounter the value «n/a», compare this with zero, and hit a type error: you can't compare a string with a number. So one processor will give you the answer true, while another gives you an error.

You can protect yourself against this error by writing the expression as:

```
if (some $a in data(@readings)[. instance of xs:decimal]
    satisfies $a lt 0)
then ...
```

Or in this case, you can mask the error by writing:

```
if (some $a in data(@readings) satisfies number($a) lt 0) then ...
```

This works because «number('n/a')» returns NaN (not-a-number), and «NaN lt 0» returns false.

Summary

This chapter covered all the various kinds of expressions in the XPath language that are designed to manipulate general sequences, specifically:

❑   The «,» operator, which appends two sequences

❑   The «to» operator, which forms a sequence of ascending integers

❑   Filter expressions, which are used to find those items in a sequence that satisfy some predicate

❑   The «for» expression, which applies an expression to every item in a sequence and returns the results, as a new sequence

❑   The «some» and «every» expressions, which test whether a condition is true for some value (or every value) in an input sequence, returning a boolean result.

Don't forget that these are not the only constructs available for manipulating sequences. For sequences of nodes, path expressions can be used, as well as the «union», «intersect», and «except» operators, as discussed in Chapter 7. And in Chapter 10 you will find descriptions of all the functions in the standard XPath library, including many functions that are useful for operating on sequences, for example, `count()`, `deep-equal()`, `distinct-values()`, `empty()`, `exists()`, `index-of()`, `insert-before()`, `remove()`, `subsequence()`, and `unordered()`.

The next chapter deals with operations involving types: operations that convert a value of one type into a value of another type, and operations that test the type of a value.

Type Expressions

This chapter is concerned with XPath expressions that involve types. This includes operations to convert a value of one type to a value of another type (which is called casting), and operations to test whether a value belongs to a particular type.

The type system for XPath was fully explained in Chapter 3. Recall in particular that there are two separate but related sets of types we are concerned with:

❑   Every value in XPath (that is, the result of every expression) is an instance of a *sequence type*. This reflects the fact that every XPath value is a sequence. A sequence type in general defines an *item type* that each of the items in the sequence must conform to, and a *cardinality* that constrains the number of items in the sequence. The items may be either nodes or atomic values, so item types divide into those that permit nodes and those that permit atomic values. There are also two special item types, the type `item()`, which permits anything, and the type `empty()`, which permits nothing.

❑   Every element and attribute node conforms to a type definition contained in a schema, or a built-in type definition that is implicit in every schema. To distinguish these clearly from sequence types (something that the spec does not always do) I will refer to these types as *schema types*. A schema type may be either a simple type or (for elements only) a complex type. A simple type may be either a list type, a union type, or an atomic type. A type definition constrains the contents of a node (that is, the value of an attribute, or the attributes and children of an element); it does not constrain the name of the node.

We need to use careful language to avoid confusing these two views of the type system. When we have an XPath value that is a node, we will speak of the node being an *instance of* a sequence type—for example, every element is an instance of the sequence type `element()`. At the same time, the node is *annotated* with a schema type—for example, an element node may be annotated as an `mf:invoice` (which will be the name of a complex type defined in some schema).

These two sets of types (sequence types and schema types) overlap: in particular, atomic types such as `xs:integer` belong to both sets. However, list types, union types, and complex types are never used as item types or sequence types, they are used only to annotate nodes. Equally, item types such as `comment()` are only used in sequence types, they are never used to annotate nodes.

The first part of this chapter is concerned with conversion of values from one type to another. These types are always atomic types; no conversions are defined for any types other than atomic types. The process of atomization, which extracts the typed value of a node, could be regarded as a conversion, but we won't treat it as such for our present purposes.

Atomic types can be referred to by the name given to them in the schema. A schema can define anonymous atomic types, but because these have no name, they can't be referenced in an XPath expression. Named atomic types are always defined by a top-level `<xs:simpleType>` element in a schema (more specifically, by an `<xs:simpleType>` element that is a child of either an `<xs:schema>` element or an `<xs:redefine>` element), and these elements always have a `name` attribute.

The final part of this chapter deals with two operators («`instance of`» and «`treat as`») that take as their "operands" an arbitrary XPath value (that is, a sequence), and a sequence type. (I've written "operands" in quotes, because a true operand is always a value, and in the XPath view of the world, types are not values). These two constructs require a special syntax for describing sequence types. For example, «`attribute(*, xs:date)?`» describes a sequence type whose item type matches any attribute node annotated as an `xs:date`, and whose cardinality allows the sequence to contain zero or one values. I will refer to such a construct as a *sequence type descriptor*, because the construct seems to need a name, and the XPath specification doesn't give it one.

Converting Atomic Values

The operation of converting an atomic value of one type into an atomic value of another type is called casting.

> *The word casting is used with the meaning that it has in the SQL language, which is subtly different from the usage in many other programming languages. In Java, the casting operation is more like the «treat as» operator described later in this chapter, which doesn't actually change the value from one type to another. But casts in Java perform a dual role, they are also used for conversions among the primitive types.*

As well as an operator to perform a cast, XPath also provides a second operator to test whether a cast is possible. This has been provided because there is no way of recovering from the error that occurs when a cast fails (if, for example, you convert a string to a date and the string does not contain a valid date). Instead of attempting the cast and then dealing with the error when it fails, XPath encourages you first to test whether it will succeed, and then to perform the conversion only if this is the case. So if $p is a user-supplied parameter that is supposed to contain a valid date, you can write:

```
if ($p castable as xs:date) then xs:date($p) else ()
```

The syntax for the «`cast as`» and «`castable as`» operators is shown below. Both operators are written as compound tokens.

Expression	Syntax
CastableExpr	CastExpr («castable as» SingleType)?
CastExpr	UnaryExpr («cast as» SingleType)?
SingleType	AtomicType «?»?
AtomicType	QName

The rule for `SingleType` is confusing at first sight. It means that the `AtomicType` may optionally be followed by a question mark.

In all these cases, the `AtomicType` must correspond to the name of an atomic type (that is, a simple type that is not a list type or a union type) in the static context for the XPath expression. Most commonly, this will be one of the built-in types such as `xs:integer` or `xs:date`, but it can also be a user-defined type. The type name is written as a `QName`, and its namespace prefix must therefore have been declared to reference the `targetNamespace` of the schema in which the type is defined. If the name has no prefix, the default namespace for elements is used; in XSLT, this will be the null namespace, unless the `xpath-default-namespace` attribute has been set to identify a different namespace.

> *The concept of the static context was described in Chapter 4. An atomic type will be present in the static context either if it is a built-in type such as `xs:date`, or if it is defined in a schema that has been explicitly imported using a host-language construct such as `<xsl:import-schema>`in XSLT.*

A question mark after the type name means that an empty sequence is allowed as the value. For example, the expression «`@A cast as xs:integer`» will fail if the attribute A does not exist, but the expression «`@A cast as xs:integer?`» will succeed, returning an empty sequence.

The «`castable as`» expression returns `true` if the corresponding «`cast as`» expression would succeed, and `false` if the corresponding «`cast as`» expression would fail. For example, the string «`2003-02-29`» is not a valid date, so the expression «`"2003-02-29" castable as xs:date`» returns `false`.

Both the «`cast as`» and «`castable as`» operators perform atomization on the supplied value. This means that if the supplied value is a node, its typed value is first extracted. If the operand (after atomization) is a sequence of more than one item, then a type error occurs in the case of «`cast as`», or the value `false` is returned in the case of «`castable as`».

There is a shorthand for a «`cast as`» expression, which is to use a constructor function. For example, the expression «`@A cast as xs:integer`» can be rewritten as a function call «`xs:integer(@A)`». There is a constructor function available for every built-in atomic type, and for every named atomic type in an imported schema, and its effect is identical to using the «`cast as`» expression. The only cases where you need to use the full «`cast as`» expression are:

- ❑   When you want to use the «`?`» after the atomic type name to indicate that an empty sequence is allowed.

- ❑   When the type name is defined in a schema with no target namespace, and the default function namespace is not the null namespace. In XSLT, the default function namespace is always the namespace holding the core library functions such as `string()`, `contains()`, and `number()`. This means that if you import a schema that has no target namespace, you will have no way of calling constructor functions for the atomic types defined in this schema, which might well clash with the names of functions in the core library. So in this situation, you have to use the more verbose «`cast as`» syntax.

The sections that follow describe all the rules for converting a supplied value to a target type. We'll start by considering the rules for converting from a primitive type to another primitive type, and then go on to consider how derived types are handled.

Converting between Primitive Types

The type conversions described in this section start with an atomic value that is labeled with a primitive type. For these purposes we consider the primitive types to be not only the primitive types defined in Part 2 of the XML Schema specification, but also the additional XPath-defined atomic types: `xdt:untypedAtomic`, `xdt:dayTimeDuration`, and `xdt:yearMonthDuration`.

The following table lists for each source type, the permitted destination types. The detailed rules for these conversions are then given in the subsequent sections, which for ease of reference are arranged alphabetically according to the type of the source value for the conversion.

Source Type	Permitted Result Types
anyURI	anyURI, string, untypedAtomic
base64Binary	base64Binary, hexBinary, string, untypedAtomic
boolean	boolean, decimal, double, float, string, untypedAtomic
date	date, dateTime, gDay, gMonth, gMonthDay, gYear, gYearMonth, string, untypedAtomic
dateTime	date, dateTime, gDay, gMonth, gMonthDay, gYear, gYearMonth, string, time, untypedAtomic
dayTimeDuration	dayTimeDuration, duration, string, untypedAtomic
decimal	boolean, decimal, double, float, string, untypedAtomic
double	boolean, decimal, double, float, string, untypedAtomic
duration	dayTimeDuration, duration, string, untypedAtomic, yearMonthDuration
float	boolean, decimal, double, float, string, untypedAtomic
gDay	gDay, string, untypedAtomic
gMonth	gMonth, string, untypedAtomic
gMonthDay	gMonthDay, string, untypedAtomic
gYear	gYear, string, untypedAtomic
gYearMonth	GYearMonth, string, untypedAtomic
hexBinary	base64Binary, hexBinary, string, untypedAtomic
NOTATION	NOTATION, string, untypedAtomic
QName	QName
string	anyURI, base64Binary, boolean, date, dateTime, dayTimeDuration, decimal, double, duration, float, gDay, gMonth, gMonthDay, gYear, gYearMonth, hexBinary, QName, string, time, untypedAtomic, yearMonthDuration
time	dateTime, time, string, untypedAtomic

Source Type	Permitted Result Types
untypedAtomic	anyURI, base64Binary, boolean, date, dateTime, dayTimeDuration, decimal, double, duration, float, gDay, gMonth, gMonthDay, gYear, gYearMonth, hexBinary, QName, string, time, untypedAtomic, yearMonthDuration
yearMonthDuration	duration, string, untypedAtomic, yearMonthDuration

At the time of writing there is some inconsistency in the specifications over casting between QNames and strings. The specs currently allow casting from a NOTATION to a string, but not from a QName to a string; and they allow casting from a string to a QName, but not from a string to a NOTATION. Since the value space of QName and NOTATION is the same, this doesn't make much sense. The difficulty with these types is that the value space includes information (the namespace URI) that can't be obtained directly from the lexical representation, and the lexical representation contains information (the namespace prefix) that can't be obtained directly from the internal value. Even if these conversions are allowed, the results may not always be useful.

Converting from anyURI

Destination Type	Rules
anyURI	The value is returned unchanged
string	The value is returned as a string containing exactly the same characters as the supplied anyURI value. No escaping or unescaping of special characters is performed
untypedAtomic	Returns the same result as converting to a string, but the result is labeled as untypedAtomic

Converting from base64Binary

Destination Type	Rules
base64Binary	The value is returned unchanged
hexBinary	A hexBinary value is constructed containing the same octets as the original base64Binary value
string	The canonical lexical representation of the base64Binary value is returned, as a string. This representation is defined in erratum E2-9 of the XML Schema specification. It arranges the value in multiple lines, with each line other than the last containing exactly 76 base-64 characters
untypedAtomic	Returns the same result as converting to a string, but the result is labeled as untypedAtomic

Converting from boolean

Destination Type	Rules
`boolean`	The value is returned unchanged
`decimal`	`true` is converted to `1.0`, `false` to `0.0`
`double`	`true` is converted to `1.0e0`, `false` to `0.0e0`
`float`	`true` is converted to `xs:float(1.0e0)`, `false` to `xs:float(0.0e0)`
`string`	Returns the string `"true"` or `"false"`
`untypedAtomic`	Returns the same result as converting to a string, but the result is labeled as `untypedAtomic`

Converting from date

Destination Type	Rules
`date`	The value is returned unchanged
`dateTime`	Returns the `dateTime` representing the instant in time at which the relevant date starts. The timezone (or the absence of a timezone) is retained unchanged. For example, the date `2004-04-04` becomes the `dateTime` `2004-04-04T00:00:00`
`gDay`	Returns a `gDay` value containing the same day component and timezone (or absence of a timezone) as the original date
`gMonth`	Returns a `gMonth` value containing the same month component and timezone (or absence of a timezone) as the original date
`gMonthDay`	Returns a `gMonthDay` value containing the same month and day components and timezone (or absence of a timezone) as the original date
`gYear`	Returns a `gYear` value containing the same year component and timezone (or absence of a timezone) as the original date
`gYearMonth`	Returns a `gYearMonth` value containing the same year and month components and timezone (or absence of a timezone) as the original date
`string`	Returns the canonical lexical representation of the date, retaining the original timezone. For example, a date with no timezone might be converted to the string «`2004-06-19`», while a date in the Pacific timezone might become «`2004-06-19-08:00`»
`untypedAtomic`	Returns the same result as converting to a string, but the result is labeled as `untypedAtomic`

Converting from dateTime

Destination Type	Rules
date	The date component of the localized `dateTime` value is returned, including the original timezone. The localized value is the value in the timezone contained with the value, for example the date component of the `dateTime` `2003-12-31T20:00:00-08:00` is `2003-12-31-08:00`. (This means you can extract the `date` part of two `dateTime` values that are equal to each other, and get different dates, because the two `dateTime` values represent the same instant in different timezones)
dateTime	The value is returned unchanged. Note that the original timezone is retained, even though it is not officially part of the value space according to the XML Schema specification
gDay	Returns a `gDay` value containing the same day component and timezone (or absence of a timezone) as the original localized `dateTime`
gMonth	Returns a `gMonth` value containing the same month component and timezone (or absence of a timezone) as the original localized `dateTime`
gMonthDay	Returns a `gMonthDay` value containing the same month and day components and timezone (or absence of a timezone) as the original localized `dateTime`
gYear	Returns a `gYear` value containing the same year component and timezone (or absence of a timezone) as the original localized `dateTime`
gYearMonth	Returns a `gYearMonth` value containing the same year and month components and timezone (or absence of a timezone) as the original localized `dateTime`
string	Returns the lexical representation of the `dateTime`, retaining the original timezone. This is not the same as the canonical lexical representation defined in XML Schema, which always normalizes the timezone to UTC
time	Returns the time component of the original localized `dateTime`, retaining its timezone
untypedAtomic	Returns the same result as converting to a string, but the result is labeled as `untypedAtomic`

Converting from dayTimeDuration

Destination Type	Rules
dayTimeDuration	The value is returned unchanged
duration	Returns a duration value whose day, hour, minute, and second components are the same as the supplied dayTimeDuration, and whose year and month components are zero
string	Returns the canonical lexical representation of the supplied dayTimeDuration. This normalizes the value so that the number of seconds is always less than 60, the number of minutes is less than 60, and the number of hours is less than 24. There is no limit on the number of days. Any component that is zero is omitted, except that the zero-length duration is represented as «PT0S». For example, a duration of 29.5 hours is represented as «P1DT5H30M»
untypedAtomic	Returns the same result as converting to a string, but the result is labeled as untypedAtomic

Converting from decimal

Destination Type	Rules
boolean	The value 0.0 is converted to false, and any other value is converted to true
decimal	The value is returned unchanged
double	The result is the closest double value to the supplied decimal. This may involve some loss of precision, because decimal values cannot usually be represented exactly in binary. The detailed rules are defined by saying that the result is equivalent to converting the decimal to a string and then converting the string to a double; this invokes rules given in XML Schema Part 2, that specify for example that if the decimal is midway between two double values, the even value is chosen. It is theoretically possible for a decimal to exceed the largest possible double value, but this is highly unlikely in practice and the specification doesn't say what should happen if it occurs: the most likely result is probably to return the special value Infinity
float	As with conversion from decimal to double, the rules are defined by saying that the decimal is converted to a string, and the string is then converted to a float. The same considerations apply

Destination Type	Rules
string	If the decimal represents a whole number (whether or not it is actually an instance of xs:integer) then it is represented on output as a string of decimal digits with no trailing zero and no decimal point. There is no truncation or rounding of significant digits, but insignificant leading or trailing zeroes are omitted. However, if the absolute value is less than one, a zero digit is included before the decimal point. The string starts with a «-» sign if the value is negative, but it never contains a «+» sign
untypedAtomic	Returns the same result as converting to a string, but the result is labeled as untypedAtomic

Converting from double

Destination Type	Rules
boolean	The values positive zero, negative zero, and NaN are converted to false, and any other value is converted to true
decimal	The result is the decimal value, within the range of decimal values that the implementation can handle, whose value is numerically closest to the value of the supplied double; if two values are equally close, the value is rounded towards zero. The range and precision of the decimal type is left to the implementor's discretion, so results may vary from one system to another. If the double is too large to be represented as a decimal, an error occurs
double	The value is returned unchanged
float	Digits are removed from the least significant end of the value to make the value fit within the precision supported by the float type. If the exponent is larger than the largest exponent allowed by a float, the result is positive or negative infinity. If the exponent is smaller than the smallest exponent allowed by a float, the result is positive or negative zero

Continues

Destination Type	Rules
string	If the value is NaN (not-a-number), it is output as the string «NaN». Positive and negative infinity are represented as «INF» and «-INF». Numbers whose absolute value is greater than or equal to 1.0e−6, and less than 1.0e+6, are represented in conventional decimal notation, for example «17.523», using the same rules as for decimal-to-string conversion. This means that if the value is a whole number, it is output without a decimal point. Numbers outside this range are output in "scientific" notation, in a form such as «1.56003E-5». There are strict rules on the precise form of this value, for example it includes no insignificant leading or trailing zeros except adjacent to the decimal point, and the «E» must be a capital «E». The value is output with as many digits (and only as many) as are needed to represent the value accurately so that the original value is recovered if the string is converted back to a double. If you want a more user-friendly representation of the number, XSLT allows you to control the formatting using the format-number() function. Outside the XSLT environment, you can trim unwanted digits using the function round-half-to-even(), which is described in Chapter 10
untypedAtomic	Returns the same result as converting to a string, but the result is labeled as untypedAtomic

Converting from duration

Destination Type	Rules
dayTimeDuration	Returns a dayTimeDuration that represents the value of the days, hours, minutes, and seconds components of the duration, ignoring the years and months. The idea is that it should be possible to convert a duration into a pair of values, a yearMonthDuration and a dayTimeDuration, which together retain the full value of the original duration
duration	The value is returned unchanged
string	The duration is output in a lexical form permitted by the XML Schema specification. There is no canonical lexical form defined, so it is not predictable whether, for example, zero-valued components will be included in the result or not. The XML Schema specification for durations regards a value such as «PT1H» (one hour) as being a distinct value from «PT60M» (60 minutes), so it is likely that the value will not be normalized in the way that yearMonthDuration and dayTimeDuration are normalized

Destination Type	Rules
untypedAtomic	Returns the same result as converting to a string, but the result is labeled as untypedAtomic.
yearMonthDuration	Returns a yearMonthDuration that represents the value of the years and months components of the duration, ignoring the days, hours, minutes, and seconds. The idea is that it should be possible to convert a duration into a pair of values, a yearMonthDuration and a dayTimeDuration, which together retain the full value of the original duration

Converting from float

Destination Type	Rules
boolean	The values positive zero, negative zero, and NaN are converted to false, and any other value is converted to true
decimal	The result is the decimal value, within the range of decimal values that the implementation can handle, whose value is numerically closest to the value of the supplied float; if two values are equally close, the value is rounded towards zero. The range and precision of the decimal type is left to the implementor's discretion, so results may vary from one system to another. If the float is too large to be represented as a decimal, an error occurs
double	The value space for float is a strict subset of that for double, so it is possible to convert every float value to a double without loss. The specification achieves this by stating that the conversion is equivalent to converting the float to a string, and then converting the string to a double
float	The value is returned unchanged
string	The rules are the same as those for double-to-string conversion: see page 270
untypedAtomic	Returns the same result as converting to a string, but the result is labeled as untypedAtomic

Converting from gDay

Destination Type	Rules
gDay	The value is returned unchanged
string	The output will be in the form ---DD, followed by a timezone if the value includes one
untypedAtomic	Returns the same result as converting to a string, but the result is labeled as untypedAtomic

Converting from gMonth

Destination Type	Rules
gMonth	The value is returned unchanged
string	The output will be in the form --MM, followed by a timezone if the value includes one. (There is an error in the XML Schema Recommendation, corrected in a published erratum, which gives the format as --MM--)
untypedAtomic	Returns the same result as converting to a string, but the result is labeled as untypedAtomic

Converting from gMonthDay

Destination Type	Rules
gMonthDay	The value is returned unchanged
string	The output will be in the form --MM-DD, followed by a timezone if the value includes one
untypedAtomic	Returns the same result as converting to a string, but the result is labeled as untypedAtomic

Converting from gYear

Destination Type	Rules
gYear	The value is returned unchanged
string	The output will be in the form YYYY, followed by a timezone if the value includes one
untypedAtomic	Returns the same result as converting to a string, but the result is labeled as untypedAtomic

Converting from gYearMonth

Destination Type	Rules
gYearMonth	The value is returned unchanged
string	The output will be in the form YYYY-MM, followed by a timezone if the value includes one
untypedAtomic	Returns the same result as converting to a string, but the result is labeled as untypedAtomic

Converting from hexBinary

Destination Type	Rules
base64Binary	A base64Binary value is constructed containing the same octets (bytes) as the original hexBinary value
hexBinary	The value is returned unchanged
string	The canonical lexical representation of the hexBinary value is returned, as a string. This representation uses two hexadecimal digits to represent each octet in the value. The digits used are 0–9 and A–F (uppercase)
untypedAtomic	Returns the same result as converting to a string, but the result is labeled as untypedAtomic

Converting from NOTATION

Destination Type	Rules
NOTATION	The value is returned unchanged
string	This conversion is currently allowed in the specifications, but it isn't entirely clear how it is supposed to work
untypedAtomic	Returns the same result as converting to a string, but the result is labeled as untypedAtomic

Converting from QName

Destination Type	Rules
QName	The value is returned unchanged

Note that casting from QName *to string is not allowed. This is because it would require the generation of a namespace declaration to represent the binding of a prefix to the namespace URI contained in the expanded* QName, *and in general there is nowhere for this namespace declaration to go.*

Converting from string

Destination Type	Rules
anyURI base64Binary boolean date dateTime dayTimeDuration decimal double duration float gDay gMonth gMonthDay gYear gYearMonth hexBinary string time yearMonthDuration	The string is converted to the destination type using the same rules as are applied during schema validation of an element or attribute declared with this type. Firstly, whitespace is normalized or collapsed as determined by the whiteSpace facet of the target type. (In most cases this means that leading and trailing whitespace is removed). Then the resulting value is tested to check that it is a valid lexical representation for the specified atomic type, and the corresponding value of that type is returned. The rules are refined in the case of the date and time data types to allow the timezone information to be retained (in XML Schema, these are lost during the process of validation)
QName	The lexical QName is converted to an expanded QName in the usual way, taking the namespace context from the static context of the XPath expression (if the value is not known at compile time, it may be necessary to retain a copy of this namespace context so that the prefix can be resolved at runtime). If the QName contains no prefix, then the default namespace for elements and types is used (in XSLT, this is the namespace declared using the xpath-default-namespace attribute)
untypedAtomic	The returned value contains the same characters as the original string, but labeled as untypedAtomic

Converting from time

Destination Type	Rules
dateTime	The result is formed by combining the supplied time value with the value of the current date. The current date is the date in the implicit timezone, which is not necessarily the same as the timezone of the supplied time value. The timezone used in the result comes from the supplied time value. This is the only example of a cast whose result depends on the dynamic context, and whose value is therefore likely to vary on different occasions
string	Returns the canonical lexical representation of the time, retaining the original timezone. For example, the value might be output as «13:20:05.012+01:00»
time	The value is returned unchanged
untypedAtomic	Returns the same result as converting to a string, but the result is labeled as untypedAtomic

Converting from untypedAtomic

The rules for conversion from an untypedAtomic value to any other type are exactly the same as the rules for converting from an equivalent string. See page 274.

Converting from yearMonthDuration

Destination Type	Rules
duration	Returns a duration value whose year and month components are the same as the supplied yearMonthDuration, and whose day, hour, minute, and second components are zero
string	Returns the canonical lexical representation of the supplied yearMonthDuration. This normalizes the value so that the number of months is always less than 12. Any component that is zero is omitted, except that the zero-length duration is represented as «P0M». For example, a duration of 18 months is represented as «P1Y6M»
untypedAtomic	Returns the same result as converting to a string, but the result is labeled as untypedAtomic
yearMonthDuration	The value is returned unchanged

Converting between Derived Types

The previous section listed all the permitted conversions between primitive atomic types. Now we need to consider what happens if the supplied value belongs to a derived type, or if the destination type is a derived type. Note that we are still only concerned with atomic types. It is not allowed for the destination type of a cast to be a list or union type. It may however be a type that is derived by restriction. This includes both built-in derived types such as xs:integer, xs:short, and xs:Name, and also user-defined derived types, provided that they are named types in a schema that has been imported in the static context of the XPath expression.

The first case, where the supplied value belongs to a derived type, is easy. As always, the principle of substitutability holds: a value of a subtype may always be used as input to an operation that accepts values belonging to its supertype. This means that conversion from a derived type to its base type is always successful. However, there is one minor caveat. In the tables in the previous section, conversion of a value to its own primitive type is always described with the rule "The value is returned unchanged." However, if the source value belongs to a subtype of the primitive type (that is, a type derived by restriction from the primitive type), this rule should be amended to read "The value is returned unchanged, but with the type label set to the destination type". For example, if you cast an xs:short value xs:short(2) to the type xs:decimal, the type label on the result will be xs:decimal. In fact, it is always a rule for casting operations that the type label on the result value is the type that you were casting to.

If the destination type of the cast is a derived type, then the general rule is "go up, then across, then down". For example, if you are converting from a subtype of xs:decimal to a subtype of xs:string, you first convert the supplied value *up* to an xs:decimal, then you convert the xs:decimal *across* to an xs:string, and then you convert the xs:string *down* to the final destination type. Of course, any of the three stages in this journey may be omitted where it isn't needed.

The last leg of this journey, the *down* part, now needs to be explained.

The rule here is (in general) that the value is not changed, but it is validated against the restrictions that apply to the subtype. These restrictions are defined by facets in the schema definition of the type. If the value satisfies the facets, then the cast succeeds and the result has the same value as the source, but with a new type label. If the value does not satisfy the facets, then the cast fails. For example, the expression «xs:positiveInteger(-5)» will cause an error, because the value −5 does not satisfy the minInclusive facet for the type (which says that the lowest permitted value is zero).

There is a slight complication with the pattern facet. This facet defines a regular expression that the value must conform to. The pattern facet, unlike all the others, is applied to the lexical value rather than the internal value. To check whether a value conforms to the pattern facet, the system must first convert it to a string. This is bad news if the pattern facet has been used to constrain input XML documents to use a form other than the canonical representation, for example to constrain an xs:boolean attribute to the values «0» and «1». The conversion to a string will produce the value «true» or «false», and will therefore fail the pattern validation. Generally speaking, using the pattern facet with data types other than string (or string-like types such as xs:anyURI) is best avoided.

There are three built-in types that are technically derived types, but that are treated almost like primitive types for the purpose of the casting rules. I have included two of these, xdt:dayTimeDuration and xdt:yearMonthDuration, in the tables in the previous section for primitive types. The other one that's special is xs:integer. I didn't include that in the previous section because there are no special rules for converting from an xs:integer to other types (it behaves just like an xs:decimal), only special rules for converting to an xs:integer. These rules are given in the next section.

Converting to an xs:integer

Generally, casting to a derived type fails if the facets of the derived type are not satisfied. The type xs:integer is derived by restriction from xs:decimal, with a facet indicating that there must not be a fractional part. Normally, this would mean that casting 12.3 to an xs:integer would fail.

However, there is a special rule for casting numeric values to integers, or to subtypes derived from xs:integer. The value is first cast to the primitive type, xs:decimal, in the usual way, and then the value is truncated towards zero. This means that «xs:integer(10 div 3)» is 3, and «xs:integer(3.5 - 8.7)» is -5.

This special rule does not apply when casting from a string to an integer. In this case xs:integer is treated like any other derived type, which means that a cast such as «xs:integer("2.5")» will fail.

Sequence Type Descriptors

The operators described in the previous section work only on atomic types, which can always be referenced by a simple QName (unless they are anonymous types, in which case they can't be referenced at all). Later in this chapter, we will be defining two important operators «instance of» and «treat as». These can be applied to any sequence type (that is, any type in the XPath type system). Sequence types cannot always be represented by a simple name; instead, XPath defines a syntactic construct for describing these types. The production rule for this is called SequenceType. I find it useful to have a name for the actual description of a type written according to this syntax, so I've coined the name *sequence type descriptor* for this.

Sequence type descriptors are used in XPath itself only in expressions involving these two operators «instance of» and «treat as». However, they are used much more widely in XSLT and XQuery, for example they can be used whenever the type of a variable or of a function parameter needs to be declared.

The syntax is quite complicated, so we'll take it in stages, explaining the semantics as we go along.

Expression	Syntax
SequenceType	(ItemType OccurrenceIndicator?) | «empty ( )»
OccurrenceIndicator	«?» | «*» | «+»
ItemType	AtomicType | KindTest | «item ( )»
AtomicType	QName
KindTest	DocumentTest | ElementTest | AttributeTest | PITest | CommentTest | TextTest | AnyKindTest

The first rule tells us that a sequence type descriptor is either an ItemType followed optionally by an OccurrenceIndicator, or it is the compound symbol «empty()».

The «empty()» construct is used very rarely in practice. The only sequence that conforms to this type is the empty sequence. This is why no occurrence indicator is allowed in this case. The only practical example I have seen where «empty()» is useful is in an XQuery «typeswitch» expression. You can use it in XPath, for example, «$x instance of empty()» means the same as «empty($x)». But it's really there only for completeness, so that every type used in expressing the formal semantics of the language is also accessible to users of the language.

Apart from «empty()», every other sequence type descriptor consists of an ItemType followed optionally by an OccurrenceIndicator. The ItemType defines what kind of items can appear in a sequence, and the OccurrenceIndicator says how many of them are allowed. The three occurrence indicators (which in computer science theory are often called Kleene operators) will be familiar from their use in regular expressions and DTDs. They are:

Occurrence Indicator	Meaning
*	Zero or more occurrences allowed
+	One or more occurrences allowed
?	Zero or one occurrence allowed

If no OccurrenceIndicator is present, then a sequence will only conform to the type if it contains exactly one item.

The rest of the syntax provides different ways of expressing an ItemType.

First of all, the compound symbol «item()» allows any kind of item, that is, any atomic value, or any node. (As with other compound symbols, you can use spaces before, between, or after the parentheses, but it's usually written without spaces so that's how I shall do it here.) You can combine «item()» with an occurrence indicator, so «item()» matches a single item, «item()?» matches a sequence that is either empty or contains a single item, «item()+» matches any non-empty sequence, and «item()*» matches any sequence whatsoever.

Every other way of writing the ItemType matches either atomic values, or nodes, but not both.

Atomic Types

Matching atomic values is easy, because atomic types have names. (You can have anonymous atomic types in a schema, but there is no way to refer to them in a sequence type descriptor). If you use a QName as the ItemType, then it must be the name of a type that is known in the static context of the XPath expression, as described in Chapter 4, and this type must be an atomic type. The way that the static context is set up depends on the host language and the API you are using to execute XPath expressions, so the set of types that are available may vary. XSLT 2.0, for example, defines a minimum set of atomic types that every processor (even one that does not support schema import) must provide, namely:

```
xs:string
xs:boolean
xs:decimal
xs:integer
xs:double
xs:date
xs:time
xs:dateTime
xdt:dayTimeDuration
xdt:yearMonthDuration
xs:QName
xs:anyURI
xdt:untypedAtomic
xdt:anyAtomicType
```

This set was chosen because it is sufficient to allow all the functions in the core function library (that is, the functions listed in Chapter 10) to be used. Many processors, however, will support the full set of built-in types defined in XML Schema as well as user-defined types declared using <xs:simpleType> declarations in an imported schema.

Most of these types were described fully in Chapter 3, but the last two are worth a special mention.

❑   xdt:untypedAtomic is the type of the atomic value that results from atomizing a node that has not been annotated (as a result of schema validation) with any more specific type. It is possible to create an xdt:untypedAtomic value by casting (and it is sometimes convenient to do so), but the most common way of getting these values is by atomizing an unvalidated node.

❑   xdt:anyAtomicType is a supertype for all atomic types. Used as an item type, this will match any atomic value (for example, a string, an integer, or a boolean), and will not match a node. It's an abstract type, in that something that is an instance of xdt:anyAtomicType will always be an instance of some other more specific type in addition. (The name is rather poorly chosen, I feel. One might expect that the instances of this type are types, just as in Java the instances of Class are classes. But the name was chosen in the tradition of xs:anyType and xs:anySimpleType, and it seems to have stuck.)

Note that the QName must be the name of an atomic type, not merely a simple type. Simple types, in the XML schema classification, also include list types and union types. Atomic values contained in an XPath sequence always belong to an atomic type, not a list or union type, and a sequence type descriptor is therefore constrained to use atomic types. This rules out types such as xs:NMTOKENS, xs:IDREFS, and xs:ENTITIES, which are list types, as well as xs:anyType, which is a complex type.

Matching Nodes

All other sorts of ItemType are used to match nodes. These all come under the umbrella of the KindTest construct.

I'll dispose of the simple kinds of node first, and then move on to elements and attributes, which is where the real complexity comes.

Expression	Syntax
KindTest	AnyKindTest | DocumentTest | ElementTest | AttributeTest | CommentTest | TextTest | PITest
AnyKindTest	«node ( )»
DocumentTest	«document-node (» ElementTest? «)»
CommentTest	«comment ( )»
TextTest	«text ( )»
PITest	«processing-instruction (» (NCName | StringLiteral)? «)»

If you're reading the book sequentially, you may have a sense of *déjà vu* about these rules. We met them before in Chapter 7, on page 224, where they appear as part of the syntax for a NodeTest in a path expression. Conveniently, the syntax for testing the type of a node in an «instance of» or «treat as» expression is exactly the same as the syntax for saying what kinds of node you are interested in within a step of a path expression. What's more, because the syntax of XSLT match patterns is defined in terms of path expressions, you can use the same constructs when defining an XSLT template rule.

The construct «node()» is the most general item type here: it matches any item that is a node.

Note, however, that if you use «node()» on its own as a step in a path expression (as described in Chapter 7), it is short for «child::node()», and will only match nodes that are found on the child axis. The only nodes that can be found on the child axis are elements, text nodes, comments, and processing instructions.

The constructs «comment()» and «text()» are straightforward: they match comment nodes and text nodes, respectively.

For matching document nodes, you can write the test «document-node()», which matches any document node, or you can be more specific. If you include an ElementTest within the parentheses, then this ItemType will only match a document node that satisfies the following two conditions:

❑   The document node must be the root of a tree that corresponds to a well-formed XML document. Specifically this means that the document node must have exactly one element node, and no text nodes, among its children. It is allowed to have comments and processing instructions before or after the element node.

❑   The element node that is a child of this document node must match the ElementTest given within the parentheses. The syntax for ElementTest is given in the next section.

This construct allows you to test what can be loosely called the "document type", for example, you can test whether an input document returned by the doc() function is an invoice, by writing:

```
if (doc("inv.xml") instance of document-node(schema-element(mf:invoice))) ...
```

This construct tests whether the document node is labeled as an invoice, as the result of previous validation. If the document has not been validated, the result will be false, whether or not validation would succeed if attempted.

The «processing-instruction()» construct can also be written with empty parentheses, in which case it will match any processing instruction. As an alternative, you can provide a name within the parentheses, in which case it will only match processing instructions with that name. For compatibility with XPath 1.0, the name can optionally be written in quotes, as a string literal. This means you can match an <?xml-stylesheet?> processing instruction using either of the constructs:

```
processing-instruction(xml-stylesheet)
processing-instruction("xml-stylesheet")
```

The two forms are precisely equivalent, except that using an invalid name is an error in the first case but not the second (you just won't select anything).

Here's the basic syntax for element and attribute tests:

Matching Elements and Attributes

The syntax for matching elements and attributes is more complex, because it allows you to take advantage of the type information attached to these nodes as a result of schema validation. The type annotation of an element or attribute node may be any type defined in an XML Schema, or a built-in type. These can be simple types or complex types, and all simple types are allowed including list types and union types. However, although any type defined in a schema can appear as a node annotation, the only types you can refer to directly are those that:

❑   have a name (that is, they are not anonymous types, which means they must be defined in top-level type definitions in the schema), and

❑   are declared in a schema that has been imported in the static context of the XPath expression. The way this is done depends on the host language you are using, and perhaps on the API of the XPath processor. In XSLT, for example, you can import schemas using the <xsl:import-schema> declaration.

Here's the basic syntax for element and attribute tests:

Expression	Syntax
ElementTest	BasicElementTest | SchemaElementTest
AttributeTest	BasicAttributeTest | SchemaAttributeTest

Continues

Expression	Syntax
BasicElementTest	«element (» (ElementNameOrWildCard («,» TypeName «?»?)?)? «)»
BasicAttributeTest	«attribute (» (AttribNameOrWildcard («,» TypeName)?)? «)»
ElementNameOrWildcard	ElementName | «*»
AttribNameOrWildcard	AttributeName | «*»
ElementName	QName
AttributeName	QName
TypeName	QName

We will come back to the SchemaElementTest and SchemaAttributeTest later. The meaning of this syntax doesn't leap out from the page, so it's best to explain it by listing all the possible cases. The general form is «element (*NAME*, *TYPE*)», where *NAME* defines conditions on the name of the element, and *TYPE* defines conditions on its type annotation.

Here are the rules for matching elements:

Test	Matches
element()	Any element node
element(*)	Any element node
element(N)	Any element node whose name is N. In a path expression this is equivalent to just writing the element name N on its own: but in contexts where a type is required, it provides a way of saying that a value must be an element with a particular name, whether or not this name is defined in any schema
element(*,T)	Any element node whose type annotation shows it to be valid according to the rules of schema type T. The type T can be a simple type or a complex type, but it must be a named type that is defined in an imported schema (this allows a built-in type, of course). If the element has the attribute «xsi:nil="true"», then it matches only if the type name T in the sequence type descriptor is followed by a question mark

Test	Matches
element(N,T)	Any element node whose name is N and that is annotated as an instance of schema type T. This combines the previous two options into a single condition

The rules for matching attributes are very similar, but they are simpler because attributes cannot be marked as nillable:

Test	Matches
attribute()	Any attribute node
attribute(*)	Any attribute node
attribute(N)	Any attribute node whose name is N
attribute(*,T)	Any attribute node whose type annotation shows it to be valid according to the rules of schema type T. The type T must always be a named simple type that is defined in an imported schema (this allows a built-in type, of course)
attribute(N,T)	Any attribute node whose name is N and that is annotated as an instance of the schema type T

Using Global Element and Attribute Declarations

The basic element and attribute tests described in the previous section allow you to test an element or attribute node according to its name and its type annotation, provided that the type annotation is a named simple or complex type in the schema. It's very common, however, to find that elements are declared in a schema using global element declarations and with an anonymous type: to take an example from the schema for XSLT 2.0 stylesheets:

```
<xs:element name="apply-imports" substitutionGroup="xsl:instruction">
  <xs:complexType>
    <xs:complexContent>
      <xs:extension base="xsl:versioned-element-type">
        <xs:sequence>
          <xs:element ref="xsl:with-param" minOccurs="0"
                                          maxOccurs= "unbounded"/>
        </xs:sequence>
      </xs:extension>
    </xs:complexContent>
  </xs:complexType>
</xs:element>
```

The syntax «element(E, T)» doesn't work in this case, because the type is anonymous. Instead, the construct «schema-element(S)» can be used. This matches any element that has been validated against the global element declaration named «S» in the schema. It's not necessary that the name of the element should be «S», it can also be an element in the substitution group of «S».

It's much less common to encounter global attribute declarations, but they are also supported in the same way, for symmetry.

The full syntax for this form of `ElementTest` and `AttributeTest` is shown below.

Expression	Syntax
SchemaElementTest	«schema-element (» ElementName «)»
SchemaAttributeTest	«schema-attribute (» AttributeName «)»

Examples

Let's try to put these different forms into context by seeing how they can be used with a real schema. I'll use as my example the schema for XSLT 2.0 stylesheets, which is published in an appendix of the XSLT 2.0 specification at `http://www.w3.org/TR/xslt20`. This example is therefore relevant if you are using XPath expressions to access an XSLT 2.0 stylesheet (which is not as esoteric a requirement as you might think), and it also assumes that the XSLT 2.0 stylesheet has been validated against this schema.

The schema starts with a couple of complex type definitions like this:

```
<xs:complexType name="generic-element-type">
  <xs:attribute name="extension-element-prefixes" type="xsl:prefixes"/>
  <xs:attribute name="exclude-result-prefixes" type="xsl:prefixes"/>
  <xs:attribute name="xpath-default-namespace" type="xs:anyURI"/>
  <attribute ref="xml:space">
  <attribute ref="xml:lang">
  <xs:anyAttribute namespace="##other" processContents="skip"/>
</xs:complexType>

<xs:complexType name="versioned-element-type">
  <xs:complexContent>
    <xs:extension base="xsl:generic-element-type">
      <xs:attribute name="version" type="xs:decimal" use="optional"/>
    </xs:extension>
  </xs:complexContent>
</xs:complexType>
```

Every element in the XSLT namespace has a type that is derived ultimately from «generic-element-type», and most of them are also derived from «versioned-element-type». If we want to use a sequence type descriptor (perhaps to declare a variable or a function argument in XSLT or XQuery) that accepts any element in the XSLT namespace that is valid against this schema, we could declare this as:

```
element(*, xsl:generic-element-type)
```

If we wanted to exclude those elements that don't allow a `version` attribute (there is only one, `<xsl:output>`, which in fact does allow a `version` attribute, but defines it differently) then we could write the sequence type descriptor as:

```
element(*, xsl:versioned-element-type)
```

The schema goes on to provide two abstract element declarations, like this:

```
<xs:element name="declaration" type="xsl:generic-element-type"
            abstract="true"/>

<xs:element name="instruction" type="xsl:versioned-element-type"
            abstract="true"/>
```

These are declared as abstract because you can't actually include an element in a stylesheet whose name is <xsl:declaration> or <xsl:instruction>. The reason these two element declarations exist is so that they can act as the heads of substitution groups. This greatly simplifies the definition of other types. For example, there are many places in XSLT where you can use a construct called a *sequence constructor*. A sequence constructor is a sequence of elements in the stylesheet that may include variable definitions, instructions, and literal result elements, and its format is defined in the schema like this:

```
<xs:group name="sequence-constructor-group">
  <xs:choice>
    <xs:element ref="xsl:variable"/>
    <xs:element ref="xsl:instruction"/>
    <xs:group ref="xsl:result-elements"/>
  </xs:choice>
</xs:group>
```

Elements that allow a sequence constructor as their content, such as <xsl:if> and <xsl:sequence>, make use of a complex type definition that refers to this structure:

```
<xs:complexType name="sequence-constructor">
  <xs:complexContent mixed="true">
    <xs:extension base="xsl:versioned-element-type">
      <xs:group ref="xsl:sequence-constructor-group"
                minOccurs="0" maxOccurs="unbounded"/>
    </xs:extension>
  </xs:complexContent>
</xs:complexType>
```

The abstract element <xsl:instruction> was introduced for convenience in defining the schema, but it is equally convenient for describing types in XPath, because we can now write:

```
schema-element(xsl:instruction)
```

to match any element that is an XSLT instruction: that is, an element that is in the substitution group of <xsl:instruction>. An example of such an element is <xsl:apply-imports>, which as we have already seen is defined like this:

```
<xs:element name="apply-imports" substitutionGroup="xsl:instruction">
  <xs:complexType>
    <xs:complexContent>
      <xs:extension base="xsl:versioned-element-type">
        <xs:sequence>
```

```
        <xs:element ref="xsl:with-param" minOccurs="0"
                                        maxOccurs= "unbounded"/>
      </xs:sequence>
    </xs:extension>
  </xs:complexContent>
 </xs:complexType>
</xs:element>
```

The schema for XSLT 2.0 stylesheets does not include any global attribute declarations, so you will never see a sequence type descriptor of the form «schema-attribute(xsl:xxxx)». This is fairly typical: attributes are most commonly declared either as part of the element declaration to which they belong, or in constructs such as xs:attributeGroup. For example, the set of «xsl:» prefixed attributes that can appear on literal result elements is defined in the schema for XSLT 2.0 in an attribute group:

```
<xs:attributeGroup name="literal-result-element-attributes">
  <xs:attribute name="extension-element-prefixes" form="qualified"
             type="xsl:prefixes"/>
  <xs:attribute name="exclude-result-prefixes" form="qualified"
             type="xsl:prefixes"/>
  <xs:attribute name="xpath-default-namespace" form="qualified"
             type="xs:anyURI"/>
  <xs:attribute name="use-attribute-sets" form="qualified"
             type="xsl:QNames" default=""/>
  <xs:attribute name="version" form="qualified"
             type="xs:decimal"/>
  <xs:attribute name="type" form="qualified"
             type="xsl:QName"/>
  <xs:attribute name="validation" form="qualified"
             type="xsl:validation-type"/>
</xs:attributeGroup>
```

This means that even these attributes (which are unusual because their names are in the target namespace of the schema) are not declared globally, and therefore not available for use in sequence type descriptors. It would be possible to change the schema to the following form (selecting just three of the attributes for brevity):

```
<xs:attribute name="version" form="qualified" type="xs:decimal"/>
<xs:attribute name="type" form="qualified" type="xsl:QName"/>
<xs:attribute name="validation" form="qualified" type="xsl:validation-type"/>

<xs:attributeGroup name="literal-result-element-attributes">
  <xs:attribute ref="version" form="qualified" type="xs:decimal"/>
  <xs:attribute ref="type" form="qualified" type="xsl:QName"/>
  <xs:attribute ref="validation" form="qualified" type="xsl:validation-type"/>
</xs:attributeGroup>
```

and you could then use «schema-attribute(xsl:version)» as a sequence type descriptor.

Much more common, I think, will be to use the form «attribute(*, T)» which matches attributes that have a particular type annotation. For example, many attributes in XSLT have the type xsl:QName. An example is the name attribute of <xsl:function>, allowing you to write, for example, <xsl:function name="math:sqrt">. This type is a variant of the built-in type xs:QName. It has the same lexical form as an `xs:QName` but is not derived from it because the validation rules are subtly different: in XML Schema, an `xs:QName` with no prefix is assumed to be in the default namespace, but in XSLT, an `xsl:QName` with no prefix is assumed to be in no namespace.

If you wanted to process a stylesheet to process all the attributes of type `xsl:QName`, perhaps to standardize the namespace prefixes that are used, you could write an XSLT template rule of the form:

```
<xsl:template match="attribute(*, xsl:QName)">
  ...
</xsl:template>
```

There is no way of writing a sequence type descriptor that matches a local element or attribute definition in a schema. Earlier working drafts defined a syntax that allowed such definitions to be referenced by means of a hierarchic name rather like a path expression, but the syntax was pulled from the final draft because of difficulties in defining its precise meaning. In many cases local element and attributes in a schema are defined by reference to a global type, and in this case you can use the syntax «element(E, T)» or «attribute(A, T)».

The «instance of» operator

The «instance of» operator is used to test whether a given value conforms to a particular type. This operator is a compound symbol; the two words must be separated by whitespace.

Expression	Syntax
InstanceOfExpr	TreatExpr («instance of» SequenceType)?

As usual, the fact that the first operand is listed as a `TreatExpr` is simply a way of indicating the operator priorities: these are summarized in Appendix A.

The «instance of» expression always returns a boolean result. The first operand is evaluated, and if it conforms to the specified sequence type (as defined by the rules in the previous section) the answer is `true`, otherwise it is `false`.

It's important to remember, whether you are testing atomic values or nodes, that the «instance of» operator is testing whether the value has a label that identifies it as a member of the specified type. It isn't testing whether the value would be a valid member of that type if the label were changed. For example:

```
5 instance of xs:positiveInteger
```

return `false` (surprisingly), because although 5 satisfies all the conditions for a positive integer, it is not labeled as such: the type label for a numeric literal of this kind is simply `xs:integer`. Similarly, given an element `<price>13.50</price>` as the context item, the expression

```
. instance of element(*, xs:decimal)
```

will return `false` unless the element has actually been validated and given a type annotation of `xs:decimal`, or some type derived from `xs:decimal`. The fact that validation against this type would succeed is not enough; the validation must actually have been done, so that the required type annotation is present on the node.

The «instance of» operator does not atomize its operand, so an expression such as «@code instance of xs:decimal» is always going to return false. You either need to atomize the value explicitly, by writing «data(@code) instance of xs:decimal», or you need to test the type annotation of the node, by writing «@code instance of attribute(*, xs:decimal)».

Note also that if an element or attribute is list-valued, then the type annotation on the node may be a list type, for example, «attribute(*, xs:IDREFS)». But when you extract the typed value of this node using the data() function, the result is a sequence of xs:IDREF values, which you can test using the sequence type descriptor «xs:IDREF*». You cannot write «data(@x) instance of xs:IDREFS», because xs:IDREFS is not an atomic type.

The «instance of» expression tests the dynamic type of a value, that is, the actual type of the value after the operand expression has been evaluated. This may or may not be the same as the static type of the operand expression. The static type of an expression (which is only of interest to users in the case of processors that implement the static typing option, as explained in Chapter 3) will always be a supertype of the dynamic type of any possible value of the expression (or the same type, of course).

Here are some examples of «instance of» expressions used in context:

Expression	Effect
$seq[. instance of node()]	Selects the items in $seq that are nodes, discarding any that are atomic values
if (some $s in $seq satisfies $s instance of node()) then ...	Tests whether the sequence $seq contains at least one node
if (not($seq instance of xdt:anyAtomicType*)) then ...	This has exactly the same effect as the previous example. If a sequence is not an instance of «xdt:anyAtomicType*», then it must contain at least one node
$p instance of item()+	This tests whether $p is a non-empty sequence. The result is the same as calling «exists($p)»

The «treat as» Operator

The «treat as» operator can be regarded as an assertion; the programmer is asserting that at runtime, the value of an expression will conform to a given type. If the assertion turns out to be wrong, evaluation of the expression will fail with a runtime error.

This is the syntax:

Expression	Syntax
TreatExpr	CastableExpr («treat as» SequenceType)?

The «`treat as`» operator is extremely important if you are using an XPath processor that does strict static type checking (or if you want to write code that is portable between processors that do such checking and those that don't). However, if you want to write robust code, there is no harm in using «`treat as`» to make explicit any assumptions you are making about data types even in a system that does all its type checking dynamically.

For example, suppose that you are using a schema that defines a union type, an attribute `quantity`, say, whose value can be either an integer or one of the two strings «`out-of-stock`» or «`unknown`». It might look reasonable to write

```
if (@quantity = "out-of-stock")
    then -2
else if (@quantity = "unknown")
    then -1
else @quantity + 2
```

Unfortunately, it's not as easy as that. The three places where `@quantity` is used all do atomization, which will produce either a string or an integer, but at compile time it's not known whether the value will be a string or an integer. The «`=`» comparison in the condition of the «`if`» will fail if the value turns out to be an integer, because you can't compare an integer to a string. The «`+`» operator would similarly fail if the value turned out to be a string. You and I can see that this will never happen, but the XPath processor is not so clever. All it knows at compile time is that the value might be either an integer or a string.

A processor that does strict static typing will throw this out with compile time errors, because it detects that the code is unsafe (meaning, it could try to do illegal things at runtime). How do you get round this?

Firstly, you could try rewriting the expression like this:

```
if (data(@quantity) instance of xs:string)
then
    if (@quantity = "out-of-stock")
        then -2
    else if (@quantity = "unknown")
        then -1
    else error()
else @quantity + 2
```

For a system that does dynamic type checking, this is good enough. It avoids the error that would otherwise occur (at runtime) when you try to compare an integer to a string.

But unfortunately this still won't persuade a static type checker that all is well, because it can't follow through the logic of this code to work out that when you take one path, the value of `@quantity` must be a string, and when you take a different path, it must be an integer. So you need to use «`treat as`», like this:

```
if (data(@quantity) instance of xs:string)
then
```

```
      if ((data(@quantity) treat as xs:string) = "out-of-stock")
         then -2
      else if ((data(@quantity) treat as xs:string) = "unknown"))
         then -1
      else error()
   else (data(@quantity) treat as xs:integer) + 2
```

This code will work both on systems that do strict static typing, and on those that don't. The «treat as» operator is essentially telling the system that you know what the runtime type is going to be, and you want any checking to be deferred until runtime, because you're confident that your code is correct.

I rather suspect that few XPath 2.0 implementations will decide to implement strict static typing, so this might all turn out to be slightly irrelevant. The enthusiasm among implementors for strict static typing is far stronger in XQuery circles, where the need for optimization is so much greater. XQuery has an additional construct, the «typeswitch» expression, to make code like that shown above much less painful to write.

There is another workaround to this problem, which is to exploit the fact that XPath also offers the chameleon xdt:untypedAtomic type, which defeats the static type checker because it takes on whatever type is required by the context. So you could write the above expression instead as:

```
for $q in xdt:untypedAtomic(@quantity) return
    if ($q = "out-of-stock")
        then -2
    else if ($q = "unknown")
        then -1
    else $q + 2
```

This approach is basically discarding the type information added as a result of schema processing, and treating the data as if it were schema-less. Some would regard it as dirty programming, but it works.

Summary

This chapter provided details of all the type-related constructs and expressions in the XPath 2.0 language.

At the beginning of the chapter we described the «cast» and «castable» operators, and constructor functions, which are used to convert an atomic value of one type to an atomic value of a different type. We provided detailed tables showing all the type conversions that are allowed by the language.

Then, moving beyond atomic types, we examined the syntax for describing sequence types. This syntax is used only in two places in XPath, the «instance of» and «treat as» expressions, but XQuery and XSLT users will use the same syntax much more widely, for example, whenever the types of variables or functions are declared.

Finally, we explained how these two expressions, «instance of» and «treat as», actually work.

We've now finished our tour of the language syntax, but an equally important part of any language is the built-in function library. The next chapter provides an alphabetical listing of all the functions in this library, which will all be available with any conformant XPath 2.0 processor.

XPath Functions

This chapter describes all the standard functions included in the XPath 2.0 specifications for use in expressions. They are all defined in the W3C specification *XPath and XQuery Functions and Operators*, and they should be available in all XPath 2.0 implementations.

For each function, I give its name, a brief description of its purpose, a list of the arguments it expects and the value it returns, the formal rules defining what the function does, and finally usage advice and examples.

These are not the only functions you can call from an XPath expression:

❑ XSLT 2.0 defines additional functions for use in XPath expressions invoked from XSLT stylesheets. These are listed in Chapter 7 of *XSLT 2.0 Programmer's Reference*.

❑ So-called *constructor functions* are available corresponding to built-in and user-defined atomic types. For example, there is a function called xs:float() to create values of type xs:float, xs:date() to create values of type xs:date, and so on. These functions are also available for user-defined atomic types. They are described in Chapter 9.

❑ User-defined functions may be available. The way these are set up depends on the host language. In XSLT 2.0, user-defined functions can be created using an <xsl:function> declaration; in XQuery 1.0, they can be declared using a «declare function» statement in the Query Prolog.

❑ Vendor-defined functions may be available. These will be in a namespace controlled by the vendor of the particular product.

The syntax of a function call is described in Chapter 5. This defines where a function call can be used in an expression, and where it can't. You can use a function call anywhere that an expression or value can be used, provided that the type of value it returns is appropriate to the context where it used. (Unlike XPath 1.0, this includes the ability to use a function call as a step in a path expression.) Within a function call, the values supplied as arguments can be any XPath expression, subject only to the rules on data types (for example, some functions require an argument that is a sequence of nodes). So a function call such as «count(..)», though it looks strange, is perfectly legal: «..» is a valid XPath expression that returns the parent of the context node (it's described in Chapter 7, on page 227).

I've arranged the functions in alphabetical order so you can find them quickly if you know what you're looking for. However, in case you only know the general area you are interested in, you may find the classification that follows in the section *Functions by Category* useful. This is followed by a section called *Notation* that describes the notation used for function specifications in this chapter. The rest of the chapter is taken up with the functions themselves, in alphabetical order.

A Word about Naming

Function names such as `current-dateTime()` seem very strange when you first come across them. Why the mixture of camelCasing and hyphenation? The reason they arise is that XPath 1.0 decided to use hyphenated lower-case names for all functions, while XML Schema decided to use camelCase for the names of built-in data types. Wherever the XPath 2.0 function library uses a schema-defined type name as part of a function name, it therefore uses the camelCase type name as a single word within the hyphenated function name.

So it may be madness, but there is method in it!

Throughout this book, I write these function names without a namespace prefix. In fact the functions are defined to be within a namespace such as `http://www.w3.org/2003/11/xpath-functions`, which is generally referred to using the namespace prefix «fn». The year and month within the namespace URI change each time a new version of the specification is published, but will stabilize when the spec reaches Candidate Recommendation status. However, in most host languages (certainly in XSLT) this is likely to be the default namespace for function names. You will therefore usually be able to write these function names without a prefix (and without declaring the namespace URI), and I have therefore omitted the prefix when referring to the names in this book. In the W3C specifications, however, you will often see the functions referred to by names such as `fn:position()` or `fn:count()`.

Functions by Category

Any attempt to classify functions is bound to be arbitrary; but I'll attempt it anyway. A few functions appear in more than one category. The number after each function is a page reference to the entry where the function is described.

Boolean Functions

`boolean()` 304, `false()` 343, `not()` 391, `true()` 439.

Numeric Functions

`abs()` 296, `avg()` 301, `ceiling()` 306, `floor()` 344, `max()` 370, `min()` 371, `number()` 393, `round()` 409, `round-half-to-even()` 411, `sum()` 431.

String Functions

`codepoints-to-string()` 308, `compare()` 310, `concat()` 312, `contains()` 314, `ends-with()` 334, `lower-case()` 366, `matches()` 368, `normalize-space()` 386, `normalize-unicode()` 388, `replace()` 400, `starts-with()` 415, `string()` 416, `string-join()` 418, `string-length()` 419, string-to-codepoints() 421, substring() 423, substring-after() 425, substring-before() 427, tokenize() 434, upper-case() 442.

Date and Time Functions

adjust-date-to-timezone() 297, adjust-dateTime-to-timezone() 297, adjust-time-to-timezone() 297, current-date() 318, current-dateTime() 318, current-time() 318, day-from-date() 322, day-from-dateTime() 322, hours-from-dateTime() 345, hours-from-time() 345, implicit-timezone() 352, minutes-from-dateTime() 373, minutes-from-time() 373, month-from-date() 374, month-from-dateTime() 374, seconds-from-dateTime() 413, seconds-from-time() 413, timezone-from-date() 433, timezone-from-dateTime() 433, timezone-from-time() 433, year-from-date() 443, year-from-dateTime() 443.

Duration Functions

days-from-dayTimeDuration() 323, hours-from-dayTimeDuration() 347, minutes-from-dayTimeDuration() 374, months-from-yearMonthDuration() 375, seconds-from-dayTimeDuration() 414, subtract-dates-yielding-yearMonthDuration() 429, subtract-dates-yielding-dayTimeDuration() 429, subtract-dateTimes-yielding-yearMonthDuration() 429, subtract-dateTimes-yielding-dayTimeDuration() 429, years-from-yearMonthDuration() 443

Aggregation Functions

avg() 301, count() 316, max() 370, min() 371, sum() 431.

Functions on URIs

base-uri() 302, collection() 309, doc() 329, document-uri() 332, escape-uri() 337, resolve-uri() 405.

Functions on QNames

expanded-QName() 342, local-name-from-QName(), namespace-uri-from-QName(), node-name() 384, resolve-QName() 403.

Functions on Sequences

count() 316, deep-equal() 323, distinct-values() 327, empty() 333, exists() 341, index-of() 353, insert-before() 356, remove() 399, subsequence() 422, unordered() 440.

Functions that Return Properties of Nodes

base-uri() 302, data() 319, document-uri() 332, in-scope-prefixes() 354, lang() 357, local-name() 363, name() 376, namespace-uri() 379, namespace-uri-for-prefix() 381, nilled() 383, node-name() 384, root() 408, string() 416.

Functions that Find Nodes

collection() 309, doc() 329, id() 347, idref() 349, root() 408.

Functions that Return Context Information

base-uri() 302, collection() 309, current-date() 318, current-dateTime() 318, current-time() 318, default-collation() 326, doc() 329, implicit-timezone() 352, last() 359, position() 396.

Diagnostic Functions

error() 336, trace() 436.

Functions that Assert a Static Type

exactly-one() 339, one-or-more() 395, zero-or-one() 444.

Notation

Technically, a function in XPath is identified by its name and arity (number of arguments). This means that there is no formal relationship between the function substring() with two arguments and the function substring() with three arguments. However, the standard function library has been designed so that in cases like this where there are two functions with different arity, the functions in practice have a close relationship, and it is generally easier to think of them as representing one function with one or more of the arguments being optional. So this is how I have presented them.

The signatures of functions are defined with a table like the one that follows:

Argument	Data type	Meaning
input	xs:string?	The containing string
start	xs:double	The position in the containing string of ...
length (*optional*)	xs:double	The number of characters to be included ...
Result	xs:string	*The required substring ...*

The first column here gives a conventional name for the argument (or *Result* to label the row that describes the result of the function). Arguments to XPath functions are supplied by position, not by name, so the name given here is arbitrary; it is provided only to allow the argument to be referred to within the descriptive text. The text (*optional*) after the name of an argument indicates that this argument does not need to be supplied: in this case, this means that there is one version of the function with two arguments, and another version with three.

The second column gives the required type of the argument. The notation is that of the SequenceType syntax in XPath, introduced in Chapter 9. This consists of an item type followed optionally by an occurrence indicator («?», «*», or «+»). The item type is either the name of a built-in atomic type such as xs:integer or xs:string, or one of the following:

Item type	Meaning
item()	Any item (either a node or an atomic value)
node()	Any node
element()	Any element node
xdt:anyAtomicType	Any atomic value
Numeric	An xs:double, xs:float, xs:decimal, or xs:integer

The occurrence indicator, if it is present, is either «?» to indicate that the supplied argument can contain zero or one items of the specified item type, or «*» to indicate that it can be a sequence of zero or more items of the specified item type. (The occurrence indicator «+», meaning one or more, is not used in any of the standard functions.)

Note the difference between an argument that is optional, and an argument that has an occurrence indicator of «?». When the argument is optional, it can be omitted from the function call. When the occurrence indicator is «?», the value must be supplied, but the empty sequence «()» is an acceptable value for the argument.

Many functions follow the convention of allowing an empty sequence for the first argument, or for subsequent arguments that play a similar role to the first argument, and returning an empty sequence if any of these arguments is an empty sequence. This is designed to make these functions easier to use in predicates. However, this is only a convention, and is not followed universally. Most of the string functions instead treat an empty sequence the same way as a zero-length string.

When these functions are called, the supplied arguments are converted to the required type in the standard way defined by the XPath 2.0 function calling mechanism. The details of this depend on whether XPath 1.0 backward compatibility is activated or not. This is determined by the host language: in XSLT it depends on the value of the [xsl:]version attribute in the stylesheet.

❑ In 2.0 mode, the standard conversion rules apply. These rules appear in Chapter 5 on page 160, under the heading *Converting the Arguments and the Result*. They permit only the following kinds of conversion:

❑ Atomization of nodes to extract their numeric values

❑ Promotion of numeric values to a different numeric type, e.g., xs:integer to xs:double

❑ Casting of a value of type xdt:untypedAtomic to the required type. Such values generally arise by extracting the content of a node that has not been schema-validated. The rules for casting from xdt:untypedAtomic values to values of other types are essentially the rules defined in XML Schema for conversion from the lexical space of the data type to the value space: more details are given in Chapter 9 (see *Converting from string* on page 274).

❑ In 1.0 mode, two additional conversions are allowed:

❑ If the required type is xs:string or xs:double (perhaps with an occurrence indicator of «?»), then the first value in the supplied sequence is converted to the required type using the string() or number() function as appropriate, and other values in the sequence are discarded.

❑ If the required type is node() or item() (perhaps with an occurrence indicator of «?»), then if the supplied value contains more than one item, all items except the first are ignored.

The effect of these rules is that even though the function signature might give the expected type of an argument as xs:string, say, the value you supply can be a node containing a string, or a node whose value is untyped (because it has not been validated using a schema). With 1.0 compatibility mode on, you can also supply values of other types, for example an xs:integer or an xs:anyURI, but when compatibility mode is off, you will need to convert such values to an xs:string yourself, which you can achieve most simply by calling the string() function.

Function Definitions

The remainder of this chapter gives the definitions of all the functions, in alphabetical order.

abs

The abs() function returns the absolute value of a number. For example, «abs(-3)» returns 3.

Changes in 2.0

This function is new in XPath 2.0.

Signature

Argument	Data type	Meaning
input	Numeric?	The supplied number
Result	Numeric?	*The absolute value of the supplied number. The result has the same type as the input*

Effect

If the supplied number is positive, then it is returned unchanged. If it is negative, then the result is «- $input».

Negative zero and negative infinity become positive zero and positive infinity. Positive zero, positive infinity, and NaN are returned unchanged. If the argument is an empty sequence, the result is an empty sequence.

The result has the same basic numeric type as the input. For example, if the input value is an xs:integer, the result will be an xs:integer, and if the input is an xs:double, the result will be an xs:double.

> *Basic here means one of the four types* xs:double, xs:float, xs:decimal, *and* xs:integer. *Clearly, if the input is an* xs:negativeInteger, *the result cannot also be an* xs:negativeInteger—*it will actually be an* xs:integer. *If the input is an* xs:positiveInteger,

you have a guarantee that the result will be an xs:integer, *but this doesn't prevent the system returning something that is actually a subtype of* xs:integer—*for example, it would be legitimate to return the original* xs:positiveInteger *unchanged.*

Examples

Expression	Result
abs(2)	2
abs(-2)	-2
abs(-3.7)	3.7
abs(-1.0e-7)	1.0e-7
abs(number('NaN'))	NaN

adjust-date-to-timezone, adjust-dateTime-to-timezone, adjust-time-to-timezone

This entry describes a collection of three closely related functions. These functions have the effect of returning a date, time, or dateTime based on a supplied date, time, or dateTime, modified by adding, removing, or altering the timezone component of the value.

Changes in 2.0

These functions are new in XPath 2.0.

Signature

Argument	Data type	Meaning
input	xs:date?, xs:dateTime?, or xs:time?	The date, time, or dateTime value whose timezone is to be adjusted. The type of this value must correspond to the name of the function invoked. For example in the case of adjust-time-to-timezone() it must be an xs:time value
timezone (*optional*)	xdt:dayTimeDuration?	Specifies the new timezone value. If this argument is omitted, the effect is the same as setting it to the result of the function implicit-timezone()
Result	xs:date?, xs:dateTime?, or xs:time?	*The adjusted date, dateTime, or time value*

Effect

If the input is an empty sequence, the result is an empty sequence.

If there is no `timezone` argument (that is, if the function is called with a single argument), the effect is the same as calling the function with a second argument of «`implicit-timezone()`». This adjusts the value to the timezone supplied in the dynamic context, which ideally will be the timezone where the user is located.

If the timezone argument is supplied, and is not an empty sequence, then it must be a duration between -50400 seconds and +50400 seconds, that is ±14 hours. To specify a timezone one hour ahead of UTC, write «`xdt:dayTimeDuration("PT1H")`».

These functions can be used to remove a timezone from a value that has a timezone, to add a timezone to a value that lacks a timezone, or to return the value that is equivalent to the supplied value, but in a different timezone. These effects are summarized in the table below:

Existing timezone	timezone argument is ()	Timezone argument is not ()
Absent	returns the input value unchanged	result has the same components as input, with the addition of the specified timezone
Present	result is the localized value of the input, with the timezone removed	result represents the same instant as the input value, but in a different timezone

The only complex case here is the one in the bottom-right cell of the table, where the supplied value already has a timezone and this is to be replaced with a new timezone. The effect varies slightly depending on which if the three functions is used:

❑ For an `xs:dateTime`, the result is an `xs:dateTime` that represents the same instant in time as the input value, but in the new timezone.

❑ For an `xs:time`, the result is an `xs:time` that represents the time in the new timezone that is simultaneous with the time provided as the input value.

❑ For an `xs:date`, the date is converted to an `xs:dateTime` representing 00:00:00 on the specified date; the requested adjustment is applied to this `xs:dateTime` value, and the result is the date part of the adjusted `xs:dateTime`.

Examples

Assume that `$CET` is set to the timezone value +01:00, represented by the `xdt:dayTimeDuration` PT1H. Assume that `$EST` is set to the timezone value -05:00, represented by the `xdt:dayTimeDuration` -PT5H. Assume also that the implicit timezone is the timezone value -08:00, represented by the `xdt:dayTimeDuration` -PT8H.

Here are some examples using `xs:time` values:

Expression	Result
`adjust-time-to-timezone(` `xs:time("15:00:00+01:00"), $EST)`	`09:00:00-05:00`

Expression	Result
adjust-time-to-timezone(xs:time("15:00:00"), $EST)	15:00:00-05:00
adjust-time-to-timezone(xs:time("15:00:00+01:00"))	06:00:00-08:00
adjust-time-to-timezone(xs:time("15:00:00+01:00"), ())	15:00:00
adjust-time-to-timezone(xs:time("15:00:00"), ())	15:00:00

The corresponding examples using xs:dateTime values are:

Expression	Result
adjust-dateTime-to-timezone (xs:dateTime("2004-03-01T15:00:00+01:00"), $EST)	2004-03-01T09:00:00-05:00
adjust-dateTime-to-timezone(xs: dateTime("2004-03-01T15:00:00"), $EST)	2004-03-01T15:00:00-05:00
adjust-dateTime-to-timezone (xs: dateTime("2004-03-01T15:00:00+01:00"))	2004-03-01T06:00:00-08:00
adjust-dateTime-to-timezone(xs:dateTime("2004-03-01T15:00:00+01:00"), ())	2004-03-01T15:00:00
adjust-dateTime-to-timezone (xs: dateTime("2004-03-01T15:00:00"), ())	2004-03-01T15:00:00

Adjusting the timezone component of a date is a less intuitive operation, but is still well defined:

Expression	Result
adjust-date-to-timezone(xs:date("2004-03-01+01:00"), $EST)	2004-02-29-05:00
adjust-date-to-timezone(xs:date("2004-03-01"), $EST)	2004-03-01-05:00
adjust-date-to-timezone(xs:date("2004-03-01+01:00"))	2004-02-29-08:00

Continues

Expression	Result
`adjust-date-to-timezone(` `xs:date("2004-03-01+01:00"), ())`	`2004-03-01`
`adjust-date-to-timezone(` `xs:date("2004-03-01"), ())`	`2004-03-01`

Usage

Values of types `xs:dateTime`, `xs:time`, and `xs:date()` either have a timezone component, or have no timezone. If they have a timezone component, it is useful to think in terms of two properties of the value, which we can call the local value and the absolute value. For example suppose you call `current-time()` and the implicit timezone is the timezone for Germany, +01:00. The value returned might be 14:54:06+01:00. The absolute value of this is the equivalent time in UTC (or "Zulu time", popularly Greenwich Mean Time or GMT). This is 13:54:06. The local value is the time in its original timezone, 14:54:06.

Converting the value to a string always gives you the local value: 14:54:06+01:00. Getting the components of the value also returns a component of the local value: `hours-from-time()` applied to this value returns 14. But comparisons between two values, or calculations such as adding a duration, use the absolute value.

You can in effect freeze a value in its current timezone by calling `adjust-X-to-timezone()` with an empty sequence «`()`» as the second argument. Applied to this value, the result will be the time 14:54:06, with no timezone component. Calling `hours-from-time()` on this value will still return 14.

You can also determine the equivalent time in a different timezone by calling `adjust-X-to-timezone()` specifying the new timezone. If the input value is 14:54:06+01:00, and the new timezone is +00:00, the result will be a time value whose absolute value and local value are both 13:54:06. When you convert this to a string, the value is «`13:54:06Z`», and when you call `hours-from-time()`, the result is «`13`». Similarly, if you adjust this value to the timezone –05:00 (New York time), the absolute value will still be 13:54:06 but the local value will be 08:54:06.

If you have a value with no timezone component, you can set a timezone, either by supplying the required timezone in the second argument, or by omitting the second argument, which sets the timezone to the implicit timezone taken from the evaluation context. When you do this, the local value of the new timezone will be the same as the timezone-less input value. For example, if the input is 14:54:06, and you set the timezone to –08:00, then the local value of the result will be 14:54:06, which means that its absolute value will be 22:54:06. When you convert the result to a string, the result will be «`14:54:06-08:00`», and when you extract the hours component, the result will be «`14`».

The functions work slightly differently for the three data types:

❑   For `xs:dateTime`, an adjustment to the time may also cause the date to change. For example, if the input time is 2004:02:29T22:00:00Z, then adjusting the timezone to +10:00 will produce the local value 2004:03:01T08:00:00+10:00.

❑   For `xs:time`, all adjustments are made modulo 24 hours.

❑   For `xs:date`, the value is treated as if it were an `xs:dateTime` representing 00:00:00 on the specified date. The adjustment is made to this `xs:dateTime`, and the time component is then removed. For example, if the input date is 2004:03:31+00:00, then adjusting the timezone to –05:00 will return the date 2004:02:29-05:00. This involves an inevitable loss of information. You can read the semantics of the function as being "tell me what the date is in a place in timezone X, at the time when the day represented by a given date has just started in timezone Y".

See also

`implicit-timezone()` on page 352

avg

The `avg()` function returns the average of a sequence of numbers or durations.

Changes in 2.0

This function is new in XPath 2.0.

Signature

Argument	Data type	Meaning
sequence	`xdt:anyAtomicType*`	The input sequence. Any untyped atomic values in the input are converted to `xs:double` values. The resulting sequence must consist entirely of numbers, or entirely of durations of the same kind
Result	`xdt:anyAtomicType?`	*The average of the values in the input sequence. This will be a value of the same primitive type as the values in the input sequence. If the input values are `xs:integer` values, the result will be an `xs:decimal`*

Effect

If the input sequence is empty, the result is an empty sequence. This is not an error, even though a literal interpretation of the rules would involve dividing by zero.

In all other cases the result is the same as «`sum($sequence) div count($sequence)`». Note that `$sequence` here is the atomized sequence generated by the function calling mechanism. If the sequence supplied in the call was a sequence of nodes, the number of atomic values is not necessarily the same as the number of nodes. For example, if «`avg(@a)`» is called to process a single attribute that is defined in the schema to contain a list of integers, then it will return the average of these integers.

The sequence of operations is as follows:

❑ The sequence supplied in the argument is atomized (this is a standard action of the function calling rules when the required type only allows atomic values).

❑ Any untyped atomic values in the resulting sequence (typically, values extracted from nodes in a schemaless document) are converted to `xs:double` values. If this conversion fails, a runtime error is reported.

❑ If the sequence now contains any NaN (not-a-number) values, the result of the avg () function is NaN.

❑ If the values are all numeric, they are summed according to the rules for the numeric «+» operator, which means that the result will depend on the types that are present in the sequence. If there is at least one xs:double, the sum will be an xs:double; otherwise, if there is an xs:float it will be an xs:float, otherwise xs:decimal or xs:integer.

❑ If the values are all durations, they are similarly summed according to the rules of the «+» operator. In consequence, it is not possible to mix the two duration types, xdt:dayTimeDuration and xdt:yearMonthDuration.

❑ Finally, the total is divided by the number of items using the «div» operator. In the case of a numeric total, this means that the average will be the same numeric type as the sum, unless the sum is an xs:integer in which case the average will be an xs:decimal. If the items are durations, the result will be a duration of the same type as the items.

Examples

Expression	Result
avg((1.0, 2.6, 3.0))	xs:decimal('2.2')
avg(())	()
avg((1, xs:float('3.5'), 5.5))	xs:float('3.0')
avg((1, 2, 3))	xs:decimal('2.0')
avg((xdt:dayTimeDuration("P1D"), xdt:dayTimeDuration("PT12H")))	PT18H

See also

count() on page 316
max() on page 370
min() on page 371
sum() on page 431

base-uri

The base-uri() function returns either the base URI from the static context of the XPath expression, or the base URI of a specific node in a document.

Changes in 2.0

This function is new in XPath 2.0.

Signature

Argument	Data type	Meaning
input-node (*optional*)	node()?	The node whose base URI is required
Result	xs:string	*If the function has no arguments, it returns the base URI from the static context of the XPath expression. If an input-node is supplied, the function returns the base URI of that node*

Effect

The effect depends on whether an input-node is supplied.

When there is no input-node

When the first argument is omitted the function returns the base URI from the static context. This is determined by the host language in which the expression appears. For an XPath expression used in an XSLT stylesheet, the base URI is the URI of the stylesheet module, unless this is modified with an xml:base attribute. In XQuery, the base URI of an expression can be specified by a declaration in the module prolog.

The base URI is used when resolving a relative URI contained in the expression, for example as an argument of the doc() function (or document() in XSLT).

It is possible that the base URI is unknown. This can happen in XSLT, for example, if the stylesheet is supplied as a DOM, or as a character string in memory with no associated URI. In this case this function returns an empty sequence.

When there is an input-node

When the first argument is present, the function returns the base URI of the input node supplied. This is a property of the node, defined in the data model. If the node was created by parsing raw XML, then the base URI is typically the URI of the resource containing the raw XML used to create the node. If the original XML used external entities, then it will be the URI of the external entity in question. The base URI of a node may also be altered by using the xml:base attribute in the XML. This attribute is defined in the W3C Recommendation *XML Base* (http://www.w3.org/TR/XMLBase/).

The base URI of a node is typically used when resolving a relative URI contained in the value of that node. By definition, relative URIs refer to files (or to be more general, resources) relative to the base URI of the file containing the relative URI.

When nodes are not created directly by parsing raw XML, the concept of base URI is not so clear-cut. XSLT defines that a node in a temporary tree derives its base URI from the base URI of the stylesheet.

If the first argument is supplied but its value is an empty sequence, the function returns an empty sequence.

Usage and Examples

The base-uri() function is useful mainly in conjunction with resolve-uri(): it gives you a base URI against which a relative URI can be resolved. For example, if you want to locate the document identified by a relative URI held in an href attribute in a source document, the following code should be used:

```
doc(resolve-uri(@href, base-uri(.)))
```

It is rarely necessary to call base-uri() explicitly without an argument, since functions like doc() will resolve a relative URI against the base URI from the static context implicitly. With a complex application containing many XPath expressions, base-uri() can sometimes be useful in diagnostic messages (for example, in the output of the trace() function, or the XSLT <xsl:message> instruction) to indicate where the message is coming from—assuming that the base URI differs from one module of the application to another.

In XSLT 2.0 and XQuery 1.0 it is well defined how the base URI in the static context is established. If you invoke XPath expressions via an API from a programming language (for example, a Java or .NET API) then there may be no explicit way of setting the base URI, especially if the API was originally designed for XPath 1.0. In this case the base-uri() function is defined to return an empty sequence.

See also

doc() on page 329
resolve-uri() on page 405

boolean

The boolean() function calculates the *effective boolean value* of the supplied argument. Every XPath value, of any data type, has an effective boolean value which is either true or false.

Changes in 2.0

The function has been generalized in XPath 2.0 so it accommodates a much wider range of possible arguments.

Signature

Argument	Data type	Meaning
value	item()*	The value whose effective boolean value is required
Result	xs:boolean	*The effective boolean value of the argument*

Effect

Every XPath 2.0 value has an effective boolean value. The boolean() function is used to calculate the effective boolean value explicitly, but it is also calculated implicitly in a number of contexts where a boolean value is required: see the *Usage* section below.

If the argument is an empty sequence, then the effective boolean value is false.

If the argument is a sequence containing two or more items, then the effective boolean value is true.

If the argument contains a node, then the effective boolean value is true.

If the argument contains a singleton atomic value, then the effective boolean value is false if this singleton value is one of:

❑   The boolean value `false`

❑   A zero-length string (or zero-length untyped atomic value)

❑   A number equal to zero (this covers all numeric data types, and includes positive and negative zero)

❑   The `xs:double` or `xs:float` value `NaN` (not-a-number).

In all other cases the effective boolean value is `true`.

Examples

Assume the source document:

```
<doc>
   <emp name="John" age="53"/>
   <emp name="Mary"/>
</doc>
```

with the variable `$John` bound to the first `<emp>` element, and `$Mary` bound to the second.

Expression	Result
`boolean(//emp[@age=21])`	false
`boolean(//emp[@age=53])`	true
`boolean(number($John/@age))`	true
`boolean(number($Mary/@age))`	false
`boolean(count($John/*))`	false
`boolean(string($John/@surname))`	false
`boolean(string($John/@name))`	true
`boolean("true")`	true
`boolean("false")`	true

Usage

In most cases conversion to an `xs:boolean` occurs automatically when the context requires it; it is only necessary to call the `boolean()` function explicitly in order to force a conversion. For example, these rules are invoked automatically when an expression is used as the condition in an «if» expression, in the «satisfies» clause of the «some» and «every» expressions, and for the operands of «and» and «or». They are also invoked in XSLT stylesheets for expressions used in `<xsl:if>` and `<xsl:when>` instructions.

The detailed rules for establishing the effective boolean value may appear somewhat arbitrary. They were defined this way in large measure for backward compatibility with XPath 1.0, which allowed sequences of nodes but did not allow sequences of strings, booleans, or numbers. The rules will probably come naturally if you are familiar with weakly-typed languages such as Perl or Python, but there are a few traps to beware of. For example, if you convert the boolean value `false` to a string, you get the string `"false"`, but the effective boolean value of this string is `true`.

The boolean() function does not always return the same result as the xs:boolean() constructor. xs:boolean() (like «cast as xs:boolean») follows the rules in XML Schema that define the lexical representations of the xs:boolean data type. This treats the strings "1" and "true" as true, and "0" and "false" as false.

XSLT Examples

The following example prints a message if the source document contains a <header> element and no <footer>, or if it contains a <footer> and no <header>.

```
<xsl:if test="boolean(//header) != boolean(//footer)">
    <xsl:message>Document must contain headers and footers,
                             or neither</xsl:message>
</xsl:if>
```

The conversion of the two node sequences «//header» (true if there are any <header> elements in the document) and «//footer» (true if there are any <footer> elements) needs to be explicit here, because we want to do a boolean comparison, not a comparison of two node sequences.

The following example sets a variable to the xs:boolean value true or false depending on whether the document contains footnotes. In this case the explicit conversion is probably not necessary, since it could be done later when the variable is used, but it is probably more efficient to retain only an xs:boolean value in the variable rather than retaining the full set of footnote nodes. An intelligent XSLT processor will recognize that the expression «//footnote» occurs in a context where a boolean is required, and scan the document only until the first footnote is found, rather than retrieving all of them.

```
<xsl:variable name="uses-footnotes" select="boolean(//footnote)"/>
```

See also

true() on page 439
false() on page 343

ceiling

The ceiling() function rounds a supplied number up to the nearest whole number. For example, the expression «ceiling(33.9)» returns 34.

Changes in 2.0

The function has been generalized to work on all numeric data types.

Signature

Argument	Data type	Meaning
value	Numeric	The supplied value
Result	Numeric	*The result of rounding $value up to the next highest integer. The result has the same primitive data type as the supplied value*

Effect

If the number is an xs:integer, it is returned unchanged.

Otherwise, it is rounded up to the next highest whole number. If the supplied value is an xs:decimal, the result will be an xs:decimal, if it is an xs:double, the result will be an xs:double, and if it is an xs:float, the result will be an xs:float.

The xs:double and xs:float data types in XPath support special values such as infinity, negative zero and NaN (not-a-number), which are described on page 84 in Chapter 3. If the argument is NaN, the result will be NaN. Similarly, when the argument is positive or negative infinity, the function will return the value of the argument unchanged.

If the argument value is an xs:double or xs:float greater than –1.0 but less than zero it will be rounded up to negative zero. For most practical purposes, negative zero and positive zero are indistinguishable; but dividing a number by negative zero produces negative infinity, while dividing by positive zero produces positive infinity.

Examples

Expression	Result
ceiling(1.0)	1.0
ceiling(1.6)	2.0
ceiling(17 div 3)	6.0
ceiling(-3.0)	-3.0
ceiling(-8.2e0)	-8.0e0
ceiling(number('xxx'))	NaN
ceiling(-0.5e0)	-0.0e0

Usage

One situation where this function is useful is when calculating the size of a table. If you have a sequence $ns and you want to arrange the values in three columns, then the number of rows needed is: «ceiling(count($ns) div 3)».

Although the result is numerically equal to an integer, it does not necessarily have the type xs:integer. You can force it to an integer by using the xs:integer() constructor function, for example, «xs:integer(count($ns) div 3)».

See also

floor() on page 344
round() on page 409
«idiv» operator on page 173 in Chapter 6

codepoints-to-string

The codepoints-to-string() function takes as input a sequence of integers representing the Unicode codepoint values of the characters in a string, and returns the corresponding string. For example, «codepoints-to-string((65,66,67))» returns the string "ABC".

Changes in 2.0

This function is new in XPath 2.0.

Signature

Argument	Data type	Meaning
codepoints	xs:integer*	The sequence of codepoints. These must represent characters that are valid in XML 1.0 or XML 1.1, depending on the version that the processor supports
Result	xs:string	*The string consisting of characters with the given codepoint values*

Effect

The function returns a string made of the characters corresponding to the Unicode codepoints in the supplied sequence.

A character whose codepoint is above xFFFF must be supplied as a single integer value, not as two code values forming a surrogate pair.

If the supplied sequence is empty, the result will be a zero-length string.

A common case, of course, is where the sequence of codepoints contains a single integer, in which case the resulting string will be of length one.

Integers that do not represent valid codepoints cause a runtime error. This includes the case of codepoints that are valid in Unicode, but not in XML (for example the integer zero).

Examples

Expression	Result
codepoints-to-string((65, 83, 67, 73, 73))	"ASCII"
codepoints-to-string(48 to 57)	"0123456789"
codepoints-to-string(())	""
codepoints-to-string(64+$n)	*The n'th letter of the English alphabet*

Usage

There are two main ways of using this function: as a way of constructing a string algorithmically, and as a complement to the function string-to-codepoints().

As an example of the first kind of application, suppose you need to construct the hexadecimal representation of an integer. This might make use of an expression to return a single hex digit representing a value in the range 0–15. Here is a possible way of writing this expression:

```
codepoints-to-string(if ($d<10) then (48+$d) else (87+$d))
```

Personally, I prefer to code this as:

```
substring("0123456789abcdef", $d+1, 1)
```

As an example of the second kind of application, suppose that you want to reverse the order of the characters in a string. One way of doing this is:

```
codepoints-to-string(reverse(string-to-codepoints($s)))
```

In this example, the two functions `string-to-codepoints()` and `codepoints-to-string()` are being used simply as a way of breaking the string into a sequence of characters, and reassembling the characters into a string; the fact that the characters are represented by Unicode codepoints is an irrelevance.

See also

`string-to-codepoints()` on page 421

collection

The `collection()` function returns a sequence of documents, or more generally a sequence of nodes, identified by a URI. The way in which a URI can be used to locate a collection of documents is entirely implementation-defined.

Changes in 2.0

This function is new in XPath 2.0.

Signature

Argument	Data type	Meaning
uri	xs:string?	A URI that identifies a collection of documents, or nodes within documents. If the argument is an empty sequence, the function returns an empty sequence
Result	node()*	*The sequence of documents, or nodes within documents, identified by the URI*

Effect

This function is specified in very abstract terms, and it's likely that its detailed behavior will vary considerably from one implementation to the next.

Many XML databases have the concept of a collection as a container for documents, and the containers generally have a name, which can be mapped into some kind of URI. Beyond that, there are many variations: for example, some systems might allow collections to be nested hierarchically, some systems might use a collection to store all the documents that are validated against one particular schema, and so on. One can also imagine mapping the concept of a collection onto a simple directory containing the documents (perhaps with a filter applied to the document names), or onto an XML catalog file that holds a list of the documents within the collection.

All that the spec really says about this function is that the supplied URI argument is resolved against the base URI from the static context, and the resulting absolute URI is used to identify a collection of documents; the result is a sequence containing the document nodes of these documents. In fact it isn't constrained to return document nodes, there might be collections that return other kinds of nodes.

The specification also says that the function is *stable*, which means that if you call it twice in the same expression (or, in the case of XSLT, in the same transformation) then you get the same answer back each time. In other words, a collection at least gives the appearance of being immutable for the duration of a query or transformation.

> *Once XQuery defines an update capability, it will have to come up with a more sophisticated definition of transactions and isolation levels, but this one is adequate for now.*

Beyond this, it's not really possible to say what the collection() function does, or what the URI that you supply to it actually means. We'll have to wait and see what implementations do. Saxon's initial implementation of the function uses a very simple XML catalog file to define a list of documents, but this certainly isn't the last word on the matter.

See also

doc() on page 329

compare

The compare() function is used to compare two strings, and to decide whether they are equal, or if not, which one sorts before the other.

For example, under most collations «compare("ALPHA", "BETA")» returns -1.

Changes in 2.0

This function is new in XPath 2.0.

Signature

Argument	Data type	Meaning
value-1	xs:string?	The first string to be compared
value-2	xs:string?	The second string to be compared
collation *(optional)*	xs:string	A URI identifying the collation to be used to perform the comparison
Result	xs:integer?	*-1 if value-1 is considered less than value-2, zero if they are considered equal, +1 if value-1 is considered greater than value-2*

Effect

If either `value-1` or `value-2` is an empty sequence, the result is an empty sequence.

If `value-1` is less than `value-2`, the function returns -1; if they are equal, it returns 0; and if `value-1` is greater than `value-2`, it returns +1. The string comparison is done using the supplied `collation` if specified; if the collation argument is omitted, the comparison is done using the default collation. For more information on collations, see the section *Collations* in Chapter 4, page 123.

Examples

These examples assume the availability of two collation URIs: `$strong`, which considers first the character value, then accents, then case (with upper case first); and `$weak`, which considers only the character value.

Expression	Result
`compare("espace", "espacer")`	-1
`compare("espace", "espacé", $strong)`	-1
`compare("espace", "espacé", $weak)`	0
`compare("espacer", "espacé", $strong)`	+1
`compare("espacer", "espacé", $weak)`	+1

Usage

Often `compare()` is followed by a three-way branch. Because XPath has no switch or case expression, it is best to assign the result of the function to a variable to avoid doing the comparison twice. For example, in XSLT:

```
<xsl:variable name="c" select="compare(A, B)"/>
<xsl:choose>
    <xsl:when test="$c = -1"> ... </xsl:when>
    <xsl:when test="$c = 0"> ... </xsl:when>
    <xsl:when test="$c = +1"> ... </xsl:when>
</xsl:choose>
```

Or, in XQuery 1.0:

```
let $c := compare(A, B) return
    if ($c = -1) then ...
    else if ($c = 0) then ...
    else ...
```

In pure XPath 2.0, you can do this rather awkwardly with a «for» expression:

```
for $c in compare(A, B) return
    if ($c = -1) then ...
    else if ($c = 0) then ...
    else ...
```

Another coding technique you could consider is to use a positional predicate:

```
("less", "equal", "greater")[compare($A,$B) + 2]
```

But I would avoid doing this if the sequence on the left contains complex expressions, because it's quite likely that more than one of the expressions will be evaluated.

See also

Collations on page 123 in Chapter 4
Value Comparisons on page 181 in Chapter 6

concat

The concat() function takes two or more arguments. Each of the arguments is converted to a string, and the resulting strings are joined together end-to-end.

For example, the expression «concat('Jane', ' ', 'Brown')» returns the string «Jane Brown».

Changes in 2.0

None.

Signature

This function is unique in that it can take any number of arguments (two or more).

Argument	Data type	Meaning
value (repeated)	xat:anyAtomicType	A string to be included in the result
Result	xs:string	The result of concatenating each of the arguments in turn

Effect

Each of the supplied strings is appended to the result string, in the order they appear.

Any argument that is an empty sequence is ignored. If all the arguments are empty sequences, the result is a zero-length string.

Note that all the arguments will automatically be cast to strings.

Examples

Expression	Result
concat("a", "b", "c")	*The string «abc»*
concat("chap", 3)	*The string «chap3»*
concat("a", (), (), "b")	*The string «ab»*
concat("a", ("b", "c"))	*In 1.0 mode: the string «ab» (when a sequence is converted to a string in backward compatibility mode, all items after the first are discarded)* *In 2.0 mode: error. The argument must be a single string, not a sequence of strings. Use the* string-join() *function instead*

Usage in XSLT

The concat() function is often a convenient alternative to using multiple <xsl:value-of> elements to construct an output string. For example:

```
<xsl:value-of select="concat(first-name, ' ', last-name)"/>
```

is equivalent to:

```
<xsl:value-of select="first-name"/>
<xsl:text> </xsl:text>
<xsl:value-of select="last-name"/>
```

However, with XSLT 2.0 it is even simpler to write:

```
<xsl:value-of select="first-name, last-name" separator=" "/>
```

Another situation where concat() is useful is in defining a key, including lookup keys (<xsl:key>), sort keys (<xsl:sort>), and grouping keys (<xsl:for-each-group>). XSLT keys cannot be multipart values, but you can get round this restriction by concatenating the parts of the key with an appropriate separator. For example:

```
<xsl:key name="full-name" match="person"
                use="concat(first-name, ' ', last-name)"/>
```

This key can then be used to retrieve the person (or persons) with a given name using an expression such as:

```
<xsl:for-each select="key('full-name', 'Peter Jones')"/>
```

See also

contains() in the section immediately below.
string-join() on page 418.
substring() on page 423.

contains

The contains() function tests whether one string contains another as a substring. For example, the expression «contains('Santorini', 'ant')» returns true.

Changes in 2.0

An optional collation argument has been added.

Signature

Argument	Data type	Meaning
value	xs:string?	The containing string
substring	xs:string?	The test string
collation (optional)	xs:string	The collation to be used
Result	xs:boolean	true if the containing string has a substring that is equal to the test string, otherwise false

Effect

If no collation is specified, then the result is true if the first string contains a consecutive sequence of characters where each character has the same Unicode value as the corresponding character of the second string.

If the second string is zero-length, the result is always true.

If the first string is zero-length, the result is false except when the second string is also zero-length.

If either of the first two arguments is an empty sequence, the effect is the same as if it were a zero-length string.

When a collation is specified, it is used to break both of the strings into a sequence of collation units, and the function returns true if the collation units generated for the test string form a subsequence of the collation units generated for the containing string.

Because this function compares substrings, rather than just performing an equality match or ordering on two strings as a whole, it imposes particular constraints on the way the collation works—it only makes sense to use a collation that considers the string character-by-character. For a function such as compare(), it would be quite viable to use a collation that sorts «January» before «February», or «5 Oak Street» before «10 Maple Drive». But a collation that does this isn't also going to be able to look for substrings of characters in a meaningful way.

This doesn't mean that each character must be considered in isolation. The collation can still consider characters in groups, as with the traditional rule in Spanish that «ch» collates as if it were a single character following «c», and «ll» as a single letter after «l». But where characters are grouped in this way, it is likely to affect the way substrings are matched, as we will see.

The XPath specification isn't completely prescriptive about how substring matching using a collation should work, and there are several possible approaches that an implementation could use. I'll describe the way the Saxon processor does it, which makes heavy use of the collation support in Java: other Java-based processors are therefore quite likely to be similar.

Firstly, let's look at a case where Java treats one character as two collation units. With a primary strength collation for German, the string «Straße» generates a sequence of seven collation units, which are exactly the same as the collation units generated for the string «strasse». This means that «contains("Straße", $t)» returns true when $t is any one of «ß», «aß», «ße», «ss», «as», «ass», or «se» (among others). Few surprises here.

Java also allows a collation to perform decomposition of combined characters. For example, the character «ç» can be decomposed into two characters, the letter «c» and a non-spacing cedilla. The advantage of doing this is that Unicode allows two ways of representing a word such as «garçon», using either six codepoints or seven, and normalizing the text so it only uses one of these forms gives better results when matching strings. For collating, Java chooses to use the decomposed form in which the accents are represented separately. (For more information on normalization, see the entry for the normalize-unicode() function on page 388.)

Under such a collation, the string «garçon» is represented as seven collation units, the same as the collation units for the string «garc̦on», in which the cedilla is represented by a separate non-spacing character. The effect of this is that the result of «contains("garçon", $t)» is true when $t is any of «ç», «rç», or «ço», and also when it is «c» or «rc», but not (and here's the surprise) when it is «co».

> I've written«garc̦on» to illustrate that the «c» and the «c̦» are two separate Unicode codepoints. But of course the cedilla is actually a non-spacing character, so in real life this string of seven codepoints would appear on the page as «garçon».

Java could instead have standardized on the composed form of the character, but the accent-blind matching would then not work: «contains("garçon", "c")» would be false.

Now let's look at a case where a pair of characters represents a single collation unit. Here we turn back to Spanish, where «ch» traditionally collates after «c» and «ll» collates after «l». We can set this up in Java by defining a RuleBaseCollator using a rule that defines «c < ch < d» and «l < ll < m». (In my tests, the default collation provided for Spanish didn't have this property. I had to set up the rules myself.)

When you do this, you find that «contains("chello", $t)» returns true if $t is «ch» or «che» or «ello», but is false if it is «c» or «h» or «l» or «hello». What is happening is that because «ch» and «ll» are being treated as single characters for collation purposes, they are also treated as single characters for the purpose of substring matching.

These rules for substring matching using a collation apply not only to the contains() function, but also to ends-with(), starts-with(), substring-before(), and substring-after(). Because collations can cause unexpected effects with these functions (as well as incurring a significant performance cost), the default collation does not apply to them: if the collation argument is not explicitly supplied, these functions match by comparing Unicode codepoints. If you want to use the default collation, you can request it explicitly. For example, «contains("ABC", "b", default-collation())» returns true if the default collation is one that ignores differences of case.

Examples

These examples use codepoint comparison, because there is no collation argument.

Expression	Result
contains("Shakespeare", "spear")	true
contains("", "a")	false
contains("Shakespeare", "")	true
contains("", "")	true
contains((), "a")	false

Usage

The contains() function is useful mainly for very simple matching, for example, testing whether a string contains a space. For more complex matching of strings, the matches() function is available in XPath 2.0 with full support for regular expressions.

See also

ends-with() on page 334
matches() on page 368
starts-with() on page 415
substring() on page 423
substring-after() on page 425
substring-before() on page 427

count

The count() function takes a sequence as its argument, and returns the number of items in the sequence. For example, the expression «count((4,5,6))» returns 3.

Changes in 2.0

The function is generalized in XPath 2.0 so it can return the number of items in any sequence.

Signature

Argument	Data type	Meaning
sequence	item()*	The sequence whose items are to be counted
Result	xs:integer	The number of items in the supplied sequence

Effect

The count() function takes any sequence as its argument, and returns the number of items present in the sequence.

If the sequence contains nodes, each node counts as one item. The function does not count the number of atomic values contained in the node's typed value, and it does not count the children or descendants of the node.

Examples

Consider the source document:

```
<doc>
   <obs at="10:42:06" colors="red green"/>
   <obs at="11:43:12" colors="green blue orange"/>
</doc>
```

and assume that this has been validated using a schema that defines the colors attribute as a sequence of strings.

Expression	Result
count(//obs)	2
count(//obs/@colors)	2
count(data(//obs/@colors))	5
count(//@*)	4
count(//obs/@date)	0
count((5 to 10))	6

Usage

Avoid using count() to test whether a sequence of nodes is empty, for example, by writing:

```
if (count(book[author='Hemingway']) != 0) then . . .
```

This can be better expressed as:

```
if (book[author='Hemingway']) then . . .
```

or, if you prefer:

```
if (exists(book[author='Hemingway'])) then . . .
```

A good processor will optimize the first expression so as to avoid counting all the books (it can stop counting books and take the then path as soon as it finds the first one that matches), but it's always best to avoid relying on such optimizations if you can.

The count() function is a useful way of finding the position of a node within a source document. In XSLT it can provide an effective alternative to using <xsl:number>, and in non-XSLT environments, it may be the only way of doing numbering. For example, if the context node is a <bullet> element, then «count(preceding-sibling::bullet)+1» returns the number of this <bullet> within the sequence of <bullet> elements. The advantages of using count() over <xsl:number>, apart from the fact that it's available in non-XSLT environments, are that it is rather more flexible in defining what you want to count, and it can be used directly in expressions. However, `<xsl:number>` gives a simple way of obtaining the sequence number, formatting it, and inserting it in the result tree in a single operation; it may also in some cases be easier for the processor to optimize.

Avoid using `count()` where `last()` would do the job just as well. This situation arises in XSLT when you are processing a sequence of nodes using `<xsl:apply-templates>` or `<xsl:for-each>`; the number of nodes in that sequence is then available from the `last()` function. For example, it is probably inefficient to write:

```
<xsl:for-each select="book[author='Hemingway']">
    <h2>Book <xsl:value-of select="position()"/> of
            <xsl:value-of select="count(../book[author='Hemingway'])"/>
    </h2>
    . . .
</xsl:for-each>
```

because—unless the XSLT processor is rather clever—it will have to re-evaluate the expression «`../book[author='Hemingway']`» each time round the loop.

Instead, write:

```
<xsl:for-each select="book[author='Hemingway']">
    <h2>Book <xsl:value-of select="position()"/> of
            <xsl:value-of select="last()"/>
        </h2>
    . . .
</xsl:for-each>
```

An alternative is to assign the sequence of nodes to a variable, so it is only evaluated once.

See also

`sum()` on page 431
`last()` on page 359

current-date, current-dateTime, current-time

These three functions are used to obtain the current date, the current time, or both.

Changes in 2.0

These functions are new in XPath 2.0.

Signature

These functions take no arguments.

	Data type	Meaning
Result	xs:date, xs:dateTime, *or* xs:time	*The current date, dateTime, or time*

Effect

The current date and time forms part of the runtime context of an XPath expression. It will normally be taken from the system clock.

The resulting value will always have an explicit timezone component. The timezone will be taken from the implicit timezone provided by the evaluation context. In practice, this means it will probably be derived from the system default timezone for the machine on which the XSLT processor is running, or from the profile of the particular user.

In XSLT 2.0 it is defined that multiple calls on current-dateTime() and the other two functions will return the same result every time they are called within a single transformation. This means you can't call the function at the beginning and the end of the transformation to measure the elapsed time. The reason for this rule is that XSLT is rather purist about being a strictly functional language, and in a strictly functional language, calling the same function twice with the same arguments always returns the same result. This property makes life much simpler for optimizers.

In XQuery 1.0, the same rule applies to multiple calls within a single query.

Examples

Expression	Possible Result
current-date()	An xs:date, say 2004-06-02Z
current-dateTime()	An xs:dateTime, say 2004-06-02T12:35:02Z
current-time()	An xs:time, say 12:35:02Z

Usage

XPath 2.0 does not provide any facilities for formatting the date and time for display. You can do this yourself by extracting the components of the value using functions such as day-from-date() and hours-from-dateTime(), or you can convert the value to a string in ISO 8601 format using the string() function.

In XSLT 2.0 the returned date and time can be formatted for display using the functions format-date(), format-dateTime(), and format-time(). These functions are described in Chapter 7 of *XSLT 2.0 Programmer's Reference*.

See also

adjust-date/time-to-timezone() functions described on page 297.

X-from-date/time() functions described in their alphabetical position in this chapter, where X is one of year, month, day, hours, minutes, seconds, or timezone.

data

The data() function returns the atomized value of a sequence. This means that any nodes in the input sequence are replaced by their typed values.

Changes in 2.0

This function is new in XPath 2.0.

Signature

Argument	Data type	Meaning
sequence	item()*	The input sequence
Result	xdt:anyAtomicType*	*A sequence based on the input sequence, in which all nodes have been replaced by their typed values*

Effect

Atomization is a process that is invoked implicitly when a sequence containing nodes is used in a context where atomic values are expected. For example, if you write «@a+42», the attribute node represented by the expression «@a» is atomized to obtain a number, which is then added to 42. The data() function invokes atomization explicitly, and is used either in a context where implicit atomization does not occur (for example, the argument to the count() function is not atomized), or in cases where you want to make it clear to the reader what is going on.

Atomization applies the following process to each item in the input sequence. The results are concatenated together retaining the original sequence order:

❑   If the input sequence contains an atomic value, the atomic value is added to the result sequence unchanged.

❑   If the input sequence contains a node, the typed value of the node is added to the result sequence.

The typed value of a node depends on its type annotation. In the absence of a schema, or when the type annotation is xdt:untypedAtomic or xdt:untyped, the typed value is the same as the string value, but the resulting atomic value remains an xdt:untypedAtomic value rather than a string, which allows it to be used in contexts (for example, as an operand of «+») where a string would not be allowed.

If the node is annotated with some other type annotation, which generally will happen only as a result of schema validation, the typed value reflects the type definition in the schema:

❑   If the schema type is a simple type, the result is, in general, a sequence of zero or more atomic values. For example, if the type is xs:NMTOKENS, the result is a sequence of atomic values of type xs:NMTOKEN. If the type is a user-defined type defined as a list of xs:unsignedInteger values, then the typed value is a sequence of atomic values of type xs:unsignedInteger. If the schema type is a union type allowing a choice of xs:integer or xs:string, then the typed value will be either an xs:integer or an xs:string.

❑   If the schema type is a complex type (which implies that the node is an element), there are four cases to consider:

❑ The type may be a complex type with simple content. This means that the type allows attributes, but does not allow child elements. In this case the element content is processed exactly as for a simple type, as described above. The attributes are ignored.

❑ The type may allow mixed content (defined using «mixed="true"» on the type definition in the schema). In this case the typed value is the same as the string value, which is the concatenation of all the text node descendants of the element. For example, the typed value of the element <chem>H₂O</chem> is the string «H2O». The result is labeled as an untyped atomic value.

❑ The type may define that the element is always empty. In this case, the typed value is an empty sequence.

❑ If the type allows element content only, then atomizing the element is an error. A system that does static type checking may report this as a compile-time error, otherwise it will be reported at runtime. You can always avoid this error by selecting the children of the complex element directly, for example by writing «$emp/*» instead of «$emp».

Examples

Suppose that the variable $x is bound to the following element, which has been validated using a schema that defines the content model of <rows> as zero or more <row> elements, and the content model of the <row> element to contain a number attribute of type xs:integer and a colors attribute whose type is xs:NMTOKENS.

```
<rows>
  <row number="1" colors="red green"/>
  <row number="2" colors="yellow purple"/>
</rows>
```

Expression	Result
data($x/row/@number)	(1, 2)
data($x/row/@colors)	("red", "green", "yellow", "purple")
data($x)	*Error. An element with element-only content does not have a typed value*
data($x/row)	()

Usage

Atomization is normally carried out automatically when an operation that expects atomic values is applied to a sequence. For example, if the argument to the sum() function is a set of nodes, then the typed values of those nodes will be extracted and totaled.

The data() function is provided so that atomization can be done explicitly in situations where it is not automatic. For example, the count() function does not automatically atomize its argument: it counts the nodes in the sequence, not the atomic values that result from atomization. The result is not the same, because if an element or attribute is declared in the schema to have a type such as list-of-integers, then atomizing the element or attribute may produce zero, one, or more atomic values.

Similarly, when testing the value of an element or attribute whose type is xs:boolean, be careful to make sure that the value is atomized: write «if (data(@married))...» rather than «if(@married)...». This is because the value of «@married» is a sequence of zero or one attribute nodes, and the effective boolean value of a sequence of nodes (which is what the «if» expression tests) is true if there is at least one node in the sequence, regardless of its contents. If the attribute exists and has the value «married="false"», the test «if(@married)...» will return true. Another way of forcing atomization is to write this as «if (@married = true())... ».

See also

The Type Matching Rules on page 107 in Chapter 3

day-from-date, day-from-dateTime

These two functions extract the day-of-the-month component from an xs:date or xs:dateTime value. For example, on Christmas Day «day-from-date(current-date())» returns 25.

Changes in 2.0

These functions are new in XPath 2.0.

Signature

Argument	Data type	Meaning
input	xs:date? or xs:dateTime?	The value from which a component is to be extracted. The data type of the supplied argument must correspond to the data type implied by the function name
Result	xs:integer?	*The day, in the range 1-31*

Effect

The function returns the day component of the supplied xs:date or xs:dateTime. The value is used in its local timezone (not normalized to UTC). If the argument is an empty sequence, the result is an empty sequence.

Examples

Expression	Result
day-from-date(xs:date("2004-02-28"))	28
day-from-dateTime(xs:dateTime("2004-02-28T13:00:00"))	28
day-from-date(xs:date("2004-07-31+01:00"))	31
day-from-dateTime(xs:dateTime("2004-07-31T23:00:00-05:00"))	31

See also

current-date(),-dateTime(),-time() on page 318.
format-date(),-dateTime(),-time() in Chapter 7 of *XSLT 2.0 Programmer's Reference*.
month-from-date(),-dateTime() on page 374
year-from-date(),-dateTime() on page 443

days-from-duration

This function extracts the value of the days component from a normalized xdt:dayTimeDuration value.

Changes in 2.0

This function is new in XPath 2.0.

Signature

Argument	Data type	Meaning
input	xdt:dayTimeDuration?	The duration whose days component is to be extracted. If an empty sequence is supplied, an empty sequence is returned
Result	xs:integer?	*The days component*

Effect

The function returns the days component of the supplied xdt:dayTimeDuration. The duration value is first normalized so that the number of hours is less than 24, the number of minutes is less than 60, and so on. The result will be negative if the duration is negative.

Examples

Expression	Result
days-from-duration(xdt:dayTimeDuration("P5DT12H"))	5
days-from-duration(xdt:dayTimeDuration("PT72H"))	3
days-from-duration(xdt:dayTimeDuration("-P1D"))	-1

See also

hours-from-duration on page 347
minutes-from-duration on page 374
seconds-from-duration on page 414

deep-equal

The deep-equal() function performs a deep comparison between two sequences:

❑   The items in corresponding positions in each sequence must be deep-equal to each other

❑   If the items are nodes, they are compared by examining their children and attributes recursively

Changes in 2.0

This function is new in XPath 2.0.

Signature

Argument	Data type	Meaning
sequence-1	`item()*`	The first operand of the comparison
sequence-2	`item()*`	The second operand of the comparison
collation (*optional*)	`xs:string`	The collation to be used for comparing strings (at any depth)
Result	`xs:boolean`	*True if the sequences are deep-equal, otherwise false*

Effect

This function may be used to compare:

- ❑ Two nodes, to see whether the subtrees rooted at those nodes have identical content at every level
- ❑ Two sequences, to see whether the items they contain are pairwise deep-equal

The function is therefore defined to operate on sequences, though in many cases it will be used to compare two singleton element or document nodes.

At the top level, two sequences are deep-equal if they have the same number of items, and if each item in the first sequence is deep-equal to the item in the corresponding position of the other sequence. A consequence of this rule is that an empty sequence is deep-equal to another empty sequence.

Where the item in a sequence is an atomic value, then the corresponding item in the other sequence must also be an atomic value, and they must compare equal using the «eq» operator, using the specified `collation` if they are strings or untyped atomic values. If two items in corresponding positions are not comparable (for example, if one is an integer and the other is a string, or if one is a date and the other is an element node) then the function returns false; it does not report an error. Nodes are not atomized.

If two items in corresponding positions are nodes, then to be deep-equal they must satisfy a number of conditions:

- ❑ They must be the same kind of node (for example, both elements or both text nodes)
- ❑ They must have the same name, that is, the same namespace URI and the same local name, or they must both be unnamed nodes such as text nodes
- ❑ In the case of document nodes, and element nodes whose type allows one or more element children, the sequences of children for the two nodes must be deep-equal to each other, after discarding any comments and processing-instructions.
- ❑ In the case of element nodes, there must be a one-to-one correspondence between the attributes of the two elements (same attribute name, and same typed value).

- ❑ In the case of attribute nodes and element nodes whose type does not allow element children, the typed values must be deep-equal to each other.

- ❑ In the case of text nodes, comments, processing instructions, and namespace nodes they must have the same string value, compared using the selected collation. (But for namespace nodes, the values—that is, the namespace URIs—are always compared using codepoint-by-codepoint comparison.) Note however that comments, processing instructions, and namespace nodes are only taken into account if they occur directly as items in the sequences supplied as arguments to the deep-equal() function. When they occur within the content of an element node, they are not considered.

Nodes can be deep-equal even if they differ in certain respects:

- ❑ When comparing elements, the namespace nodes of the elements do not need to be the same, and contained comments and processing instructions are not taken into consideration. (The fact that the namespace nodes can be different also means that one element can pass validation while the other fails validation, if they happen to contain xs:QName values in their content.)

- ❑ Type annotations are not taken into account: for example two attributes can be equal if one is annotated as an xs:decimal with value 3.0 and the other is annotated as xs:integer with value 3.

- ❑ The order of attributes within an element can vary. (But the order of attribute nodes in the top-level sequence is significant.)

- ❑ The base URI can vary.

- ❑ When comparing document nodes, the document URI and unparsed entities are ignored.

Surprisingly, however, whitespace text nodes are taken into account even within an element that has an element-only content model.

Examples

Expression	Result
deep-equal((1,2,3), (1,2,3))	true
deep-equal((1,2,3), (3,2,1))	false
deep-equal((1,2), (1.0, 2.0))	true
deep-equal((), ())	true

In the following examples, assume that $doc refers to the following document:

```
<doc>
   <e att1="a" att2="b" att3="c"><f/><g/></e>
   <e att3="C" att1="a" att2="b"><f/></e>
   <e att3="C" att1="a" att2="b"><f/><g/></e>
</doc>
```

and assume that $weak refers to a collation under which «c» and «C» compare equal. Then:

Expression	Result
deep-equal($doc/e[1], $doc/e[2])	false
deep-equal($doc/e[1], $doc/e[3], $weak)	true
deep-equal($doc/e[1]/@*, $doc/e[2]/@*, $weak)	*undefined (the result depends on the order of attribute nodes, which is unpredictable)*

Usage

The deep-equal() function represents one particular way of deciding whether two nodes or sequences are equal to each other. In practice there are probably two common ways it is likely to be used:

- ❏ To compare two sequences of atomic values: the result is true if the two sequences are the same length, and the sequences are pairwise equal to each other.

- ❏ To compare two element or document nodes to see if they have the same content at every level of the hierarchy.

Note that comparing two element nodes using the «=» or «eq» operators fails if the elements are defined in the schema to have a complex type, unless this is a complex type allowing mixed content, in which case the elements are compared by comparing their string values.

The definition of deep equality for nodes is one that will suit some tastes and not others. For example, it treats comments and processing instructions within an element as insignificant, but whitespace between elements as significant. It also treats the order of child elements (but not attributes) as significant. If you don't like this definition, the answer is simple: define your own function, and use that instead.

default-collation

The default-collation() function returns the URI of the default collation, that is, the collation that is used when no collation is explicitly specified in a function such as compare().

Changes in 2.0

This function is new in XPath 2.0.

Signature

This function takes no arguments.

	Data type	Meaning
Result	xs:string	*The URI of the default collation from the runtime context*

Usage

The default-collation() function is useful when you want to assign a collation conditionally, for example:

```
compare($x, $y, if ($param-uri) then $param-uri else default-collation())
```

When you call a function that expects a collation, you can always omit the argument to request the default collation, but you cannot supply a value such as an empty sequence or a zero-length string: if the argument is present, then it must be a valid collation.

Remember that for the five functions contains(), ends-with(), starts-with(), substring-before(), and substring-after(), the default when you don't supply the collation argument is not the default collation from the runtime context, but the Unicode codepoint collation.

See also

compare() on page 310
deep-equal() on page 323
distinct-values() on page 327
index-of() on page 353
max() on page 370
min() on page 371
Value Comparisons on page 181 in Chapter 6

distinct-values

The distinct-values() function eliminates duplicate values from a sequence.

For example, «distinct-values((3, 5, 3, 6))» might return «(5, 6, 3)».

Changes in 2.0

This function is new in XPath 2.0.

Signature

Argument	Data type	Meaning
sequence	xdt:anyAtomicType*	The input sequence
collation (*optional*)	xs:string	The collation to be used when comparing values that are strings
Result	xdt:anyAtomicType*	*The input sequence, with duplicate values removed*

Effect

If a sequence containing nodes is supplied as the argument, the nodes are first atomized as part of the standard function calling rules.

An untyped atomic value in the sequence is treated as a string.

If two or more values in the sequence are equal to each other (according to the rules of the «eq» operator, using the specified collation when comparing strings) then only one of them is included in the result sequence. It is not defined which of them will be retained (for example, if the input sequence contains the xs:integer 3 and the xs:decimal 3.0 then it is unpredictable which of these two values will be present in the result). In addition, the order of the values in the result sequence is undefined.

If the sequence contains two values that are not comparable using the «eq» operator (for example, an integer and a string) then these values are treated as distinct; no error is reported.

For the purpose of this function, NaN is considered equal to itself, and distinct from any other value.

Examples

Assume that the default collation is case-blind, that is, that it treats the strings «A» and «a» as equal. The table below gives one possible result for each expression; a particular XPath processor might return some permutation of this result, or might include different items from a set that are equal to each other (such as «A» and «a»).

Expression	Possible Result
distinct-values((1, 2, 3, 3.5, 2.0, 1.0))	3.5, 2.0, 1, 3
distinct-values(("A", "B", "C", "a", "b", "c"))	"B", "c", "a"
distinct-values((xs:time("12:20:02Z"), xs:time("13:20:02+01:00")))	xs:time("13:20:02+01:00")
distinct-values((1, "a", current-date()))	"a", 1, 2004-05-08Z

Usage

The distinct-values() function is the only way provided for eliminating duplicate values in XPath 2.0 and in XQuery 1.0. In XSLT 2.0, however, richer functionality is available in the form of the <xsl:for-each-group> instruction.

If you apply the function to a sequence of nodes, the result will be the distinct values present in those nodes, not the nodes themselves. To process the nodes, you will have to find the nodes having each value. The typical logic is the following, which returns a sequence of integers representing the number of employees in each department:

```
for $x in distinct-values(//employee/@dept)
    return count(//employee[@dept = $x])
```

In practice the processing of the result will probably be done in XSLT, XQuery, or some other host language, because it will usually involve generating nodes in the output, which XPath cannot do on its own.

Having found the distinct values that appear in a sequence, it is possible to determine the positions of each of these values using the index-of() function. For example, if you are using XQuery then you can sort the distinct values in order of their first appearance in the sequence by writing:

```
(: XQUERY 1.0 EXAMPLE :)
for $d in distinct-values($sequence)
order by index-of($sequence, $d)[1]
return $d
```

Alternatively, you could sort them in order of their frequency of occurrence by writing:

```
(: XQUERY 1.0 EXAMPLE :)
for $d in distinct-values($sequence)
order by count(index-of($sequence, $d))
return $d
```

XPath 2.0 has no sorting capability, so this operation can only be done in the host language. In XSLT, it is usually more convenient to use the <xsl:for-each-group> instruction.

See also

index-of() on page 353.
<xsl:for-each-group> in Chapter 5 of *XSLT 2.0 Programmer's Reference*.

doc

The doc() function retrieves an external XML document by means of a URI, and returns the document node at the root of the tree representation of that XML document.

Changes in 2.0

This function is new in XPath 2.0. It is a simplified version of the document() function that was provided in XSLT 1.0 and which remains available in XSLT 2.0. When combined with functions such as resolve-uri() and base-uri(), the doc() function provides most of the capability of the XSLT 2.0 document() function, but with a much simpler interface.

Signature

Argument	Data type	Meaning
uri	xs:string?	The URI of the document to be loaded
Result	document-node()?	*The document node of the document identified by this URI*

Effect

The doc() function gives XPath a window on the outside world, by allowing it to retrieve documents identified by a URI. Potentially this makes any XML document anywhere on the Web available for processing.

However, because the doc() function is an interface between the XPath processor and the world outside, many aspects of its behavior depend on the implementation, or on the way that the implementation is configured. XPath 2.0 is expected to be used in a great variety of environments (for example, some XPath processors might only work with XML documents that have been preloaded into a purpose-designed database) and the spec therefore gives a great deal of freedom to implementors. In fact, the formal specification of this function simply says that the evaluation context for processing an XPath expression provides a mapping of URIs to document nodes; if you specify a URI for which a mapping exists, then you get back the corresponding document node, and if you specify a URI for which no mapping exists, you get back an empty sequence.

The term *mapping* here is deliberately abstract. It actually allows the implementation to do anything it likes to get from the URI you specify to the tree that comes back. Many implementations will allow users to control the process, either by implementing user hooks like the URIResolver in Java's JAXP interface and the XmlResolver in .NET, or by setting options in configuration files or command line parameters.

Before the URI is used, it is first resolved into an absolute URI. You can resolve the URI yourself using the resolve-uri() function, in which case you have a free choice of the base URI to use, but if you pass a relative URI to the doc() function then it will always be resolved against the base URI from the static context of the XPath expression. In XSLT 2.0 this generally means the URI of the containing stylesheet module; in XQuery it means the base URI given in the query prolog. If the relative URI was read from a source document, then it should normally be resolved against the base URI of the document from where it was read, but this is left to the application to do.

One rule that the implementation must enforce is that if you call doc() twice with the same absolute URI, you get the same document node back each time. In XSLT, this rule applies for the duration of a transformation, not just for a single XPath expression evaluation.

Another rule is that the URI must not contain a fragment identifier (the part after the «#» sign). (This rule is currently under review by the Working Groups.)

What is likely to happen in a typical implementation is this:

❑ The URI (once resolved into an absolute URI) is checked against a list of documents that are already loaded. If the URI is in the list, the same document node is returned again.

❑ Otherwise, the absolute URI is used to identify and fetch an XML document, for example, by using the file or http URI schemes.

❑ The XML document is parsed, and optionally validated using a DTD validator or schema processor.

❑ A tree representation of the document is built in memory, and the document node at the root of this tree is returned as the result of the function.

Many processors are likely to allow users to control aspects of this process, including:

❑ Locating the physical resource containing the source XML (if indeed it is source XML). Mechanisms such as catalogs or user hooks (like the JAXP URIResolver) might be used to provide an indirection between the URI and the location of the resource.

❑ Selecting an XML parser, and setting options to determine whether it performs DTD and/or schema validation.

- ❑ Setting options that define whether XInclude directives in the source document are expanded, and whether any information in the source document (such as insignificant whitespace, comments, processing-instructions, or unused namespaces) is to be excluded from the tree representation.

- ❑ Setting tuning options, for example, parameters that control space/time tradeoffs in the way the tree is built.

- ❑ Setting error handling options, for example, whether a parsing error is to be treated as fatal, or whether an empty sequence (or perhaps a fallback document) should be returned in such cases.

If a schema is used to validate the document, then it must be compatible with any schema that was used when compiling the XPath expression. Here again, the detailed rules have been left to the implementation. The processor may require that the input document is validated against a schema that was known at compile time; or it may allow validation using a different schema, provided that the tree that comes back contains enough information to allow the type definitions to be located at runtime. The processor is supposed to ensure that there is no version incompatibility between the compile time and runtime schemas, but it wouldn't be surprising to come across a processor that simply passes this responsibility back to the user.

Usage and Examples

There are three main ways an XPath expression can access nodes in input documents.

- ❑ The input document (or a node within it) can be supplied as the context node.

- ❑ A node can be included in the value of a variable available in the context.

- ❑ The XPath expression can invoke the doc() function (or the collection() function) to access the document by URI.

Which of these three approaches is used is a matter of application convenience, and may be influenced by the facilities available in the host language or the processor API for configuring the behavior of the different options.

The following example shows an expression that uses a lookup table in an external document. The lookup table might have the form shown below, and be held in a document called «countries.xml»:

```
<countries>
  <country name="Andorra" code="ad"/>
  <country name="United Arab Emirates" code="ae"/>
  <country name="Afghanistan" code="af"/>
  <country name="Antigua and Barbuda" code="ag"/>
  ...
</countries>
```

A query that uses this table to display the number of employees located in each country might look like this:

```
string-join(
  for $c in doc("countries.xml")/country return
    concat($c/@name, ": ",
           count(//employee[location/country = $c/@code]))
  "&#x0a;")
```

This will return a string of the form:

```
Andorra: 0
United Arab Emirates: 12
Afghanistan: 1
Antigua and Barbuda: 25
...
```

See also

base-uri() on page 302
collection() on page 309
document-uri() on page 332
resolve-uri() on page 405
document() in Chapter 7 of *XSLT 2.0 Programmer's Reference*.

document-uri

The document-uri() function returns a URI associated with a document node.

Changes in 2.0

This function is new in XPath 2.0.

Signature

Argument	Data type	Meaning
input	node()?	The document node whose URI is required. If the node is not a document node, or if an empty sequence is supplied, the empty sequence is returned
Result	xs:string?	The URI of the document node

Effect

The URI that is returned is always an absolute URI, and it has the property that if you passed it as an argument to the doc() function, you would get the input node back.

If no absolute URI is known for the supplied document node, the empty sequence is returned.

Usage

This function is provided to allow a reference to a particular document to be constructed, either in the result document of an XSLT transformation or XQuery function, or simply in error messages. It is particularly useful where the transformation or query is processing a large batch of similar input documents, accessed perhaps using the collection() function, or perhaps supplied as a parameter to the transformation or query in a global variable.

To take an XSLT example, you might be producing a result document that acts as an index to a collection of input documents. This might include code such as:

```
<xsl:for-each select="collection('dataset.xml')">
  <xsl:sort select="/doc/title"/>
  <p><a href="document-uri(.)">
      <xsl:value-of select="/doc/title"/>
    </a>
  </p>
</xsl:for-each>
```

See also

base-uri() on page 302
collection() on page 309
doc() on page 329

empty

The empty() function returns true if and only if the argument is an empty sequence.

For example, the expression «empty(//a)» returns true if the context document contains no <a> elements.

Changes in 2.0

This function is new in XPath 2.0.

Signature

Argument	Data type	Meaning
sequence	item()*	The input sequence
Result	xs:boolean	true *if the input sequence is empty, otherwise* false

Effect

The function returns true if and only if the supplied sequence is empty.

Examples

Assume the source document:

```
<para>See also <a ref="elsewhere.xml" style=""/>.</para>
```

Expression	Result
empty(/para)	false
empty(/para/a)	false
empty(/para/a/@style)	false
empty(/para/b)	true
empty(/para/a[2])	true

Usage

Note that empty() is used only to test whether the number of items in a sequence is zero. As the examples above illustrate, it is *not* used to test whether a node is empty, in the sense of an element that has no children, or an attribute whose string value is a zero-length string.

To test whether an element $E has no element or text node children (or comments or processing instructions), you can write «if (empty($E/node()) ...».

To test whether the string value of a node $N is the zero-length string, you can write «if (string($N) eq "") ...».

Remember also that a test on any value in the condition of an «if» expression is done by taking the effective boolean value of the expression, as defined under the boolean() function on page 304. For example, if the expression is a path expression then the condition is true if the path expression selects one or more nodes; if it is a string, then the condition is true if the string is not zero-length. So, for example:

```
if (not(*)) then X else Y
```

has the same effect as:

```
if (empty(*)) then X else Y
```

and similarly, if @a refers to a list-valued attribute, then:

```
if (string(@a)) then X else Y
```

is equivalent to:

```
if (empty(data(@a))) then Y else X
```

See also

boolean() on page 304
exists() on page 341
not() on page 391

ends-with

The ends-with() function tests whether one string ends with another string. For example, the expression «ends-with('17cm', 'cm')» returns true.

Changes in 2.0

This function is new in XPath 2.0.

Signature

Argument	Data type	Meaning
input	xs:string?	The containing string
test	xs:string?	The test string
collation (*optional*)	xs:string	A collation URI
Result	xs:string?	*True if the input string ends with the test string, otherwise false*

Effect

If there is no collation argument, then the system tests to see whether the last N characters of the input string match the characters in the test string (where N is the length of the test string). If so, the result is true; otherwise it is false. Characters match if they have the same Unicode value.

If the test string is zero-length, the result is always true. If the input string is zero-length, the result is true only if the test string is also zero-length. If the test string is longer than the input, the result is always false.

If either the input or the test argument is an empty sequence, it is treated in the same way as a zero-length string.

If a collation is specified, this collation is used to test whether the strings match. See the description of the contains() function on page 314 for an account of how substring matching works with a collation. If the collation argument is omitted, the function matches characters according to their Unicode codepoint values.

Examples

Expression	Result
ends-with("a.xml", ".xml")	true
ends-with("a.xml", ".xsl")	false
ends-with("a.xml", "")	true
ends-with("", "")	true
ends-with((), ())	true

Usage

The ends-with() function is useful when the content of text values, or attributes, has some internal structure. For example, the following code can be used to strip an unwanted «/» at the end of an href attribute:

```
doc(if (ends-with(@href, '/')
    then substring(@href, 1, string-length(@href)-1)
    else @href)
```

Many string manipulations that can be done using ends-with() (but not those that rely on collations) can also be achieved using the matches() function, which allows regular expressions to be used.

See also

contains() on page 314
matches() on page 368
starts-with() on page 415
string-length() on page 419
substring() on page 423

error

The error() function can be called when the application detects an error condition; it causes evaluation of the XPath expression as a whole to fail. (In XSLT, this will cause the entire transformation to fail.)

Changes in 2.0

This function is new in XPath 2.0.

Signature

Argument	Data type	Meaning
value (*optional*)	item()?	The value can be used to identify the error, in an implementation-defined way. If the value is a string, it will probably be used as an error message
Result	None	*This function does not return a result; it always raises an error*

Effect

The error() function always reports an error, it never returns a result.

Calling the error() function causes the XPath expression as a whole to fail, since XPath provides no try/catch mechanism for catching errors.

Under XSLT, calling the error function causes the whole transformation to fail: the effect is the same as `<xsl:message terminate="yes"/>`.

The optional value argument can be used to identify the error. The exact way in which this is used depends on the implementation.

Examples

Expression	Result
error()	*causes termination, with no explanation*
error(xs:QName ("docbook:invalid-page-ref"))	*causes termination, with an error code «invalid-page-ref» in the namespace associated with the «docbook» prefix*

Usage

The `error()` function is useful when the application encounters a condition that it is not designed to handle, for example, invalid arguments passed to a function.

Every runtime error defined by the XPath specification itself has a short code, such as XP0120. The specification suggests that this code might be made available to applications via the API of the XPath processor, though there is nothing prescriptive about this. It also suggests that these codes could be regarded as being `xs:QName` values with no namespace, and that it makes sense for vendor-defined and user-defined error codes to fit into the same scheme of things by using `xs:QName` values as error values, with an explicit namespace. An implementation that allows error messages to be localized will typically provide some way of using the `xs:QName` as a code to look up a message in a file of message texts appropriate to the user's language.

This error-handling scheme is fine for product-quality applications that need to be delivered to a large number of users, localized to different languages, and so on. If you're just writing a simple stylesheet that's going to be used once and thrown away, it's all rather over the top. In this case, you can just pass a message that says what's gone wrong in the form of a string.

See also

trace() on page 436
<xsl:message> in Chapter 5 of *XSLT 2.0 Programmer's Reference*

escape-uri

The `escape-uri()` function applies the URI escaping conventions defined in RFC 2396 to an input string.

For example, «escape-uri("my doc.xml", true())» returns the string «my%20doc.xml».

Changes in 2.0

This function is new in XPath 2.0.

Signature

Argument	Data type	Meaning
value	xs:string	The input string, to which URI escaping is to be applied
escape-reserved	xs:boolean	Set to true if characters with a reserved meaning in URIs (for example «/» and «#») are to be escaped
Result	xs:string	*The URI in its escaped form, as a string*

Effect

The result string is formed from the input string by escaping special characters according to the rules defined in RFC 2396, (http://www.ietf.org/ref/rfc2396.txt). It also takes into account changes defined in RFC 2732 (http://www.ietf.org/ref/rfc2732.txt), which introduces the use of square brackets to support Internet Protocol version 6 (IPv6). Special characters are escaped by first encoding them in UTF-8, then representing each byte of the UTF-8 encoding in the form %HH where HH represents the byte as two hexadecimal digits. The digits A–F are always in upper case.

The characters that are escaped depend on the setting of the escape-reserved argument. If this is set to true, then all characters except A-Z, a-z, 0-9 and «-», «_», «.», «!», «~», «*», «'», «(», and «)» are escaped. If it is set to false, then the characters «;», «/», «?», «:», «@», «&», «=», «+», «$», «,», «[», «]», and «#» are not escaped.

A «%» character is never escaped: it is assumed that «%» characters already form part of an escape sequence.

Examples

Expression	Result
escape-uri("simple.xml", true())	"simple.xml"
escape-uri("simple.xml", false())	"simple.xml"
escape-uri("my doc.xml", true())	"my%20doc.xml"
escape-uri("my doc.xml", false())	"my%20doc.xml"
escape-uri("f+o.pdf", true())	"f%2Bo.pdf"
escape-uri("f+o.pdf", false())	"f+o.pdf"
escape-uri("Grüße.html", true())	"Gr%C3%BC%C3%9Fe.html"
escape-uri("Grüße.html", false())	"Gr%C3%BC%C3%9Fe.html"

Usage

This function is designed for use by applications that need to construct URIs.

The name escape-uri() is slightly misleading, in that it suggests that the input is a URI. In fact, the rules for URIs (given in RFC2396, http://www.ietf.org/ref/rfc2396.txt) make it clear that a string in which special characters have not been escaped is not a valid URI. In many contexts where URIs are required, both in XPath functions such as the doc() function and in places such as the href attribute of the <a> element in HTML, the URI must be fully escaped according to these rules. In practice, software is very often tolerant and accepts unescaped URIs, but applications shouldn't rely on this.

The rules for escaping special characters are rather peculiar. To escape a character, it is first encoded in UTF-8, which in general represents a character as one or more octets (bytes). Each of these bytes is then substituted into the string using the notation «%HH» where HH is the value of the byte in hexadecimal. For example, the space character is represented as «%20», and the euro symbol as «%E2%82%AC». Although RFC 2396 allows the hexadecimal digits «A-F» to be in either upper or lower case, the escape-uri() function mandates upper case, to ensure that escaped URIs can be compared as strings.

Historically, the same algorithm has been used to escape URLs and URIs using character encodings other than UTF-8. However, in most environments where XPath is used UTF-8 is the recommended encoding for URIs, and this is therefore the only encoding that the escape-uri() function supports.

Which characters need to be escaped? The answer to this depends on context. Essentially, characters fall into three categories: those that can be used freely anywhere in a URI, those that cannot be used anywhere and must always be escaped, and those that have a special meaning in a URI and must be escaped if they are to be used without this special meaning. The characters in this last category are referred to as *reserved* characters.

The table below shows the characters in each category:

Category	Characters
allowed anywhere	A-Z, a-z, 0-9 «-» «_» «.» «!» «~» «*» «'» «(» «)»
reserved	«;» «/» «?» «:» «@» «&» «=» «+» «$» «,» «[» «]» «#»
disallowed everywhere	all other characters, including all non-ASCII characters

One or two characters deserve special mention:

❑ The «#» character is not listed in RFC 2396 as a reserved character. This is because (technically speaking) it cannot appear within a URI. However, it is allowed within a *URI Reference*, to separate the URI part from the fragment part. The escape-uri() function is actually concerned with escaping a URI Reference rather than a URI proper, so «#» is added to the reserved category.

❑ The «%» character is a disallowed character, so it should always be escaped as «%25». However, RFC 2396 says that implementations should be careful not to apply escaping to a URI that is already escaped, which would result in a single space being represented not as «%20» but as «%2520». The specification for escape-uri() therefore stipulates that «%» should be left alone. If you do need to replace «%» characters by «%25», you can always call the replace() function to do this, before calling escape-uri().

❑ The characters «[» and «]» were defined in RFC 2396 as disallowed characters, but their status was changed to reserved by RFC 2732, which extended the URI syntax to support IPv6 addresses.

In theory, the right way to construct a URI is to apply escaping to each of its components individually (for example, the URI scheme, the authority, the path components, the query parameters, and the fragment identifier), and then to assemble the components by adding the appropriate delimiters. This is the only way of ensuring, for example, that an «=» sign is escaped if it appears as an ordinary character in a path component, but not if it appears between a keyword and a value in the query part. When a URI is constructed this way, the escape-reserved argument should be set to true(), so that reserved characters appearing within a component are properly escaped.

But often in practice the unescaped URI (so called—as we have seen, if it isn't escaped then technically it isn't a URI) arrives in one piece and escaping needs to be applied to the whole string. In this case it's a reasonable assumption that characters such as «/» and «:» appearing within the string have their special meanings, and should not be escaped. In this situation, the escape-reserved argument should be set to false().

See also

escape-uri-attributes option in <xsl:output>: *XSLT 2.0 Programmer's Reference*, Chapter 5.

exactly-one

The exactly-one() function returns its argument unchanged, provided that it is a sequence containing exactly one item. In other cases, it reports an error.

Changes in 2.0

This function is new in XPath 2.0.

Signature

Argument	Data type	Meaning
value	item()*	The input value. Although the function signature says that any sequence of items is allowed, a runtime error will occur if the number of items is not exactly one
Result	item()	*The same as the supplied value, after checking to ensure that it contains a single item*

Effect

The exactly-one() function returns its argument unchanged, provided that it is a sequence containing exactly one item. In other cases, it reports an error.

This function is useful with XPath processors that perform static type-checking, as described in Chapter 3. Calling this function acts as a promise by the programmer that the argument will be a sequence containing exactly one item. This allows the expression to be used in contexts that require a single value (for example, the operands of the «is» operator) when the processor might otherwise have reported a static type error. The XPath expression is still type-safe, because the check that the sequence does indeed contain a single item will be done at runtime, just as it would with a processor that does not enforce static type checking.

Examples

Assume the source document

```
<list separator=";"/>
```

with a schema that defines the separator attribute to be optional.

Expression	Result
string-join(("a", "b", "c"), /list/@separator)	*Succeeds unless the processor is doing static type checking, in which case it gives a compile time error because the second argument of string-join() must not be an empty sequence*
string-join(("a", "b", "c"), exactly-one(/list/@separator))	*Succeeds whether the processor is doing static type checking or not, because the check that the typed value of @separator contains a single item is deferred until runtime*

Usage

This function is never needed unless you are using a processor that does static type checking.

However, you may still find it useful as a way of inserting runtime checks into your XPath expressions, and documenting the assumptions you are making about the input data.

See also

`one-or-more()` on page 395
`zero-or-one()` on page 444
«`treat as`» expression on page 288 in Chapter 9.

exists

The `exists()` function returns true if and only if a supplied sequence contains at least one item.

Changes in 2.0

This function is new in XPath 2.0.

Signature

Argument	Data type	Meaning
sequence	`item()*`	The input sequence
Result	`xs:boolean`	`true` *if the input sequence is non-empty, otherwise* `false`

Effect

The function returns true if and only if the supplied sequence contains at least one item.

Examples

Assume the source document:

```
<para>See also <a ref="elsewhere.xml" style=""/>.</para>
```

Expression	Result
`exists(/para)`	true
`exists(/para/a)`	true
`exists(/para/a/@style)`	true
`exists(/para/b)`	false
`exists(/para/a[2])`	false

Usage

This function is largely cosmetic: when testing to see if nodes exist, some people prefer to write an expression such as «author[exists(child::element())]» over the more cryptic «author[*]». But they have the same meaning.

Writing exists() explicitly is good practice when you are testing to see whether a sequence of atomic values (rather than nodes) is non-empty. This is because the effective boolean value of an atomic sequence is false not only when the sequence is empty, but also when it contains a single numeric zero, zero-length string, or boolean false value.

Writing «exists(X)» is precisely equivalent to writing «not(empty(X))».

See also

boolean() on page 304
empty() on page 333
not() on page 391

expanded-QName

The expanded-QName() function returns a value of type xs:QName, given a namespace URI and a local name.

Changes in 2.0

This function is new in XPath 2.0.

Signature

Argument	Data type	Meaning
namespace	xs:string?	The namespace URI part of the xs:QName. To construct a QName that is in no namespace, supply either a zero-length string or an empty sequence
local-name	xs:string	The local part of the xs:QName. This must conform to the XML rules for an NCName
Result	xs:QName	*The newly constructed xs:QName*

Effect

A value of type xs:QName has two parts: a namespace URI, and a local name. This function constructs an xs:QName value from these two components.

XPath uses the term *lexical QName* to refer to a QName in the form prefix:local-name, and *expanded QName* to refer to the underlying value of the QName, in which the prefix has been resolved to a namespace URI. This function creates an expanded QName directly, without going through the stage of writing a prefix and then converting this to a namespace URI.

Examples

Expression	Result
expanded-QName("http://www.w3.org/ XML/1998/namespace", "space")	*The* xs:QName *usually written as* «xml:space»
expanded-QName("http://www.w3.org/ 2001/XMLSchema-instance", "type")	*The* xs:QName *usually written as* «xsi:type»

Usage

The expanded-QName() is useful when you want to compare node names against a specified name, especially one determined at runtime. This is done by using it in conjunction with the node-name() function.

For example, suppose that you are dealing with source documents for which several variants of the schema exist, all using different namespace URIs; and suppose that the actual namespace URI to be used in a particular run is passed in as a parameter. This makes it difficult to use path expressions in the natural way, because path expressions can only refer to names that are fully known (that is, both the namespace URI and local name are known) at compile time.

Suppose you are using XSLT and define a set of global variables like this:

```
<xsl:variable name="address" select="expanded-QName($ns, 'address')"/>
<xsl:variable name="postalcode"
              select="expanded-QName($ns, 'postalcode') "/>
```

and so on.

It is then possible to use path expressions such as:

```
select="*[node-name()=$address]/*[node-name()=$postalcode]"
```

to locate nodes.

See also

local-name-from-QName() on page 365
namespace-uri-from-QName() on page 382
node-name() on page 384

false

This function returns the boolean value false.

Changes in 2.0

None.

Signature

There are no arguments.

	Data type	Meaning
Result	xs:boolean	*The* xs:boolean *value false*

Usage

There are no boolean constants available in XPath expressions, so the functions true() and false() can be used where a constant boolean value is required.

The most common usage is when passing an argument to a function that expects a boolean value.

XSLT Example

The following code calls a named template, setting the parameter «verbose» to false:

```
<xsl:call-template name="do-the-work">
   <xsl:with-param name="verbose" select="false()"/>
</xsl:call-template>
```

See also

true() on page 439

floor

The floor() function returns the largest integer value that is less than or equal to the numeric value of the argument. The result has the same data type as the supplied value. For example if the supplied value is an xs:double then the result is returned as an xs:double.

For example, the expression «floor(11.3)» returns 11.0 (this is displayed as "11", but it is actually a decimal value).

Changes in 2.0

The function has been generalized to work with all numeric data types.

Signature

Argument	Data type	Meaning
value	Numeric?	The supplied number. If an empty sequence is supplied, an empty sequence is returned
Result	Numeric?	*The result of rounding down the supplied number to the integer below. The result has the same data type as the supplied value*

Effect

If the number is an xs:integer, it is returned unchanged.

Otherwise, it is rounded down to the next lowest whole number. If the supplied value is an xs:decimal, the result will be an xs:decimal, if it is an xs:double, the result will be an xs:double, and if it is an xs:float, the result will be an xs:float. In the case of negative numbers, the rounding is away from zero.

The xs:double and xs:float data types in XPath support special values such as infinity, negative zero and NaN (not-a-number), which are described on page 84 in Chapter 3.

If the argument is NaN (not-a-number), the result will be NaN. Similarly, when the argument is positive or negative infinity, the function will return the value of the argument unchanged.

Examples

Expression	Result
floor(1.0)	1.0
floor(1.6e0)	1.0e0
floor(17 div 3)	5.0
floor(-3.0)	-3.0
floor(-8.2e0)	-9.0e0
floor(number('NaN'))	NaN

Usage

Like round() and ceiling(), this function is useful when calculating sizes of HTML tables.

Two alternatives you may want to consider are:

❑ Using the xs:integer() constructor function. This differs from floor() in that it always truncates (rounds towards zero); also, it returns an actual integer, rather than returning a value of the same type as the argument

❑ Using the expression «$x idiv 1». This produces the same result as the xs:integer() constructor function, but saves you having to declare the XML Schema namespace.

See also

ceiling() on page 306
round() on page 409
Converting to an xs:integer in Chapter 9, page 277
The «idiv» operator, under *Arithmetic Operators* in Chapter 6, page 173.

hours-from-dateTime, hours-from-time

These two functions extract the hour component from an `xs:date` or `xs:dateTime` value. For example, at noon local time both these functions return 12.

Changes in 2.0

These functions are new in XPath 2.0.

Signature

Argument	Data type	Meaning
input	`xs:time?` or `xs:dateTime?`	The value from which the hour component is to be extracted. The data type of the supplied argument must correspond to the data type implied by the function name
Result	`xs:integer`	*The hour, in the range 0 to 23 (midnight is represented as 0)*

Effect

The function returns the hour component of the supplied `xs:time` or `xs:dateTime`. The value is from the time as expressed in its local timezone (not normalized to UTC). This means that if the time (or dateTime) has a timezone, the value is the time in that timezone; if it has no timezone, it is the value as written.

If an empty sequence is supplied, an empty sequence is returned.

Examples

Expression	Result
`hours-from-time(xs:time("12:35:03.142"))`	12
`hours-from-dateTime(xs:dateTime("2004-02-28T13:55:30"))`	13
`hours-from-time(xs:time("23:59:59+01:00"))`	23
`hours-from-dateTime(xs:dateTime("2004-07-31T22:10:00-05:00"))`	22

See also

`current-date()`, `-dateTime()`, `-time()` on page 318.
`format-date()`, `-dateTime()`, `-time()` in Chapter 7 of *XSLT 2.0 Programmer's Reference*.
`day-from-date()`, `-dateTime()` on page 322
`year-from-date()`, `-dateTime()` on page 443

hours-from-duration

This function extracts the value of the hours component from a normalized xdt:dayTimeDuration value.

Changes in 2.0

This function is new in XPath 2.0.

Signature

Argument	Data type	Meaning
input	xdt:dayTimeDuration?	The value from which the component is to be extracted. If an empty sequence is supplied, an empty sequence is returned
Result	xs:integer?	*The hours component*

Effect

The function returns the hours component of the supplied xdt:dayTimeDuration. The duration value is first normalized so that the number of hours is less than 24, the number of minutes is less than 60, and so on. The result will be negative if the duration is negative. The result will therefore be in the range −23 to +23.

Examples

Expression	Result
hours-from-duration(xdt:dayTimeDuration("P5DT12H30M"))	12
hours-from-duration(xdt:dayTimeDuration("PT72H"))	0
hours-from-duration(xdt:dayTimeDuration("-PT36H15M"))	-12

See also

days-from-duration on page 323
minutes-from-duration on page 374
seconds-from-duration on page 414

id

The id() function returns a sequence containing all the elements in a given document with given ID attribute values.

For example, if the code attribute is defined as an ID attribute, then the expression «id('A321-780')» might return the single element <product code="A321-780">.

Changes in 2.0

A second optional argument has been added, to define which document is to be searched. The semantics of the function have been redefined in terms of the XPath 2.0 type system.

Signature

Argument	Data type	Meaning
values	xs:string*	Specifies the required ID values
node *(optional)*	node()	Identifies the document to be searched
Result	element()*	*A sequence of nodes, in document order, containing the nodes with the required ID values*

Effect

The function is designed to make it easy to find all the elements referenced in an element or attribute of type xs:IDREF or xs:IDREFS, but there is no requirement that it should be used this way. The rules are defined so that the supplied argument can be any of the following:

- ❑ A string containing an ID value
- ❑ A string containing a space-separated sequence of ID values
- ❑ A node containing an ID value
- ❑ A node containing a space-separated sequence of ID values
- ❑ A sequence of any of the above

Any nodes in the sequence are atomized as part of the function calling mechanism. The resulting strings are then tokenized by splitting their contents on whitespace boundaries. Each token is used as a candidate ID value, if there is a node in the selected document that has an ID attribute or ID content equal to this candidate ID value: this node is included in the result of the function.

The rules for this function are strict about the type annotation of the nodes that are selected: the identifying attribute or element content must be annotated as being of type xs:ID. The specification is a little open-ended about how this works in a non-schema-aware processor, but it's likely that most processors will recognize attributes declared in a DTD as ID attributes.

By contrast, it is not necessary for the candidate IDs to be declared as type IDREF or IDREFS, though the function is designed to produce the expected result when they are, that is, it finds the nodes referenced by the IDREF or IDREFS values in the argument sequence.

It is not an error if there is no element with an ID equal to one of the candidate ID values. In this situation, there will simply be no node in the resulting sequence corresponding to this value. In the simplest case, where there is only one candidate ID value supplied, the resulting sequence will be empty if the ID is not present.

The second argument, if supplied, identifies the document to be searched. This does not have to be the document node, it can be any node within the target document. This argument defaults to the context node. Whether the argument is explicit or implicit, it must be a node in a tree whose root is a document node. If the argument is omitted, then a runtime error is reported if the context item is undefined, or if it is not a node. The nodes in the supplied `values` argument will often come from the same document, but this is not required.

IDs and Validation

`ID` values only really work properly if the source document is valid (in the XML sense: meaning, loosely, that it obeys the rules in its own DTD or Schema). However, XPath is designed to allow invalid documents as well as valid ones to be processed. One possible kind of validity error is that `ID` values are not unique within the document. This is explicitly covered in the specification: the first node with that `ID` value is located. Other validity errors may also be present, for example an `ID` attribute may contain embedded spaces. In this case it will not be retrieved.

When no schema is used, a non-validating XML parser isn't required to read attribute definitions from an external DTD. In this situation the XSLT processor will assume there are no `ID` attributes present, and the `id()` function will always return an empty result. If this appears to be happening, try a different XML parser. Most good parsers will report the attribute type, even though it isn't absolutely required by the XML standard.

Usage and Examples

The `id()` function provides an efficient means of locating nodes given the value of an ID attribute.

In a sense it is a convenience function, because if the attribute named `id` is always an `ID` attribute, then the expression:

```
id('B1234')
```

is equivalent to the path expression:

```
//*[@id='B1234']
```

However, the chances are that in most implementations, the `id()` function will be much more efficient than the straightforward path expression with a predicate, because the processor is likely to build an index rather than doing a sequential search.

In XSLT it is also possible to use `key()` in place of `id()`. The main advantage of the `id()` function over using `key()` is that it handles a whitespace-separated list of IDs in one go. The `key()` function cannot do this, because there is nothing to stop a key value containing a space.

The `id()` function when used with a single argument locates elements in the same document as the context node. XPath 2.0 provides two ways to locate elements in a different document. You can either use the `id()` function on the right-hand side of the «/» operator, for example «doc("lookup.xml")/id($param)», or you can supply a second argument, like this: «id($param, doc("lookup.xml"))».

Where the source document includes an `IDREFS` attribute, it is possible to locate all the referenced elements at once. For example, if the <book> element has an attribute `authors` which is an `IDREFS` attribute containing a whitespace-separated list of author ids, the relevant <author> elements can be retrieved and processed using a construct such as:

```
string-join(id(@authors)/surname), ', ')
```

See also

key() in *XSLT 2.0 Programmer's Reference*, Chapter 7
idref() in the following section

idref

The idref() function performs the inverse operation to the id() function: it locates all the nodes in a document that contain IDREF or IDREFS values referencing a given ID value.

Changes in 2.0

This function is new in XPath 2.0.

Signature

Argument	Data type	Meaning
target	xs:string*	A sequence of ID values. The function finds all element and attribute nodes of type IDREF or IDREFS that contain a reference to at least one of the ID values in this argument
node *(optional)*	node()	Identifies the document to be searched
Result	node()*	*The element and attribute nodes that were found, in document order, without duplicates*

Effect

If the idrefs argument is supplied as a node, or a sequence of nodes, then the values of the nodes are automatically atomized by the function calling mechanism. The argument can thus be supplied as any of the following:

- ❑ A string containing an ID value
- ❑ A node containing an ID value
- ❑ A sequence of either of the above

The function locates element and attribute nodes of type xs:IDREF or xs:IDREFS that contain an ID value equal to one of the supplied strings. Note that when an attribute node is matched, it is the attribute node that is returned by the function, not the containing element.

In a schema-aware processor, both elements and attributes can be marked as xs:IDREF or xs:IDREFS values. In a non-schema-aware processor, only attribute values can be recognized as IDREF or IDREFS attributes, and they are recognized as a consequence of validation using a DTD.

It is not an error if there is no node that references one of the target ID values (or even if there is no node that has this ID value). In this situation, there will simply be no node in the resulting sequence corresponding to this value. In the simplest case, where there is only one candidate ID value supplied, the resulting sequence will be empty if the document contains no reference to this ID value.

If the second argument is supplied, the nodes that are returned will come from the same document as the node supplied in this argument. This must be a node in a tree whose root is not a document node. The default for this argument is the context node: a runtime error is then reported if the context item is undefined, or if it is not a node. The nodes in the supplied `target` argument will often come from the same document, but this is not required.

IDs and Validation

`ID` and `IDREF` values only really work properly if the source document is valid (in the XML sense: meaning, loosely, that it obeys the rules in its own DTD or Schema). However, XPath is designed to allow invalid documents as well as valid ones to be processed. One possible kind of validity error is that an attribute of type `IDREF` or `IDREFS` may contain a value that is not a legal `ID` value. This situation is not an error as far as XPath is concerned; it just means that this function will never retrieve that node.

When no schema is used, a non-validating XML parser isn't required to read attribute definitions from an external DTD. In this situation the XSLT processor will assume there are no `IDREF` or `IDREFS` attributes present, and the `idref()` function will always return an empty result. If this appears to be happening, try a different XML parser. Most good parsers will report the attribute type, even though it isn't absolutely required by the XML standard.

Example

Consider the following data, representing part of a family tree:

```
<person id="I001">
  <name="Queen Elizabeth II"/>
  <spouse ref="I002"/>
</person>
<person id="I003">
  <name="Prince Charles"/>
  <mother ref="I001"/>
  <father ref="I002"/>
</person>
```

Given a `<person>` element as the context node, and assuming that the `ref` attributes have type `xs:IDREF`, it is possible to find the children of a person as:

```
idref(@id)/(parent::father|parent::mother)/parent::person
```

Note the need to check the names of the parent and grandparent elements. Without this check, one would find relatives other than the children, for example the spouse. This is because an `IDREF` in XML doesn't capture any information about which relationship is being modeled; that is implicit in the context in which the `IDREF` appears.

Sorry about the confusion here between family trees and XML trees. A family tree is of course not a tree at all in the computer science sense, because people (unlike nodes) have two parents. This means that the parent-child relationship in the family tree cannot be represented by a parent-child relationship in the XML tree; instead, it is represented here by an ID/IDREF relationship. Of course, it could have been modeled in either direction, or redundantly in both directions, but the representation chosen above works well because it is in relational third normal form.

351

See also

id() on page 347

implicit-timezone

The implicit-timezone() function returns the value of the implicit timezone from the runtime context. The implicit timezone is used when comparing dates, times, and dateTimes that have no explicit timezone.

Changes in 2.0

This function is new in XPath 2.0.

Signature

This function takes no arguments.

	Data type	Meaning
Result	xdt:dayTimeDuration?	*The value of the implicit timezone*

Effect

Timezones are represented as values of type xdt:dayTimeDuration, in the range PT14H to +PT14H. This function simply returns the value of the implicit timezone from the runtime XPath context. The way that the value is initialized is determined by the implementation; it might be set using an API, or it might simply be taken from the system clock. The idea is that the implicit timezone should be the timezone in which the user is located; but of course, when users are scattered around the world, it is not always possible to achieve this.

There are a number of operators and functions that make use of the implicit timezone. The most obvious is when comparing an xs:dateTime that has a timezone to one that does not; in this case, the xs:dateTime without an explicit timezone is assumed to represent a time in the implicit timezone. This means that an expression such as:

```
if (current-time() gt xs:time('12:00:00')) then . . .
```

can be read as "if the current time in the user's timezone is after midday...". (The result of the current-time() function will always be in the implicit timezone.)

The specification allows for implicit-timezone() to return an empty sequence if the implicit timezone is undefined. However, it's not clear that it really makes sense for the implicit timezone to be undefined: many other operations that use the implicit timezone do not allow for this possibility.

Example

If the system is correctly configured for a user situated in New York, with no daylight savings time in operation, the function implicit-timezone() will return «PT05:00».

See also

`adjust-date/time/dateTime-to-timezone()` family of functions on page 297
`current-date/time/dateTime()` family of functions on page 318
`timezone-from-date/time/dateTime()` family of functions on page 433

index-of

The `index-of()` function returns a sequence of integers indicating the positions within a particular sequence where items equal to a specified value occur.

For example, «`index-of(("a","b","c"), "b")`» returns 2.

Changes in 2.0

This function is new in XPath 2.0.

Signature

Argument	Data type	Meaning
sequence	`xdt:anyAtomicType*`	The sequence to be searched
value	`xdt:anyAtomicType`	The value to be found
collation (*optional*)	`xs:string`	The collation to be used when comparing strings
Result	`xs:integer*`	*A list containing the positions within the supplied sequence where items that are equal to the specified value have been found*

Effect

If either the `sequence` or the `value` is supplied as a node, the nodes are atomized (to extract their values) as part of the function calling rules. This function therefore operates on a sequence of atomic values. It finds all the items in the atomized sequence that compare equal to the supplied value under the rules of the «eq» operator, using the specified collation when comparing strings, or the default collation if none is specified. It then returns the positions of these items in ascending numeric order, using the usual convention of numbering positions starting at 1.

This means that if a sequence of nodes is supplied, and the nodes are list-valued (for example, a node whose type is `xs:NMTOKENS`) then the positions returned are the positions in the atomized sequence, which may not be the same as the positions of the nodes in the original sequence.

If no matching items are found, the result is an empty sequence.

Another way of writing this function, assuming that the default collation is used and that the values have already been atomized, would be:

```
for $i in 1 to count($sequence) return
    if ($sequence[$i] eq $value) then $i else ()
```

Examples

Consider the source document:

```
<doc>
   <obs at="10:42:06" colors="red green"/>
   <obs at="11:43:12" colors="green blue orange"/>
</doc>
```

and assume that this has been validated using a schema that defines the `colors` attribute as a sequence of strings.

Expression	Result
index-of(//@colors, "red")	1
index-of(//@colors, "green")	(2, 3)
index-of(//@colors, "pink")	()

in-scope-prefixes

The `in-scope-prefixes()` function returns a sequence of strings, representing all the namespace prefixes that are in scope for a given element.

Changes in 2.0

This function is new in XPath 2.0. It is provided as a replacement for the namespace axis, which is now deprecated.

Signature

Argument	Data type	Meaning
element	element()	The element whose in-scope namespaces are to be returned
Result	xs:string*	The prefixes of the in-scope namespaces

Effect

In the XPath data model, the namespaces that apply to a particular element are modeled as a set of namespace nodes: the name of the namespace node represents a namespace prefix, and the string value of the namespace node represents the namespace URI.

In XPath 1.0 it was possible to find the namespace nodes for a given element using the namespace axis. In XPath 2.0 the namespace axis has become deprecated. This was done because many implementations did not physically represent namespaces as nodes in memory, for efficiency reasons, and presenting the information as "virtual nodes" could be expensive, because of the overhead that nodes carry to maintain information about their identity, their parentage, their base URI, and so on. XPath 2.0 has therefore provided a new mechanism to allow applications to obtain the namespace information when it is needed.

The `in-scope-prefixes()` function returns all the prefixes of the in-scope namespaces for an element, or to express it in terms of the data model, the names of all the namespace nodes for that element. The order in which the names appear is unpredictable. The list will always include the name «xml», since the XML namespace is in scope for every element. If there is a default namespace in force for the element, the list will also include the zero-length string to represent the default namespace.

The namespace URIs corresponding to each of these prefixes can be determined using the function `namespace-uri-for-prefix()`.

Examples

Consider the source document below. Note that this includes a namespace undeclaration for the «soap» namespace, as permitted by XML Namespaces 1.1:

```
<?xml version="1.1"?>
<soap:Envelope
       xmlns:soap="http://schemas.xmlsoap.org/soap/envelope/">
       xmlns:xs="http://www.w3.org/2001/XMLSchema"
  <soap:Body>
   <echoString xmlns="http://example.com/soapdemo"
              xmlns:xsi="http://www.w3.org/2001/XMLSchema-instance"
              xmlns:soap="">
     <inputString xsi:type="xs:string">Hello</inputString>
   </echoString>
  </soap:Body>
 </soap:Envelope>
```

Expression	Result
`in-scope-prefixes(/soap:Envelope)`	`("xs", "soap", "xml")` *(in any order)*
`in-scope-prefixes(//*:inputString)`	`("xs", "", "xsi", "xml")` *(in any order)*

Usage

Like the namespace axis that it replaces, this function is unlikely to be needed every day of the week. It is generally needed only when dealing with documents that use namespace prefixes as part of the content of elements and attributes (and not only in forming the names of elements and attributes). I have also seen situations where it is necessary simply to detect whether a particular namespace is declared, regardless whether or not it is actually used. For example, you might want to find all your stylesheets that declare the namespace `http://icl.com/saxon` because you have decided to migrate from Saxon 6.5 (which uses this namespace) to Saxon 7.x (which does not). You could find these using the query:

```
collection("stylesheets")//*["http://icl.com/saxon" =
                        for $p in in-scope-prefixes(.)
                        return namespace-uri-for-prefix($p, .)]
```

See also

`namespace-uri-for-prefix` on page 381

insert-before

The `insert-before()` function returns a sequence constructed by inserting an item, or a sequence of items, at a given position within another sequence.

For example, «`insert-before(("a","b","c"), 2, "X")`» returns «`("a", "X", "b", "c")`».

Changes in 2.0

This function is new in XPath 2.0.

Signature

Argument	Data type	Meaning
sequence-1	`item()*`	The original sequence
position	`xs:integer`	The position in the original sequence where the new items are to be inserted
sequence-2	`item()*`	The items that are to be inserted
Result	`item()*`	*The constructed sequence*

Effect

The returned sequence consists of all items in `sequence-1` whose position is less than the specified `position`, followed by all items in `sequence-2`, followed by all remaining items in `sequence-1`. Positions, as always, are numbered starting at one. It's not an error if `position` is outside the actual range of positions in the sequence.

In other words, the result is the same as the value of the expression:

```
$sequence-1[position() lt $position],
$sequence-2,
$sequence-1[position() ge $position]
```

Examples

Expression	Result
`insert-before(1 to 5, 4, (99, 100))`	`(1, 2, 3, 99, 100, 4, 5)`
`insert-before(1 to 5, 0, 99)`	`(99, 1, 2, 3, 4, 5)`
`insert-before(1 to 5, 10, 99)`	`(1, 2, 3, 4, 5, 99)`

Usage

Although functions are provided to insert and remove items into a sequence, there is no function to replace the item at a given position $p. To achieve this, you can write:

```
insert-before(remove($seq, $p), $p, $new-item)
```

or perhaps more simply,

```
$seq[position() lt $position],
$new-item,
$seq[position() gt $position]
```

See also

remove() on page 399

«,» operator on page 240 in Chapter 8

lang

The lang() function tests whether the language of a given node, as defined by the xml:lang attribute, corresponds to the language supplied as an argument.

For example, if the context node is the element <para lang="fr-CA"> (indicating Canadian French), then the expression «lang('fr')» would return true.

Changes in 2.0

An optional second argument has been added to allow nodes other than the context node to be tested.

Signature

Argument	Data type	Meaning
language	xs:string	The language being tested
node *(optional)*	node()	The node being tested. If omitted, the context node is tested
Result	xs:boolean	true *if the language of the selected node is the same as, or a sublanguage of, the language being tested*

Effect

The function tests the node identified by the second argument if present, or the context node if it is omitted. When the second argument is absent, a runtime error occurs if there is no context item, or if the context item is not a node.

The language of the selected node is determined by the value of its xml:lang attribute, or if it has no such attribute, by the value of the xml:lang attribute on its nearest ancestor node that does have such an attribute. If there is no xml:lang attribute on any of these nodes, the lang() function returns false.

The xml:lang attribute is one of the small number of attributes that are given a predefined meaning in the XML specification (in fact, you could argue that it is the only thing in the XML specification that has anything to say about what the contents of the document might mean to its readers). The value of the attribute can take one of the following four forms:

❑ A two-letter language code defined in the international standard ISO 639. For example, English is «en» and French is «fr». This can be given in either upper-case or lower-case, though lower-case is usual. The second edition of the XML specification also anticipates the introduction of three-letter language codes in a revision of Internet RFC 1766.

❑ A two letter language code as above, followed by one or more subcodes: each subcode is preceded by a hyphen «-». For example, US English is "en-US"; Canadian French is "fr-CA". The first subcode, if present, must be either a two-letter country code from the international standard ISO 3166, or a subcode for the language registered with IANA (Internet Assigned Numbers Authority). The ISO 3166 country codes are generally the same as Internet top-level domains, for example "DE" for Germany, "CZ" for the Czech Republic, but with the notable exception of the United Kingdom, whose ISO 3166 code (for some reason) is "GB" rather than "UK". These codes are generally written in upper case. The meaning of any subcodes after the first is generally not defined (though a few have been registered with IANA), but they must contain ASCII letters (a–z, A–Z) only.

❑ A language code registered with the IANA (see http://www.isi.edu/in-notes/iana/assignments/languages/), prefixed "i-", for example, "i-Navajo".

❑ A user-defined language code, prefixed "x-", for example, "x-Java" if the element contains a Java program.

The xml:lang attribute defines the language of all text contained within the element it appears on, unless it is overridden by another xml:lang attribute in an inner element. So if a document is written in English but contains quotations in German, the xml:lang language code on the document element might say «xml:lang="en"», while an element containing a quotation specifies «xml:lang="de"».

The lang() function allows you to test whether the language for the context node is the one you are expecting. For example «lang('en')» returns true if the language is English, while «lang ('jp')» returns true if it is Japanese.

Specifically, the rules are as follows:

❑ If the value of xml:lang for the context node is equal to the string supplied in the argument, ignoring differences of case, the function returns true.

❑ If the value of xml:lang for the context node, ignoring any suffix starting with a hyphen «-», is equal to the string supplied in the argument, again ignoring differences of case, the function returns true.

❑ Otherwise, the function returns false.

Examples

Expression	Result
`boolean(//*[lang('de')])`	*true() if the document contains any elements marked as being in German*
`/*/msg[@code="$p"][lang('fr')]`	*the <msg> element with a required code value that is marked as being in French*

Usage

This function provides a convenient way of testing the language used in a source document. Assuming that the source document has been properly marked up using the `xml:lang` attribute as defined in the XML specification, the `lang()` function allows you to do language-dependent processing of the data.

The `lang()` function only allows you to test whether the language is one of the languages you are expecting; if you want to find out the actual language, you will need to read the `xml:lang` attribute directly. You can find the relevant attribute using the expression «`(ancestor-or-self::*/@xml:lang)[last()]`».

last

The `last()` function returns the value of the context size. When processing a sequence of items, if the items are numbered from one, `last()` gives the number assigned to the last item in the sequence.

Changes in 2.0

None.

Signature

This function takes no arguments.

	Data type	Meaning
Result	`xs:integer`	*A number, the value of the context size. As the name implies, this is context dependent*

Effect

The XPath specification defines the value of the `last()` function in terms of the *context size*.

The context size is part of the *focus*, which is described in the spec as having three components: the context item, the context position, and the context size. However, it may be easier to think of the focus as being a bit like an `Iterator` object in a language such as Java. Behind the iterator is a list of items that are processed individually (though not necessarily in any particular order). The context item, position, and size can be thought of as three methods provided by this iterator object: the context position is a number than ranges from 1 to the size of the list, the context item is the item found at the context position, and the context size is the number of items in the list.

When a top-level XPath expression is evaluated (that is, an XPath expression that is not part of another expression), the context size is set by the host language. In XSLT, it is set from the XSLT context. For example:

❑ When a global `<xsl:variable>` declaration is being evaluated, or in certain other contexts such as evaluating the `use` expression in `<xsl:key>`, or evaluating the initial template that matches the root node, it is normally set to 1 (one).

❑ When `<xsl:apply-templates>` is called to process a sequence of nodes, the context size is the number of nodes selected in the call of `<xsl:apply-templates>`.

❑ When `<xsl:for-each>` is called to process a sequence of items, the context size is the number of items selected in the call of `<xsl:for-each>`.

This means that within an `<xsl:for-each>` iteration, the test `<xsl:if test="position()= last()">` succeeds when the last item in the sequence is being processed.

Many APIs that enable XPath expressions to be executed from languages like Java or JavaScript allow the caller to set the context item, but not the context position or size. In such cases, the context position and size on entry to the XPath expression will normally both be one.

Within an XPath expression, the context size changes within a predicate and on the right-hand-side of the «/» operator.

❑ In a predicate, `last()` refers to the number of items in the sequence that is being filtered using the predicate. For example, «`$seq[last()]`» selects the last item in a sequence (this is short for «`$seq[position()=last()]`»), while «`$seq[ceiling(last() div 2)]`» selects the item at the midway position of the list (the fourth item in a list of eight, the fifth item in a list of nine).

❑ It's less common to find `last()` being used on the right-hand-side of a «/» operator. It refers to the number of items in the sequence selected by the left-hand operand of the «/». I can't find a very plausible way of using this, but it can be done. For example, «`$a/remove($b, last())`» returns all items from `$b` except the one at position P, where P is the number of items in `$a`. But there are simpler ways of writing this!

Usage

When `last()` is used within a predicate in a filter expression, the focus refers to the sequence of items being filtered. If the filter is used within a step of a path expression, then the context size is the number of nodes selected by the current step of the expression, after applying any previous filters. For example, suppose the source document is as follows:

```
<countries>
    <country name="France" capital="Paris" continent="Europe"/>
    <country name="Germany" capital="Berlin" continent="Europe"/>
    <country name="Spain" capital="Madrid" continent="Europe"/>
    <country name="Italy" capital="Rome" continent="Europe"/>
    <country name="Poland" capital="Warsaw" continent="Europe"/>
    <country name="Egypt" capital="Cairo" continent="Africa"/>
    <country name="Libya" capital="Tripoli" continent="Africa"/>
    <country name="Nigeria" capital="Lagos" continent="Africa"/>
</countries>
```

Then:

❑ The expression «`countries/country[last()]`» returns the `<country>` element for Nigeria

❑ The expression «`countries/country[@continent='Europe'][last()]`» returns the `<country>` element for Poland

❑ The expression «countries/country[@continent='Europe'][last()-1]» returns the
    <country> element for Italy

❑ The expression «countries/country[@continent='Africa'][position() !=
    last()]» returns the <country> elements for Egypt and Libya.

> An easy mistake is to think that **last()** returns a boolean value. You can use
> **last()** in a predicate to match the last node, for example «**para[last()]**». This is
> a shorthand for the predicate «**[position()=last()]**», because in a predicate, a
> numeric value X is equivalent to a test for the condition «**position()=X**».
> However, this doesn't extend to other contexts, for example if you write:
>
>   **if (last()) then ...**
>
> then the numeric value of the **last()** function is simply converted to a boolean as if
> the **boolean()** function were used. The result will always be true, because **last()**
> can never be zero.

Usage in XSLT

The last() function can be called in XSLT as a free-standing XPath expression, or in simple tests such as
<xsl:if test="position() = last()">. This kind of usage is frequent in XSLT, because XSLT
makes heavy use of the focus. To understand the effect of calling last(), you need to know how
different XSLT instructions set the focus.

When last() is used as a top-level expression within an <xsl:template> (and not within <xsl:
for -each>), it returns the number of nodes selected by the relevant <xsl:apply-templates> select
expression. This is because <xsl:apply-templates> sets the focus to refer to the sequence of nodes
selected by the select expression, after sorting them into the order in which they are processed.

For example, the following code can be used to number all the figures in a document. The last()
function prints the number of figure elements in the document.

```
<xsl:apply-templates select="//figure"/>
. . .
<xsl:template match="figure" version="2.0">
   <div align="center">
   <img src="{@href}"/>
   <p>Figure <xsl:value-of select="position(), 'of', last()"/></p>
   </div>
</xsl:template>
```

(The «version="2.0"» setting is used to ensure that <xsl:value-of> displays the whole sequence in
its select attribute, not just the first item.)

Similarly, when last() is used as a top-level expression within <xsl:for-each>, it returns the
number of items selected by the relevant <xsl:for-each> select expression. Again, this is because

<xsl:for-each> sets the focus to refer to the sequence of items selected by the select expression, after sorting into the correct order.

If the last() function is used within the select expression of an <xsl:sort> element, then it refers to the number of items being sorted. For example, specifying the following sort key:

```
<xsl:sort select="position() mod (ceiling(last() div 3))"/>
```

will sort the nodes A, B, C, D, E, F, G, H into the sequence A, D, G, B, E, H, C, F, which might be useful if you want to arrange them in a table with three columns.

The last() function can be used as a qualifier in a pattern when the last child of a given element is to be treated differently from the others. For example:

```
<xsl:template name="normal-p" match="p">
    <xsl:copy>
        <xsl:apply-templates/>
    </xsl:copy>
</xsl:template>

<xsl:template match="p[last()]">
    <xsl:call-template name="normal-p"/>
    <hr/>
</xsl:template>
```

However, this may not perform well on all processors, because in principle each <p> element needs to be tested to see if it is the last one, which may involve looking at all the children of the parent of the <p> element. Some processors may optimize this construct, but it's best not to assume it will (in Saxon, as it happens, «match="p[last()]"» is quite efficient, but «match="p[last()-1]"» is rather expensive).

Using <xsl:if> will often achieve the same effect more economically:

```
<xsl:template match="p">
    <xsl:copy>
        <xsl:apply-templates/>
    </xsl:copy>
    <xsl:if test="position()=last()">
        <hr/>
    </xsl:if>
</xsl:template>
```

However, note that these two examples are not strictly equivalent. If the <p> elements are processed by a call on <xsl:apply-templates> with no <xsl:sort> specification, they will have the same effect; but if a sort key is specified, then the second template will output an <hr/> element after the last <p> element in the order of the output, whereas the first will output the <hr/> element after the last <p> element in document order.

See also

count() on page 316
position() on page 396
<xsl:number> in Chapter 5 of *XSLT Programmer's Reference*

local-name

The `local-name()` function returns the local part of the name of a node, that is, the part of the name after the colon if there is one, or the full name otherwise.

For example, if the context node is an element named `<title>` the expression «`local-name()`» returns «`title`»; for an element named `<ms:schema>` it returns «`schema`».

Changes in 2.0

Under XPath 2.0 it is an error to supply a sequence containing more than one node, unless running in backward compatibility mode.

Signature

Argument	Data type	Meaning
node *(optional)*	`node()?`	Identifies the node whose local name is required. If the argument is an empty sequence, the function returns a zero-length string.
		If the argument is omitted, the target node is the context node. It is then an error if there is no context item, or if the context item is not a node
Result	`xs:string`	*A string value: the local part of the name of the target node*

Effect

The local name of a node depends on the kind of node, as follows:

Node kind	Local name
document	None, a zero-length string is returned
element	The element name, after any colon
attribute	The attribute name, after any colon
text	None, a zero-length string is returned
processing instruction	The *target* used in the processing instruction to identify the application for which it is intended
comment	None, a zero-length string is returned
namespace	The namespace prefix; or the zero-length string if this is the default namespace

Examples

Consider the source document:

```
<my:doc xmlns:my="some.uri" security="high"/>
```

Expression	Result
local-name(/)	""
local-name(/*)	"doc"
local-name(/*/@*)	"security"

Usage

This function can be useful if you need to test the local name without also testing the namespace URI. For example, if you want to select both `<title>` and `<html:title>` elements, you could do this by writing:

```
*[local-name()='title']
```

However, XPath 2.0 allows you to achieve this more directly by writing:

```
*:title
```

In some ways this can be seen as a misuse of the XML Namespaces facility. The names in one namespace are supposed to bear no relation to the names in another, so any similarity between the names `<title>` and `<html:title>` is a pure coincidence.

In practice, this isn't always true. What often happens is that one namespace is adapted from another. For example, the US Post Office might devise a schema (and associated namespace) for representing US names and addresses, and the Canadian Post Office might then create a variant of this, with a different namespace URI, for Canadian names and addresses. The two schemas will have many elements in common, and it's quite reasonable to try to write a stylesheet that can handle either. If you want to write template rules that match on both a `<us:address>` and a `<canada:address>`, there are two ways of doing it:

Either list both possibilities:

```
<xsl:template match="us:address | canada:address">
```

or match on the local name only:

```
<xsl:template match="*[local-name()='address']">
```

or equivalently:

```
<xsl:template match="*:address">
```

It's not a good idea to use this construct simply to avoid the hassle of declaring the namespace prefix. Your code will almost certainly be less efficient, and it runs the risk of producing incorrect results because it can match elements in namespaces you weren't expecting.

XSLT Example

The following stylesheet fragment outputs an HTML table listing the attributes of the current element, sorted first by namespace and then by local name:

```
<xsl:template match="*" mode="tabulate">
   <table>
      <xsl:for-each select="attribute::node()">
      <xsl:sort select="namespace-uri()"/>
      <xsl:sort select="local-name()"/>
         <tr>
         <td><xsl:value-of select="namespace-uri()"/></td>
         <td><xsl:value-of select="local-name()"/></td>
         <td><xsl:value-of select="."/></td>
         </tr>
      </xsl:for-each>
   </table>
</xsl:template>
```

See also

name() on page 376
namespace-uri() on page 379

local-name-from-QName

The function local-name-from-QName() returns the local-name part of an xs:QName value.

Changes in 2.0

This function is new in XPath 2.0.

Signature

Argument	Data type	Meaning
value	xs:QName?	The xs:QName value whose local-name part is required. If the supplied value is an empty sequence, an empty sequence is returned
Result	xs:string?	*The local-name part of the xs:QName*

Effect

Given an expanded QName (that is, an instance of type xs:QName), this function returns the local-name part of the value.

Examples

Expression	Result
local-name-from-QName(expanded-QName('some.uri', invoice))	invoice
local-name-from-QName(node-name(@xml:space))	space

The second example assumes that the context node has an attribute called xml:space.

See also

expanded-QName() on page 342
namespace-uri-from-QName() on page 382

lower-case

The lower-case() function converts upper-case characters in a string to lower-case.

For example, «lower-case("McAndrew")» returns "mcandrew".

Changes in 2.0

This function is new in XPath 2.0.

Signature

Argument	Data type	Meaning
value	xs:string?	The string to be converted
Result	xs:string?	*The string with upper case letters converted to lower case*

Effect

For those whose only language is English, the matter of converting characters between upper case and lower case is straightforward: there is a direct one-to-one mapping between the 26 upper-case letters A–Z and the 26 lower-case letters a–z. In other languages, the relationship is not always so simple. In many Oriental scripts there is no concept of case at all. Even with Western languages there are many complications. To take a few examples:

❑ The upper-case equivalent of the German «ß» character is the character pair «SS».

❑ In most languages, the lower-case equivalent of «I» is «i», but in Turkish, it is «ı» (known as "dotless I").

❑ Some characters have multiple lower-case forms, depending on context: for example the lower-case version of the Greek «Σ» (sigma) is «σ» or «ς» depending on where in the word it appears.

❑ Some accented characters exist in both upper-case and lower-case forms, but the upper-case form is usually written without accents when it appears in running text.

Fortunately, the Unicode consortium has defined a mapping from upper-case to lower-case characters, and the XPath specification refers to this mapping. An outline of the principles can be found in Unicode Technical Report #21 (`http://www.unicode.org/unicode/reports/tr21/`). This material has been merged into Unicode 4.0, but in my view the original technical report is easier to read. The actual character mappings can be extracted from the database of Unicode characters found on the Unicode Web site.

The effect of the function is as follows:

❑ If the input is an empty sequence, the result is the zero-length string.

❑ Otherwise, every character in the input string is replaced by its corresponding lower-case character (or sequence of characters) if there is one, or it is included unchanged in the result string if it does not.

The function does not implement case mappings that Unicode defines as being locale-sensitive (such as the Turkish dotless I). A good implementation will support the mappings that are context-sensitive (such as the choice between the two lower-case sigma characters) but it would be unwise to rely on it.

Examples

Expression	Result
`lower-case("Sunday")`	sunday
`lower-case("2+2")`	2+2
`lower-case("CÉSAR")`	césar
`lower-case("ΕΛΛΑΣ")`	ελλας

Usage

With simple ASCII keywords, it's safe to use the `lower-case()` or `upper-case()` functions to do a case-blind comparison, for example:

```
if (lower-case($param) = "yes") then ...
```

With a more extensive alphabet, it's better to use a specific collation for this purpose. The reason is that converting two strings to lower-case for comparison doesn't always work («STRASSE» will be mapped to «strasse», while «Straße» will be mapped to «straße»). Converting both to upper-case is better, though there are still a few problems that can crop up.

So it's best to use this function only if you genuinely need to convert a string to lower case, not just in order to perform comparisons.

Note also that the «i» flag can be used to achieve case-blind matching in regular expressions used by the `matches()`, `replace()`, and `tokenize()` functions.

See also

translate() on page 437
upper-case() on page 442

matches

The matches() function tests whether a supplied string matches a regular expression.

Changes in 2.0

This function is new in XPath 2.0.

Signature

Argument	Data type	Meaning
input	xs:string?	The string to be tested against the regular expression. If an empty sequence is supplied, an empty sequence is returned
regex	xs:string	The regular expression
flags (*optional*)	xs:string	One or more letters indicating options on how the matching is to be performed. If this argument is omitted, the effect is the same as supplying a zero-length string, which defaults all the option settings
Result	xs:boolean?	*True if the input string matches the regular expression, false if not*

Effect

Regular expressions provide a powerful pattern-matching capability for strings.

The syntax of regular expressions supported by this function is described in Chapter 11. The syntax is based on the regular expression syntax defined for the pattern facet in XML Schema, which, in turn, is based on the established conventions used in languages such as Perl.

Note that whereas the pattern facet in XML Schema uses a match that is implicitly anchored to the ends of the string, this function does not. A pattern specified in XML Schema must match the entire string to be successful; the regex specified in this function only needs to match some substring. For example, «#[0-9]+» will match a string if it contains as a substring a «#» character followed by one or more digits. If you want to test whether the entire string takes the form of a «#» character followed by one or more digits, use the regex «^#[0-9]+$».

The options that may be specified in the flags argument are:

Option	Effect
i	Use case-insensitive mode. In this mode, a letter used in the regular expression matches characters in the input string regardless of their case, for example, the regex «Monday» matches the strings «Monday» or «monday» or «MONDAY». Without this flag, characters must match exactly. Note that collations are not used for regex comparisons
m	Use multiline mode. In the default mode (called string mode) the meta-characters «^» and «$» match the beginning and end of the input string. In multiline mode, the input string is treated as a sequence of individual lines separated by a newline (x0A) character. The meta-characters «^» and «$» then match the beginning and end of any line
s	Use dot-all mode. By default, the meta-character «.» in a regular expression matches any character in the input except a newline (x0A) character. In dot-all mode, «.» matches any character, including a newline
x	Ignore whitespace. By default, whitespace characters in a regular expression represent themselves, for example, the regex « *» matches a sequence of zero or more spaces. If the «x» flag is set, whitespace in the regex is ignored, and can be used to make the layout more readable. Whitespace characters can always be matched using character escapes such as «\s» and «\n»

Multiple flags can be specified in any order, for example «mx» and «xm» are both allowed.

If the regular expression does not conform to the specified syntax, a fatal error is reported at runtime.

Examples

Assume that $e is the following element:

```
<verse>A grand little lad was young Albert
All dressed in his best, quite a swell
With a stick with an horse's head handle
The finest that Woolworth's could sell.</verse>
```

Expression	Result
matches($e, "grand")	true
matches($e, "^The finest", "m")	true
matches($e, "(^.*$){4}", "m")	true
matches($e, "Albert.*Woolworth's", "s")	true
matches($e, "with", "i")	true
matches("banana", "^(.a)+$")	true
matches("23 May 2003", "^[0-9]+\s[A-Z][a-z]+\s[0-9]+$")	true
matches("", "a*")	true

Usage

The matches() function provides a much more powerful alternative to the contains(), starts-with(), and ends-with() functions. It might be more expensive, but this is only likely to make a difference if searching a large amount of text.

See also

contains() on page 314
ends-with() on page 334
replace() on page 400
starts-with() on page 415
tokenize() on page 434

max

The max() function returns the maximum value in a sequence. The input sequence may contain any items that can be compared using the «lt» and «gt» operators.

Changes in 2.0

This function is new in XPath 2.0.

Signature

Argument	Data type	Meaning
sequence	xdt:anyAtomicType*	The input sequence
collation (*optional*)	xs:string	Collation used for comparing strings
Result	xdt:anyAtomicType?	*The maximum value found in the input sequence*

Effect

If the sequence supplied in the function call contains nodes, then the nodes will automatically be atomized (to extract their typed values) as part of the function call mechanism.

Any untyped atomic values in the atomized sequence (which will typically result from atomizing a node in a schema-less document) are converted to xs:double values. A runtime error is reported if there are values that cannot be converted. If there are NaN (not-a-number) values in the sequence, which might happen if you do the conversion to numbers yourself using the number() function, then the result of the max() function is NaN.

If the input sequence is empty, the result is an empty sequence. If the input sequence contains a single value, that value is returned.

If the input sequence contains two or more values, then the values must be comparable using the «lt» operator. This rules out values of types such as xs:QName and xs:anyURI for which no ordering is defined, and it rules out sequences that mix values such as integers and strings. The function then returns a value that is greater than or equal to every other value in the sequence.

If there are two values that both satisfy this condition (for example the xs:integer 10 and the xs:double 10e0, or two xs:dateTime values in different timezones) then it is not predictable which of them will be returned.

If the collation argument is supplied, then it is used when comparing strings. If the sequence contains strings and no collation is supplied, then the default collation is used.

Examples

Expression	Result
max((10, 20, -5, 13))	20
max(("a", "x", "b"))	"x"
max(2)	2
max(())	()

Usage

Note that max() returns an atomic value. If you supply a sequence of nodes, the nodes are atomized, and the highest atomic value is returned. If you actually want to know which node contained the highest value, you will have to search for it, using a predicate. For example:

```
for $n in max($nodes/size) return $nodes[size=$n]
```

Because of this limitation, it may sometimes be better to use the technique of sorting the nodes and selecting the last. For example, in XQuery:

```
(for $n in $nodes order by $n/size return $n)[last()]
```

or in XSLT 2.0:

```
<xsl:for-each select="$nodes">
  <xsl:sort select="size"/>
  <xsl:if test="position() = last()">
    <xsl:sequence select="."/>
  </xsl:if>
</xsl:for-each>
```

See also

min() in the following section.

min

The min() function returns the minimum value in a sequence. The input sequence can contain any items that can be compared using the «lt» and «gt» operators.

Changes in 2.0

This function is new in XPath 2.0.

Signature

Argument	Data type	Meaning
sequence	`xdt:anyAtomicType*`	The input sequence
collation (*optional*)	`xs:string`	Collation used for comparing strings
Result	`xdt:anyAtomicType?`	*The minimum value found in the input sequence*

Effect

If the sequence supplied in the function call contains nodes, then the nodes will automatically be atomized (to extract their typed values) as part of the function call mechanism.

Any untyped atomic values in the atomized sequence (which will typically result from atomizing a node in a schemaless document) are converted to `xs:double` values. A runtime error is reported if there are values that cannot be converted. If there are NaN (not-a-number) values in the sequence, which might happen if you do the conversion to numbers yourself using the `number()` function, then the result of the `min()` function is NaN.

If the input sequence is empty, the result is an empty sequence. If the input sequence contains a single value, that value is returned.

If the input sequence contains two or more values, then the values must be comparable using the «lt» operator. This rules out values of types such as `xs:QName` and `xs:anyURI` for which no ordering is defined, and it rules out sequences that mix values such as integers and strings. The function then returns a value that is less than or equal to every other value in the sequence.

If two values both satisfy this condition (for example the `xs:integer` 10 and the `xs:double` 10e0, or two `xs:dateTime` values in different timezones), then it is not predictable which of them will be returned.

If the `collation` argument is supplied, then it is used when comparing strings. If the sequence contains strings and no `collation` is supplied, then the default collation is used.

Examples

Expression	Result
`min((10, 20, -5, 13))`	-5
`min(("a", "x", "b"))`	"a"
`min(2)`	2
`min(())`	()

See also

max() on page 370

minutes-from-dateTime, minutes-from-time

The two functions minutes-from-dateTime() and minutes-from-time() extract the minutes component from an xs:date or xs:dateTime value. For example, at 16:30 local time both these functions return 30.

Changes in 2.0

These functions are new in XPath 2.0.

Signature

Argument	Data type	Meaning
input	xs:time or xs:dateTime?	The value from which the minutes component is to be extracted. The data type of the supplied argument must correspond to the data type implied by the function name
Result	xs:integer	The minutes component, in the range 0 to 59

Effect

The function returns the minutes component of the supplied xs:time or xs:dateTime. The value is from the time as expressed in its local timezone (which will be the same as the minutes component of the time in UTC except in the rare case where the timezone offset is not a multiple of one hour).

Examples

Expression	Result
minutes-from-time(xs:time("12:35:03.142"))	35
minutes-from-dateTime(xs:dateTime("2004-02-28T13:55:30"))	55
minutes-from-time(xs:time("00:30:02+01:00"))	30
minutes-from-dateTime(xs:dateTime("2004-07-31T03:10:00+08:30"))	10

See also

current-date(), -dateTime(), -time() on page 318.
format-date(), -dateTime(), -time() in Chapter 7 of *XSLT 2.0 Programmer's Reference*.
day-from-date(), -dateTime() on page 322
year-from-date(), -dateTime() on page 443

minutes-from-duration

This function extracts the value of the minutes component from a normalized `xdt:dayTimeDuration` value.

Changes in 2.0

This function is new in XPath 2.0.

Signature

Argument	Data type	Meaning
input	`xdt:dayTimeDuration?`	The value from which the component is to be extracted. If an empty sequence is supplied, an empty sequence is returned
Result	`xs:integer?`	*The minutes component*

Effect

The function returns the minutes component of the supplied `xdt:dayTimeDuration`. The duration value is first normalized so that the number of hours is less than 24, the number of minutes is less than 60, and so on. The result will be negative if the duration is negative.

Examples

Expression	Result
`minutes-from-duration(xdt:dayTimeDuration("PT12H20M"))`	20
`minutes-from-duration(xdt:dayTimeDuration("PT210S"))`	3
`minutes-from-duration(xdt:dayTimeDuration("-PT75M"))`	-15

See also

`days-from-dayTimeDuration` on page 323
`hours-from-dayTimeDuration` on page 347
`seconds-from-dayTimeDuration` on page 414

month-from-date, month-from-dateTime

These two functions extract the month component from an `xs:date` or `xs:dateTime` value. For example, on Christmas Day «`month-from-date(current-date())`» returns 12.

Changes in 2.0

These functions are new in XPath 2.0.

Signature

Argument	Data type	Meaning
input	`xs:date?` or `xs:dateTime?`	The value whose month component is to be extracted. The data type of the supplied argument must correspond to the data type implied by the function name. If an empty sequence is supplied, an empty sequence is returned
Result	`xs:integer?`	*The month, in the range 1 (January) to 12 (December)*

Effect

The function returns the month component of the supplied `xs:date` or `xs:dateTime`. The value is used in its local timezone (not normalized to UTC).

Examples

Expression	Result
`month-from-date(xs:date("2004-02-28"))`	2
`month-from-dateTime(xs:dateTime("2004-02-28T13:00:00"))`	2
`month-from-date(xs:date("2004-07-31+01:00"))`	7
`month-from-dateTime(xs:dateTime("2004-07-31T23:00:00-05:00"))`	7

See also

`current-date()`, `-dateTime()`, `-time()` on page 318.
`format-date()`, `-dateTime()`, `-time()` in Chapter 7 of *XSLT 2.0 Programmer's Reference*.
`day-from-date()`, `-dateTime()` on page 322
`year-from-date()`, `-dateTime()` on page 443

months-from-duration

This function extracts the value of the months component from a normalized `xdt:yearMonthDuration` value.

Changes in 2.0

This function is new in XPath 2.0.

Signature

Argument	Data type	Meaning
input	`xdt:yearMonthDuration?`	The value from which the component is to be extracted. If an empty sequence is supplied, an empty sequence is returned
Result	`xs:integer?`	*The months component, in the range −11 to +11*

Effect

The function returns the months component of the supplied `xdt:yearMonthDuration`. The duration value is first normalized so that the number of months is less than 12. The result will be negative if the duration is negative.

Examples

Expression	Result
`months-from-duration(xdt:` `yearMonthDuration("P1Y3M"))`	3
`months-from-duration(xdt:` `yearMonthDuration("P15M"))`	3
`months-from-duration(xdt:` `yearMonthDuration("-P1Y3M"))`	-3

See also

`years-from-duration` on page 443

name

The `name()` function returns a string in the form of a lexical `QName` that represents the name of a node. Typically, this will be the name of the node as written in the original XML source document, but the namespace prefix may differ.

For example, if the context node is an element named `<ms:schema>`, then the expression «`name()`» will normally return the string «`ms:schema`».

Changes in 2.0

Under XPath 2.0 it is an error to supply a sequence containing more than one node, unless running in backward compatibility mode.

There has been some clarification of the rules for choosing a namespace prefix.

Signature

Argument	Data type	Meaning
node *(optional)*	`node()?`	Identifies the node whose name is required. If the argument is an empty sequence, the function returns a zero-length string.
		If the argument is omitted, the target node is the context node. It is then an error if there is no context item, or if the context item is not a node
Result	`xs:string`	*A string value: a QName representing the name of the target node*

Effect

The name of a node depends on the kind of node, as follows:

Node kind	Name
document	None, a zero-length string is returned
element	The element name (a lexical QName), normally as it appears in the source XML, though a different prefix that maps to the same namespace URI may be substituted
attribute	The attribute name (a lexical QName), normally as it appears in the source XML, though a different prefix that maps to the same namespace URI may be substituted
text	None, a zero-length string is returned
processing instruction	The *target* used in the processing instruction to identify the application for which it is intended
comment	None, a zero-length string is returned
namespace	The namespace prefix; or the zero-length string if this is the default namespace. (This is *not* prefixed with «xmlns:»)

Except for element and attribute nodes, name() returns the same value as local-name().

The QName returned will normally use the same prefix as appeared in the original XML source. However, this is not guaranteed: the only guarantee is that it will use a prefix that maps to the same namespace URI. If the source document contains multiple prefixes that map to the same namespace URI the implementation can choose which one to use.

With XSLT 2.0 and XQuery 1.0, it becomes possible to apply the name() function to a node in a temporary tree constructed by the stylesheet or query, rather than a node obtained by parsing a source XML document. The same considerations apply; the processor is free to choose any prefix that maps to the right namespace URI, including if necessary a prefix that it has invented itself. To find a suitable prefix, it searches the namespace nodes associated with the element (when the name of an element is requested), or the element containing the attribute (when the name of an attribute is requested).

If you apply the name() function to a parentless attribute node then there are no namespace nodes that can be used to locate a suitable namespace prefix. In this case, if the attribute is in a non-null namespace then the system is required to invent an arbitrary prefix.

Usage

The name() function is useful when you want to display the element name, perhaps in an error message, because the form it takes is the same as the way in which users will generally write the element name.

So, for example, you could use name() in the output of the diagnostic trace() function:

```
for $e in child::* return
   trace(string(.), concat("contents of element ", name()))
```

You can also use the `name()` function to test the name of a node against a string, for example, «`doc:title[name(..)='doc:section']`». However, it's best to avoid this if you can:

❑   Firstly, this fails if the document uses a different prefix to refer to the namespace. There's nothing here to tell the system to treat «`doc:section`» as a QName, so if the writer of a particular document chose to use the prefix «DOC» instead of «doc» for this namespace, the test would fail, even though the names are equivalent.

❑   Secondly, there is usually a better way of doing it: this particular example can be written as «`doc:title[parent::doc:section]`». In fact, in most cases where you want to test whether a node has a particular name, you can do it using a predicate of this form. The «`self`» axis is particularly useful. For example, to test whether the current node is a `<figure>` element, write «`if (self::figure) then ...`». This doesn't work for attribute nodes (because the principal node kind of the self axis is element nodes; see *Name Tests* in Chapter 7, page 221), but for attributes you can write «`if (. is ../@figure) then...`».

One common requirement, in both XSLT and XQuery, is to sort data on the value of a sort key that is supplied as a runtime parameter (this might be because the user has asked interactively for a table to be sorted on a particular column). Neither XSLT nor XQuery allows the expression that defines the sort criteria to be completely dynamic. But very often the possible sort keys are all element children of the elements that represent the rows being sorted. In this situation it is possible to define the sort key like this (in XSLT):

```
<xsl:for-each select="row">
    <xsl:sort select="*[name()=$sortkey]"/>
```

or like this (in XQuery):

```
for $r in row
order by *[name()=$sortkey]
```

If you are using namespaces it is safer to do such tests using the `node-name()` function, which gives you an `xs:QName` as its result: an `xs:QName` represents an expanded name (namespace URI plus local name) and is not sensitive to the choice of prefix. Alternatively, use the `namespace-uri()` and `local-name()` functions to test the two components of the expanded name separately.

If you want to select all attributes except the `description` attribute, you can write:

```
@*[name() != 'description'
```

This is namespace-safe, because an unprefixed attribute name always represents a name in no namespace. But in XPath 2.0, I prefer:

```
@* except @description
```

In XSLT, avoid using `name()` to generate a name in the result document, for example, by writing `<xsl:element name="{name()}">`. The problem is that any prefix in `name()` is interpreted in the light of namespace declarations appearing in the stylesheet, not namespace declarations in the original source document. The correct tool for this job is `<xsl:copy>`. There are cases where `<xsl:copy>` won't do the job, for example, you may want to use the name of an attribute in the input document to generate the name of an element in the output document. In this case use `local-name()` and `namespace-uri()` separately, for example:

```
<xsl:element name="{local-name()}" namespace="{namespace-uri()}">
```

Examples

Consider the source document:

```
<my:doc xmlns:my="some.uri" security="high"/>
```

Expression	Result
`name(/)`	`""`
`name(/*)`	`"my:doc"`
`name(/*/@*)`	`"security"`

See also

`local-name()` on page 363
`namespace-uri()` on page 379
`node-name()` on page 384

namespace-uri

The `namespace-uri()` function returns a string that represents the URI of the namespace in the expanded name of a node. Typically, this will be a URI used in a namespace declaration, that is, the value of an `xmlns` or `xmlns:*` attribute in the source XML.

For example, if you apply this function to the outermost element of an XSLT stylesheet by writing the expression «`namespace-uri(doc('')/*)`», the result will be the string «`http://www.w3.org/1999/XSL/Transform`».

Changes in 2.0

None.

Signature

Argument	Data type	Meaning
node *(optional)*	`node()?`	Identifies the node whose namespace URI is required. If the argument is an empty sequence, the function returns a zero-length string.
		If the argument is omitted, the target node is the context node. It is then an error if there is no context item, or if the context item is not a node
Result	`xs:string`	*The namespace URI of the expanded name of the target node*

Effect

The namespace URI of a node depends on the kind of node, as follows:

Node kind	Namespace URI
document	None, a zero-length string is returned
element	If the element name as given in the source XML contained a colon, the value will be the URI from the namespace declaration corresponding to the element's prefix. Otherwise, the value will be the URI of the default namespace. If this is null, the result will be a zero-length string
attribute	If the attribute name as given in the source XML contained a colon, the value will be the URI from the namespace declaration corresponding to the attribute's prefix. Otherwise, the namespace URI will be a zero-length string
text	None, a zero-length string is returned
processing instruction	None, a zero-length string is returned
comment	None, a zero-length string is returned
namespace	None, a zero-length string is returned

Except for element and attribute nodes, `namespace-uri()` returns an empty string.

Examples

Consider the source document:

```
<my:doc xmlns:my="some.uri" security="high"/>
```

Expression	Result
`namespace-uri(/)`	`" "`
`namespace-uri(/*)`	`"some.uri"`
`namespace-uri(/*/@security)`	`" "`
`namespace-uri(/*/namespace::my)`	`" "`

Usage

Let's start with some situations where you *don't* need this function.

If you want to test whether the context node belongs to a particular namespace, the best way to achieve this is using a NameTest of the form «prefix:*». For example, to test (in XSLT) whether the current element belongs to the «`http://ibm.com/ebiz`» namespace, write:

```
<xsl:if test="self::ebiz:*" xmlns:ebiz="http://ibm.com/ebiz">
```

If you want to find the namespace URI corresponding to a given prefix the best solution is to use namespace nodes. You might need to do this if namespace prefixes are used in attribute values: the XSLT standard itself uses this technique in attributes such as `extension-element-prefixes`, and there is no reason why other XML document types should not do the same. If you have an attribute «`@value`» which you know takes the form of a namespace-qualified name (a `QName`), you can get the associated namespace URI using the expression:

```
namespace-uri-for-prefix(substring-before(@value, ':'), .)
```

The `namespace-uri()` function, by contrast, is useful in display contexts, where you just want to display the namespace URI of the current node, and also if you want to do more elaborate tests. For example, you may know that there is a whole family of namespaces whose URIs all begin with `urn:schemas.biztalk`, and you may want to test whether a particular element is in any one of these. You can achieve this by writing:

```
if (starts-with(namespace-uri(), 'urn:schemas.biztalk')) then ...
```

See also

`local-name()` on page 363
`name()` on page 376

namespace-uri-for-prefix

The function `namespace-uri-for-prefix()` returns the namespace URI corresponding to a given namespace prefix, in the in-scope namespaces of a particular element node.

Changes in 2.0

This function is new in XPath 2.0. Together with `in-scope-prefixes()`, it provides a replacement for the namespace axis, which is deprecated in XPath 2.0.

Signature

Argument	Data type	Meaning
prefix	`xs:string`	The namespace prefix whose corresponding namespace URI is required, or the zero-length string to get the default namespace URI
element	`element()`	The element node to be examined to find an in-scope namespace declaration for this prefix
Result	`xs:string?`	*The namespace URI corresponding to the given prefix*

Effect

The in-scope namespaces for an element are represented in the data model as namespace nodes, and the behavior of this function is therefore described in terms of a search of the namespace nodes.

This function searches the namespace nodes of the given element. If it finds a namespace node whose name matches the given prefix, then it returns the string value of this namespace node. If it doesn't find one, then it returns the empty sequence.

Examples

Consider thesource document below. Note that this includes a namespace undeclaration for the «soap» namespace, as permitted by XML Namespaces 1.1:

```
<soap:Envelope
      xmlns:soap="http://schemas.xmlsoap.org/soap/envelope/">
      xmlns:xs="http://www.w3.org/2001/XMLSchema"
   <soap:Body>
      <echoString xmlns="http://example.com/soapdemo"
                  xmlns:xsi="http://www.w3.org/2001/XMLSchema-instance"
                  xmlns:soap="">
         <inputString xsi:type="xs:string">Hello</inputString>
      </echoString>
   </soap:Body>
</soap:Envelope>
```

Expression	Result

`for $n in`
`in-scope-prefixes(`
`//demo:inputString)`
`return`
`namespace-uri-for-prefix(`
`$n,`
`//demo:inputString)`
	`("http://www.w3.org/2001/XMLSchema",`
	`"http://example.com/soapdemo",`
	`"http://www.w3.org/2001/XMLSchema-instance",`
	`"http://www.w3.org/XML/1998/namespace")`
	
	(in any order)

Usage

This function is often used in conjunction with `in-scope-prefixes()`, which finds the prefixes of all the in-scope namespaces for an element as a sequence of strings.

See also

`in-scope-prefixes` on page 354.

namespace-uri-from-QName

The function `namespace-uri-from-QName()` returns the namespace URI part of an `xs:QName` value.

Changes in 2.0

This function is new in XPath 2.0.

Signature

Argument	Data type	Meaning
value	xs:QName?	The xs:QName value whose namespace URI part is required. If the supplied value is an empty sequence, an empty sequence is returned. An empty sequence is also returned if the namespace URI part of the value is null, that is, if the QName is in no namespace
Result	xs:string?	*The namespace URI part of the xs:QName*

Effect

Given an expanded QName (that is, an instance of type xs:QName), this function returns the namespace URI part of the value. If the xs:QName is in no namespace, it returns the empty sequence.

Examples

Expression	Result
namespace-uri-from-QName(expanded-QName('some.uri', invoice))	«some.uri»
namespace-uri-from-QName(node-name(@xml:space))	«http://www.w3.org/XML/1998/namespace»

The second example assumes that the context node has an attribute called xml:space.

See also

expanded-QName() on page 342
local-name-from-QName() on page 365

nilled

The nilled() function returns true if applied to an element that (a) specifies «xsi:nil="true"», and (b) has been successfully validated against a schema.

Changes in 2.0

This function is new in XPath 2.0.

Signature

Argument	Data type	Meaning
input	node()	The node being tested
Result	xs:boolean?	*True for an element that has the nilled property*

Effect

If the input is an element node that has the attribute «xsi:nil="true"» and that has been subjected to schema validation, the function returns true.

If the input is an element node that does not have an «xsl:nil» attribute, or that has the value «xsi:nil="false"», or if it is an element node that has not been assessed against a schema, the function returns false.

If the function is applied to a node other than an element, it returns the empty sequence.

Examples

Assume the context node is the element:

```
<person>
   <title xsi:nil="true"/>
   <first>Samuel</first>
   <middle xsi:nil="false"/>
   <last>Johnson</last>
</person>
```

Expression	Result
nilled(title)	True
nilled(first)	False
nilled(middle)	False
nilled(last)	False

Usage

The xsi:nil attribute is an explicit way of saying that a value is absent. Although its meaning is entirely up to the application, the intended purpose is to distinguish unknown data (a person's title is unknown) from data known to be empty (a person is known to have no middle name). When an element that has xsi:nil set to true is validated, it is given the *nilled* property in the data model, and this function allows this property to be tested. For most practical purposes, using the nilled() function achieves the same as testing the xsl:nil attribute directly, so long as you are sure that the element has been validated.

The *nilled* property is present in the data model primarily to support the rules for type matching: a *nilled* element will not match a type of the form «element(N, T)», but it will match «element (N, T?)». These rules are given in Chapter 9, in the section *Matching Elements and Attributes* on page 281. This function is provided to allow direct access to this property.

node-name

The node-name() function returns a value of type xs:QName containing the expanded name of a node, that is, the namespace URI and local name.

Changes in 2.0

This function is new in XPath 2.0.

Signature

Argument	Data type	Meaning
input	node()?	The node whose name is required
Result	xs:QName?	*The name of the node if it has a name, or an empty sequence if it has no name*

Effect

If the node is an element or attribute, then the function returns an xs:QName whose components are the namespace URI and local name of this node. If the node is not in a namespace, then the namespace URI component of the xs:QName will be absent (the function namespace-uri-from-QName() will return the empty sequence).

If the node is a processing instruction, the function returns an xs:QName whose local name is the name of the processing instruction, and whose namespace URI is absent.

If the node is a text node, comment, or document node, or if an empty sequence is supplied, then the function returns an empty sequence.

If the node is a namespace node, then the function returns an xs:QName whose local name represents the namespace prefix and whose namespace URI part is null; except when the namespace node represents the default namespace, in which case the function returns an empty sequence.

Examples

It's difficult to illustrate function calls that return xs:QName values, because there's no way to display an xs:QName conveniently as a string. In these examples I'll display the value in so-called Clark notation (after James Clark, the editor of the XSLT 1.0 and XPath 1.0 specifications), which uses the format «{uri}local-name».

Assume the following source document:

```
<soap:Envelope
     xmlns:soap="http://schemas.xmlsoap.org/soap/envelope/">
     xmlns:xs="http://www.w3.org/2001/XMLSchema"
  <soap:Body>
    <echoString xmlns="http://example.com/soapdemo"
                xmlns:xsi="http://www.w3.org/2001/XMLSchema-instance"
                xmlns:soap="">
      <inputString xsi:type="xs:string">Hello</inputString>
    </echoString>
  </soap:Body>
</soap:Envelope>
```

Expression	Result
`node-name(/*)`	`{http://schemas.xmlsoap.org/soap/envelope/}Envelope`
`node-name(/*/*/*)`	`{http://example.com/soapdemo}echoString`
`node-name (//@*:type)`	`{http://www.w3.org/2001/XMLSchema-instance}type`

Usage

To access the components of the `xs:QName` returned by the `node-name()` function, you can use the functions `local-name-from-QName()` and `namespace-uri-from-QName()`. Alternatively, if you don't like long function names, you can use the `local-name()` and `namespace-uri()` functions to get these two components directly from the node itself.

See also

local-name-from-QName() on page 365
namespace-uri-from-QName() on page 382
local-name() on page 363
name() on page 376
namespace-uri() on page 379

normalize-space

The `normalize-space()` function removes leading and trailing whitespace from a string, and replaces internal sequences of whitespace with a single space character.

For example, the expression «`normalize-space(' x&#x9; y ')`» returns the string «x y».

Changes in 2.0

None.

Signature

Argument	Data type	Meaning
value (*optional*)	`xs:string?`	The input string. If the argument is omitted, it defaults to the string value of the context item. If an empty sequence is supplied, the function returns a zero-length string
Result	`xs:string`	*A string obtained by removing leading and trailing whitespace from the input string, and replacing internal sequences of whitespace by a single space character*

Effect

Whitespace is defined, as in the XML specification, as a sequence of space, tab, newline, and carriage return characters (#x9, #xA, #xD, and #x20).

Examples

Expression	Result
normalize-space(" the quick 	 brown fox ")	"the quick brown fox"
normalize-space(" ")	" "
normalize-space("piano")	"piano"
normalize-space(())	" "

Usage

It is often a good idea to apply the normalize-space() function to any string read from the source document before testing its contents, as many users will assume that leading and trailing whitespace has no significance and that within the string, multiple spaces or tabs are equivalent to a single space.

Don't imagine that the XSLT <xsl:strip-space> declaration does this for you. The only thing it does is to remove text nodes that contain whitespace only.

Using normalize-space() shouldn't be necessary when accessing structured information in a schema-validated document. The schema should specify for each data type (in the xs:whiteSpace facet) how whitespace is to be treated, and this will normally ensure that redundant whitespace is removed automatically when nodes are atomized. Note that the action of the normalize-space() function is equivalent to the option <xs:whiteSpace value="collapse"/> in XML Schema. This removes whitespace more vigorously than the schema data type xs:normalizedString, which uses the option <xs:whiteSpace value="replace"/> (this doesn't replace runs of spaces with a single space, it only replaces individual newlines, carriage returns or tabs with single space characters.)

However, if you access the string value of an element with a mixed content type (typically by calling the string() function explicitly, or by accessing the text nodes of an element explicitly) then schema-defined whitespace normalization will not be applied, so using normalize-space() is a good idea.

The normalize-space() function can be particularly useful when processing a whitespace-separated list of values. Such lists are used in some document designs. With a schema processor, the system can deliver the value as a sequence of strings, but in the absence of a schema you have to tokenize the sequence yourself. You can call normalize-space() to ensure that there is a single space between each string, and it is then possible to use substring-before() to get the next token. To make this easier still, I usually add a space at the end of the string after normalization, so that every token is followed by a single space.

One situation where it isn't safe to use normalize-space() is where you are processing mixed element content containing character-level formatting attributes. For example, if you process the nodes that result from the element:

```
<p>Some <i>very</i> traditional HTML</p>
```

then the spaces after «Some» and before «traditional» are significant, even though they appear respectively at the end and the beginning of a text node.

XSLT Example

The following key declaration indexes the titles of books with whitespace normalized:

```
<xsl:key name="book-title" match="book" use="normalize-space(title)"/>
```

This may then be used to locate books by title as follows:

```
<xsl:for-each select="key('book-title', normalize-space($title))">
```

The effect is that it will be possible, without knowing how many spaces and newlines there are, to retrieve a book appearing in the source document as:

```
<book>
    <title>Object Oriented Languages -
                Basic Principles and Programming Techniques</title>
</book>
```

See also

concat() on page 312
substring-after() on page 425
substring-before() on page 427

normalize-unicode

The normalize-unicode() function returns a canonical representation of a string in which different ways of representing the same Unicode character have been reduced to a common representation. This makes it possible to compare two strings accurately.

Changes in 2.0

This function is new in XPath 2.0.

Signature

Argument	Data type	Meaning
input	xs:string?	The string to be normalized. If an empty sequence is supplied, the function returns a zero-length string
normalization-form (*optional*)	xs:string	The normalization algorithm to be used
Result	xs:string	*The result of normalizing the string*

Effect

The function applies a Unicode normalization algorithm to the input string, and returns the normalized string as its result. If the normalization-form argument is omitted, the default is NFC. The only normalization form that all implementations must support is NFC. Other normalization forms can be requested (including but not limited to «NFC», «NFD», «NFKC», «NFKD», «fully-normalized») using the `normalization-form` argument; a runtime error is reported if the requested normalization form is not supported by the implementation. For the meanings of these normalization forms, see the *Usage* section below.

The value supplied for the `normalization-form` argument is converted to upper case, and leading and trailing spaces are removed.

Examples

In these examples I have used the two separate characters «c» and «ˏ» to indicate the Unicode codepoints x0063 x0327. In practice, when you actually use these two codepoints together the character you will see displayed looks like «ç».

Expression	Result
`normalize-unicode("garcˏon")`	garçon
`normalize-unicode("garçon", "NFD")`	garcˏon

Usage

The subject of character normalization has a long, tortured history. There have always been two interest groups concerned with character encoding: those primarily interested in data processing have favored fixed-length encodings of each character, with composite characters treated as a single unit, while those more concerned with publishing and printing have favored variable-length encodings in which the separate parts of a composite character (for example, a base letter and a diacritical mark) were encoded separately. Inevitably, the only way both communities could be satisfied was by a standard that allowed both, and that is exactly what Unicode does. The letter «Å» for example (which is widely used in Swedish) can be encoded either using the single codepoint x00C5 (called LATIN CAPITAL A WITH RING ABOVE) or by the two codepoints x0041 (LATIN CAPITAL LETTER A) followed by x030A (COMBINING RING ABOVE). To make matters even worse, there is also a separate code x212B (ANGSTROM SIGN), which is visually indistinguishable from the letter «Å» but has a separate code because it is considered to have its own meaning.

This means that unless special precautions are taken, when you search for text containing the character «Å», you will not find it unless you choose the same representation as is used in the text you are searching. This applies not only to the textual content, but also to the markup: both representations of this character are acceptable in XML names, and if you use one representation in the source XML, and a different representation in a path expression, then they won't match.

Unicode normalization is an algorithm that can be applied to Unicode strings to remove these arbitrary differences.

The *Character Model for the World Wide Web*, a W3C Working Draft, specifies that documents on the Web should be subject to "early normalization": that is, they should be normalized at the time they are created; and it advocates the use of a particular normalization algorithm called NFC (further details below). If everyone followed this advice, there would be no need for a `normalize-unicode()` function in XPath. But unfortunately, there is little chance of this happening.

The normalization algorithms have been published in Unicode Technical Report #15 (`http://www .unicode.org/unicode/reports/tr15`). There are several, notably normalization forms C, D, KC, and KD, and "fully normalized". (Why have one standard when you can have five?) The default used by the `normalize-unicode()` function is NFC (normalization form C), but the other forms can be requested using the second parameter to the function, provided that the implementation supports them—they aren't mandatory.

Normalization forms C and KC replace decomposed characters by composed characters; in our example using «Å», they choose the single-codepoint representation x00C5 in preference to the two-codepoint representation x0041x030A. Normalization forms D and KD prefer the decomposed representation, that is x0041x030A.

As a general rule, most software that produces Unicode text (for example, text editors) will produce NFC output most of the time. This is useful, and explains why you don't hear of many people having real-world XPath expressions that fail because of normalization issues. But it's certainly a possibility, and one of the concerns is that it is also a security risk—using the "wrong" representation of characters could be a way of getting round validation software.

The K variants (NFKC and NFKD) differ from NFC and NFD in that they normalize further, specifically, they normalize away distinctions between "compatibility variants" of characters. These compatibility variants exist because Unicode was created as the union of many different pre-existing character sets. The designers had to make the decision whether two characters in different character sets were really representations of the same character. The problem in merging two characters into one is that it would lose information when data is converted into Unicode and then back again—the original data stream could not necessarily be reconstituted. So Unicode adopted the approach of allowing multiple representations of a character as *compatibility variants*. The distinction between the letter «Å» and the Ångstrom symbol is an example of this phenomenon; normalization forms NFKC and NFKD eliminate the distinction between these two characters. Another example is the distinction between the two characters «f» «i» and the single character «fi» (really just a graphical visualization of the two separate characters, but recognized as a single character for the benefit of typesetting applications). Another one (and here the "loss of information" argument starts to become significant) is the distinction between the superscript digits «^{2}» and «^{3}» and the ordinary digits «2» and «3».

When you take a substring of a normalized string, the substring will always be normalized, and this is true for all the normalization forms discussed here. Splitting a string between a letter «c» and a non-spacing cedilla that follows it may not produce a very meaningful result, but the result is normalized, in the sense that the normalization algorithm will not change it. However, concatenating two normalized strings is not guaranteed to produce a normalized string. This is true whether you choose a composed form (NFC) or a decomposed form (NFD):

- ❑ With NFC, concatenating a string that ends with letter «c» and a string that starts with a non-spacing cedilla produces a string that is not in normalized form NFC.

- ❑ With NFD, concatenating a string that ends with a non-spacing modifier and a string that starts with a non-spacing modifier may produce a string that is not in normalized form NFD, because this normalization form requires multiple non-spacing modifiers applying to the same letter to be in a standard order.

This means that the concat() function, and other XPath functions that concatenate strings such as string-join(), as well as node construction instructions in XSLT and XQuery, are not guaranteed to produce normalized output even if they are given normalized input. Another place where string concatenation occurs implicitly is in forming the string value of an element with mixed content. The W3C policy of early normalization means that this problem should be corrected as soon as possible. One way of doing this is to call the normalize-unicode() function on the results of the string concatenation; another is to do the normalization at the time the result of a transformation or query is serialized (see the normaliation-form option of <xsl:output>, described in *XSLT 2.0 Programmer's Reference*).

The term fully-normalized refers to an additional normalization format defined by W3C (see *Character Model for the World Wide Web: Normalization*, http://www.w3.org/TR/charmod-norm/). A string is defined to be fully normalized if it is in NFC and if it doesn't start with a combining character. The significance of this is that if you concatenate two fully normalized strings the result is guaranteed to be fully normalized as well. The specification isn't very explicit about how you get a string into fully-normalized form, but the idea is apparently that if it starts with a combining character, you add a space in front of it.

See also

<xsl:output> in Chapter 5 of *XSLT 2.0 Programmer's Reference*.

not

The not() function returns true if the effective boolean value of the argument is false, and vice versa.

For example, the expression «not(2+2=4)» returns false.

Changes in 2.0

This function has been generalized to accept a wider range of data types.

Signature

Argument	Data type	Meaning
value	item()*	The input value
Result	xs:boolean	true *if the effective boolean value of the argument is false, otherwise* false

Effect

In effect, the argument is converted to a boolean using the rules of the boolean() function, and the return value is then true if this is false, false if it is true.

The rules for determining the effective boolean value are described under the boolean() function on page 304.

Examples

Expression	Result
not(*)	true *if the context node has no child elements*
not(normalize-space(@a))	true *if attribute @a is absent, is zero-length, or consists entirely of whitespace*
not(author="Kay")	true *if the context node does not have an author child element whose typed value is* "Kay"

Usage

Note that writing «not($A=2)» is not the same thing as writing «$A!=2». The difference arises when $A is a sequence: «not($A=2)» will be true if $A does not contain an item that is equal to 2, while «$A!=2» is true only if A *does* contain an item that is *not* equal to 2. For example, if $A is an empty sequence, «not($A=2)» will be true, while «$A!=2» will be false.

It is easy to forget this when testing attribute values, for example, the following two examples behave the same way if the attribute go is present (they output «go» if the value is anything other than «no»), but they behave differently if the attribute is absent the second one outputs «go», but the first one outputs nothing.

```
1: if (@go!='no') then "go" else ""
2: if (not(@go='no')) then "go" else ""
```

When used with sequences, the comparison operators such as «=» and «!=» are subject to an implicit *if there exists* qualifier: «$X=$Y» is true *if there exists an item* x *in* $X *and an item* y *in* $Y *such that* x eq y. If you want to achieve an *if all* qualifier, for example, *if all nodes in* $N *have a* size *attribute equal to 0*, then you can achieve this by negating both the condition and the expression as a whole: «not($N/@size!=0)». But it XPath 2.0, it is probably clearer to write this out explicitly:

```
if (every $s in $N/@size satisfies $s eq 0) . . .
```

XSLT Examples

The following test succeeds if the context node has no children:

```
<xsl:if test="not(node())">
```

The following test succeeds if the context node has no parent (that is, if it is a root node):

```
<xsl:if test="not(parent::node())">
```

The following <xsl:for-each> statement processes all the child elements of the context node except the <notes> elements:

```
<xsl:for-each select="*[not(self::notes)]">
```

The following test succeeds if the string-value of the context node is zero-length:

```
<xsl:if test="not(.)">
```

The following test succeeds if the name attribute of the context node is absent or is a zero-length string:

```
<xsl:if test="not(string(@name))">
```

The following test succeeds if the name attribute of the first node in node-set $ns is different from the name attribute of each subsequent node in the node-set (we assume that this attribute is present on all nodes in the node-set):

```
<xsl:if test="not($ns[1]/@name = $ns[position()!=1]/@name)">
```

See also

boolean() on page 304
false() on page 343
true() on page 439

number

The number() function converts its argument to a value of type xs:double.

For example, the expression «number('-17.3')» returns the xs:double value –17.3e0.

Changes in 2.0

A leading «+» sign is allowed in the number, and exponential notation is permitted, to align the rules with XML Schema.

Signature

Argument	Data type	Meaning
value *(optional)*	item()?	The value to be converted. If the argument is omitted, the context item is used
Result	xs:double	*A double-precision floating point number: the result of converting the given* value. *If the argument cannot be converted to a number, the function returns NaN (not-a-number)*

Effect

The conversion rules used are the same as the rules for casting to an xs:double (and therefore, the same as the xs:double() constructor function), with the exception that if the value is not convertible to a number, the result is NaN (not-a-number) rather than an error.

If the value supplied is a node, then the node is first atomized in the usual way.

The only atomic types that can be converted to a number are booleans, strings, and other numbers. The conversion is as follows:

Supplied data type	Conversion rules
xs:boolean	false becomes zero; true becomes one
xs:string	The rules are the same as the rules for writing an xs:double value in XML Schema
xs:integer, xs:decimal, xs:float	The result is the same as converting the value to a string, and then converting the resulting string back to an xs:double

Examples

Expression	Result
number(12.3)	12.3e0
number("12.3")	12.3e0
number(true())	1.0e0
number("xyz")	NaN
number("")	NaN

Usage

In XPath 1.0, conversion to a number was generally implicit so it was rarely necessary to use the number() function explicitly. This remains the case if XPath 1.0 backward compatibility mode is used. When this mode is not enabled, however, type errors will be reported when strings or booleans are supplied in contexts where a number is expected, for example as operands to numeric operators such as «+». You still get implicit conversion when you supply an untyped node as the operand (for example, «@code + 1» is okay), but not when the value is explicitly typed. For example, if the date-of-birth attribute is an untyped string in the format of an ISO 8601 date, the following is an error under XPath 2.0 rules:

```
substring(@date-of-birth, 1, 4) < 1970
```

This is because substring() returns a string, and you cannot compare a string to a number. Instead, write:

```
number(substring(@date-of-birth, 1, 4)) < 1970
```

There is one important situation where conversion needs to be explicit: this is in a predicate. The meaning of a predicate depends on the data type of the value, in particular, a numeric predicate is interpreted as a comparison with the context position. If the value is not numeric, it is converted to a boolean.

So for example, if a value held in an attribute or in a temporary tree is to be used as a numeric predicate, you should convert it explicitly to a number, thus:

```
$sales-figures[number(@month)]
```

To test whether a value (for example, in an attribute) is numeric, use `number()` to convert it to a number and test the result against NaN (not-a-number). The most direct way to do this is:

```
if (string(number(@value))='NaN') then ...
```

Alternatively, use the «`castable as`» operator described in on page 262 in Chapter 9.

See also

boolean() on page 304
string() on page 416
cast expression in Chapter 9 on page 262

one-or-more

The `one-or-more()` function returns its argument unchanged, provided that it is a sequence containing one or more items. If the input is an empty sequence, it reports an error.

Changes in 2.0

This function is new in XPath 2.0.

Signature

Argument	Data type	Meaning
value	item()*	The input value. Although the function signature says that any sequence of items is allowed, a runtime error will occur if the number of items is zero
Result	item()	The same as the supplied value, after checking to ensure that it is not an empty sequence

Effect

The `one-or-more()` function returns its argument unchanged, provided that it is a sequence containing at least one item. If an empty sequence is supplied, it reports an error.

This function is useful with XPath processors that perform static type-checking, as described in Chapter 3. Calling this function acts as a promise by the programmer that the argument will be a sequence containing at least one item. This allows the expression to be used in contexts that require a single value (for example, a call to a function that has a parameter with the required type «`item()+`») when the processor might otherwise have reported a static type error. The XPath expression is still type-safe, because the check that the sequence does indeed contain at least one item will be done at runtime, just as it would with a processor that does not enforce static type checking.

Examples

Expression	Result
one-or-more(1)	1
one-or-more((1,2,3))	1,2,3
one-or-more(())	*Error*

Usage

As it happens, functions in the core library do not generally have a required type such as «item()+», even in cases like min(), max() and avg() where there is no meaningful result that can be returned for an empty sequence. This is because the designers decided that rather than reporting an error for these functions when the argument is an empty sequence, it made more sense to return an empty sequence as the result. However, if you do want to make a runtime check that a sequence is not empty before calling a function such as avg(), then calling one-or-more() is a simple way to do the check.

See also

exactly-one() on page 339
zero-or-one() on page 444
«treat as» expression on page 288 in Chapter 9.

position

The position() function returns the value of the context position. When processing a list of items, position() gives the number assigned to the current item in the list, with the first item being numbered as 1.

Changes in 2.0

None.

Signature

This function takes no arguments.

	Data type	Meaning
Result	xs:integer	*A number, the value of the context position. As the name implies, this is context-dependent*

Effect

The XPath specification defines the value of the position() function in terms of the context position.

The context position is part of the *focus*, which is described in the spec as having three components: the context item, the context position, and the context size. However, it may be easier to think of the focus as being a bit like an `Iterator` object in a language such as Java. Behind the iterator is a list of items that are processed individually (though not necessarily in any particular order). The context item, position, and size can be thought of as three methods provided by this iterator object: the context position is a number that ranges from 1 to the size of the list, the context item is the item found at the context position, and the context size is the number of items in the list.

When a top-level XPath expression is evaluated (that is, an XPath expression that is not part of another expression), the context position is set by the host language. In XSLT, it is set from the XSLT context. For example:

❑   When a global `<xsl:variable>` declaration is being evaluated, or in certain other contexts such as evaluating the use expression in `<xsl:key>`, or evaluating the initial template that matches the root node, it is normally set to 1 (one).

❑   When `<xsl:apply-templates>` or `<xsl:for-each>` is called to process a sequence of nodes, the nodes are numbered 1 to N in their sorted order, and while each node is being processed the context position is the number assigned to that node. (There is no implication that node 1 is processed before node 2, incidentally.)

This means that within an `<xsl:for-each>` iteration, the test `<xsl:if test="position() =last()">` succeeds when the last item in the sequence is being processed.

Many APIs that enable XPath expressions to be executed from languages like Java or JavaScript allow the caller to set the context item, but not the context position or size. In such cases, the context position and size on entry to the XPath expression will both be one.

Within an XPath expression, the context size changes within a predicate and on the right-hand-side of the «/» operator.

❑   In a predicate, `position()` refers to the position of the item that is being filtered using the predicate within the sequence of items being filtered. For example, «$seq[position()!=1]» selects all items except the first in a sequence, because the first item is the only one for which the predicate is false.

❑   It's less common to find `position()` being used on the right-hand-side of a «/» operator. It refers to the position of the context item in the sequence selected by the left-hand operand of the «/». For example, you could write «./(para, subsequence($notes, position(), 1))» to select the `<para>` element children of the context node, with each `<para>` pulling in the item at the corresponding position in the $notes sequence. (But the final results will be sorted in document order.)

Remember that the focus is not changed within a «for» expression. If you need to know within the body of a «for» expression what the position of the item being processed is, you need to rewrite it. Instead of doing:

```
for $s in $sequence
return EXPR
```

write:

```
for $i in 1 to count($sequence),
    $s in $sequence[$i]
return EXPR
```

You can then use $i within EXPR to refer to the position of $s within the sequence.

Usage in XSLT

The position() function is often used as a complete XPath expression within an XSLT stylesheet. The function has particular significance in XSLT because it gives the position of the item currently being processed by an <xsl:for-each> instruction (as well as other instructions such as <xsl:apply-templates> and <xsl:for-each-group>). The two main uses of the position() function in XSLT are to *display* the current position, and to *test* the current position.

Displaying the Current Position

In this role the position() function can be used for simple numbering of paragraphs, sections, or figures.

In XSLT this provides an alternative to the use of <xsl:number>. There is much less flexibility to control how the numbering is done than when using <xsl:number>, but the position() function has two important advantages:

❑   It is generally faster.

❑   It numbers items in the order they are output, whereas <xsl:number> can only allocate a number based on the position of a node in the source document. This means <xsl:number> is of little use when a list has been sorted using <xsl:sort>.

If you use position(), you can still exploit the formatting capabilities of <xsl:number> by writing, for example:

```
<xsl:number value="position()" format="(a)"/>
```

This determines the position of the node and formats the result according to the given format pattern; the resulting sequence will be « (a) », « (b) », « (c) », and so on.

Testing the Current Position

It is possible to test the position of the current item either in a boolean expression in an <xsl:if> or <xsl:when> element, or in a predicate within a filter expression or pattern.

A common requirement is to treat the first or last item in a list differently from the rest. For example, to insert a horizontal rule after every item except the last, the following logic might be used:

```
<xsl:for-each select="item">
<xsl:sort select="@name"/>
    <p><xsl:value-of select="@name"/>:
        <xsl:value-of select="description"/></p>
    <xsl:if test="position() != last()">
        <hr/>
    </xsl:if>
</xsl:for-each>
```

Within a predicate in an expression or pattern, a numeric value represents an implicit test against the result of `position()`, for example, «`item[1]`» is equivalent to «`item[position()=1]`», and «`item[last()]`» is equivalent to «`item[position()=last()]`».

> You can only use this shorthand in a predicate; that is, within square brackets. If you use a numeric value in other contexts where a Boolean is expected, the number is converted to a boolean on the basis that 0 is false; everything else is true. So `<xsl:if test="1">` does *not* mean `<xsl:if test="position()=1">`; it means the same as `<xsl:if test="true()">`.

See also

`last()` on page 359
`<xsl:number>` in Chapter 5 of *XSLT 2.0 Programmer's Reference*

remove

The `remove()` function returns a sequence that contains all the items in an input sequence except the one at a specified position.

Changes in 2.0

This function is new in XPath 2.0.

Signature

Argument	Data type	Meaning
sequence	item()*	The input sequence
position	xs:integer	The position of the item to be removed
Result	item()*	*A sequence containing all the items in the input sequence except the item at the specified position*

Effect

The effect is the same as the expression:

```
$sequence[position() ne $position]
```

This means that if the `position` parameter is less than one or greater than the number of items in the input sequence, the input sequence is returned unchanged.

Examples

Expression	Result
remove((1 to 5), 4)	1, 2, 3, 5
remove((1 to 5), 10)	1, 2, 3, 4, 5
remove((), 1)	()

Usage

A common requirement, especially in recursive functions, is to get the *tail* of a sequence, that is, all items except the first. There are several ways of doing this in XPath 2.0, all equivalent. Take your pick:

- ❑ $sequence[position() ne 1]
- ❑   subsequence($sequence, 2)
- ❑   remove($sequence, 1)

See also

insert-before() on page 356
subsequence() on page 422

replace

The replace() function constructs an output string from an input string by replacing all occurrences of substrings that match a supplied regular expression with a given replacement string. The replacement string may include references to captured groups within the input string.

Changes in 2.0

This function is new in XPath 2.0.

Signature

Argument	Data type	Meaning
input	xs:string?	The input string. If an empty sequence is supplied, an empty sequence is returned
regex	xs:string	The regular expression, written according to the rules given in Chapter 11
replacement	xs:string	The replacement string

Argument	Data type	Meaning
flags (*optional*)	xs:string	One or more letters indicating options on how the matching is to be performed. If this argument is omitted, the effect is the same as supplying a zero-length string, which defaults all the option settings
Result	xs:string?	*The string produced by replacing substrings of the input string that match the regular expression*

Effect

The rules for the syntax of regular expressions are given in Chapter 11, and the rules for the flags attribute under the entry for the matches() function on page 368.

The input string is processed from left to right, looking for substrings that match the regular expression supplied in the regex argument. Characters that don't participate in a match are copied unchanged to the output string. When a substring is found that does match the regex, the substring is not copied to the output, but the replacement string is copied instead. The search then resumes at the character position following the matched substring. For example, the result of «replace("banana", "a", "A")» is «bAnAnA».

It can happen that two substrings starting at the same position both match the regex. There are two ways this situation can arise.

Firstly, it happens when part of the regex is looking for repeated occurrences of a substring. For example, if the regex is «(an)*a» then immediately after the «b» of «banana», there are three possible matches, the matched substrings being «a», «ana», and «anana». The rule here is that «*» is a greedy quantifier: it matches as long a substring as it can. So the result of the expression «replace("banana", "(an)*a", "#")» is «b#». If you want to match the shortest possible substring, add a «?» after the quantifier to make it non-greedy: «replace("banana", "(an)+?a", "#")» is «b#na». Note that the final three characters of «banana» don't result in a replacement, because two matches never overlap: the middle «a» cannot participate in two different matching substrings.

Another situation that can cause two different substrings to match at the same position is where the regex contains two alternatives that both match. For example, the regex «a|ana» could match the second character of «banana», or it could match characters 2 to 4. The rule here is that the first (leftmost) alternative wins. So the result of «replace("banana", "a|ana", "#")» is «b#n#n#», whereas the result of «replace("banana", "ana|a", "#")» is «b#n#».

The replacement string supplied in the replace argument can contain the variables «$1» to «$9» to refer to parts of the input string that were matched by parts of the regular expression. If you want to include a «$» sign in the replacement string, you must write it as «\$», and if you want to include a «\» character, you must write it as «\\». (These rules might seem bizarre. But it was done this way for compatibility with other languages, and to allow other features to be added in the future.)

The variable $N refers to the substring of the input that was matched by the Nth parenthesized sub-expression of the regex. You can find out which the Nth subexpression is by simply counting «(»

characters from the first character of the regex. For example, in the regex «`([0-9]+)([A-Z]+)`
`([0-9]+)`», $1 refers to the digits at the start of the string, $2 to the group of letters in the middle, and
$3 to the digits at the end. So if you want to insert a hyphen between the groups of letters and digits, you
can write:

```
replace($input, "^([0-9]+)([A-Z]+)([0-9]+)$", "$1-$2-$3")
```

If you run this with the input string «`23MAR2004`», the result will be «`23-MAR-2004`». (Note the use of
an anchored regex here to match and replace the entire string.)

If the replacement string contains a variable that hasn't been matched, perhaps because the relevant
parenthesized subexpression was in a branch that wasn't used, then a zero-length string is substituted for
the variable. If the subexpression was matched more than once, then it's the last one that is used.

If the regex does not match the input string, the `replace()` function will return the input string
unchanged. If this is not the effect you are looking for, use the `matches()` function first to see if there is a
match.

If the regex is one that matches a zero-length string, that is, if «`matches("", $regex)`» is true, the
system reports an error. An example of such a regex is «`a*`». Although various interpretations of such a
construct are possible, the Working Group decided that the results were too confusing and decided not to
allow it.

Examples

Expression	Result
`replace("banana", "a", "o")`	bonono
`replace("banana", "(ana|na)", "[$1]")`	b[ana][na]
`replace("banana", "(an)+", "**")`	b**a
`replace("banana", "(an)+?", "**")`	b****a

Usage

The `replace()` function provides a much-needed string replacement capability for XPath. In XPath 1.0
it was possible to do simple one-for-one character replacement using the `translate()` function, but
anything more complex required the use of cumbersome recursive templates in XSLT.

One limitation of the `replace()` function, however, is that the result is always a string: this function
cannot be used directly for so-called *up-conversion* applications where the aim is to generate markup
within the string (a typical example of such a conversion is the requirement to replace newlines in a
string by empty <br> elements). For such applications, the XSLT <xsl:analyze-string> instruction
is more powerful. In a non-XSLT application, an alternative might be to use `tokenize()` to split the
string into a sequence of substrings, leaving the calling application to insert the element tags at the
boundaries.

See also

<xsl:analyze-string> in *XSLT 2.0 Programmer's Reference*, Chapter 5.
matches() on page 368
tokenize() on page 434
translate() on page 437

resolve-QName

The resolve-QName() function returns a value of type xs:QName (that is, an expanded QName consisting of a namespace URI and a local name), taking as input a lexical QName (a string in the form «prefix:local-name» or simply «local-name»), by resolving the prefix used in the lexical QName against the in-scope namespaces of a given element node.

Changes in 2.0

This function is new in XPath 2.0.

Signature

Argument	Data type	Meaning
lexical-qname	xs:string?	The lexical QName whose prefix is to be resolved. It must conform to the syntax of a QName as defined in the XML Namespaces specification (which is the same as the lexical space for an xs:QName defined in XML Schema)
element	element()	An element node whose in-scope namespaces are to be used to resolve the namespace prefix used in the lexical QName
Result	xs:QName?	*The expanded xs:QName, containing the namespace URI corresponding to the prefix supplied in the lexical QName*

Effect

If the first argument is an empty sequence, the function returns an empty sequence.

The local-name part of the resulting xs:QName value will always be the same as the local-name part of the supplied lexical QName: that is, the part after the colon, if there is a colon, or the whole string otherwise.

If the lexical QName has no prefix, then the system looks for an unnamed namespace node of the given element (representing the default namespace for that element). If it finds one, then the namespace URI component of the result is taken from the string value of this namespace node. If there is no unnamed namespace node, then the namespace URI component of the resulting xs:QName value will be null.

If the lexical QName does have a prefix, then the system looks for a namespace node of the given element whose name matches this prefix. If it finds one, then the namespace URI component of the result is taken from the string value of this namespace node. If there is no matching namespace node, then the function reports an error.

Examples

Consider the source document:

```
<doc xmlns:one="one.uri" xmlns="default.uri">
  <chap xmlns="" att-one="text">
    <data-one>one:value</data-one>
    <data-two>value</data-two>
  </chap>
</doc>
```

And suppose that the following variables are bound:

```
$chap  /doc/chap
$data1 /doc/chap/data-one
$data2 /doc/chap/data-two
```

Expression	Result
resolve-QName($chap/@att-one, $chap)	{default.uri}text
resolve-QName(string($data1), $data1)	{one.uri}value
resolve-QName(string($data2), $data2)	{}value

In these examples I have shown the resulting URI in *Clark notation*, named after James Clark, the lead designer of XSLT 1.0 and XPath 1.0. This notation represents an expanded QName in the form «{namespace-uri}local-name».

Note that all these examples resolve a lexical QName found in the content of the document against the element node that contains the value. This is the normal and probably the only sensible way to use this function, since the prefix of a QName only has meaning in the context of the element where it is used.

Usage

The purpose of this function, as the examples show, is to resolve QName values found in the content of elements or attributes within a document.

It's never necessary to use this function to resolve QNames used as element and attribute names, because the system does that for you.

It's also unnecessary to use this function if you have a schema-aware processor, and a schema that declares the relevant elements and attributes as having type xs:QName. In this case the schema processor will do the work for you, and you can access the expanded QName as the typed value of the element or attribute, using the data() function.

The function is needed when you have lexical QNames in the document content and they aren't declared as such in the schema. This can happen for a number of reasons:

❑   You are using a processor that isn't schema-aware, or a source document for which no schema has been written.

❑   The lexical QName doesn't make up the whole of the element or attribute value, for example, it might be buried inside an XPath expression.

❑   The value of the attribute isn't always a QName (an example is the `default` attribute of the `<xs:element>` element in XML Schema itself, whose type depends on the type of the element being defined).

❑   You don't want to use the rules that XML Schema uses for handling the default namespace (an example is the `name` attribute of the `<xsl:variable>` element in XSLT, where an unprefixed name uses the null namespace rather than the default namespace).

Let's look at this last example more closely. If your source documents are XSLT stylesheets (it is actually quite common to process stylesheets using XSLT) then there are many lexical QNames used within the content of the document (for example, in the `name` attribute of templates, keys, and functions, the `mode` attribute of `<xsl:apply-templates>`, and myriad other places. These aren't declared as `xs:QName` values in the schema for XSLT, however. The reason is subtle: although an XML Schema would do the correct validation if these attributes had type `xs:QName`, it would not do the conversion from the lexical space to the value space correctly. This is because XSLT specifies that when there is no prefix, these names are in the null namespace, regardless of any default namespace declaration, while XML Schema when it processes `xs:QName` values decides that the absence of a prefix implies use of the default namespace (if you want to find this rule, look in the second edition of *XML Schema Part 2*, or in the errata to the first edition).

This means that you can only use this function for names found in XSLT stylesheets if you handle the unprefixed case yourself. Fortunately, this is easy enough:

```
if (contains(@name, ':'))
then resolve-QName(@name, .)
else expanded-QName("", @name)
```

Rather surprisingly, it's also possible to come across QNames that aren't declared as such when you run XPath expressions against an XML Schema document. This is because values of any data type can appear in places such as the `xs:enumeration` facet of a simple type, or the `default` attribute of an element or attribute declaration. Because these constructs might contain values of any data type, their declared type in the schema for schemas is simply `xs:string`. The only way you can work out that one of these strings needs to be treated as a QName is by rather complex analysis of the schema.

See also

expanded-QName() on page 342
in-scope-prefixes() on page 354

resolve-uri

The `resolve-uri()` function converts a relative URI into an absolute URI by resolving it against a specified base URI.

Changes in 2.0

This function is new in XPath 2.0.

Signature

Argument	Data type	Meaning
relative	xs:string	The URI to be resolved. If this is an absolute URI, it is returned unchanged; otherwise, it is resolved against the specified base URI
base-uri (*optional*)	xs:string	The base URI against which the relative URI is to be resolved. If this argument is omitted, the base URI from the static context is used. This must be an absolute URI
Result	xs:string	*The resulting absolute URI*

Effect

The process of URI resolution takes a relative URI such as «details.html» and resolves it against an absolute URI such as «http://example.com/index.html» to produce an absolute URI such as «http://example.com/details.html». Note that this process is done purely by analyzing the two character strings, it doesn't require any access to the network to find out whether these files actually exist. This means that it is quite legitimate to apply the operation to things like collation URIs that don't necessarily represent real resources on the Web.

The actual algorithm for URI resolution is described in section 5.2 of Internet RFC 2396 (http://www.ietf.org/rfc/rfc2396.txt). In essence, the relative URI is appended after the last «/» in the path component of the base URI, and some tidying-up is then done to remove redundant «/./» and «/../» components.

The rules in the RFC allow the base URI to be itself a relative URI, in which case the result will also be a relative URI. The resolve-uri() function, however, does not allow this; it requires the base URI to be absolute. The RFC is fairly permissive in defining how implementations should handle edge cases, or cases that are strictly speaking invalid, and it's likely that different implementations of the resolve-uri() function will also show some variability in these situations.

If the second argument of resolve-uri() is omitted, the effect is the same as using the function call «resolve-uri($relative, base-uri())»: this means that the base URI is taken from the static context of the XPath expression. The way this is set up is (as the name implies) very context-dependent.

❑   In the case of XPath expressions within an XSLT stylesheet the base URI is reasonably well-defined: the base URI of the stylesheet module is used, unless the stylesheet contains xml:base attributes, or is split into multiple XML external entities. But the base URI of the stylesheet module may be unknown, for example, if the XSLT code was read from a string constructed in memory rather than from a file.

❑   In the case of XPath expressions constructed programmatically, for example, by a Java or JavaScript application, all bets are off. Your XPath API may provide a way of setting the base URI, but it's more likely in my experience that it won't. In this situation relative URIs are rather meaningless, and it's best to avoid them.

Examples

Most of these examples are taken from Appendix C of RFC 2396, and assume a base URI of «`http://a/b/c/d;p?q`». The RFC includes other more complex examples that are worth consulting.

Expression	Result
`resolve-uri("g")`	`http://a/b/c/g`
`resolve-uri("./g")`	`http://a/b/c/g`
`resolve-uri("g/")`	`http://a/b/c/g/`
`resolve-uri("/g")`	`http://a/g`
`resolve-uri("?y")`	`http://a/b/c/?y`
`resolve-uri("g?y")`	`http://a/b/c/g?y`
`resolve-uri("")`	`http://a/b/c/d` (*but see Note*)
`resolve-uri("#s")`	`http://a/b/c/d#s` (*but see Note*)
`resolve-uri("../g")`	`http://a/b/g`

The RFC is rather coy in its description of how a relative URI of "" (the zero-length string) is supposed to behave. For a start, its BNF rules don't actually allow "" as a relative URI, though the accompanying text makes it clear that it has a meaning. But where it discusses zero-length relative URIs, it always speaks of resolving them relative to "the current document" rather than relative to the base URI. It doesn't actually define the term "current document", but I think it is trying to make a careful distinction that makes sense in a browser, but not elsewhere. Certainly in XPath and XSLT, there is no concept of a current document as something distinct from the base URI, and the only sensible way to interpret a zero-length relative URI is as a reference to the base URI itself, which is what I have done in the examples above. The only exception to this might arise when the XSLT or XPath processor is running client-side, in the browser.

Usage

The most likely place you will need to use the `resolve-uri()` function is in conjunction with the `doc()` function, described on page 329. By default, a relative URI passed to the `doc()` function is resolved relative to the base URI from the static context of the XPath expression. If the relative URI was read from a source document, it makes much more sense to resolve it against the base URI of the node that contained it. The code usually looks something like this:

```
doc(resolve-uri(@href, base-uri(.)))
```

See also

reverse

The reverse() function returns a sequence in reverse order. For example, «reverse(1 to 5)» returns the sequence «5, 4, 3, 2, 1».

Changes in 2.0

This function is new in XPath 2.0.

Signature

Argument	Data type	Meaning
sequence	item()*	The input sequence
Result	item()*	*A sequence containing the same items as the input sequence, but in reverse order*

Effect

The result of the function contains exactly the same items as the input sequence, but the order is reversed. The effect is the same as the expression:

```
for $i in 1 to count($sequence) return
    $sequence[count($sequence) - $i + 1]
```

Examples

Expression	Result
reverse(1 to 5)	5, 4, 3, 2, 1
reverse(1)	1
reverse(())	()
reverse(ancestor::*)	*A list of ancestor elements, in reverse document order (that is, innermost first)*

See also

unordered() on page 440

root

The root() function returns the root node of the tree containing a specified start node, or the root of the tree containing the context node.

Changes in 2.0

This function is new in XPath 2.0.

Signature

Argument	Data type	Meaning
start-node (*optional*)	node()?	A node in the tree whose root is required. If the argument is omitted, it defaults to the context node. It is then an error if the context item is not a node (for example, if it is an atomic value, or if it is undefined)
Result	node()?	*The root of the tree containing the start node*

Effect

If the `start-node` argument is supplied and its value is an empty sequence, then the result of the function is an empty sequence.

In other cases, the function returns the root node of the tree containing the `start-node`. The result is the same as the path expression «(ancestor-or-self::node())[1]». This node is not necessarily a document node, since it is possible in the XPath 2.0 data model to have elements or other nodes that are parentless. The system follows the parent axis until it finds a node that has no parent, and then it returns that node. If the start node has no parent, then the start node itself is returned as the result of the function.

Examples

Expression	Result
root()	*The root node of the tree containing the context node*
root($x)	*The root node of the tree containing the node $x*
$seq/root()	*A sequence containing the root nodes of all the trees containing nodes in $seq, in document order with duplicates removed*

Usage

The effect of the `root()` function, when called with no argument, is very similar to the effect of the expression «/». However, «/» will return the root node of the tree containing the context node only if the root is a document node; in other cases, it reports a runtime error.

See also

The Root Expression «/» on page 205 in Chapter 7.

round

The `round()` function returns the closest integer to the numeric value of the argument, as an instance of the same data type as the argument

For example, the expression «round(4.6)» returns the xs:decimal value 5.0.

Changes in 2.0

The function has been generalized to accept arguments of any numeric type.

Signature

Argument	Data type	Meaning
value	Numeric?	The input value. If an empty sequence is supplied, an empty sequence is returned
Result	Numeric?	*The result of rounding the first argument to the nearest integer, but expressed as a value of the same data type as the input value*

Effect

The XPath specification is very precise about the results of round(). The rules are given in the tables below. The first table applies regardless of the data type:

If the argument is...	Then the result is...
Equal to an integer N	N
Between N and N + 0.5	N
Exactly N + 0.5	N + 1
Between N + 0.5 and N + 1	N + 1

Note that this rounds +3.5 to +4.0, but -3.5 to -3.0.

For values of type xs:float and xs:double, there are additional rules to cover the special IEEE values. The concepts of positive and negative zero, positive and negative infinity, and NaN are explained in the section on the xs:double data type in Chapter 3, page 83.

If the argument is...	Then the result is...
Between −0.5 and zero	*Negative zero*
Positive zero	*Positive zero*
Negative zero	*Negative zero*
Positive infinity	*Positive infinity*
Negative infinity	*Negative infinity*
NaN (not-a-number)	*NaN*

Examples

Expression	Result
round(3.2)	3.2
round(4.6e0)	5.0e0
round(7.5)	8.0
round(-7.5)	-7.0
round(-0.0e0)	-0.0e0

Usage

The round() function is useful when you want the nearest integer, for example, when calculating an average, or when deciding the geometric coordinates for an object to be displayed. If you want to convert the result to a value of type xs:integer, use the xs:integer() constructor function, or the construct «round($x) idiv 1».

See also

ceiling() on page 306
floor() on page 344
round-half-to-even() in the next entry
«idiv» operator on page 173 in Chapter 6

round-half-to-even

The round-half-to-even() function performs rounding to a specified number of decimal places. The rounding algorithm used is to round to the nearest value that has the required precision, choosing an even value if two values are equally close.

Changes in 2.0

This function is new in XPath 2.0.

Signature

Argument	Data type	Meaning
input	Numeric?	The number to be rounded. If an empty sequence is supplied, an empty sequence is returned
precision (*optional*)	xs:integer	If positive, the number of significant digits required after the decimal point. If negative, the number of zeroes required at the end of the integer part of the result. The default is zero
Result	Numeric?	*The rounded number. This will have the same data type as the supplied number*

Effect

The precision argument indicates the number of decimal digits required after the decimal point. More generally, the function rounds the supplied number to a multiple of 10^{-p} where p is the requested precision. So if the requested precision is 2, the value is rounded to a multiple of 0.01; if it is zero, the value is rounded to a multiple of 1 (in other words, to an integer), and if it is –2, the value is rounded to a multiple of 100.

If the precision argument is not supplied, the effect is the same as supplying the value zero, which means the value is rounded to an integer.

The value is rounded up or down to whichever value is closest: for example, if the required precision is 2, then 0.123 is rounded to 0.12 and 0.567 is rounded to 0.57. If two values are equally close then the round-to-even rule comes into play: 0.125 is rounded to 0.12, while 0.875 is rounded to 0.88.

This function is designed primarily for rounding of xs:decimal values, but it is also available for other numeric types. For xs:integer, the behavior is exactly the same as if the value were an xs:decimal (which, in fact, it is). For xs:double and xs:float it may be less obvious that this works. The specification states that the floating-point value should first be adjusted so that it has an exponent of zero (for example, 1.5e-3 is rewritten as 0.0015e0) and the rounding is then applied to the mantissa as if it were a decimal number. This works well for most numbers in a reasonable range, though there may be rounding errors when you use it with numbers that are extremely small or extremely large.

Examples

Expression	Result
round-half-to-even(1.1742, 2)	1.17
round-half-to-even(1.175, 2)	1.18
round-half-to-even(2.5, 0)	2.0
round-half-to-even(273, -1)	270
round-half-to-even(-8500, -3)	-8000

Usage

Most of us were probably taught at school that when numbers are rounded, 0.5 should be rounded upwards. Professional accountants and statisticians, however, often prefer the "half-to-even" rule because it avoids creating bias: it means that on average, the total of a large set of numbers will remain roughly the same when all the numbers are rounded.

This function is useful when you want to display the results of a numerical calculation to a certain number of decimal places. Floating point arithmetic often produces rounding errors because decimal values cannot be represented exactly in binary: for example, the result of «0.3e0 div 3» is «0.09999999999999999» rather than «0.1». Rounding the result say to six decimal places by writing «round-half-to-even(0.3e0 div 3,6)» corrects this error, and produces the result «0.1».

In XSLT, you can also achieve this rounding by using the `format-number()` *function, described in Chapter 7 of* XSLT 2.0 Programmer's Reference.

See also

`ceiling()` on page 306
`floor()` on page 344
`round()` on page 409

seconds-from-dateTime, seconds-from-time

The two functions `seconds-from-dateTime()` and `seconds-from-time()` extract the seconds component (including fractional seconds) from an `xs:dateTime` or `xs:time` value.

Changes in 2.0

These functions are new in XPath 2.0.

Signature

Argument	Data type	Meaning
input	`xs:time?` or `xs:dateTime?`	The value from which the seconds component is to be extracted. The data type of the supplied argument must correspond to the data type implied by the function name. If an empty sequence is supplied, an empty sequence is returned
Result	`xs:decimal?`	*The seconds component, normally in the range 0 to 59.999...Exceptionally, a value greater than 60 can be returned because some days include a leap second to compensate for variations in the earth's rotation*

Effect

The function returns the seconds component of the supplied `xs:time` or `xs:dateTime`. The value is from the time as expressed in its local timezone (not normalized to UTC).

Examples

Expression	Result
`seconds-from-time(xs:time("12:35:03.142"))`	`3.142`
`seconds-from-dateTime(xs:dateTime ("2004-02-28T13:55:30-01:00"))`	`30.0`

See also

`current-date(),-dateTime(),-time()` on page 318.
`format-date(),-dateTime(),-time()` in Chapter 7 of *XSLT 2.0 Programmer's Reference.*

hours-from-dateTime(),-time() on page 345
minutes-from-dateTime(),-time() on page 372
timezone-from-dateTime(),-time() on page 433

seconds-from-duration

This function extracts the value of the seconds component (including fractional seconds) from a normalized xdt:dayTimeDuration value.

Changes in 2.0

This function is new in XPath 2.0.

Signature

Argument	Data type	Meaning
input	xdt:dayTimeDuration?	The value whose seconds component is to be extracted. If an empty sequence is supplied, an empty sequence is returned
Result	xs:decimal?	*The seconds component, including any fractional seconds*

Effect

The function returns the seconds component of the supplied xdt:dayTimeDuration. The duration value is first normalized so that the number of hours is less than 24, the number of minutes is less than 60, and so on. The result will be negative if the duration is negative. The result is therefore a decimal number in the range – 60.0 to +60.0, exclusive.

XPath processors are required to maintain duration values to a precision of three decimal places (one millisecond). Some processors may maintain a finer precision than this, but it is optional.

Examples

Expression	Result
seconds-from-duration(xdt:dayTimeDuration("PT1M30.5S"))	30.5
seconds-from-duration(xdt:dayTimeDuration("PT150S"))	30
seconds-from-duration(xdt:dayTimeDuration("-P0.0055S"))	-0.0055

See also

days-from-duration on page 323
hours-from-duration on page 347
minutes-from-duration on page 374

starts-with

The `starts-with()` function tests whether one string starts with another string.

For example, the expression «`starts-with('$17.30','$')`» returns `true`.

Changes in 2.0

An optional collation argument has been added.

Signature

Argument	Data type	Meaning
input	`xs:string?`	The containing string
test	`xs:string?`	The test string
collation *(optional)*	`xs:string`	A collation URI
Result	`xs:boolean`	*True if the containing string starts with the test string, otherwise false*

Effect

If there is no `collation` argument, then the system tests to see whether the first N characters of the input string match the characters in the `test` string (where N is the length of the `test` string). If so, the result is `true`; otherwise it is `false`. Characters match if they have the same Unicode value.

If the `test` string is empty, the result is always `true`. If the `input` string is empty, the result is `true` only if the `test` string is also empty. If the `test` string is longer than the `input`, the result is always `false`.

If either the `input` or the `test` argument is an empty sequence, it is treated in the same way as a zero-length string.

If a `collation` is specified, this collation is used to test whether the strings match. See the description of the `contains()` function on page 314 for an account of how substring matching works with a collation. If the `collation` argument is omitted, the function matches characters according to their Unicode codepoint values.

Examples

Expression	Result
`starts-with('#note', '#')`	true
`starts-with('yes', 'yes')`	true
`starts-with('YES', 'yes')`	false
`starts-with('yes', '')`	true

Usage

For more sophisticated string matching, use the matches() function, which provides the ability to match against a regular expression. However, the matches() function does not give the ability to use a collation.

See also

contains() on page 314
ends-with() on page 334
matches() on page 368
string-length() on page 419

string

The string() function converts its argument to a string. When the argument is a node, it extracts the string value of the node; when the argument is an atomic value, it converts the atomic value to a string in a similar way to the xs:string() constructor function.

For example, the expression «string(4.00)» returns the string "4".

Changes in 2.0

The function has been generalized to take a wider range of data types as its input.

In XPath 1.0, when a sequence containing several nodes was supplied, the string() function returned the string value of the first node, and ignored the rest. This behavior is retained in XPath 2.0 when running in 1.0 backward compatibility mode; but in 2.0 mode, supplying more than one item in the argument is an error.

Signature

Argument	Data type	Meaning
value (*optional*)	item()?	The value to be converted. If the argument is omitted, it defaults to the context item
Result	xs:string	*The result of converting the argument to a string*

Effect

Values of most data types can be converted to a string.

If the function is called with no arguments, the effect is the same as supplying «.» (the context item) as the first argument.

If the supplied value is an empty sequence, the result is a zero-length string. (Don't confuse supplying an argument whose value is «()» with not supplying an argument—the effect is different.)

If the supplied value is a single node, the result is the string value of that node. The string value of a node is defined as follows:

- ❑ For a document node or element node, the string value is the concatenation of all the descendant text nodes.

- ❑ For an attribute, the string value is the attribute value.

- ❑ For a text node, the string value is the textual content.

- ❑ For a comment, the string value is the text of the comment.

- ❑ For a processing instruction, the string value is the *data* part of the processing instruction, that is, the part after the name that forms the *target* of the processing instruction.

- ❑ For a namespace node, the string value is the namespace URI.

If the supplied value is a single atomic value the result is the same as the result of casting the atomic value to a string. The casting rules are given in Chapter 9. There are two cases where casting is not well defined in the current specifications, namely when the value is an `xs:QName` or an `xs:NOTATION`. In these two cases there is not enough information available to construct a lexical representation of the value, because there is no context information available to provide a namespace prefix.

Note that taking the string value of a node is not the same as taking the typed value and converting it to a string. For example, the typed value might be a sequence of integers, but no conversion is defined from a sequence of integers to a string. In some cases a node has no typed value, notably in the case where the schema defines it as having element-only content (as distinct from mixed or empty content). Such an element has no typed value, but it still has a string value that is the concatenation of the desendant text nodes.

The type signature does not allow a sequence of more than one item to be supplied. However, if XPath 1.0 compatibility mode is enabled, any items in the sequence after the first are ignored.

Examples

Assume that the context node is the element:

```
<e example="yes"><first>17</first><second>blue</second></e>
```

Expression	Result
string()	"17blue"
string(first)	"17"
string(second)	"blue"
string(@example)	"yes"
string(+47.20)	"47.2"
string(2=2)	"true"
string(*)	*In 1.0 mode:* "17" *In 2.0 mode: error*

Usage

When converting atomic values to strings, there isn't really anything to choose between using the `string()` function and using the `xs:string()` constructor function.

When the argument is a node, the two functions behave differently. The `string()` function extracts the string value of the node, while `xs:string()` extracts the typed value and converts it to a string. In the absence of a schema, they do exactly the same thing. But with a schema, here are two cases where they can give different results:

- ❑ Where the node has a list-valued simple type (for example, a list of integers), `string()` will give the textual content of the node (a space-separated list of numbers), whereas `xs:string()` will fail if the list contains more than one item, or is empty.

- ❑ Where the node is an element with an element-only content model, `string()` will give the concatenation of the descendant text nodes of the element, while `xs:string()` will fail.

See also

`boolean()` on page 304
`number()` on page 393
Converting Atomic Values on page 262 in Chapter 9

string-join

The `string-join()` function returns a string constructed by concatenating all the strings in a supplied sequence, with an optional separator between adjacent strings.

For example, «`string-join(("a","b","c"), "|")`» returns «a|b|c».

Changes in 2.0

This function is new in XPath 2.0.

Signature

Argument	Data type	Meaning
sequence	`xs:string*`	The supplied sequence of strings
separator	`xs:string`	The separator to be used between adjacent strings. If no separator is required, supply a zero-length string for this argument
Result	`xs:string`	*The result of concatenating the supplied strings and inserting separators*

Effect

Each of the strings in the supplied sequence is appended to the result string, retaining the order in which the strings appear in the sequence. Each string except the last is followed by the requested `separator` string.

If the supplied sequence is empty, the result is always a zero-length string.

Examples

Expression	Result
string-join(("a", "b", "c"), ", ")	a, b, c
string-join(("A", "B", "C"), "")	ABC
string-join("Z", "+")	Z
string-join((), "~")	()

Usage

The expression:

```
string-join(for $a in ancestor-or-self::* return name($a), "/")
```

will return a path such as:

```
book/chapter/section/title
```

Note that there is no implicit conversion of the items in the sequence to strings, even in XPath 1.0 compatibility mode. If the items are not strings, you need to convert them explicitly. For example, given a sequence of numbers, you can write:

```
string-join(for $i in $seq return string($i), ", ")
```

The `string-join()` function is often a handy alternative to `concat()`, because you can in effect give it a sequence of sequences to output. For example:

```
string-join(("debits:", $debits, "credits:", $credits), " ")
```

might produce the string:

```
debits: 23.40 18.50 67.00 credits: 17.00 5.00 4.32
```

See also

concat() on page 312

string-length

The `string-length()` function returns the number of characters in a string value.

For example, the expression «`string-length('Beethoven')`» returns 9.

Changes in 2.0

None.

Signature

Argument	Data type	Meaning
value (*optional*)	xs:string?	The string whose length is required.
		If the argument is omitted, the string-value of the context item is used. If the argument is an empty sequence, the result of the function is 0 (zero)
Result	xs:integer	*A number: the number of characters in the value of the argument*

Effect

Characters are counted as instances of the XML Char production. This means that a Unicode surrogate pair (a pair of 16-bit values used to represent a Unicode character in the range #x10000 to #x10FFFF) is treated as a single character.

It is the number of characters in the string that matters, not the way they are written in the source document. A character written using a character reference such as «ÿ» or an entity reference such as «&» is still one character.

Unicode combining and non-spacing characters are counted individually, unless the implementation has normalized them. The implementation is allowed to turn strings into normalized form, but is not required to do so. In normalized form, accents and diacriticals will typically be merged with the letter that they modify into a single character. To assure yourself of consistent answers in such cases, the normalize-unicode() function should be called to force the string into normalized form.

Examples

These examples assume that the XPath expression is used in a host language that expands XML entity references and numeric character references, for example, XSLT or XQuery.

Expression	Result
string-length("abc")	3
string-length("<>")	2
string-length("""")	1
string-length("")	0
string-length('&#xFFFD;')	1
string-length('𠀀')	1

Usage

The string-length() function can be useful when deciding how to allocate space on the output medium. For example, if a list is displayed in multiple columns then the number of columns may be determined by some algorithm based on the maximum length of the strings to be displayed.

It is *not* necessary to call `string-length()` to determine whether a string is zero-length, because converting the string to an `xs:boolean`, either explicitly using the `boolean()` function, or implicitly by using it in a boolean context, returns `true` only if the string has a length of one or more. For the same reason, it is not usually necessary to call `string-length()` when processing the characters in a string using a recursive iteration, since the terminating condition when the string is empty can be tested by converting it to a boolean.

See also

`normalize-unicode()` on page 388
`substring()` on page 423.

string-to-codepoints

The `string-to-codepoints()` function returns a sequence of integers representing the Unicode codepoints of the characters in a string.

Changes in 2.0

This function is new in XPath 2.0.

Signature

Argument	Data type	Meaning
input	xs:string?	The input string
Result	xs:integer*	*The codepoints of the characters in the input string*

Effect

If an empty sequence or a zero-length string is supplied as the input, the result is an empty sequence.

In other cases, the result contains a sequence of integers, one for each character in the input string. Characters here are as defined in Unicode and XML: a character above xFFFF that is represented as a surrogate pair counts as one character, not two. The integers that are returned will therefore be in the range 1 to x10FFFF (decimal 1114111).

Examples

Expression	Result
string-to-codepoints("ASCII")	65, 83, 67, 73, 73
string-to-codepoints("𘚠")	100000
string-to-codepoints("")	()

See also

`codepoints-to-string()` on page 308

subsequence

The subsequence() function returns part of an input sequence, identified by the start position and length of the sub-sequence required.

For example the expression «subsequence(("a", "b", "c", "d"), 2, 2)» returns «("b", "c")».

Changes in 2.0

This function is new in XPath 2.0.

Signature

Argument	Data type	Meaning
sequence	item()*	The input sequence
start	xs:double	The position of the first item to be included in the result
length *(optional)*	xs:double	The number of items to be included in the result. If this argument is omitted, all items after the start position are included
Result	xs:string	*The sequence of items starting at the start position*

Effect

The two-argument version of the function is equivalent to:

```
$sequence[position() >= round($start)]
```

The three-argument version is equivalent to:

```
$sequence[position() >= round($start)
          and position() < (round($start) + round($length))]
```

A consequence of these rules is that there is no error if the start or length arguments are out of range. Another consequence is that if the start or length arguments are NaN, the result is an empty sequence.

The arguments are defined with type xs:double for symmetry with the substring() function, which itself uses xs:double arguments for backward compatibility with XPath 1.0, which did not support any numeric type other than double. If you supply an integer, it will automatically be converted to a double. The fact that they are doubles rather than integers is occasionally convenient because the result of a calculation involving untyped values is a double. For example:

```
subsequence($seq, 1, @limit + 1)
```

works even when the limit attribute is untyped, in which case the value of «@limit + 1» is an xs:double.

Examples

Expression	Result
subsequence(3 to 10, 2)	4, 5, 6, 7, 8, 9, 10
subsequence(3 to 10, 5, 2)	7, 8
subsequence(1 to 5, 10)	()
subsequence(1 to 10, 2.3, 4.6)	2, 3, 4, 5, 6

See also

insert-before() on page 356
remove() on page 399
Filter Expressions on page 244 in Chapter 8

substring

The substring() function returns part of a string value, determined by character positions within the string. Character positions are counted from one.

For example, the expression «substring('Goldfarb', 5, 3)» returns the string «far».

Changes in 2.0

None.

Signature

Argument	Data type	Meaning
input	xs:string?	The containing string. If an empty sequence is supplied, the result is a zero-length string
start	xs:double	The position in the containing string of the first character to be included in the result string
length (*optional*)	xs:double	The number of characters to be included in the result string. If the argument is omitted, characters are taken from the start position up to the end of the containing string
Result	xs:string	*The required substring of the containing string*

Effect

Informally, the function returns a string consisting of the characters in the input string starting at position start; if a length is given, the returned string contains this many characters, otherwise, it contains all characters up to the end of the value.

Characters within a string are numbered 1, 2, 3 . . . *n*. This will be familiar to Visual Basic programmers but not to those accustomed to C or Java, where numbering starts at zero.

Characters are counted as instances of the XML Char production. This means that a Unicode surrogate pair (a pair of 16-bit values used to represent a Unicode character in the range #x 10000 to #x 10FFFF) is treated as a single character.

Combining and non-spacing characters are counted individually, unless the implementation has normalized them into a single combined character. The implementation is allowed to turn strings into Unicode normalized form, but is not required to do so. In normalized form, accents and diacritics will typically be merged with the letter that they modify into a single character.

It is possible to define this function in terms of the subsequence() function. With two arguments, the function has the same result as:

```
codepoints-to-string(
        subsequence(string-to-codepoints($input), $start)))
```

With three arguments, the definition becomes:

```
codepoints-to-string(
        subsequence(string-to-codepoints($input), $start, $length)))
```

These rules cover conditions such as the start or length being negative, NaN, fractional, or infinite. The comparisons and arithmetic are done using IEEE 754 arithmetic, which has some interesting consequences if values such as infinity and NaN, or indeed any non-integer values are used. The rules for IEEE 754 arithmetic are summarized in Chapter 2.

The equivalence tells us that if the start argument is less than one, the result always starts at the first character of the supplied string, while if it is greater than the length of the string, the result will always be an empty string. If the length argument is less than zero, it is treated as zero, and again an empty string is returned. If the length argument is greater than the number of available characters, and the start position is within the string, then characters will be returned up to the end of the containing string.

Examples

Expression	Result
substring("abcde", 2)	"bcde"
substring("abcde", 2, 2)	"bc"
substring("abcde", 10, 2)	""
substring("abcde", 1, 20)	"abcde"

Usage

The substring() function is useful when processing a string character-by-character. One common usage is to determine the first character of a string:

```
substring($filename, 1, 1)
```

Or when manipulating personal names in the conventional American format of first name, middle initial, last name:

```
string-join((first-name, substring(middle-name, 1, 1), last-name), " ")
```

The following example extracts the last four characters in a string:

```
substring($s, string-length($s)-3)
```

Using substring() as a Conditional Expression

The technique outlined in this section is thankfully obsolete, now that XPath 2.0 offers «if» expressions, as described in Chapter 5. But you may encounter it in XSLT 1.0 stylesheets, and you may still have to use it if you write code that has to run under both XPath 1.0 and XPath 2.0, so it's worth a mention here.

Suppose that $b is an xs:boolean value, and consider the following expression:

```
substring("xyz", 1, $b * string-length("xyz"))
```

Under XPath 1.0 rules, the xs:boolean $b when used in an arithmetic expression is converted to a number: 0 for false, 1 for true. So the value of the third argument is 0 if $b is false, 3 if $b is true. The final result of the substring() function is therefore a zero-length string if $b is false, or the string "xyz" if $b is true. The expression is equivalent to «if ($b) then "xyz" else ""» in XPath 2.0.

In fact the third argument doesn't need to be exactly equal to the string length for this to work, it can be any value greater than the string length. So you could equally well write:

```
substring("xyz", 1, $b * (1 div 0))
```

exploiting the fact that «1 div 0» under XPath 1.0 is infinity, and zero times infinity is NaN. This obscure construct provided XPath 1.0 programmers with a substitute for a conditional expression.

In fact if you try to run this code under XPath 2.0, it will fail: «1 div 0» is an xs:decimal division rather than an xs:double division, and the xs:decimal data type has no infinity value. If you need to rewrite this so that it works under both XPath 1.0 and XPath 2.0, the simplest way is to replace the «1 div 0» by a very large but finite number. In XSLT, you can define this as a global variable. Remember, though, that exponential notation for numbers is not available in XPath 1.0.

See also

substring-after() in the section immediately below
substring-before() on page 427
string-length() on page 419
contains() on page 314

substring-after

The substring-after() function returns that part of a string value that occurs after the first occurrence of some specified substring.

For example, the expression «substring-after('print=yes', '=')» returns «yes».

Changes in 2.0

An optional collation argument has been added.

Signature

Argument	Data type	Meaning
value	xs:string?	The containing string
substring	xs:string?	The test string
collation (*optional*)	xs:string	Identifies the collation to be used for comparing strings
Result	xs:string	*A string containing those characters that follow the first occurrence of the test substring within the containing string*

Effect

If the containing string does not contain the test substring, the function returns a zero-length string. Note that this could also mean that the containing string ends with the test substring; the two cases can be distinguished by calling the ends-with() function.

If the containing string does contain the test substring, the function returns a string made up of all the characters that appear in the containing string after the first occurrence of the test substring.

If either of the first two arguments is an empty sequence, it is treated as if it were a zero-length string.

If the test substring is zero-length, the function returns the containing string.

If the containing string is zero-length, the function returns a zero-length string.

If a collation is specified, this collation is used to test whether the strings match. See the description of the contains() function on page 314 for an account of how substring matching works with a collation. If the collation argument is omitted, the function matches characters according to their Unicode codepoint values.

Examples

Expression	Result
substring-after("my.xml", ".")	"xml"
substring-after("my.xml", "m")	"y.xml"
substring-after("my.xml", "xml")	""
substring-after("my.xml", "#")	""
substring-after("", "#")	""
substring-after("my.xml", "")	"my.xml"

Usage

The `substring-after()` function was often used in XPath 1.0 to analyze a string that contains delimiter characters. For example, when the string is a whitespace-separated list of tokens, the first token can be obtained using

```
substring-before($s, ' ')
```

and the rest of the string using

```
substring-after($s, ' ')
```

With XPath 2.0, this can be done more robustly using the `tokenize()` function. However, there are still many cases where it is more convenient to use `substring-after()`. For example, to extract the local part of a lexical QName, you can write:

```
substring-after($qname, ':')
```

XSLT Example

The following example shows a recursive template that takes a whitespace-separated list as input, and outputs each token separated by an empty `<br/>` element.

```
<xsl:template name="output-tokens">
    <xsl:param name="list" as="xs:string" required="yes"/>
    <xsl:variable name="nlist"
        select="concat(normalize-space($list),' ')"/>
    <xsl:variable name="first" select="substring-before($nlist, ' ')"/>
    <xsl:variable name="rest" select="substring-after($nlist, ' ')"/>
    <xsl:value-of select="$first"/>
    <xsl:if test="$rest">
        <br/>
        <xsl:call-template name="output-tokens">
            <xsl:with-param name="list" select="$rest"/>
        </xsl:call-template>
    </xsl:if>
</xsl:template>
```

See also

contains() on page 314
substring() on page 423
substring-before() in the next section

substring-before

The `substring-before()` function returns that part of a string value that occurs before the first occurrence of some specified substring.

For example, the value of «`substring-before('print=yes', '=')`» is the string «print».

Changes in 2.0

An optional `collation` argument has been added.

Signature

Argument	Data type	Meaning
value	xs:string?	The containing string
substring	xs:string?	The test string
collation (*optional*)	xs:string	Identifies the collation to be used for comparing strings
Result	xs:string	*A string containing those characters that precede the first occurrence of the test substring within the containing string*

Effect

If the containing string does not contain the test substring, the function returns a zero-length string. Note that this could also mean that the containing string starts with the test string; the two cases can be distinguished by calling the starts-with() function.

If the containing string does contain the test substring, the function returns a string made up of all the characters that appear in the containing string before the first occurrence of the test substring.

If either the test substring or the containing string is an empty sequence or a zero-length string, the function returns a zero-length string.

If a collation is specified, this collation is used to test whether the strings match. See the description of the contains() function on page 314 for an account of how substring matching works with a collation. If the collation argument is omitted, the function matches characters according to their Unicode codepoint values.

Examples

Expression	Result
substring-before("my.xml", ".")	"my"
substring-before("my-xml.xml", "xml")	"my-"
substring-before("my.xml", "")	""
substring-before("my.xml", "#")	""

Usage and Examples

An example of the use of substring-after() and substring-before() to process a whitespace-separated list of tokens is given under substring-after() on page 427.

If the only reason for using substring-before() is to test whether the string has a given prefix, use starts-with() instead. You could write:

```
if (substring-before($url, ':')='https') then ...
```

but the following is simpler:

```
if (starts-with($url, 'https:')) then ...
```

In XPath 1.0, the substring-before() and substring-after() functions were often used in conjunction to find and replace portions of a string. In XPath 2.0, this kind of string manipulation is much easier using regular expressions, as offered by the replace() function.

See also

contains() on page 314
replace() on page 400
starts-with() on page 415
substring() on page 423
substring-after() on page 425

subtract-dates, subtract-dateTimes

This entry describes four related functions:

```
subtract-dates-yielding-dayTimeDuration()
subtract-dateTimes-yielding-dayTimeDuration()
subtract-dates-yielding-yearMonthDuration()
subtract-dateTimes-yielding-yearMonthDuration()
```

The first two determine the interval between two dates (or dateTimes) in days, hours, minutes, and seconds. The result of these two functions is exactly the same as the result of using the subtraction operator «-». The effect of the subtraction operator when applied to dates and times is described in the section *Date/Time minus Date/Time* on page 179 in Chapter 6.

The other two functions determine the interval between two dates (or dateTimes) in years and months.

Changes in 2.0

These functions are new in XPath 2.0.

Signature

Argument	Data type	Meaning
value-1	xs:date? or xs:dateTime?	The first operand: generally the later of the two dates or dateTimes
value-2	xs:date? or xs:dateTime?	The second operand: generally the earlier of the two dates or dateTimes
Result	xdt:dayTimeDuration? *or* xdt:yearMonthDuration?	*A duration representing the elapsed time between value–2 and value-1. If value–1 is earlier than value–2, the result will be a negative duration*

Effect

If either of the arguments is an empty sequence, the result is an empty sequence.

The effect of the two forms that return a dayTimeDuration is described in Chapter 6 under the heading *Date/Time minus Date/Time* on page 179.

The rules for the two forms that return a yearMonthDuration are as follows.

If `value-1` is the later of the two dates or dateTimes, the result is the largest yearMonthDuration that can be added to `value-2` to produce a date or dateTime that is not greater than `value-1`. This definition relies on the rules for adding a duration to a date, which are given in Chapter 6 under the heading *Date/Time plus Duration* on page 177.

If `value-2` is the later of the two dates or dateTimes, the result can be obtained by subtracting `value-1` from `value-2` and making the resulting duration negative.

> *Actually, the specification at the time of writing is vague on the details, especially for the second case. There are other ways of defining it, and they don't all give the same answer. On this rule 31 March minus 30 April is minus one month. But it's also possible to justify the answer zero months, on the grounds that adding the negative duration –P1M to 30 April gives you 30 March. It depends whether you start with the earlier date and walk forward, or whether you start with the later date and walk backward. At the time of writing, the W3C specification doesn't say which is right.*

Simple cases give reasonably intuitive results, for example, subtracting `2004-09-30` from `2005-03-31` gives a duration of six months, as does subtracting `2005-03-31` from `2005-09-30`. However, the variable length of the month can still give surprises: if you add six months to the date `2004-03-31`, you get `2004-09-30`; if you add another six months you get `2005-03-30`, and if you then subtract the starting date `2004-03-31`, the answer is 11 months.

Examples

Expression	Result
`subtract-dates-yielding-dayTimeDuration(` `xs:date("2005-01-01"), xs:date("2004-07-01"))`	P184D
`subtract-dates-yielding-dayTimeDuration(` `xs:date("2004-02-28"), xs:date("2004-03-01"))`	–P2D
`subtract-dates-yielding-yearMonthDuration(` `xs:date("2005-01-01"), xs:date("2004-07-01"))`	P6M
`subtract-dates-yielding-yearMonthDuration(` `xs:date("2005-12-31"), xs:date("2004-06-30"))`	P1Y6M
`subtract-dates-yielding-yearMonthDuration(` `xs:date("2005-03-31"), xs:date("2004-02-29"))`	P1Y1M
`subtract-dates-yielding-yearMonthDuration(` `xs:date("2004-11-01"), xs:date("2004-12-15"))`	–P1M

`subtract-dateTimes-yielding-yearMonthDuration(`
`xs:dateTime("2005-01-01T12:00:00Z"),`
`xs:dateTime("2004-01-01T18:00:00Z"))`
	–P11M

Usage

Note that if you want to manipulate the resulting duration as a numeric value, for example, as an integer number of months, you can convert it to an integer by dividing by a unit duration, such as the yearMonthDuration `P1M`.

For example, if you want to calculate the compound interest due on an account since a given date, when interest is calculated on a monthly basis, you will first need to know the number of complete months that the account has been open, as an integer value. You can get this as the result of the expression:

```
subtract-dates-yielding-yearMonthDuration(current-date(), @date-opened)
    div xdt:yearMonthDuration("P1M") idiv 1
```

The purpose of the final «`idiv 1`» is to convert the `xs:double` that results from dividing the two durations to an integer.

See also

Arithmetic using Durations in Chapter 6, page 176

sum

The `sum()` function calculates the total of a sequence of numeric values or durations.

For example, if the context node is the element `<rect x="20" y="30"/>`, then the expression «`sum(@*)`» returns 50. (The expression «`@*`» is a sequence containing all the attributes of the context node.)

Changes in 2.0

This function is generalized in XPath 2.0 so that it can sum over all the numeric data types, and also over durations.

In XPath 1.0 the function returned NaN if the sequence contained a value that could not be converted to a number. In XPath 2.0 (even under backward compatibility mode) this situation causes a failure.

Signature

Argument	Data type	Meaning
sequence	`xdt:anyAtomicType*`	The set of items to be totaled
zero-value (*optional*)	`xdt:anyAtomicType`	The value to be returned when the sequence is empty
Result	`xdt:anyAtomicType`	*The total of the values in the sequence*

Effect

Although the function signature states that the input sequence must consist of atomic values, the function calling rules ensure that the actual argument can be a sequence of nodes—the nodes in this sequence will be atomized, which extracts their typed values. If the source document has been validated using a schema, then the type of the resulting values depends on the schema, while if it has not been validated, the result of atomization will be untyped atomic values.

Any untyped atomic values in the sequence are converted to xs:double values. A runtime error is reported if this conversion fails. If the sequence contains any NaN (not-a-number) values, which might happen if you do the conversion yourself by calling the number() function, then the result of the function is NaN.

The values in the sequence are added using the «+» operator. An error is reported if there are values that cannot be added using the «+» operator. This will happen if the sequence contains values of types other than the numeric types, the duration types, and xdt:untypedAtomic, or if it contains a mixture of durations and other types. If you are totaling durations, all the durations must either be of type xdt:dayTimeDuration or they must all be of type xdt:yearMonthDuration—you cannot mix the two, and you cannot use duration values that don't match one of these subtypes.

If the input sequence is empty, then the value returned is the value specified in the zero-value argument. If this argument is omitted, the return value for an empty sequence is the xs:integer value 0. The purpose of this argument is to allow a return value to be specified that has the appropriate type, for example, an xs:double 0.0e0 for use when totaling doubles, or the value PT0S when totaling xdt:dayTimeDuration values. This is needed because there is no runtime type information associated with an empty sequence—an empty sequence of xs:double values does not look any different from an empty sequence of xdt:dayTimeDuration values.

Examples

Expression	Result
sum((1, 2, 3, 4))	10 (xs:integer)
sum((1, 2, 3, 4.5))	10.5 (xs:decimal)
sum((1, 2, 3.5e0, 4.5))	11.0e0 (xs:double)
sum(())	0 (xs:integer)
sum((), 0.0e0)	0.0e0 (xs:double)
sum((xdt:dayTimeDuration("P3D"), xdt:dayTimeDuration("PT36H")))	P4DT12H
sum((), xdt:dayTimeDuration("PT0S"))	PT0S

Usage

The sum() function can be used to create totals and subtotals in a report. It is also useful for calculating geometric dimensions on the output page.

A problem that sometimes arises is how to get a total over a set of values that aren't present directly in the source file, but are calculated from it. For example, if the source document contains <book> elements with attributes price and sales, how would you calculate the total sales revenue, which is obtained by multiplying price by sales for each book, and totaling the result over all books? Or, how would you total a set of numbers if each one has a leading «$» sign which you need to strip off first? In XPath 1.0 this was difficult to achieve, but the solution in XPath 2.0 is simple:

In the first case:

```
sum(for $b in //book return ($b/price * $b/sales))
```

In the second case:

```
sum(for $p in //price return number(substring-after($p, '$'))
```

See also

avg() on page 301
count() on page 316

timezone-from-date, timezone-from-dateTime, timezone-from-time

These three functions extract the timezone component from an xs:date, xs:time, or xs:dateTime value. For example, for a user in California, «timezone-from-dateTime(current-dateTime())» typically returns the dayTimeDuration «-PT8H».

Changes in 2.0

These functions are new in XPath 2.0.

Signature

Argument	Data type	Meaning
input	xs:date?, xs:time?, or xs:dateTime?	The value from which the timezone component is to be extracted. The data type of the supplied argument must correspond to the data type implied by the function name
Result	xdt:dayTimeDuration?	The timezone, expressed as a duration

Effect

The function returns the timezone component of the supplied xs:date, xs:time, or xs:dateTime.

If the argument is an empty sequence, or if it is a date, time, or dateTime containing no timezone, then the result is an empty sequence. Otherwise, the function returns the timezone from the specified value. The timezone is returned in the form of an xdt:dayTimeDuration value giving the offset from UTC (or Greenwich Mean Time, in common language).

If you want the timezone as a numeric value in hours, divide it by «xdt:dayTimeDuration("PT1H")».

Examples

Expression	Result
timezone-from-date(xs:date("2004-02-28"))	()
timezone-from-dateTime(xs:dateTime("2004-02-28T13:00:00-06:00"))	-PT6H
timezone-from-time(xs:time("13:00:00+01:00"))	PT1H
timezone-from-dateTime(xs:dateTime("2004-07-31T23:00:00Z"))	PT0S

See also

adjust-date/time-to-timezone on page 297
current-date(), -dateTime(), -time() on page 318.
format-date(), -dateTime(), -time() in Chapter 7 of *XSLT 2.0 Programmer's Reference*.
implicit-timezone() on page 352

tokenize

The tokenize() function splits a string into a sequence of substrings, by looking for separators that match a given regular expression.

For example, «tokenize("12, 16, 2", ",\s*")» returns the sequence «("12", "16", "2")».

Changes in 2.0

This function is new in XPath 2.0.

Signature

Argument	Data type	Meaning
input	xs:string?	The input string. If an empty sequence or zero-length string is supplied, the function returns an empty sequence
regex	xs:string	The regular expression used to match separators, written according to the rules given in Chapter 11
flags (*optional*)	xs:string	One or more letters indicating options on how the matching is to be performed. If this argument is omitted, the effect is the same as supplying a zero-length string, which defaults all the option settings
Result	xs:string*	*A sequence whose items are substrings of the input string*

Effect

The rules for the syntax of regular expressions are given in Chapter 11, and the rules for the flags attribute under the entry for the matches() function on page 368.

The input string is processed from left to right, looking for substrings that match the regular expression supplied in the regex argument. A consecutive sequence of characters that don't participate in a match is copied as a string to form one item in the output sequence. A sequence of characters that does match the regex is deemed to be a separator and is discarded. The search then resumes at the character position following the matched substring.

It can happen that two substrings starting at the same position both match the regex. There are two ways this situation can arise.

Firstly, it happens when part of the regex is looking for repeated occurrences of a substring. For example, suppose the regex is «\n+», indicating that any sequence of one or more consecutive newlines acts as a separator. Then clearly, if two adjacent newline characters are found, the regex could match on the first one alone, or on the pair. The rule here is that «+» is a greedy quantifier: it matches as long a substring as it can, in this case, both newline characters. In this case this is what you want to happen. But if you were trying to remove comments in square brackets by using a regex such as «\[.*\]», this would have the wrong effect—given the input «Doolittle [1] and Dalley [2]», the first separator identified would be «[1] and Dalley [2]». If you want to match the shortest possible substring, add a «?» after the quantifier to make it non-greedy, thus: «\[.*?\]».

Another situation that can cause two different substrings to match at the same position is where the regex contains two alternatives that both match. For example, when the regex «#|##» is applied to a string that contains two consecutive «#» characters, both branches will match. The rule here is that the first (leftmost) alternative wins. In this case this is almost certainly not what was intended: rewrite the expression as «##|#», or as «##?».

If the input string starts with a separator, then the output sequence will start with a zero-length string representing what was found before the first separator. If the input string ends with a separator, there will similarly be a zero-length string at the end of the sequence. If there are two adjacent separators in the middle of the string, you will get a zero-length string in the middle of the result sequence. In all cases the number of items in the result sequence is the number of separators in the input string plus one.

If the regex does not match the input string, the tokenize() function will return the input string unchanged, as a singleton sequence. If this is not the effect you are looking for, use the matches() function first to see if there is a match.

If the regex is one that matches a zero-length string, that is, if «matches("", $regex)» is true, the system reports an error. An example of such a regex is «\s*». Although various interpretations of such a construct are possible, the Working Group decided that the results were too confusing and decided not to allow it.

Examples

Expression	Result
tokenize("Go home, Jack!", "\W+")	("Go", "home", "Jack", "")
tokenize("abc[NL]def[XY]", "\[.*?\]")	("abc", "def", "")

Usage

A limitation of this function is that it is not possible to do anything with the separator substrings. This means, for example, that you can't treat a number differently depending on whether it was separated from the next number by a comma or a semicolon. The solution to this problem is to process the string in two passes: first, do a `replace()` call in which the separators «,» and «;» are replaced by (say) «,#» and «;#»; then use `tokenize()` to split the string at the «#» characters, and the original «,» or «;» will be retained as the last character of each substring in the tokenized sequence. Another alternative, if you are using XSLT, is to use the `<xsl:analyze-string>` instruction.

A similar technique is possible when there are no separators available. For example, suppose that the input is alphanumeric, and you want to break it into a sequence of alternating alphabetic and numeric tokens, for example, the input «W151TBH» needs to be split into the three strings «("W", "151", "TBH")». Here's how to do this:

```
tokenize(replace($input, "([0-9]+|[A-Za-z]+)", "$1#"), "#")[.]
```

The predicate «[.]» at the end of this expression causes zero-length strings in the result to be filtered out (there will be a zero-length string at the end of the sequence).

See also

`<xsl:analyze-string>` in *XSLT 2.0 Programmer's Reference*, Chapter 5
`matches()` on page 368.
`replace()` on page 400
Regular Expressions: Chapter 11

trace

The `trace()` function is used to produce diagnostic output. The format and destination of the output is implementation-defined.

Changes in 2.0

This function is new in XPath 2.0.

Signature

Argument	Data type	Meaning
value	item()*	A value that is to be displayed in the diagnostic output
message	xs:string	A message that is to be output along with the displayed value
Result	item()*	*The function returns the displayed* value, *unchanged*

Effect

The detailed effect of this instruction depends on the implementation; some implementations might ignore it entirely. The idea of the function is that when it is evaluated, a message should be produced to some diagnostic output stream (perhaps a log file, or perhaps an interactive console) showing the message string and the contents of the supplied value. The function then returns this value, and execution continues normally.

Note that since the order of execution of different expressions is undefined, the trace output will not necessarily be strictly sequential, and it may be difficult to see what is going on when the same trace() expression is evaluated repeatedly. This problem can be reduced if the message, rather than being a simple literal string, is constructed from variables that provide some context.

The specification doesn't say whether the presence of the trace() function should or should not affect the optimizer's evaluation strategy. Some implementors may decide that to make the trace output intelligible, certain optimizations should be suppressed; others may decide that the execution strategy with tracing should be as close as possible to the execution strategy without tracing, to reduce the risk of so-called Heisenbugs, in which the behavior of the expression changes when debugging is switched on.

Usage and Examples

Suppose you are having problems understanding why the function call «sum(//@price)» is returning NaN. Try changing it to

```
«sum(//trace(@price, "price value"))»
```

to see the price values that are being used in the computation.

In the current Saxon implementation, when you trace a sequence, you get one message for each item in the sequence. Saxon pipelines the evaluation of sequences, and tracing doesn't change the pipeline, so you might find that the evaluation of different sequences is interleaved. This can be confusing, but it gives you a faithful picture of what is happening internally. Other implementations might give you one message for the entire sequence, and might break the evaluation pipeline in order to output the message.

Sometimes you might just want to output a value that is not actually used in the computation. In this case you can usually use an empty sequence as the value, and put the required value into the message—just remember that the trace() function will then return an empty sequence. For example, you could write:

```
«sum(//(trace((),concat("reading price for ", string(@code)), @price)»
```

See also

error() on page 336.
<xsl:message> in Chapter 5 of *XSLT 2.0 Programmer's Reference*.

translate

The translate() function substitutes characters in a supplied string with nominated replacement characters. It can also be used to remove nominated characters from a string.

For example, the result of «translate('ABC-123', '-', '/')» is the string «ABC/123».

Changes in 2.0

An empty sequence is not accepted for the second and third arguments.

Signature

Argument	Data type	Meaning
value	`xs:string?`	The supplied string
from	`xs:string`	The list of characters to be replaced, written as a string
to	`xs:string`	The list of replacement characters, written as a string
Result	`xs:string?`	*A string derived from the supplied string, but with those characters that appear in the second argument replaced by the corresponding characters from the third argument, or removed if there is no corresponding character*

Effect

For each character in the supplied string, one of three possible actions is taken:

❑   If the character is not present in the list of characters to be replaced, the character is copied to the result string unchanged

❑   If the character is present at position P in the list of characters to be replaced, and the list of replacement characters is of length P or greater, then the character at position P in the list of replacement characters is copied to the result string

❑   If the character is present at position P in the list of characters to be replaced, and the list of replacement characters is shorter than P, then no character is copied to the result string

Note that the third argument must be present, but it can be a zero-length string. In this case any character present in the second argument is removed from the supplied string.

If a character appears more than once in the list of characters to be replaced, the second and subsequent occurrences are ignored, as are the characters in the corresponding position in the third argument.

If the third argument is longer than the second, excess characters are ignored.

In these rules a *character* means an XML character, not a 16-bit Unicode code. This means that a Unicode surrogate pair (a pair of 16-bit values used to represent a Unicode character in the range `#x10000` to `#x10FFFF`) is treated as a single character, whichever of the three strings it appears in.

Examples

Expression	Result
`translate("aba12", "abcd", "ABCD")`	`"ABA12"`
`translate("aba121", "12", "")`	`"aba"`
`translate("a\b\c.xml", "\", "/")`	`"a/b/c.xml"`
`translate("5,000.00", ".,", ",.")`	`"5.000,00"`

Usage and Examples

Many of the XPath 1.0 use cases for the `translate()` function can now be achieved more conveniently in XPath 2.0 by other more powerful functions, such as `matches()` and `replace()`.

In an XSLT stylesheet you might see the `translate()` function being used to perform simple case conversion, for example:

```
translate($X,
       'abcdefghijklmnopqrstuvwxyz',
       'ABCDEFGHIJKLMNOPQRSTUVWXYZ')
```

This can now be done much better using the `upper-case()` and `lower-case()` functions.

The `translate()` function is useful to remove extraneous punctuation or whitespace: for example to remove all whitespace, hyphens, and parentheses from a telephone number, write:

```
translate($X, '&#x20;&#x9;&#xA;&#xD;()-', '')
```

Another use for `translate()` is to test for the presence of a particular character or range of characters. For example, to test whether a string contains a sequence of three or more ASCII digits, write:

```
contains(translate($X, '0123456789', '9999999999'), '999')
```

Of course, you could do this equally well using «`matches($X, '[0-9]{3}')`».

The `translate()` function can be surprisingly powerful. For example, to remove all characters other than digits from a string, you can write:

```
translate($X, translate($X, '0123456789', ''), '')
```

The inner call on `translate()` strips the digits from `$X`, thus building a list of characters that appear in `$X` and are not digits. The outer call processes `$X` again, this time removing the non-digit characters.

See also

contains() on page 314
matches() on page 368
replace() on page 400
substring() on page 423
substring-after() on page 425
substring-before() on page 427

true

This function returns the boolean value `true`.

Changes in 2.0

None.

Signature

This function takes no arguments.

	Data type	Meaning
Result	xs:boolean	*The* xs:boolean *value* true.

Effect

There are no boolean constants available in XPath expressions, so the functions true() and false() can be used where a constant boolean value is required.

Usage

The most common occasion where constant boolean values are required is when supplying an argument to a function or to an XSLT template. See the example below.

XSLT Example

The following code calls a named template, setting the parameter «verbose» to true:

```
<xsl:call-template name="do-the-work">
   <xsl:with-param name="verbose" select="true()"/>
</xsl:call-template>
```

See also

false() on page 343

unordered

The formal definition of the unordered() function is that it returns a sequence that is an arbitrary re-ordering of the sequence provided as its argument. In practice, this is really a pseudo-function: wrapping an expression in a call of unordered() tells the XPath processor that you don't care what order the results of that expression are in, which means that the processor might be able to avoid the cost of sorting them into the right order.

For example, «unordered(ancestor::*)» returns the ancestor elements in whatever order the system finds most convenient. (In Saxon, it currently returns them in reverse document order, that is, innermost ancestor first.)

Changes in 2.0

This function is new in XPath 2.0.

Signature

Argument	Data type	Meaning
sequence	item()*	The supplied sequence
Result	item()*	*A sequence that contains the same items as the supplied sequence, but in an arbitrary order*

Effect

The ordering of the items in the result is arbitrary, which means the processor can choose any order it likes. This doesn't mean it has to be a randomized order; on the contrary, the system might well choose to return the original order unchanged. In fact, it would be completely conformant with the specification for this function to be implemented as a no-operation. It's really best to think of it as an optimization hint.

Note that although the `unordered()` function allows the system to return the results of the argument expression in any order, it doesn't absolve it from the need to eliminate duplicates. In practice this reduces the possibilities available to an optimizer considerably: for example in forming a union between two sequences of nodes «$A|$B», the system is required both to sort the result in document order and to remove duplicates. Writing it as «unordered($A|$B)» removes the requirement to sort the results, but not the requirement to eliminate duplicates. Since the system is very likely to eliminate duplicates as a by-product of sorting, this might not result in any changes to the execution strategy chosen by the optimizer.

Usage and Examples

Because the XPath data model is defined in terms of sequences rather than sets, the ordering of the results of an expression is usually well-defined. For example, the results of a path expression are always in document order, and the results of the `index-of()` function are defined to be in ascending numeric order. By enclosing such expressions in a call of `unordered()`, you can tell the system that you don't care about the order. For example, «unordered(preceding-sibling::*)» returns the preceding siblings of the context node in an arbitrary order, rather than in document order as usual. In the current version of Saxon, the preceding siblings will be returned in reverse document order, because that is the fastest way of finding them, but you should not rely on this behavior as it may vary from one product to another and might depend on other circumstances.

Some functions take a sequence as an argument, and produce a result that doesn't depend on the order of the items in the sequence. Obvious examples are `count()` and `sum()`. In such cases, it's reasonable to assume that the optimizer will insert a call on `unordered()` automatically, and that you don't need to do it yourself: «count(unordered(X))» gives the same result as «count(X)», and removes the need to sort the items in X into the right order.

The place where the `unordered()` function really comes into its own is in handling joins, for example:

```
//customer/order[@prod-code = //product[supplier=$s]/@code]
```

or equivalently,

```
for $o in //customer/order,
    $p in //product[supplier=$s][@code=$o/@prod-code]
return
    $o
```

There are many different ways of writing join expressions in XPath, just as there are in SQL, and it's often the case that you are only interested in knowing which elements are selected, not in getting them back in a particular order. If you make it clear that you don't care about the order, by wrapping the join expression in a call on the `unordered()` function, then the system can select from a wider choice of possible access paths to retrieve the data. This is particularly true if there are indexes to the data, which is likely if it is stored in an XML database.

upper-case

The upper-case() function converts lower-case characters in a string to upper case.

Changes in 2.0

This function is new in XPath 2.0.

Signature

Argument	Data type	Meaning
value	xs:string?	The string to be converted
Result	xs:string?	*The string with lower case letters converted to upper case*

Effect

See the entry for lower-case() on page 366 for a description of how this function is defined in terms of Unicode case mappings.

The effect of the function is as follows:

❑ If the input is an empty sequence, the result is the zero-length string.

❑ Otherwise, every character in the input string is replaced by its corresponding upper-case character (or sequence of characters) if there is one, or is included unchanged in the result string if not.

The function does not implement case mappings that Unicode defines as being locale-sensitive (such as the Turkish dotless I).

Examples

Expression	Result
upper-case("Sunday")	SUNDAY
upper-case("2+2")	2+2
upper-case("césar")	CÉSAR
upper-case("ελλας")	ΕΛΛΑΣ

Usage

See lower-case() on page 366.

See also

lower-case() on page 366
translate() on page 437

year-from-date, year-from-dateTime

These two functions extract the year component from an `xs:date` or `xs:dateTime` value. For example, «`year-from-date(current-date())`» might return 2004.

Changes in 2.0

These functions are new in XPath 2.0.

Signature

Argument	Data type	Meaning
input	`xs:date?` or `xs:dateTime?`	The value from which the year component is to be extracted. The data type of the supplied argument must correspond to the data type implied by the function name. If an empty sequence is supplied, an empty sequence is returned
Result	`xs:integer`	*The year. The range of values is implementation-defined; negative years (representing BC dates) are allowed*

Effect

The function returns the year component of the supplied `xs:date` or `xs:dateTime`. The value is used in its local timezone (not normalized to UTC).

Examples

Expression	Result
`year-from-date(xs:date("2004-02-28"))`	2004
`year-from-dateTime(xs:dateTime("1969-07-20T16:17:00-04:00"))`	1969

See also

`current-date()`, `-dateTime()`, `-time()` on page 318
`format-date()`, `-dateTime()`, `-time()` in Chapter 7 of *XSLT 2.0 Programmer's Reference*
`day-from-date()`, `-dateTime()` on page 322
`month-from-date()`, `-dateTime()` on page 374

years-from-duration

This function extracts the value of the years component from a normalized `xdt:yearMonthDuration` value.

Changes in 2.0

This function is new in XPath 2.0.

Signature

Argument	Data type	Meaning
input	xdt:yearMonthDuration	The value from which the component is to be extracted
Result	xs:integer	*The years component*

Effect

The function returns the years component of the supplied xdt:yearMonthDuration. The duration value is first normalized so that the number of months is less than 12. The result will be negative if the duration is negative.

Examples

Expression	Result
years-from-duration(xdt:yearMonthDuration("P1200Y"))	1200
years-from-duration(xdt:yearMonthDuration("P18M"))	1
years-from-duration(xdt:yearMonthDuration("-P1M"))	0

See also

months-from-duration on page 375

zero-or-one

The zero-or-one() function returns its argument unchanged, provided that it is a sequence containing no more than one item. In other cases, it reports an error.

Changes in 2.0

This function is new in XPath 2.0.

Signature

Argument	Data type	Meaning
value	item()*	The input value. Although the function signature says that any sequence of items is allowed, a runtime error will occur if the number of items is not zero or one
Result	item()	*The same as the supplied value, after checking to ensure that it is either an empty sequence or contains a single item*

Effect

The `zero-or-one()` function returns its argument unchanged, provided that it is a sequence containing no more than one item. In other cases, it reports an error.

This function is useful with XPath processors that perform static type-checking, as described in Chapter 3. Calling this function acts as a promise by the programmer that the argument will be a sequence that is either empty, or contains exactly one item. This allows the expression to be used in contexts that require an optional single value (for example, the argument of a function such as `root()`) when the processor might otherwise have reported a static type error. The XPath expression is still type-safe, because the check that the sequence does indeed contain a single item will be done at runtime, just as it would with a processor that does not enforce static type checking.

Examples

Assume the source document

```
<paint colors="red"/>
```

with a schema that defines the colors attribute with type `xs:NMTOKENS` (that is, it allows a list of colors to be specified, but our sample document only specifies one).

Expression	Result
`string(@colors)`	*Succeeds unless the processor is doing static type checking, in which case it gives a compile-time error because the argument to `string()` must be a sequence of zero or one items*
`string(zero-or-one(@colors))`	*Succeeds whether the processor is doing static type checking or not, because the check that the typed value of `@colors` contains at most one item is deferred until runtime*

Usage

This function is never needed unless you are using a processor that does static type-checking.

However, you may still find it useful as a way of inserting runtime checks into your XPath expressions, and documenting the assumptions you are making about the input data.

See also

`exactly-one()` on page 339
`one-or-more()` on page 395

Summary

Much of the power of any programming language comes from its function library, which is why this chapter explaining the function library is the longest one in the book. The size of the function library has grown greatly since XPath 1.0, largely because of the richer set of data types supported.

One chapter remains. Chapter 11 defines the syntax of the regular expressions accepted by the three functions `matches()`, `replace()`, and `tokenize()`.

Regular Expressions

This chapter defines the regular expression syntax accepted by the XPath functions `matches()`, `replace()`, and `tokenize()` which were described in the previous chapter.

This regular expression syntax is based on the definition in XML Schema, which in turn is based on the definition in the Perl language, which is generally taken as the definitive reference for regular expressions. However, all dialects of regular expression syntax have minor variations. Within Perl itself there are features that are deprecated, there are features that differ between Perl versions, and there are features that don't apply when all characters are Unicode.

XML Schema defines a subset of the Perl regular expression syntax; it chose this subset based on the requirements of a language that only does validation (that is, testing whether or not a string matches the pattern) and that only deals with Unicode strings. The requirements of the `matches()` function in XPath are similar; but XPath also uses regular expressions for tokenizing strings and for replacing substrings. These are more complex requirements, so some of Perl's regular expression constructs that XML Schema left out have been added back in for XPath.

The XPath regular expression syntax explained in this chapter is also used (without any further modifications!) by the XSLT `<analyze-string>` instruction, which is described in Chapter 5 of *XSLT 2.0 Programmer's Reference.*

In the grammar productions in this chapter, as elsewhere in the book, I generally enclose characters of the target language (that is, the regex language) in chevrons, for example «|». I have avoided using the more consise notation «[abcd]» because I think it is confusing to use regular expressions when defining regular expressions. If a character is not enclosed in chevrons, then it is either the name of another non-terminal symbol in the grammar, or a symbol that has a special meaning in the grammar.

The description of the syntax of regular expressions closely follows the description given in the XML Schema Recommendation. (You can find this in Appendix F of Schema Part 2. A second edition is in preparation, which corrects numerous errors in the original. At the time of writing the current draft of the second edition is at `http://www.w3.org/TR/2004/PER-xmlschema-2-20040318/`).

Remember that the syntax rules given here apply to the regular expression after it has been preprocessed by the host language. If a regular expression is used within an XML document (for example, an XSLT stylesheet), then special characters such as «&» must be escaped using XML entity or character references such as «&». If it appears within an XSLT attribute value template, then curly braces must be doubled. If it appears within an XPath string literal, then any apostrophe or quotation mark that matches the string delimiters must be doubled. And if your XPath expression is written as a string literal within a host language such as Java or C#, then a backslash will need to be written as «\\» (which means that a regular expression to match a single backslash character becomes «\\\\»).

Branches and Pieces

Construct	Syntax
regex	branch («|» branch)*
branch	piece*
piece	atom quantifier?

A regular expression consists of one or more *branches*, separated by «\|» characters. For example, «abc|def» matches either of the strings «abc» or «def». A regex matches a string if any of the branches matches the string. If more than one branch leads to a match, then the one that is chosen is the first one that matches.

A *branch* consists of one or more *pieces*, concatenated together. A branch consisting of two pieces A and B matches a string if the string can be split into two substrings, with the first substring matching A and the second matching B. For example, «def» is the concatenation of three pieces, «d», «e», and «f», and it matches a string consisting of a «d» followed by an «e» followed by an «f». The regex «[a-z][0-9]» consists of two pieces, «[a-z]» and «[0-9]», and it matches any string that consists of a letter in the range «[a-z]» followed by a digit in the range «[0-9]».

A *piece* is an *atom*, optionally followed by an optional *quantifier*. Quantifiers are described in the next section.

Unlike content models in XML Schema, there are no rules preventing ambiguities or backtracking in a regular expression. It is perfectly legal to have a regex with two branches that both match the same string, or to have two branches that start with the same characters, for example «abc|abd».

Quantifiers

Construct	Syntax
quantifier	indicator «?»?
indicator	«?» | «*» | «+» | («{» quantity «}»)
quantity	quantRange | quantMin | quantExact
quantRange	quantExact «,» quantExact

Construct	Syntax
quantMin	quantExact «,»
quantExact	Digit+
Digit	«0»|«1»|«2»|«3»|«4»|«5»| «6»|«7»|«8»|«9»

A quantifier is either one of the symbols «?», «*», or «+», or a quantity enclosed between curly braces. A quantifier may be followed by «?» to indicate that it is a non-greedy quantifier.

A quantity is either a number, or a number followed by a comma, or two numbers separated by a comma: *number* here means a sequence of one or more digits.

The piece «A?» matches a single «A» or a zero-length string; «A*» matches a sequence of zero or more «A»s, while «A+» matches a sequence of one or more «A»s.

The piece «A{3}» matches a sequence of exactly three «A»s; «A{3,}» matches a sequence of three or more «A»s, and «A{3,5}» matches a sequence of at least three and at most five «A»s.

By default, quantifiers are greedy: they match as many occurrences of the relevant characters as they can, subject to the regex as a whole succeeding. For example, given the input string «17(c)(ii)», the regular expression «\(.*\)» will match the substring «(c)(ii)». Adding a «?» after the quantifier makes it non-greedy, so the regex «\(.*?\)» will match the substring «(c)». This doesn't affect the matches() function, which is only concerned with knowing whether or not there is a match, but it does affect replace() and tokenize(), and XSLT's <xsl:analyze-string>, which also need to know which characters matched the regex.

Atoms

Construct	Syntax
atom	Char | charClass | («(» regex «)»)
Char	*Any XML character except* . \ ? * + ( ) | < >^$[]
charClass	charClassEsc | charClassExpr | «.» | «^» | «$»
charClassExpr	«[» charGroup «]»

An atom is either a *normal character*, a *character class*, or a *regex enclosed in parentheses*.

A *normal character* (Char) is any character except «.», «\», «?», «*», «+», «|», «<», «>», «^», «$», «[» and «]». A normal character matches itself, and if the «i» flag is used, it also matches upper- and lower-case variants of itself.

A *character class* (charClass) is either a *character class escape* or a *character class expression*, or one of the metacharacters «.», «^» or «$». We will see what a *character class escape* is later, on page 45.

The metacharacter «.» in a regex matches any single character except a newline character (x0A), except when the «s» (dot-all) flag is set, in which case it matches any character including a newline.

The metacharacters «^» and «$» match the beginning and end of the input string, respectively, except when the «m» (multiline) flag is set, in which case they match the beginning and end of each line. The beginning of a line is either the start of the entire string, or the position immediately after a newline (x0A) character; the end of a line is either the end of the entire string, or the position immediately before a newline character. So (with multiline mode off) the regex «^The» matches a string that begins with the characters «The», while the regex «\.xml$» matches a string that ends with the characters «.xml».

A *character class expression* is a *character group* enclosed in square brackets. Character groups are described in the next section. A character group matches a single character.

Character Groups

Construct	Syntax
charGroup	posCharGroup | negCharGroup | charClassSub
posCharGroup	(charRange | charClassEsc)+
negCharGroup	«^» posCharGroup
charClassSub	(posCharGroup | negCharGroup) «-» charClassExpr

Character groups always appear within square brackets. A character group is either a *positive group*, a *negative group*, or a *subtraction*. Examples of the three kinds are «[a-z]», «[^0-9]», and «[a-z-[pqr]]».

A *positive group* (posCharGroup) consists of a sequence of one or more parts, each of which is either a *character range* or a *character class escape*. A positive group matches a character if any one of its parts matches the character. For example, «[a-zA-Z0-9%#]» matches any character that falls in one of the ranges «a» to «z», «A» to «Z», or «0» to «9», as well as the «%» and «#» characters.

A *negative group* (negCharGroup) consists of a circumflex «^» followed by a *positive group*. A negative group matches any character that is not matched by the corresponding positive group. For example, the negative group «[^abc]» matches any character except «a», «b», or «c».

A *subtraction* (charClassSub) consists of either a positive group or a negative group, followed by the «-» symbol, followed by a character class expression (which, as we saw earlier, is a character group enclosed in square brackets). A subtraction matches any character that matches the group preceding the «-» operator, provided it does not also match the character class expression following the «-» operator. For example, «[0-9-[5]]» matches any digit except the digit «5».

Character Ranges

If you are comparing these rules with the ones in XML Schema Part 2, be sure to look at the second edition; the original XML Schema Recommendation got this syntax badly wrong. I have changed the names of the productions slightly.

Construct	Syntax
charRange	codepointRange | SingleChar
codepointRange	charOrEsc «-» charOrEsc
charOrEsc	SingleChar | SingleCharEsc
SingleChar	*Any XML character except* «-» «[» «]» «\»

A *character range* is either a *codepoint range* or a *single character*.

A *codepoint range*, for example, «a-z», consists of two characters, or *single character escapes*, separated by a «-» character. The Unicode codepoint for the second character must be greater than or equal to the codepoint for the first. Specifying a codepoint range is equivalent to listing all the Unicode characters with codepoints in that range, for example «[0-9]» is equivalent to «[0123456789]».

A *single character* is any character permitted by the XML specification, other than the four characters listed: «-», «[», «]», and «\». There is an additional rule not shown in the grammar: if «^» appears at the start of a character group, then it is taken to indicate that the group is a negative character group. This means that it can't appear at the start of a positive character group, except in the case where the positive character group is part of a negative character group. (You can't have a double negative: «[^^]» matches any character except a circumflex.)

> *The original XML Schema Recommendation allowed a character range such as* «[+-]», *and in fact this construct is used in the published schema for XHTML. According to the revised syntax published in the XML Schema Errata, this is not valid. This has caused a certain amount of friction, to put it politely.*

Single character escapes are described in the following section.

Character Class Escapes

Construct	Syntax
charClassEsc	SingleCharEsc | MultiCharEsc | backReference | catEsc | complEsc
SingleCharEsc	«\» («n»|«r»|«t»|«\»|«|»|«.»|«?»| «*»|«+»|«(»|«)»|«{»|«}»|«-»|«[»| «]»|«~»|«^»|«$»)
MultiCharEsc	«\» («s»|«S»|«i»|«I»|«c»|«C»|«d»| «D»|«w»|«W»)
backReference	«\» Digit+
catEsc	«\p{» charProp «}»
complEsc	«\P{» charProp «}»

Continues

Construct	Syntax
charProp	Category | IsBlock
Category	*One of the two-character codes listed in the section* Character Categories *on page 455*
IsBlock	«Is» BlockName *where BlockName is the name of one of the Unicode code blocks listed in the section* Character Blocks *on page 453*

A *character class escape* can appear at the top level of a regular expression (as an atom); a *single character escape* (which is one kind of character class escape) can also appear at either end of a codepoint range, as we saw in the previous section.

There are five kinds of character class escapes: *single character escapes, multicharacter escapes, back references, category escapes,* and *complementary escapes.*

A *single character escape* (SingleCharEsc) consists of a backslash followed by one of the characters shown below. The single character escape matches a single character, as shown in the table.

Single character escape	Matches
«\n»	newline (x0A)
«\r»	carriage return (x0D)
«\t»	tab (x09)
«\\» «|» «\.» «\?» «*» «\+» «\(» «\)» «\{» «\}» «\-» «\[» «\]» «\ ~» «\^» «\$»	The character following the backslash, for example, «\?» matches a question mark

A *multicharacter escape* (MultiCharEsc) is a «\» followed by one of the characters shown below. Each multicharacter escape matches one of a number of different characters (but it only matches one character at a time).

Multi character escape	Matches
«\s»	space (x20), tab (x09), newline (x0A), or carriage return (x0D)
«\i»	an initial name character: specifically, a character that matches «\p{L}» or «:» or «_»
«\c»	a name character, as defined by the NameChar production in the XML specification
«\d»	a decimal digit: anything that matches «\p{Nd}»

Multi character escape	Matches
«\w»	a character considered to form part of a word, as distinct from a separator between words: specifically a character that does not match «\p{P}» or «\p{Z}» or «\p{C}»
«\S»	Any character that does not match «\s»
«\I»	Any character that does not match «\i»
«\C»	Any character that does not match «\c»
«\D»	Any character that does not match «\d»
«\W»	Any character that does not match «\w»

A *backReference* consisting of «\» followed by one or more digits is a reference to the substring that matched the n'th parenthesized subexpression within the regex. Thus, the regex «(['"])[^'"]*\1» matches a string consisting of a single or double quote, then an arbitrary sequence of non-quote characters, then a reappearance of the same quote character that started the string. A single digit following a «\» is always recognized as part of the *backReference*; subsequent digits are recognized as part of the backreference only if there are sufficiently many parenthesized subexpressions earlier in the regex. For example, «\15» is recognized as a *backReference* only if there are at least fifteen parenthesized subexpressions preceding it in the regular expression; if this is not the case, then it is interpreted as a *backReference* «\1» followed by the digit «5».

A *category escape* «\p{prop}» matches any character with the property *prop*, as defined in the Unicode character database. A complementary escape «\P{prop}» matches any character that does not have the property *prop*. The *prop* may either represent the block of characters being matched, or a character category. The next two sections define the character blocks and categories.

Character Blocks

Character blocks are simply names for ranges of characters in Unicode. For example, «\p{IsHebrew}» matches any character in the range x0590 to x05FF, while «\P{IsHebrew}» matches any character that is not in this range.

The names of the blocks are listed in the table below. The name of the block is preceded by «Is» in the regular expression, which then matches any character in the block. Note that some of the blocks (such as PrivateUse) map to several ranges of codes.

Range	Name	Range	Name
x0000-x007F	BasicLatin	x2460-x24FF	EnclosedAlphanumerics
x0080-x00FF	Latin-1Supplement	x2500-x257F	BoxDrawing
x0100-x017F	LatinExtended-A	x2580-x259F	BlockElements

Continues

Range	Name	Range	Name
x0180-x024F	LatinExtended-B	x25A0-x25FF	GeometricShapes
x0250-x02AF	IPAExtensions	x2600-x26FF	MiscellaneousSymbols
x02B0-x02FF	SpacingModifierLetters	x2700-x27BF	Dingbats
x0300-x036F	CombiningDiacriticalMarks	x2800-x28FF	BraillePatterns
x0370-x03FF	Greek	x2E80-x2EFF	CJKRadicalsSupplement
x0400-x04FF	Cyrillic	x2F00-x2FDF	KangxiRadicals
x0530-x058F	Armenian	x2FF0-x2FFF	IdeographicDescriptionCharacters
x0590-x05FF	Hebrew	x3000-x303F	CJKSymbolsandPunctuation
x0600-x06FF	Arabic	x3040-x309F	Hiragana
x0700-x074F	Syriac	x30A0-x30FF	Katakana
x0780-x07BF	Thaana	x3100-x312F	Bopomofo
x0900-x097F	Devanagari	x3130-x318F	HangulCompatibilityJamo
x0980-x09FF	Bengali	x3190-x319F	Kanbun
x0A00-x0A7F	Gurmukhi	x31A0-x31BF	BopomofoExtended
x0A80-x0AFF	Gujarati	x3200-x32FF	EnclosedCJKLettersandMonths
x0B00-x0B7F	Oriya	x3300-x33FF	CJKCompatibility
x0B80-x0BFF	Tamil	x3400-x4DB5	CJKUnifiedIdeographsExtensionA
x0C00-x0C7F	Telugu	x4E00-x9FFF	CJKUnifiedIdeographs
x0C80-x0CFF	Kannada	xA000-xA48F	YiSyllables
x0D00-x0D7F	Malayalam	xA490-xA4CF	YiRadicals
x0D80-x0DFF	Sinhala	xAC00-xD7A3	HangulSyllables
x0E00-x0E7F	Thai	xD800-xDB7F	HighSurrogates
x0E80-x0EFF	Lao	xDB80-xDBFF	HighPrivateUseSurrogates
x0F00-x0FFF	Tibetan	xDC00-xDFFF	LowSurrogates
x1000-x109F	Myanmar	xE000-xF8FF	PrivateUse
x10A0-x10FF	Georgian	xF900-xFAFF	CJKCompatibilityIdeographs
x1100-x11FF	HangulJamo	xFB00-xFB4F	AlphabeticPresentationForms
x1200-x137F	Ethiopic	xFB50-xFDFF	ArabicPresentationForms-A
x13A0-x13FF	Cherokee	xFE20-xFE2F	CombiningHalfMarks
x1400-x167F	UnifiedCanadianAboriginalSyllabics	xFE30-xFE4F	CJKCompatibilityForms
x1680-x169F	Ogham	xFE50-xFE6F	SmallFormVariants

Range	Name
x16A0-x16FF	Runic
x1780-x17FF	Khmer
x1800-x18AF	Mongolian
x1E00-x1EFF	LatinExtendedAdditional
x1F00-x1FFF	GreekExtended
x2000-x206F	GeneralPunctuation
x2070-x209F	SuperscriptsandSubscripts
x20A0-x20CF	CurrencySymbols
x20D0-x20FF	CombiningMarksforSymbols
x2100-x214F	LetterlikeSymbols
x2150-x218F	NumberForms
x2190-x21FF	Arrows
x2200-x22FF	MathematicalOperators
x2300-x23FF	MiscellaneousTechnical
x2400-x243F	ControlPictures
x2440-x245F	OpticalCharacterRecognition

Range	Name
xFE70-xFEFE	ArabicPresentationForms-B
xFEFF-xFEFF	Specials
xFF00-xFFEF	HalfwidthandFullwidthForms
xFFF0-xFFFD	Specials
x10300-x1032F	OldItalic
x10330-x1034F	Gothic
x10400-x1044F	Deseret
x1D000-x1D0FF	ByzantineMusicalSymbols
x1D100-x1D1FF	MusicalSymbols
x1D400-x1D7FF	MathematicalAlphanumeric Symbols
x20000-x2A6D6	CJKUnifiedIdeographs ExtensionB
x2F800-x2FA1F	CJKCompatibilityIdeographs Supplement
xE0000-xE007F	Tags
xF0000-xFFFFD	PrivateUse
x100000-x10FFFD	PrivateUse

Character Categories

Characters in the Unicode character database are assigned to a category and sub-category. For example, category «L» denotes letters, and within this «Lu» denotes upper-case letters. Within a regular expression, «\p{L}» matches any letter, and «\p{Lu}» matches any upper-case letter. The complementary sets can also be selected: «\P{L}» matches any character that is not a letter, and «\P{Lu}» matches any character that is not an upper-case letter.

The list of categories, with a few examples of characters found in each, is listed in the table below.

Category	Description	Examples
L	Letters	
Lu	Uppercase	A, B, Ø, φ
Ll	Lowercase	a, b, ö, λ
Lt	Titlecase	Dz (x01C5)

Continues

Category	Description	Examples
Lm	Modifier	
Lo	Other	Hebrew ALEF (x05D0)
M	**Marks**	
Mn	Nonspacing	Combining acute accent (x0301)
Mc	Spacing	Gujarati vowel sign AA (x0ABE)
Me	Enclosing	Combining enclosing circle (x20DD)
N	**Numbers**	
Nd	decimal digits	1, 2, 3, 4, ١, ٢, ٣, ٤
Nl	numeric letters	Roman numeral ten thousand (x2182)
No	Other	^{2} ^{3} (x00B2, x00B3)
P	**Punctuation**	
Pc	Connector	_ (x005F)
Pd	Dash	em dash (x2014)
Ps	Open	([{
Pe	Close	)] }
Pi	initial quote	« (x00AB)
Pf	final quote	» (x00BB)
Po	Other	! ? ¿ (x00BF)
Z	**Separators**	
Zs	Space	space (x0020), non-breaking space (x00A0)
Zl	Line	line separator (x2028)
Zp	Paragraph	paragraph separator (x2029)
S	**Symbols**	
Sm	Mathematical	+ < = > | ~ ¬ ±
Sc	Currency	$ ¢ £ ¥ €
Sk	Modifier	acute accent « ′ », cedilla « ¸ »
So	Other	¦ § © ° ¶
C	**Others**	
Cc	Control	tab (x0009), newline (X000A)
Cf	Format	soft hyphen (x00AD)

Category	Description	Examples
Co	private use	
Cn	not assigned	

Disallowed Constructs

Finally, here are some examples of constructs that might be familiar from other regular expression dialects that have not been included in the XPath 2.0 definition. A conformant XPath 2.0 processor is expected to reject any attempt to use these constructs.

Disallowed Construct	Meaning in other languages
`[a-z&&[^oi]]`	intersection: any character in the range «a» to «z», except for «o» and «i»
`[a-z[A-Z]]`	union: same as «`[a-zA-Z]`»
`\0nn`, `\xnn`, `\u nnnn`	character identified by Unicode codepoint in octal or hexadecimal
`\a`, `\e`, `\f`, `\cN`	various control characters not allowed in XML 1.0
`\p{Alpha}`, `\P{Alpha}`	character classes defined in POSIX
`\b`, `\B`	word boundary
`\A`, `\Z`, `\z`	beginning and end of input string
`\g`, `\G`	end of the previous match
`X*+`	non-backtracking or possessive quantifiers (in Java, these force the matching engine down this path even if this results in the match as a whole failing)
`(?...)`	expressions that set various special options; non-capturing sub-expressions; comments

Summary

This chapter provided a rather technical definition of the regular expression syntax provided for use in the XPath functions `matches()`, `replace()`, and `tokenize()`, and in the XSLT `<analyze-string>` instruction.

This regular expression syntax is not very different from the regular expressions supported in languages such as Perl and Java. In practice, you may find that some implementations cut corners by exposing a regular expression library that does not conform exactly to these rules. Caveat emptor!

XPath 2.0 Syntax Summary

This appendix summarizes the entire XPath 2.0 grammar. The tables in this appendix also act as an index: they identify the page where each construct is defined.

The grammar is presented in this book in a slightly less formal style than is used in the W3C specifications. The W3C specification goes to some effort to write the grammar rules in such a way that the syntax can be parsed without backtracking. This is important if you are developing a parser for the language, but my intended audience is users of the language, not implementors. There are therefore a few differences both in the way the rules are organized, and in the notation used for individual rules.

The way that the XPath grammar is presented in the W3C specification is also influenced by the need to support the much richer grammar of XQuery. In this book, I have tried to avoid these complications.

An interesting feature of the XPath grammar is that there are no reserved words. Words that have a special meaning in the language, because they are used as keywords («if», «for»), as operators («and», «except») or as function names («not», «count») can also be used as the name of an element in a path expression. This means that the interpretation of a name depends on its context. The language uses several techniques to distinguish different roles for the same name:

❑ Operators such as «and» are distinguished from names used as element names or function names in a path expression by virtue of the token that precedes the name. In essence, if a word follows a token that can appear at the end of an expression then the word must be an operator; if it follows a token that cannot appear at the end of an expression then it must be another kind of name. Some operators such as «instance of» use a pair of keywords. There are some cases in XQuery where this is essential to disambiguate the grammar, but it's not needed for parsing XPath.

❑ Function names, together with the «if» keyword, are recognized by virtue of the following «(» token.

❑ Axis names are recognized by the following «::» token.

❑ The keywords «for», «some», and «every» are recognized by the following «$» token.

❑   If a name follows «/» or «//», it is taken as an element name, not as an operator. To write «/ union /*», if you want the keyword treated as an operator, you must write the first operand in parentheses: «(/) union /*».

Whitespace

I have organized the rules in the appendix to make a clear distinction between tokens, which cannot contain internal whitespace, and non-terminals, which can contain whitespace between their individual tokens. This separation is not quite so clear in the W3C specification, which is another result of the complications caused by XQuery. Because XQuery uses element constructors that mimic XML syntax, it does not have such a clear separation between the lexical level of the language and the syntactic level.

Whitespace is defined here as any sequence of space, tab, linefeed, and carriage return characters, and comments.

A comment in XPath starts with «(:» and ends with «:)». Comments may be nested, so any «(:» within a comment must be matched by a closing «:)».

Tokens

The definition of a token that I am using here is a symbol that cannot contain separating whitespace. This means that my classification of which symbols are tokens is slightly different from the classification that appears in the W3C specification.

Simple tokens such as «+» and «and» are not included in this table; they simply appear anonymously in the syntax productions.

Symbol	Syntax	Page
IntegerLiteral	Digit+	page 142
DecimalLiteral	(«.» Digit+) | (Digit+ «.» Digit*)	page 142
DoubleLiteral	((«.» Digit+) | (Digit+ («.» Digit*)?)) («e» | «E») («+» | «-»)? Digit+	page 142
Digit	[0-9]	page 142
StringLiteral	(«"» ([^"]) * «"») + | («'» ([^']) * «'») +	page 144

Symbol	Syntax	Page
Wildcard	«*» | NCName «:*» | «*:» NCName	page 222
NCName	*See XML Namespaces Recommendation*	page 146
QName	*See XML Namespaces Recommendation*	page 146
Char	*See XML Recommendation*	page 146

Syntax Productions

These rules mainly use familiar notations: «*» for repetition, parentheses for grouping, «?» to indicate that the preceding construct is optional, «|» to separate alternatives.

Simple tokens are represented using chevrons, for example «,» in the first rule represents a literal comma.

Sometimes multiple tokens are grouped inside a pair of chevrons, for example «for $» in the third rule. This notation indicates that there are two tokens (whitespace may appear between them) but that the parser needs to recognize both tokens together in order to proceed. The keyword «for» on its own is not enough to recognize a ForExpr, because it might equally well be an element name appearing as a step in a path expression: the parser is therefore looking for the composite symbol consisting of the token «for» followed by the token «$».

Whitespace is always allowed between two tokens, whether these are grouped using chevrons or not. Whitespace is required between two tokens in cases where the second token could otherwise be taken as a continuation of the first token. For example, in the expression «$a - $b» whitespace is required before the «-» (but not after it). But whitespace is optional before the «:» that follows an axis name, because «child::» would not be a legal as part of a QName.

Symbol	Syntax	Page
Expr	ExprSingle («,» ExprSingle)*	page 137
ExprSingle	ForExpr | QuantifiedExpr | IfExpr | OrExpr	page 137
ForExpr	«for $» VarName «in» ExprSingle («,» «$» VarName «in» ExprSingle)* «return» ExprSingle	page 247

Continues

461

Symbol	Syntax	Page
QuantifiedExpr	(«some $» | «every $») VarName «in» ExprSingle («,» «$» VarName «in» ExprSingle) * «satisfies» ExprSingle	page 255
IfExpr	«if (» Expr «)» «then» ExprSingle «else» ExprSingle	page 165
OrExpr	AndExpr («or» AndExpr) *	page 198
AndExpr	ComparisonExpr («and» ComparisonExpr) *	page 198
ComparisonExpr	RangeExpr ((ValueComp | GeneralComp | NodeComp) RangeExpr) ?	page 182
ValueComp	«eq» | «ne» | «lt» | «le» | «gt» | «ge»	page 182
GeneralComp	«=» | «!=» | «<» | «<=» | «>» | «>=»	page 182
NodeComp	«is» | ««» | «»»	page 182
RangeExpr	AdditiveExpr («to» AdditiveExpr) ?	page 242
AdditiveExpr	MultiplicativeExpr ((«+» | «-») MultiplicativeExpr) *	page 170
Multiplicative Expr	UnionExpr ((«*» | «div» | «idiv» | «mod») UnionExpr) *	page 170
UnionExpr	IntersectExceptExpr ((«union» | «|») IntersectExceptExpr) *	page 235
IntersectExcept Expr	InstanceOfExpr ((«intersect» | «except») InstanceOfExpr) *	page 235
InstanceofExpr	TreatExpr («instance of» SequenceType) ?	page 287
TreatExpr	CastableExpr («treat as» SequenceType) ?	page 282
CastableExpr	CastExpr («castable as» SingleType) ?	page 262
CastExpr	UnaryExpr («cast as» SingleType) ?	page 262

Symbol	Syntax	Page
UnaryExpr	(«+» | «-») * PathExpr	page 170
PathExpr	(«/» RelativePathExpr?)	(«//» RelativePathExpr)	RelativePathExpr	page 204
RelativePathExpr	StepExpr ((«/» | «//») StepExpr)*	page 208
StepExpr	AxisStep	FilterExpr	page 208
AxisStep	(ForwardStep | ReverseStep) PredicateList	page 212
FilterExpr	PrimaryExpr PredicateList	page 244
PredicateList	Predicate*	page 231
Predicate	«[» Expr «]»	page 231
PrimaryExpr	Literal	VarRef	ParenthesizedExpr	ContextItemExpr	FunctionCall	page 152
Literal	NumericLiteral	StringLiteral	page 152
NumericLiteral	IntegerLiteral	DecimalLiteral	DoubleLiteral	page 152
VarRef	«$» VarName	page 153
Parenthesized Expr	«(» Expr? «)»	page 155
ContextItemExpr	«.»	page 156
FunctionCall	FunctionName «(» (ExprSingle («,» ExprSingle)*)? «)»	page 158
FunctionName	QName	page 158
ForwardStep	(ForwardAxis NodeTest)	AbbrevForwardStep	page 212
ReverseStep	(ReverseAxis NodeTest)	AbbrevReverseStep	page 212
Abbrev ForwardStep	«@»? NodeTest	page 227
Abbrev ReverseStep	«..»	page 227

Continues

Symbol	Syntax	Page
ForwardAxis	«child ::»| «descendant ::»| «attribute ::»| «self ::»| «descendant-or-self ::»| «following-sibling ::»| «following ::»| «namespace ::»	page 213
ReverseAxis	«parent ::»| «ancestor ::»| «preceding-sibling ::»| «preceding ::»| «ancestor-or-self ::»|	page 213
NodeTest	KindTest | NameTest	page 220
NameTest	QName | Wildcard	page 222
SingleType	AtomicType «?»?	page 262
SequenceType	(ItemType OccurrenceIndicator?) | «empty ( )»	page 277
AtomicType	QName	page 262
ItemType	AtomicType | KindTest | «item ( )»	page 277
Occurrence Indicator	«?» | «*» | «+»	page 277
KindTest	DocumentTest | ElementTest | AttributeTest | PITest | CommentTest | TextTest | AnyKindTest	page 224
ElementTest	BasicElementTest | SchemaElementTest	page 281
AttributeTest	BasicAttributeTest | SchemaAttributeTest	page 281
Basic ElementTest	«element (» (ElementNameOrWildCard («,» TypeName «?»?) ?) ? «)»	page 282
Basic AttributeTest	«attribute (» (AttributeNameOrWildcard («,» TypeName) ?) ? «)»	page 282

Symbol	Syntax	Page
ElementName OrWildcard	ElementName | «*»	page 282
AttributeName OrWildcard	AttributeName | «*»	page 282
ElementName	QName	page 282
AttributeName	QName	page 282
TypeName	QName	page 282
Schema ElementTest	«schema-element (» ElementName «)»	page 284
Schema AttributeTest	«schema-attribute (» AttributeName «)»	page 284
PITest	«processing-instruction (» (NCName | StringLiteral)? «)»	page 224
DocumentTest	«document-node (» ElementTest? «)»	page 224
CommentTest	«comment ( )»	page 224
TextTest	«text ( )»	page 224
AnyKindTest	«node ( )»	page 224

Operator Precedence

The following table lists the precedence of the XPath operators.

Precedence	Operator
1	«,»
2	«for», «some», «every», «if»
3	«or»
4	«and»
5	«eq», «ne», «lt», «le», «gt», «ge», «=», «!=», «<», «<=», «>», «>=», «is», «<<», «>>»
6	«to»
7	infix «+», infix «-»
8	«*», «div», «idiv», «mod»
9	«union», «|»
10	«intersect», «except»
11	«instance of»
12	«treat as»
13	«castable as»
14	«cast as»
15	unary «+», unary «-»
16	«/», «//»
17	«[]»

Operators lower down the table bind more tightly than operators further up the table. So «A or B and C» means «A or (B and C)».

It two operators appear in the same row, then they are evaluated from left to right. So «A - B + C» means «(A - B) + C».

Compatibility with XPath 1.0

This appendix describes the main areas where XPath 2.0 is incompatible with XPath 1.0, that is, constructs that gave a result under XPath 1.0 and that either fail, or give a different result, under XPath 2.0.

The level of incompatibility depends on exactly how you run XPath 2.0. The best compatibility is achieved if you run without validating your source documents against a schema, and with the XPath 1.0 compatibility mode enabled. Additional incompatibilities arise if XPath 1.0 compatibility mode is switched off, and further problems can occur if at the same time as you switch to XPath 2.0 you also start validating your source documents. These three scenarios are discussed in the three sections of this appendix.

With Compatibility Mode Enabled

Even with the XPath 1.0 compatibility mode in the static context enabled, there are some constructs that were permitted in XPath 1.0 that either fail in XPath 2.0, or produce a different result. These are described in the following sections, with examples.

Syntax Changes

The only known syntactic incompatibility between XPath 2.0 and XPath 1.0 is that constructs such as «A = B = C», or «A < B < C» were allowed in XPath 1.0, but are disallowed in XPath 2.0.

If you have written such an expression in XPath 1.0, the chances are that it doesn't mean what you intended. The interpretation is «(A = B) = C», or «(A < B) < C». So, for example, «1 = 2 = 0» is true, because «(1 = 2)» is false, and «false() = 0» is true.

These expressions are disallowed in XPath 2.0 because their actual meaning is so wildly different from their intuitive meaning, making them a probable cause of errors.

There is one other change that may give a syntax error under some XPath 2.0 implementations. Support for the namespace axis is now optional: XPath 2.0 processors can choose whether or not to support it. The chances are that vendors enhancing their 1.0 products to support XPath 2.0 will continue to support the namespace axis, while vendors developing new products from scratch are more likely to leave it out.

Comparing Strings

This is probably the most likely source of incompatibility in real applications.

In XPath 1.0, any expression involving the operators «<», «<=», «>», and «>=» was handled by converting both operands to numbers, and comparing them numerically. If the operands were non-numeric strings, the conversion produced the value NaN (not a number), and the comparison then always produced false, regardless of the other operand. But a comparison such as «"10" > "2"» was treated as a numeric comparison and produced the answer true.

In XPath 2.0, these operators can be used to compare values of any data type for which an ordering is defined, including strings. If at least one of the operands is a number, then the other operand is converted to a number and the result will generally be the same as with XPath 1.0. But if both operands are strings, or if they are untyped values (which will happen with a comparison such as «@discount < @rebate»), then they are compared as strings, using the default collation. This means that the comparison «"10" > "2"» will now return false.

To get round this problem, if you want a numeric comparison, you should explicitly convert either or both of the operands to numbers, which you can do by calling the number() function.

When two strings are compared for equality, XPath 1.0 always compared them codepoint-for-codepoint, so, for example «"a" = "A"» would be false. If you want this to be the result under XPath 2.0, take care to select the Unicode codepoint collation as your default collation.

Formatting of Numbers

When very small or very large numbers are converted to strings, XPath 1.0 always used conventional decimal notation, never scientific notation. For example, the value one billion would be output as «1000000000». If the number is an xs:double rather than an xs:decimal or xs:integer, XPath 2.0 will output this value in scientific notation as «1.0E9». If you want the old format, use the xs:decimal() constructor function to convert the value to a decimal before converting it to a string. In XSLT you can get more precise control over the format by using the format-number() function.

There have also been some minor changes in the rules for converting strings to numbers, to align the rules with XML Schema. The representations of positive and negative infinity are now «INF» and «-INF» rather than «Infinity» and «-Infinity». Converting a string containing a leading plus sign to a number with XPath 1.0 produced NaN (not a number); with XPath 2.0 this format is recognized.

Numeric Precision

XPath 1.0 supported only one numeric data type, namely double-precision floating point. XPath 2.0 also supports xs:decimal, xs:integer, and xs:float. Numeric literals that were interpreted as double values under XPath 1.0 will be interpreted as decimal or integer values under XPath 2.0.

One effect of this is that division by zero is likely to produce an error under XPath 2.0, whereas with XPath 1.0 it produced the result positive or negative infinity.

The other effect is that the precision of the result of a numeric computation may be different. For example, every conformant XPath 1.0 processor would produce as the result of the division «1 div 7» the answer «0.14285714285714285», as a double. With XPath 2.0, the result of this division is an xs:decimal, and the precision of the result is implementation-defined. Saxon 7.9 produces the result «0.142857142857142857», but a different processor might legitimately produce more digits or fewer digits in the answer.

Comparisons with a Boolean

The rules for comparing a boolean to a boolean are unchanged; but comparing a boolean to any other type can create problems.

In XPath 1.0, when a node-set was compared to a boolean, the node-set was first converted to a boolean (false if the node-set was empty, otherwise, true), and the two booleans were then compared. In XPath 2.0, when you compare a sequence of nodes to a boolean, the nodes are first atomized. In the absence of a schema, the resulting atomic values will all be of type xdt:untypedAtomic. These untyped values are converted to booleans for the purposes of comparison. The conversion uses the casting rules, so «0» and «false» are treated as false, «1» and «true» are treated as true, and any other value causes an error. If any of these booleans is equal to the other operand, the result is true, otherwise, the result is false.

The most likely outcomes are:

❑   If the node-set is empty, XPath 2.0 will always return false (regardless of the boolean operand)
❑   If the node-set is non-empty, the comparison is likely to fail, unless all the nodes happen to contain one of the string values «0», «1», «true», or «false».

When comparing a number to a boolean, XPath 1.0 converted the number to a boolean and then performed a boolean comparison. XPath 2.0 converts the boolean to a number and performs a numeric comparison. If the number is «0» or «1», this produces the same result. In other cases the result may be different, as the following examples illustrate.

Expression	XPath 1.0 Result	XPath 2.0 Result
1 = true()	true	true
1 = false()	false	false
2 = true()	true	false
2 = false()	false	false

When comparing a string to a boolean, XPath 1.0 converted the string to a boolean and then performed a boolean comparison. XPath 2.0 always rejects this comparison as a type error.

The Empty Sequence

In XPath 1.0, if an empty node-set was used as an operand to a function or operator that expected a string, it was automatically converted to the zero-length string. Similarly, if the operator or function expected a number, it was automatically converted to NaN (not-a-number).

In XPath 2.0 the functions in the core library that expect a string argument reproduce this behavior (this was a late change to the specification before the November 2003 draft was issued). This is not a built-in feature of the language, it is simply part of the way these particular functions are specified, but this is sufficient to prevent compatibility problems.

However, the corresponding change for numeric operators and functions has not been made. For example, if the attribute A does not exist, then the expression «@A+1» returned NaN under XPath 1.0, but returns an empty sequence under XPath 2.0. If you output this value by converting it to a string, the result will be a zero-length string instead of the string "NaN".

Although the empty sequence plays a significant role as a null value in XPath 2.0, most practical expressions are unaffected by the change.

Error Semantics

In XPath 1.0 it was defined, in the case of an expression such as «A and B», that B would not be evaluated if A was false. Similarly, with «A or B», B would not be evaluated if A was true.

This meant that you could safely write an expression such as:

```
($cols = 0) or ($n div $cols > 100)
```

XPath 2.0 no longer gives this guarantee. The operands of «and» and «or» can now be evaluated in either order, or in parallel. In the example above, this means that the division might be evaluated, and cause an error, in the case where $cols is zero.

To be sure of avoiding this failure, you need to rewrite the expression as:

```
if ($cols = 0)
then true
else ($n div $cols > 100)
```

The reason this change was made is that changing the order of evaluation of expressions within a predicate is a common technique used by database optimizers to take maximum advantage of indexes present in a database. The existing rule in XPath 1.0 prevented many such optimizations. This of course is more likely to affect XQuery than XPath implementations, but the rule was changed in both languages to keep them consistent. A vendor who wishes to offer the maximum level of backward compatibility can of course continue to implement boolean expressions in the same way as XPath 1.0.

I think it's unlikely that many existing stylesheets or freestanding XPath expressions will be affected by this change, if only because runtime errors in XPath 1.0 are extremely rare: most programming mistakes in XPath 1.0 produce either a syntax error, or wrong answers, but not a runtime failure.

With Compatibility Mode Disabled

The provision of XPath 1.0 compatibility mode is best regarded as a transition aid to help you make the move to XPath 2.0, rather than as a feature you will want to keep switched on for ever. This section therefore looks at what further changes you may need to make to your XPath expressions when you decide that the time has come to switch compatibility mode off.

(In XSLT 2.0, you can do this by using the version attribute in the stylesheet. Remember that you can set this on any element in the stylesheet, so if you really need to, you can keep compatibility mode on in some parts of the stylesheet, but switch it off in others. However, my own experience is that moving the whole stylesheet over to 2.0 is rarely difficult, so you might just as well bite the bullet and do it all at once.)

There's a description of the effect of 1.0 compatibility mode in Chapter 4, on page 116. In summary, this is what happens when you switch compatibility mode off:

- ❑ Sequences are no longer truncated to their first item when you call a function or operator that requires a single value.

- ❑ Values are no longer automatically cast to xs:string or xs:double when you call a function or operator that requires a string or number.

For both these changes, something that worked with compatibility mode switched on will stop working when you switch compatibility mode off. If your code relies on this feature, it will fail with an error message, rather than producing different results. So it's easy to find out where you need to make the changes.

What"s more, the changes are very easy to make, and they won't stop your code continuing to work with an XPath 1.0 processor if that's something you need to do. If your code is relying on sequences being truncated to their first item, simply add the predicate «[1]». If your code is relying on implicit conversion of values to a number or string, simply wrap the expression in the number() or string() function to make the conversion explicit.

Compatibility when using a Schema

XPath 1.0 was not schema-aware. You could validate your source documents if you wanted to, but this would make no difference to the result of any XPath expression (other than the fact that schema validation expands defaulted elements and attributes, which would therefore become visible to your XPath expressions).

With XPath 2.0, there can be considerable differences in the behavior of an XPath expession depending on whether the source document is validated against a schema or not.

The first difference you are likely to notice is that untyped data (specifically, atomic values of type xdt:untypedAtomic, which most often arise as a result of atomizing a node that has not been subjected to schema validation) can be implicitly cast to the type required by the expression in which it is used, whereas typed data cannot. For example if the attribute value @chapterNr holds an untyped value, then it is perfectly okay to write «string-join(11 @chapter Nr, ",")». But if the attribute is validated as an integer, then this expression will fail, because the string-join() function expects its arguments to be strings. You will have to convert the integer to a string explicitly, by calling the string() function.

Some operations are likely to lose the original lexical form of the data once you apply schema validation. For example, if an attribute is defined in the schema to be numeric, then copying the attribute may cause the numeric value to be normalized, which means that insignificant leading or trailing zeroes and spaces may be lost. With some processors you may be able to avoid this effect by applying the `string()` function to the attribute node, which means that the string value of the node will be used rather than its typed value. However, processors are not required to retain the original lexical form of the value, so this won't always work. If the distinction between «5» and «5.00» is important to you, then it's best not to describe the value in the schema as an «xs:decimal», because the definition of the «xs:decimal» data type says that these are two different representations of the same value.

If the schema declares the type of an element or attribute as a list type, then comparisons applied to that node will behave completely differently. For example given the attribute «colors="red green blue"», in the absence of a schema the predicate «@colors="green"» will return false, but if the schema defines the value as a list, this predicate will return true.

Atomizing an element with element-only content is an error. This error can only arise when you have a schema, because without a schema, all elements are considered to have mixed content. An example of an expression that does this is «contains(invoice, "overdue")» which checks for the presence of the string «overdue» anywhere in the text of an invoice. To make this work after applying a schema, you need to extract the string value of the invoice explicitly, by writing «string(invoice)».

As this book went to press, the XSL working group was finalizing a new XSLT feature that allows stylesheets to discard the type information added to input documents by a schema processor. This feature is designed to improve compatibility between schema-aware and non-schema-aware XSLT processors. For details of this feature, see the latest WC3 language specifications.

Error Codes

The XPath specification associates error codes with each error condition. There is an implicit assumption here that although the W3C specification defines no API for invoking XPath expressions, there will be such APIs defined elsewhere, and they will need some way of notifying the application what kind of error has occurred. The error codes may also appear in error messages output by an XPath processor, though there is no guarantee of this.

Technically, these error codes are QNames with no namespace prefix. This is to allow additional error codes defined by a vendor to be allocated in a different namespace.

The text of the messages associated with each error code is not intended to be normative: hopefully real products will give error messages that are much more helpful than those in the specification, including an indication of where the error occurred.

The errors listed here include those defined in the XPath language specification, and those defined in the definitions of functions in the core function library.

It's likely that there will be last-minute changes in the detailed list of error conditions after this book goes to press, since it's exactly this sort of detail that tends to be subject to change in the final stages before a specification becomes a Recommendation. It's also likely, I think, that many products will not trouble themselves too much with matching their error codes exactly to the ones specified. Time will tell. But despite these caveats, I thought that it would be useful to summarize the codes currently listed in the specifications, and to explain their meaning.

These codes fall into two groups: codes defined in the XPath language specification itself, and codes defined in the Functions and Operators specification for the core function library.

XPath Language Errors

For each error, the heading gives the error code. This is followed by the error description from the XPath language specification, and an explanation of the meaning.

XP0001

It is a static error if analysis of an expression relies on some component of the static context that has not been assigned a value.

For example, using an unprefixed function name is an error if there is no default namespace for functions, and using the «=» operator is an error if there is no default collation.

The initialization of the static context depends on the host language or the XPath API, and it's entirely possible that the host language will define default values for all components of the static context, in which case this error can never occur.

XP0002

It is a dynamic error if evaluation of an expression relies on some part of the dynamic context that has not been assigned a value.

For example, it's an error to perform operations on a time that has no timezone if no implicit timezone has been defined.

This error might also be used if the evaluation of an expression depends on some part of the static context that has not been assigned a value, for example, the base URI.

As with the static context, it's up to the host language to define whether the various parts of the dynamic context are given default values.

XP0003

It is a static error if an expression is not a valid instance of the XPath grammar.

This is an umbrella code that covers all XPath syntax errors.

XP0004

During the analysis phase, it is a type error if the static typing feature is in effect and an expression is found to have a static type that is not appropriate for the context in which the expression occurs.

For example, a processor that supports the static typing feature will raise a static error when you write:

```
@price * 1.1
```

if the price attribute is defined in the schema to have a union type that allows either numbers or strings. A system that does dynamic type checking will raise an error only if the expression is actually applied to a non-numeric value.

XP0005

During the analysis phase, it is a type error if the static typing feature is in effect and the static type assigned to an expression other than the expression () is the empty type.

This error is designed primarily to catch incorrect path expressions. For example, if the schema definition for element «para» does not allow it to contain element «head», then a processor that does static typing will reject the path expression «para/head» as an error.

It's possible that this error may catch things that you actually consider reasonable expressions to write. For example, you may want to write an expression that anticipates an extension to the schema which would allow new elements to appear. Unlike most errors raised when doing static typing, there is no easy way round this one.

XP0006

During the evaluation phase, it is a type error if a value does not match a required type as specified by the matching rules in SequenceType Matching.

This generally means that the argument to a function call is not the type required by the signature of that function; it might also apply to operands of operators such as «is» and «to».

For example, this error will occur if you call «ends-with($n, "00")», when $n is numeric. You need to convert the number to a string before you can use it as an argument to the ends-with($n, "00") function.

XP0007

It is a type error if the data() function is applied to a node whose type annotation denotes a complex type with non-mixed complex content.

Although this error is expressed in terms of the data() function, it doesn't necessarily require an explicit call on this function, because the data() function is called implicitly whenever nodes are atomized. So you will get this error, for example, if you write «contains(invoice, "overdue")», if the «invoice» element is defined in the schema to have element-only content.

The remedy is to call the string() function to take the string value of the node explicitly, write «contains(string(invoice), "overdue")».

XP0008

It is a static error if an expression refers to a type name, function name, namespace prefix, or variable name that is not defined in the static context.

This error means that you haven't declared the object that is referenced in the expression. This might be because you misspelt the name, or it might be because you got the namespace prefix wrong—if the name has a prefix, check that it refers to the correct namespace URI, and if it doesn't, check what the default namespace for that kind of name is.

This error might also be used if the expression refers to an element name or attribute name in a NodeTest, in a context where the element or attribute name is required to be present in the static context.

In the case of undeclared functions, the error XP0017 (defined below) will probably be used in preference.

XP0017

It is an error (the host language environment may define this error as either a static or a dynamic error) if the expanded QName and number of arguments in a function call do not match the name and arity of an in-scope function in the static context.

This error either means that the function you are calling has not been declared, or that you are calling it with the wrong number of arguments. Normally, this will be reported as a static error, but the phrase in parentheses is a let-out clause for XSLT, which (under some circumstances) makes this a dynamic error, allowing a stylesheet to contain conditional logic to run under different XSLT processors that provide different vendor extensions.

XP0018

It is a static error for an expression to depend on the focus when the focus is undefined.

The focus here means the context item, context position, or context size. In XPath 1.0 these always had a value, but in 2.0 they may be undefined. For example, in XSLT the focus is undefined when evaluating a global variable if no source document has been supplied, and it is always undefined on entry to a stylesheet function.

XP0019

It is a type error if the result of a step expression is not a (possibly empty) sequence of nodes.

This error description is not quite accurate: the context in the specification makes it clear that by *step expression* it is actually referring to the operands of the «/» operator in a path expression. This is really just a special case of the rule that the operands of any operator must have the correct type for that operator.

The error probably means that you've attempted something like «item/name()» to get the names of all the «item» elements. To do this, you need a «for» expression: «for $i in item return name($i)».

XP0020

It is a type error if in an axis expression, the context item is not a node.

When you use an expression such as «title» or «@code» or «..» or «ancestor::chap», you are selecting nodes relative to the context node. If the context item is an atomic value then these expressions can't be evaluated.

An example of how this situation can occur is if you write in XSLT:

```
<xsl:analyze-string select="text" regex="[^,]*">
  <xsl:matching-substring>
    <xsl:value-of select="name"/>
  <xsl:matching-substring>
</xsl:analyze-string>
```

Within the `<xsl:matching-substring>` instruction, the context item is a string (the string that was matched). This means that there is no context node, so any path expression will fail with this error.

Note that even absolute path expressions (those starting with «/») require a context node, because they always select nodes within the same document that contains the context node.

XP0021

It is a dynamic error if a value in a cast expression cannot be cast to the required type.

Not all casts are allowed. For example, you cannot cast from an integer to a date. This error message means that you have attempted one of these disallowed casts. The casts that are allowed are described in Chapter 9 of this book.

XP0029

It is a dynamic error in a cast expression if the input value does not satisfy the facets of the target type.

This error means that the cast you are attempting is allowed in principle, but that it doesn't work with the specific value supplied. For example, you can cast a string to a date, but you can't cast the string «2003-02-29» to a date because it isn't a valid date.

XP0050

It is a dynamic error if the dynamic type of the operand of a treat expression does not match the type specified by the treat expression.

The «treat as» expression is an assertion: when you say «$x treat as xs:integer», you are asserting that at runtime, the variable «$x» will contain an xs:integer. If you get it wrong, and the variable contains some other value, this is the error that will be reported.

XP0051

It is a static error if a QName that is used as an AtomicType in a SequenceType is not defined in the in-scope type definitions as an atomic type.

This means you have used an expression such as «$x instance of mf:invoice» where the type «mf:invoice» is either not defined at all, or is a complex type, a list type, or a union type. (The case where it is not defined at all is also covered by error XP0008).

If the type is a complex type, then what you probably meant to write was «$x instance of element(*, mf:invoice)». The type used here is an item type rather than a schema type: the distinction is explained in Chapter 3.

If the type is a list type, for example, xs:IDREFS, then you should instead write «$x instance of xs:IDREF*»: that is, you should test whether all the items are instances of the item type of the list type.

Errors in Functions and Operators
FOAR0001

Division by zero

This error is raised whenever an attempt is made to divide by zero using integer or decimal arithmetic. It may also occur when dividing durations. The error can occur when using any of the operators «div», «idiv», or «mod». With floating point arithmetic, division by zero results in positive or negative infinity.

FOAR0002

Numeric operation overflow/underflow

This error is raised whenever numeric operations result in an overflow or underflow. With floating point arithmetic, overflow and underflow conditions generally produce infinity or zero, but the implementation has the option of raising this error instead. With integer and decimal arithmetic, an implementation must produce this error if the result is out of the range of values that can be represented. The capacity of a decimal or integer value is implementation-defined, so an operation that succeeds with one implementation might raise this error with another.

FOCA0001

Error in casting to decimal

Despite its rather general description, this error has a very specific meaning: it is used when casting to a decimal value from a float or double that is outside the implementation-defined limits supported by the xs:decimal data type.

FOCA0002

Invalid lexical value

This error, although it is described very broadly, is used specifically for a small number of situations: specifically, when the first argument to resolve-QName() is not a valid lexical QName; and when the second argument to expanded-QName() is not a valid NCName.

FOCA0003

Input value too large for integer

This error is raised when casting from an xs:decimal, xs:float, or xs:double to an xs:integer, if the value is outside the implementation-defined limits for the xs:integer data type.

FOCA0004

Error in casting to integer

This error is raised when casting from one of the `xs:float` or `xs:double` values NaN, positive infinity, and negative infinity, to the type `xs:integer`.

FOCA0005

NaN supplied as float/double value

This error is raised when multiplying or dividing a duration by a number, if the number supplied is NaN.

FOCH0001

Codepoint not valid

This error is raised by the `codepoints-to-string()` function if the sequence of integers supplied includes a value that does not represent a legal XML character.

FOCH0002

Unsupported collation

This error is raised if a collation specified in the collation argument of any function that allows such an argument is not one of the collations defined in the static context. It is also raised if a collation defined in the static context (including the default collation) is not one that is supported by the implementation.

FOCH0003

Unsupported normalization form

This error means that the normalization form requested in a call to the `normalize-unicode()` function is one that the implementation does not support.

FOCH0004

Collation unsuitable for this function

Some collations can be used for comparing strings, but not for extracting substrings. This error is reported if you use a collation with one of the functions `contains()`, `starts-with()`, `ends-with()`, `substring-before()`, or `substring-after()`, when the collation is not able to split a string into substrings.

FODC0001

No context document

The functions `id()` and `idrefs()` operate within the document containing the context node. If there is no context item, or if the context item is not a node, or if the tree containing the context node is not rooted at a document node, then this error is raised.

FODC0004

Resource cannot be retrieved by collection()

This error means that the URI passed to the *collection()* function is not a valid URI, or does not correspond to the URI of any collection available in the dynamic context.

FODC0005

Invalid URI argument

This error is raised if the string passed as an argument to the `doc()` function is not a valid URI, according to the rules for the `xs:anyURI` type. (Actually, it is far from clear what these rules are, and many products simply accept any string as a legitimate URI.) The same error is raised if (in the formal language of the specification) there is no mapping in the dynamic context from this URI to a document node. In practice, this may mean that no document can be located with the specified URI, or that the resource found at that URI cannot be parsed as an XML document.

FODT0001

Overflow in date/time arithmetic

This error occurs when adding a duration to an `xs:date` or `xs:dateTime` value (or when subtracting), if the result of the operation is outside the implementation-defined range supported for dates. The error does not occur with `xs:time` values because arithmetic with `xs:time` values is always modulo one day.

FODT0002

Overflow in duration arithmetic

This error occurs when multiplying or dividing a duration by a number, if the resulting duration is outside the implementation-defined limits for the relevant duration data type.

FONC0001

Undefined context item

This error is raised by functions that depend on the context item, or that take the context item as an implicit argument (for example `number()`) if the context item is undefined. It is also raised by the functions `position()` and `last()` if the context position or size are undefined.

FONS0003

No prefix defined for namespace

This error is raised when casting from a string to a QName if there is no namespace binding in the static context for the prefix used in the lexical QName.

FONS0004

No namespace found for prefix

This error is raised by the `resolve-QName()` function if the element node used to resolve the lexical QName has no namespace node that binds a namespace URI to the namespace prefix used in the lexical QName.

FONS0005

Base URI not defined in the static context

This error is raised by the single-argument form of the `resolve-URI()` function if no base URI has been established in the static context. Such a base URI is needed to resolve relative URIs appearing in the XPath expression. The way in which you set a base URI in the static context depends on the host language; in XSLT, for example, it is taken from the base URI of the stylesheet module containing the XPath expression.

FORG0001

Invalid value for cast/constructor

This error means that the value passed to a constructor function or «cast as» expression is not a legal value (and cannot be converted to a legal value) for the target data type.

FORG0002

Invalid argument to resolve-uri()

This error occurs when either the base URI or the relative URI passed to the `resolve-URI()` function is not a valid URI.

FORG0003

zero-or-one() called with a sequence containing more than one item

When you call the `zero-or-one()` function, you are asserting that the value of the argument is a sequence containing at most one item. If the assertion proves to be wrong, this error is raised.

FORG0004

one-or-more() called with a sequence containing no items

When you call the `one-or-more()` function, you are asserting that the value of the argument is a sequence containing at least one item. If the assertion proves to be wrong, this error is raised.

FORG0005

exactly-one() called with a sequence containing zero or more than one item

When you call the `exactly-one` function, you are asserting that the value of the argument is a sequence containing exactly one item. If the assertion proves to be wrong, this error is raised.

FORG0007

Invalid argument to aggregate function

This error means that the sequence supplied to one of the functions `avg()`, `min()`, `max()`, or `sum()` contains inappropriate values. For example, it might contain values that are not numbers or durations, or it might contain both numbers and durations within the same sequence.

FORG0009

Base URI argument to resolve-uri() is not an absolute uri

The specification of the `resolve-uri()` function requires that the second argument, if supplied, should be an absolute URI.

FORX0001

Invalid regular expression flags

The relevant argument of the functions `matches()`, `replace()`, and `tokenize()` must contain zero or more of the letters «s», «m», «i», and «x», in any order.

FORX0002

Invalid regular expression

This error message indicates that the regular expression passed to the function `matches()`, `replace()`, or `tokenize()` is not valid according to the rules given in Chapter 11.

FORX0003

Regular expression matches zero-length string

The functions replace() and tokenize() disallow use of a regular expression that would match a zero-length string. This rule exists because there are various interpretations of what such a regular expression would mean, none of which is obviously correct, and users will have different expectations of the results depending on other programming languages that they are familiar with.

FORX0004

Invalid replacement string

This message means that there is an error in the string supplied as the third argument of the replace() function. Check firstly that if the string contains a «\» character, this is followed by either another «\» or a «$», and secondly, that if the string contains a «$» that is not preceded by a «\», then it is followed by a digit.

FOTY0011

Context item is not a node

The root() function raises this error if it is called when there is no context item, or when the context item is not a node.

FOTY0012

Items not comparable

This error is raised by the function index-of() if the sequence being searched contains an item that cannot be compared with the item used as the search key. For example, this will happen if you search a sequence of strings when looking for an integer. The items are said to be comparable if you could use the «eq» operator to compare them without getting a type error.

Glossary

This glossary gathers together some of the more common technical terms used in this book. Most of these terms are defined in the XPath specifications, but some of them are borrowed from XML or other standards in the XML family, and one or two have been invented for the purposes of this book. So for each definition, I also tell you where the term comes from.

The definitions in all cases are my own; in some cases the original specifications have a much more formal definition, but in other cases they are surprisingly vague.

Where a definition contains references to other terms defined in the glossary, these terms are written in italic.

ANCESTOR AXIS (XPATH)

The ancestor *axis* selects the *parent* of the *context node*, its *parent*, and so on up to and including the *root node*. This *axis* is a *reverse axis*.

ANCESTOR-OR-SELF AXIS (XPATH)

The ancestor-or-self *axis* selects the *context node* followed by all the *nodes* on the *ancestor axis*. This axis is a *reverse axis*.

ARITY (XPATH)

The arity of a function is the number of parameters defined in the function signature: for example, the arity of the function `true()` is zero, while the two versions of the `contains()` function have arity two and three respectively.

ATOMIC VALUE (XPATH)

An atomic value is an item such as an integer, a string, a date, or a boolean. Specifically, it is an instance of the class `xdt:anyAtomicType`, which includes all *simple types* (as defined in XML Schema) that are not *list types* or *union types*.

ATOMIZATION (XPATH)

Atomization is a process that takes an arbitrary *sequence*, containing a mixture of *nodes* and *atomic values*, and creates a new *sequence* in which each of the nodes is replaced by its *typed value*. The resulting sequence consists entirely of *atomic values*.

Attribute (*XML*)

A name=value pair appearing in an element's start tag, for example «`category="grocery"`».

Attribute Axis (*XPath*)

The attribute *axis* selects all the *attributes* of the *context node*. If the *context node* is not an *element*, the *axis* will be empty.

Attribute Declaration (*Schema*)

An attribute declaration is a *schema component* corresponding to an `<xs:attribute>` element in a schema: it defines constraints on the values of *attributes* having a particular name. It may be a global attribute declaration (if it is defined at the top level of a schema) or a local attribute declaration (if defined within the structure of a *complex type*).

Attribute Node (*XPath*)

A *node* in a tree that represents an *attribute* in an XML document. There will be an attribute node attached to an element node for each *attribute* defined in the start tag of the corresponding element in the original XML document, other than an attribute acting as a namespace declaration. There will also be attribute nodes for attributes given a default value in the *document type definition*. The *string value* of the node is the value of the attribute; its *typed value* is the result of *validating* the string value against the relevant *type definition* in a *schema*.

Axis (*XPath*)

An axis is a direction of travel through the *tree*. Starting from a particular *context node*, an axis defines a list of *nodes* reached from that origin. For example, the *ancestor axis* returns the parent, grandparent, and so on up to the root of the tree, while the *following-sibling* axis returns all the nodes that appear after the context node and share the same parent.

Base URI (*XML Base*)

Every *node* has an associated base URI. For an *element node* this is the absolute URI of the XML external entity containing the element's start and end tags (most often, of course, this will be the document entity). For other *node kinds*, it is defined by reference to an associated element node, typically its parent. The base URI of an element can also be set explicitly by using the `xml:base` attribute. The base URI of a node is used when expanding a relative URI defined in that node; for example, a relative URI in an `href` attribute is considered to be relative to the base URI of the parent element.

Every XPath expression also has a base URI defined as part of its static context. For an XPath expression contained in a stylesheet, this is the base URI of the stylesheet element containing the XPath expression. In non-XSLT contexts, it's up to the host environment to specify a base URI for the expression.

Boolean (*XPATH*)

One of the allowed data types for the value of an XPath expression. It takes the value true or false.

Built-In Type (*Schema*)

The XML Schema specification defines a number of built-in *simple types* that are available for use without any need to declare them in a schema. These include 19 *primitive types* (such as xs:string and xs:date), 20 built-in derived *atomic types* (including xs:integer and xs:ID), and 3 built-in *list types* (xs:NMTOKENS, xs:IDREFS, and xs:ENTITIES).

Cast (*XPATH*)

An expression that converts an *atomic value* of one type to an *atomic value* of a different type.

CDATA Section (*XML*)

A sequence of characters in an XML document enclosed between the delimiters «<![CDATA[» and «]]>»; within a CDATA section all characters represent text content rather than markup, except for the sequence «]]>». CDATA sections don't appear in the XPath data model: they are purely a conventional way of entering text that avoids the need to escape special characters such as «&» and «<».

Character Reference (*XML*)

A representation of a character using its decimal or hexadecimal Unicode value, for example «
» or «↤». Normally used for characters that are difficult or impossible to enter directly at the keyboard. Character references appear in lexical XML documents, but in the XPath data model they are replaced by the characters that they represent.

Child Axis (*XPATH*)

The child axis selects all the immediate children of the *context node*. These can include *element nodes, text nodes, comments,* and *processing instructions,* but not *attributes* or *namespace nodes.* This is a *forwards axis.*

Codepoint (*Unicode*)

A numeric value identifying a Unicode character.

Codepoint Collation (*XPATH*)

A *collation* that compares and sorts strings strictly according to the numeric values of the *codepoints* making up the characters of the string.

COLLATION (*XPATH*)

A set of rules for comparing strings. A collation can be used to decide whether two strings are equal, to decide how they should be ordered, and to decide whether one string is a substring of another. Different collations are needed to satisfy the needs of different languages or different applications. In XPath and XSLT a collation is identified by a URI. Except for the *codepoint collation*, the URIs used to identify collations are defined by the implementation.

COMMENT (*XML*)

Markup in an XML document that is conventionally used to carry extraneous information that is not part of the document proper. Written between the delimiters «<!--» and «-->».

COMMENT NODE (*XPATH*)

A *node* in a tree representing an XML *comment*. The *string value* of the node is the text of the comment.

COMPLEX TYPE (*SCHEMA*)

A *schema type* that describes the structure of *elements* that may have child elements or attributes. If the type permits attributes but no child elements, it is referred to as a complex type with simple content.

CONSTRUCTOR FUNCTION (*XPATH*)

A function that constructs an *atomic value* of a particular type. The function has the same name as the target atomic type, and always takes a single argument. A constructor function is created automatically for every *atomic type*, including user-defined atomic types. An example of a call on a constructor function is «xs:date("2004-02-29")». The semantics of constructor functions are defined by reference to the rules for *cast* expressions.

CONTEXT ITEM (*XPATH*)

The *item* currently being processed, part of the *dynamic context*. Certain XSLT instructions and XPath expressions place a new context item on the stack, and revert to the previous context item when the instruction or expression has been evaluated. The XSLT instructions <xsl:apply-templates> and <xsl:for-each> change the context item, as do the XPath expressions «E1/E2» and «E1[E2]». The context item can be referenced using the expression «.».

CONTEXT NODE (*XPATH*)

If the *context item* is a *node*, then the context node is the same thing as the context item. If the context item is not a node, then the context node is undefined.

Context Position (*XPath*)

When a *sequence* of *items* is processed in an expression of the form «E1/E2» or «E1[E2]», or by an `<xsl:for-each>` or `<xsl:apply-templates>` instruction in XSLT, each item in the sequence in turn becomes the *context item*, and the context position identifies the position of the context item in the sequence being processed. The context position determines the value of the `position()` function, and is also used in evaluating a numeric predicate such as «[1]».

Context Size (*XPath*)

When a *sequence* of *items* is processed in an expression of the form «E1/E2» or «E1[E2]», or by an `<xsl:for-each>` or `<xsl:apply-templates>` instruction in XSLT, each item in the sequence in turn becomes the *context item*, and the context size identifies the number of items in the sequence being processed. The context size determines the value of the `last()` function.

Data Model (*XPath*)

The data model is a description of the kinds of object that can be manipulated by XPath expressions, and their properties and relationships. Examples of such objects are *sequences*, *items*, *atomic values*, *nodes*, and *trees*. (Sometimes the phrase *a data model* is used incorrectly to refer to a specific object, such as a tree representing a particular document).

Default Namespace Declaration (*XML*)

This takes the form of an XML attribute `xmlns="uri"`. It declares that within its scope, an element name with no explicit *prefix* will be associated with a particular *namespace URI*. The default namespace is used only for element names; other objects with no prefix (for example, attributes) have a null namespace URI.

Descendant Axis (*XPath*)

The descendant axis selects all the children of the *context node*, their children, and so on, in *document order*. This is a *forwards axis*.

Descendant-or-Self Axis (*XPath*)

The descendant-or-self axis selects the *context node* followed by all the *nodes* on the *descendant axis*. This is a *forwards axis*.

Document Element (*XML*)

The outermost *element* of a *document*, the one that contains all other elements. The XML standard also refers to this as the root element, but it must not be confused with the *root node* in the XPath tree model: the *root node* is usually the *document node* that is the parent of the document element, which represents the document itself.

Document Order (*XPath*)

The *nodes* in a sequence can always be sorted into document order. For elements from the same *document*, document order is the same as the order of the start tags in the original source. In terms of the tree structure, a node is ordered after its preceding siblings, and these are ordered after their parent node. The ordering of attribute and namespace nodes, and of nodes from different source documents, is only partially defined.

Document Type Definition (*XML*)

The definition of the structure of an XML document, or a collection of XML documents. May be split into an external subset, held in a separate file, and an internal subset, embedded within the document itself.

Document (*XML*)

A parsed entity that conforms to the XML syntax for a *document* is said to be a well-formed document; a document that also obeys the rules in its *document type definition* is said to be valid. In XSLT and XPath the term *document* is often used to refer to the *tree* representation of a document: that is, a *document node* together with all the nodes that have this document node as an *ancestor*.

Document Node (*XPath*)

If the *tree* represents a well-formed XML *document* the *root node* will be a *document node* with exactly one *element node* as a child, representing the *document element*, and no *text nodes* as children. In other cases it may have zero or more *element node* children, and zero or more *text node* children: I refer to such a document as being *well-balanced*. In both cases the *root node* may also have *comment nodes* and *processing instruction nodes* as children.

Document Order (*XPath*)

An ordering of nodes. Within a single document, this order reflects the order of the markup in the original source XML: the document node comes first, elements precede their attributes, which in turn precede the children of the element. Across multiple documents, document order is unpredictable but stable.

Dynamic Context (*XPath*)

The dynamic context of an XPath *expression* is the total collection of information available to the XPath engine at evaluation time. This includes the *context item*, *context position*, and *context size*, the values of all *variables*, and the contents of all documents that can be accessed by their *URI* using functions such as `doc()` and `document()`.

Dynamic Error (*XPath*)

A dynamic error is an error detected during the evaluation phase, as distinct from a *static error* which is detected at compile time. Technically, *type errors* (which may be detected either at compile time or at runtime) form a separate third category.

EFFECTIVE BOOLEAN VALUE (*XPATH*)

The effective boolean value of an expression is used when the expression is used in a context where a choice needs to be made: for example the condition in an XPath conditional *expression* or an XSLT `<xsl:if>` *instruction*. The effective boolean value of a *sequence* is `false` if the sequence is empty, or if it contains a singleton atomic value that is the boolean `false`, a zero-length string, a number equal to zero, or NaN; in all other cases, the effective boolean value is `true`.

ELEMENT (*XML*)

A logical unit within an XML document, delimited by start and end tags, for example `<publisher>Wrox Press</publisher>`; an empty element may also be written in abbreviated form, for example `<publisher name="Wrox"/>`.

ELEMENT DECLARATION (*SCHEMA*)

An element declaration is a *schema component* that corresponds to an `<xs:element>` element in a schema: it defines the structure of elements having a particular name. It may be a global element declaration (if it is defined at the top level of a schema) or a local element declaration (if defined within the structure of a *complex type*).

ELEMENT NODE (*XPATH*)

A *node* in a *tree* that represents an *element* in an XML *document*. The parent of the element node is either the containing element or the *document node* of the tree; its children are the element nodes, *text nodes, comment nodes*, and *processing instruction nodes* derived from the immediate content of the XML *element*.

EMPTY SEQUENCE (*XPATH*)

An empty sequence is a *sequence* containing no *items*.

ENTITY REFERENCE (*XML*)

A reference to an internal or external *entity*, generally in the form «&name;». Note that numeric references of the form « » are correctly referred to as *character references* rather than entity references.

ENTITY (*XML*)

A physical unit of information that may be referenced within an XML document. Internal entities are embedded within the document in its *Document Type Definition*; external entities are generally held as a separate file. A parsed entity contains text with XML markup; an *unparsed entity* contains binary data. A general entity contains material for inclusion in the document; a parameter entity contains material for inclusion in the Document Type Definition.

EXPANDED QNAME (*XPATH*)

The term QName is sometimes used to mean a QName as written in source XML documents, that is, a construct of the form «prefix:local-name», and it is sometimes used to mean the (namespace-uri, local-name) pair that this represents. Within the XSLT 2.0 and XPath 2.0 specifications the preferred usage is *lexical QName* for the first construct, and *expanded QName* for the second. These terms are not consistent across the full range of XML specifications.

There is no standard convention for displaying an expanded QName, though in some interfaces such as JAXP, expanded QNames are written in the form «{namespace-uri}local-name». This is sometimes referred to as Clark notation.

EXPRESSION (*XPATH*)

An XPath construct that can be evaluated to yield a value, which will always be a *sequence* (of *nodes* and/or *atomic values*). In XSLT, expressions are used in many contexts such as the select attribute of <xsl:for-each>, <xsl:value-of>, and <xsl:variable>, and the test attribute of <xsl:if> and <xsl:when>. Expressions are also used between curly braces in *attribute value templates*.

FACET (*SCHEMA*)

A facet is a constraint placed on the values of a *simple type* in the *schema*. For example, the pattern facet (not to be confused with XSLT patterns) constrains the value to match a given regular expression, while the maxInclusive facet defines the largest permitted value.

FOLLOWING AXIS (*XPATH*)

The following *axis* selects all the nodes that follow the *context node* in *document order* with the exception of *attribute* and *namespace nodes*, and the node's own descendants. This is a *forwards axis*.

FOLLOWING-SIBLING AXIS (*XPATH*)

The following-sibling axis selects all the *nodes* that follow the *context node* and that share the same parent node. This is a *forwards axis*.

FORWARDS AXIS (*XPATH*)

An *axis* containing a sequence of *nodes* that follow the *context node* in *document order*. Within a *predicate* of an axis *step* that uses a forwards axis (for example, «following-sibling::x[3]»), position numbers count the nodes in *document order*.

FUNCTION (*XPATH*)

A procedure that can be called from within an XPath *expression*; it takes arguments and returns a result. Functions cannot be defined using XPath, only invoked from XPath. A function is either a core function

defined in the XPath or XSLT recommendations, or a *stylesheet function* defined using an
`<xsl:function>` declaration in XSLT, or an *extension function* provided by the vendor or the user.
Functions may also be defined using XQuery. A function has a name (which is a *QName*), a signature
defining the types expected for its arguments and the return type, and an implementation.

ID (*XML*)

An *attribute* of type ID has a value which is unique within the document (that is, different from any other
ID attribute). It is an ID by virtue of being declared as such in the *DTD* or *Schema*. It is only guaranteed
unique if the document is valid (XPath is not constrained to operate only on valid documents). *Elements*
can be accessed using their ID by means of the `id()` function.

IN-SCOPE NAMESPACES (*XPATH*)

Any *element node* has a set of *namespace declarations* that are in scope for the element: these are represented
by the *namespace nodes* for that element. An XPath *expression* also has a set of in-scope namespaces in its
static context. For XPath expressions in an XSLT stylesheet, the in-scope namespaces for the expression are
the namespaces that are in-scope for the element in the stylesheet that contains the XPath expression,
augmented with the namespace defined in the `[xsl:]xpath-default-namespace` attribute if
present. In non-XSLT contexts, it is up to the host environment to define how the static context for an
XPath expression is established.

ITEM (*XPATH*)

An item is either an *atomic value* or a *node*.

ITEM TYPE (*THIS BOOK*)

An item type describes the type allowed for *items* within a *sequence*. This is either `item()`, which allows
any item, `empty()`, which allows nothing, an *atomic type*, or a node type. Node types define the kind of
node (for example element, attribute, or comment) plus optionally, constraints on the name of the node
and on its *type annotation*, which will always be a *schema type*.

LEXICAL QNAME (*XPATH*)

A *QName* written in its lexical form: either a simple unprefixed name, or a construct of the form
«`prefix:local-name`». See also *expanded QName*.

LIST TYPE (*SCHEMA*)

A *simple type* that allows a space-separated sequence of values to be written. For example, the type
`xs:NMTOKENS` permits the value `"red green blue"`. When an *element* or *attribute* is annotated with a
list type, its *typed value* in XPath is a *sequence* containing the individual *items*.

NAMESPACE (*XML NAMESPACES*)

A named collection of names. The namespace is named using a *URI* (or in the 1.1 specification, an IRI), which is intended to be formed in such a way as to ensure global uniqueness, but which, in practice, may be any string. Within a particular region of a document, a namespace is also identified by a local name called a prefix; different prefixes can be used to refer to the same namespace in different documents or even within the same document. A name (of an element or attribute in XML, and of a variable, template, function, mode etc. in XSLT) belongs to a specific namespace, and two names can be considered equivalent only if they belong to the same namespace.

NAMESPACE AXIS (*XPATH*)

The namespace *axis* selects all the *namespace nodes* belonging to the *context node*. If the context node is not an *element node*, the axis will be empty. For element nodes, there is one *namespace node* for every *namespace* that is in scope for the element, whether it relates to a *namespace declaration* that was defined on this element or on a containing element. This is a *forwards axis*. The namespace axis is retained in XPath 2.0, but is deprecated: applications requiring namespace information should instead use the functions `in-scope-prefixes()` and `namespace-uri-for-prefix()`.

NAMESPACE DECLARATION (*XML NAMESPACES*)

A construct in an XML *document* that declares that within a particular region of the document, a given *namespace prefix* will be used to refer to the namespace with a particular *URI*. There are two forms of namespace declaration: `xmlns="uri"` to declare the default namespace (the one with a null prefix), and `xmlns:prefix="uri"` to declare a namespace with a non-null prefix. Both are written in the form of XML attributes and apply to the element they are on and all descendant elements, unless overridden.

NAMESPACE NODE (*XPATH*)

A node in a tree that represents the binding of a namespace prefix to a namespace URI. A namespace node belongs to an element called its parent: it applies only to that element and not to any descendant elements.

NAMESPACE PREFIX (*XML NAMESPACES*)

A short name used to identify a namespace within a particular region of a stylesheet, so called because it is most often used as the prefix of a *lexical QName* (the part before the colon). Different prefixes can be used to identify the same namespace, and in different contexts the same prefix can be used to identify different namespaces.

NAMESPACE URI (*XML NAMESPACES*)

A URI used to identify a namespace. Namespace URIs are unusual in that there is no actual resource that can be obtained using the URI; the URI is simply a unique identifier. In practice, any string can be used as a namespace URI, though «`http://`» URLs are often used to give some prospect of uniqueness. Technically, the XML Namespaces specification refers to this concept as a *namespace name*, and in version 1.1 the namespace name can be an IRI, which unlike a URI allows non-ASCII characters. However, the term namespace URI is in widespread use despite the fact that practical products allow any string to be used.

NaN (*XPath*)

Not-a-Number. This is one of the possible values of a *variable* whose data type is float or double. It results from an operation whose result is not numeric, for example, «`number('apple')`».

Node (*XPath*)

An object forming part of a *tree*. There are seven kinds of node: *attribute nodes, comment nodes, document nodes, element nodes, namespace nodes, processing instruction nodes,* and *text nodes*. Nodes have properties including a name, a *string value*, a *typed value*, and a *base URI*. Every kind of node except a document node may have a parent node; document nodes and element nodes may have children; element nodes may have attributes and namespaces.

Node Kind (*XPath*)

Nodes are classified into seven kinds: *attribute nodes, comment nodes, document nodes, element nodes, namespace nodes, processing instruction nodes,* and *text nodes*.

Number (*XPath*)

In XPath 2.0, the term *number* is used as a generic term for the three primitive types `decimal`, `double`, and `float`, and their subtypes (including `integer`).

Parent Axis (*XPath*)

The parent *axis* selects the *node* that is the parent of the *context node*, assuming it has a parent. Since this axis selects at most one node, it doesn't matter whether it is considered as a *forwards axis* or as a *reverse axis*.

Particle (*Schema*)

In the language of XML Schema, a particle is a component part of the definition of the structure of a *complex type*. A particle may be an *element declaration*, or a wildcard that allows elements from defined namespaces, or a sequence or choice compositor with a defined substructure.

Path Expression (*XPath*)

A path expression is an *expression* that selects a *sequence* of *nodes* in a *tree*. It defines a sequence of *steps* which define navigation paths from the *context node* to further nodes. The final result is the sequence of nodes reached by following each of the steps in turn. For example, the path expression «`../@code`» has two steps: the first step selects the parent of the context node, and the second step selects the «code» attribute of the selected parent. The nodes in the result of a path expression are always returned in *document order*, with duplicates removed.

PRECEDING AXIS (*XPATH*)

The preceding *axis* selects all the *nodes* that precede the *context node* within the same *tree*, with the exception of attribute and namespace nodes, and the node's own ancestors. This is a *reverse axis*.

PRECEDING-SIBLING AXIS (*XPATH*)

The preceding-sibling *axis* selects all the *nodes* that precede the *context node* and that share the same parent node. This is a *reverse axis*.

PREDICATE (*XPATH*)

An *expression* used to filter which *nodes* are selected by a particular *step* in a *path expression*, or to select a subset of the *items* in a *sequence*. A boolean expression selects the items for which the predicate is true; a numeric expression selects the item at the position given by the value of the expression, for example, «[1]» selects the first item.

PREFIX (*XML NAMESPACES*)

See *Namespace Prefix*.

PRIMITIVE TYPE (*SCHEMA*)

The XML Schema specification defines 19 primitive types. In the XPath model these are defined as subtypes of the abstract type xdt:anyAtomicType, which contains all atomic values. The 19 primitive types are boolean, string, decimal, double, float, QName, anyURI, hexBinary, base64Binary, date, time, dateTime, gYear, gYearMonth, gMonth, gMonthDay, gDay, duration, and NOTATION. XPath in effect adds untypedAtomic to this list, representing values that have not been validated against any schema.

PRINCIPAL NODE KIND (*XPATH*)

Every *axis* has a principal *node kind*. For most axes, the principal nodes are *elements*. For the *attribute axis*, the principal node kind is *attribute*, and for the *namespace axis*, it is *namespace*. The principal node kind determines the kind of nodes selected by the node test «*»: for example, «following-siblings::*» selects elements, while «namespace::*» selects namespace nodes.

PROCESSING INSTRUCTION (*XML*)

An item in an XML *document* that is conventionally used to carry instructions to the software that receives the document and processes it. Written between the delimiters «<?» and «?>». Note that the XML declaration at the start of a document, and the text declaration at the start of an external parsed entity, are not processing instructions even though they use the same delimiters.

PROCESSING INSTRUCTION NODE (*XPATH*)

A *node* in a *tree* representing an XML *processing instruction*.

PROMOTION (*XPATH*)

The type-checking rules for *function* calling in XPath, and also for arithmetic operators and comparison operators, allow numeric values to be used where a different numeric type is expected. The operation of converting the supplied *number* to the required type (for example, integer to double) is known as promotion.

QNAME (*XML NAMESPACES*)

A qualified name. It is either a simple name (an NCName) or a name preceded by a namespace prefix and a colon. See also *lexical QName* and *expanded QName*.

RANGE VARIABLE (*XPATH*)

A variable declared in a «for», «some», or «every» expression, which is bound to each item in a sequence in turn, for example the variable $i in «for $i in 1 to 5 return $i*$i».

REGULAR EXPRESSION (*XPATH*)

A regular expression is a pattern that strings may or may not match. Regular expressions can be used in the three functions matches(), replace(), and tokenize() defined in XPath, and in the <xsl:analyze-string> instruction in XSLT.

REVERSE AXIS (*XPATH*)

An *axis* containing a sequence of nodes that precede the *context node* in *document order*. Within a *predicate* of an axis step that uses a reverse axis (for example, «preceding-sibling::x[position() = 1 to 3]»), position numbers count the nodes in reverse document order. However, as with any other axis *step*, the result of the expression is in forwards document order. So this expression returns the last three «x» nodes before the context node, in document order.

ROOT NODE (*XPATH*)

The top-most *node* in a *tree*; any *node* that has no parent. In XPath 2.0, any kind of node may be a root node. A root node that represents a complete XML document is now referred to as a *document node*.

Schema (Schema)

In this book the term *schema* always means a schema defined using the W3C XML Schema language. A schema can be regarded as a collection of *element declarations*, *attribute declarations*, and *type definitions*. A *schema document*, by contrast, is the XML *document* rooted at an <xs:schema> element (which one might regard as containing one module of a schema).

Schema Component (Schema)

A generic term for *element declarations*, *attribute declarations*, and *type definitions*.

Schema Type (this book)

A type as defined in XML Schema: either a *complex type* or a *simple type*. The type may be named, or it may be anonymous. The term includes both *built-in types* (such as xs:integer) and user-defined types.

Self Axis (XPath)

The self *axis* contains a single node, the *context node*. It makes no difference whether it is regarded as a *forwards axis* or a *reverse axis*. The *principal node kind* of the self axis is *elements*, which means that when the context node is an *attribute*, an axis *step* of the form «self::*» or «self::xyz» will not select that attribute.

Sequence (XPath)

A sequence in the XPath *data model* is an ordered collection of *items*. The items may be *atomic values* or references to *nodes* in a *tree*. A sequence containing no items is referred to as the *empty sequence*. Sequences have no identity of their own; two sequences containing the same items cannot be distinguished.

Sequence Type (XPath)

A sequence type is a definition that constrains the permitted values of a *sequence*. It has two parts: an *item type*, which constrains the type of the *items* in the sequence, and a cardinality, which constrains the number of items in the sequence. The cardinality may be zero-or-one, exactly-one, zero-or-more, or one-or-more.

Serialization (XSLT)

Serialization is the reverse of parsing: it takes a *document* represented as a *tree* in the XPath *data model*, and converts it into a lexical XML document.

Simple Type (Schema)

A simple type in XML Schema describes values that can be written as text, with no embedded markup. Simple types divide into atomic types, *list types*, and *union types*. Attributes always have a simple type;

the content of an element may be either a simple or a *complex type*. XML Schema defines a number of built-in simple types, but further simple types can be defined in a user-written schema.

STATIC CONTEXT (*XPATH*)

The static context of an XPath *expression* is the total collection of information available to the XPath engine at compile time. This includes the *namespace declarations* that are in scope, the names and types of declared *variables*, the *base URI* of the expression, and the *collations* that are available.

STATIC ERROR (*XPATH*)

A static error is an error detected during the analysis phase, that is, at compile time.

STATIC TYPE (*XPATH*)

Every *expression* (and subexpression) has a static type. This is a *sequence type*, representing the best possible inference that can be made about the dynamic type of the value that will be returned when the expression is evaluated. For example, the static type of the expression «@*» might be «attribute()*». In an XPath processor that implements strict static typing, a *type error* will be reported if the static type of an expression is not a subtype of the type required by the context in which the expression is used.

STEP (*XPATH*)

A step is used within a *path expression* to navigate from one node to a sequence of related nodes. The most common kind of step is an axis step, which is defined by an *axis*, giving the direction of navigation, a node test, which defines constraints on the type of and names of the target nodes, and zero or more *predicates*, which define arbitrary constraints that the target nodes must satisfy.

STRING (*XPATH*)

One of the allowed data types for the value of an XPath expression. It is a sequence of zero or more Unicode characters (the same character set as is used in XML).

STRING VALUE (*XPATH*)

Every node has a string value. For a text node the string value is the textual content; for an element it is the concatenation of the string values of its descendant text nodes (that is, the textual content of the element after stripping all markup). The string value of a node can be obtained using the string() function.

TEXT NODE (*XPATH*)

A *node* in a *tree* representing character data (called PCDATA in XML) within an XML *document*. Adjacent text nodes will always be merged into a single node. *Character references* and *entity references* occurring within the original text will have been replaced by their expansions.

TREE (*XPATH*)

An abstract data structure representing the information content of an XML document. The tree always has a single *root node* (which contrary to the botanical analogy, is always depicted at the top). The structure of nodes in the tree need not follow the rules for a *well-formed* document in XML, for example, there may be several *element nodes* as children of the root. In XPath 2.0 the root of a tree need not be a *document node*. It is possible to have an element node as the root. It is also possible for any other kind of node (for example, an attribute node) to be parentless, in which case it acts as the root of a tree in which it is the only node.

TYPE (*XPATH*)

In the context of XPath values, the term type means *sequence type.* In the context of nodes validated against a schema, it means *schema type.*

TYPE ANNOTATION (*XPATH*)

Every *element node* and *attribute node* has a type annotation. The type annotation identifies a *schema type,* which may be a *simple type* or a *complex type.* Type annotations are added to nodes as a consequence of validation against a *schema.* An element node that has not been validated against any schema is annotated with the special type `xdt:untyped`, while an attribute node that has not been validated is annotated as `xdt:untypedAtomic`.

TYPE DEFINITION (*SCHEMA*)

A type definition is a *schema component* that defines a *simple type* or a *complex type.*

TYPED VALUE (*XPATH*)

The typed value of a node is in general a *sequence* of *atomic values.* It represents the result of analyzing the textual content of the *node* against the *schema definition* for that node, during the process of *validation.*

TYPE ERROR (*XPATH*)

A type error occurs when the value used as input to some operation is not of the type required by that operation: for example, when a string is used as an argument to an arithmetic operator. Type errors may be detected either at compile time or at runtime. A system that implements strict *static type* checking will report type errors at compile time pessimistically: that is, it will report an error if there is any possibility that the runtime value will have the wrong type.

UNPARSED ENTITY (*XML*)

An unparsed entity is an *entity* declared in the *document type definition* with an associated notation. Such entities are unparsed because they generally contain binary data such as images, rather than XML. Two functions, `unparsed-entity-uri()` and `unparsed-entity-public-id()` are available in XSLT to access the unparsed entities associated with a source document. However, it is not possible to create unparsed entities in a result document.

UNION TYPE (*SCHEMA*)

A union type is a *simple type* that allows a choice of alternatives. For example a union type might allow an attribute to contain either a decimal value, or the string `"N/A"`.

URI (*RFC 2396*)

Uniform Resource Identifier: a generalization of the URLs (Uniform Resource Locators) used to uniquely address resources such as Web pages on the Internet.

VARIABLE (*XPATH*)

A named value. Variables in XPath and XSLT differ from variables in procedural programming language in that there is no assignment statement.

VARIABLE REFERENCE (*XPATH*)

A reference to a *variable* within an *expression*, in the form `$name`.

WELL-BALANCED (*XML FRAGMENT INTERCHANGE*)

An XML fragment is well-balanced if there is an end tag that matches every start tag. This is a less strict constraint than being *well-formed*: a well-balanced fragment does not have to have a single element that encloses all the others. XSLT and XPath are defined so they will work on any *trees* representing a well-balanced XML fragment. The XML and XSLT standards don't use this terminology; instead they refer to the rules for an *external general parsed* entity.

WELL-FORMED (*XML*)

A *document* is well-formed if it follows the syntax rules in the XML specification. These include the rule that there must be a single outermost *element* that encloses all others. The XML output of an XSLT stylesheet is not required to be well-formed, only to be *well-balanced*.

WHITESPACE (*XML*)

Whitespace is any contiguous sequence of tab, carriage return, newline, and space characters. A whitespace node is a *text node* whose *string value* consists solely of whitespace. (The XML specification spells this as two words, *white space*, but I prefer a single word, because using *white* as an adjective suggests that white space is to be contrasted with red space and green space, which of course is not the case.)

XPATH 1.0 COMPATIBILITY MODE (*XPATH*)

A mode of executing XPath 2.0 expressions that attempts to provide the maximum possible level of backwards compatibility with XPath 1.0. In XSLT, this mode is selected by specifying «version="1.0"» in the stylesheet.

Index

F